D1827427

Building A Successful Plant In China 2002/3

An Insider's Guide

China Knowledge Press

RUSSIA

•Manzhouli

HEILONGJIANG

•Daqing

⊚Ulaan baatar

◎ **Harbin**

•Jilin

Tongliao• **Changchun**   Yanji•
•Xilinhot   **JILIN**

⊚ **Shenyang**

INNER MONGOLIA   **LIAONING**   NORTH
◎**Huhhot**   Jinzhou Anshan•   KOREA
Baotou• •Jining Qinhuangdao•
BEIJING
YELLOW RIVER •Datong Tangshan• Dalian•
Ordos•   Baoding•   ◎Pyongyang
            ◎**TIANJIN**
         HEBEI   **BOHAI SEA**
Yinchuan   Yantai• •Weihai
NING   ◎   ◎   Weifang•   ◎Seoul   JAPAN
XIA   **Taiyuan** **Shijiazhuang** **Jinan**   SOUTH
  Yan'an•   Handan• ◎ •Zibo Qingdao• KOREA

      SHANXI   **SHANDONG**   **YELLOW SEA**

•Baoji   Kaifeng•   Xuzhou• Lianyungang•
Xianyang• ◎ Luoyang• ◎**Zhengzhou**
Tianshui• **Xi'an**   **JIANGSU**
SHAANXI   **HENAN**   **ANHUI**   Nantong•
        •Nanyang **Nanjing** Changzhou•
Nanchong• Xiangfan•   **Hefei** ◎ Wuxi•◎Suzhou•
        HUBEI **Wuhan** Anqing• Wuhu• ◎**SHANGHAI**
       ◎   ◎   **Hangzhou**
    Yichang• Jingzhou• Huangshan• Ningbo• •Zhoushan
CHONGQING YANGTZE RIVER Jiujiang• •Jinhua   **EAST**
◎   Yueyang•   Yingtan• **ZHEJIANG**   **CHINA**
    •Zhangjiajie **Nanchang**   Wenzhou•   **SEA**
Changsha◎ ◎ •Ji'an
•Zunyi Zhuzhou• **JIANGXI** **Fuzhou**◎
    HUNAN Yingtan
◎**Guiyang** •Huaihua Henyang• Ganzhou• **FUJIAN**
GUIZHOU   Quanzhou•
•Anshun   Xiamen•   **Taipei**
  Guilin•   **GUANGDONG**   **TAIWAN**
    •Liuzhou   Shantou•   Kaohsiung•
GUANGXI   **Guangzhou**
◎**Nanning** Foshan•◎•Dongguan
    Beihai• Zhuhai• Shenzhen• **HONG KONG**
◎Hanoi   **MACAU**
         SOUTH
Haikou◎   CHINA   PHILIPPINES
HAINAN   SEA
  Sanya•

Western Region
Central Region
Coastal Region
HK SAR, Macau SAR,
and Taiwan Province

Published by China Knowledge Press Pte Ltd.

© 2002 China Knowledge Press Pte Ltd.

We would appreciate it if readers could alert us as to errors and omissions by writing to:

China Knowledge Press Pte Ltd
Robinson Road
P. O. Box 1362
Singapore 902712
Email: info@chinaknowledge.com
www.chinaknowledge-press.com

ISBN 981-04-6766-4

Printed in Singapore

FOREWORD

The emergence of China being the world's manufacturing base is an awakening fact to most businesses globally today; and, this new paradigm and cost equation of producing goods have surfaced. Early foreign entrants who tapped upon this advantage have gained success in both domestic and international markets. China is world's top producer in making apparel, footwear, TV sets, disk drive, cellular phones … the list seems unexhausted – it is no wonder why foreign investors are jumping into the bandwagon of tremendous growth and business opportunities.

Ever since the success of first Special Economic Zone in Shenzhen, Guangdong, two decades ago, the concept of industrial park to attract investors has evolved, and it offers foreign businesses a menu of wide selections – a new phenomenon the developed economies have not encountered over centuries of industrialization. To exemplify early success in Shenzhen, more than 100,000 component manufacturers, mostly from Japan and Taiwan, have relocated to the inner regions of Pearl River Delta – an extension of Shenzhen. To date, there are over 3,000 industrial and technological parks mushroomed and scattered across the country, with different scale, emphasis of industry, local government policy and location.

In terms of human resources, China is equipped with high quality professionals and skilled workers. Last year, China churned out 1.03 million full-time university graduates, about one million adult education qualifiers, and 9.88 millions of students having acquired vocational and technical trainings. As reported in Financial Times (April 2002), China's rich manpower resources have attracted Indian businessmen, too. Indian diamond cutters, with 70% of world's market share worth some USD7 billion, are setting up workshops in China to tap on a combination of cheaper labor costs, better design skills, and operational ease.

Beside lower costs of production, enormous domestic market presents market opportunities that foreign businesses find hard to resist. To quote what Nokia's Chairman & CEO says: "No China, no today's Nokia" – with a USD3 billion of hand phones bought by the Chinese in 2001 alone, and an even larger figure of USD5 billion achieved by Motorola.

The recent entry into World Trade Organization reflects China's commitment to cast away protectionism and to play by international rules and regulations in conducting trades and investment. This facilitates the imports and exports of goods and services that equate the size of developed nations. In fact, China has already overtaken many top places by its world rankings.

Coupled with high quality, diligent workforce, competitive wages, and rapidly growing consumer market, China has captured a bigger share of foreign investments than Japan with Southeast Asian countries combined, with nearly USD45 billion of foreign direct investment inflows landed. This also fuels the ever increasing cadres of nouveau riche in the country.

The first consideration of setting up a plant in China, be it manufacturing, warehousing, R&D, or, even a trading office, is to select an industrial park. It is our aim to assist foreign investors in making better decisions from our in-depth and independent analyses. Beyond a directory and reference guide, we have painstakingly researched, analyzed and constructed a rating system to offer readers a quick, unbiased yet reliable rating allocated to over two hundred selected industrial parks. Unlike most property evaluations that are mainly based on quantitative factors, we take into accounts elements like industrial park's management, accessibility, local authority's administration efficiency, macroeconomic performance of host area, and availability of human resources - given AAA as the highest rating and least attractive with a C grade.

With the proliferation of industrial parks, foreign investors have the advantages of tapping on the 'special treatments' of tax relieves and other incentives – some city and county governments welcome investment of as low as USD50,000 – not bad a sum for a foothold in one of the largest markets in the world.

When this guide was first conceptualized in 2001, our research in the world's markets showed that there is a huge demand for such a guide. Even, in the Chinese literary market, a comprehensive listing and well-researched guide on China's industrial and technological parks were either too narrow in comparisons or, specifically, based on geographic coverage. We hope our efforts will benefit users when doing their sums in riding the waves of China's growth.

Charles Chaw Chong Loong
Research Director
September 2002

Our Rating System

Our rating system certainly provokes contention and disagreement. But rating goes on. So does controversy. The beauty of a rating system is, rather a human nature of comparison, that readers are able to make a quick judgement, albeit a preliminary one, upon the first glance of the hierarachy.

Whenever China discussed, complexity and diversity become the norm for any well sought research. This is in particular true in this publication that covers a widespectrum of industrial parks in China. Given all sorts of names, scales, prominences and functionalities, those spatial cum administrative formations intrigue every ambitious investor who is readily willing to invest in China.

In this regard, the research team of China Knowledge Press has innovated a rating system after broad and in-depth analysis of the issue. Categorization has been done on most of the industrial parks where crucial data are available and the application of the system proves to be meaningful. Although every method has been cautiously applied to ensure accuracy and representativeness of the ratings, we are not, however, responsible for any loss, damage or inconvenience caused whatsoever, as a result of using the ratings in this book.

Being the first edition, the book cannot list a full range of industrial parks in China - it is simply impossible given the country's context. Therefore, those included are usually not necessarily, of greater importance and enjoy better priviledges than the others; and exclusion should not be automatically interpreted into criticism or neglectfulness. In fact, we welcome all relevant Chinese authorities to contribute to make future editions of this Guide more comprehensive and complete.

For any suggestions or corrections, we would appreciate if you could contact us by email at info@ChinaKnowledge.com

Qian Yiqi
Senior Analyst

contents

INDUSTRIAL PARKS IN SARs

BUSINESS DIRECTORY

中 盛 资 讯

China Knowledge Press

China Economy

GENERAL INFORMATION ON CHINA

GEOGRAPHY

Location
East Asia, bordering East China Sea, Bohai Sea, Yellow Sea, and South China Sea

Area
9.6 million sq km

Climate
China is divided into two main climatic regions. The north and west are semi-arid or arid, with extreme temperature variations. The south and southeast are warmer and more humid, with year-round rainfall.

Topography
Land is higher in the west and lower in the east: 33.3% mountain areas, 26% plateaus, 18.8% basins, 12% plains and 9.9% hills.

Natural resources
Coal, iron ore, petroleum, natural gas, mercury, tin, tungsten, antimony, manganese, molybdenum, vanadium, magnetite, aluminum, lead, zinc, uranium, hydropower potential (world's largest)

PEOPLE

Population
Total population: 1,273,111,290 (July 2001 est.)
Mainland: 1.26 billion
Hong Kong SAR: 6.8 million
Macau SAR: 440 thousand
Taiwan: 22.3 million

Population growth
12.79 million persons/year, or a growth rate of 1.07%

Population of family households
Total family households: 348.37 million family households (mainland)

Average size of family household
3.44 persons

Population breakdown

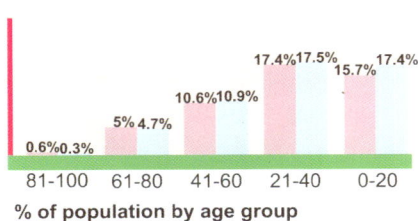

17.4% 17.5% 15.7% 17.4%
10.6% 10.9%
5% 4.7%
0.6% 0.3%

81-100   61-80   41-60   21-40   0-20

% of population by age group
■ Female   ■ Male

Urban and rural composition	Urban: 456 Million (36.09%) Rural: 807 Million (63.91%)
Languages	Standard Chinese or Mandarin (Putonghua, based on the Beijing dialect), Yue (Cantonese), Wu (Shanghainese), Minbei (Fuzhou), Minnan (Hokkien-Taiwanese), Xiang, Chuan, Qian, Dian, Gan, Hakka dialects, minority languages.

Urban/rural population split

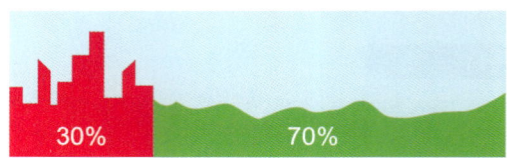

Religious persuasion

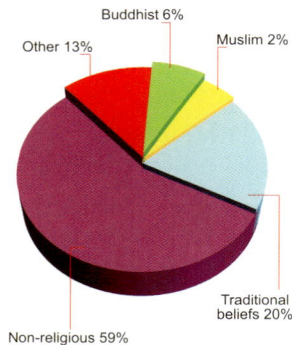

Literacy (mainland)	Illiteracy definition: cannot read and write at age 15 and above Illiteracy Rate: 6.72% Primary School: 35.7% Secondary School: 45.1% College and above: 3.6% (Nov. 2000, est.)

Ethnic makeup

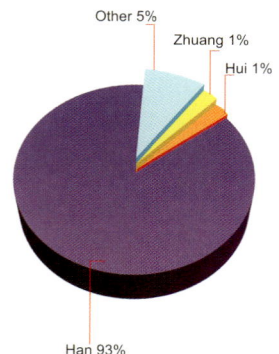

GOVERNMENT

Currency	Renminbi (RMB), usually called the Yuan (CNY)
Official name	People's Republic of China
Capital	Beijing

Administrative divisions

23 provinces
Anhui, Fujian, Gansu, Guangdong, Guizhou, Hainan, Hebei, Heilongjiang, Henan, Hubei, Hunan, Jiangsu, Jiangxi, Jilin, Liaoning, Qinghai, Shaanxi, Shandong, Shanxi, Sichuan, Taiwan, Yunnan, Zhejiang
(Note: Taiwan is still under an independent government)

Four municipalities
Beijing, Chongqing, Shanghai and Tianjin

Five autonomous regions
Guangxi, Inner Mongolia, Ningxia, Tibet and Xinjiang

Two Special Administrative Regions (SAR)
Hong Kong (since 1 July 1997)
Macau (since 20 December 1999)

Legal system

A complex amalgamation of custom and statute, largely criminal law; rudimentary civil code in effect since 1 January 1987; new legal code in effect since 1 January 1980; continuing efforts are being made to improve civil, administrative, criminal, and commercial laws

Legislative branch

National People's Congress (2,979 seats; members elected by the people's congresses in municipalities, autonomous regions and provinces to serve five-year terms)

Judicial branch

Supreme People's Court (judges appointed by the National People's Congress); Local People's Courts (comprising higher, intermediate and local courts); Special People's Courts (primarily military, maritime and railway transport courts)

Political leader

Chinese Communist Party or CCP [Jiang Zemin, General Secretary of the Central Committee]

Public holidays

New Year's Day: 1-2 January
Chinese New Year: January in lunar calendar, normally in Jan or Feb (1-3 February 2003, 22-24 January 2004)
International Labor Day: 1-3 May
National Day: 1-3 October

Economic fact sheet

GDP	RMB9,593 billion (USD1.162 billion) (2001 est.)
GDP – real growth rate	7.3% (2001 est.), 8% (2000 est.)
GDP – composition by sector	Primary Industry: 15.2% Secondary Industry: 51.1% Tertiary Industry: 33.6% (2001 est.)
Total Investment in Fixed Assets	RMB3,690 billion (USD447.3 billion) (2001 est.) 12.1% (Increased over 2000)
Total Retail Sales of Consumer Goods	RMB3,760 billion (USD455.7 billion) (2001 est.) 10.1% (Increased over 2000)
Consumer Price Index (2000=100)	Urban: 100.7 Rural: 100.8 (2001 est.)
Per Capita Disposable Income of Urban Households	RMB6,860 (USD831.5) (2001 est.), 8.5% (over 2000)
Per Capita Net Income of Rural Households	RMB2,366 (USD286.8) (2001 est.), 4.2% (over 2000)
Savings Deposit Balances of Urban and Rural Residents	RMB7,376 billion (USD894 billion) (2001)
Government Revenue	RMB1,637 billion (USD198.4 billion) (2001)
Government Expenditure	RMB1,884 billion (USD228.4 billion) (2001)
Money Supply	M2: RMB15,830 billion (USD1,918.79 billion) M1: RMB5,987 billion (USD725.7 billion) M0: RMB1,569 billion (USD190.2 billion) (2001 est.)
FDI Actually Utilized	USD46.85 billion (2001), 14.9% (over 2000)
Foreign Exchange Reserves	USD212.17 billion (2001)
Unemployment rate	Urban: 3.6% (2001 est.)
Industries	Iron and steel, coal, machine building, armaments, textiles and apparel, petroleum, cement, chemical fertilizers, footwear, toys, food processing, automobiles, consumer electronics and telecommunications
Exports	USD266.2 billion (2001), 6.8% (over 2000)
Main export commodities	Machinery and equipment, textiles, clothing, footwear, toys, sporting goods and mineral fuels
Imports	USD243.6 billion (2001), 8.2% (over 2000)
Main import commodities	Machinery and equipment, mineral fuels, plastics, iron and steel and chemicals
Main trading partners	Japan (17.2%), US (15.8%), EU (15%), Hong Kong SAR (11%), ASEAN countries (8.2%), South Korea (7%), Taiwan (6.3%), Russia (2.1%), Australia (1.8%), Canada (1.4%) (2001)
Exchange Rate	USD1 to RMB 8.2776 (January 2001), 8.2785 (2000), 8.2783 (1999), 8.2790 (1998), 8.2898 (1997), 8.3142 (1996)

Comparison of Major Economies in 2000

Country	GDP (USD trillion)	GDP growth	GNI (USD billion)	GNI rank	GNI/capita (USD)	GNI/capita rank
US	9.81	4.2	9,601.5	1	34,100	7
Japan	4.76	2.4	4,519.1	2	35,620	5
Germany	1.86	3.0	2,063.7	3	25,120	17
UK	1.43	3.1	1,459.5	4	24,430	21
France	1.29	3.1	1,438.3	5	24,090	23
Italy	1.07	2.9	1,163.2	6	20,160	30
China	1.08	7.9	1,062.9	7	840	141
Canada	0.70	4.5	649.8	8	21,130	26

THE ECONOMY

After stagnating for three decades under the rigid authoritarianism of early Communist rule, China has emerged in recent years as one of the world's leading powers, its influence growing in the economic rather than military sphere. In early 1980s, it dismantled collective farming and allowed private enterprise again. Now it is one of the world's top exporters and is attracting record amounts of foreign investment. According to the World Competitiveness Yearbook (WCY) 2002 issued by the Lausanne Institute of Management and Development of Switzerland, China's competitiveness has raisen to 31st position from 33rd in 2001. China could soon undergo what some see as another revolution, and now that it has gained admission to the World Trade Organization. It will benefit from increased access to foreign markets but in return will have to expose itself to competition from abroad.

Review and outlook

Prior to 1978, China maintained a central planning economy. A large share of the country's economic output was controlled and directed by the Central Government, which set production goals, controlled prices and allocated resources throughout most of the economy.

In late 1978, China began to change from

this central planning economy to a more market oriented system. Over the past two decades, China has become one of the world's fastest growing economies. From 1979-2001, China's GDP grew at an average annual rate of 9.5%. (refer to *"China's annual GDP growth rate 1990 - 2001"*).

In 2000, with its 1.2 billion people and Gross National Income (GNI) of USD1,062.9 billion, China stood as the seventh largest economy in the world, according to the World Bank economic report (refer to *"Comparison of Major Economies in 2000"*).

Along with rapid growth and impressive achievements, the ownership structure has also changed substantially.

Ownership structure

China has a mixed economic structure. The economy comprises three major sectors: namely state-owned, collective-owned and private-owned include individually-owned enterprises and those with foreign capital. (refer to *"Composition of National Industrial Output"* and *"Composition of National Retail Sales"*).

Formerly, China's economy was mainly controlled by large state-owned enterprises (SOEs), many of which were inefficient and unprofitable. However, due to the economic

China's annual GDP growth rate 1990 - 2001

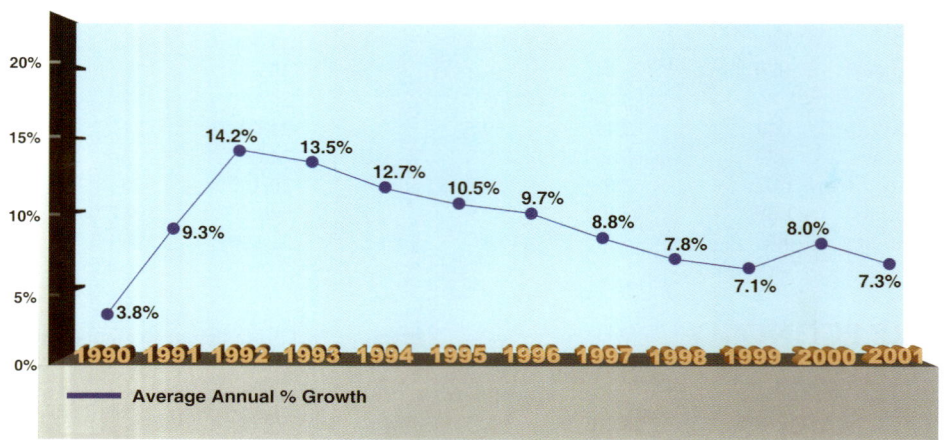

Average Annual % Growth

Composition of National Industrial Output

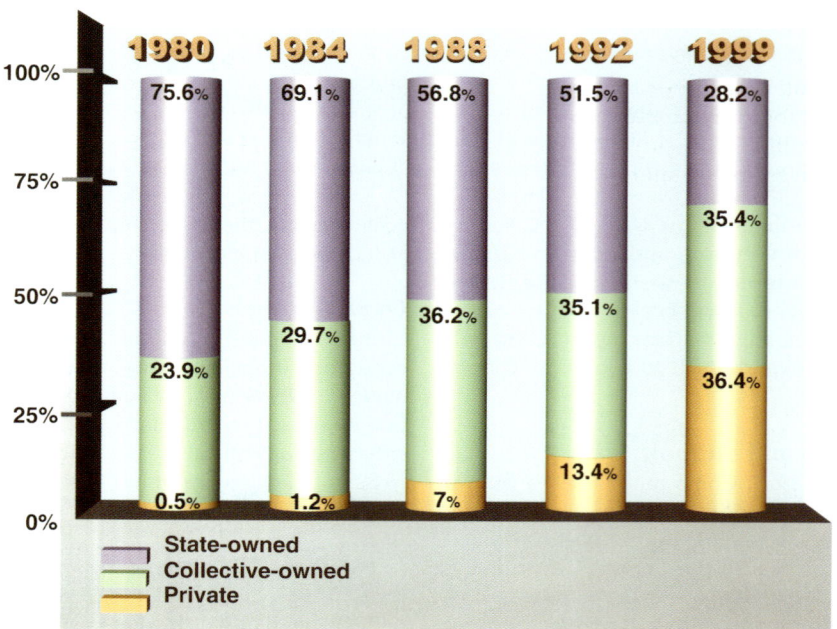

State-owned
Collective-owned
Private

Composition of National Retail Sales

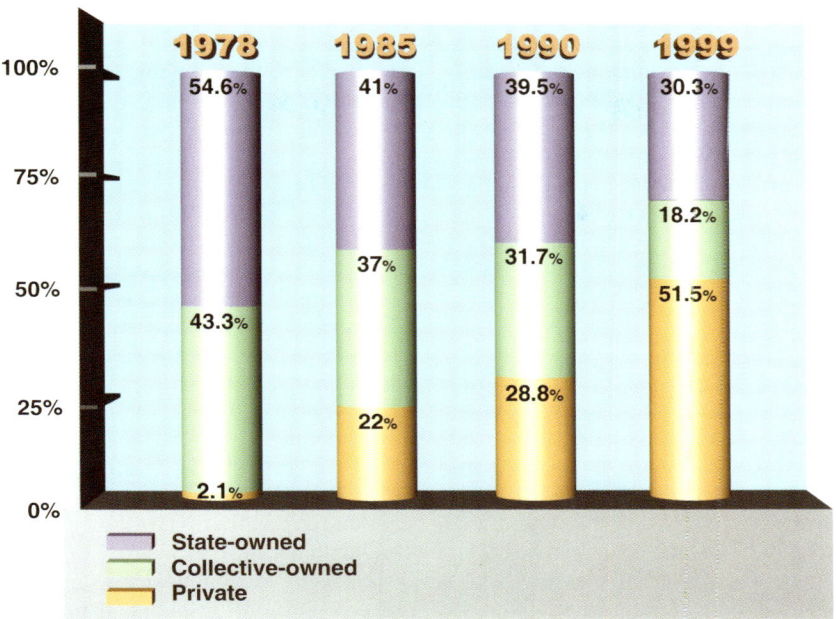

	1978	1985	1990	1999
State-owned	54.6%	41%	39.5%	30.3%
Collective-owned	43.3%	37%	31.7%	18.2%
Private	2.1%	22%	28.8%	51.5%

reforms, the proportion of the state sector in the overall economy has been decreasing sharply. Today, restructuring of the SOE sector, including the privatization of some enterprises, is a major priority of the government. An important recent reform has been the conversion of selected state-owned enterprises into limited shareholding companies, and the issue of shares to public and private investors (including employees) and even foreign investors. A significant number of these state-owned enterprises, after being converted into limited liability shareholding companies, have been granted approval to list domestically in two stock exchanges: the Shanghai Stock Exchange and the Shenzhen Stock Exchange. Since 1993, it has also been possible to list PRC companies on the mainboard stock exchanges in Hong Kong and New York.

In general, the SOE sector has performed better over the past few years after taking cost-cutting measures to prepare for privatization. According to the State Economic and Trade Commission (SETC), 66.5% of SOEs were profitable in 2000, but there were doubts as to the accounting standards on which this figure is based. Unemployment is one of the major social concerns which have accompanied the reforms, as SOEs have shed redundant employees.

Partly due to the state-owned enterprise (SOE) reforms, the urban unemployment rate rose to 3.1% at the end of 1999. To help ease the deteriorating unemployment situation, the government has taken measures to create more jobs, speeding up the development of the private sector and providing training to the displaced workers. By the end of September 1999, more than 668 cities and 1,638 counties established a minimum-income guarantee system. To alleviate the social pressure of rising unemployment, the central government will continue to accelerate its social security system reforms.

Collective-owned enterprises are mostly located in rural areas and are concentrated in industries with lower demands for capital and technology, or those which are more consumer oriented. These enterprises are not subject to strict control, and are only under the guidance of the State Plan. This allows them more operational flexibility than state-owned enterprises, but entitles them to fewer state subsidies. In 1999, collective-owned enterprises accounted for 38.5% of total industrial production output and 18.2% of national retail sales.

China's private sector expanded rapidly and experienced healthy development in recent years. At the end of 1999, there were more than 1.1 million private-owned enterprises and three million individually run businesses, which employed more than 80 million workers. In 1999, about 51.5% of the country's retail sales of consumer goods and 33% of industrial output were generated by the private sector (including domestic individually-owned and foreign-owned enterprises). The status and economic contribution of private enterprises are officially recognized after the constitutional amendment endorsed in the 9th National People's Congress held in March 1999. Private firms are increasingly being treated equally as state firms in terms of obtaining bank credits and acquiring state assets.

Industrial structure

Since the establishment of the People's Republic of China in 1949, great efforts have been made to carry out the industrialization process and the eradication of poverty, based upon a former Soviet model of the central planning system and industrialization process, although there were some modifications of the system since the 1960s. Prior to early 1980s, development effort on industrialization was focused on the establishment of a heavy industrial base as

well as a comprehensive range of modern industries. As China entered a new economic stage since 1978, she has adopted a series of policies and measures to develop light industry, expanding the import of high-quality consumer goods, strengthening the basic industries and facilities and devoting to the development of tertiary industries, so as to make China's economic structure more coordinated and balanced (Note: The traditional approach to industrial classification sees the economy made up of a hierarchy of sectors, industries and firms. The primary sector consists of agriculture, forestry, fishing and mining industries. The secondary sector consists of manufacturing industries; and the tertiary sector consists of service industries. (refer to *"Share of GDP of Economic Sectors"* and *"Share of Employment of Economic Sectors"*).

The relations between different industries and within industries in terms of proportion have been clearly improved since the start of economic reforms. The proportion of primary industry has declined, while those of the secondary and tertiary industries have grown. Formerly, growth of the overall national economy was mainly driven by the primary and secondary industries, but now it is being driven by the secondary and tertiary industries. Actually, the growth of secondary industries is now the main growth engine of China's economy.

The internal structure of each industry category has also changed greatly. In the total output value of agriculture, forestry, animal husbandry and fisheries, the proportion of pure agriculture has declined, while that of forestry, animal husbandry and fisheries has grown. The structure of light and heavy industries has shifted from the light-pattern structure stressing "consumption compensation" to the heavy-pattern structure of "investment guidance".

Within the tertiary industry, the proportion of the traditional industries, such as communications, transportation and

Share of GDP of Economic Sectors

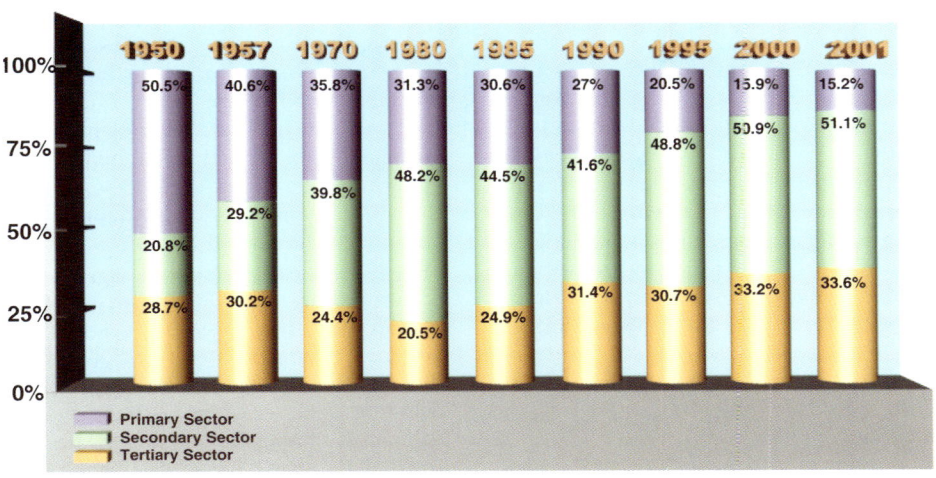

Share of Employment of Economic Sectors

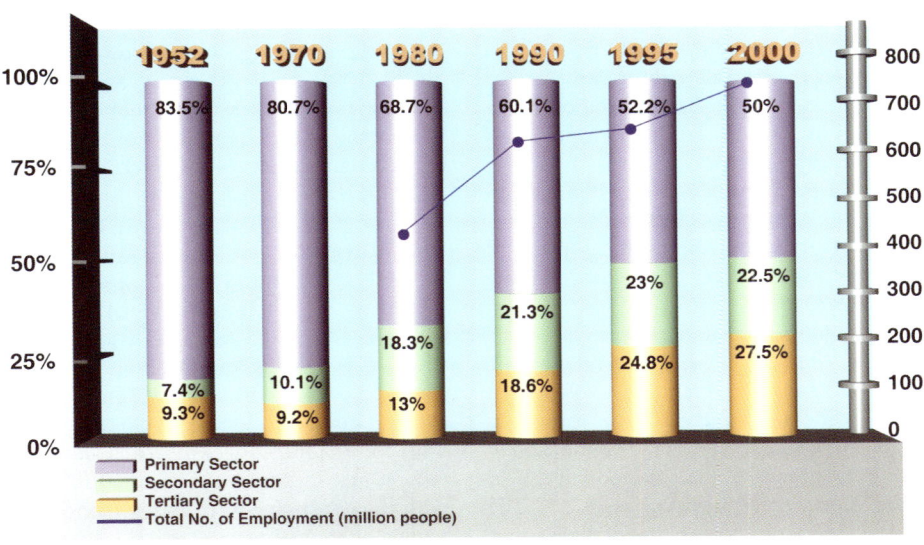

commerce, has declined, while real estate, banking, insurance and telecommunications, have developed rapidly.

Economic development in different regions

Since 1986, China has been classified into three parts: Eastern, Middle and Western regions. The Eastern region includes relatively developed coastal provinces and municipalities such as Beijing, Tianjin, Shanghai, Hebei, Liaoning, Zhejiang, Jiangsu, Fujian, Shandong, Guangdong and Hainan. The Middle region includes Shanxi, Jilin, Heilongjiang, Anhui, Jiangxi, Henan, Hubei, Hunan and Inner Mongolia. The Western region includes Chongqing, Sichuan, Guizhou, Yunnan, Shaanxi, Gansu, Qinghai, Guangxi, Ningxia, Tibet and Xinjiang.

Industrial and manufacturing sectors were distributed nationwide. In 1999, the GDP of the industrial sector in the Eastern, Middle and Western regions accounted for 50.7%, 45.5% and 41.1% of the national total respectively. The share of primary sector in the Western region (23.5%), is higher than that in the Eastern region (12.5%). The Western region has a higher share of production of raw materials and some heavy industries, while the Eastern region has a higher share of high value-added manufacturing goods.

During the Ninth Five-Year Plan period (1996-2000), China has made great achievements in narrowing the social and economic gaps between its Eastern, Middle and Western areas.

Due to the central government's favorable policies, the Middle and Western areas, which are considered under-developed in China, witnessed rapid economic growth in the past five years. The average annual GDP growth rate in western areas stood at 9.77%. In the Middle areas the rate was 10.10%. The growth rates were close to that of the Eastern region, which stood at 10.43%.

Countrywide, 13 provinces and autonomous regions in the Middle and Western regions achieved higher economic growth than the national average during the Ninth Five-Year Plan period, while only eight provinces and autonomous regions managed to exceed the average during the Eighth Five-Year Plan period (1991-95).

Many of the newly prosperous provinces and regions are located in the middle and western parts of China. A few cities such as Xi'an, Chongqing, Chengdu, Urumqi and Kunming have become economic powerhouses in these areas.

Accounting for 34.7% of the country's total in 1996, fixed assets investment in western China accounted for 38.8% of the total in 1999. A number of key projects, including the Three Gorges Dam project, the Nanning-Kunming Railway and the Beijing-Kowloon Railway, have been launched since 1996. These key projects have greatly improved the infrastructure in central and western areas, which help the areas' economic development.

Macroeconomic policies

In the past two decades, China succeeded in obtaining an average annual growth rate of about 10%, while the average annual inflation rate has been kept under 3% during most of the years. One of the most important contributing factors is macroeconomic regulation of the Chinese government.

Monetary policies

In 1991, the country's GDP growth rate picked up to 9.5% from 3.8% in 1990, when China registered the lowest GDP growth rate since 1978. During the 8th Five-Year Plan Period (1991-1995), China achieved an average annual economic growth rate of 12%, with tremendous success. Yet at the same time it also experienced serious inflation, with the consumer price index rising at an annual average rate of 12.9%.

In the middle of 1993, the government began to tighten its macroeconomic policy to clamp down on inflation. The measures include: (1) Clearing and withdrawing unauthorized loans, (2) Raising the interest rate and pegging the returns on long-term deposits to inflation to encourage the public to hold more illiquid savings deposit, (3) Controlling the growth of bank credits (the counterpart of the money supply), administrative orders were issued to restrain construction works and investment in real estate and property development.

As a result, the growth rate of M1 declined from 34% in the first half of 1993 to about 20% later in the year. However, the growth rate of M2 was still high and the inflation continued to worsen, and even reached a peak of 24.1% in 1994. It was attributable to three factors. The first was the laggard effect of previous years' excess demand which had resulted from excessive growth of the money supply. The second was price liberalization, implemented by the government in the middle of 1994. The third was related to the sterilization policy adopted by the central bank, the People's Bank of China (PBC).

In view of this problem, the government began to pursue moderately tight fiscal and monetary policies from 1995. The PBC adopted a variety of monetary policies to exercise strict controls over the total currency credit. The increase in broad money hit 34.5% in 1994, but it began to fall year by year after 1995, dropping to 17.3% in 1997. Moreover, the retail price and the consumer price plunged to 0.8% and 2.8% respectively in 1997. Yet China still maintained an 8.8% economic growth rate that year. The moderately tight monetary policy played a significant role in curtailing inflation.

However, in late 1997, signs of lack of effective demand became prevalent. Many surveys showed that there were excess supplies of goods in almost all markets, and capacity utilization rates were low for almost all industries. In 1998, China encountered a situation never before experienced— deflation. China's export dropped due to the impact of the Asian financial crisis and the price level continued to fall. To deal with the rapid deterioration of the domestic economy, the government made adjustments to its monetary policies, making comprehensive use of various types of monetary policy instruments and appropriately increasing money supply. These measures included reducing interest rates seven times, lowering the deposit reserve ratio twice, expanding open market operations, vigorously adjusting credit policy and expanding commercial banks credit scope.

These ensured a moderate increase in money supply and loans. In 1998 and 1999, the broad money supply shot up 15.3% and 14.7% respectively, and loans extended by financial institutions surged to RMB1.1 trillion and RMB1.08 trillion respectively. The increased money supply and loans were basically compatible with economic growth. The monetary policy contributed to warding off deflation and ensuring sustained and rapid growth of the national economy.

Meanwhile, efforts were made to promote the reform of the monetary policy mechanism. Marked primarily by relaxing management of the loan scale and the expansion of open market operations, the monetary policy had shifted from direct to indirect control within three years of the regulation. In 1998, RMB192 billion of base money was issued via open market operations, accounting for 52% of the increased amount of base money that year. In 2000, more than RMB300 billion of net base money was withdrawn via open market operations. This practice played a major role in controlling the issue of base money and money supply. Open market operations have now become a principal instrument of the routine operation of the central bank to pursue.

Moreover, efforts were made to reform the deposit reserve system and the mechanism for forming the rediscount rate, relaxing the rediscount rate, realizing the market oriented issue of financial bonds of policy-based banks and national debts, deregulating interest rates on foreign currency loans and reforming the system of interest rates on foreign currency deposits. Work was also done to increase the floating range of interest rates on RMB loans extended to small and medium-sized enterprises, to improve the re-lending administration procedures and to perfect a series of rules, regulations and systems regarding management of money markets, all of which led to a great change in the monetary policy's transmission mechanism.

Despite these positive changes, the reform of the country's monetary policy mechanism is far from complete. The central bank's ability to use indirect policy instruments such as open market operations is still very limited; the relaxation of interest rate is still on the agenda; commercial banks are still overburdened by the large volume of non-performing loans made by state-owned enterprises and prudential regulations are not yet fully in place.

Fiscal policies

In 1993, the government decided to strengthen its macro-control to cool down the overheated economy and fight inflation. After three years, the economy achieved a soft landing. But at the end of the first quarter in 1998, the impact of the Asian financial turmoil coupled with the domestic economic downturn exerted great pressure to expand domestic demand. Since the second half of 1998, while maintaining the monetary policy to ensure appropriate money supply, the authority has shifted the emphasis of macroeconomic mechanism from monetary policy to fiscal policy. A series of proactive expansionary fiscal policies were employed to stimulate economic growth and expand domestic demand. These measures include:

• Issuing long-term treasury bonds to sponsor a number of large scale infrastructure projects that are fundamental to long term economic development, for example, agriculture, forestry and water conservancy facilities, transport and communications, urban infrastructure, environmental protection, reparation and technical upgrading of key industries.

• Granting preferential taxation policies to expand domestic demands and spur exports. Priorities were given to the projects already under construction and the projects in the middle and western areas in order to avoid recurrence of repetitive construction and increase the efficiency of capital use.

From 1998, the export tax rebate rate has been raised several times. It has been raised to more than 15%. In 2000, the total tax rebate amounted to RMB81.1 billion, a 29.2% increase compared with that of the previous year. From the second half of 1999, the tax to adjust the fixed asset investment propensity has been cut by half. Starting from 2000, it was halted to encourage investment. In addition, from 1 August 1999, a tax cut was implemented in the business tax, contract tax and the land value added tax of the real estate sector. From 1 January 2000, the business tax rate for foreign enterprises investing in those preferred sectors in the middle and western areas was also reduced to 15% for another three years after the legal tax holiday expires and the tax rate for export oriented foreign funded enterprises was reduced to 10%, if their export volume accounted for over 70% of their total value of output.

• Since 1999, the State has adjusted the income distribution to increase the income of urban and rural residents and expand domestic demand. The focus was to increase the income of medium-and low-income residents by raising the bottom line of the social security network and increasing the salary of public servants. At the same time, the old age pension level was raised and the problem of defaulting the pension handing out for State-owned enterprise retirees was solved. The State has also found various ways to lessen farmers' financial burden and increase their income to expand the stagnant rural market.

Due to the adoption of expansionary fiscal policy, China's budget deficit/GDP ratio at the end of 2001 jumped by 3.3 times, compared with the end of 1997 (refer to "The Chinese Government's Fiscal Position").

In 2000, while the government continued its expansionary fiscal policy, a new feature emerged. The tax revenue increased dramatically. Government revenue rose to RMB1,338 billion (USD162.2 billion), a 17.6% increase over the previous year. This rapid increase in tax revenue was attributable to an improved macroeconomic situation, the improvement in tax collection, the increase in exports and imports and the increase in stamp tax on transactions in the stock markets.

In considering China's fiscal sustainability, one important factor must be taken into consideration, that is, the savings behavior of Chinese households. One of the most important features of the Chinese economy is the high savings rate of Chinese households. Its 37.4% gross national savings rate since 1978 has been supported by cultural tradition and rising personal incomes. As long as this savings behavior does not change much, the government will encounter no serious problem in selling government bonds.

On the whole, the proactive policy has produced remarkable effects. Starting from 1998, the accumulated RMB360 billion (USD43.6 billion) long-term treasury bonds issued and the RMB750 billion (USD90.9 billion) matching funds raised by localities, departments and enterprises and loans granted by banks have played a big role in accelerating economic growth. A total of 6,620 projects have been budgeted with a

The Chinese Government's Fiscal Position

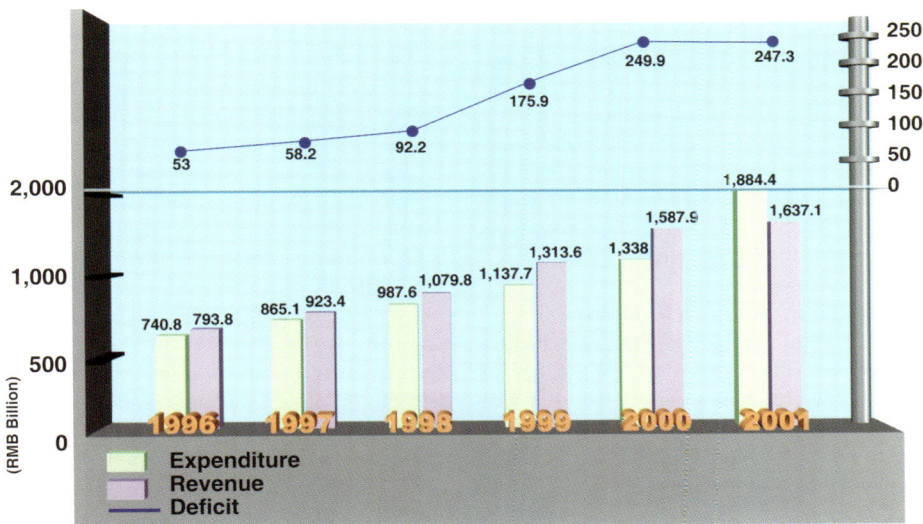

total investment of RMB2,400 billion (USD290.9 billion). In 1998, the projects financed with treasury bonds contributed 1.5% to the economic growth rate. In 1999, the figure was 2% and in 2000, it was 1.7%.

Assisted by the treasury bonds, more embankment projects along major lakes and rivers were built and the projects that were destroyed by floods have been repaired. From 1998 to 2000, 16,369 km of dykes and dams were reinforced, 25 multi-purpose water controlling projects were completed, 75 flawed reservoirs were repaired, and 22 security zones in the flood ridden areas were built. Besides, the bonds also helped develop 4.3 million hectare water-saving irrigation areas, which helped local campaigns of returning some cultivated land to lake to maintain the ecological balance along the Yangtze River and building towns for displaced people.

The treasury bonds also greatly improved the transportation system. The period from 1998 to the present has witnessed the fastest development of highways, railways and civil aviation. About 174,000 kilometers of highway have been built, including 10,230 km express highway. Now China's total highway mileage is 1.7 million km and the express highway mileage is 19,300 km. The expansion of domestic investment also promoted technical innovation and industrial upgrading. Projects on high-tech industrialization, new materials, information network and high-tech industrialization projects have made great progress. By the end of 2000, 68 high-tech industrialization projects had been completed.

Macroeconomic policy outlook

In the National People's Congress (NPC) opened in March 2002, China's Finance Minister Xiang Huaicheng delivered the report on the implementation of the Central and Local Budgets for 2001 and on the Draft Central and Local Budgets for 2002.

The report stated that, in 2001, both China's fiscal revenue and expenditure exceeded the budget targets, and the deficit of the central authorities was kept within the budgeted size. In t h e same year, China continued to implement a proactive fiscal policy, issued a total of RMB150 billion (USD18.18 billion) of long-term treasury bonds. The use of the funds from treasury bonds helped to ensure the timely construction of some major development projects in the western region, such as the Qinghai-Tibet Railway and projects to transport electricity from the west to the east. In addition, some of these funds were used to accelerate a number of major projects under construction. Deficit in the central budget for 2001 totaled RMB259.8 billion (USD31.49 billion), accounting for 2.7% of GDP, and outstanding debts totaled RMB1.56 trillion, 16.3% of GDP, all of which are still within safe limits.

The report also made it clear that China will continue to stimulate domestic demand by following a proactive fiscal policy, appropriately increase expenditures and strive to promote sustained, rapid and sound development of the national economy in 2002. About RMB150 billion (USD18.18 million) of treasury bonds will be issued in 2002.

Meanwhile, the report of the People's Bank of China (PBC) on the implementation of the monetary policy in 2001 said that China's monetary policy also attained its stated goals. By the end of 2001, there were RMB15.8 trillion in outstanding broad money (M2), up 14.4% from the previous year; RMB6 trillion in narrow money (M1), up 12.7%; and money in circulation (M0) reached RMB1.6 trillion, up 7.1%. At the same time, outstanding deposits stood at RMB14.4 trillion, up 16% from the previous year. Of these, corporate deposits made up RMB5.2 trillion, while individual savings were RMB7.4 trillion. The outstanding loans were RMB11.2 trillion, up 11.6% from the previous year. Loans to agriculture, individual consumption and note discount saw big increases, which helped to rationalize loan structures. The report also revealed that the country's foreign exchange reserves in 2001 were USD212.2 billion, up USD46.6 billion from the previous year.

The PBC's report also announced that it will continue pursuing steady monetary policies while maintaining the exchange rate of the Renminbi (RMB) in 2002. The supply amount of M2 and M1 is targeted to be increased by about 13%, while investment of M0 is not to exceed RMB150 billion and credit amount of all financial institutions to be increased by about RMB1,300 billion (USD157.66 billion). The main tasks of monetary policies in 2002 are to "ensure a proper growth money supply, give a full play to the guiding function of credit policies so as to direct credit flow and promote the adjustment of economic structure, further reform state-owned commercial banks, enhance the concept of credit sales and straighten out the transmitting system of monetary policies, strengthen investigations and study, and exchange and transmit related information of the implementation of currency credit in time".

FOREIGN TRADE

Economic reforms have made China a major trading power. Chinese exports rose from USD13.6 billion in 1979 to nearly USD249.2 billion in 2001, while imports grew from USD15.6 billion to USD225.1 billion. Among world nations, China's rank as a trading power rose from 27th in 1979 to 7th in 2001 — after the US, Japan, Germany, the UK and France. Historically, China has run trade deficits in some years, but during the past eight years, China's foreign trade continued the momentum of rapid growth and enjoyed surplus despite the impact of the Asian

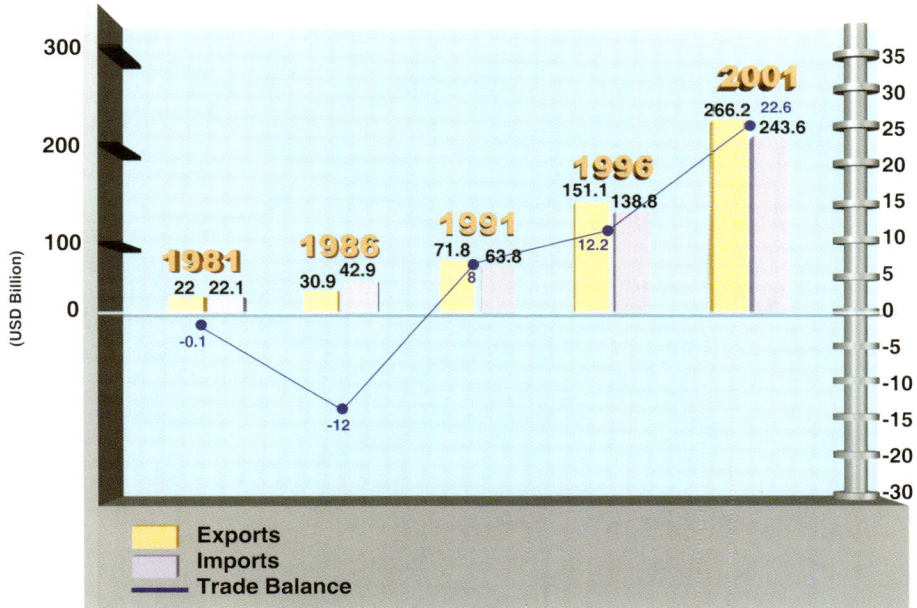

China's Foreign Commodity Trade

financial crisis (refer to *"China's Foreign Commodity Trade"*). Merchandise trade surplus and large scale foreign investment have enabled China to accumulate the world's second largest foreign exchange reserves, USD233.8 billion in total by the end of April 2002.

The rapid growth of foreign trade further promoted the integration of the Chinese economy with the world economy. The index of economic dependence on trade rose from 40.2% in 1995 to 44.5% in 2000, rising 4.3 % points.

China's major trading partners
China's trade data often differ significantly from those of its major trading partners. This is due to the fact that a large share of China's trade (both exports and imports) passes through Hong Kong (which reverted back to Chinese rule in July 1997, but is treated as a separate customs area by most countries, including China and the United States). China treats a large share of its exports through Hong Kong as Chinese exports to Hong Kong for statistical purposes, while many countries that import Chinese products through Hong Kong generally attribute their origin to China for statistical purposes.

In 2001, China's top five trading partners were Japan, the United States, the European Union nations, Hong Kong, and ASEAN countries (refer to *"China's Major Trading Partners 2001"*).

Foreign trade structure
Over the past two decades, China's import and export commodity trade has gone through great changes.

Constant improvement

China's Major Trading Partners 2001

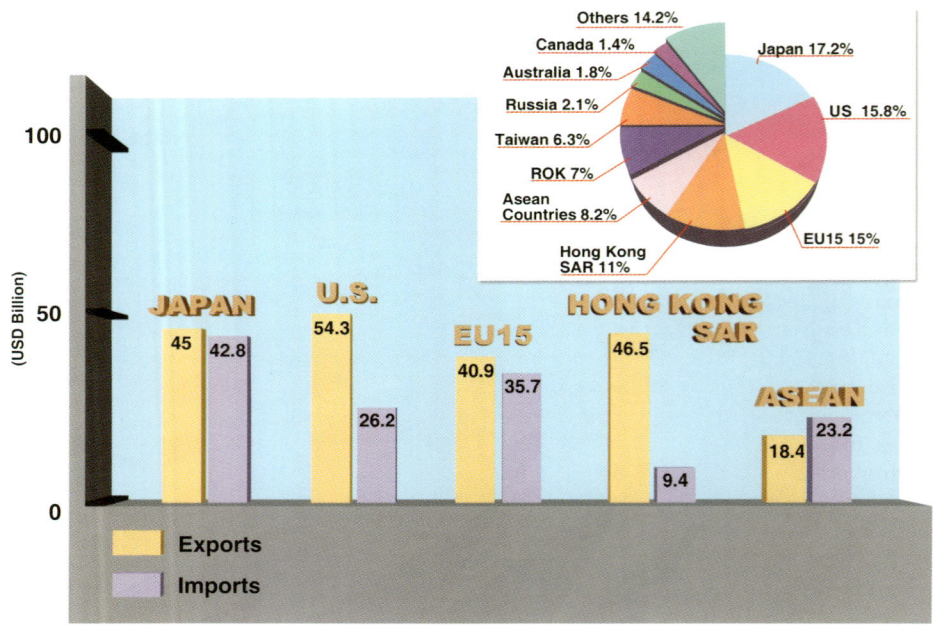

BUILDING A SUCCESSFUL PLANT IN CHINA

The structure of import and export commodities has been constantly improved. China's abundance of cheap labor has made it internationally competitive in many low cost, labor-intensive manufactures. As a result, manufactured products comprise an increasingly large share of China's trade. The share of Chinese manufactured exports to total exports rose from 50% in 1980 to 91% in 2001, while manufactured imports as a share of total imports rose from 65% to 82%. A large share of China's manufactured imports consists of intermediates (e.g., chemicals, electronic components and textile machinery) used in manufacturing products in China, while its major exports are finished products (e.g., apparel and clothing, electrical machinery, equipment and toys).

The export volume of primary products, with food, agricultural and sideline products, and crude oil as the mainstay, has been greatly reduced — from 53.5% of the total export volume in 1978 to 9.0% in 2001; and the proportion of industrial products increased from 46.5% in 1978 to 91% in 2001.

Remarkable progress has been achieved in the export of machinery and electrical products, rising from USD1.41 billion in 1980 to USD8.7 billion in 2001. For six consecutive years since 1995, machinery and electronic equipment have been China's largest exports, helping the country make big strides towards becoming one of the world's major manufacturers.

Customs statistics show that between January and October 2001, exports and imports of electromechanical products stood at USD194.47 billion, 15.6% up compared with the same period in 2000, and making up about 46.59% of China's total foreign trade value. In the breakdown, gross exports of electromechanical products went up 12.2% to USD96.24 billion, in comparison to the 6.1% growth rate of total exports.

Electromechanical products have contributed much to China's improvement in world ranking for foreign trade from 32nd in 1978 to 7th in 2001. In addition, among all imports of electromechanical products, 97.8% were technology-intensive products including machinery, electronic products and equipment. The proportion for exports of such products was 91.18%.

New factors

Foreign-invested enterprises have become new factors contributing to the growth of China's foreign commodity trade. In 1981, the export value of foreign-invested enterprises (FIEs) made up only 0.1% of China's total exports, and 0.5% of the total import volume. In 2000, the export of FIEs stood at USD119.44 billion, making up 47.9% of China's total exports, while the imports made by FIEs reached USD117.27 billion, 52.1% of total imports.

Diversification and expansion

China's international trade market is becoming more diversified. In 1980, nearly 180 countries and regions had trade relationships with China. This figure rose to 228 in 1999. Along with the recovery of the Asian economy, China's exports to other Asian countries restored growth, and its exports to North America, Europe, Oceania and Africa also grew.

New trading forms

Foreign trade has been expanded through various trading forms. Processing trade and small-scale border trade have increased by a large margin. Ordinary trade, processing and assembling with supplied or imported materials, and small-scale border trade are competing with each other for development.

China's major foreign trade relations

Canada

There have been non-governmental trade activities between China and Canada since the 1950s, and the formal trade relationship started with the China-Canada Wheat

Agreement signed in 1961. Canada is one of the earliest western countries to establish a diplomatic relationship with China. In a period of two decades, the original simple bilateral trade relationship has grown into an all-dimensional economic and technical cooperation. On 26 November 1999, the two parties signed the China-Canada Agreement on Bilateral Market Access for China's accession to the World Trade Organization (WTO).

According to the statistics of China Customs in 2001, the volume of China-Canada bilateral trade was USD7,375 million, 6.7% higher than that in the previous year; China exported USD3,346 million, up 6.0%, and imported USD4,028 million, up 7.4%. Canada ranks tenth among China's trade partners.

Canada began to invest in China directly in 1980. By the end of 1999, there were 4,328 approved Canadian direct investment projects in China. The committed Canadian amount was USD7,041 million, out of which USD2,057 million has been paid up. From January to June 2000, Canada set up 180 new investment projects in China, the contractual volume was USD463 million, out of which USD150 million has been paid up.

The Canadian fund enterprises are scattered in more than 20 provinces, municipalities and autonomous regions. The major industries are petroleum, machinery, electronics, communication, chemicals, light industry, food, textile, farming, aquiculture, real estate, finance and assurance and public service, etc. Production-oriented projects account for around 80%.

European Union (EU)

The EU has all along been one of the major suppliers of funds and technology in China's economic development. Since early 1990s, EU-China trade relations have entered a new stage, thanks to the EU-China political relations. In 1994, the EU launched its new Asia strategy and adopted a series of China-oriented policies. The landmark 1998 "Building a Comprehensive Partnership with China," raised China's trade status with the EU to the same level as the United States, Russia and Japan. Due to the mutual efforts made by the two sides, bilateral trade has increased 29-fold. The EU has become China's third largest trading partner, while China has also become the EU's third largest trade partner, behind the United States and Japan.

According to the statistics of China Customs in 2001, the volume of China-EU bilateral trade was USD76.6 billion, 11% higher than that in the previous year, with China exporting USD40.9 billion, up 7.1%, and importing USD35.7 billion, up 15.8%.

EU's investment in China has grown steadily since early 1990s. By October 1999, the number of EU-invested projects reached 10,025, involving a total contractual investment of USD39.61 billion, and materialized investment was USD20.74 billion.

Between January and October 1999, the EU invested in 695 projects in China, but the contractual investment dropped 35.2% to USD3.26 billion, and the arrived investment slipped 4.4% to USD3.33 billion.

One feature of the EU's investment is that most of EU-invested projects involve huge investments and are of high technical standards. In addition, the EU is a major source of China's technology imports. In the first nine months of 1999, the country imported a total of 280 items of technology from EU member nations, with a contractual value of USD2.457 billion and accounting for 65.8% of all technology imports in the period.

Japan

Sino-Japanese economic and trade relation plays an essential role in the economic and trade relations between the two nations. As key economic and trade partners to each other, Japan has, for the past eight years, been China's biggest trade partner. China is the second largest trade partner to Japan. Japan is also the main source nation from which China absorbs foreign investment and introduces technologies. Japan is also the biggest provider of governmental loan and gratuitous assistance to China.

In 2001, bilateral merchandise trade value hit a record of USD87.7 billion, up 5.5% from that of the previous year, of which exports accounted for USD44.9 billion, up 7.9% and imports USD42.8 billion, up 3.1%.

The major commodities exported to Japan are electronic and machinery products, shoes, garments and accessories, textile yarn, vegetable, aquatic products, raw oil, tourist products etc, while the major imports from Japan were electronic and machinery products, integrated circuit and microelectronic components, steel, primary shaped plastics, automatic data processing equipment and components, etc.

Japanese investment in China reached its peak in 1995 and then went on a downward slide. The total investment in 1999 was, on a yen basis, at 83.8 billion, less than a fifth of what it was at its peak. But this downward trend has seen a shift since the fall of 1999. According to Chinese statistics, direct Japanese investment in the first quarter of 2000 increased by 20% over the previous year, a sign that the investment decrease that had started in 1996 was coming to an end. By the end of 2000, the realized investment value from Japan is USD27.8 billion, 7.98% of the total foreign investment in China, which made Japan the third largest investment source for China.

Republic of Korea (ROK)

Since the establishment of diplomatic relations between China and ROK in 1992, the bilateral trade has seen rapid developing growth. In 2001, the total volume of China-ROK bilateral trade reached USD35.9 billion, 4.1% higher than that of 2000, of which China's export accounted for USD12.5 billion, up 10.9%, and import USD23.4 billion, up 0.8%. ROK now is China's sixth largest trading partner.

As to the export and import commodity structure, for many years, China's principal exports to ROK focused on textiles, raw materials, crude oil and finished products, corn, coal and other raw materials. Other large commodities included raw materials for chemical industry, steel, leather products, footwear, foodstuff, machinery and electric facility. In recent years, high value-added products account more in export to ROK, such as electronic parts. China's principal imports from ROK include chemical products, electronic products, paper sheets, steel, etc.

Since the outbreak of the financial crisis at the end of 1997, ROK investment to China has seen a continuous decline. With the alleviation of the crisis, newly signed ROK investment contracts to China increased dramatically, but the fulfillment of investment is still sliding. From January to April 2000, the number of approved ROK investment projects coming into China reached 623, contractual investment USD543 million, fulfilling USD306 million, the increasing rates are respectively 46.24%, 21.3% and -28.68%, compared to the same period of the previous year. By the end of April 2000, the total approved ROK investment projects entering China reached 13,448, with a contractual investment of USD16.92 billion and utilized investment of USD9.05 billion. ROK investment mainly focuses on the areas of manufacture (fiber, costume, electronic and appliance assembling, footwear making, petrochemical product, food and beverage industry), transportation, mining and construction, trade, real estate, etc.

Singapore

In 1979, China and Singapore signed a trade agreement under which Singapore revoked a trade licensing system imposed on China, which signaled that the bilateral economic and trade relation between the two countries had entered a new era. Over the past years, trade between China and Singapore developed rapidly. The bilateral trade volume was USD7.35 billion in 1996 and rose to USD12.47 billion in 2000, of which imports from China accounts for USD7.10 billion while exports to China are USD5.37 billion. Being the largest trading partner of China among ASEAN countries, Singapore is a traditional market for Chinese export of textiles, cereals, edible oils, foodstuff, native produce and petrochemical products. In recent years, China has increased its export of mechanical and electrical products, telecom equipment, electronic components, metals, minerals, vessels, foodstuff, textiles and garments to Singapore.

Since the establishment of diplomatic relations in 1990, Singapore has been keeping up a good momentum of investment in China. In 2000, Singapore is the fifth largest foreign investment source for China in terms of actual investment. With the robust economic recovery of Southeast Asian countries in 1999, the down trend of the investment of Singapore to China since 1995 was reversed. By the end of 2000, the number of investment projects in China totaled 9,111 with a contractual amount of USD35.29 billion and an actual amount of USD16.9 billion. Investment covers areas such as machinery manufacturing, industrial and agricultural production and food processing, rubber production, textile and electronics.

The major projects invested in China include Suzhou Industrial Park (SIP), Wuxi Industrial Park, Shanghai Sanlincheng Housing Development project and Dalian Container Wharf. By the end of January 2001, SIP had attracted a contractual amount of foreign investment of USD7.9 billion and an actual investment amount of USD4.04 billion. Average investment value of these projects exceeded USD30 million.

The United States

In 1972, President Nixon made his historic visit to China and opened the door for China-US relationship. The two countries established diplomatic ties in 1979. In early 1980s, a series of industrial cooperation agreements were signed and the framework of ministerial dialogues, namely, the Joint Commission on Commerce and Trade, the Joint Economic Commission and the Joint Commission on Science and Technology, were also established.

In 2001, China-US bilateral trade reached USD80.5 billion, over 30 times of that in 1979, of which China's exports accounted for USD54.3 billion and imports USD26.2 billion. The United States is now the second largest trading partner and import source of China, while China is the fourth largest trade partner of the US.

Chinese imports from the United States include agricultural products, aircraft, power generation equipment, oil equipment, machinery and electronics, etc. US imports from China include textiles and garments, footwear, toys, home appliances, general machinery tools, hardware, lighting products, furniture, etc. Apart from commodity trade, China also imported technology from the US, mainly in auto-making technology, complete set of power generation and telecommunication equipment.

The scale and fields of US direct investment in China is expanding year by year. By the end of 2000, the number of approved projects involving US investment totaled 31,181, with a contractual US capital of USD60.3 billion and actual input of USD30.1 billion. Fields of US investment in China range from machinery, power generation, oil exploration, petrochemicals, pharmaceuticals, real estate, as well as newly opened up sectors, such as banking, insurance, foreign trade, accounting and freight transport.

Chinese companies are also active in

investments in the United States. Fields of Chinese investment in the US range from garment manufacturing, home appliance manufacturing, restaurants, transportation, travel service, etc.

Influences of WTO Entry on China's Foreign Trade

China's foreign trade is administered by the Ministry of Foreign Trade and Economic Relations (MOFTEC). A major function of MOFTEC is to exercise macro-control and economic adjustment to China's foreign trade. Like the country's economy, China's foreign trade is in the period of changing from a planned economy to a market economy. Under the planned economy, foreign trade was operated exclusively by the state. The prices of import and export commodities were set by the state. Profits and losses in the foreign trade had nothing directly to do with the interests of export companies. With the opening-up and reform of China's economy, more and more companies, enterprises, institutes and other entities, even private sectors have obtained MOFTEC approval to autonomously engage in international business, as long as they meet certain criteria. Those business entities are fully self-governed, and the government now does not subsidize any company which loses in business.

China's WTO entry gives new impetus to China's foreign trade. The WTO rules stipulate that its members should abide by the principle of non-discrimination and most-favored nation treatment. As a result, the entry into WTO has several impacts on China's foreign trade administration, including tariff reduction, a lift of import quota restrictions and easing of market entry criteria. China's WTO membership will push the country to further open its markets, improve investment environments and provide foreign investors with national treatment.

Import tariffs

After WTO accession, China will lower the import tariff barriers to fulfill its WTO commitments. In fact, since the 1990s, China has already cut tariffs five times between 1992 and 1999, lowering the average import tariff level from 43% to 17%. If various kinds of tariff concessions are taken into consideration, the country's actual tariff level is far below 15%.

In December 2001, when the Chinese government signed the protocol on China's accession to the WTO, more solid steps were announced, including cutting the country's general level of tariff duties from the previous 15.3% to 12%, starting from 1 January 2002. The average tariff rate of industrial products is lowered to 11. 6%. The average tariff rate of agricultural products, excluding aquatic products, is lowered to 15.8%, while that of aquatic products is lowered to 14.3%.

In 2002, the tariff rates of 5,300 items, or 73% of the total items of tariffs, are to be cut, that of crude oil and refined oil is lowered to 6.1%, timber, paper and paper products to 8.9%, textile and garments to 17.6%, chemical products to 7.9%, transport vehicles to 17.4%, machinery to 9.6% and electronic products to 10.7%. By 1 July 2006, the tariff on automobiles will be cut from the current 80%-100% to 25%, and automobile parts to an average of 10%. As a member of Information Technology Agreement (ITA), China is also committed to lower the present tariff of high-tech products, such as PC, telecommunication equipment, semi-conductor and else, from 13.3% to 0% by 2005.

China promised that the general tariff level would be reduced to 10% by 2005. The average tariff level of all WTO members is now about 6%. It stands at 3% in developed countries and 10% in developing ones.

Non-tariff barriers

Non-tariff measures on imports are to be

reduced after China's entry into WTO. China will gradually revoke quota requirements from foreign trade products and export subsidies within three to five years after WTO accession. Imported quotas of industrial products, automobiles and automotive components, for example, are to be phased out by 2005. Quotas of textile will also be eliminated by 31 December 2004. Average quotas of agriculture products will be reduced to 15% by January 2004. Quotas will be reserved to wheat, corn, cotton, barley and rice. Other than state trading, private enterprises can also share the imported quota. Export subsidies of agricultural products will be eliminated. Government's support to agriculture industry cannot exceed 8.5% of the total product value of the same year. State-controlled bean oil trading will be phased out. In addition, import and export quotas on all products covered by ITA were eliminated upon WTO accession.

Only eight sensitive products, including crude oil, finished oil, chemical fertilizer, basic food, cotton, vegetable oil, sugar, tobacco etc, are reserved to state trading management, which is limited to a few designated companies for import and export.

Export subsidies

After becoming a full member of WTO, most of the export subsidies adopted by China to encourage exports will be eliminated, more agricultural produce, agricultural production goods, chemical fiber, automobiles, iron and steels and other products will be imported, and the export by related industries will be restrained, which will exert influence on the export of related foreign trade enterprises. At present, foreign businesses are mostly concerned about industries such as iron and steel, raw coal, and simple finished products (such as bicycles and hardware), which have been granted export subsidies for a long time.

Import and distribution rights

By joining the WTO, China will see the opening up of import and distribution rights. Currently, the granting of operational rights in foreign trade is somewhat liberal. The traditional foreign trade companies are confined to such products as light industrial products, light textiles, staple raw materials, petrochemicals, and monopolized products. Within three years after WTO accession, the restrictions on trading rights will be phased out, while distribution rights will first be granted for wholesale, transportation and maintenance. Restriction of distribution service in most other areas will be also eliminated within three years. China is also committed to phasing out limitation in leasing, carrier, cargo shipment, advertisement, consulting and packaging services in three to four years.

Commodity inspection

China is expected to improve its commodity inspection system with its entry into WTO. In March 1998, the State Council announced that the former State Administration for the Inspection of Import and Export Commodities, the former Animal & Plant Quarantine Service under the Ministry of Agriculture, and the former Health & Quarantine Bureau under the Ministry of Health, were combined to form the State Administration for Entry-Exit Inspection and Quarantine. A new "Law on Inspection of Commodity Imports and Exports" was promulgated on 28 April 2002 and will come into force on 1 October 2002. The amended law provides for a system of certification for imports and exports. Domestic and foreign inspection organizations are to be licensed instead of accredited. The amendments add a new provision on confidentiality duties of commodity inspection staff. In addition, the rules on the standards have been changed.

Without
China knowledge

Your Business Grows

With
China knowledge

CHINA KNOWLEDGE PRESS PTE LTD

Website: www.chinaknowledge-press.com Email: info@chinaknowledge.com

Beijing◆Chengdu◆Chongqing◆Dalian◆Guangzhou◆Hong Kong◆London◆Shanghai◆Singapore◆Suzhou◆Tianjin

Over the past two decades, China has been actively seeking foreign direct investment (FDI) and advanced technologies to promote its modernization. Meanwhile, remarkable improvements have been made, especially in recent years with entry into WTO, on its infrastructure environment, financial and legislative system to create a favorable investment environment.

TRANSPORTATION

Railway transport

Railways have led China's transportation system. By the end of 2000, China's total railway length was 68,000 km. They cover the entire area of China except Tibet. However, they are mainly in northeast and east (coastal) China. Other parts of China rely more on trunk lines. More than 80% of freight comprises raw materials and staple material, including coal, iron and steel, non-ferrous metals, metals and non-metallic ore, building materials and grain, with coal exceeding 40%. Over 1,000 passenger trains are dispatched daily.

In 2001, China's railways transported 1.78 billion tons of goods and yielded 1,424 billion ton/km in cargo turnover, up 7.6% and 6.8% respectively on the previous year. The railway sector also transported 1.016 billion passengers. The revenue from railway transportation totaled RMB134 billion, up 11.3% on the previous year.

The railway sector raised the speed limit of trains for the fourth time in 2001, extended the express lines by 4,257 km and increased the total mileage of express railways to 13,000 km. The average speed of passenger trains has reached 61.9 km/hr, and that of express trains has been increased to 92.8 km/hr. The operation time of major trains has been reduced considerably, with the highest speed of express trains hitting 160-200 km/hr.

Aside from improving the transport capacity in northeast areas, China is speeding up construction and upgrading of trunk lines in the central and western regions, where railway coverage is still poor. Major projects under construction include Xi'an-Hefei, Chongqing-Huaihua, and Qinghai-Tibet Railways. These projects have been launched successively over the past few years.

Highway transport

By the end of 2001, China had more than 1.69 million km of highways, including 19,437 km of expressways, the second longest road network in the world. Today, 99.3% of towns and 91.8% of villages have roads. Construction of eight inter-provincial gateways in the western region has been accelerated. In the first 11 months of 2001, investment in highway construction in west

China's Transportation Scale in Cargo Volume (Units: million tons)

Year	Waterways	Highways	Railways	Pipelines	Airways
1997	1,134.06	9,765.36	1,697.34	160.02	1.25
1998	1,095.55	9,760.04	1,612.43	174.19	1.40
1999	1,146.00	9,904.00	1,569.00	202.00	2.00
2000	1,223.91	10,388.13	1,744.4	187.00	1.97

China rose by 23% compared to the same period in the previous year.

Waterway transport
The coastline of mainland China is more than 18,000 km, and the rivers total 220,000 km in length. Excellent natural conditions provide convenience for developing inland river transport and ocean shipping.

Inland river transport
China's inland rivers totaled 110,300 km by end-2000, including 5,800 km of channels which can accommodate ships of 1,000 DWT. Major inland river harbors had 8,525 wharves and berths, including 44 for ships over 10,000 DWT. The Yangtze River, the Pearl River, the Heilongjiang and Huaihe Rivers and the Jinghang (Beijing-Hangzhou) Grand Canal are major inland river shipping routes.

Ocean transport
Ocean transport remains a dominant mode of transport in China, with ocean cargo turnover comprising 70% of waterway transport cargo turnover. More than 85% of China's foreign trade goods utilize ocean transport with a total cargo volume of 520 million tons in 2000.

China has more than 60 ports with 33,441 berths, of which 3,718 are located along the coast, 29,723 are at inland rivers and 810 are deep-water berths able to accommodate 10,000-tonnage ships. Goods handled in 2001 registered 2.4 billion tons, with foreign trading goods making up 25%. The top ports with an annual handling capacity exceeding 50 million tons are (in order of handling capacity) Shanghai, Ningbo, Guangzhou, Qinhuangdao, Dalian, Qingdao and Tianjin. China's top coastal ports are usually linked with the hinterland through high-grade roads or trunk railways, forming an international container system consisting of ocean transport, port loading and unloading, and inland transport.

More than 40 ports can handle container loading and unloading, and 16 have special berths for 10,000 -tonnage containers. The capacity of container ports in 2000 was 18.05 million TEUs, and China's container fleet was among the world's top four.

Shipping routes are available from China to 1,100 ports in 150 countries and regions worldwide. Since 1989, China has been elected Class A Council Country in the International Maritime Organization.

Civil aviation transport
China has 143 domestic airports and 1,115 regular air routes (including 987 international air routes) that connect to more than 132 domestic cities. Its international air routes connect to 60 cities in 34 countries and regions.

In 2001, Chinese domestic airports handled 75.2 million passengers and 1.7 million tons of cargo. 28 of these airports can each handle more than a million passengers annually. Beijing Capital International Airport, Guangzhou Baiyun International Airport, and Shanghai Hongqiao International Airport accounted for 37% of total passenger throughput. The airports can handle 3.47 million tons of mail, of which these three airports accounted for 52.7%.

COMMUNICATION
China's post and telecommunications industry has developed rapidly in recent years. Many advanced methods are used, including optical cables, high-speed networks, satellites, submarine cables, program-controlled exchanges, mobile telecommunications and data telecommunications. By the end of 2001, the total number of telephone subscribers reached 190 million, of which 61.6% were urban inhabitants. The population of mobile telephone users had reached 160 million, according to Chinese Ministry of Information Industry. The mobile roaming service covers 325 cities within China as well as 56 overseas

Fact Sheet	2001
Telephones	
fixed line	190 million
mobile	160 million
Internet international exit bandwidth	6032 MHz
Internet users	36 million
Dial-in	17 million
DDN users	436,000
Optical cable length	1.58 million km
Internet country code	cn

countries. By the end of 2001, China's overall scale of telecommunication network and users, in terms of the total number of mobile and telephone users (350 million), ranked the first in the world.

In terms of state public service telecommunications networks, by the end of 2001, the total length of optical cables reached 1.58 million km, of which long-distance cables account for 25%, linking all provincial capitals. The total capacity of program-controlled exchange system reached 200 million lines. The total number of ports for IP dial-in servers had reached 2.51 million and the number of ports for broadband service 140,000.

In addition, China has taken efforts to boost its broadband networks with advanced technologies and new cables. Notable projects include an integrated broadband multi-service network offering internet-based voice and data service, a new broadband Internet access network designed for apartment building, the manufacturing of PCs with built-in cable modems and projects involving Digital Subscriber Line (DSL), Asymmetric Digital Subscriber Line (ADSL), and High-bit-rate Digital Subscriber Line (HDSL) technology.

As for the post service, China has 102,000 post offices nationwide, and the total length of postal routes and rural mail delivery routes reaches 6.215 million km. China had direct post relations with over 150 countries and regions. All large and medium-sized cities provide international express mail service, and have developed international automatic telex, data transmission, express fax, and TV program transmission services. Besides, various services via the Internet, including e-mail and e-commerce, are now available.

Internet infrastructure in China has developed very fast too. China's Internet bandwidth of international exit has reached 5,724 megahertz in September 2001, increased significantly from 2,799 megahertz at the beginning of the year. The domestic Internet backbone and the inter-connection bandwidth between the ISPs have also been improved. The Internet users also increased quickly. It is reported by CNNIC that by the end of June 2001 there were 26.5 million Internet users in China with access through 10.02 million Internet hosts. The Second-Level Domain Name (SLD) under '.cn', China's Top-Level Domain Name (TLD), reached more than 128,000, of which '.com.cn' accounted for 78%. Local Chinese websites increased to about 243,000, of which 79% were owned by '.com.cn'.

ENERGY

Energy is an important basis for social development as well as a potential pollution source, which has great impact on the environment. Since the 1990s, the Chinese economy has sustained rapid growth rate and the scale for energy production and consumption has been continuously expanded.

Coal industry

China is the world's largest coal producer and second largest electricity producer. Coal is China's primary energy source with 988 million tons of standard coal utilized in 2000. China's reserves of high quality coal are estimated at 5,059.2 billion tons, and are mostly in north, northwest, northeast, east, and southwest China. In 2001, China's raw coal production totaled 1,110 million tons.

Power industry

By end-2001, China generated 1,478 billion kWhr of electrical power, an increase of 9.0% over 2000. The total production capacity of energy amounted to 1.17 billion ton standard coal. China's power resources are unevenly distributed. The central and western regions have large hydropower and coal reserves, whereas the eastern coastal region is relatively energy deficient. China will accelerate energy production in the central and western regions, and distribute power to the east.

Petroleum industry

In 2000, the production of crude oil and natural gas were 162.6 million tons and 27.5 billion cubic meters respectively. Its land oilfields are mainly in the east, such as Daqing, Shengli, Liaohe, Jilin, Dagang and Jianghan. Western regions are the new concentration for development, such as Xinjiang, Tarim, Turpan, Hami, Changqing and Qinghai. China's natural gas mainly comes from Sichuan, Shaanxi, Gansu, Ningxia, the Tarim Basin, the Jungar Basin, and offshore gas fields.

China's rapid economy growth has outstripped its crude oil production and China has been importing crude oil since the mid-1990s.

ENVIRONMENTAL PROTECTION

The Chinese government has been attaching greater importance to environmental protection. In the past decades, China has developed 670,000 sq km of soil-eroded areas, and the forest coverage rate has increased to 13.9%. Some achievements have also been made in natural environmental protection, with 151 model ecological zones nationwide. There are 1,146 nature reserves all over the country, including 137 national nature reserves. The largest project for the transformation of ecological environment is the "Three-Norths" (Northwest, North and Northeast) Shelterbelt Project. Following the beginning of the development of this 7,000-km "Green Great Wall" in 1978, more than 18 million hectares of areas had been afforested, 21 million hectares of fields had been protected by trees and about 20% of desertified land had been improved by 1996.

The construction of another two projects — the shelterbelts at the middle and lower reaches of the Yangtze River and the coastal shelterbelts — is being accelerated. At present, the Chinese natural ecological environment is still very weak. Water erosion, desertification and degeneration of grasslands are worsening increasingly. Hence, the Chinese government is taking measures to implement the National Program for the Construction of the Ecological Environment in an all-round way, while paying great attention to the prevention and control of pollution, and the protection of ecological environment.

Rapid growth of environmental protection industry

Over the past decades, Chinese government has been committed to controlling industrial pollution and improving the urban environment in an all-round way. China completed 22,258 scheduled environmental improvement projects, involving a total investment of RMB12.31 billion (USD1.49 billion). There are 2,364 smoke-and-dust control districts being set up in 536 cities; and 2,040 noise standardized areas were established in 431 cities.

In recent years, China has witnessed a rapid growth of its environmental protection industries. According to State Economic and Trade Commission, by 2000, there were over 10,000 enterprises in the industry employing 1.8 million workers with total output value reaching RMB108 billion (USD13.1 billion). Compared with the situation of 10 years ago, enterprises engaging in environmental protection increased by four-fold and the population of employees rose six-fold, while the annual output value grew 25 times, making the industry a new growth engine in the national economy. It is estimated that by 2005, the output value of the environmental protection industry will reach RMB200 billion (USD24.2 billion), with an annual growth rate of about 15%.

The central government has outlined the goal for ecological construction and environmental protection in the 10th Five-Year Plan (2001-2005) for national economic development. The goal is to stop further ecological deterioration in China in five years, to improve the environmental quality in cities, reduce the emission of pollutants by 10% from 2000 onwards, and make progress in conserving and protecting natural resources. According to the plan, the focus of environmental protection industry will be the development of advanced technologies, equipment, and materials for environmental protection, e.g. for desulphurization and exhaust treatment. It will also give priority to the comprehensive utilization of resources, and to the development of information, consulting and technology services.

To reach that goal, China will greatly develop the environmental protection industry. It is estimated that about RMB700 billion (USD84.8 billion), or 1.3% of the GDP, will be put into the environment sector in the period of 2001-2005, of which RMB550 billion (USD 66.6 billion) will be used for air and water pollution prevention and treatment.

The development of China's environmental protection industry will not only upgrade the overall level of Chinese enterprises in this field, but also provide a huge market and many opportunities for foreign companies. The Chinese government is committed to establish a diversified investment and financing mechanism for the industry and encourage businesses with multiple ownership.

It can be expected that, with the implementation of the plan and with Beijing's preparation for the 2008 Olympic Games, China will have a rapidly expanding market in environmental protection.

SCIENCE & TECHNOLOGY

A comprehensive network of science and technology research bodies has been established in China, comprising the Chinese Academy of Sciences (CAS), Chinese Academy of Engineering (CAE), research organizations functioning under departments of the State Council, and the local governments, research organizations operating under institutions of higher education. There are 1,319 universities and colleges all over China and over 160 academic organizations under the jurisdiction of the Chinese Science and Technology Association, with branches in large and medium-sized cities. Various kinds of research organizations are also run by industrial enterprises. There are also many national defense research organizations. Taken as a whole, these organizations form a nationwide scientific and technological network.

The Chinese Academy of Sciences, with its headquarters in Beijing, is the main research organization for the natural sciences. The divisions of mathematics, physics, chemistry, earth sciences, biology and technology have 123 research institutes in total, with over 60,000 scientific and technical personnel. Throughout the country, there are many research organs affiliated to the Chinese Academy of Sciences. In provinces, autonomous regions and municipalities where there is a concentration of such affiliates, branch academies have been set up. The 630 fellows are all high-profile scientists, professors and engineers who have made significant contributions in respective fields. The Chinese Academy of

Engineering, comprising 439 fellows, was founded in June 1994. It is the most respected academic and advisory body in the country's engineering community. In 1986, the State Natural Science Foundation Committee was established. Its task is to provide financial assistance to basic and applied research projects. Funds are allocated from the state treasury. To date, the Committee has subsidized more than 40,000 projects in various field of natural science. The Committee is presently made up of 26 members, most of whom are academics from the Chinese Academy of Sciences and the Chinese Academy of Engineering. The National Committee for Scientific and Technological Awards (NCSTA) was founded in 1999. Its main functions are to organize the National Appraisal Committee for Scientific and Technological Awards.

High and new technology

The State High-Tech Research and Development Plan, also known as the "863" plan, was implemented in 1986. It is a medium and long term plan that aims to develop technologies in the areas of biology, space, information, laser, automation, energy, new materials and oceanology on a large scale and in an organized fashion.

The Spark Program was established in 1986 with the mission of rejuvenating the rural economy with science and technology. There was a strong need to popularize scientific and technological findings in the rural areas and to apply them to villages and townships. Pilot projects included the development of crop cultivation, animal husbandry, aquaculture and the processing of agricultural products and by-products. Advanced breeding and cultivation techniques have been introduced and popularized. The program also aimed to alleviate poverty in the rural areas.

Launched in 1988, the Torch Program is meant to put research findings in advanced technologies into practical use. Since its inception, 53 state high-tech parks and nearly 100 service centers, so called incubators, have been set up. The establishment of these parks and incubators greatly facilitated the transfer of research findings into production, and spawned enterprises and servicing entrepreneurs utilizing advanced technologies. In the meantime, some development belts for high-tech industries to renovate traditional industries and speed up the development of local economy have gradually developed in some more developed regions.

FINANCIAL SYSTEM

Banking industry

In the past two decades of adopting reform and open-up policy, China's banking industry has developed from a simple banking system to a macro regulation and control system with commercial banks as the foundation. Today, China's banking system consists of the central bank – the People's Bank of China (PBC), three policy banks, 114 commercial banks, and a large number of city and rural credit cooperatives. At the end of 2001, over 190 foreign banks have been established in the Special Economic Zones (SEZs) and coastal open cities as well as in major inland cities. China's commercial banks also set up many branches abroad. Among them, the Bank of China has the largest network of overseas. In 1980, China resumed its membership status in World Bank, and rejoined the International Monetary Fund. In 1984, it established business relations with the Bank for International Settlements. In 1986, China became an official member of Asian Development Bank.

The central bank — the People's Bank of China (PBC)

The PBC is the nation's central bank. Compared to its pre-reform role as both a central bank and a unique business bank,

China's Banking System

People's Bank of China (Central Bank)

3 State Policy banks
- China Development Bank (CDB)
- Agricultural Development Bank of China (ADBC)
- Export & Import Bank of China (EIBC)

114 Commercial banks

4 Wholly State-owned Commercial Banks
- Industrial and Commercial Bank of China (ICBC)
- Bank of China (BOC)
- Agricultural Bank of China (ABC)
- China Construction Bank (CCB)

10 Nationwide or Regional Shareholding Commercial Banks

6 Nationwide
- Bank of Communications
- CITIC Industrial Bank
- China Everbright Bank
- China Merchants Bank
- China Mingsheng Bank
- Huaxia Bank

4 Regional
- Shenzhen Development Bank (SDB)
- Shanghai Pudong Development Bank (SPDB)
- Guangdong Development Bank (GDB)
- Fujian Industrial Bank (FIB)

100 City Shareholding Commercial Banks

Such as
- Bank of Shanghai
- Beijing City Commercial Bank
- Nanjing City Commercial Bank

42,000 Credit unions
- 3 rural commercial banks have been established in Jiangsu.
- Credit unions are spread in rural areas nationwide

190 Foreign banks

Such as
- Standard Chartered
- HSBC
- Citibank
- Bank of East Asia
- ABN AMRO
- Credit Agricole
- DBS
- BNP
- Bangkok Bank

TRUSTS: WHY ARE THEY SO POPULAR?

With the rapid growth in Asian wealth, SG Trust (Asia) Ltd, part of the Societe Generale Group, believes that high net worth Asians now have a need for structured solutions to preserve this new found wealth.

The changing nature of wealth creation in Asia has brought with it the need to employ more sophisticated structures, many encompassing the use of trusts. Why is their use becoming more popular in Asia, and why only now given the long history of trusts?

Wealth structuring for major families has been popular in the West for many years. Wealth creation in Asia has a relatively short history and familiarity with the use of trusts has been a recent phenomenon. Traditionally wealth in Asia was not created through inheritance nor through international investment but rather through business acumen and the success of a business. Planning for a future event such as disability or their demise was itself considered unlucky. Traditional families tended to rely on the family environment and with low rates of tax or inefficient collection of tax felt that informal arrangements were effective enough.

Today the world is changing and the values and personalities of the new generation of wealth creators are very different. Many have been educated in the West; the UK, USA, Canada and Australia and are more Western-orientated and internationalised.

As a result Asian investors have become increasingly global in their investment outlook and such exposure to global markets provides the risk diversification and opportunity that they are now looking for and expecting. However, hand in hand with this there are foreign taxes and legal systems that one must need to provide for. Tax regimes can be very different; one country may charge capital gains tax when a property is sold another may not. This fact alone may impact on whether a good or mediocre investment has been made. Other taxes have to be considered such as estate taxes, income taxes, stamp duties VAT etc. Thus sound financial planning is necessary and is of paramount importance in ensuring that your beneficiaries are not having a large part of their inheritance swallowed up through taxes paid unnecessarily to a foreign government.

SG is aware that today, many wealthy Asian families are exposed to multiple jurisdictions at family, business and investment levels. Perhaps your children are studying overseas in the US or UK; maybe it looks a good time to buy property in London or New York; perhaps there are business opportunities in China. All these, as well as the wider use of alternative passports; Canadian, Australian, US and UK, mean that the assets and the family members of wealthy Asians are touched by the customs and laws of many countries that are very different from their own. Legal process and tax enforcement is becoming stronger and more efficient. Sadly this means that traditional unstructured arrangements are now no longer as effective as they once were. As such, SG advises that it is essential that proper wealth planning and structuring is implemented to ensure efficient wealth management.

Asians in general do not have the experience of being highly taxed. Tax rates in Asia generally are low and where this is not the case there has been a marked inefficiency in collecting taxes from certain jurisdictions. As a result until recently the tax factor has not been a major focus of the typical Asian entrepreneur or investor in his investment decision making. In addition today's modern investor has to consider the complications posed a variety of legal systems. For example you may have assets in a Common Law country i.e. the US and you may live in a Civil Law country i.e. Taiwan and be subject to forced heirship. You may be a Muslim and be exposed to Sharia Law requirements. To counter these differences a proper structure should be in place to provide for your family should the legal status of your will be in dispute and your assets frozen until resolution. Even a properly drafted will cannot prevent delays caused by going through the normal probate process. Other problems can arise with disability, illness, business misfortune, divorce, re-marriage etc.

What, therefore are the solutions to avoid such problems? Our trust experts at SG believe that special circumstances require special remedies and here the Common Law Trust and the use of companies in a myriad of offshore/onshore locations can provide the building block for optimal wealth planning. Other products such as certain specialised insurance products can assist in this.

Today many offshore locations such as the Bahamas, the Cayman Islands, Jersey, Guernsey, the B.V.I. and Bermuda are used as jurisdictions for these structures. However over the next 10 years, we will see the emergence of jurisdictions such as Singapore, Hong Kong and New Zealand as jurisdictions of choice for these structures.

What is a trust? A trust is created when a person (the settlor) transfers assets to a third party (the trustee) to be administered for the benefit of persons chosen by the settlor (the beneficiaries). It is the transfer of legal title of property to the trustee to be held and administered for the benefit of others; the separation of legal and beneficial ownership of trust property, which gives rise to the many advantages of the trust.

The trust structure with underlying companies will provide both tax and administrative efficiencies. It will provide confidentiality in asset ownership; protection against foreign estate taxes and capital gains tax; tax treaty benefits. Trusts can provide security for future generations; provide a fund for education and protect the vulnerable. The trust funds are out of reach of all other than the beneficiaries. They can avoid undue delays occasioned by probate and the enforced freezing of assets where a will is contested.

To an Asian investor the fear of giving control to a faceless institution is perhaps their greatest fear and a Trustees greatest obstacle. This is perfectly natural given the short history of trusts in Asia and hearing "horror stories" of trustees misappropriating trust funds. Today a Settlor is well protected through legal provisions where a trustee does not properly carry out its fiduciary responsibilities. Always use a Trustee who is part of a well-known institution and has the experience in administering these structures. Today most trustees are regulated to ensure that they carry out their responsibilities in a proper manner. Dealing with several institutions for estate planning, investments and tax planning may give raise to conflicting advice and an unstructured approach to your wealth management strategy. It can be an advantage to use a corporate trustee that has access to a wide array of capabilities including investment vehicles, investment products, investment advisors and asset managers.

There is no doubt that the importance of private wealth structuring is coming to be accepted now in Asia. It is an enormous growth business. Wealthy Asians need it, but the skills to provide the right advice in multi-jurisdictional situations is relatively scarce. Organisations such as SG Trust (Asia) Ltd that position themselves to do it properly will be doing themselves and the high net worth market in Asia a great service.

Contributed by:

Daniel Truchi

Chairman & CEO, SG Trust (Asia) Ltd

SG TRUST (ASIA) LTD

SG Trust (Asia) Ltd (SGTA) is a wholly owned subsidiary of the Societe Generale Group. Staffed by legal, banking and trust professionals with extensive experience in Asia, SGTA is familiar with intricacies and regulatory environment of doing business both in Asia as well as in the global context. Operating under strict rules of confidentiality, SGTA offers a complete range of trust services that include Personal Trust, Company Management & Corporate Trust, Custodian & Escrow Services and Wills & Estate Management. But more than value-added solutions, SGTA provides you the highest level of professionalism and discretion, to assure you complete peace of mind even as it helps you build upon your assets for the future.

with rural credit cooperatives providing supplement financial services in rural areas the PBC now does not handle loans and savings. It only acts as the central bank to exercise macro-control and supervision over the nation's banking business. It is also authorized to issue currency, and regulate the borrowing and lending activities in the private sector.

Its main responsibilities include financial supervision, investigation, state treasury management, public finance, and foreign exchange management. It implements and manages monetary policy through adjustments of interest rates.

Policy banks
The policy banks include China Development Bank (CDB), Export-Import Bank of China (EIBC) and Agricultural Development Bank of China (ADBC). The chief creditors of CDB are policy projects in infrastructure and key industries, large and medium-sized projects, and technical innovation. ADBC offers relevant financial services according to agricultural policy. EIBC provides financial support for export of large machinery and electrical products. The policy banks support government policy. They are backed by the state budget, and their loans are for long-term financing, with interest rates generally lower than rates of commercial banks.

Commercial banks and incorporated commercial banks
Wholly state-owned banks include Industrial and Commercial Bank of China (ICBC), Agricultural Bank of China (ABC), China Construction Bank (CCB) and Bank of China (BOC). These four state commercial banks are originated from the four former state specialized banks, which actually had been the four major business divisions of the PBC before it changed the role, the 90 city shareholding commercial banks are mainly established after the restructuring of former city credit cooperatives while 10 nation-wide or regional shareholding commercial banks were all newly established in late 1980s and early 1990s. These commercial banks are financially strong and have outlets nationwide. They currently account for over 80% of China's total banking assets. The incorporated commercial banks include Bank of Communications, China Merchants Bank, CITIC Industrial Bank, China Everbright Bank, China Minsheng Banking Corporation, Huaxia Bank, Shanghai Pudong Development Bank, Shenzhen Development Bank, Guangdong Development Bank and Fujian Industrial Bank.

Foreign banks
By the end of September 2001, there had been nearly 190 business agencies of foreign-funded banks in China, including all the top 50 banks in the world with 158 branches. Most of these branches are concentrated in cities such as Shanghai, Shenzhen, Beijing, Guangzhou and Tianjin. In China, foreign banks have total assets of USD44 billion, accounting for 1.5% of total assets in China's banking sector. The loans and deposits of foreign banks were USD18.6 billion and USD6.5 billion respectively, representing around a 2% market share. But in terms of international settlement business and foreign currency lending, they account for 40% and 23% respectively. The latter is especially high in Shanghai, reaching 60%. At the end of September 2001, the total assets of the 53 business-oriented foreign banks in Shanghai had reached USD23.1 billion, which accounted for half of the total assets of foreign banks in China.

Geographically foreign banks' assets are concentrated in large and developed cities, particularly in Shanghai, Beijing, Shenzhen, Dalian, Guangzhou and Tianjin (refer to *"Geographical Distribution of Foreign Banks' Assets in China"*).

Geographical Distribution of Foreign Banks' Assets in China

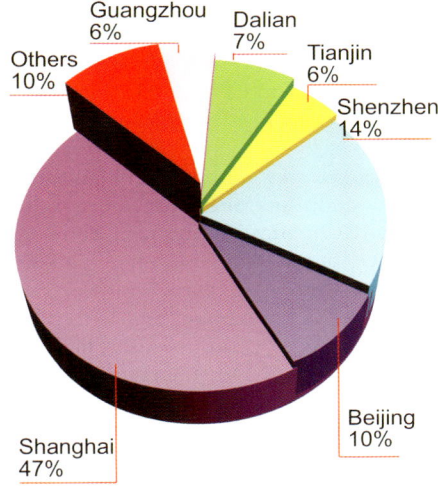

Guangzhou 6%
Dalian 7%
Others 10%
Tianjin 6%
Shenzhen 14%
Beijing 10%
Shanghai 47%

WTO and China's banking industry

China's WTO accession has accelerated the opening of China's banking industry. The Chinese government will gradually expand the regions where foreign-invested banks may establish business operation, from the present 23 cities and Hainan province to all major cities. Foreign banks now are mostly in the form of joint venture, and most of the partners they look for are small and medium-sized banks. As these Chinese banks have relatively larger market share in specific markets, they will help foreign banks to obtain useful market information. For the Chinese banks, it is in way of expanding their capital and strengthening capacity quickly. At the end of November 2001, the International Finance Corporation (IFC) signed an agreement in Beijing on making equity investment in Nanjing City Commercial Bank. According to the agreement, the International Finance Corporation will spend USD27 million to buy

180 million shares of Nanjing City Commercial Bank or 15% of its share capital after expansion. This made IFC the largest foreign shareholder in China's banking industry by the end of 2001.

Currently, foreign banks' main business is to provide foreign currency services for foreign-funded enterprises and a limited number of Chinese enterprises. But according to Sino-US WTO Agreement, China will gradually lift the regional restriction on foreign banks in handling Renminbi business:

- Shanghai, Shenzhen, Dalian and Tianjin upon China's accession to the WTO;
- Guangzhou, Zhuhai, Qingdao, Nanjing and Wuhan after 11 December 2002;
- Jinan, Fuzhou, Chengdu and Chongqing after 11 December 2003;
- Kunming, Beijing, and Xiamen after 11 December 2004;
- Shantou, Ningbo, Shenyang and Xi'an after 11 December 2005;
- After 11 December 2006, all geographic restrictions will be removed.

In addition, China will gradually abolish client restrictions on foreign banks in relation to Renminbi.

- After 11 December of 2003, China will allow foreign banks to handle Renminbi service for Chinese enterprises;
- After 11 December of 2006, China will permit foreign banks to provide services for all Chinese clients, it will also permit them to set up business outlets in the same region, requirements of examination and approval are the same with Chinese-funded banks.
- After 11 December of 2006. China will abolish all existing non-cautious measures regarding restrictions imposed on foreign banks in their ownership, forms of operation and establishment, including their branch offices and the issue of licenses.

Foreign non-banking financial institutions

are allowed to be established to provide automobile consumption credit business, which enjoy equal treatment with the same type of Chinese financial institutions. Foreign banks can, within five years after WTO entry, provide automobile credit service for individual Chinese residents. Foreign-funded financial leasing companies are allowed to provide financial leasing service with in the same period of time as that of Chinese firms.

Securities

After more than a decade of development, China's securities market has reached a sizeable scale. The two stock exchanges, Shanghai Stock Exchange and Shenzhen Stock Exchange, were established in 1990 and 1991 respectively. Two types of shares are traded in the market. A shares are exclusively for Chinese nationals, and B shares, until early 2001, were limited to foreign investors. By October 2001, there were 1,152 domestic listed companies, with market capitalization of RMB4.37 trillion (about USD533 billion). At that time, the total China's domestic market capitalization plus the USD623 billion in the Hongkong market made China the sixth largest stock market in terms of market capitalization.

Insurance

Currently, China has 25 insurance companies, of which four companies are state-owned, nine are joint stock companies, three are joint ventures and nine are foreign-funded. Eight of the 25 companies have nationwide operations, while 17 are regionally based companies. The 25 companies work in four business fields: three companies offer comprehensive insurance, 12 focus on property insurance, nine provide life insurance, and one does reinsurance.

China's insurance sector has registered 10 to 15% revenue growth in recent years. According to the China Insurance Regulatory Commission (CIRC), in 2000, China's insurance industry brought in USD19.27 billion in premiums, an increase of 14.5% over 1999. The total assets of China's insurance companies reached USD40.75 billion, an increase of 19.3% over 1999. Of the total premiums income in 2000, property insurance accounted for USD7.23 billion, a 14.8% increase over 1999. Life insurance income increased 14.4% to USD12.05 billion in 2000, accounting for 62.5% of the total premium income.

The major players in China's insurance market include the People's Insurance Company, China Pacific Insurance Company, Ping An Insurance Company, Taikang Insurance Company, China Life Insurance, Huatai Insurance Company and Xinhua Life Insurance. Among the foreign insurance groups in China, the American International Group (AIG) enjoys the largest market share and its insurance arm, AIA, has set up branches in Shanghai, Shenzhen, Guangzhou and Foshan.

By 2005, the total value of insurance premiums is expected to reach USD33.82 billion, constituting 2.3% of China's total GDP. The average premium per person will be USD27.78. Despite such rapid growth, the insurance industry is still a very small part of the entire economy. Compared with 11% in Japan and 8% in the United States, the insurance industry only represents less than 2% of China's GDP. China will attract more global insurance companies in the coming years.

In November 2001, CIRC released the procedure details for foreign investors to join China's insurance market. Eight foreign-funded insurance companies were approved by the Chinese government to start business in life and property or enlarge business scales. The eight companies are Germany-based Gerling-Konzern Allgemeine Versicherungs AG and Allianz; Swiss Zurich Insurance Company; the CNP from France; Transamerica Occidental Life from the United States; the Commercial Union

Assurance Co PLC and Royal & Sun Alliance Insurance Group PLC, both from Britain; and a Shanghai-based joint-venture with investment from French AXA.

LEGAL & POLICY ENVIRONMENT

Major regulation adjustment for WTO entry

As a WTO member, China has already amended dozens of laws and rules. The most important amendments were made to the three major laws that regulate foreign equity joint ventures, cooperative joint ventures, and Wholly-Owned Foreign Enterprises (WOFEs).

Restrictions on foreign-funded enterprises relaxed

In October 2000, the National People's Congress (NPC) ratified the amendment to the country's foreign-funded enterprises laws. Restrictions and regulations imposed on WOFEs in areas such as foreign exchange balance, export obligation, priority of domestic sourcing, and the reporting requirements for production and operation plans have been either deleted or amended.

- Export obligation

  Under the revised law, WOFEs no longer have to export all or the majority of their products. According to the original law, enterprises with foreign capital shall be established in such a manner to help promote the development of China's national economy and they shall adopt advanced technology and equipments, and market all or most of their products outside China. But the amended laws stated that foreign enterprises are "encouraged" (not "shall") to market their products outside China and use advanced technologies. This change gives a greater degree of autonomy to WOFEs to sell their products in China's domestic markets.

- Priority of Chinese sources

  According to the old regulations, WOFEs should purchase their production equipments and raw materials in domestic markets. The revised law now stipulates that when purchasing raw materials within the permitted scope of its operation, a joint venture "may purchase the goods in China and may also buy them in international markets." With these new amendments, WOFEs in China can enjoy greater freedom in purchasing.

- Foreign exchange balance

  The original regulation on Sino-Foreign Contractual Joint Ventures requires a contractual joint venture to achieve the balance of foreign exchange income and expenditures. If a contractual joint venture is unable to achieve the balance of its foreign exchange income and expenditures on its own, it may, in accordance with State provisions, apply to relevant authorities for assistance. In the current amendments, the provisions on "foreign exchange balance" requirement for WOFEs have been removed.

- Filing system for reporting production and operation plans to authorities

  According to the previous regulations, WOFEs are required to submit their production and operation plans to the authorities for filing. This requirement has, to a certain extent, impeded the daily operation and management of WOFEs. The revised laws on Foreign Capital Enterprises and Sino-foreign Equity Joint Ventures have deleted this item. WOFEs can enjoy greater autonomy in operation.

Restrictions on service industries lifted

In accordance with China's entry into WTO, the China market will be gradually liberalized in the next few years. Most foreign-owned joint ventures and wholly foreign-owned companies will be allowed, with quantitative and geographical restrictions progressively removed. Foreign investment restrictions on many service industries, including financial, distribution, telecommunication, professional services, commerce and tourism will be relaxed.

Industrial preferential policies

To align foreign investment with national industrial development, the Chinese Government had in June 1995 formulated and published the Interim Provisions for Directing Foreign Investment and Guidance Catalogue of Industries for Foreign Investment, to outline industrial policies for foreign investment. The industrial items are divided into four categories: the encouraged, permitted, restricted and prohibited industries. The Guidance Catalogue has been revised in December 1997 to broaden the scope of foreign investment encouraged by the state.

On 11 March 2002, the latest version of "Foreign Investment Industrial Guidance Catalogue" was released with effect from 1 April 2002. In addition, another regulation titled "The Regulation on Guiding Direction of Foreign Investment" was also released and implemented with effect from the same date.

In the new "Catalogue", the "Permitted" category is removed. There are now a total of 371 line items covering the three categories, namely "Encouraged", "Restricted" and "Prohibited".

Regional preferential policies

China's market liberalization policy focused initially on the eastern coastal region. Most reform measures were initiated there in a fairly favorable investment environment with many preferential policies. Today, the region has five Special Economic Zones, 14 coastal open cities, and the Pudong New Area in Shanghai. The subsidiaries of foreign companies were mostly established in the region.

Rapid development in the eastern regions has brought up important social and economic issues such as income disparity between people in the eastern and western regions. To address these issues, China has recently shifted its focus of economic development gradually westward. Policies have been formulated to develop the central and western regions through increased investment (through fiscal spending and foreign investment) and accelerated infrastructure development.

To encourage the flow of foreign direct investment into the central and western regions, the Chinese government formulated a set of preferential policies for foreign investors in central and western regions.

Greater investment scope

On 16 June 2000, the State Economic and Trade Commission (SETC), State Planning and Development Commission (SPDC) and Ministry of Foreign Trade Economic Cooperation (MOFTEC) jointly issued the Catalogue of Advantageous Industries in Central and Western Regions (C&W Catalogue).

In combination with the Industrial Catalogue, restrictions on foreign investment in the central and western regions will be further relaxed. For example, foreign investment in the following sectors are encouraged only if they are located in the central and western regions:

- Manufacturing of high quality glass with a daily melting capacity of more than 500 tons;
- New method dry-processing cement production (using cement clinker) with a daily production capacity of more than 2,000 tons.

If the following projects are located in central and western region, wholly-owned foreign enterprises will be allowed. Otherwise, they are only limited to joint ventures.

- Mining, extraction and processing of low grade and hard to extract gold mines;
- Exploration and mining of copper, lead and zinc ores;
- Exploration and mining of aluminum ores.

Different forms of foreign investment will be encouraged. In addition to traditional forms of investment, such as equity and cooperative joint ventures, and wholly foreign-owned enterprises, efforts will be made to promote project financing, project management and fund-raising in the stock market. Foreign-invested enterprises in eastern China will also be allowed to go west and contract domestic enterprises for management.

More tax concessions

The central and western regions, which can enjoy preferential tax policies, include 19 provinces, autonomous regions, and municipalities, namely, Shanxi, Inner Mongolia, Jilin, Heilongjiang, Anhui, Jiangxi, Henan, Hubei, Hunan, Chongqing, Sichuan, Guizhou, Yunnan, Tibet, Shaanxi, Gansu, Qinghai, Ningxia and Xinjiang.

- Income Tax

In accordance with the December 1999 Notice Regarding Foreign Investment Enterprises Established in Western and Central China, foreign investment enterprises (FIEs) engaged in "Encouraged" and "Restricted" projects in accordance with the Foreign Investment Industrial Guidance Catalogue will enjoy reduced enterprise income tax rate of 15% for 3 years after the expiry of existing preferential tax rate. This means that FIEs can enjoy preferential tax treatment for up to 8 years compared to the current 5-year period.

In addition, the October 2000 Notice on Several Policies for Implementing Large Scale Western Development extends the preferential enterprise income tax rate of 15%

to both foreign and domestic investors. Newly established enterprises engaged in fields such as transportation, power and water resources will be eligible for a 2-year exemption and a 3-year 50% reduction.

Furthermore, the Notice on Preferential Taxation Policies for Large-Scale Development of Western China issued on 30 December 2001 set the rules governing application of the reduced 15% Enterprise Income Tax (EIT) for qualified enterprises in Western China. It also set the rules governing exemptions from customs duty and import-stage value-added tax for equipment imports by qualifying enterprises in Western China. It also addressed the 2-year exemption, 3-year 50% reduction for special types of enterprise in Western China as well as exemptions from Special Local Agricultural Product Tax and Occupation of Cultivated Land Tax for certain special types of projects.

FIEs engaging in high-tech industries that are recognized by the relevant government departments will also enjoy two-year income tax exemption and three-year 50% income tax reduction. Farms which are involved in transforming cultivated land to forest or grassland for the purpose of environmental protection will enjoy exemption of tax on special agricultural products for 10 years.

FIEs which are designated as export enterprises with exports exceeding 70% of their total output value in the current year are eligible for a further 50% reduction with a minimum rate of 10% in the extended 3-year period. Before this, FIEs established in the central and western regions had to pay a 30% enterprise income tax.

- Import Duty

FIEs engaged in the "Encouraged" industries will be able to import equipments for their own use as well as accessories and spare parts free of import stage value-added tax in import-stage and customs duties, except for those expressly excluded from such exemptions in accordance with the 1997

Notice on Adjusting Policies for the Collection of Duties on Imported Equipments. However, the imported equipments must be those types that either cannot be produced in China or the types made in China do not meet the needs of the FIEs.

• Reinvestment

Currently, FIEs who reinvest their profits to increase registered capital or to establish another FIE with an operation period of at least 5 years will enjoy a 40% refund on the tax already paid on the invested amount. Reinvestment in export-oriented or technologically advanced projects are eligible for full refund on tax already paid on the invested amount. Furthermore, if 25% of the registered capital in the new subsidiary is directly foreign-owned, the enterprise will enjoy FIE status and other preferential policies that extended to FIEs, including preferential tax treatment. This rule applies to reinvestment in all regions. However, with the Go West campaign, it seems that the rule for determining whether new subsidiaries located in the central and western regions is considered an FIE has been expanded to include indirect foreign investment through an FIE, depending upon the interpretation of relevant provincial governments.

• Land tax

Both domestic and foreign investors will be exempted from land tax on cultivated land used for constructing national highways in the west.

Inspection and quarantine policy concessions

To accelerate the construction of the western region, the State Administration for Entry-Exit Inspection and Quarantine has recently announced a series of supporting measures.

• A system of enterprise management by category and exemption from inspection has been introduced to encourage export. Export-oriented enterprises in western China that are well-managed and excellent in keeping product quality are classified as Category I or II enterprises by inspection and quarantine authorities. Fewer spot checks will be conducted on their goods to facilitate export.

• Assistance will be given to export-oriented production enterprises in western China in making better use of the Generalized System of Preferences (GSP). Efforts will be made to publicize the GSP scheme to enterprises and keep them informed of how this scheme works.

• Steps will also be taken to urge the EU to extend the graduation deadlines for western China so that enterprises in the region can benefit more from this scheme. Export-oriented enterprises in western China will be encouraged to obtain management and product quality certifications. Certification agencies will open special hotlines to provide enterprises in the region with advice and training. Each year, a number of export-oriented mechanical and electronic products in the western region will be chosen and assistance will be granted to them to obtain international certification for their products. Assistance will also be given to agricultural and animal product processing enterprises and food production enterprises to obtain hygienic and management accreditation.

• Support will be given to key projects in western China. Priority will be given to the inspection of equipment imported for key development projects, including major infrastructure projects, environmental protection projects, local resources exploitation projects, special native products processing projects, high-tech projects, and education projects. Encouragement will be given to agricultural development and environmental protection in western China. To promote the export of agricultural products, better supporting services will be provided for the export of beef, mutton, nuts, beans, seeds and fruits. Efforts will also be made to create the necessary conditions for the improvement of local ecological environment, animal species and plant species, and the adjustment of the agricultural structure. Fine species of poultry, animals, seeds and saplings from other countries will be more actively introduced to China. Inspection and quarantine-related technical support will also be offered.

Latest moves to encourage foreign investment

The Chinese government will continue to adopt a series of policies and measures that encourage foreign investment. The new measures to attract foreign investment include:

Technical development and innovation preferred

Foreign-invested research and development centers will further be exempted from tariff and tax when they import self-use matching technology, fittings and spare parts within the total investment capital amount; foreign firms transferring technology to China will be exempted from business tax and corporate income tax after being approved; foreign firms will be exempted from business tax on their income from technology transfers; and with approval, foreign firms that report over 10% growth of the investment in technological development may offset 50% of their capital investment in technological development against their tax for the year. Furthermore, foreign-invested research and development centers, high-tech and export-oriented foreign-funded firms will be

exempted from tariff and tax when they import technology, equipments and components for technical upgrading purpose. If they purchase China-made equipments, they may get back all the incremental tax and have business income offset according to relevant rules.

Central and Western Regions preferred

Foreign investors investing in projects listed in the "Priority Industrial Catalogue of Foreign Investment in the Central and Western Region" will enjoy preferential policies. Enterprises investing in these regions will not be required to pay tariff and import linkage tax on equipments, supporting technology, accessories and spare parts imported for self-use.

In addition, the geographical coverage to receive foreign investment in middle and western areas will be expanded, conditions for the establishment of foreign firms will be relaxed and the foreign side will be allowed to hold larger share proportions. The FIEs in central and western China will receive an extended reduction and exemption period for corporate income tax. Reinvested projects in the central and western region by FIEs with foreign capital exceeding 25% can enjoy the same treatment as FIEs. The FIEs in the coastal areas are allowed to contract the operation and management of FIEs and domestic enterprises in the central and western regions.

Service sectors encouraged

The service sector has become a new attraction for investment. Service industries such as foreign trade, finance, insurance, transportation, legal, tourism, advertising, healthcare, accounting, property, education, engineering design, consultancy, etc. have been opened to foreign investors at varying degrees. Take commerce as an example, after China's accession to WTO, the Chinese Government will, in three years, gradually abolish restrictions on locations, quantity, percentage of shares and the existing mode of enterprises, and this will speed up the process of foreign capital penetrating the commercial sector.

Issue of A and B shares allowed

The business scope of investment companies launched by multinationals in China will be expanded. The procedure of approving foreign-funded firms will be simplified; provincial governments will have the right to approve various foreign-funded firms except those that will influence the balance of economic development; no more value appraisals will be conducted on equipments imported by wholly foreign-owned firms; and policies and regulations unfavorable to the introduction of foreign capital will be eliminated.

FOREIGN INVESTMENT IN CHINA: THE CURRENT TREND

Despite the world economic downturn in 2001, China's economy maintained a robust development momentum that has attracted an inflow of large amounts of overseas funds and demonstrated China's appeal as a rising "global factory".

Statistics show that by the end of 2001, direct overseas investment to the country totaled USD69.2 billion in terms of contractual value, up 10.4% from the previous year. The realized overseas investment added up to USD46.8 billion, up 14.9%, the highest in history.

China registered an average economic growth rate of 8% on a yearly basis since it launched the reform and opening-up policy in 1979. The nation has been the largest recipient of foreign direct investment (FDI) among developing countries for eight straight years, with annual FDI over USD40 billion.

The total number of overseas-invested firms in China now stands at about 390,000, involving a total overseas investment of USD745.9 billion in contractual value. Realized overseas investment added up to USD395.5 billion (refer to "Foreign Direct Investment in China as of 2001").

Location preference

In terms of contractual FDI value, the top ten provinces and municipalities in 2001 are: Guangdong, USD15.80 billion; Jiangsu, USD15.11 billion; Shanghai, USD7.37 billion; Zhejiang, USD7.18 billion, Shandong, USD7.16 billion; Fujian, USD5.00 billion, Tianjin, USD4.63 billion, Beijing, USD3.31 billion; Hubei, USD2.21 billion; Hunan, USD1.33 billion.

When it comes to the regional distribution, foreign capital is mainly invested in eastern China. In the eastern region, newly-established FIEs numbered 18,840 in 2000 alone; contractual FDI rose to USD54.7 billion; and realized FDI stood at USD35.3 billion. The three figures are up by 37.2%, 59.1% and 1.4% respectively over 1999.

As to the central region, the number of newly established FIEs and contractual FDI value grew to 2,100 FIEs and USD4.472 billion respectively, 3.4% and 13.5% higher than those of 1999. But the central region saw a slight drop in terms of actual investment value, down by 2.4% to USD3.6 billion.

In 2000, the western region saw marked growth of FDI in terms of the number of newly established FIEs, and the value of contractual and realized investment. A total number of 1, 407 new FIEs were established, an amount of USD3.2 billion was pledged, and an investment of USD1.9 billion arrived, a rise of 21.7%, 10.9% and 0.8% over 1999 respectively.

Investment form preference

With regard to the investment form, by the end of 2001, Equity Joint Venture (EJV) was the most popular form. In terms of both contractual FDI value and realized FDI value, EJV took up a share of 55.3% and 44.6% respectively. Wholly-Owned Foreign

Enterprises saw rapid growth in 2001 with 115,640 new WOFEs were set up and contractual value of USD43.0 billion. By contrast, only 8,895 cooperative joint ventures were set up, with realized value of USD17.5 billion (refer to *"FDI in China by Form as of 2001 (USD billion")*.

Industrial sector preference
With regard to FDI flow into the primary, secondary and tertiary industries in 2000, secondary industry accounted for the largest

share. In terms of the total number of approved foreign invested enterprises (FIEs), the secondary industry captured 73% while the primary and tertiary industries took up 2.9% and 24.2%. In terms of accumulated value of contractual FDI, the secondary industry accounted for 60.9% while the primary and tertiary industries represented 1.8% and 37.3% respectively.

In the secondary industry, manufacturing sector remains the major investment sector for FDI, accounting for 98.4%, 96.2% and

FDI in China by Form as of 2001 (USD billion)

Form	Projects	Contractual Value	Realized Value
Total	390,183	744.88	394.3
EJV	215,640	308.02	175.76
CJV	51,368	157.04	77.63
WOFE	122,995	274.99	133.77
Joint Exploration	180	4.84	7.15

Foreign Direct Investment in China as of 2001

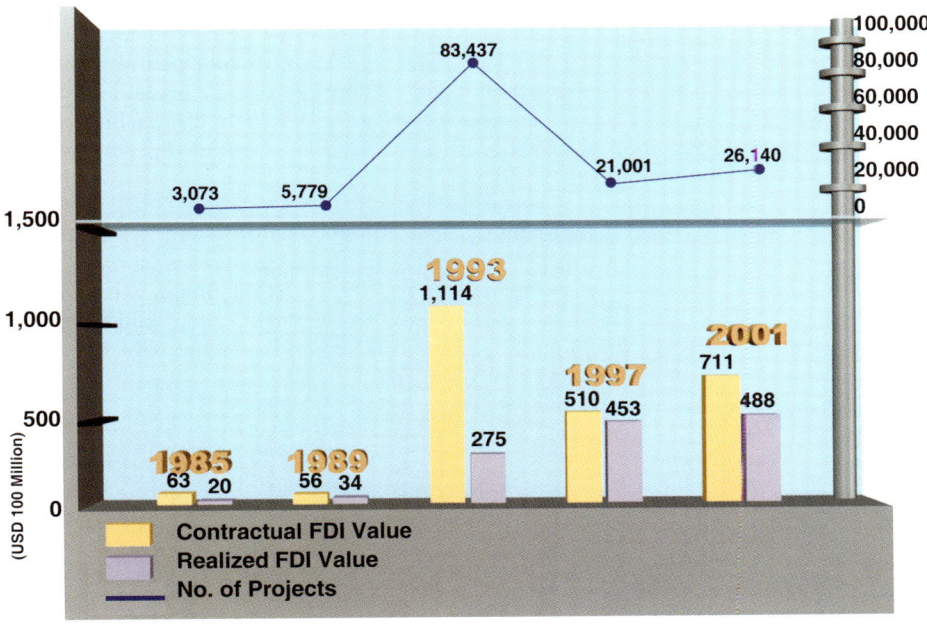

90.2% in terms of the number of newly established FIEs, the value of contractual and realized FDI respectively.

Within the manufacturing sector, there was a remarkable growth in FDI inflows into the electronics and telecommunication equipments manufacturing. In 2000, there are 1,529 newly-established FIEs engaging in telecommunications equipment manufacturing, with contractual and realized FDI standing at USD11.4 billion and USD4.6 billion, increasing 188.03% and 46.04% respectively, accounting for 24.7% and 16% of total FDI in the secondary industry and representing 18.2% and 11.28% of the nation's FDI.

In 2000, the tertiary industry witnessed a growth with 5,269 new FIEs and the attraction of USD14.9 billion in contractual FDI, expanding by 36.2% and 19.6% respectively from the year before; the value of realized foreign investment stood at USD 11.4 billion, declining by 10.8%. In terms of the nation's FDI, the tertiary industry accounted for 23.6%, 23.9% and 27.9% respectively, among which contractual and realized FDI dropped by 6.3% and 3.7% from 1999.

In the tertiary industry, the real estate development and management sector associated with the renovation of existing urban districts showed a significant growth margin, with contractual FDI reaching USD5.1 billion, a rise of 61.1% over the previous year. The hotel sector witnessed a drop in FDI inflows, with its contractual FDI reaching USD0.3 billion, shrinking by 21.3%.

Source of foreign investments

By the end of 2000, in terms of realized investment value, the top 10 investors in China were the following countries and territories: Hong Kong (USD170.3 billion, 48.9%), the United States (USD30.0 billion, 8.6%), Japan (USD27.8 billion, 8.0%), Taiwan Province (USD26.2 billion, 7.5%), Singapore (USD17.0 billion, 4.9%), the Virgin Islands (USD13.2 billion, 3.8%), South Korea (USD10.3 billion, 3.0%), the United Kingdom (USD 8.7 billion, 2.5%), Germany (USD 5.8, 1.7%) and Macau (USD 4.9 billion, 1.4%).

Asia

As a whole, ten Asian countries and territories (Hong Kong, Macau, Taiwan Province, Japan, the Philippines, Thailand, Malaysia, Singapore, Indonesia and South Korea) serve as the major sources of foreign investment absorbed by China. In 2000, these Asian countries and territories established 15,981 enterprises in China and put in USD30.5 billion as contractual FDI, a rise of

Statistics of Foreign Direct Investment by Sector in 2000 (USD billion, %)

Sector	Projects	Contractual Value	Realized Value
Total	22,347	62.3	40.7
Agriculture*	821	2.38%	1.66%
Mining	162	0.81%	1.43%
Manufacturing	15,988	71.01%	63.48%
Construction	233	1.33%	2.22%
Logistics	306	2.27%	2.49%
Wholesale & Retailing	852	2.30%	2.11%
Real Estate	684	8.40%	11.44%
Social Service	2,679	6.83%	5.37%
Others	622	4.67%	9.8%

* Including agriculture, forestry, animal husbandry & fishing

30.2% and 25.6% respectively over the previous year; and their actual Investment was USD25.4 billion, down by 5.3% from the previous year. Among these countries and territories, the biggest five investors, in terms of realized investment, were Hong Kong, Japan, Taiwan Province, Singapore and South Korea.

EU

In 2000, the total number of investment projects by EU nations in 2000 reached 1,390, an increase of 27.2% over 1999. While the realized value of investment only stood at USD4.8 billion, slightly down from that of 1999, the contractual investment value jumped by 110.8%, rising from USD4.3 billion in 1999 to USD9.1 billion. Among the 15 members of the European Union, the top five investors in China, ranked by realized investment value, were the United Kingdom, Germany, France, the Netherlands and Italy.

North America

The United States saw a marked growth of contractual investment from USD6.0 billion in 1999 to USD8.0 billion in 2000, a jump of 33.0%. Approved US-invested projects totaled 2,609, an annual increase of 28.7%; and the realized investment stood at USD4.4 billion, a slight rise of 4.0%.

FDI trend in China

China's easing restrictions on foreign investment and improved transparency of investment policies, both markedly boosted by its entry into the World Trade Organization (WTO), have reduced the need of foreign investors to find a local partner to handle the issues of taxation, application procedures and policy interpretation. As a result, three important investment trends are to emerge:

- Among the three major investment modes available for foreign investors, WOFEs are expected to become the most popular form for foreign investment. With the lifting of

a ban on 100% foreign ownership in certain sectors, WOFEs have become increasingly popular because of the greater freedom in management.

- More joint stock limited companies are to be set up. This mode is attractive to foreign investors because it carries limited liabilities and a clearer ownership structure with voting rights based on the number of shares held by each partner. In existing joint ventures, Chinese partners could sometimes veto management decisions even though they were just minority shareholders. A joint stock company is also easier for transfer of assets and eventual listing on the stock market.

- Mergers and acquisitions. According to the new foreign investment regulations, foreign investors are allowed to acquire equity interest of other enterprises, including domestic enterprises provided that certain conditions are satisfied.

Opportunities

China's reform and market liberalization will open up tremendous opportunities for foreign investors:

- China's economic restructure will release enormous domestic consumer demand, particularly in agriculture, water conservancy, energy, transport, communications, raw material, environmental protection and advanced technologies etc.

- China's Western Regions Development Program, supported by the existing industrial base, technical strength, and rich natural and human resources, provides favorable conditions for foreign investors to explore market opportunities in Central and Western China.

- Foreign partners of Chinese enterprises, with their advanced technologies and sophisticated management expertise, can play important roles helping Chinese enterprises improve management, marketing and technical practice. These needs are particularly urgent for Chinese state-owned enterprises.

- Multinational companies can leverage on China's technology and quality workforce to set up R&D centers, invest in high-tech industries, and participate in the technological transformation process of traditional industries, while enjoying favorable policies.

- The service industry will continuously grow. Foreign investors are expected to help develop the key service sectors, such as banking, insurance, commercial retail, foreign trade and accounting.

唐山高新技术开发区
Tangshan New & High Tech Development Zone

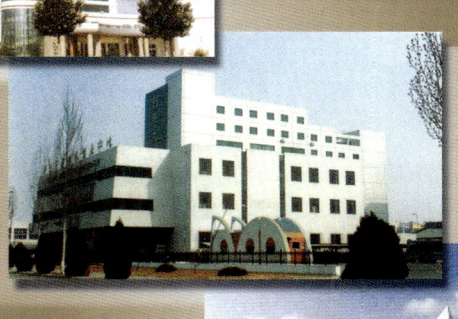

China:

**Business Promoting Bureau
Administrative Committee of TSDZ
Torch Building, Jianshebei Road
Tangshan, China
Tel: 86-315-3179735 / 3178029
Fax: 86-315-3178031
Email: yanny@tsdz.net
Website: www.tsdz.net**

Singapore:

**China Knowledge Press
Tel: 65-63108737
Fax: 65-63108738
Email: info@chinaknowledge.com**

www.sportiv.com.sg

We provide full comprehensive services. You simply give us a brief description of your missions and goals. With this initial contact point, you attain peace of mind and indirectly enhance your productivity as you channel more of your time to trouble shoot your organization's performance whilst we do all your leg work as follow:

Research & Development -
We identify the latest trends in colors, fabrications, trims, raw materials, etc thru' extensive global market research.

Design Concepts -
We create Orginal, Creative & Ingeniously funtional design concepts for each season. We even help to design your product catalogues.

Sourcing -
we explore the latest fabrics & accessories to offer your products a competitive edge.

Manufacturing Services -
We ensure factories are soundly assessed and passed Human Rights Requirements. Premium quality workmanship is our motto.

Logistics -
We assist in export documentation, customs clearance, shipments consolidation, and timely deliveries to final recipient countries.

Sportiv (Singapore) Pte Ltd
119 Genting Lane #05-01 H&H Industrial Building Singapore 349570
Tel: (65)(67417233) Fax: (65)(67411796) Email: mail@sportif.com.sg

Guidelines For Foreign Investors

Foreign-funded enterprises can independently operate their businesses, once approved by the relevant authorities and registered with administrations for industry and commerce. There is no administrative affiliation between the Chinese government and foreign-funded enterprises, but foreign-funded enterprises, in their production and business operations, must accept the guidance and supervision by the Chinese government in line with law, regulations and relevant policies.

MAJOR LAWS ON FOREIGN INVESTMENT

Equity joint venture, contractual joint venture and wholly-owned foreign enterprises are the three major forms of foreign direct investment in China. Equity joint ventures used to be the most dominant form, but in recent years, there has been a growing trend for FDI to take the form of wholly-owned operation. This is particularly evident among large multinational corporations (MNCs). To accommodate this trend, the three major foreign investment laws have been revised since October 2000.

Wholly-Owned Foreign Enterprise (WOFE) Law

The revised regulations for the WOFE law were approved in April 2001. The amendments of WOFE law and implementing regulations (State Council Order no. 301) were generally positive. The key revisions include the following:

- elimination of export performance requirements (i.e., rules that required companies to export certain percentages of product). Exports are encouraged, but not required. (It is unclear whether export performance requirements contained in existing contracts remain valid.)
- Deletion of advanced technology and import substitution requirements. The law had previously specified that a WOFE must use advanced technology and equipment to develop new products, promote conservation, and upgrade products for import substitution. Under the amended law, those activities are encouraged, but not required.
- Deletion of foreign exchange balancing requirements. The law had previously required that WOFEs balance their foreign exchange receipts and expenditures. However, The State Administration of Foreign Exchange (SAFE) had not seriously enforced the balancing requirement in recent years, reflecting China's relatively strong foreign exchange reserves.
- Deletion of prohibition against WOFE direct domestic sales of products without prior government approval.
- Deletion of requirement that raw materials and fuel for WOFEs be obtained solely within China unless unavailable from the domestic market. The amended law also lifted prohibitions on imports of capital equipment and technology that could be obtained in the domestic market.
- Deletion of requirement that WOFEs submit production and operation plans to local authorities.
- Deletion of requirements that WOFEs sell products in accordance with China's price control regulations or file the prices with price control and tax authorities.
- Deletion of specific limitations or

prohibitions on WOFE investment in certain business sectors, including media, real estate, communications and transportation, and public utilities. Limitations or prohibitions on WOFE investment will instead be indicated in the industrial catalogue guiding foreign investment. The catalogue is scheduled to be published in 2002.

Several provisions require additional scrutiny.
- WOFEs are permitted to adjust the scale of their registered capital with government approval.
- China may reject an application to establish a WOFE for any of the five specified reasons. Permission may be denied if approval would endanger China's national security or violate China's laws and regulations. These conditions are consistent with international norms. The other three bases for permission denial, however, seem overly broad. They are: (1) detriment to China's sovereignty or public interest; (2) nonconformity with the requirements of the development of China's national economy; and (3) possibility of environmental pollution.
- WOFEs must draft and submit import/export plans and renew import/export licenses every six months.
- State Administration for Foreign Exchange (SAFE) continues to be actively involved in the approval process for foreign exchange bank accounts related to WOFE production and business operations in China.

Equity Joint Venture (EJV) Law

EJVs are currently the most popular form for foreign investment in China. China had traditionally favored JV investment, as such investment was perceived as a way to rescue poorly performing domestic industries. In March 2001, the National People's Congress (NPC) approved revisions of the Chinese-foreign equity joint venture law. Most changes were fairly minor, but more detailed and comprehensive amendments are expected to be introduced soon. The amended law deleted:
- Requirements that JVs either procure raw materials, fuel and some capital goods from the domestic market or source from the international market using on hand foreign currency. The amended law does not restrict sourcing from the international market, although it specifies that procurement must be consistent with the principles of "fairness and reasonableness."
- Requirements that JVs file production and business plans with government agencies and implement the plans through business contracts.

Contractual Joint Venture Law

Foreign investors have not traditionally demonstrated significant interest in Sino-foreign cooperative enterprises. The NPC passed minor revisions to the cooperative enterprises law in October 2000. The Ministry of Foreign Trade and Economic Cooperation (MOFTEC) stated that it did not contemplate amendments to regulations.

Intellectual Property Rights (IPR) Law

In connection with its accession to the WTO, China has strengthened its legal framework considerably by amending its IPR Law, including patent, trademark and copyright laws, as well as by issuing judicial interpretations and other administrative regulations to make them more compliant with the Trade-related Aspects of Intellectual Property Rights (TRIPS) Agreement and international standards.

Patent Law

The Patent Law was amended in June and August 2000 and came into effect from 1 July 2001. The new law increased the number of items for the preliminary examination. New grounds for rejecting an invention patent are introduced.

The patent revocation procedure is removed because it was considered that the function of the revocation procedure could be fully achieved by means of the invalidation procedure. New grounds for invalidating a patent were thus introduced. A lengthy chapter was added on "international patent applications" made pursuant to the provisions of the Patent Cooperation Treaty that China joined in 1994. Numerous other modifications were made, including changes to the rules governing fees, documentation procedures of patent application, and special rules on compulsory licenses.

Trademark Law

The new Trademark Law was ratified on 27 October 2001 with effect from 1 December 2001. The key areas of amendment include trademark registration, counterfeiting, enforcement, judicial review as well as definition of "well-known" trademarks. According to the new law, natural persons have the right to apply for trademark registration. Apart from the characters and graphics, the symbols applicable for registration as trademarks also include letters, numbers, 3D signs, and color combinations. Geographic names are protected as collective trademarks or certification trademarks.

In addition, the new Trademark Law now clearly states that copies, imitations or translations of a well-known trademark, registered or unregistered, that are used on identical or similar goods, shall not be registerable or allowed for use.

Copyright Law

The new Copyright Law was ratified on 27 October 2001 and took effect from the same date. The amendments include an enhanced scope of protection and an enlarged scope of remedies. The Law now includes more items to be protected, such as dance, acrobatic, and architectural works.

In addition, it provides the descriptions of property rights and includes more rights to be protected, such as rental rights of computer programs and movies, mechanical performance rights, rights of assignment for copyright properties, and the right to disseminate within information networks. The assignment of property rights now requires a written contract, and the Law gives a format of the main contents to be included. Also, China's radio and television stations will be required to get the permission of and pay remuneration to copyright owners for broadcasting published audio or video products.

Noticeably, copyright protection of the Internet (known as "information network-based publication rights"), computer programs and compilations of data, were enforced by separate legislation promulgated by the National Copyright Administration. The Measures for Registration of Copyright in Computer Software came into force on 20 February 2002. The Measures apply to the registration of copyright in software and the registration of exclusive license contracts and assignment contracts for copyright in software.

According to the Measures, the Copyright Protection Center of China is the software registration authority. Upon approval from the National Copyright Administration, the Copyright Protection Center of China may establish software registration offices at the local level. Software to be registered must be independently developed or significantly improved in terms of function or performance after making changes to existing software with permission from the original copyright holder. The Measures set forth the detailed requirements for making applications for registration.

Despite remarkable progress in improving its intellectual property regime, IPR protection in China remains a problem. IPR enforcement, through either judicial or administrative means, leaves much to be desired.

ENCOURAGED, PERMITTED AND PROHIBITED AREAS

The Industrial Catalogue for Directing Foreign Investment is the major regulation that foreign investors should consult before making any investment decision. It is one of the important criteria for determining whether the proposed projects will benefit from customs duty and related VAT exemption, or whether they fall within the "prohibited" category for foreign investment. The latest version of the Industrial Catalogue was promulgated by Ministry of Foreign Trade and Economic Cooperation (MOFTEC) on 11 February 2002 with effect from 1 April 2002. It replaced the 1995 and 1998 Industrial Catalogues. The new Catalogue sets out a list of industry sectors falling within three categories, that is, "Encouraged", "Restricted" and "Prohibited". Industry sectors which do not fall within any of these three categories will be allowed for investment.

The release of this new list is aimed at bringing foreign investment in line with China's WTO commitments. In this new Industry Catalogue, the Chinese government demonstrated a much more open attitude towards foreign investment. The number of "encouraged" items for investment has increased from 186 to 262, while prohibited items are reduced from 112 to 75.

Service industries experienced the greatest change. Many industrial sectors that are traditionally not encouraged by the government are now new additions to the "Encouraged" category. Examples include wholesale and retail, real estate, public services, health, sports and social welfare services, education, culture and art, broadcasting, movie and television.

In addition, industries such as telecom services and the supply of water, gas and heat in cities have been moved from the "Prohibited" category to the "Restricted" category. Similarly, the manufacturing of general consumer goods has been moved from the "Restricted" category to the "Encouraged" category.

On the whole, foreign investors are generally encouraged to:

- Transform traditional agriculture to modern agriculture and promote agricultural industrialization,
- Invest in communications, energy, raw materials, infrastructure and other fundamental industries,
- Invest in electronic information, biological engineering, new material, aeronautics and astronautics and other high-tech industries,
- Use new and advanced technology to help China improve machinery, light industries and textiles so as to upgrade the manufacturing industry,
- Invest in projects for comprehensive utilization of resources, recycling, environmental protection and infrastructural construction,
- Invest in China's western regions,
- Promote exports of all the permitted items.

Apart from a relaxation of restrictions on investment, the foreign shareholding caps for various industries, for instance, telecom, wholesale and retail, will be gradually lifted in accordance with the WTO market access timetable.

Meanwhile, with an introduction of the concept of "relative Chinese majority shareholding", more flexibility was accorded to foreign investors. In some industries such as water supply, the aggregate shareholding of foreign investors may exceed the shareholding of Chinese partners, provided that the shareholding of Chinese partners is larger than the share of any one foreign investor.

Despite favorable developments, the new Catalogue also announced a list of areas prohibited to foreign investment. For example, foreign investment is banned in strategic parts of the economy, including construction and operation of power grids and aviation transport. Media industries such as broadcasting and television are also closed to foreign investment.

However, this new Industrial Catalogue is not the only guide for foreign investors who plan to invest in Central and Western China. There is another catalogue, the Catalogue of Advantageous Industries in Central and Western China (C&W Catalogue), which sets out an additional list of industry sectors where foreign investment is encouraged in the western and central China regions. Since the issue of the C&W Catalogue in 16 June 2000, conflicting requirements between the two Catalogues have arisen. A new version of the C&W Catalogue is expected to be released soon.

REGULATIONS FOR FDI IN NEWLY-OPENED SECTORS

With entry into the WTO in December 2001, China has embarked on a series of steps to reform its trade and business environment. Hundreds of PRC laws and regulations are being reviewed and amended, and many crucial contradictions have been removed and the details made clear. These new laws and regulations will open up China's economy to foreign investment in financial services, banking, insurance, professional services, and other key sectors.

Financial institutions

The Regulations of the People's Republic of China on Administration of Foreign-Invested Financial Institutions was passed by the State Council on 12 December 2001. It was promulgated on 20 December 2001 and came into force on 1 February 2002.

Regulations cover wholly-owned foreign banks, branches of foreign banks, equity joint venture banks, wholly-owned foreign financial companies and equity joint venture financial companies in China. The minimum registered capital for wholly-owned foreign banks and equity joint venture banks is equivalent to RMB300 million. For wholly-owned foreign financial companies and equity joint venture financial companies, it is equivalent to RMB200 million. Parent companies should allocate at least the equivalent of RMB100 million to their branches in China as operating funds.

The total assets of a party applying to establish a wholly-owned foreign bank or wholly-owned foreign finance company must not be less than USD10 billion at the end of the year preceding the application. The total assets of a party that applies to establish a foreign bank branch must be at least USD20 billion at the end of the year preceding the application. The total assets of a foreign joint venture partner applying to establish a joint venture bank or joint venture finance company must be USD10 billion at the end of the year preceding the application.

Banking services

Wholly foreign-owned banks, branches of foreign banks and equity joint venture banks may:
- Issue short-, medium- and long-term loans;
- Accept bills and discount;
- Purchase and sell government and financial bonds and securities in foreign currencies other than shares;
- Engage in credit and guarantee services;
- Handle domestic and foreign account settlements;
- Purchase and sell foreign exchange;
- Engage in foreign currency conversion;
- Execute inter-bank call loans;
- Engage in bank card services;
- Handle safe keeping services;
- Offer credit investigation and consulting services; or
- Engage in operations approved by People's Bank of China (PBC).

Industrial Catalogue for Directing Foreign Investment in China 2002

Encouraged

(1) Agriculture, forestry, animal husbandry, fishery (11 items);
(2) Mining (11 items);
- Exploration and development of oil and gas;
- Development of low-permeation oil and gas fields (deposits);
- Development and application of new technology in oil exploration and development;
(3) Manufacturing (196 items);
- Food processing (6 items);
- Tobacco processing (2 items);
- Textile (2 items);
- Leather and fur products (2 items);
- Timber processing, and bamboo, rattan and grass products (1 item);
- Paper making and paper products (2 items);
- Petroleum processing and coking industry (3 items);
- Chemical feedstock and chemical product manufacturing (29 items);
- Medicine (16 items);
- Chemical fiber manufacturing (3 items);
- Plastics products (3 items);
- Non-metal mineral products (9 items);
- Non-ferrous metal smelting and rolling processing (4 items);
- Ferrous metal smelting and rolling processing (5 items);
- Metal products (3 items);
- Ordinary machinery manufacturing (7 items);
- Specialized equipment manufacturing (42 items);
- Transportation equipment manufacturing (18 items);
- Manufacturing of complete automobiles and motorcycles;
- Automobile and motorcycle engine production;
- Design and manufacturing of diesel engines for ships, auxiliary machines, wireless communication, navigation equipment and parts (Chinese party holding relative majority);
- Electric machinery and equipment manufacturing (4 items);
- Electronics and communications equipment manufacturing (29 items);
- Satellite navigation receiving equipment and key parts manufacturing (limited to JVs)
- Apparatus, instruments, and cultural and office appliance manufacturing (7 items) and
- Other manufacturing industries (2 items).
(4) Generation and supply of electricity, gas and water (8 items);
(5) Water conservation management;
(6) Transportation, storage, post and telecommunications (13 items);
- Construction and operation of railway trunk line networks (Chinese party holding majority);
- Air transportation companies (Chinese party holding majority);
- Periodic and non-periodic international sea transportation business;
- International multi-mode container transportation business;
(7) Wholesale and retail (1 item);
- Logistics/delivery of ordinary commodities
(8) Real estate (1 item);
- Development and construction of ordinary residential housing

(9) Public services (5 items);
  - Information & Consultation Professional Services: accounting and auditing services
(10) Health, sports and social welfare services (1 item);
  - Services for elderly and handicapped people
(11) Education, culture & art, and broadcasting, movie & television (1 item);
  - Institutions of education (limited to EJVs and CJVs)
(12) Scientific research and comprehensive technological services (12 items);
(13) Permitted sectors where all products are directly exported (1 item).

Restricted

(1) Agriculture, forestry, animal husbandry and fishery (2 items);
(2) Mining (6 items);
  - Exploration and mining of precious non-metal such as diamonds
(3) Manufacturing (33 items);
  - Food Processing (4 items)
  - Tobacco processing (1 item)
  - Textile (2 items)
  - Publishing and photocopy (1 item)
(4) Generation and supply of electricity, gas and water (1 item);
(5) Transportation, storage, post and telecommunications (7 items);
(6) Wholesale and retail (8 items);
(7) Finance and insurance (6 items);
  - Insurance companies
  - Securities
(8) Real estate (2 items);
(9) Public services (2 items);
(10) Health, sports and social welfare services (2 items);

(11) Education, broadcasting, culture & art, movie & television (2 items);
(12) Scientific research and comprehensive technological services (2 items); and
(13) Permitted sectors where all products are directly exported (1 item).

Prohibited

(1) Agriculture, forestry, animal husbandry and fishery (3 items);
(2) Mining (2 items);
(3) Manufacturing (5 items);
  - Food Processing (1 item)
  - Medicine (2 items)
  - Ferrous metal smelting and rolling processing (1 item)
  - Weapon & ammunition
  - Others (6 items)
(4) Generation and supply of electricity, gas and water (1 item);
(5) Transportation, storage, post and telecommunications (2 items);
(6) Finance and insurance (1 item);
  - Futures
(7) Public services (4 items);
(8) Education, culture and art, and broadcasting, movie and television (8 items);
  - Primary educational institutions
  - Publishing, wholesale distribution and importation of books, newspapers and magazines
  - Production and publishing of video/audio products and electronic publication
(9) Other sectors (1 item); and
(10) Sectors prohibited by international treaties entered into by China (1 item).

This catalogue includes major items only.

Other financial services

Wholly foreign-owned financial companies and equity joint venture financial companies may:

- Accept deposits of no less than RMB1 million or equivalent in freely convertible foreign currencies for no less than three months;
- Grant short-, medium- and long-term loans;
- Accept bills and discount;
- Purchase and sell government and financial bonds and securities in foreign currencies other than shares;
- Guarantee services;
- Engage in foreign currency conversion;
- Offer call loans within the trade;
- Offer credit investigation and consulting services;
- Engage in foreign exchange trust services; or
- Engage in other PBOC-approved operations.

The Regulations provide that a foreign-invested financial institution must meet the following requirements in order to carry out Chinese currency-related businesses:

- It must be operating in China for at least three years before the application.
- It must have made a profit in the two successive years preceding the application.
- It must meet other prudential requirements stipulated by the People's Bank of China.

As for the fund management sector, foreign investors may either invest in an existing fund management company or jointly create a new enterprise. Initially the investment must be more than 25% and less than 33%; that percentage of ownership may increase to 49% in three years.

Insurance

The State Council issued the Administrative Rules on 12 December 2001, and they became effective on 1 February 2002. The Administrative Rules apply to Sino-foreign equity joint venture insurance companies, wholly foreign-owned insurance companies and branches set up by foreign insurance companies in China.

Following China's entry into WTO, foreign non-life insurers may set up their branches or joint ventures in China. Foreign equity in a joint venture can amount to 51%. Within two years of China's entry, wholly foreign-owned subsidiaries of life insurers will be permitted with no limitation on business models. Foreign life insurers can set up joint ventures in China but foreign equity should be no more than half. Within five years of entry, wholly foreign-owned subsidiaries for life insurers could be set up.

Foreign life and non-life insurers will be permitted to provide services in Shanghai, Guangzhou, Dalian, Shenzhen and Foshan after China's entry. Within two years, such companies' businesses could be expanded to another ten cities. Within three years, the geographic restriction for these foreign companies will be lifted.

Foreign non-life insurers will be permitted to provide identified services in specified areas on China's entry to WTO, and business limitation will be abolished within two years. Within two years, foreign life insurers may only provide individual insurance to foreigners and Chinese. Within three years, they will be permitted to provide health insurance, group insurance and pension/annuities insurance to foreigners and Chinese. Approved business licenses will be issued to foreign insurers with no quantitative limits upon China's entry to the WTO.

Qualifications

Minimum registered capital for an equity joint venture insurance company and a wholly-owned foreign insurance company should be RMB200 million or the equivalent in a freely convertible currency. A foreign insurance company branch must have operating capital equivalent to at least RMB200 million in a freely convertible currency allocated by its parent company without any charges.

A foreign insurance company wishing to set up a foreign funded insurance company in China must have been operating in the insurance business for at least 30 years, has maintained a representative office in China for at least two years, and, at the end of the year prior to the filing of the application, have total assets amounting to USD5 billion. A foreign-funded insurance company may not engage in both property insurance (property damage insurance, liability insurance and credit insurance) and personal insurance (including life insurance, health insurance, accidental injury insurance).

Securities

At the end of 2001, China Securities Regulatory Commission (CSRC) announced the contents of opening securities market in five aspects after China's WTO entry. They are:

- China will allow foreign securities institutions to directly deal in B shares through special seats set up in stock exchanges;
- More domestic enterprises are encouraged to list overseas. While these enterprises are encouraged to list in the Hong Kong stock exchange, global securities markets such as New York, London, Tokyo, Singapore and Australia are also to be tapped;
- China will gradually permit qualified foreign-funded enterprises to issue stocks and be listed in China when conditions are mature;
- Sino-foreign joint ventures of securities and fund management are to be set up;
- In time, foreign capital will be allowed to enter the Chinese securities market in a controlled way;
- Foreign service suppliers will be permitted to establish joint ventures with foreign

investment up to 33% to conduct domestic securities investment fund management businesses. Within three years, foreign investment shall be increased to 49%;
- Within three years, foreign securities institutions will be permitted to establish joint ventures, with foreign minority ownership not exceeding one-third, to engage (without a Chinese intermediary) in underwriting A shares, and in underwriting and trading of B and H shares as well as government and corporate debts and launching of funds.

Telecommunication

The Regulations for Administration of Foreign-Invested Telecommunication Enterprises (Regulations) was issued on 21 December 2001 with effect from 1 January 2002.

The Regulations provide that the shares of foreign investors' in a foreign-invested telecom enterprise that provides basic telecommunication services (other than wireless paging services) in China do not exceed 49%, and shares of foreign investors in a foreign-invested telecom enterprise that provides value-added telecommunication services (or wireless paging services) in China do not exceed 50%.

According to the Regulations, the minimum registered capital of a foreign-invested telecommunication enterprise that provides nationwide basic telecommu-nication services should be RMB2 billion. In the case of nationwide value-added telecommunication services, the minimum registration capital should be RMB10 million; the minimum registered capital of a foreign-invested telecommunication enterprise that provides in-province basic telecommu-nication services should be RMB200 million, and in the case of in-province value-added telecommunication services, the minimum registration capital should be RMB1 million.

The Regulations also state that the department of the State Council in charge of the information industry should decide geographic areas in which foreign-invested telecommunication enterprises may operate.

Road transportation

On 20 November 2001, the Ministry of Communications and the MOFTEC jointly published the Administrative Regulations on Foreign Investments in Road Transportation Industry ("Administrative Regulations"), which replaced the Provisional Regulations of the PRC Ministry of Communications on Examination of Project Proposals of Foreign Investment in Road Transportation Industry (issued by Ministry of Communications in 1993).

According to the Administrative Regulations, a foreign investor may be permitted access to the China road transportation industry by setting up a joint venture or a wholly foreign-owned enterprise. The Administrative Regulations stipulate that a Sino-foreign equity joint venture road transportation enterprise may engage in passenger transportation, cargo transportation, loading and unloading of cargo, cargo storage, vehicle repairs and other services related to road transportation; a Sino-foreign cooperative joint venture or a wholly foreign-owned road transportation enterprise may engage in the aforesaid services except passenger transportation.

According to the Administrative Regulations, the term of a foreign-invested road transportation enterprise is usually not longer than 12 years. If a foreign-invested road transportation enterprise uses 50% of its investment in the construction of passenger transportation infrastructure facilities, however, its term may be extended to 20 years.

Printing

The Provisional Regulations on the Establishment of Foreign-Invested Printing Enterprises were issued by the State Press and Publications Administration and MOFTEC on 29 January 2002, with effect from the same date.

According to the Provisional Regulations, Sino-foreign equity or cooperative joint ventures may be set up to engage in the printing of publications, packaging articles and other printed materials, and wholly foreign-owned enterprises may be set up to engage in the printing of packaging articles and other printed materials. The Provisional Regulations provide that the minimum registered capital of a foreign-invested printing enterprise engaged in the printing of publications and packing articles should be RMB10 million, and RMB5 million for foreign-invested printing enterprises engaged in the printing of other printed materials. It is also stated that in a Sino-foreign equity or cooperative enterprise that is engaged in the printing of publications and packaging articles, the Chinese partner must be a majority shareholder, and particularly, in the case of a Sino-foreign equity or cooperative enterprise that engages in the printing of publications, the Chairman of the board of directors should be appointed by the Chinese partner, and the number of board directors appointed by the Chinese partner should exceed those appointed by the foreign partner. According to the Provisional Regulations, another limitation to foreign-invested printing enterprises is that they are not permitted to open branches or offices. Also, the term of a foreign-invested printing enterprise generally may not be longer than 30 years.

Audio visual product distribution

The Regulations for the Administration of Sino-Foreign Cooperative Audio-visual Product Distribution Joint Ventures (Regulations) was jointly issued on 10 December 2001 by Ministry of Culture and MOFTEC.

According to the Regulations, a Sino-foreign cooperative audio-visual product distribution joint venture may engage in wholesale, retail or rental of audio-visual products in China, including magnetic tapes, video tapes, discs, etc.

The Regulations state that the Chinese partner in such joint ventures should hold at least a 51% interest, and the term of the joint venture should not exceed 15 years. An important limitation specified in the Regulations states that such a joint venture may not engage in the import of audio-visual products.

Employment agencies

The Ministry of Labor and Social Security and the State Administration for Industry and Commerce (SAIC), with the consent of MOFTEC, promulgated The Provisional Regulations for Administration of the Establishment of Sino-foreign Equity and Cooperative Joint Venture Employment Agencies ("Provisional Regulations") on 9 October 2001 with effect from 1 December 2001.

According to the Provisional Regulations, China permits the establishment of Sino-foreign equity and cooperative joint venture employment agencies ("joint venture employment agencies"). The establishment of wholly foreign-owned employment agencies is still prohibited.

The Provisional Regulations stipulate the conditions and procedures for setting up joint venture employment agencies. Two major conditions are: (i) the minimum registered capital of a joint venture employment agency is USD300,000, and (ii) a joint venture employment agency has to maintain at least three full-time employees with employment agent qualifications.

The Provisional Regulations provide the business scope, which includes providing recruiting services for Chinese or foreign job seekers and employers; providing employment guidance and consulting, collecting and publishing employment information, hosting of job fairs.

Tourism

A special charter on foreign-invested travel agencies was added to the Regulations on the Administration of Travel Agencies and enacted by the State Council. The amended regulation came into effect on 1 January 2002. The regulation provided:

- Upon WTO accession, foreign services suppliers that meet certain qualifications are allowed to form joint venture travel agencies and tour operators in holiday resorts designated by the Chinese government and in the cities of Beijing, Shanghai, Guangzhou and Xi'an;
- The prescribed qualifications are: the foreign investor shall be a travel agency and tour operator engaged mainly in the travel business; and its annual worldwide turnover should exceed USD40 million;
- Foreign majority ownership (over 51% ownership) and a 100% foreign ownership shall be allowed within three years and six years respectively. There will be no geographical restriction or restriction on setting up branches.
- The registered capital of a joint venture travel agency/tour operator shall be no less than RMB4 million, with the requirement being lowered to RMB2.5 million within three years. Full national treatment will be granted within six years.
- Foreign-invested travel agencies are permitted to operate the business of inbound travel to China and domestic travel services. They are not permitted to engage in outbound travel including Hong Kong SAR, Macau SAR and Taiwan.

At present, a few international travel agencies have business operations in China. An example is CITS-AE Travel Agency, started in March 2002, was jointly established by China International Travel Service and American Express Company. Another is Comfort-Rosenbluth, which was set up by China Comfort Travel Co. and Rosenbluth International.

Law firms

On 1 January 2002, the Regulations on the Administration of Foreign Law Firms' Representative Offices in China stipulating the administration of representative offices of foreign law firms in China came into force. Under the Regulations, a representative office of a foreign law firm may be set up if it meets the following requirements:

- The representative office must be affiliated with a foreign law firm that is legally registered in its home country.
- The representative must be a legally registered attorney, having been qualified as a member of the bar association in the country where his/her license was issued, and exercising his/her license for no fewer than two years outside China.
- The chief representative is required to have practised as a registered attorney for at least three years outside China, be a partner of the firm or holds an equivalent position there.

Any representative offices of foreign law firms legally established in China cannot be involved in any Chinese legal business, but they can:

- Provide clients with legal consultation with regard to the laws and regulations of the country, where its attorneys have been licensed to practice legal business, and consultation on any relevant international conventions and treaties or common practice;
- Handle the legal affairs in the country, where its attorneys have been licensed to practice legal business, as entrusted by the interested parties or Chinese law firms;
- Entrust Chinese attorneys to handle Chinese legal affairs, on behalf of foreign clients;
- Maintain long-term cooperative relationship with Chinese law firms by entering into contracts; and
- Provide information on the Chinese legal environment.

The representative office should be named "Representative Office in (city name in Chinese) of the (Chinese translation of its foreign name) Law Firm". Any foreign law firm or organization may be involved in legal services in China in the name of a consulting company or others. The representative office may not employ any Chinese attorney, and the assistants hired cannot provide legal services to clients. All service charges must be settled in China. To set up such a representative office, a foreign law firm shall apply to the local judicial department at the provincial level where its representative office is planned to be located.

Law firms in Hong Kong, Macau or Taiwan shall refer to other rules made in accordance with the major principles of the Regulations for setting up their representative offices in mainland China.

Pharmaceuticals

After January 2003, China will open pharmaceutical distribution services to foreign operators. Within one year before the opening of pharmaceutical distribution services, China will allow the establishment of pilot foreign-invested pharmaceutical distribution enterprises. The State Economic and Trade Commission (SETC) and MOFTEC will approve the establishment of foreign-invested pharmaceutical distribution enterprises. Foreign-invested pharmaceutical distribution enterprises will be as Sino-foreign equity joint ventures or Sino-foreign cooperative joint ventures. Foreign-invested pharmaceutical distribution enterprises can engage in the retail of pharmaceuticals. The foreign party in enterprise should have an average annual sales turnover of at least USD2 billion during the three years prior to the application, and assets worth USD200 million in a year prior to the application.

The Chinese party in such JVs must be an enterprise engaged in the circulation of merchandise with an annual average sales turnover of at least RMB300 million (RMB200

Top 20 Foreign Joint Venture Enterprises in China, 2001 (Unit: RMB million)

Rank Value	Enterprises	Sales
1	Motorola (Tianjin) Electronics Ltd.	31,289
2	Shanghai Volkswagen Automotive Company Ltd.	28,698
3	Guangdong Mobil Communication Co. Ltd.	25,513
4	China National Offshore Oil Corp. China Ltd.	18,910
5	SAIC-Volkswagen Sales Co. Ltd	15,867
6	FAW-Volkswagen Automotive Co. Ltd.	15,797
7	Dalian West Pacific Petrochemical Co. Ltd	13,000
8	Nanjing Ericsson Mobile Communication Co. Ltd.	9,873
9	Zhejiang Mobile Communication Co., Ltd	9,718
10	Konka Group Co. Ltd.	9,017
11	China International Marine Containers (Group) Co. Ltd.	8,954
12	Shanghai General Motors Co. Ltd	8,847
13	TPV Electronics (Fujian) Co. Ltd	7,791
14	Shanghai Siemens Mobile Communication Ltd.	7,717
15	Guangzhou Honda Automobile Co., Ltd.	7,545
16	Great Wall International Information Products (Shenzhen) Company Ltd.	7,224
17	Guangdong Nuclear Power JV Co. Ltd.	6,974
18	Shandong International Power Development Co. Ltd	6,863
19	TCL King Electronics (Huizhou) Co. Ltd.	6,860
20	Dongguan Nokia Mobile Telecommunications CO. Ltd.	6,829

million for those located in central or western China) during the three years prior to the application and assets worth at least RMB50 million (RMB30 million for those located in central or western China) in one year prior to the application. If the Chinese party is a foreign trading company, its annual average trading volume in its own account during the three years prior to the application shall be at least USD50 million (of which exports shall account for at least USD30 million). The share of the capital contribution by the Chinese party in a foreign-invested pharmaceutical wholesale and distribution enterprise shall not be less than 51%.

OPERATIONAL MATTERS

Taxation

Tax incentives serve as one of the most important factors to foreign investors. Currently, there are 13 types of taxes applicable to foreign-funded enterprises, foreign enterprises and foreigners. These include enterprise income tax, value-added tax, consumption tax, business tax, personal income tax, resource tax, land value-added tax, stamp tax, tax on urban real estate, tax for use of car and ship license plates, slaughter tax, contract tax and construction tax for cultural undertakings. Various tax concessions or breaks are available to foreign-invested enterprises (FIEs) under certain circumstances.

Enterprise income tax (EIT)

So far, China maintains two sets of enterprise income tax (EIT) laws, one for FIEs and the other for domestic enterprises. For domestic enterprises, the EIT is 33%, while for FIEs, the EIT is 30% plus 3% local surtax when no preferential tax treatments are applicable. In fact, most of the FIEs can enjoy a far more favorable average rate of 15%.

- FIEs located in the coastal open cities/areas, open cities along the Yangtze River, open cities along the border, and provincial capitals can enjoy an EIT rate of 24%. FIEs enjoy a preferential EIT rate of 15% in Special Economic Zones (SEZs), High-tech Parks (HTPs), Economic and Technological Development Zones (ETDZs) and Shanghai Pudong New District.
- Some special industrial sectors and regions also enjoy a favorable income tax rate of 15%. They include: energy, transportation, pier and port construction; enterprises located in old urban areas of coastal open areas; FIEs acknowledged as high and new–technology enterprises that are set up in approved High-tech Parks or in Beijing; foreign banks located in special economic zones and in areas authorized by the State Council with capital not less than USD10 million; and qualifying FIEs in Western China.

However, it is widely expected that China will gradually eliminate preferential tax treatment for foreign investors in order to create a nationwide level playing field pursuant to the WTO principle of "national treatment". **China's State Administration of Tax (SAT) indicated that the domestic and foreign tax regimes will be unified under one system in 2003.**

Tax exemption and reduction

Preferential tax exemption and reduction are available to FIEs

- FIEs in the manufacturing industry can enjoy income tax exemption in the first two years after making profits and income tax reduction by half in the following three years.
- High-tech FIEs can enjoy a further three-year extension of half reduction after expiry of the basic tax holiday with a minimum tax rate of 10%.
- Export-oriented FIEs with annual exports exceeding 70% of total sales can enjoy the income tax reduction by half but not less than the minimum tax rate of 10%.
- If FIEs purchase domestically made equipment within the volume of the total investment which are entitled to Category of Tariff Exemption, they can enjoy the tax credit according to some regulations.
- FIEs engaged in production scheduled to operate for no fewer than 10 years are eligible for a two-year exemption and three years' half reduction.
- Port and wharf construction projects scheduled to operate for no fewer than 10 years are eligible for five years' exemption and five years' half reduction.
- Foreign banks scheduled to operate for no fewer than 10 years are eligible for a one-year exemption and two years' half reduction.

However, the above forms of tax exemptions are likely to be abolished in accordance with the "national treatment" principle.

Reinvestment

A foreign investor may obtain a refund of 40% of taxes paid on its share of income, if the profit is reinvested in China for at least five years. Where profits are reinvested in high technology or export-oriented enterprises, the foreign investor may receive a full refund. Many foreign companies that have invested in China have adopted a strategic plan to reinvest profits for growth and expansion.

Urban maintenance and construction tax

China levies an urban maintenance and construction tax on FIEs, which so far has only been levied on domestic enterprises.

Import Stage Value Added Tax (VAT)

The import of equipment for foreign or domestic-invested projects encouraged and supported by the state shall be exempted from tariff and import stage value-added tariff. As long as a foreign-invested project is subject to the categories of "Encouraged" or "Restricted", all equipment imported for self-use within its aggregated investment, except for those listed in the "Catalogue of Imports for Foreign-invested Projects not Entitled to Tariff Exemption", shall be exempted from tariff and import-stage value-added tax. The aims and significance are in further expanding the utilization of foreign investment, encouraging inflow of foreign advanced technology and equipment, promoting the industry structural improvement and technological advancement as well as maintaining a continuous, rapid and healthy development of the economy.

(Refer to "Industrial Preferential Policies" & "Regional Preferential Policies" in Investment Environment for more details).

Finance

China imposes a highly regulated system of foreign exchange control and strictly monitors foreign debt levels. FIEs are free to take foreign currency loans from foreign banks under certain conditions. However, when borrowing from overseas parties (including offshore branches of foreign banks and other parties such as foreign shareholders) or from foreign banks in China (such as PRC branches of foreign banks or joint venture banks), FIEs are required to undertake foreign debt registration at State Administration for Foreign Exchange (SAFE). Failure to do so may mean penalties

for the borrower and the inability to remit money or to repay the debt.

FIEs can also seek Chinese currency financing, which has been a growing trend since foreign exchange controls were tightened and concerns regarding exchange rate risks were raised. Chinese currency financing is available from Chinese banks and, subject to some geographic and other restrictions, from foreign banks in China licensed to carry out Chinese currency businesses.

When lending to FIEs, banks usually require some credit support. The most common forms include guarantees from foreign shareholders, bank guarantees, standby letters of credit (particularly in RMB borrowings) and mortgages of real estate and equipment. Security given by FIEs in favor of foreign banks (including PRC branches of foreign and JV banks) must be registered at SAFE.

FIEs in China are permitted to apply for loans from Chinese capital banks with overseas assets of their foreign partners as mortgages. Inter-company loans (i.e. loans between PRC companies) are not permitted except through a financial intermediary. FIEs are permitted to apply for A- or B-stock issues. Insurance services may be provided to foreign investments in certain areas.

Sources of financing

The International Finance Corporation (IFC)
Asian Development Bank (ADB)

Foreign exchange

The Chinese currency or Renminbi has so far not been freely convertible. China regulates the flow of foreign exchange in and out of the country, and sets exchange rates through a "managed float" system. To better control this flow, almost all Chinese enterprises and agencies are required to exchange their foreign currency earnings to the banks for Renminbi (large exporters were allowed to retain up to 15% of their earnings beginning from late 1997). When foreign exchange is required for import and other authorized transactions, they then apply to designated banks that are members of the interbank foreign exchange market.

FIEs are permitted to keep foreign exchange in foreign currency accounts at commercial banks by following specific procedures.

Procedures for opening a foreign exchange account

For FIEs whose establishment has been approved by competent authorities i.e. they have obtained the business license issued by the authorities for industry and commerce, they are required to contact local authorities to have their foreign exchange registered. The local authorities will examine and check the basic conditions of the FIEs, including their investment forms and ratios, sources of funds, sources of revenue and expenditure of operating foreign exchange, proportions of products for domestic sales and exports, forms of sharing foreign exchange profits and so on. After examining and approving all these conditions, the local authorities will register and issue the Certificate on Foreign Exchange Registration to the FIEs.

With the Certificate, FIEs may open their foreign exchange accounts directly with a foreign exchange bank designated by Chinese authorities or a foreign-funded bank in China. According to relevant official regulations, all activities of foreign exchange receipts and disbursements of a foreign-funded enterprise must be conducted through its foreign exchange account with a bank in China, except for those otherwise approved by the State.

Payment and remittance of foreign exchange

New regulations have recently been made which govern the remittance of profits, dividends, and bonuses abroad. Companies must now submit the following documents to the designated foreign-exchange bank:
- Tax payment certificate and tax return (or evidence of tax exemption);
- Auditor's report on the profits, dividends or bonuses for the current year, issued by an accounting firm;
- Board of directors' resolution concerning distribution of profits, dividends, or bonuses;
- Foreign exchange certificate ;
- Capital verification report by an accounting firm;
- Other documents requested by the State Administration of Foreign Exchange (SAFE);

If a company intends to remit the profits, dividends and bonuses abroad of previous years, it must, in addition to these documents, present to the designated foreign exchange bank an accounting firm's audit report of the company's financial situation for the relevant years. Only enterprises with registered capital that is completely paid up in accordance with the contract terms will be permitted to make such remittances.

With relevant certificates and documents, current payment of foreign exchange within the business scope of the foreign-funded enterprise can be directly remitted through the bank of deposit.

The remittance of foreign exchange under the capital account, such as the capital transfer of foreign-funded enterprises, recovery of investment, and the remittance of outlay of the enterprise's branches outside China, must be approved by the Administration of Foreign Exchange Control.

Limited convertibility

China distinguishes between current account items and capital account items. China's currency, Renminbi (RMB), is convertible only in the current account.

Current account items are ordinary transaction items involving international receipts and payments. They include payments and receipts in respect of trade, labor services and unilateral remittances. For such items, conversion can usually be made on the strength of the relevant documents and after the relevant transaction has been verified.

Capital account items are items where debt or equity changes as a result of the inflow or outflow of capital involving international receipts and payments. They include direct investment and all types of loans and investments in securities. For such items, specific approval from SAFE is required before conversion.

An example of how the distinction works is foreign currency loan payments. The payment of interest is treated as a current account item, and borrowers can convert RMB into foreign exchange at their bank after the transaction has been verified by SAFE. The repayment of principal, however, is treated as a capital account item, and conversion for this purpose requires SAFE approval.

Imports & exports

In line with Chinese laws and government regulations, foreign-funded enterprises have the right to import and export from the date of their establishment. They are eligible to import machines, equipment, raw materials, fuel, spare parts and components, auxiliary equipment, elements, devices, means of transportation, office equipment and other supplies needed for their operation independently within their scope of approved business, and also export their products independently. They may also commission other foreign trade enterprises to import and export the supplies and products on their behalf. Presently, China does not allow foreign-funded enterprises to import goods which are not needed by themselves or export products which are not produced by them. Foreign-funded investment companies may act on behalf of the enterprises in China, in which they have

invested, to import goods for their own use, and export products produced by themselves as well. Foreign-funded commercial retail enterprises may purchase part of the products produced in China and export them to earn hard currency, with the approval of competent authorities.

As for the trading commodities restricted by the State (including commodities whose export is restricted under bilateral agreements), foreign-funded enterprises shall have to apply for quotas and obtain import and export licenses.

Land use rights

For FIEs, particularly those which want to engage in manufacturing or processing, it is important to consider land use rights when they choose their locations. There are certain key points a foreign investor should be aware of. Three types of land use rights are available – collectively owned rights, allocated rights and granted land use rights.

- Collectively owned rights are related to land owned by a township or rural collective and are mostly agricultural. They cannot be used for industrial purposes without special approval. Collectively owned land must first be converted into state-owned land to be convertible into granted land use rights.
- Allocated rights are those given by the state to a user, usually state owned enterprises, the army, schools, etc. There is no time limit attached to these rights, but the land may be repossessed by the state at any time. Allocated rights are non-transferable.
- Granted land use rights involve land which the state allows to be used for a specific purpose in a fixed term, for which a fee must be paid to the Government. Granted rights are freely transferable on the open market and may not be repossessed by the Government within the term, except in exceptional circumstances for which compensation must be paid. The

term for granted rights is generally a maximum of 70 years for residential use, 50 years for industrial use, and 40 years for commercial use. The term may be extended upon expiry.

A foreign investor should be aware of the difference between allocated and collectively owned land. Except in some cities, such as Shanghai and Wuxi, which have special regulations, allocated land has to be converted into granted land before a local party contributes its allocated land to a joint venture.

A foreign investor seeking to obtain land use rights in a suburban area should check if it is collectively owned land. Rights pertaining to such land must be transferred from the relevant township to the central Government before it can be transferred to a third party.

Foreign investors can obtain land use rights in several ways: by transfer from a joint venture partner; by direct transfer or lease from domestic parties, development zones or authorities; or directly from the Government by auction, tender or agreement with the Government. If existing land use rights are acquired, the term is the remainder of the original term granted to the original grantee. Land use fees are payable to the Government for all granted land and a premium is also payable for new grants of land.

Foreign investors should check that the land they propose to obtain land use rights for is designated for their intended purpose. Land is categorized into agricultural, construction or unused land. The State Council is the only body which can change land use designations and it rarely approves using agricultural land for industrial purposes.

Local land bureaus are permitted to grant land use rights on behalf of the State, and to receive fees and premiums relating to the use and grant of land. They are also responsible for approving transference of land use rights

and conversion of allocated rights into granted rights.

Arbitration

Arbitration in China is different from that in other countries in some important aspects. Most importantly, ad hoc arbitration is not generally recognized in PRC law. Arbitration may only be conducted by officially recognized arbitration institutions. As a result, parties selecting China as an arbitration venue may be constrained in their choice of applicable procedural and substantive rules, and will be required to choose arbitrators from lists maintained by the arbitration institution.

Chinese arbitration institutions have traditionally been divided into two sets handling foreign-related disputes and purely domestic disputes respectively, although now each kind of institution may handle the other set of disputes. There are two recognized foreign-related arbitration institutions: China International Economic and Trade Arbitration Commission (CIETAC) and China Maritime Arbitration Commission (CMAC). CIETAC handles disputes arising from international economic and trade activities, while CMAC deals with maritime disputes.

CIETAC

CIETAC, established in Beijing, has chapters in Shenzhen and Shanghai, and liaison offices in Dalian, Fuzhou, Changsha, Chengdu and Chongqing. The commission and chapters accept arbitration cases according to arbitration rules and regulations. The liaison offices are responsible for providing arbitration consultation services, helping arrange arbitration tribunal, doing promotion work for arbitration publicity and promotion, collecting related arbitration information, developing arbitration research work and carrying out work appointed or entrusted by the arbitration commission.

CIETAC handles cases relating to:

- International or foreign-related disputes;
- Disputes related to Hong Kong, Macau or Taiwan regions;
- Disputes among foreign-invested enterprises and/or with Chinese legal persons, physical persons or economic organizations;
- Disputes arising from project financing, invitation for tender, bidding, construction and other activities conducted by Chinese legal persons, physical persons and/or other economic organizations through utilizing the capital, technology or service from foreign countries, international organizations or from the Hong Kong, Macau and Taiwan regions;
- Disputes that may be handled by the Arbitration Commission in accordance with special provisions of or upon special authorization from the law or administrative regulations of PRC.

China International Economic and Trade Arbitration Commission
6F Gaolan Building, 32 Liangmaqiao Road, Chaoyang District, Beijing
P. R. China 100016
Tel: (86)(10) 64646688
Fax: (86)(10) 64643500 / 64643520

CMAC

China Maritime Arbitration Commission (CMAC), established in Beijing, has liaison offices in Shanghai and Guangzhou. CMAC accepts arbitration cases according to arbitration rules and regulations. The liaison offices are responsible for providing arbitration consultation services, helping to arrange arbitration tribunals, carrying out arbitration publicity and promoting arbitration negotiations, collecting arbitration information, developing arbitration research and doing work appointed and entrusted by the arbitration commission.

CMAC handles maritime cases relating to the following:

- Dispute arising from salvage and general average;
- Dispute arising from collision between vessels or from damage caused by a vessel to the structure and installation on the sea, waterways connected with sea, and in the harbor as well as the submarine or underwater installation;
- Dispute arising from management, operation, chartering, mortgage, agency, towage, raising, sale, repair, building, dismantling of seagoing/river vessels, as well as transportation by sea or by river by virtue of contracts of affreightment, bill of lading or other documents, and marine insurance;
- Dispute regarding exploitation and utilization of sea resources and pollution damage to the sea environment;
- Dispute arising from contract of freight forwarding, supply of ship stores, employment of seamen aboard a foreign vessel, fishery production and fishing;
- Other maritime dispute submitted for arbitration by agreement between the parties.

China Maritime Arbitration Commission
6F Gaolan Building, 32 Liangmaqiao Road, Chaoyang District. Beijing
P. R. China 100016
Tel: (86)(10) 64646688
Fax: (86)(10) 64643500 / 64643520

FORMS OF INVESTMENT

At present, there are three main types of foreign direct investment in China: Equity Joint Venture (EJV), Cooperative Joint Venture (CJV), and Wholly-Owned Foreign Enterprises (WOFEs). Collectively, they are referred to as "Foreign Investment Enterprises" (FIEs).

By definition, joint ventures (including EJV and CJV) refer to separate corporate entities, usually with limited liability status, jointly invested and established by one or more Chinese entities together with one or more foreign business entities (including individuals) in accordance with the EJV Law/EJV Regulations or CJV Law/CJV Regulations. The fundamental feature of a joint venture in China is that the foreign party or parties hold 25% or more in the ownership of the JV. In contrast, a Wholly-Owned Foreign Enterprise refers to a separate legal entity with limited liability status set up in China pursuant to WOFE Law/WOFE Regulations. In such an entity, one or more of the foreign investors hold 100% ownership.

Equity Joint Venture (EJV) vs. Cooperative Joint Venture (CJV)

Sino-foreign EJV companies are legal persons under PRC law, and may own assets, sue and be sued. In addition, the liability of the partners is limited to their contribution to the company's registered capital. This is similar to limited companies elsewhere in the world.

Cooperative joint ventures, or contractual joint ventures, are usually but not necessarily set up as legal persons. Non-legal person cooperative JVs may be attractive to investors from some countries (such as USA or Germany) for tax reasons.

EJV and CJV are different in the following aspects:

- Unlike CJV, EJV allows investors to limit their liabilities.
- CJVs enjoy much greater flexibility in ways of establishment and the relationship between the parties, such as sharing profits in proportions differing from their respective contributions to the joint venture capital.
- Foreign investors can recover their capital prior to the termination of a CJV provided the Chinese partner receives all the joint venture assets on its termination. Investors in Sino-foreign EJVs can normally recover their capital only in a liquidation (if the company is solvent) or if they sell their interest to the Chinese partner or a third party.

Wholly-Owned Foreign Enterprises (WOFE)

Since its introduction in 1986, WOFEs had only been an alternative to JVs in certain specific economic sectors. However, with the amendments of WOFE Law in 2001, WOFEs are expected to become increasingly popular. According to the 2002 Industrial Catalogue, WOFEs can be set up in all the "Encouraged" and "Restricted" sectors except those specified as "limited to joint ventures".

The areas in the "Encouraged" category that are only limited to joint ventures are:

- Construction and operation of municipal light railways;
- Construction and operation of civic airports;
- Construction and operation of nuclear power plants;
- Exploitation and mining of copper, lead, zinc and aluminum;
- Repair, design and manufacture of special type or high quality ships;
- Manufacture of nuclear power units (more than 600 megawatts);
- Construction and operation of comprehensive water irrigation systems;
- Construction and operation of trunk railway line networks;
- Air transportation companies;
- Post-graduate level education institutions;
- Manufacture of air transportation control network equipment;
- Design and manufacture of civilian airplanes and airplane engines;
- Design and manufacture of satellites for civilian use; and
- Design and manufacture of rocket launchers for civilian purposes.

The areas in the "Restricted" category that

are only limited to joint ventures are:
- Development and production of grain, cotton and oil seeds;
- Processing of wood from precious trees;
- Exploration and mining of special and rare types of coal;
- Printing of publications;
- Smelting and separation of rare earth;
- Manufacture of automobile cranes with capacity under 50 tons;
- General services (used in areas such as photography, mineral exploration and industries)
- Air transportation companies;
- Development of large tracts of land;
- Medical facilities;
- Senior high secondary education institutions;
- Construction and operation of cinemas.

Other forms available for foreign investment

In addition to setting up traditional forms of FIEs (i.e. EJV, CJV, WOFE), foreign investors can also set up holding companies and foreign invested joint stock limited companies in China. These new forms of investment are expected to become popular – with the Chinese government's relaxing of the laws and regulations in accordance with the WTO entry.

Foreign invested holding companies

Foreign invested holding companies refer to those EJVs or wholly-owned subsidiaries engaging in direct investment activities set up in China by foreign investors. They are set up as separate legal entities with limited liability status and independent from enterprises in which they invest in (i.e. their subsidiaries).

Unlike manufacturing and trading FIEs, which are restricted to only carry on business in the place of its business registration, foreign invested holding companies are able to invest in projects all over China without the need for further registration in the location of project.

However, there is the capitalization requirement for foreign invested holding companies. A foreign invested holding company is required to have a registered capital of at least USD30 million. The total loan amount that a foreign invested holding company can borrow shall not be more than four times its actual paid up registered capital unless it is specifically approved by MOFTEC. This is clearly different from the case of the general forms of FIEs where the limit of debt financing is determined by the total investment of the relevant FIE.

Foreign invested joint stock companies

A foreign invested joint stock company refers to an enterprise or a legal person that meets the following conditions:
- Its capital consists of shares of equal denomination;
- The liabilities of its shareholders are limited to the respective subscription of the share by such shareholders;
- Its liabilities are limited to the value of all its assets; and
- Its shares are held by Chinese as well as foreign shareholders and the foreign investors together hold more than 25% of its shares.

A foreign-invested joint stock company is considered as a type of FIE. Accordingly, all laws and regulations (including industrial sector control), with regard to foreign investment in China are applicable. In other words, it would be legally impossible to set up a foreign invested joint stock company in the industrial sectors that are prohibited to foreign investment.

The minimum capitalization requirement for registering a foreign invested joint stock company is at least RMB30 million, of which foreign investors must subscribe and contribute more than 25%.

INVESTMENT PROCEDURES

Foreign investors need to prepare required documents and go through the approval and registration process before establishing their businesses in China. The required procedures and documents are different for joint ventures and WOFEs, but in general, there are five stages FIEs have to go through.

Stage 1: Letter of Intent (LOI) / Memo of Understanding (MOU) (For JV only)

This stage is only for foreign investors who want to establish a joint venture in China. They need to reach a preliminary understanding (LOI / MOU) with their Chinese partners. These documents provide a basic description of the project contemplated, planned equity distribution between the partners, the amount of planned capitalization (which will determine the government level to which the project approval application will be directed) etc. Although LOI / MOU does not have any legal binding effect on the parties, it should nevertheless expressly provide that provisions concerning exclusivity and confidentiality are legally binding on the parties.

The preliminary agreement is attached to a project proposal which the Chinese partner is required to submit to appropriate planning commissions, the Ministry of Foreign Trade Economic Cooperation (MOFTEC) or the Commission on Foreign Trade and Economic Cooperation (COFTEC) officials for approval – the next stage.

Stage 2: Preliminary Approval — Project Proposal (For both JV and WOFE)

For JVs, the next stage is to submit a project proposal to the local or provincial government departments in charge of planning or, in some instances, MOFTEC / COFTEC. The project proposal is prepared and submitted by the Chinese partner and will include the LOI / MOU as an attachment. This step in the approval process is entirely the responsibility of the Chinese partner. Foreign investors monitoring this process have, at times, found "errors" in the translation of the preliminary agreement attached to the project proposal (all of which are in Chinese); this would, of course, alter the terms of the project. In addition, Chinese partners have sometimes drafted the project proposals to facilitate speedy approval and included export requirements, which were not part of the original agreement.

For WOFEs, this is their first step. The project proposal is prepared and submitted by the foreign investor directly to the planning commission, COFTEC or MOFTEC offices. The foreign investor sometimes contracts with a designated agent to serve as a liaison with local authorities. The foreign investor will sign an agreement with the agent stipulating the agent's scope of authority, areas of responsibility, and fees.

Generally, the Planning Commission or MOFTEC/COFTEC offices will provide a preliminary approval of the project within 20-30 days of the submission of the project proposal and preliminary agreement. An approval document will be issued to the investor, if a WOFE, or directly to the Chinese partner, if a JV. The foreign investor in a JV should request a copy of this document from the Chinese partner to confirm that the approval is consistent with the agreed terms of the project.

Stage 3: Submission of Feasibility Study Report (For both JV and WOFE)

Once the preliminary approval, the project proposal, is obtained, a feasibility study is prepared by the WOFE foreign investor or, for a JV, jointly by the joint venture partners. A feasibility study is in essence a more detailed and expanded version of project proposal.

INVESTMENT PROCEDURES

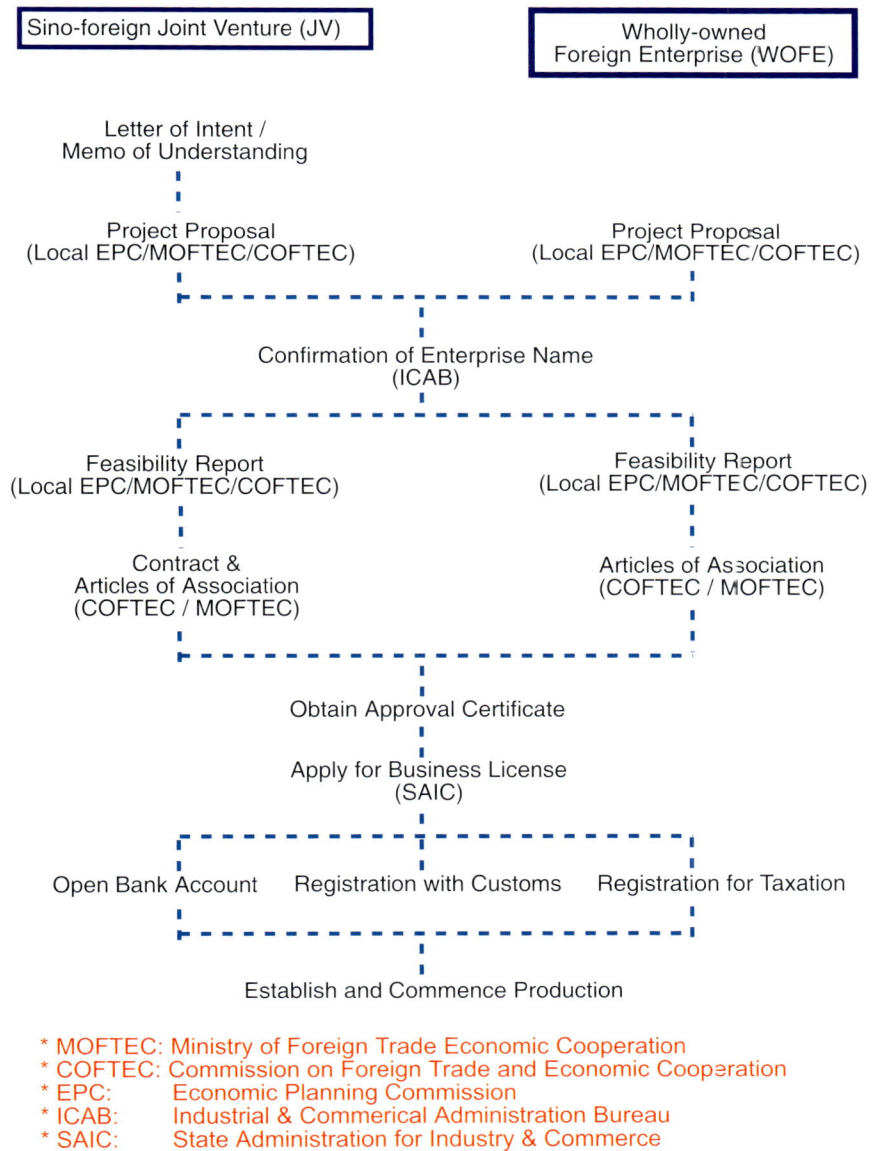

Sino-foreign Joint Venture (JV)

Wholly-owned
Foreign Enterprise (WOFE)

Letter of Intent /
Memo of Understanding

Project Proposal
(Local EPC/MOFTEC/COFTEC)

Project Proposal
(Local EPC/MOFTEC/COFTEC)

Confirmation of Enterprise Name
(ICAB)

Feasibility Report
(Local EPC/MOFTEC/COFTEC)

Feasibility Report
(Local EPC/MOFTEC/COFTEC)

Contract &
Articles of Association
(COFTEC / MOFTEC)

Articles of Association
(COFTEC / MOFTEC)

Obtain Approval Certificate

Apply for Business License
(SAIC)

Open Bank Account   Registration with Customs   Registration for Taxation

Establish and Commence Production

* MOFTEC: Ministry of Foreign Trade Economic Cooperation
* COFTEC: Commission on Foreign Trade and Economic Cooperation
* EPC: Economic Planning Commission
* ICAB: Industrial & Commerical Administration Bureau
* SAIC: State Administration for Industry & Commerce

The feasibility study must include:

- A general description of the project and the parties involved in the venture;
- Production plans and a simple marketing study;
- Location of the project and reasons for the selection;
- Description and explanation of purposes of equipment and technology to be utilized;
- Organizational structure of the enterprise;
- Environmental protection, labor arrangements, construction plans and timetable;
- Capital sourcing and the calculation thereof;
- Plus a number of attachments such as certificate of incorporation and business license, certificates of legal representation, and power of attorney and financial reports of the investors.

One important issue in the drafting of the feasibility study is the "scope of business" for the enterprise. The scope of business should be carefully defined as it will likely be repeated in the JV contract, articles of association and on the enterprise's business license. The scope of business entry on a Chinese business license delineates what activities the company is authorized to conduct; the language is usually narrowly construed. Thus, investors must be sure that the scope of business covers all categories of business activities planned for the enterprise. However, Chinese authorities will reject overly broad or vague language, so the scope must be described in precise terms. In addition, broad or ambiguous wording in the scope of business will almost certainly be interpreted narrowly by Chinese authorities. This could prevent the enterprise from engaging in business activities that the investor believed authorized at the time of approval.

Another key issue to be addressed in the feasibility study is capital contributions.

Chinese authorities have a series of guidelines that must be followed with respect to the minimum amount of capitalization for each type of FIE. There is also a timetable, based on the size of investment, for foreign partners to fulfill commitments for capital contributions. In addition, depending on the size of investment, there is a maximum ratio of debt/equity allowed for a JV. There are also regulations requiring audits to confirm the valuation of state-owned assets when used as the Chinese partners' contributions to capital. Finally, foreign investors' contributions of equipment or other kinds of contributions require appraisals by Chinese import/export authorities.

The feasibility study is to be approved by the local planning commission, COFTEC, SPC, MOFTEC, or the State Council (depending on the size of investment).

Stage 4: Formal Approval – Contracts, Articles of Association (For JVs and WOFEs)

For JVs, the next step is the completion of contract, articles of association and the formal application for approval. While the feasibility study is under review, JV partners can work to complete negotiations on the actual contract. The contract incorporates all understandings and terms from the preliminary agreement, project proposal and feasibility study, though there may be some modifications by mutual agreement between the parties. Chinese law views the joint venture contract as the fundamental document for the establishment of joint venture. The contract must meet the requirements spelt out in China's joint venture law (for equity JVs) or cooperative enterprise law (for cooperative JVs). The feasibility study and preliminary project approval document are included as attachments when the contract is submitted for formal approval.

For WOFEs, the contract is not needed. All relevant documents included a written application for the establishment of WOFE, a feasibility study report, the articles of association, a list of board members and the legal representatives, the foreign investor's incorporation documents and evidence of credit standing, the written approval of the project proposal, and other necessary documents.

For both JVs and WOFEs, articles of association must be drawn up and submitted as part of the formal application process. Under Chinese law, the articles of association are viewed as the code of company governance – similar to the company by-laws or memorandum of association in other legal jurisdictions. Chinese law (JV regulations) contains detailed provisions regarding issues that must be addressed in the joint venture contract and articles of association. The articles of association include basic information about the enterprise: the enterprise's name and address, scope of business, total capital and organizational framework. The JV regulations require that the JV contract and articles of association be written in Chinese. However, a foreign language version of the documents is frequently prepared in conjunction with the Chinese and the parties may agree that both language versions have equal validity.

According to Chinese regulations, COFTEC / MOFTEC will approve the formal application within 90 days. Approval will be in the form of a certificate issued by COFTEC / MOFTEC.

The joint venture regulations require that the JV contract be governed by Chinese law. However, disputes under the contract may be resolved through arbitration outside of China. Foreign investors are often able to convince the Chinese partner to accept the arbitration of disputes in places such as Stockholm, Zurich, London, or Singapore.

Stage 5: Apply for Business License

After obtaining the approval certificate, the WOFE or JV must apply for a business license within one month to State Administration for Industry & Commerce (SAIC) or its local delegate. The SAIC will require a nominal fee (regulations mandate that it not exceed 1/1000th of the total capital of the investment) and will usually issue a business license within two to four weeks. The enterprise will be considered to have come into existence on the date of issue of business license.

Worldwide Economic & Commercial Counselor's Offices of PRC

As China's official business institutions stationed abroad, the Economic and Commercial Counselor's Offices of PRC Embassies are in charge of trade and economic cooperation affairs between China and host countries. One of the main functions of the Economic and Commercial Office is to organize, coordinate and manage all sorts of trade and economic cooperation affairs between China and host countries. They also provide investors consulting services on the general policies, laws, regulations and application procedures regarding investment, trade, and other economic activities.

Foreigners intending to invest in China may first inquire at the Economic & Commercial Counselor's Office of the Chinese Embassy/Consulate in their countries/cities about the guide principles, policies and development strategies. A list of these is found in the Directory Section of this book.

BUSINESS TRAVEL & ETIQUETTE

Foreign investors may find it frustrating if they are not aware of the differences between Western and Chinese business culture. Understanding important business etiquette in China may help foreign investors with their businesses in China.

Greetings

Chinese names appear in a different order from Western names. The Chinese family name comes first and is usually one syllable. For example, in the case of "Wang Xiaobing", "Wang" is the family name and "Xiaobing" is the given name. For business purposes, it is traditionally acceptable to call a Chinese person by the surname, together with a title, such as "Director Wang" or "Chairman Li." Avoid using someone's given name unless you have known him or her for a long period of time. Formality is a sign of respect, and it is advisable to clarify how you will address someone very early in a relationship, generally during your first meeting.

The Chinese way of greeting is a nod or slight bow. However, when interacting with Westerners, Chinese usually shake hands. Bear in mind that a soft handshake and a lack of eye contact do not necessarily indicate timidity. It only implies that the person is not accustomed to the firm handshakes commonly used in the West.

Business meetings

In China, it is assumed that the first person that enters the room is the head of the group. Westerners should observe this convention so as not to confuse the Chinese. Important guests are usually escorted to their seats. If the meeting room has a large central table, the principal guest is likely to be seated directly opposite the principal host.

When exchanging business cards, hold out your card using both hands with the writing facing the recipient. Cards should always be exchanged individually (one-on-one). Never toss or "deal" your business card across the table, as this is considered extremely rude. Receive a business card with both hands and scan it immediately for vital information. Then lay the card in front of you on the table. It is demeaning to put someone's card directly into your pocket without looking at it first.

Meetings begin with small talk. Resist the temptation to get down to business right away. Also, avoid telling Western-style jokes, because jokes sometimes do not translate across cultures and can cause confusion or hurt feelings.

Social events

At a formal banquet, be prepared to give a brief and friendly speech in response to the host's speech. When inviting Chinese to a party, serve a "real" meal rather than snacks and drinks. When invited for dinner, it is considered proper etiquette to sample every dish served. Your host may serve some food for you, and it is nice to reciprocate, if you feel comfortable doing so. Always leave something on your plate at the end of the meal or your host might think that you are still hungry.

Gift giving

It is appropriate to bring a gift, particularly something representative of your town or region, to a business meeting or social event. Gifts indicate that you are interested in building a relationship. A gift should always be wrapped, but avoid plain black or white paper because these are the colors of mourning. Present the gift with both hands as a sign of courtesy and always mention that this is only a small token of appreciation. Do not expect your gift to be opened in your presence. This indicates that it is the thought that counts more than the material value.

Never give a clock, handkerchief, umbrella or white flowers, specifically chrysanthemums, as a gift, as all of these signify tears and/or death. Never give sharp objects such as knives or scissors as they would signify the cutting of a relationship. Lucky numbers are six and eight (especially in a series, such as 66 or 888). An unlucky number is four.

Survival tips

Welcomed topics during conversation are Chinese scenery, landmarks, weather,

Do learn a few words of Chinese. This shows an interest in your host's language and culture. It also is a very good icebreaker.

One	yi	Credit card	xin yong ka
Two	er	Delicious	hao chi
Three	san	Foot the bill	jie zhang
Four	si	Go straight	zhi zou
Five	wu	Goodbye	zai jian
Six	liu	Hello	ni hao
Seven	qi	Hot weather	tian qi re
Eight	ba	Hotel	jiu dian
Nine	jiu	How much	duo shao
Ten	shi	Mister	xian sheng
Twenty	er shi	Miss	xiao jie
Thirty	san shi	Please	ma fan ni
Hundred	bai	Shopping center	gou wu zhong xin
Thousand	qian	Take a cab	da di
Apology	dui bu qi	Thank you	xie xie
Bank	yin hang	Thanks for praising	duo xie kua jiang
Cheers	gan bei	Tips	xiao fei
Chinese currency	ren mi bi	Turn left	wang zuo
Cold weather	tian qi leng	Turn right	wang you
Congratulations	gong xi	You are most welcome	bie ke qi

climate, geography, your travels in other countries, your positive experiences traveling in China, Chinese art, etc. Avoid talking about politics or religion.

Patience is an important element in doing business in China. Respect is another: a condescending attitude is difficult to hide. Chinese are proud of their cultural heritage and generally respond sympathetically to those who take an interest in it.

Chinese business partners usually prefer long-term relationship to "one-off deals". They would only enter into such relationships when they have developed confidence in their would-be partners. So it is advisable for foreign investors to take time in developing a good relationship ("guanxi") with their Chinese partners.

If a Chinese person gives you a compliment, it is polite to deny it graciously. Modesty is highly valued in China.

The Chinese point at objects with an open hand instead of the index finger. Beckoning to someone is done with a palm facing down. Avoid beckoning with your index finger facing up.

When making a call to China from abroad, dial 86 (China's county code) + Area code (e.g. 10 for Beijing) + fixed phone number. But when making a call within China, 0 should be added before Area code, that is, 0 + Area code (e.g. 10 for Beijing) + fixed phone number. In the case of mobile phones, no area code is needed.

Visa

Any foreign investor who wishes to visit China on business requires a visa. One way to apply for a visa is for the foreign investor to first contact its Chinese trading partner directly, stating the purpose and date of the visit. If the Chinese trading partner agrees, it may on behalf of the foreign investor, apply to its local foreign affairs department for a visa notice fax. Once the foreign investor receives the fax from the Chinese domestically authorized unit, it must take the fax to the Chinese Embassy (Consulate) in its country to apply for a visa to enter China.

Another easy way is to stop off in Hong Kong on the way to the mainland destination, and apply there for a business visa either through China Travel Service (an agent) or directly with the China Visa Office. Visas are often issued within a day. A few different types of visas are issued to visitors, including the tourist visa (Type L) that allows the bearer one to two entries to stay up to one month each time. Consult the Chinese Embassy or Consulate General on obtaining the right type of visa or apply through a travel agent.

Those who wish to work and stay in China for extended periods of time need to apply for an employment visa (Type Z), which allows multiple entries into China and is valid for up to one year and is renewable. The various types of visa are:

- Visa D: Issued to aliens who are to reside permanently in China.
- Visa F: Issued to foreigners who are invited to China to visit, study, lecture, on business, scientific, technological and cultural exchanges, short term refresher courses or job training, for a period of not more than six months.
- Visa G: Issued to foreigners passing through China.
- Visa L: Issued to foreigners who come to China for tourism, visit relatives or other private purposes.
- Visa X: Issued to foreigners who come to China for study or job training for a period of six months or more.
- Visa Z: Issued to foreigners who come to China to take up posts or employment, and their accompanying family members

Established in 1967, Lee Seng Chan & Co has grown over the past 3 decades to become a diversified firm of Certified Public Accountants. Given the broad perspective of our practice, and our knowledge of and access to the global network of UHY*, our fully dedicated partners and professional staffs have extensive experience to provide clients with value-added advice and solutions demanded in today's business world. Our professional services include:

Audit:
Statutory audit, special audit, internal audit assistance, company accounts examination.

Accounting:
Outsourcing services include bookkeeping, accounting supervision, financial reporting and payroll administration.

Tax:
Tax returns preparation, tax planning, assistance in tax inquiries.

Corporate Secretarial:
Formation of companies, filing of returns, provision of registered office facilities, nominee services, maintenance of register of members, processing share transfers and allotments.

Insolvency & Business Resuscitation:
Liquidations, judicial management, receiverships.

Business Advisory:
Restructuring, business valuation, M&A, private market capital advisory, divestiture & exit strategies, business matching, IPO grooming and executive search.

China Business:
Assistance in negotiation, establishing businesses in China, special audit, tax planning, liquidation, feasibility study, M&A and student recruitment program (from China).

Information Technology:
Provision of payroll and HR software applications.

* UHY is an international network of accounting and consulting firms with 3,500 people in 120 business centres to offer professional and personal services.

Frequent travellers in China prefer staying with Novotel

Novotel provides the smart alternative to luxury accommodation, offering the astute traveller comfort, convenience and professional hospitality in key cities throughout China:

- **Novotel Peace Beijing**
- **Novotel Atlantis Shanghai**
- **Novotel Century Hong Kong**
- **Novotel Xin Hua Wuhan (Opening August 2002)**
- **Novotel Xinqiao Beijing**
- **Novotel Qi Yun Hefei**

We know you enjoy our level of service. After all, we're the business class of hotels.

For reservations call China 1 0800 610 0171*, Hong Kong 800 962 509*, Singapore 800 6161 367*, Taiwan 008 061 1216*(fax), Thailand 02 237 6064, Japan 00531 61 6353*, USA Canada 1 800 221 4542*, France 0825 88 0000, Germany 0 6995 307 595, UK 08 5 601 4768. (*toll free)

If calling from countries other than those listed please phone: (61-2) 8584 8666, fax: (61-2) 8584 8699, e-mail: Accorres_BKK@accor-hotels.com or check our website: www.accorhotels-asia.com

A worldwide leader in Hotel, Tourism and Services

Special Economic Zones

INTRODUCTION

Ever since the launch of the Open Policy, China has witnessed tremendous changes in its economy, and to a lesser degree, in the social and political ecosystem as well. The policy was actually the brainchild of the late paramount Chinese leader Deng Xiaoping and endorsed by a milestone meeting of the Third Plenary Session of the 11th Central Committee of Chinese Communist Party in December 1978.

The first step of the reforms was to establish Special Economic Zones (SEZs) in China to attract inward foreign capital. The initial four SEZs, namely, Shenzhen, Xiamen, Zhuhai and Shantou, were launched in the early 1980s, followed by Hainan, an entire province established as the largest SEZ, in 1988.

The endorsement of the first four SEZs was largely intended to attract investment from overseas Chinese with various ethnic backgrounds, in particular, Cantonese, Hokkien and Teochew dialect groups in Hong Kong, Macau, Taiwan and Southeast Asian countries. The strategy proved to be so successful that in 1984 another 14 Coastal Open Cities were singled out, followed by the establishment of five Coastal Economic Open Regions between 1985-1988 and Pudong New District of Shanghai in 1990.

Today, the five SEZs have all developed into booming export-oriented economies, with Shenzhen, Xiamen and Zhuhai taking the lead. They account for nearly one-sixth of China's total import and export volume, and one-tenth of total foreign direct investment (FDI) in China.

General preferential policies

Typically, foreign-invested enterprises (FIEs) in the SEZs are able to enjoy tax holidays and incentives that are not available or less favored elsewhere in China. This was obvious particularly in the early years of the Open Policy. However, recent trends have shown that, with more regions competing for foreign investment and offering equally attractive local concessions, such advantages of the SEZs have become gradually scaled down. Listed below are some of the general preferential policies granted by the SEZs for FIEs, although similar terms may be found in many other development zones.

- While corporate income tax rate stands at 33% nationwide for all FIEs, a 15% income tax is applicable to all FIEs located in the SEZs.
- FIEs engaged in production with more than 10 years operational terms shall be exempted from income tax in the first and second profit-making years and granted a 50% reduction of income tax in the third, fourth and fifth years. Upon maturity of these said tax exemptions, income tax for those certified as export enterprises is a reduced rate of 10%. For FIEs certified as technologically advanced, the 50% reduction in income tax rate is extended for another three years.
- Enterprises in the service sector with an investment of more than USD5 million and with operational terms of more than ten years shall be exempted from income tax in the first profit-making year and extended a 50% reduction of income tax in the second and the third year upon application and approval.
- Sino-foreign joint ventures engaged in port and wharf construction with operational terms of more than 15 years are exempted from income tax in the first five profit-making years and allowed a 50% reduction of income tax in the next five profit-making years upon application and approval.
- Foreign-funded financial institutions, such as foreign-funded banks, with foreign investment exceeding USD10 million or with operation funds of at least USD10 million appropriated from headquarters, and with operational terms of more than ten years, are exempted from income tax in the first profit-making year and granted a 50% reduction of income tax in the second and third year upon application and approval.
- Foreign investors who reinvest their after-tax profits with operational terms of no fewer than five years may apply for a 40% refund of the income tax that has been paid on the sum reinvested. Foreign investors who reinvest their after-tax profits to set up or enlarge export-oriented or technologically-advanced enterprises with operational terms of five years may apply for full refund of the income tax that has been paid on the sum reinvested.

SHENZHEN
SPECIAL ECONOMIC ZONE

Introduction

Shenzhen Special Economic Zone, the first of its kind in China, is widely known for its "Shenzhen speed" and economic vitality. The only mainland city bordering Hong Kong, Shenzhen was initially selected as an experimental site for China's economic reforms in 1979 – at that time it was a mere fishing village in the remote South. However, it was after Deng Xiaoping's 1992 southern tour calling for bolder reforms that FDI significantly increased. Driven by vigorous inflows of foreign investment, the economy has since registered astonishing two-digit growth over the past two decades.

Geography

Located at Guangdong Province's Pearl River Delta along the South China Sea, Shenzhen covers a total area of 1,949 sq km and has a population of 4.69 million. The municipal city

Shenzhen Fact Sheet

Total Land Area	1,949 sq km
Area of SEZ	391.71 sq km
Year Established	1980
Population	4.69 million
GDP	RMB190.8 billion or USD23.13 billion (2001)
Total Industrial Output	RMB288.0 billion or USD34.91 billion (2001)
Total Foreign Trade	USD68.59 billion (2001)
FDI Contracted	USD4.00 billion (2001)
FDI Utilized	USD3.60 billion (2001)

of Shenzhen consists of six districts, namely Luohu, Nanshan, Futian, Yantian, Bao'an, and Longgang, among which the first four make up the SEZ covering 391.71 sq km.

Facing Dapeng Bay in the east, Shenzhen stretches to the mouth of Pearl River in the west. To the south lies Hong Kong; Dongguan and Huizhou are at the north border. Shenzhen's topography is mostly low hilly land ascending from northwest to southeast. Wutong Moutain, standing at 943.7 m high above sea level, is the highest peak in the SEZ.

Shenzhen is famous for its mild subtropical oceanic climate. Spring is comfortable and sunny, summer is hot, rainy and windy, autumn is clear and fine and winter is short, dry and a little cold. Annual temperature ranges from 14.1°C to 28.2°C and averages at 22.4°C. Rainy season normally starts from May and ends in September. The average precipitation is 1,948 mm yearly. Southeasterly wind prevails all year round. Typhoons in the summer and fall occur less than once a year on average.

Travel information

Shenzhen is a great all-season destination for tourists. While travelers need to prepare an umbrella for the heat of summer and the rain of the rainy season, in the winter they can enjoy the luxuriant trees and blooming flowers not commonly seen then elsewhere in China. The city, which is 45% green, has been elected as the "Garden City of the State" and the "Environmental Star City" for several consecutive years. In November 2000, it won the honor of "International Garden City" at the "Green Oscar" contest in Washington; and in June 2002, it was added into the UN Environment Program's Global 500 Roll of Honor for Environmental Achievement.

Shenzhen's Bao'an International Airport lies 20 km west of the downtown. It has 76 routes and flights connecting 41 major cities domestically. Shuttle buses and taxis are readily available for commuting to downtown.

Passengers from Guangzhou, Zhuhai, Shantou and Hong Kong can go directly to Shenzhen's Shekou Port by sea. Alternatively, visitors may also reach Shenzhen by rail from Beijing, Changsha (Hunan), Jiujiang (Jiangxi), Wuhan (Hubei), or transferring at Guangzhou to express service with 40 trains scheduled every day. Overseas visitors may also take trains from Hong Kong via the Guangzhou-Kowloon Railway, which would take about 35 minutes.

Shenzhen boasts a well-developed road system with numerous bus services linking Hong Kong and many inland cities. It is a pleasant journey by express buses heading straight for attractions in the city such as China Folk Culture Villages, Window of the World, Splendid China and the Safari etc.

Economic performance

Shenzhen is the fastest developing city in China. During the period of 1980-2001, its annual increase in GDP averaged 29.5%, that in industrial total output was 45.4%, and that in total foreign trade volume was 39.1%. In 2001, its GDP exceeded USD23 billion, or 295 times the figure in 1979, ranking it fourth among all Chinese cities; GDP per capita reached USD4,900, ranked at the top. By 2001, its annual inland revenue has ranked third for five consecutive years, and total import and export volume (USD68.6 billion) top for nine consecutive years, surpassing Shanghai and Beijing. In terms of economic strength, Shenzhen is now equivalent to a medium-sized mainland province.

Built from a small agricultural town, Shenzhen now features a wide range of manufacturing and service industries. The proportion of primary sector has declined to be less than one percent. In recent years, the city's high-tech industries have seen tremendous growth. Such industrial clusters include computer and its accessories, tele-communication and networks, micro-electronic and basic devices, optical electromechanical integration, digital audio-visual devices, biotechnology and new materials. In 2001, the total industrial output of the high-tech sector accounted for 45.9% of the city's total. The development of the tertiary sector is also rapid. Financial services, including banking, securities and insurance, information service, tourism, real estate and logistics have become important components of the local economy.

Infrastructure

Shenzhen Port comprises nine harbors, 82 cargo terminals, and 39 deepwater berths of 10,000-ton capacity. It has 69 overseas routes with a monthly run of 417 ships, and in 2001 it handled over 66.43 million tons of freight. Shenzhen has the second largest container terminal, Yantian, in China, and after handling over 5.08 million TEUs in 2001, it is now the eighth largest in the world. Ten more berths expected to open before 2005 will increase the port's annual handling capacity by another 1.6 million TEUs.

Bao'an Huangtian International Airport is ranked the fourth largest airport in the mainland and handled 77.75 million people in 2001. It owns a unique passenger-cum-cargo terminal, the only airport in mainland

China that can transport goods in and out of the country directly.

Shenzhen is situated at the intersection of two Chinese trunk railways – Beijing-Kowloon Railway and the Beijing-Guangzhou-Kowloon Railway, boosting its accessibility to many hinterland cities. A 19.5 km Shenzhen Metro System is also under construction, and is expected to go into operation by the end of 2003. The first phase alone costs a total investment of USD1.3 billion.

Shenzhen has daily water supply of 3.64 million tons and an installed generating capacity of 3.020 mW to suit domestic and industrial requirements. Switchboard volume totals 1.78 million lines and IT services are available for the growing demand from high-tech industries.

Climate of foreign investment

In terms of foreign trade and investment, Shenzhen has undoubtedly stimulated overseas businessmen's strongest interest since its conversion to an SEZ in 1980.

As an export-oriented economy, its exports has reached USD37.5 billion, of which mechanical and electronic products contribute a combined proportion of 64.0% and high-tech products contribute 29.4%. Among others, FDI has played a pivotal role in the process. Currently, FIEs account for over three quarters of the city's total industrial output and half of its total exports.

In 2001 alone, Shenzhen has registered new contracted foreign investment worth USD4.0 billion and utilized foreign investment worth USD3.6 billion. Shenzhen is now home to more than a tenth of the world's top 500 enterprises including IBM, Dupont, DEC, Lucent Technologies, Microsoft, Emerson, Compaq, HP, Intel, Walmart, Xerox, Hitachi, Sanyo, Mitsubishi, Matsushita, Mitsui, Fujitsu, Sumitomo, Toshiba, Komatsu, Shell, Samsung, Hyundai, Siemens and Nortel etc. Foreign invested capital averages USD1.8 million per project in 2001. However, there are increasingly large projects being signed – with 97 exceeding USD5 million and 49 above USD10 million.

Foreign investors engage in a wide range of industries such as electronics, pharmaceuticals, foodstuff, textile and garments, metals, plastics, real estate and hotels. While roughly 64% of total FDI has flowed into manufacturing, the rest is put into tertiary industries. Recently, trends have been shown in the high-tech sectors like optical fiber and integrated chips (ICs) as well as in the previously rather restrictive sectors such as finance, logistics, wholesale and retail.

Noticeably, foreign financial institutions are mushrooming in Shenzhen SEZ, for example HSBC, UFJ Bank, Bank of East Asia, Bank of Tokyo-Mitsubishi, Societe Generale, BNP, Citibank, Standard & Chartered Bank and Merrill Lynch.

Preferential policies

Playing a vanguard role in China's economic reforms, Shenzhen offers exclusive incentives to foreign investors besides general preferences given nationwide.

- While corporate income tax stands at 15%, 3% local income tax is exempted.
- Export companies at the expiry of their tax exemption and reduction period still enjoy a reduced rate of 10% for income tax, provided the export volume accounts for 70% of their total industrial output.
- Foreign invested high-tech enterprises are exempted from income tax for two years and enjoy a 50% reduction for the subsequent eight years. High-tech projects are given an income tax exemption period of three years on the profit hitherto made regardless of previous tax incentives.
- The value added tax (VAT) of foreign invested high-tech projects is computed against last year's figure and 50% of the local portion of the newly added VAT is returned to the enterprise by the municipal financial department.

- Newly established export oriented FIEs need pay only half of the land use fee for industrial purposes. This also applies to certified projects with technological innovations for five years. As for high-tech businesses, no fee is payable on the transfer of land use rights.
- High-tech enterprises are exempted from property tax for five years for newly built or purchased sites.
- Technology contributed by companies with limited liability can take up a maximum of 35% in the total registered capital, provided its high-tech status is approved by the Municipal Bureau of Science and Technology.
- Technological enterprises set up by Chinese students and professionals abroad are not limited by requirements on shareholders' residential status. Payment of registered capital can be in installments in two years.
- Venture capital companies are welcomed in Shenzhen. With a minimum investment of 70% in the high-tech sector, they are equally eligible for all the abovementioned tax holidays and incentives. About 3% to 5% of the current year's profit can be set as risk compensation fee to make up for the investment loss incurred before.
- High-tech enterprises invested by overseas investors can be registered as domestic companies if their capital contribution is below 25% of the total registered capital.
- FIEs in the service sector with investment exceeding USD5 million and operational terms of at least 10 years are entitled to income tax exemption for the first profit-making year and a 50% reduction for the second and third years.
- Foreign banks or Sino-foreign equity joint venture banks in Shenzhen are exempt from business tax for five years commencing from the date of opening.
- Goods made and sold within the SEZ are free from VAT in the production process.

- FIEs and expatriates in Shenzhen enjoy national treatment. This means that FIEs may decide and re-adjust the shares between its domestic and overseas sales, if not restricted by State quota or permits. Utility charges for FIEs are based on the same rates as for their Chinese counterparts. Expatriates in Shenzhen have equal access to domestic housing, medical or traveling services and pay the same rates as local citizens.

Areas for foreign investment

Shenzhen has three forms of industrial estates for foreign investors to choose from.

Modeling on the free trade zone (FTZ) concept, Shenzhen SEZ contains three such bonded areas: Shatoujiao, Futian and Yantian FTZs, where imported materials such as equipments, components and packaging needed for export processing or consumption within the bonded areas are exempt from tariffs, VAT and consumption tax. Goods shipped into these FTZs from overseas are also free from license and customs duty. Entrepot trade, transportation and warehousing, financial and insurance services are highlighted by the local developer. The sizes of the FTZs are 0.3 sq km (Shatoujiao), 0.85 sq km (Yantian Port) and 1.35 sq km (Futian).

An 11.5 sq km state-level Shenzhen High-tech Park is situated in the west of Shenzhen SEZ. It aims to be a high profile industrial park of international standards and Shenzhen's key economic growth base as well. Industries that are given priority by the high-tech park include information technologies, bio-engineering, new materials and optical electromechanical integration.

Longgang Greater Industrial Estate covers 174.4 sq km of land, or one fifth of the total area of Longgang District. Though outside Shenzhen SEZ, it has been the most dynamic area in Shenzhen city. With manufacturing as the core part of the economy, it promotes the use of state of the art technology and competes with the SEZ in attracting FDI

inflows. Local authorities encourage foreign investment to be channeled into industries such as computer products and software, microelectronics, refined chemicals, pharmaceuticals, bio-engineering, automobile, metals, textiles and machinery. There are four sub-level industrial districts.

Shenzhen Municipal Government
Website: www.sz.gov.cn

Information Center of Shenzhen Bureau of Foreign Trade
5th Floor, Design Building
8 Zhenhua Road
Shenzhen, Guangdong
P. R. China 518031
Fax: (86)(755) 3786296
Website: www.szinvest.com
www.sztdb.gov.cn

Shenzhen High-tech Park
Website: www.shipgov.net

XIAMEN
SPECIAL ECONOMIC ZONE

Introduction

Xiamen is just a stone's throw from Taiwan, another important source of FDI fueling China's economy in the early days. Following Shenzhen SEZ, Xiamen SEZ was approved by the central government in October 1980 and established a year later on a humble export processing industrial zone in the northwestern corner of Xiamen Island. It was in March 1984 that the SEZ expanded from a mere 2.5 sq km to the whole 133 sq km island.

Geography

Xiamen City is situated on the southeast coast of Fujian Province, at the estuary of Jiulong River. At the back of Xiamen lies the Xia-Zhang-Quan Plain. It faces the Penghu Islands and Taiwan Island over the Taiwan Straits. Xiamen comprises Xiamen Island,

Xiamen Fact Sheet

Total Land Area	1,565 sq km
Area of SEZ	133 sq km
Year Establishe	1980
Population	1.31 million
GDP	RMB55.64 billion or USD6.74 billion (2001)
Total Industrial Output	RMB80.05 billion or USD9.70 billion (2001)
Total Foreign Trade	USD11.08 billion (2001)
FDI Contracted	USD1.27 billion (2001)
FDI Utilized	USD1.15 billion (2001)

Gulang Islet and some coastal parts of north Jiulong River. The municipality of Xiamen administers seven districts: Siming, Kaiyuan, Gulangyu, Huli, Jimei, Xinglin and Tong'an. The former four form the SEZ which is less than a tenth of the total land area of Xiamen city. At the end of 2001, the population of the whole city was 1.31 million. The language spoken predominantly in Xiamen is the South Fujian dialect.

The topography of Xiamen is characterized by a gradual descent from the south to the north, with the northwestern part being relatively flat and the southern part mountainous and hilly. The Yunding Rock, standing 339.6 m above sea level, is the highest within the territory. The strait-type Xiamen Port has a zigzagging coastal line 234 km long. As the deepwater port is not frozen all year round, Xiamen has been a famous seaport for foreign trade in China since ancient times.

The climate of Xiamen is typically subtropical, mild and temperate with abundant rainwater. Winter in Xiamen is not harsh, while summer is free from extreme heat. Rainfall is common from May to August. The annual temperature averages 21°C and annual precipitation 1,200 mm. Northeast wind dominates in Xiamen and typhoons normally occur three to four times in summer.

Travel information

Xiamen is a well-known tourist port city in the Southeast coast of China. It is one of the "Cleanest Cities of China", the "Garden Cities of China", the "National Environmental Star Cities", and the best sightseeing cities in China.

In ancient times, there were "Eight Major Landscapes", "Eight Minor Landscapes" and eight "Landscapes Beyond Landscapes" in Xiamen. Some of the 24 scenic spots can still be traced today. Xiamen now has five main tourist resorts – Gulangyu Island Tourist Area, Nanputuo Temple Tourist Area, Wangshi Rock Tourist Area, Huangcuo Tourist Area and Jimei Tourist Area.

Xiamen's fast and convenient transportation and communication, combined with complete travel facilities, make it very accessible. Xiamen port ranks among the top 10 in China and has shipping routes to over 60 ports in more than 40 countries. Passengers may arrive in Xiamen from Shanghai, Wenzhou, Shantou, Guangzhou and Hong Kong by sea. Xiamen International Airport serves 22 airlines linking major mainland cities as well as Singapore, Hong Kong, Macau, Kuala Lumpur, Manila, Seoul, Tokyo, Osaka and Bangkok. Well-developed highway and expressway systems connect Xiamen with other Chinese cities and Hong Kong. Visitors may also choose trains as Xiamen is at one end of Yingtan-Xiamen Railway.

Economic performance

In 2001, Xiamen's GDP increased by another 12.0% to USD6.74 billion, doubling that of 1995 or 31.9 times that of 1980. Since its inception as an SEZ, Xiamen has maintained fast and sustainable economic growth. The average annual growth is 18.4%, and GDP per capita has become comparable to that of Shenzhen. Total inland revenue in 2001 reached USD1.11 billion, which is 49 times higher than that in 1980. An ever occlusive seaport has already been turned into a bustling modern metropolis.

The proportions of three sectors of the local economy are 3.81%, 53.2% and 43.0% for the primary, secondary and tertiary industries respectively. The service sector has recently registered accelerated growth. Previously, Xiamen's economy was largely driven by investment on fixed assets. The scenario has been greatly changed, as exports and fast expanding consumption have become the main force. In 2001, Xiamen's total industrial output rose by 15.4% to USD9.7 billion or 78.6 times that of 1980. Foreign trade amounted to USD11.08 billion, confirming Xiamen as an export-driven economy.

High-tech enterprises are recently giving new momentum to Xiamen's economy. Their industrial output now accounts for 29.8% in total. Electronics, communication equipment, and photosensitive materials have become

the leading industries in Xiamen.

Infrastructure

Relying on its favorable location as a main import harbor historically, Xiamen has developed into a regional hub of transportation and communication. The transportation system includes the sixth largest container terminal in the country, an international airport and a highway-expressway-railway network. In 2001, Xiamen Port, with its seven harbors and eighteen 10,000-ton-capacity berths, has handled over 20.99 million tons of cargo, including 1.29 million TEUs. Shipping routes have been extended to Hong Kong, Japan, Korea, Singapore, Taiwan, the Mediterranean and European regions, and the west coast of the US.

The second phase of the Gaoqi International Airport was completed in 2000. With a 3,400 m runway and a 3,300 m taxiway, the airport is now able to serve up to 10 million passengers per year. The parking apron is 250,000 sq m and is able to accommodate 40 large airplanes at a time. The airport is connected to 54 domestic and overseas destinations by 102 air routes with 1,326 flights scheduled weekly.

Transportation companies in Xiamen provide various passenger and cargo services by road or by rail, and a regular Xiamen-Shenzhen-Hong Kong container truck service is scheduled.

IDD services can be easily found in Xiamen as public telephones and IC telephones are found everywhere. Local mobile, public multimedia communication, and public digital data networks (DDN) have also been set up. Travelers may choose internet, express mail, or collect call services as well.

The daily capacity of water supply is 915,000 tons. The electric network in Xiamen is safe and reliable with a capacity of 4.3 billion kWh. Eligible applicants will be equipped with separate meters and supplied electricity within ten working days after completion of necessary electrical work.

Climate of foreign investment

FIEs have contributed immensely to Xiamen SEZ and municipality. Year 2001 saw contractual FDI soaring by 26.7% to USD1.27 billion. By the end of 2001, Xiamen had in total approved 5,334 contracts with foreign investors; contractual and utilized FDI amount to USD18.8 billion and USD12.7 billion, respectively. MNCs such as GE, ABB, Linde, Kodak, Dell, Matsushita, Itochu, TDK and Taikoo have already set up their operations in Xiamen. In 2000, FIEs generated an industrial output of USD7.2 billion and total export and import value of USD6.6 billion, taking a share of 84.8% and 65.8% in the city's total, respectively. Foreign investment covers a range of industries, such as electronics, chemicals, textile, foodstuff, electric power, real estate and finance, etc.

More than 600 financial institutions are currently operating in Xiamen, a number of which are from overseas. Besides many state owned banks, there is a Sino-foreign joint venture Xiamen International Bank and a wholly foreign owned Xiamen Commercial Bank. Among others, Chiyu Bank and the Bank of East Asia from Hong Kong, HSBC and Standard Chartered Bank from the United Kingdom, United Overseas Bank from Singapore, Bank of the Orient from the United States, Credit Lyonnais from France, ING Bank from the Netherlands and Bangkok Bank from Thailand have opened branches in Xiamen. Meanwhile, representative offices have been set up by Hang Seng Bank from Hong Kong, Citibank and the Hartford Fire Insurance from the US and the Mizuho Bank from Japan etc.

Preferential policies

Taxation incentive schemes in Xiamen SEZ basically include:

- Corporate income tax rate for FIEs is 15%. FIEs are exempted from local income tax.
- FIES engaged in manufacturing, logistics, agricultural development with an operational period of more than ten years are entitled to a tax holiday for the first two profit-making years and a 50% tax concession for the following three years; FIEs engaged in port construction with an operation period of more than 15 years are entitled to a tax holiday for the first five profit-making years and a 50% tax concession for the following five years.
- At the maturity of the above-mentioned tax holidays and concessions, such enterprises can enjoy a preferential tax rate of 10% in the year when they export 70% or above of their industrial output and generate a foreign exchange surplus, and FIEs with advanced technology shall be eligible for the same preferential tax rate of 10% for the following three years.

- FIEs engaged in the service sector with FDI exceeding USD5 million and an operational period of more than ten years qualify for the tax exemption for the first profit-making year and a 50% tax concession for the following two years.
- When a company suffers loss in one year, it may cover such loss by drawing a corresponding sum from the income of the next year. Should the income of the next year be inadequate to make up for the loss, the enterprise may continue to draw from the income of the subsequent years but within a period not exceeding five years.
- An FIE which has reinvested the profits in the same enterprise or in establishing another enterprise with an operational period of over five years shall enjoy a 40% refund of the tax on the reinvested profits. If such profits are re-invested in establishing or expanding an export-oriented enterprise or a technologically advanced enterprise with an operational period of five years, the foreign investor shall enjoy a 100% refund instead.
- Corporate income tax is levied on a yearly basis and paid in advance in quarterly instalments. Full payment of taxes will be settled within five months after each accounting year.
- Foreign-funded projects that transfer technology and fall within the categories of Encouraged or Restricted Projects (B) in the Industrial Catalogue for Foreign Investment are exempted from customs duties and import VAT on imported equipment for own usage within the investment amount, except those commodities listed in the Catalogue of Non-Duty-Free Imported Commodities of Foreign Invested Projects.

Areas for foreign investment

Xiamen SEZ was first started as Huli Industrial Zone for Export Processing with a small area of 2.5 sq km. Since the expansion of the SEZ to the current size in 1984, the city has also nominated a few areas to further attract overseas investors, especially Taiwanese. These consist of Investment Zones in Haicang, Xinglin and Jimei, the Xiangyu Free Trade Zone, the Xiamen Torch High-tech Industrial Development Zone and other zones.

The State-level Haicang Investment Zone is the biggest within the SEZ. The 100 sq km area is committed to become a new urban district, a new harbor district and two new industrial districts in the 21st century as an extension to Xiamen Island proper. Though located outside the SEZ, it is going to be the key region for Xiamen's economic development. Haicang Bridge has already been completed to link Xiamen Island. Capital or technology-intensive projects in petrochemical, mechanical engineering and building materials are welcomed. The investment zone itself contains Xiamen Export Processing Zone, the only one of its kind in Fujian Province.

To the northwest of the SEZ lie the two new Taiwanese Investment Zones – Jimei and Xinglin. The Xiamen Torch High-tech Industrial Development Zone was founded in 1990 to carry out the nation's Torch Plan by promoting technological application in new material, optical and electromechanical integration and biotech industries. It is made up of a few high-tech parks, including the Torch High-tech Park, Siming Software Park, Luqiao High-tech Park etc.

Currently, priority has been given to foreign investment involved in the following projects:

- Infrastructure construction in roads, bridges, wharfs and environment protection etc;
- High and new technological industries or those applying advanced technologies, especially those in electronics and IT, mechanical, chemical and pharmaceutical industries;
- Reforms of traditional light industries, textiles and building materials;

- Supporting industries such as new material and component manufacturing;
- Export-oriented projects that will increase local foreign exchange reserves;
- Import-substitute projects that meet domestic demand;
- Development of tourist resources;
- Projects in the tertiary sector that meet the central government's guidelines;
- Comprehensive agricultural development.

Xiamen Municipal Government
Website: www.xm.gov.cn

Xiamen Foreign Investment Bureau
14-15th Floor, Foreign Trade Building
North Hubin Road
Xiamen, Fujian
P. R. China 361012
Tel: (86)(592) 5054866, 5054856
Fax: (86)(592) 5054859, 5043092
Email: xmfiecip@xm.fj.cn
Website: www.fdi-xiamen-cn.com

ZHUHAI
SPECIAL ECONOMIC ZONE

Introduction
While the establishment of Shenzhen and Xiamen SEZs was primarily targeting at overseas Chinese investors in Hong Kong and Taiwan, Zhuhai SEZ was established to leverage on the then Portuguese governed city of Macau. Upgraded to a City in 1979 and subsequently founded as a Special Economic Zone a year later, Zhuhai has since totally changed its landscape of an economically disadvantaged fishing village.

Geography
Zhuhai sits on the west bank of the Pearl River estuary, 36 nautical miles away from Hong Kong and Shenzhen and 140 km to the south of Guangzhou, the capital of

Zhuhai Fact Sheet

Total Land Area	1,600 sq km
Area of SEZ	121 sq km
Year Established	1980
Population	1.25 million
GDP	RMB36.72 billion or USD4.45 billion (2001)
Total Industrial Output	RMB71.64 billion or USD8.68 billion (2001)
Total Foreign Trade	USD9.06 billion (2001)
FDI Contracted	USD710 million (2001)
FDI Utilized	USD860 million (2001)

Guangdong Province. The urban area of the city borders Macau. Facing South China Sea, Zhuhai has a vast water area three times more than its land area of 1,600 sq km. There are 146 islets scattered around that form the Wanshan Archipelago. The city of Zhuhai has a population of 1.25 million and three districts – Xiangzhou, Doumen and Jinwan.

The area of Zhuhai SEZ is about 121 sq km.

Zhuhai's topography ranges from hills, plains, lakes to sea. Its subtropical oceanic climate is mild. The temperature averages 22.1°C annually and reaches its lowest in January and February. It is hot and rainy between May and September. The yearly average precipitation is 1,700 – 2,300 mm. Southeasterly wind prevails in summer and northeasterly wind in winter. Typhoons occur commonly in summer and autumn.

Travel information

Endowed with good weather conditions, Zhuhai is a coastal tourist city in South China. The whole city of Zhuhai is listed in the "Top 40 Tourist Attractions in China" and has been elected as the "Garden City of State" and the "Environmental Star City" as well. It is the only Chinese city that has won the "Dubai International Award for Best Practices to Improve the Living Environment" by the United Nations Center for Human Settlements in 1998.

As the expressway-highway system is highly developed, travelers may take coaches and buses to reach Zhuhai from adjacent provinces. The airport is 40 km away from downtown and has 100 flights weekly flying to and from more than 30 destinations all over China. Passengers transferring in Guangzhou, Shenzhen, or Hong Kong may also choose to arrive by sea via Jiuzhou Port.

Economic performance

When Zhuhai was founded as a city in 1979, it had only a small population of 100,000 with industrial output of less than USD20 million. In 2001, the city's industrial output skyrocketed to USD8.68 billion and GDP USD4.45 billion. Zhuhai has been built into a dynamic export-oriented economy with an array of comprehensive industries led by electronics and electromechanical equipment manufacturing, supported by commerce, trade, tourism, finance, real estate, IT, transportation, agriculture and fishery. The total foreign trade volume amounted to USD9.06 billion in 2001. Electromechanical products accounted for 68.3% of the total export, and high-tech products took a 34.9% share.

Infrastructure

Zhuhai has the 10th biggest container terminal in China – Jiuzhou Port. With a total of 17 berths, the handling capacity of the port is 0.45 million TEUs per year. Gaolan Port has two ready-built berths and the maximum berthing capacity is 20,000 tons. Passenger ferries from Zhuhai to Hong Kong run on a daily basis. Zhuhai Airport occupies an area of four square kilometers in the southwest of Zhuhai and has 32 air routes connecting domestic destinations. Guangzhou-Shenzhen-Zhuhai Expressway was open for traffic in the end of December 1999.

Zhuhai has a daily water supply capacity of 1.5 million tons and power supply of 650,000 kWh. The 3.72-million-kw Zhuhai Power Plant will also be functional soon.

Climate of foreign investment

By the end of 2001, investors from 46 countries or regions have already set up their establishments there. There are 6,597 FIEs currently operating in Zhuhai, including BP-Amoco, Mobil, AT&T, Coca-Cola, Concord, MTU of Daimler-Chrysler, Celanese, Flextronics, Bell, Matsushita, Canon, Iwatani, Fujikura, Mitsubishi Electric, Carrefour, Phillips and Foster's, etc. Among the Fortune 500 MNCs, 30 have a presence in Zhuhai. FIEs have become the most important part of local economy, contributing nearly 70% to the city's total economic volume.

Year 2001 saw 646 new foreign-invested projects signed, with a total committed investment amounting to USD1.37 billion, increasing by 38.6% over the previous year, of which more than half are foreign funds. Wholly owned foreign enterprise (WOFE) becomes the dominant form of FDI, as 85% of such newly-signed projects fall into this category. The actually paid-up FDI in 2001 was USD864.7 million.

A few foreign banks have already entered Zhuhai, such as Standard Chartered Bank, Bank of East Asia, Xiamen International Bank and Banco Nacional Ultramarino. Currently, the foreign investors community in Zhuhai has two major platforms. Founded in 1989, Zhuhai Association of Foreign Investment Enterprises has more than 1,800 members and two sub-branches in the city's two districts. Zhuhai Association of Taiwanese Investment Enterprises was set up in 1993 and now has 160 member enterprises and one sub-association.

Preferential policies

FIEs located in Zhuhai SEZ enjoy all the taxation holidays and incentives currently available in the five SEZs. As China enters the World Trade Organization (WTO) and national treatment for FIEs looms large, preferential policies are being adjusted and inclined to show the emphasis on industrial sectors and specific locations rather than on ownership of a business entity. The major concessional terms are:

- For the land use of high-tech industry, land prices are reduced by a significant margin of 10% to 50%, based on the standards for industrial land use.
- For projects with a total investment of at least RMB100 million (equivalent to USD12.1 million) and a registered capital of RMB50 million (except the development of commercial property), land use prices can be further granted a 50% reduction and land use fees are exempted.
- For large projects of public welfare like education and sports, the land use prices can be reduced by 100%.
- For scientific and technological projects in high-tech zones, land use prices can be charged on the basis of state-level advanced high-tech projects, at RMB153 or USD18.5 per sq m, even before they are verified for such ratings.
- When projects in high-tech zones start operation, a recalculation of their land use prices and refunds are available, provided their products or technology in use are verified to have reached international technological levels, or their products are import substitutes and meet domestic demand. The land use prices are thereby charged at RMB99 or USD12.0 per sq m for the projects of this category.
- Projects in high-tech zones whose investment per unit area and annual tax contribution exceed certain levels may enjoy up to 50% rebate or refund of paid land use fees.
- For all the industrial, warehousing, and scientific and technological projects that have acquired the lease of the land through the assignment system, they are qualified for a five-year installment plan with a

minimum down payment of 30%. For those with a higher-level amount of investment or technology, the minimum is 15%. For projects renewing their lease on a yearly basis, the lease term can be up to 50 years, but no fewer than 10 years, and the prices can be based on the current terms.

- Software companies in high-parks zones and Technical Innovation Beach may enjoy another 30% discount on land use prices based on the technological level of these projects verified. The down payment of land use may reduce further to 15% when approval from the administration committee is given–on a case-by-case basis.
- Land may be provided for free when it is used for establishing educational institutions by key domestic universities. Foreign institutions for higher learning or research institutes can also enjoy the privilege after they get State approval.
- There is no installation fee involved for additional capacity of electricity and water supply in high-tech parks. A 20% discount in electricity and water prices is applied to all companies in such high-tech parks.
- The local financial department allocates a certain amount of subsidy for high-tech projects with promising prospects. Funds for software industry development and biological pharmaceuticals are also available in Zhuhai.

Areas for foreign investment

Apart from the SEZ, the city of Zhuhai has allocated five main industrial zones to accommodate foreign investments, the most prominent one being Zhuhai State-level High-tech Park. However, it is by no means a spatially continuous single zone. It is composed of six subsidiary parks all over the municipal territory: four Science and Technology Industrial Parks in Nanping (4.2 sq km), Sanzao (2.66 sq km), Xinqing (3.44 sq km) and Baijiao (4 sq km), Guangdong Zhuhai Base for Industrialization of Technological Achievements, and Zhuhai Technological Innovation Beach.

Projects welcomed to reside in the parks are those in the industries of electronics, information technologies, biological pharmaceuticals, new energy, new materials, photomechatronics, computer software development and network communications.

Zhuhai Free Trade Zone (FTZ) is a three square kilometer bonded zone situated in the southern part of Zhuhai Special Econmic Zone. It was established in 1996 to boost export processing activities.

Just opposite the free trade zone lies the Province-level Hengqin Development Zone, an island of 96 sq km, which aims to develop its rich tourism resources.

Located in the west part of the city is Zhuhai Port Industrial Zone. It has a total planned area of 64.44 sq km. The grade-A port has two 20,000-ton-capacity berths for bulky cargo and containers plus another six berths with varied sizes for liquefied gas, chemicals and coal. This zone is keen to develop large-scale industries such as energy, petrochemical, machinery and warehousing.

Approved by the provincial government in 1998, Wanshan is committed to develop the 76 islets – spanning 3,200 sq km – into the fields of fishery, tourism and warehousing.

Zhuhai Municipal Government
Website: www.zhuhai.gov.cn

Zhuhai Bureau of Foreign Trade and Economic Cooperation
Website: www.zhuhai-trade.gov.cn

Zhuhai Service Center for Foreign Investment
Nanyou Hotel, Shuiwan Ave.
Zhuhai, Guangdong
Tel: (86)(756) 3372472, 3372478
Website: www.zhuhai.com.cn

SHANTOU
SPECIAL ECONOMIC ZONE

Introduction

Shantou has had a long history of foreign trade since it was made one of the open seaport cities in 1861. Eight foreign countries had set up their consulates there in the 1930s. As emigration surged since the middle of Qing Dynasty, Shantou now boasts a large population of 2.16 million ethnic Chaozhou-Shantou people living abroad in more than 40 countries and regions all over the world, of which most are residing in Southeast Asian countries. There are 80,000 "Chao-shan people" in Hong Kong, Macau and Taiwan. In 1981, Shantou became the last of the first four Special Economic Zones in China and stepped into a new era of development.

Geography

Shantou City consists of five districts of Longhu, Jinyuan, Shengping, Dahao and Hepu, and also administers Nan'ao County, Chaoyang City and Chenghai City on behalf of the province. In total, Shantou covers an area of 2,064 sq km with a population of 4.59 million, of which 1.19 million live in Shantou's urban area. Shantou Special

Economic Zone covers 234 sq km.

Bordering South China Sea, Shantou is located in the southeast of Guangdong Province. With a meandering coastline and a lot of islets, Shantou has many natural harbors.

As the Tropic of Cancer runs through the entire city, Shantou enjoys a subtropical oceanic climate with annual average temperature of 21.3°C and annual sunshine time of 2,000-3,000 hours. Rainfall is abundant and gives the city an annual precipitation of 1,514 mm.

Shantou Fact Sheet	
Total Land Area	2,064 sq km
Area of SEZ	234 sq km
Year Established	1981
Population	4.59 million
GDP	RMB46.10 billion or USD5.59 billion (2001)
Total Industrial Output	RMB77.19 billion or USD9.36 billion (2001)
Total Foreign Trade	USD2.73 billion (2001)
FDI Contracted	n.a.
FDI Utilized	USD180 million (2001)

Travel information

Being one of the "Best Tourist Cities of China" and an "Environmental Star City of the State", Shantou is famous for its seashore landscape and moderate weather. Tourist sites include the Queshi Scenic Area, Dahao Qingyun Rock, Chaoyan Linshan Temple, Chenghai Zhanglin Ancient Port, Overseas Chinese Park, Beishanwan and Donghu Resort. The Qing'ao Gulf in Nan'ao County is praised as the "Hawaii of the Orient". Thirty-nine hotels in Shantou provide accommodation for foreign guests, three being five-star hotels.

Travelers may enter Shantou by all means of transportation. Shantou International Airport has air routes linking to over 40 major domestic cities as well as Hong Kong and Bangkok. Passenger ships sail between Shantou and Hong Kong everyday, and also reach Guangzhou and Xiamen. Visitors can take trains from Guangzhou, Shenzhen, Jiujiang and Wuhan to get there. The newly built Shenzhen-Shantou Expressway and two state-level highways make Shantou easily accessible by coach from major cities in the south, east and southwest of China.

Economic performance

In 2001, the city's total GDP was USD5.59 billion and the GDP per capita is RMB10,017.

Shantou is among the top 50 Chinese cities in terms of economic development. The total industrial output was USD9.36 billion in 2001, and the total foreign trade was USD2.73 billion. Year 2001 saw significant decreases in most of the economic indicators compared to 2000 when Shantou was suffering from a "creditability crisis" and a global economic setback. The total exports in 2001 went down by 48.3% to USD1.34 billion.

The structure of the local economy is represented by a ratio of 9.6:45.9:44.5 for the primary, secondary and tertiary sectors, respectively. Light industry is the mainstay for Shantou, and includes electronic and ultrasonic industry, chemistry, pharmaceuticals, textiles and garments, and mechanical industries. Currently, Shantou is carrying out plans to enhance exports, science, education and sustainable development. Modern agriculture is also highlighted by the local authority.

An important feature of Shantou's economy is indicated by the thriving private sector. The private sector accounts for more than 70% of the total industrial output of the city and some 40% in total exports. Private enterprises are even more prominent in the local high-tech industries.

Infrastructure

Shantou Port is assigned as one of the 20 pivotal ports of China. Cargo ships sail from Shantou to more than 210 ports in 53 countries and regions. There are 31 berths of 5,000-ton capacity scale or above, nine of which are 10,000-ton capacity deepwater berths including a 35,000-ton capacity coal wharf, a 20,000-ton capacity multifunction berth, and a 15,000-ton capacity dry freight berth. The annual handling capacity of Shantou Port is 24.70 million tons of cargo and 0.725 million TEUs of containers.

With annual capacity of handling three million passengers, Shantou Airport had served 1.04 million passengers in 2000. It provides 44 routes and is the home to Shantou Airline of China Southern Airlines Group.

Guangzhou-Meizhou-Shantou Railway started operation in 1995. It starts from Guangzhou, via Dongguan, Huizhou, Meizhou and finally reaches Shantou. With Meizhou-Kanshi Railway newly completed, Shantou is now joining Beijing-Kowloon Railway and Beijing-Guangzhou Railway to the west, and Yingtan-Xiamen Railway to the northeast, presenting itself as a pivotal Southeast seaport in the railway networks of China. Shantou-Shenzhen Coastal Railway is also under construction.

Land transportation in Shantou is among the most developed. Highways connect Shantou with Hong Kong, Guangzhou, Shenzhen, Meizhou, Zhangzhou and Xiamen. Container trucks run between Shantou and Hong Kong every day. Shenzhen-Shantou Expressway, which stretches 286 km and is dubbed "the Golden Corridor" of eastern Guangdong, has already been completed and opened to traffic.

The Asia-Europe, Sino-US and Asia-Pacific II international optical cables have landed in Shantou, positioning Shantou as an important hub in the world telecommunication network. Shantou is linked to the power supply network of Guangdong Province and has an installation capacity of 826,300 kW at the end of 2000. It has four water works with a daily supply capacity of 0.92 million tons.

Climate of foreign investment

As an SEZ and an overseas Chinese hometown, Shantou has been one of the hottest Chinese locations for FDI. The overseas Chao-shan people have played an important role in the economic construction of their hometown. Among others, Li Ka-shing, the famous Hong Kong business tycoon, has alone committed about USD870 million worth of investments in nine projects in Shantou. Taiwan is the second largest source region of FDI, injecting USD620 million of pledged investment by end August 2001.

So far, 47 transnational companies have made their way to Shantou, including Shell, Eastman Kodak, Caltex and Walmart etc. By the end of 2001, 5,255 FIEs have been set up in Shantou with total accumulated utilized FDI amounting to USD7.46 billion.

Foreign investment covers a lot of areas, not only in manufacturing, but also in agriculture, commerce, finance, infrastructure, real estate and even urban redevelopment.

Preferential policies

- Besides the 15% preferential corporate income tax rate, the general terms of tax holidays and incentives in SEZs shall apply to all FIEs involved in production or services in Shantou SEZ.
- Upon application and approval by the Administration of Foreign Exchange Control, the FIEs in Shantou may open accounts with Chinese banks or foreign-funded banks in Shantou. The foreign exchange, transferred into the SEZ or earned from export business, may be retained by the FIEs for ordinary business expenses. Upon examination and approval, the remaining may be used to raise a mortgage for an RMB loan with People's Bank of China Shantou Branch. The after-tax net profits of the FIEs and the legitimate income of the foreign staff after paying tax may be remitted according to the relevant regulations.
- The term of land use for industrial purpose in Shantou SEZs is 50 years, and for dwelling is 70 years. After expiry the contract may be extended upon application and approval from Shantou

Land Administration or its relevant subordinate bodies.

Areas for foreign investment

Three districts are allocated by Shantou SEZ to accommodate FDI – Shantou Free Trade Zone, Shantou High-tech Park and Nan'ao Island Development Experimental Zone.

The FTZ is situated in the southeast part of Shantou Dahao peninsula. Specialized berths have been built there with a regular cargo line to Hong Kong, and its highways connect to the Shenzhen-Shantou Expressway. The bonded area concentrates on the development of international trade, logistic business, export processing, finance and IT industry.

The High-tech Park is a province-level developing district set up in 1993, covering four square kilometers. A group of industries such as electronic data, optical electro-mechanical integration, biological engineering, pharmaceuticals and new energy, has been developed in the eastern part. With an area of three square kilometers, the western part is located to the south of Shantou University and still in initial stage.

Nan'ao is the only island county in Guangdong Province, covering 130 sq km and a maritime area of 4,600 sq km. It boasts beautiful bay and beach resorts, cultural relics, great wind force, unique aquatic resources and a grade-A seaport. It is selected by the province to develop an ecologically sustainable area.

Shantou Municipal Government
Website: www.gdst.gov.cn

Shantou Development Planning Bureau
Website: www.stdp.gov.cn

Shantou Bureau of Foreign Trade and Economic Cooperation
Foreign Trade Building
47 East District, Jintaozhuang
Shantou, Guangdong

Tel: (86)(754) 8931830
Fax: (86)(754) 8931831
Website: www.stfet.gov.cn

Shantou Free Trade Zone
Email: ftzst@pub.shantou.gd.cn
Website: www.stftz.gov.cn

HAINAN
SPECIAL ECONOMIC ZONE

Introduction
The second largest island of China, the youngest province, and the largest SEZ in China, Hainan deserves a unique place in the country's economic development history. It was founded as the nation's 31st Province and the 5th Special Economic Zone in April 1988 to further its independent pursuit of an open economy. However, in terms of economic achievement, Hainan is still the least developed vis-à-vis other four SEZs.

Geography
Traditionally called "the Remotest Cape of the Earth", Hainan lies to the southernmost of the mainland, opposite Leizhou Peninsula. The island has a total land area of 34,000 sq km with a coastline as long as 1,585 km. The entire Hainan territory covers two million sq km of South China Sea, stretching 1,800 km from north to south and 900 km from east to west, adjoining Vietnam to the west, Taiwan and Philippines to the east and Malaysia, Brunei and Singapore to the far south. Administratively, Hainan Province is divided into Hainan Island, Xisha, Zhongsha and Nansha Islands (Spratly Islands). It has two major cities, Haikou in the north and Sanya in the far south. The island's 7.87 million population is made up of Han race, totaling 82.7%, and 37 minority groups in which the Li (16%) and Miao (0.7%) are the most populous.

Located between 4°-21° north latitude, about the same as Hawaii, Hainan enjoys a monsoon tropical oceanic climate with plenty of sunshine. Temperatures range between 16°C and 21°C in January and February and between 25°C and 29°C in July and August. Annual precipitation is between 1,500 mm and 2,000 mm, occurring mostly in the east and central areas. Hainan Island is mountainous at its center and features extensive forests (forest coverage of 51.5%) in addition to natural beaches along much of its coastline. Wuzhi Mountain is the highest, with its peak reaching 1,867 m.

Travel information
Rather than an SEZ, Hainan is more reputable for its sightseeing resources, like Yalong Bay, Tianya Haijiao (the End of Heaven and Corner of the Sea), Dadong Sea, Luhuitou (Turn-round Deer), Sanya Bay, Xiao Tongtian, Folk Village, etc. It has 72 natural reserves, five of which are state-level ones.

By the end of 2001, Hainan has 77 star hotels in total, of which six are five-star hotels, 20 four-star hotels and 67 three-star hotels.

Though separated from the mainland by the Qiongzhou Straits, Hainan is by no means an isolated island. With international and domestic flights on 108 air routes, getting to Hainan is comfortable and convenient. Two international airports are in operation, Meilan in Haikou, the provincial capital, and Phoenix in Sanya. Passengers may reach Hainan directly from Hong Kong, Seoul, Osaka, Tokyo, Macau, Thailand, Singapore and Bangkok as well as from 49 key Chinese cities.

In addition, Hainan is served by ferries to and from Guangzhou, Shenzhen, Shantou, Zhanjiang, Beihai and Hong Kong. It is also crisscrossed by a network of inland expressways, highways and roads.

Hainan Fact Sheet	
Total Land Area	34,000 sq km
Area of SEZ	34,000 sq km
Year Established	1988
Population	7.87 million
GDP	RMB56.61 billion or USD6.86 billion (2001)
Total Industrial Output	RMB26.56 billion USD3.22 billion (2000)
Total Foreign Trade	USD1.76 billion (2001)
FDI Contracted	n.a.
FDI Utilized*	USD0.47 billion (2001)

Economic performance

In 2001, the province-cum-SEZ registered GDP of USD6.86 billion, increased by 8.9% on a year-on-year basis. Most noticeably, 35.4% of it was contributed by value added in the primary sector composed of tropical fruits, aquatic and livestock products. Though the industrial output since the establishment of SEZ has kept on increasing at a 16.7% average margin, the secondary sector still accounts for less than a quarter of the provincial economy. Food and beverage, pharmaceuticals, chemicals and sugar manufacturing are the local leading industries. Recently, production of automobiles and motorcycles has also shown signs of robust growth.

The tourism-led service sector is the most significant component in the island's economy, taking up a 41.4% share in 2001. Being one of the national seven key tourist attractions, Hainan attracts more than 10 million visitors every year. As a result, commerce, transportation and finance are booming. Sanya and Haikou are the two major sightseeing cities with a total of 300 hotels. In 2001, Hainan recorded an income of USD1.05 billion from 11 million tourists.

Infrastructure

Infrastructure in Hainan has been largely improved after its inception as a province in 1988. Haikou Meilan International Airport was opened in 1999, which has an annual loading and unloading capacity of 150,000 tons of freight and six million passengers. It is now among the top ten airports in China and home to two regional airlines.

Hainan has developed 24 seaports of varied sizes, 15 of them being 10,000-ton-capacity. Cargo ships sail from Haikou to nearly every coastal port of China and Hong Kong, Macau and Singapore. In 2001, the ports of the province handled over 21.4 million tons of cargos, up 8.4% from the last year. Vehicle ferries are operated on a 24-hour basis to connect the island with the mainland.

With a total installed capacity of 1.57 million kWh, Hainan is among the few Chinese provinces that is rich in power supply.

Climate of foreign investment

Though it's the newest SEZ since 1988, Hainan does not seem to benefit much from such an advantage. At the very beginning, the biggest SEZ had to compete for FDI inflows with other coastal open cities as well as the four established SEZs. Recently, it has to compete with inland regions, as preferential policies are no longer exclusive to SEZs and coastal regions. Furthermore, Hainan's vast hinterland with relatively less developed infrastructure, its relatively less convenient island geography, disadvantageous industrial structure and fewer connections to overseas Chinese have also hindered FDI influx into Hainan to some extent. The real estate bubble of early 1990s eventually burst, making 60% of the province's total loans non-performing.

In 2001, actually utilized FDI in Hainan decreased by nearly 30% to USD467 million, compared to the previous year, marking the fifth consecutive year of decline.

However, the recent establishment of the Boao Forum for Asia (BFA) in 2001 has attracted much international spotlight onto the island. A high profile non-government and non-profit international organization, BFA was initiated to prompt the economic exchanges and cooperation within the region, especially when East Asia cooperation (10+3) has already entered into a substantive stage. Permanently based in Boao, a small city in Eastern Hainan, BFA may further catch foreign investors' interest as well as FDI.

Preferential policies

The preferential policies in Hainan are characterized by "three lows" and "three freedoms", i.e., low tax, low labor costs and low land prices; free movement of foreigners, capitals and goods. The incentives package exclusive to Hainan includes:

- VAT is exempted for products made by enterprises in Hainan and sold in the island, except in the case of mineral oils, tobacco and alcoholic products where the VAT is reduced by half.
- For IT companies engaged in service sector with a total investment exceeding USD5 million and operational terms of more than ten years, corporate income tax is exempted for the first profit-making year and granted a 50% reduction for the following two years. If their total investment and operational period do not meet that threshold requirement, they are still eligible for the exemption for the first profit-making year and a 50% reduction in the second year.
- The products of IT companies are subsidized by 60% of local paid VAT for the first three years and by 40% for the next three years if products are sold outside Hainan.
- High-tech companies enjoy full refund of business tax in intellectual property transfers or selling fixed assets, provided their high-tech projects are approved by relevant authorities.

- Land used by IT companies and high-tech projects for production is exempted from fees payable on the transfer of land use rights.

Areas for foreign investment

Hainan is ambitious in developing three industrial bases in the west, north and east of the island. Yangpu Economic and Technological Development Zone forms the core part of the planned west base for heavy industries. It is co-developed by investors from Hong Kong and Taiwan, and the provincial government and endorsed by the State Council in 1992 as a 3-in-1 zone, that is, combining SEZ, ETDZ and free trade zone status. Aiming to be a modern industrial port city, it will gradually expand to an area of 18 sq km.

Efforts are concentrated on offshore petroleum and natural gas processing, high-tech industries, and supporting services. Three berths with a capacity of one million tons and an expressway to Haikou have been completed and put into operation. A one-million-ton rice refinery, an optical fiber project, factories of marbleize vitrified tiles and vegetable oil are either in operation or near completion.

Surrounding Haikou city, the northern industrial base is the island's most dynamic growth area. It has a comprehensive range of industries, in particular, food and beverage, automobiles and motorcycles, polyester, IT, pharmaceuticals, chemicals and plastics etc. accounting for half the provincial economy. Emphasis is to be given in light, export-oriented and high-tech industries in future.

As eastern Hainan is the traditional agricultural base of the island, the eastern industrial base is to become the industrial base for deep processing of farm and sideline products, sea farming and fishing, and developments of other marine resources.

There is also a state-level Yalong Bay Tourist District located near Sanya city in the south, which is largely meant for development of tourist resources and relevant traveling facilities.

Hainan Provincial Government
Website: www.hainan.gov.cn

Hainan Department of Foreign Trade and Economic Cooperation
Website: doftec.hainan.gov.cn

Yangpu Economic Zone
Website: www.yangpu.hainan.gov.cn

Our Rating System

INTRODUCTION

China has witnessed many kinds of industrial parks mushrooming across the country since the mid-1980s, after the establishment of Special Economic Zones (SEZs) in the early 1980s. Among others, Economic and Technological Development Zone, High and New Technological Development Zone (or High-tech Park), Export Processing Zone, Free Trade Zone (or Bonded Zone), and Border Trade Cooperation Zone are the most common names used. Apart from those zones where industries are rather comprehensive, specific Software Development Parks and University Science Parks are designated to further the efforts on original R&D. The general term of "industrial park" in this study thus covers the various types of such spatial formations, regardless whether they physically span a few hectares or tens of square kilometers.

China Knowledge Press has devised a rating system to assess the investment environment of various industrial parks. It is intended to give potential investors some insight, albeit preliminary, into the attractiveness of these development zones.

INDUSTRIAL PARKS

Economic and technological development zones (ETDZ)

At the end of 1984, the state government named 13 coastal cities, such as Dalian, Tianjin, Shanghai, Guangzhou etc., to set up 14 Economic and Technological Development Zones (ETDZs). The second batch of 18 state-level ETDZs were approved between 1992-1993, following the inception of Shanghai Pudong New District in 1990, Daxie Development Zone in 1993, and Suzhou Industrial Park in 1994. In 2000 and 2001, the State Council endorsed another 11 ETDZs, all located in western and central regions of China. Some of these were upgraded from provincial level zones.

Number of state-level industrial parks in China

Category	Total	Coastal Regions	Inland Regions
Economic and Technological Development Zones	51	29	22
High and New Technological Development Zones	53	27	26
Export Processing Zones	15	12	3
Free Trade Zones	17	17	0
Border Trade Cooperation Zones	14	1	13
University Science Parks	22	11	11
Software Development Parks	17	11	6
Grand total	**189**	**108**	81

According to MOFTEC, the number of state-level ETDZs has grown to 54, with coastal regions taking 32 and inland regions taking 22. The total developed area is estimated to be 400 sq km, with a share of 10% in China's total accumulated foreign direct investment (FDI).

As quasi-SEZ preferential policies were established in ETDZs and the host cities normally had sound infrastructures and established industrial structures, the state-level ETDZs have enjoyed great advantages in attracting FDI inflows. One such privilege is that foreign invested enterprises (FIEs) are taxed at a preferential rate of 15% on corporate income, the same as in SEZs. Their objectives are similar, which is to attract FDI, to encourage industrial projects, to further promote export-oriented processing, and to improve traditional industries with advanced technologies.

Inspired by the success stories of these ETDZs, provinces and municipality-level cities all followed suit. Today, local ETDZs, estimated at 4,000 with various sizes and capacities, have spread all over China. Although local incentives and conditions vary, they have become the most dynamic and fastest growing areas in China.

State-level economic and technological development zones

COASTAL REGIONS (32)		INLAND REGIONS (22)	
Regions	**ETDZ names**	**Regions**	**ETDZ names**
Shanghai	Minhang, Hongqiao, Caohejing, Jinqiao	Chongqing	Chongqing
		Anhui	Wuhu, Hefei
Beijing	Beijing	Gansu	Lanzhou
Tianjin	Tianjin	Guangxi	Nanning
Liaoning	Dalian, Yingkou, Shenyang	Guizhou	Guiyang
		Heilongjiang	Harbin
Hebei	Qinhuangdao	Henan	Zhengzhou
Shandong	Yantai, Qingdao, Weihai	Hubei	Wuhan
		Hunan	Changsha
Jiangsu	Lianyungang, Nanjing, Nantong, Kunshan, Suzhou Industrial Park	Inner Mongolia	Hohhot
		Jiangxi	Nanchang
Zhejiang	Ningbo, Hangzhou, Xiaoshan, Wenzhou, Daxie (Ningbo)	Jilin	Changchun
		Ningxia	Yinchuan
		Qinghai	Xining
Fujian	Fuzhou, Dongshan (Xiamen), Rongqiao (Fuqing), Haicang	Shaanxi	Xi'an
		Shanxi	Taiyuan
Guangdong	Zhanjiang, Guangzhou, Nansha (Guangzhou), Dayawan (Huizhou)	Sichuan	Chengdu
		Tibet	Lhasa
		Xinjiang	Urumqi, Shihezi
Hainan	Yangpu	Yunnan	Kunming

High-tech parks (HTPs)

In the early 1990s, the state government approved the first group of High and New Technological Development Zones, or High-tech Parks, to implement the Torch Program, an ambitious national plan to develop and commercialize high technologies from 1988.

By the end of 2001, there were 53 state-level High-tech Parks in China, half of which are in the coastal regions. The total output of HTPs skyrocketed to approximately USD114.6 billion in 2001, which is 137 times that in 1991. It is estimated that one fourth of China's total industrial value added and one seventh of China's export increment are now contributed by these high-tech parks. The workforce in high-tech parks was 2.94 million as in 2001. Zhongguancun in Beijing and Zhangjiang in Shanghai have become the most powerful and promising high-tech parks in China.

The focus of these industrial parks is primarily on the continuous introduction and innovation of advanced technologies, and to eventually explore the global market. FIEs in these high-tech parks enjoy national tax incentives. For instance, corporate income tax can be reduced by half or totally exempted, provided such FIEs are approved enterprises with "advanced technology".

State-level high-tech parks

COASTAL REGIONS (27)		INLAND REGIONS (26)	
Regions	**HTP names**	**Regions**	**HTP names**
Shanghai	Zhangjiang	Chongqing	Chongqing
Beijing	Zhongguancun	Anhui	Hefei
Tianjin	Tianjin	Gansu	Lanzhou
Liaoning	Shenyang, Anshan, Dalian	Guangxi	Guilin, Nanning
		Guizhou	Guiyang
Hebei	Shijiazhuang, Baoding	Heilongjiang	Harbin, Daqing
Shandong	Jinan,Weihai, Weifang, Zibo, Qingdao	Henan	Zhengzhou, Luoyang
Jiangsu	Nanjing, Suzhou New District, Wuxi New District, Changzhou	Hubei	Wuhan East Lake, Xiangfan
		Hunan	Zhuzhou, Changsha
Zhejiang	Hangzhou	Inner Mongolia	Baotou
Fujian	Xiamen Torch, Fuzhou	Jiangxi	Nanchang
Guangdong	Guangzhou, Shenzhen, Zhuhai, Foshan, Zhongshan Torch, Huizhou Zhongkai	Jilin	Jilin, Changchun
		Shaanxi	Xi'an, Yangling Agriculture (Xi'an), Baoji
Hainan	Haikou	Shanxi	Taiyuan
		Sichuan	Chengdu, Mianyang
		Xinjiang	Urumqi
		Yunnan	Kunming

Arguably, however, technology transfer by foreign investors and innovativeness by domestic enterprises still leave much to be desired. The high-tech parks are said to be entering their second phase of development now.

Free trade zones (FTZs)

It is still a controversial question whether Free Trade Zones in China are actually Bonded Zones. The first free trade zone was set up in Waigaoqiao, Shanghai, in May 1990. By now, 15 such FTZs are present in 12 coastal cities with a total planned area of 42.39 sq km, of which 80.4% has already been bonded. Given freer trade policies, if not an FTZ status as defined by the Kyoto Protocol, they have since been the prime choices for many foreign investors. By now, there are 12,038 (FIEs) currently operating in these zones, with contractual FDI totaling USD13.9 billion. Around 134 of the world's top 500 MNCs are now having a presence there.

State-level free trade zones

COASTAL REGIONS (15)

Regions	FTZ names
Shanghai	Waigaoqiao
Tianjin	Tanggu
Liaoning	Dalian
Shandong	Qingdao
Jiangsu	Zhangjiagang
Zhejiang	Ningbo
Fujian	Fuzhou, Xiangyu (Xiamen)
Guangdong	Shantou, Futian (Shenzhen), Yantian (Shenzhen), Shatoujiao, (Shenzhen), Guangzhou, Zhuhai
Hainan	Haikou

Though FTZs originally have three basic functions — export processing, entrepot trade, and bonded warehousing. It seems that focus has largely been put on export processing by those FTZ administrations. Generally, FIEs resident in these zones are eligible for tax refunds on exports, concessionary VAT, and other preferential policies in trading and foreign exchange. FTZs in China are still trying to fully conform to international practices.

Export processing zones (EPZs)

To curb rampant smuggling involved in export processing trade since China's opening, the state government of China started to reform the administration, especially in customs supervision. Since April 2000, when Kunshan EPZ in Jiangsu Province was set up, it has approved 15 Export Processing Zones nationwide with a total planned area of 43.41 sq km. In early 2002, 247 companies, including 164 FIEs, were running in 14 already bonded EPZs, with a total investment of USD2.84 billion. Another 249 companies with committed investment of USD4.7 billion are expected to move in soon.

The establishment of EPZs was initially intended to closely manage previously dispersed export processing enterprises and to better conform to international routines. All EPZs are located within the existing state-level development zones to avoid redundant infrastructure construction. The sole function of EPZ is to process and trade export products. Spatially, it is a bonded special area under customs jurisdiction.

Border economic cooperation zones (BECZs)

To expedite the economic exchanges along its 22,800 km long national boundary, the state government assigned a number of state-level Border Economic Cooperation Zones (BECZs) in the frontier areas with countries like Russia, North Korea, Kazakhstan,

State-level export processing zones

COASTAL REGIONS (12)		INLAND REGIONS (3)	
Regions	**EPZ names**	**Regions**	**HTP names**
Shanghai	Songjiang	Hubei	Wuhan
Beijing	Tianzhu	Jilin	Hunchun
Tianjin	Tianjin	Sichuan	Chengdu
Liaoning	Dalian		
Shandong	Yantai, Weihai		
Jiangsu	Kunshan, Suzhou Industrial Park		
Zhejiang	Hangzhou		
Fujian	Xinlin (Xiamen)		
Guangdong	Guangzhou, Shenzhen		

Myanmar and Vietnam.

University science parks (USPs)

In order to capitalize on universities' research capabilities, the State Council decided to develop about a hundred University Science Parks (USPs) by the end of 2005 as the incubators for promising enterprises. Among them, 50 will become exemplary USPs and 20 will be developed into first-class USPs in China. So far, there are 22 state-level USPs supported by 67 Chinese universities and research institutes in China. In May 2002, the development of other 21 new University Science Parks were started in more provinces.

Software development parks (SDPs)

As software development is the core part of information technology and a push factor for other high-tech industries, the national Torch Program has nominated 17 state-level software development centers or parks nationwide since October 1995. Top-notch software enterprises were born and have already developed some reputable customized operating systems or applications for the China market. These include

PKU Founder's laser publishing system, Stone Rich Sight's Chinese platform, NEU Soft's Openbase, UFSoft's accounting system etc.

State-level border economic cooperation zones

NORTHEAST AND NORTH (6)	
Regions	**BECZ names**
Liaoning	Dandong
Heilongjiang	Heihe, Suifenhe
Jilin	Hunchun
Inner Mongolia	Manzhouli, Erenhot

NORTHWEST (3)	
Regions	**BECZ names**
Xinjiang	Yining, Tacheng, Bole

SOUTHWEST (5)	
Regions	**BECZ names**
Guangxi	Pingxiang, Dongxing
Yunnan	Ruili, Wanting, Hekou

State-level university science parks

COASTAL REGIONS (11)		INLAND REGIONS (11)	
Regions	**USP names**	**Regions**	**USP names**
Shanghai	Shanghai Jiaotong University, Fudan University	Chongqing	Chongqing University
		Anhui	Hefei
Beijing	Tsinghua University, Peking University	Heilongjiang	Harbin Institute of Technology,
Tianjin	Tianjin University	Hubei	Wuhan East Lake
Liaoning	Northeast University (Shenyang),	Hunan	Yuelushan (Changsha)
		Shaanxi	Xi'an Jiaotong University, Northwest Polytechnical University (Xi'an), Northwest Sci-tech University of Algriculture and Forestry (Yangling, Xi'an)
Shandong	Shandong University (Jinan),		
Jiangsu	Southeast University (Nanjing), Nanjing Gulou		
Zhejiang	Zhejiang University (Hangzhou)		
Guangdong	South China University of Technology (Guangzhou)	Sichuan	University of Electronic Science and Technology (Chengdu), Sichuan University (Chengdu)
		Yunnan	Yunnan University (Kunming)

State-level software development parks

COASTAL REGIONS (11)		INLAND REGIONS (6)	
Regions	**SDP names**	**Regions**	**SDP names**
Shanghai	Shanghai	Anhui	Hefei
Beijing	Beijing	Hubei	Hubei (Wuhan)
Tianjin	Tianjin Huayuan	Hunan	Powerise (Changsha)
Liaoning	NEU (Shenyang), Dalian	Jiangxi	Jinlu (Nanchang)
		Jilin	Changchun
Shandong	Qilu (Jinan)	Shaanxi	Xi'an
Jiangsu	Nanjing	Sichuan	West (Chengdu)
Zhejiang	Hangzhou		
Fujian	Fuzhou, Xiamen		
Guangdong	Guangzhou		

OUR RATING SYSTEM

Introduction

As seen above, industrial parks in China are at different levels and various stages of development.

Some are located within another development zone. For example, FTZs and EPZs are usually a part of ETDZs to leverage on them for investment and more concentrated administration. In some cases, they were allocated a piece of land in an established ETDZ. Whilst SDPs and USPs are commonly located within high-tech parks because many HTPs were formerly founded based on proximity to talent pools or universities.

Parks with specific functions are generally small in size, and not comprehensive in industrial structure. For example, EPZs are uniquely meant for export processing related companies whose production is mostly of the labor-intensive type, which may not be convenient for many potential investors who are more concerned about the Chinese domestic market. Parks identified as bases for software companies or for overseas Chinese students obviously exclude investors in other categories.

Moreover, since it has not been long since the inception of FTZs, EPZs, SDPs and USPs in China, the infrastructure of some parks is still under development.

In view of that, to avoid repetitiveness and to maintain accuracy in our rating, those industrial parks temporarily not suitable for assessment are excluded in this study. The list will be reviewed and amended in due course.

Selection of factors

There are many existing factors relevant to an enterprise's performance at a specific industrial park. For foreign investors who are not acquainted with the local context, an evaluation of industrial parks in China becomes particularly critical. With reference to different approaches to regional compe-

Factors of investment environment of an industrial park

1. Locational advantage and macroeconomic performance of the host area
   - Accessibility (transportation, logistics)   0.0743
   - GDP per capita   0.0414
   - GDP growth rate   0.0414
   - Industrial structure   0.0429
2. Development of the industrial park
   - Infrastructure   0.0875
   - IT facilities   0.0357
   - Level of prominence (state, province or city)   0.0393
   - Land and utility cost   0.0554
   - Size of development area   0.0321
3. Existing investment in the industrial park
   - Existing establishments (number, investment, output)   0.0786
   - Foreign investment (number, investment, output)   0.1214
4. Human resources
   - Professionals   0.0461
   - Universities and colleges   0.0396
   - Labor cost   0.0386
   - Population   0.0257
5. Management and services
   - Local administration (efficiency and quality)   0.0786
   - Preferential policies   0.0357
   - Business support services   0.0500
   - Marketing   0.0357

titive advantage evaluation, credit and risk analysis, and a plethora of literature available on FDI in China, a holistic rating system has been conceptualized and finally developed to assess the investment environment of various industrial parks in China.

Attributes for a successful business can be economic, social and even behavioral, and are just too many to be entirely included in any single study. It is particularly true when China — a land that remains mysterious and unpredictable to many potential foreign investors — is under discussion or assessment. Therefore, this book concentrates on key elements that have significant impact on investment decisions, that is, with regard to a specific industrial park in China, what are businessmen most concerned about vis-à-vis other possible locations?

We divide business environmental variables into five main categories or factors: locational advantage and macroeconomic performance of the host area, development of the industrial park, existing investment in the industrial park, human resources, and management and services.

Each category comprises several factors. A distribution of weight in percentage terms for all factors was decided, based on careful comparison, normalization and calculation. For example, when the first category is considered as of x% importance to an industrial park's investment climate, and one component factor, say, "accessibility", contributes y% importance to the category, an aggregate weight of importance (w) is derived as w= x%y%. We list below all the factors examined and their respective weights in our total evaluation.

Rating mechanism

After the factors and their respective weights are determined, necessary criteria are adopted to complete the rating system. Economic and demographic statistics are sought and grouped. For normalization, they are converted into standard scores of 1-5 scale by criteria defined by China Knowledge Press (CKP), 1 for the least desirable, 5 for the most favored. Some factors may require consideration of several indicators to arrive at a single score.

Apart from the quantifiable factors, however, factors like accessibility and administration efficiency are implicit or difficult to measure. Therefore, besides seeking substitutes, all statistically obtainable data and qualitative information are transformed into scores using CKP's professional assessment.

Given the weights of each factor and its corresponding scores, we then calculate the actual aggregate sum of the industrial park. All results are sorted, grouped and translated into the standard ratings defined below. An ideal industrial park may get as high as AAA rating on our scale. The rationale for adopting such a descriptive system is to show the results more vividly and to adjust for any inaccuracy in our scoring.

Rating definition
AAA

This is CKP's highest rating. We consider the investment environment of an AAA industrial park as the best, and highly recommend it to potential investors.

AA

Industrial parks rated AA are highly attractive and are strongly recommended. They are of lower rank than AAA rated ones, as certain areas still need improvement.

A

Industrial parks rated A are recommended as upper-medium level ones appealing to potential investors. Their basic conditions are adequate, but some elements suggest their competitiveness appears lower than the AA industrial parks.

BBB

Industrial parks rated BBB are considered as

attractive at a medium level. Their conditions are less adequate and may contain flaws at a moderate level, or they may be promising industrial parks but are still under construction.

BB

Industrial parks rated BB are considered fairly attractive or only attractive to specific investors. The business environment there leaves much to be improved.

B

Industrial parks rated B lack in attractiveness to investors. There either exists significant weaknesses or the industrial park is not yet ready for investment.

C

We believe industrial parks rated C to be least attractive to most investors. One or more components are missing, or their current conditions are not suitable for foreign investment.

SUMMARY

The individual ratings will be displayed in each of the following chapters introducing individual industrial parks. For quick reference, a complete list of rated industrial parks is provided at the end of this book, in descending order.

This book rates some 130 major industrial parks in China, varying in level, developmental stage and capacity. This coverage will be constantly extended and updated to mirror foreseeable changes in the near future, as China enters WTO and calls for the Great Development of Western Regions.

Given the structure of our rating system, it is observed that industrial parks in the coastal regions normally have an advantageous status over their counterparts in the inland regions. This is because the cities they reside in are many steps ahead of the inland cities in terms of economic reforms and infrastructure development. Transport conditions and GDP indicators are essential attributes in this assessment.

Similarly, industrial parks hosted by capital cities in the central or western regions of China generally get higher ratings than those in secondary-level cities, as provincial capitals in inland China traditionally enjoy the most political, financial and human resources in the previous centrally planned economy.

Our results show that industrial parks with comprehensive economic activities and functions seem to be more popular. As high-tech parks are intrinsically more selective of industries and tenants, our ratings reflect these limitations. However, a lower rating shouldn't be necessarily interpreted as being poor in attracting FDI into a certain sector.

Much remains contentious, as factors included in our rating system are by no means complete and values given remain arguably assertive. Although every possible means have been taken to make the rating system reflect reality, it is still subject to our researchers' limited capabilities and preoccupations. The ratings in this book are therefore just indicative, and serve only as a reference to help foreign and domestic investors choose their business locations. As a continued commitment, our research team will revise and refine it on a regular basis.

Ministry of Foreign Trade and Economic Cooperation
Website: www.moftec.gov.cn

Association of Chinese Development Zones
Website: www.cadz.org cn

China Torch Program
Website: www.chinatorch.gov.cn

RATINGS OF INDUSTRIAL PARKS IN CHINA

AAA

AA

A

BBB

BEIJING

Industrial Parks in Beijing

1. Beijing Economic & Technological Development Zone
2. Tianzhu Airport Industrial Park
3. Tianzhu Export Processing Zone
4. Zhongguancun Science Park
5. Peking University Science Park
6. Tsinghua University Science Park

INTRODUCTION

Beijing, also known as Peking by the western world before 1949, is the capital city of China. The history of the city can be dated back more than 3,000 years ago. It has been the capital of the dynasties of Jin (1115-1234), Yuan (1271-1368), Ming (1368-1644) and Qing (1644-1911).

Beijing is also the nation's political and cultural center, and it boasts abundant cultural heritages such as the Great Wall, the Forbidden City, the Summer Palace and the Tian'anmen Square. It is a place that has

witnessed the pride and humiliation of many Chinese empires. Being the second largest city in China, Beijing is now developing its economic prowess as well.

GEOGRAPHY

Situated in the northern part of China, Beijing covers an area of 16,808 sq km and had 16 urban and suburban districts and two counties in 2002. Hilly area occupies 62% of the total territory. It borders Tianjin in the east and is surrounded by Hebei Province.

Beijing has a temperate continental monsoon climate, with cold and dry winters and wet and hot summers. The average temperature in January is between -7°C and -4°C and in July between 25°C to 26°C. The annual precipitation averages 600 mm.

TRAVEL INFORMATION

Beijing is a transportation hub in northern China, with highly developed railway, expressway and highway network connecting major Chinese cities directly. Located 26 km northeast to downtown Beijing, the Capital International Airport is one of the nation's gateways.

From Capital Airport to:

Shanghai Pudong	1 hr 40 mins
Chicago	13 hrs
Hong Kong	3 hrs 10 mins
Singapore	6 hrs
Seoul	1 hr 50 mins
Tokyo	3 hrs 10 mins
Sydney	13 hrs 30 mins
Paris	10 hrs 25 mins
London	10 hrs 45 mins
Vancouver	10 hrs 30 mins
New York	15 hrs
Los Angeles	12 hrs 15 mins
San Francisco	14 hrs 30 mins
Frankfurt	9 hrs

Fact Sheet	2001
Area (sq km)	16,808
Population (million)	13.8
GDP (RMB billion)	281.8
GDP Growth Rate	11%
Consumption Expenditure (RMB billion)	
• Government	41
• Household	81
Per capita annual	
• disposable income of urban residents (RMB '000)	11.6
• net income of rural households (RMB '000)	5.1
Contractual FDI (USD million)	3,310
Industrial Value Added (RMB bn)	84.57
Imports (USD million)	39,750
Exports (USD million)	11,791
Universities & Colleges	62

CLIMATE OF FOREIGN INVESTMENT

In 2001, Beijing's GDP reached USD34.2 billion, an increase of 11% over 2000. The increase was largely brought by the rapid development of urban infrastructure and real estate and steady growth of consumption. Beijing's industrial structure has been improved. The value added of high-tech enterprises accounted for 31.2% of the total industrial output.

In 2001, the city handled 305.4 million tons of freight and welcomed 2.86 million overseas tourists, The which the airport alone handled 24.2 million passengers.

The total foreign trade in 2001 saw a modest 3.9% increase and stood at USD51.5 billion. The city approved 1,149 foreign invested projects in 2001, with USD3.31 billion contractual FDI. The utilized FDI was USD1.77 billion.

By the end of 2001, 14,489 FIEs were located in various industrial parks of Beijing, more than 30 of them being Fortune Global 500 MNCs. Zhongguancun Science Park, located in the northwest of Beijing urban area and with many Chinese key universities and research institutes within its proximity, is the most dynamic area in China for high-tech developments. It has attracted more than 9,000 high-tech enterprises to date, with value added of RMB45.6 billion.

The Municipal Government of Beijing
Website: www.beijing.gov.cn

Beijing Municipal Foreign Economic Relations and Trade Commission
Website: www.bjfetc.gov.cn

Beijing Investment Platform
Website: www.bjinvest.gov.cn

Beijing Foreign Investment Service Center
3-4th Floor, Tower F, Fuhua Mansion
8 Chaoyangmen North Street
Dongcheng District, Beijing
P. R. China 100027
Tel: (86)(10) 65543151, 65543172
Fax: (86)(10) 65543161
E-mail: bfisc@bjchina.com
Website: www.fdibeijing.org.cn

BEIJING ECONOMIC AND TECHNOLOGICAL DEVELOPMENT AREA

Our Rating:	AA
Year of Establishment:	1994
Location:	Beijing
Size:	15 sq km (first phase), 143 sq km (planned)
Major Investors:	Bayer, Lucent, NCR, Lotte, National, Sanyo, Shiseido, Unilever, ABB, Coca Cola, Cummins, GE, Ronabranc, Nokia and BMW
Total Foreign Direct Investment:	USD2.95 billion (June 2002)
Major Industries Encouraged:	Pharmaceuticals, information technologies, optical-mechanical-electronic integration technologies, new materials and service industries

INTRODUCTION

Beijing Economic and Technological Development Area (BDA) was approved by the State Council to be the only state-level development zone in Beijing on 25 August 1994, and part of the Area is the well-known Yizhuang Science Park. With new international management systems, BDA enjoys the preferential policies of both the coastal open regions and the national high-tech parks.

Geographic location

BDA lies in the southeast suburb, west to the start of the Beijing-Tianjin Expressway, and south to the planned 5th Ring Road. It is 3.5 km from the South 4th Ring Road, seven km to the South 3rd Ring Road, and 16.5 km from Tian'anmen Square.

Key statistics

In 2001, the GDP of BDA was RMB6.97 billion, an increase of 139.2% over 2000. The GNP per capita was RMB193,000. Annual realized sales revenue was USD5.66 billion, an increase of 375% over 2000. Annual realized fiscal income was RMB2.68 billion, an increase of 148.4% over 2000.

At the end of June 2002, 1044 enterprises had registered in BDA, with total investment of USD3.96 billion. Among them were 762 domestic enterprises, with total investment of RMB8 billion. According to the statistics at Beijing's Customs House, annual import-export amounted to US3.58 billion, an increase of 495.4% over 2000. Import values were USD2.34 billion, an increase of 406% over 2000 while export values were USD1.24 billion, an increase of 794.5% over 2000.

INVESTMENT CLIMATE

Infrastructure

BDA is able to process sewage and provide quality natural gas etc. A central heating system is adopted to supply saturated steam for manufacturing, heating, cooling and daily life. BDA is connected with the North China Power Network. 100,000 lines cabled with optical fibers provide wired, wireless, microwave, digital services, IDD, DDD, telegram, facsimile, computerized data network, satellite TV, video-phone, cable TV and Internet facilities.

Foreign-invested enterprises

It has 282 foreign-invested enterprises. Hong Kong, Macau and Taiwan enterprises have invested a total of US2.696 billion, with average of USD9.87 million for every project.

Key projects

Major industries include pharmaceuticals, information technology, optical-mechanical-electronics, construction new materials, light industries and service industries. Major foreign investors in the zone include Bayer, Lucent, NCR, Lotte, National, Sanyo, Shisheido, Unilever, ABB, Coca Cola, Cummins, GE, Ronabranc, Nokia and BMW.

Economic Development Bureau of Beijing Economic & Technological Development Area
Tel: (86) 10) 67881209

Foreign Investors Service Center
Tel: (86)(10) 67881236, 67881126
Fax: (86) 10) 67880226
Website: www.bda.gov.cn

TIANZHU AIRPORT INDUSTRIAL PARK

Our Rating:	AA
Year of Establishment:	1994
Location:	Capital International Airport, Beijing
Size:	6.6 sq km
Major Investors:	JVC, Panasonic, MuRata, Ericcson, Citizen, LG, Sony, Goldwin, Hanmi, Drager, Rosenberger, Domino, Fenefine, Blue Star Cleaners, Sinotrans, Air China and Vanke
Total Foreign Direct Investment:	USD1.55 billion
Major Industries Encouraged:	electronics, telecommunication, warehousing, aviation, medicine, machinery, fine chemical engineering, bioengineering and new materials

INTRODUCTION

Beijing Tianzhu Airport Industrial Park (TZAIP) is located 1 km from the Capital International Airport, which is China's largest airport. With total development area of 6.6 sq km, the development zone was established in January 1994. The first development stage of TZAIP is around 3 sq km. It is 17 km to downtown Beijing, 20 km to Beijing Railway Station and 150 km to Tianjin Port.

By June 2002, 179 enterprises have joined TZAIP and the total investment was USD1.55 billion. Fifteen companies of the 50 over MNCs were among Fortune 500 companies. These include JVC, Panasonic, MuRata, Ericcson, Citizen, LG, Sony, Goldwin, Hanmi, Drager, Rosenberger, Domino, Fenefine, Blue Star Cleaners, Sinotrans, Air China and Vanke etc.

DEVELOPMENT

According to the master plan of Beijing municipality, the region where TZAIP is located will emerge as an international airport city which can accommodate 300,000 people together with villas, star hotels, golf course, horse racing field, an international conference center and other quality entertainment facilities.

The Administrative Committee of Tianzhu Airport Industrial Park is responsible for the planning, development and coordination affairs of the development zone.

The Administrative Committee of Tianzhu Airport Industrial Park
4F Lantian Building
West, Capital International Airport
Shunyi District, Beijing
P. R. China
Tel: (86)(10) 80489922
Fax: (86)(10) 80489568
Email: baizinfo@public.bta.net.cn
Website: www.chinabaiz.com

TIANZHU EXPORT PROCESSING ZONE

Year of Establishment:	2000
Location:	Beijing
Size:	2.726 sq km (first phase is 1.251 sq km)
Major Investor:	SMC
Major Industries Encouraged:	Export processing, warehousing, transportation, electronics, information technologies, bio-pharmaceuticals and new materials

INTRODUCTION

Beijing Tianzhu Export Processing Zone (TEPZ) was approved by the State Council in April 2000 to be one of the first 15 export processing zones in China. It remains the only state-level export processing zone in Beijing.

TEPZ is located within Tianzhu Airport Industrial Park, only 1 km west to the Capital International Airport, with total planned area of 2.726 sq km and 1.251 sq km for the first phase development.

INVESTMENT CLIMATE

Groundwater from Chaobai River system is supplied to TEPZ, the same source of water for the embassy districts and Capital International Airport.

At present there are two 110 kV sub-stations, of which 10 kV cables are led to each switching station to power enterprises in the zone.

The telecommunication facilities in the zone can supply 80,000 program-controlled telephones. Optical fiber cables have been introduced to the zone for wide-band data transmission.

TEPZ will furnish the processing-oriented enterprises with a more flexible and facilitated operation environment by its advantageous location, sound infrastructure, preferential policies, high quality and efficient services, and operation in line with international practice.

The Administrative Committee of Tianzhu Export Processing Zone (Tianzhu Airport Industrial Park)
Website: www.chinabaiz.com/ckjgq/

ZHONGGUANCUN SCIENCE PARK

Year of Establishment:	May 1988
Location:	Haidian and other Districts of Beijing
Size:	355 sq km (75 sq km for the core zone)
Major Investors:	Legend Group, Stone Group, Founder Group, Tsinghua Unisplendour, Datang Telecom, Tsinghua Tongfang, Nokia, HP, UTStarcom, Matsushita, Mitsubishi, Microsoft, Oracle, Norvatis, SMC, Ericcson and Bell etc.
Total Foreign Direct Investment:	USD3.26 billion (1999)
Major Industries Encouraged:	software, information service, IT products, optical-mechanical-electronic integration technologies, bio-engineering, new medicine, new materials, environment protection technologies, education and commerce

INTRODUCTION

As one of China's most famous and developed state-level high-tech parks, Zhongguancun Science Park (ZSP) is located in Haidian district, northwest of Beijing. It was approved by the State Council in May 1988.

During the past ten years, ZSP has maintained an average economic growth rate of 30% annually. In 2001, the total sales of all enterprises in the park was RMB201.4 billion (USD24.35 billion), total value added was RMB45.57 billion (USD5.5 billion) and total industrial output was RMB128.7 billion (USD15.6 billion). About 17.7% of the total enterprises or over 1,100 are wholly owned foreign enterprises or joint ventures. It is estimated that in 2010, the annual GDP will reach RMB130 billion (USD15.76 billion).

INVESTMENT CLIMATE

The actually utilized foreign direct investment has accumulated to USD3.26 billion. Many world top 500 companies have joined ZSP, among which more than 20 have set up research centers in the Park. Major foreign investors such as Nokia, HP, UTStarcom, Matsushita, Mitsubishi, Microsoft, Oracle, Norvatis, SMC, Ericcson, Sun, Schlumberger and Bell have established operations in the park. Some prestigious domestic enterprises are also located here, for example the Legend Group (legend.com.cn), the Stone Group (stonegroup.com), the Founder Group (founder.com.cn), Datang Telecom (dtt.com.cn), Tsinghua Unisplendor (thunis.com) and Tsinghua Tongfang (thtf.com.cn) and others.

Various incubators in ZSP have become cradles for the commercialization of scientific achievements and development of high-tech enterprises. In the park, there are Fengtai Innovation Center, Haidian Innovation Center for Overseas Chinese Scholars and Tsinghua Innovation Center. Encouraged by the Technological Innovation Fund, as many as 3,000 new enterprises have been set up during the period of 1999-2001. Over 20 venture investment institutions are cooperating with ZSP. More than 120 companies in the park have revenues of above RMB100 million or USD12.1 million.

According to the master plan, the development focus of ZSP are software, information service, IT products, optical-mechanical-electronic integration technologies and products, bio-engineering, new pharmaceuticals, new materials, environment protection technologies, education and commerce.

The park consists of five subsidiary zones, namely the Haidian zone, the Changping Zone, the Fengtai Zone, the Yizhuang S & T Park and the Electronics City S & T Park. The Haidian Zone is located in Haidian District, in which there are the 1.8 sq km Shangdi Information Industrial Base and the 4 sq km Yongfeng Experimental Base.

The 5 sq km Changping Zone is located in Changping District, a northern suburb of Beijing. It has over 1,000 high-tech enterprises and gross industrial output of RMB40 billion. It is focused on bio-technology, telecommunication, optical-mechanical-electronic technology and new material etc.

The Fengtai Zone is located in Fengtai District, the southern suburb of Beijing. It covers an area of 5 sq km; Yizhuang S & T Park covers an area of 7 sq km and is located near the starting point of the Beijing-Tianjin-Tanggu Expressway.

The 0.5 sq km Electronics City S & T Park is located in the Jiuxianqiao area in the northeastern part of Beijing, hosted by Chaoyang District. Beijing aims to become the microelectronics production base in North China. It has set up six software colleges to train more professionals.

HUMAN RESOURCES

ZSP has some of China's most prestigious universities, Peking University and Tsinghua University. Peking University, an institution with over 100 years of history, is famous for its strength in arts, humanities, natural sciences and social sciences. Tsinghua University, which is China's best polytechnic university, is an incubator for teams of top scientists and engineers. People's University of China is very strong in business, political science, economics, journalism and humanities. The Chinese Academy of Sciences (CAS), China's national research institution, is also located in ZSP.

In the past two years, more than 3,000 overseas Chinese students back from foreign nations, including Australia, Canada, France, Germany, Japan, the United Kingdom and the United States, have started their own ventures or joined major companies in the park.

The Administrative Committee of Zhongguancun Science Park
2nd Level, Haidian Technologies Building
Zhongguancun South Avenue
Haidian District, Beijing
P. R. China 100081
Tel: (86)(10) 68915118
Fax: (86)(10) 68915214
Email: zgc@zgc.gov.cn
Website: www.zgc.gov.cn

PEKING UNIVERSITY SCIENCE PARK

Year of Establishment:	1992
Location:	Haidian District, Beijing
Major Supporting Institutions:	Peking University and the People's Government of Haidian District
Major Investors:	Founder Group, Tsinghua Tongzhou, Lian Chuang Hang Li, Royal Stone, PKU Pioneer, PKU Xifei, PKU Zoteq and Yunnan PKU Resources
Major Industries Encouraged:	Information technologies, bio-pharmaceuticals, optical-mechanical-electrical integration technologies, new materials, new energy, environmental protection technologies, consulting, finance and publishing

INTRODUCTION

Established in 1992, Peking University Science Park (PKUSP) was authorized as a National University Science Park by Chinese Ministry of Education and Ministry of Science & Technology jointly in May, 2001. Among China's 22 national university science parks, PKUSP had the largest group of member enterprises and largest sales revenue, 390 and RMB15 billion (USD1.82 billion) at the end of 2000 respectively. The member enterprises enjoy preferential policies of the country, of Beijing Municipality as well as of Zhongguancun Science Park. So far, Peking University and Huaxia Bank have invested RMB500 million (USD60.6 million) and RMB100 million (USD12.1 million) in joint development of PKUSP. The total construction area to be finished by 2003 will be around 550,000 sq m, of which 100,000 sq m were already in use at the end of 2000.

Located in the northwest of Beijing urban area, about 35 minutes by taxi to the city's central business district, the 20 ha PKUSP is composed of three parts – the Eastern Chengfu Zone, the South Street Zone and the Western Loudouqiao Zone. The Park faces the western part of Zhongguancun, China's Silicon Valley, in the south, and adjoins Shangdi Information Industrial Base in the north.

DEVELOPMENT

Among the 390 enterprises that have joined at PKUSP, more than 80% are engaged in high-tech industries, for instance Founder Group, Tsinghua Tongzhou, Lian Chuang Hang Li, Royal Stone, PKU Pioneer PKU Xifei, PKU Zoteq and Yunnan PKU Resources. The range of their technologies covers electronics, information technologies, bio-pharmaceuticals, optical-mechanical-electrical integration technologies, new materials, new energy and environmental protection. Among these enterprises, the development of PKU Founder Group (founderpku.com) is most impressive. With around 5,000 employees, it now owns three listed companies, namely Founder Holdings, Founder Digital and Shanghai Founder Yanzhong Science & Technologies Group, and other 17 subsidiaries. The total assets of the whole group are around RMB6 billion (USD727.3 million).

One particular attraction of PKUSP is Peking University (www.pku.edu.cn) itself. The university was established in 1898 and is now recognized as one of the most prestigious Chinese universities, particularly in natural science and social science. In April 2000, Peking University merged with Beijing Medical University . The R&D strength of the university is strong: 46 CAS (Chinese Academy of Science) fellows, seven CAE (Chinese Academy of Engineering) fellows, and over 1,600 professors and associate professors. Their research covers a wide range of areas, including life science, government administration, international relations, economics, management, foreign languages, physics, law, education, journalism, medicine, physics, electronics, urban planning, psychology, information management and sociology etc. Peking University today owns 42 State Key Subjects - research programs authorized by the Ministry of Education in top university, 42 research institutes, 52 research centers and 15 State Key Laboratories. University researchers have achieved major honors — such as National Natural Science Award, National Invention Award and National Science & Technology Advancement Award. In 2000, Peking University ranked top among all Chinese universities in contributing articles to SCI (Science Citation Index). In addition, the university has established international cooperation with 174 overseas universities, such as Harvard University, Princeton University, Stanford University, Cambridge University, Oxford University, University of Tokyo and UC-Berkeley.

As a member of the PKU affiliated enterprises group, PKUSP enjoys active support from other major group members, such as PKU Founder Group (www.founderpku.com), Jade Bird Group (www.jadebird.com.cn), PKU Weiming (www.weiming.com.cn), PKU Resources Group, WBL PKU Biotech (www.wpu.com.cn), PULEAD Technology Industry (www.-pulead.com.cn) and PKU High-tech (www.-pkuht.com). Their R&D and industrial fields cover electronics, information technology, broadband and mobile communication, computer network, software, POS system, gene engineering and natural medicine etc.

Overall, Peking University, together with other 60 plus Beijing-based universities and colleges, including Tsinghua University, People's University of China, Beijing Institute of Technology and hundreds of national, ministry-affiliated and municipal research institutes, for example the Chinese Academy of Sciences (CAS) and the Chinese Academy of Engineering (CAE), provides abundant research and management talents for companies that enter PKUSP.

At present, with registered capital of RMB100 million (USD12.1 million), the PKUSP Development Corporation provides one-stop service for member enterprises and continuous support in the incubation stage and later development periods. Companies such as PKU Zhengyuan Science & Tech, PKU New Century, PKU Pioneer, PUK Royal Stone, PKU Xifei and Yunnan PKU Resources have been successfully incubated in PKUSP.

Peking University Science Park Development Co. Ltd
17th Floor
PKU Pacific Technologies Plaza
52 Haidian Road, Haidian District
Beijing 100871
Tel: (86)(10) 82667188
Fax: (86)(10) 82667840
Email: inf@pkusp.com.cn
Website: www.pkusp.com.cn

TSINGHUA UNIVERSITY SCIENCE PARK

Year of Establishment:	1993
Location:	Haidian District, Beijing
Major Supporting Institutions:	Tsinghua University and the People's Government of Haidian District
Major Investors:	Unisplendour, Tongfang, P&G Technologies and OMNERC
Major Industries Encouraged:	electronics, information technology, environmental protection, new materials, new energy, bio-engineering, fine chemical engineering, optical-mechanical-electrical integration and pharmaceuticals etc.

INTRODUCTION

Tsinghua University Science Park (THUSP) has long been recognized as an important R&D base for the capital's high-tech industries by the Beijing municipal government. The 22 ha park is located at the southeastern part of the university campus and in the northwest of Beijing, with a total planned building area of 50 ha and is about 40 minutes by taxi to the central business district.

DEVELOPMENT

The development of THUSP started in 1993 and the start-up zone, the Entrepreneur sector of THUSP, was opened in August 1998 to be a key base for the development of high-tech industries in Beijing. In May 2001, with authorization from Ministry of Science & Technology and Ministry of Education, THSUP became one of the first 22 National University Science Parks. Till now, Tsinghua University and the government of Haidian District have invested RMB500 million (USD60.6 million) to co-establish the Beijing THUSP Development Corporation. At the same time, Bank of China provided credit support of RMB1 billion (USD121.2 million).

Since its establishment, many enterprises have joined the park. Among them, there are prestigious high-tech enterprises and MNCs such as Tsinghua Unisplendour (www.thunis.com), Tisnghua Tongfang (www.thtf.com.cn) and Beijing P&G Technologies, major research institutes such as Optical Memory National Engineering Research Center (OMNERC) and National Engineering Research Center for CAD Supporting Software, and other organizations such as Tsinghua Exhibition Hall for Science & Technology, National University Science & Technology Collaboration Network, Beijing Tsinghua Industrial Development Research Institute, THUSP Entrepreneur Service Center and Guo Chuang Venture Capital Fund.

A special advantage of THUSP is Tsinghua University (www.tsinghua.edu.cn) itself. The university is widely recognized as one of China's most prestigious universities, particularly in natural science, engineering and advanced technology. The R&D strength of the university is particularly strong: 26 CAS (Chinese Academy of Science) fellows, 25 CAE (Chinese Academy of Engineering) fellows, 1,035 professors, 1,740 associate professors and 446 postdoctoral fellows.

Their research cover a wide range of areas,

including architecture, civil engineering, hydraulic and hydropower engineering, environmental science, mechanical engineering, precision instruments, optical engineering, material science, power engineering, electrical engineering, computer science, chemical engineering, nuclear science, physics, mathematics, information and communication technology, biomedicine and management science. At the university, there are 13,861 undergraduate students, and there are 6,927 master students as well as 3,275 doctoral students.

Altogether, Tsinghua University owns 29 State Key Subjects, 49 National University Key Subjects, 39 research institutes, 15 State Key Laboratories and 10 Education Ministry Key Laboratories. University researchers have been awarded prestigious honors including National Natural Science Award, National Invention Award and National Science & Technology Advancement Award. In addition, the university has established international cooperation with 130 overseas universities in 26 countries and regions worldwide and strategic alliances with more than 130 top Chinese enterprises including Beijing Electronic Information Industry, Eastcom, Guangdong Nuclear Power, Haier, Hongta Group, Huawei Technologies, Jilin Chemicals, Shanghai Auto Industry, Shanghai Baosteel and Three Gorges Development Corporation and 30 major MNCs such as AT&T, General Motors, Hitachi, HP, IBM, Mitsubishi, Motorola, Rockwell, Shell and Sun Microsystem etc.

In 2001, many international guests visited the university, including three presidents, 19 ministers and vice-ministers, 11 Noble Prize winners, 84 university presidents and vice-presidents, 14 ambassadors and 20 CEOs of major MNCs.

As a joint venture between Tsinghua University and Beijing Municipal Government, THUSP is a member enterprise of Tsinghua University Enterprise Group, which owns more than 30 member enterprises such as Unisplendour group, Tongfang group, Tongli Instruments, Sunshine energy, Venture Investment, Industrial Arts Corporation, Huayuan Electronics and Wanbo Internet Technologies. Their R&D and industrial fields cover electronics, information technology, environmental protection, civil nuclear technology, communication, new materials, new energy, bio-engineering, fine chemicals, optical-mechanical-electrical integration and pharmaceutical. In 2001, the assets and sales revenue of the whole enterprise group reached RMB16 billion (USD1.94 billion) and RMB10 billion (USD1.21 billion) respectively, with average growth rate of more than 50% annually.

So far, municipal-level THUSP Development Council has been established to manage and supervise the development of the park. The THUSP Development Corporation is responsible for providing full-range services for tenants as well as the planning, construction, development and daily operation of the park.

With preferential policy treatment in corporate and personal income tax rates, R&D costs and business operation, the enterprises investing in THUSP are in fact highly integrated with the vibrant Beijing economy and the goal of Tsinghua University to become a leading world-class university in the coming decades.

Tsinghua University Science Park Development Corporation
Huaye Building, Tsinghua University
Haidian District, Beijing
P. R. China 100084
Tel: (86)(10) 62785888
Fax: (86)(10) 62772777
Email: thsp@tsinghua.edu.cn
Website: www.tsinghua.edu.cn/docsn/ kjy/ahead.htm

BEIJING SOFTWARE DEVELOPMENT BASE

Year of Establishment:	1998
Location:	Beijing
Size:	139 ha
Major Investors:	IBM, Microsoft, Oracle, CA, SUN, Legend, Founder, Tongfang, UFSOFT, Tsinghua Unis, PKU Jadebird, Stone Group, Hope Computer, CASS, Sinosoft Group, Da Heng Information Technologies, Federal Software and Great Wall Computer Software.
Major Industries Encouraged:	Software products and services

INTRODUCTION

The development of Beijing Software Development Base is closely related to the comprehensive advantages of Beijing in R&D strength, human resources, information and market. Over 60,000 software professionals, about one third of China's total, are working with the 1,300 plus software companies in Beijing.

DEVELOPMENT

Apart from major MNCs including IBM, Microsoft, Oracle, SUN and CA, many major Chinese IT enterprises and their software divisions have joined the base, including Legend Group (legend.com.cn), Founder Group (founderpku.com), Tongfang Group (thtf.com.cn), China National Computer Software & Technology Service Corporation (css.com.cn), UFSOFT Corporation (ufsoft.com.cn), Tsinghua Unis Group (thunis.com), PKU Jadebird Co. Ltd. (jbcase.com), Stone Group (stonegroup.com), Hope Computer (hope.com.cn), CASS Group (cass.ac.cn), Clever Group (clever.com.cn), Sinosoft Group (sinosoft.com.cn), Federal Software (federal.com.cn), Hunan Computers (hcc.com.cn), Da Heng Info Technologies (dahengit.com.cn) and Great Wall Computer Software and System

(gwssi.com.cn). The incubation center is to promote small and medium sized software companies.

By the end of 2001, 723 software firms have joined in Beijing Software Development Base. The population of software professionals has reached 70,000. The annual growth rate in output of those enterprises has been above 35% for consecutive years.

The Promotion Center of Beijing Software Development Base
16 Xizhimen South Street
Beijing, P. R. China 100035
Tel: (86)(10) 68026999
Fax: (86)(10) 66153423
Website: www.bsw.gov.cn/rjjd/rjjd.jsp

CHONGQING

Industrial Parks in Chongqing

1. Chongqing Economic & Technological Development Zone
2. Chongqing High-tech Park

INTRODUCTION

Chongqing is famous for its agriculture, light industry and natural resources. It became the fourth municipality on 14 March 1997. The establishment of the youngest municipality shows a breakthrough of China's initiatives to speed up economic development of the central and western regions, as well as the emphasis on the Three Gorges Dam project.

GEOGRAPHY

Formerly a part of Sichuan Province, Chongqing is located at the upper reaches of Yangtze River in Southwest China. Being the largest municipality among the four, in terms of area and population, Chongqing's administrative jurisdiction covers 6 urban districts, 8 suburban districts, 26 counties and county-level cities. Among the nearly 31 million people of Chongqing, 65% are still living in rural areas.

Situated in the east of Sichuan Basin, the land of Chongqing is largely mountainous and hilly. It has a subtropical humid monsoon climate. The city of Chongqing is known as one of the three "Stoves" in China for its extreme hot weather in summer. The annual precipitation is about 1,100-1,300 mm. The 200 km long Three Gorges rides on the borders between Chongqing and Hubei Province, making Chongqing a renowned tourist destination in China.

Fact Sheet	2001
Area (sq km)	82,300
Population (million)	30.97
GDP (RMB billion)	175.0
GDP Growth Rate	9.0%
Consumption Expenditure (RMB billion)	
• Government	25.6
• Household	69.9
Per capita annual	
• disposable income of urban residents (RMB '000)	6.72
• net income of rural households (RMB '000)	1.97
Utilized FDI (USD million)	256
Industrial Value Added (RMB bn)	57.7
Imports (USD million)	731
Exports (USD million)	1,103
Universities & Colleges	29

TRAVEL INFORMATION

Though visitors may enjoy sightseeing by taking river steamers or trains to get into Chongqing, the fastest way is by air.

From Chongqing Airport to:

Beijing	2 hrs 5 mins
Guangzhou	1 hr 40 mins
Shanghai Hongqiao	2 hrs 10 mins
Xi'an	1 hr 5 mins
Kunming	1 hr 10 mins
Shenzhen	1 hr 40 mins
Hong Kong	1 hr 40 mins
Bangkok	2 hrs 50 mins
Seoul	3 hrs 30 mins
Tokyo	4 hrs 10 mins
Nagoya	3 hrs 40 mins

CLIMATE OF FOREIGN INVESTMENT

In 2001, Chongqing realized GDP of USD21.2 billion, up 9.0% from the previous year, and the total industrial output increased 14.3%

to USD12.9 billion. There were 191 newly signed foreign investment projects in 2001 and utilized FDI increased by 5.0% to USD256 million.

Chongqing is a transportation hub in inland China. Three major railways of western China converge on its territory. Seven national highways and an expressway to Chengdu also go through the municipality. Chongqing also boasts a well-developed inland river transportation system.

Under the national policy for the Great Western Development, priority is given to foreign investors engaged in the development of infrastructure, natural resources, agriculture, environmental protection as well as projects in machinery, metallurgy, electronics and light industries.

The two prominent areas for investment are Chongqing Economic and Technological Development Zone and Chongqing High-tech Park.

Chongqing Municipal Government
Website: www.cq.gov.cn

Chongqing Foreign Investment Center
248 Renmin Road
Yuzhong District, Chongqing
P. R. China 400015
Tel: (86)(23) 69039083, 69039084
Fax: (86)(23) 63615852
Email: investcq@investcq.gov.cn
Website: www.investcq.gov.cn

Chongqing Foreign Trade & Economic Relations Commission
65 Jianxin North Road, Chongqing
P. R. China 400020
Tel: (86)(23) 69018014
Fax: (86)(23) 67523458
Website: www.ft.cq.cn

CHONGQING ECONOMIC AND TECHNOLOGICAL DEVELOPMENT ZONE

Our Rating:	A
Year of Establishment:	April 1993
Location:	Chongqing
Size	93.3 sq km
Major Investors:	Ford, Visteon, Ericsson, BP, Metro, Honda, Daikin, Suzuki, Denso, Kansai and Formosa Plastics
Total Foreign Direct Investment:	USD1.5 billion (end 2001)
Major Industries Encouraged:	Electronics, information technology, bio-pharmaceuticals, automobiles, motorcycles, fine chemicals, new materials, food and clothes

INTRODUCTION

Chongqing Economic and Technological Development Zone (CQETDZ) was set up in the early 1990s, and was approved by the State Council in April 1993 to be the first state-level economic and technological development zone in western China.

INVESTMENT CLIMATE

CQETDZ comprises a 9.6 sq km Southern Zone that is already built and a 83.7 sq km Northern Zone whose infrastructure is now under development. The Southern Zone has a planned area of 9.6 sq km, and is located in Chongqing City's Nanping. It is 3 km away from Chongqing Railway Station, 5 km away from Chongqing Passenger Pier and 28 km away from Chongqing Airport.

An Information Industrial Zone, Dangui Industrial Zone and Huilong Industrial Zone have been established, combining a commercial district and Nanhu, Luochang-wan residential district. The Northern Zone has a planned area of 83.7 sq km and is located at Chongqing's Yuanyang Town and Lijia Town It is 1 km away from Chongqing's largest container port and enjoys the advantages of convenient transportation, leveled land and excellent geographical position. An export processing zone, an automobile industrial zone, an environmental industrial zone, a technology industrial zone and a central commercial district will be built.

In 2001, the GDP of CQETDZ was RMB3.26 billion (USD 461 million), an increase of 16.35%.

At the end of 2001, there were 1,225 enterprises in CQETDZ, among which there were 304 foreign enterprises from 22 countries with total investment of USD1.5 billion and an average investment of USD4.97 million per project. There are 29 large projects of more than USD10 million. Major enterprises include Ford and Visteon from the US; Ericsson from Sweden; BP from UK; Metro from Germany; Honda, Suzuki, Denso, Kansai and Daikin from Japan; Formosa Plastics and Ting Hsin from Taiwan, etc. The number of domestic enterprises was 925, with contractual investment of RMB3.327 billion.

CQETDZ has developed a few key industries of electronics, information technologies, bio-pharmaceuticals, manu-facturing of automobiles and motorcycles, fine chemicals, new materials, food and clothes.

The Administrative Committee CQETDZ
2 Wanshou Road
Nanping, Chongqing
P. R. China 400060
Tel: (86)(23) 62802780, 62982932
Fax: (86)(23) 62982636
Website: www.cqetdz.gov.cn

CHONQING HIGH-TECH PARK

Our Rating:	A
Year of Establishment:	March 1991
Location:	Chongqing
Size:	20 sq km
Major Investors:	Yazaki and Chiatai
Total Foreign Direct Investment:	USD520 million
Major Industries Encouraged:	electronics, telecommunication, optical-electro-mechanical integration, bio-engineering, precise instruments and environmental technologies

INTRODUCTION

Chongqing High-tech Park (CQHTP) is located in southwest Chongqing. It was approved by the State Council in March 1991. The park covers 20 sq km, and is divided into a few subsidiary zones.

The industrial focus of CQHTP is on electronics, telecommunication, optical-electro-mechanical integration, bio-engineering, precise instruments and environmental technologies.

Among the 4,000 enterprises that had joined the park by the end of 1999, there were 334 high-tech enterprises and over 300 foreign enterprises. The total capital of these foreign enterprises was USD520 million. The major investors include several famous international companies such as Yazaki and Chiatai. The main fields of those foreign enterprises are automobile components, electronics, telecommunication equipments, new materials and bio-engineering etc.

INVESTMENT CLIMATE

There are two important subsidiary parks within CQHTP, Shiqiaopu High-tech Zone and Erlang Science & Technology Zone. The former is near the entrance of State Chengyu Expressway. It is 36 km from Chongqing Airport, 8 km from Chongqing Railway Station, 10 km from Chongqing Port and 13 km from the container terminal. Erlang Science & Technology Zone is a new project under construction. It aims to become an incubation center for high-tech ventures.

HUMAN RESOURCES

Over 400,000 researchers and professionals are working in the municipality. Chongqing University, the Third Military Medical University, Southwest University of Political Science & Law, Sichuan Foreign Studies University and Chongqing University of Medical Sciences are located around the high-tech park.

The Administrative Committee of Chongqing High-tech Park
5 Keyuan First Road
Shiqiaopu, Chongqing
P. R. China 410039
Tel: (86)(23) 68601972
Fax: (86)(23) 68606272
Email: hnzcqw@public.cta.cq.cn
Website: www.hnzcq.com.cn

CHONGQING UNIVERSITY SCIENCE PARK

Year of Establishment:	2001
Location:	Chongqing
Major Supporting Institutions:	Chongqing University
Major Investors:	CQU High Technologies, Yuanshen Molecule Pharmaceutical,Chongqing Magnesium, Xinwang Intelligence and Lifan Electric Spraying Software
Major Industries Encouraged:	Information technologies, bio-medicine, environmental engineering, new materials, fine chemical engineering, software development and internet security products

Relying on the intellectual and human resources of Chongqing University (www.cqu.edu.cn), the Third Military Medical University (www.tmmu.com.cn) and Chongqing University of Posts and Telecommunications (www.cqupt.edu.cn), the Chongqing University Science Park (CQUSP) was formally established in June 2001.

According to the master plan, the science park will comprise a core zone, a bio-medicine base and an extended zone. In the next ten years, the Chongqing municipal government plans to invest about RMB6.8 billion in the park. So far, more than 70 enterprises such as CQU High Technologies, Yuanshen Molecule Pharmaceutical, Chongqing Magnesium, Xinwang Intelligence and Lifan Electric Spraying Software have joined the park.

Merged with Chongqing Architecture University and Chongqing College of Architecture, the current Chongqing University owns four State Key Subjects, one State Key Laboratory and four Education Ministry Key Laboratories. Together, three CAE (Chinese Academy of Engineering) fellows, 353 professors and 1,066 associate professors are working with the university. Their academic fields cover economics, business administration, humanities and social sciences, arts, natural science and engineering. The number of students is around 35,000, with 3,178 students pursuing master degree and 1,066 students pursuing doctorate degree.

Now, Chongqing University has established academic exchange links with 74 overseas universities in USA, UK, Russia, Japan, Canada, Australia, Netherlands, Italy, France, etc. At the same time, cooperative relationships have been developed with major MNCs such as IBM, Microsoft, Omron, Rockwell, Siemens, etc.

Chongqing
P. R. China
Tel: (86)(23) 65102345

SHANGHAI

Railway
Expressway

Chongming

JIANGSU

Baoshan
Jiading
Anting **8**
Waigaoqiao **11**
Jinqiao
Shanghai
Qingpu **2 1**
Pudong **3**
Minhang **12**
Nanhui
4
Songjiang
10

Fengxian
7

6
ZHEJIANG
Jinshan

Industrial Parks in Shanghai

1. Caohejing Economic & Technological Development Zone
2. Hongqiao Economic & Technological Development Zone
3. Jinqiao Export Processing Zone
4. Minhang Economic & Technological Development Zone
5. International Automobile City
6. Chemical Industrial Park
7. Comprehensive Industrial Development Zone
8. Jiading Industrial Park
9. Qingpu Industrial Park
10. Songjiang Industrial Park
11. Waigaoqiao Free Trade Zone
12. Zhangjiang High-tech Park

INTRODUCTION

Shanghai is called in Chinese "Hu" for short and "Shen" as a nickname. It has been an important trading port of China since the 13th century. Sitting at the mouth of the Yangtze River and the center of China's coastline, it offers tremendous opportunities for foreign investors to explore the vast Chinese hinterland .

GEOGRAPHY

Shanghai covers an area of 6,340.5 sq km that extends 120 km longitudinally and 100 km in latitude. It borders Jiangsu in the northwest and Zhejiang in the southwest, forming the so-called Great Shanghai Area at the Yangtze River Delta that is the economically most advanced and dynamic area in China. It is administratively divided into 17 districts and three counties. Shanghai has a urban area of 2,057 km and a population of 16.7 million, making it the largest metropolis in China.

TRAVEL INFORMATION

Shanghai has the most developed transportation system in China. Passengers may reach the city by air, expressway, railway or sea. Currently it has two international airports, the Hongqiao International Airport and Pudong International Airport.

From Hongqiao Airport to:

Beijing	1 hrs 40 mins
Hong Kong	2 hrs 25 mins
Osaka	2 hrs
Tokyo	2 hrs 40 mins
Singapore	5 hrs
Seoul	1 hr 40 mins

From Pudong Airport to:

Paris	11 hrs 30 mins
Frankfurt	11 hrs
Los Angeles	11 hrs
New York	16 hrs
Chicago	14 hrs

Fact Sheet	2001
Area (sq km)	6,341
Population (million)	16.7
GDP (RMB billion)	495
GDP Growth Rate	10.2%
Consumption Expenditure (RMB billion)	
• Government	72.6
• Household	186.1
Per capita annual	
• disposable income of urban residents (RMB '000)	12.9
• net income of rural households (RMB '000)	5.8
Contractual FDI (USD million)	737.3
Industrial Value Added (RMB bn)	756.7
Imports (USD million)	33,267
Exports (USD million)	27,628
Universities & Colleges	50

INVESTMENT CLIMATE

In the early 1990s, the central government decided to turn Shanghai into a world economic, financial and trade center with the development of Pudong New District. With population of only 1% and land area of 0.06% of the nation's total, Shanghai contributes one twelfth of industrial output, one sixth of port cargo volume, one fourth of exports and one eighth of fiscal revenue.

In 2001, Shanghai achieved RMB495 billion (USD60 billion) in GDP, up 10.2% from 2000, marking the 10th consecutive year of double-digit growth. Shanghai's GDP per capita is the highest among all municipalities, provinces and autonomous regions.

Shanghai owns the biggest port in China. In 2001, it handled 221 million tons of freight and 6.34 million TEUs. The multi-dimensional transportation system moved 63.24 million passengers in 2001, in which two airports handled 20.66 million passengers.

The total foreign trade of Shanghai increased by 11.3% to USD60.9 billion in 2001. Contractual and utilized FDI amounted to USD7.37 billion and USD4.39 billion respectively. In the first 7 months of 2002, 1,595 new investment projects were approved and the contractual value is USD6.03 billion.

The city's financial sector has been opening wider for overseas investors. By the end of 2000, the city had 66 foreign financial institutions, of which 24 foreign banks have been authorized to deal in Chinese RMB business.

Various development zones in Shanghai are ideal places for foreign investors. They include Lujiazui Finance and Trade Zone, Jinqiao Export Processing Zone, Zhangjiang HTP, Waigaoqiao FTZ, Caohejing HTP, Minhang ETDZ, Hongqiao ETDZ, Shanghai Chemical Industrial Park, Shanghai International Automobile City, Songjiang Industrial Park, Qingpu Industrial Park, Jiading Industrial Park and Shanghai Comprehensive Industrial Development Zones etc.

In addition, Shanghai has 50 universities and colleges and 258 independent research institutions. Over 15,000 overseas students have come back to work in Shanghai.

The Municipal Government of Shanghai
Website: www.shanghai.gov.cn

Shanghai Foreign Economic Cooperation and Trade Commission
Website: www.smert.gov.cn

Shanghai Foreign Investment Commission
Tel: (86)(21) 62752200
Fax: (86)(21) 62754200
Website: www.investmert.gov.cn

Shanghai Foreign investment Development Board
Tel: (86)(21) 62368800
Fax: (86)(21) 62368024, 62368026

Fly in style, because you deserve it.

At Shanghai Airlines we endorse the philosophy that private air travel is no longer just for the rich and famous, it has become an essential tool for the serious business traveler, too.

Long check-ins, inconvenient timetables and many others using the airlines can take so much time.
Let's face it-your time is valuable.
By choosing Shanghai Airlines Business Jet, your trips can be tailor-made to fit your itinerary, and to allow you to control your time.

In the comfort of your 'own' private jet, our professional attention ensures a smooth and efficient flight.

SHANGHAI AIRLINES

Business Jet Operation Department
Address:18F,No.212,Jiangning Road, Shanghai,China   Tel: 0086-21-62555000   Fax: 0086-21-62555333
E-mail:charter@shanghai-air.com   Web:www.shanghai-air.com

CAOHEJING HIGH-TECH PARK

Our Rating:	AA
Year of Establishment:	1986
Location:	Shanghai
Size:	189 ha
Major Investors:	GE, Lucent Technologies, 3M, Intel, Emerson, AMP, Raychem, DuPont, Agilent, Tandem, Lattice, Foxboro; Air Liquid, Schneider, Philips, Clariant, Mettler-Toledo, Bell, Spirax Sarco, NTT, Toshiba, Mitsui, Epson, Ricoh and Nortel
Total Foreign Direct Investment:	N.A.
Major Industries Encouraged:	Microelectronics, IT products, software, telecommunication, laser technology, bio-engineering, new materials and aerospace technology

INTRODUCTION

Caohejing High-tech Park (CHJHTP) is the only state-level development zone enjoying the preferential policies granted for both economic & technological development zones and high-tech parks.

By the end of 1999, there were more than 800 domestic and foreign high-tech enterprises in the park, among which were more than 300 foreign-invested, 186 high-tech enterprises and 40 top MNCs.

CHJHTP is located in the southwest part of Shanghai. It is only 11 km from downtown Shanghai, 4 km from Xujiahui Commercial District and 7 km from Hongqiao International Airport.

INVESTMENT CLIMATE

Major domestic enterprises include Datang Mobilecom, Zhongxin Telecommunication, China Unicom, China Netcom, Fuxin Group and Huaxin Bio-technology, while Taiwanese enterprises include Acer, Inventech, Microtek, Sinowealth Electronics, Kimpo Electronics etc.

Over 40 world-renowned enterprises have set up subsidiaries in the zone, for example, GE, Lucent Technologies, 3M, Intel, Emerson, AMP, Raychem, DuPont, Agilent, Tandem, Lattice and Foxboro from the USA; Air Liquid and Schneider from France; Philips from Holland; Clariant and Mettler-Toledo from Switzerland; Bell from Belgian; Spirax Sarco from Britain; NTT, Toshiba, Mitsui, Epson and Ricoh from Japan and Nortel from Canada etc.

The zone is dedicated to the development of high technologies in the fields of microelectronics, IT products, software, telecommunication, laser technology, bio-engineering, new materials and aerospace technology.

CHJHTP Development Corporation
Tel: (86)(21) 64859900, 64850000
E-mail: contact@caohejing.com
Website: www.e-caohejing.com

HONGQIAO ECONOMIC AND TECHNOLOGICAL DEVELOPMENT ZONE

Our Rating:	AA
Year of Establishment:	1983
Location:	Shanghai
Size:	65.2 ha
Major Investors:	3M, GE, Nokia, Ericsson and LG
Total Foreign Direct Investment:	USD2.26 billion
Major Industries Encouraged:	Exhibition, office, residential estate, food & beverage and shopping centers

INTRODUCTION

Hongqiao Economic & Tech-nological Development Zone (HQETDZ), established in 1983, is a new commercial and business area which combines exhibition, office, residence, food & beverage amenities and shopping centers. At HQETDZ, there are several plots of land allocated to foreign consulates in Shanghai to build their premises.

HQETDZ is located in the west part of Shanghai urban area, 5.5 km away from Hongqiao International Airport.

INVESTMENT CLIMATE

HQETDZ covers 65.2 ha, with construction area of 31.09 ha, greenery area of 19.54 ha and road area of 14.39 ha.

The total volume of contractual invest-ments has almost reached USD2.8 billion, with foreign utilized investment totaling USD2.26 billion. Investors come from different countries and regions: Hong Kong and Taiwan (55%), Japan (16%), Singapore (8%) and the United States (8%). big multinational companies have set up offices in the Zone such as 3M and GE from the United States, Nokia from Finland, Ericsson from Sweden and LG from South Korea etc.

In addition, India, Denmark, Holland, Switzerland, Argentina, Romania, Israel and Cuba have established consulates in HQETDZ.

HQETDZ United Development Corporation
34-35th Floor, New Town Center
83 Loushanguan Road, Shanghai
P. R. China 200336
Tel: (86)(21) 62756888
Fax: (86)(21) 62194505
Website: www.shudc.com

JINQIAO EXPORT PROCESSING ZONE

Our Rating:	AAA
Year of Establishment:	1990
Location:	Pudong, Shanghai
Size:	20 sq km
Major Investors:	General Motors, HP, Bell, Siemens and Nestle
Total Foreign Direct Investment:	USD8.963 billion (end-June 2001)
Major Industries Encouraged:	Electronics, information technology, vehicles and automobile components, home electronic appliances, bioengineering and pharmaceuticals

INTRODUCTION

Jinqiao Export Processing Zone (JQEPZ) was among the first state-level development zones approved by the State Council in 1990 to be named as "Export Processing Zone". The eastern area is the Jinqiao High-tech Park approved by China Ministry of Science & Technology in April 1998 while the western area is a residential district, the Biyun International Community.

JQEPZ is located in the middle of Pudong New District with planned area of 20 sq km. It connects Lujiazui Finance & Trade Zone in the west, Waigaoqiao Free Trade Zone in the north and is near Zhangjiang High-tech Park in the south. It is 25 km away from Hongqiao International Airport, 15 km away from Pudong International Airport and 9 km from Waigaoqiao Harbor.

JQEPZ's gross industrial output for the first half of 2001 was RMB29.74 billion, one-third of the gross industrial output of Pudong; an increase of 50.3% over the previous year, twice the average growth rate of the whole Pudong. High-tech industry accounted for 92% of the total output.

INVESTMENT CLIMATE

By June 2001, JQEPZ had attracted 398 projects, with committed foreign investment of USD8.963 billion. On average, each project is more than USD22.5 million. Industrial projects accounted for 70%, of which 50 projects were more than USD30 million each. Today, 51 multinational companies from 18 countries and regions have set up 60 projects in JQEPZ. 21 of Fortune Global 500 have invested here, such as General Motors, Siemens, Nestle, Hewlett-Packard, Bell, etc. The development focus at JQEPZ includes electronics, information technology, vehicles and automobile components, electrical home appliances, bioengineering and pharmaceuticals.

In August 2000, JQEPZ was conferred the title of "ISO14000 State-level Model Zone", the country's third, and Shanghai's first of its kind.

JQEPZ Administrative Committee
28 New Jinqiao Road
Pudong, Shanghai
P. R. China 201206
Tel: (86)(21) 58991818
Fax: (86)(21) 58991812

MINHANG ECONOMIC AND TECHNOLOGICAL DEVELOPMENT ZONE

Our Rating:	AA
Year of Establishment:	1983
Location:	Minhang District, Shanghai
Size:	3.5 sq km
Major Investors:	Coca Cola, Ingersoll Rand, Bristol-Myers Squibb and Fuji-Xerox
Total Foreign Direct Investment:	USD2.1 billion
Major Industries Encouraged:	Mechanical equipments, electronics, bio-engineering, pharmaceuticals and food & beverage

INTRODUCTION

Minhang Economic and Technological Development Zone (MHETDZ), established in 1983, was one of the first 14 development zones approved by the State Council in 1986. It has a total development area of 3.5 sq km.

The zone is located in Minhang District. It is 30 km away from the downtown, 27 km away from Hongqiao International Airport and 15 km away from Longwu Port.

By the end of 2001, MHETDZ had attracted 154 projects, of which 28 were Fortune 500 corporations. Contractual investment value amounted to USD2.1 billion, and average investment of these projects was over USD13.5 million. Major foreign investors include Bristol-Myers Squibb, Coca Cola, Fuji-Xerox and Ingersoll Rand etc.

INVESTMENT CLIMATE

By the end of 2000, Shanghai Minhang United Development Corporation (SMUDC) had invested about RMB800 million in MHETDZ's infrastructure development.

Major industries include mechanical equipments, electronics, bio-engineering & pharmaceuticals and food & beverage.

About 25% of enterprises in MHETDZ have been awarded the ISO14000 certification. SMUDC itself is planning for ISO14000 certification.

The International Education Joint College of Shanghai Foreign Languages University and a branch of Shanghai Normal University were also set up within MHETDZ.

Minhang United Development Corporation
1251 Jiangchuan Road
Minhang, Shanghai
P. R. China 200245
Tel: (86)(21) 64300888
Fax: (86)(21) 64300789
Email: smudc@online.sh.cn
Website: www.smudc.com

SHANGHAI INTERNATIONAL AUTOMOBILE CITY

Our Rating:	AA
Year of Establishment:	2001
Location:	Jiading District, Shanghai
Size:	68 sq km
Major Investors:	Volkswagen, Shanghai Auto Group, Jia'an Group, Shanghai Materials Group, China Automobile Association and Akzo Nobel
Total Foreign Direct Investment:	USD6 billion
Major Industries Encouraged:	Automobile trade, automobile exhibition, automobile logistics, automobile tourism, auto racing, auto services, education, real estate and entertainment facilities.

INTRODUCTION

Shanghai International Automobile City (SHIAC) is located at Anting town, northwest of Shanghai Municipality. It is also the location of Shanghai Volkswagen Co. Ltd., which has been continuously listed as one of the largest and most successful joint venture enterprises in Mainland China. Since its establishment in 1985, Shanghai Volkswagen has been taking the lead in China's automobile market. In 2001, the turnover of Shanghai Volkswagen was over RMB32 billion.

Automobile industry has been developing fast, and became one of the pillar industries of Shanghai. The municipal government has thus implemented the strategy to develop Shanghai International Automobile City in Anting town. It is now among the four key industrial bases of Shanghai. The SHIAC Development Corporation has been established by Shanghai Automobile Industry Group, Jia'an Group, Shanghai Materials Group and China Automobile Association to look after the project.

INVESTMENT CLIMATE

With co-efforts from German AS&P GmbH, McKinsey and Debenham Tie Leung, the development plan of the city expects that the total investment commitment will be RMB50 billion (USD6.06 billion). Hopefully, SHIAC will become one of the largest comprehensive automobile industrial bases in Asia Pacific. SHIAC will consist of Automobile Manufacturing Zone, Automobile Trade Zone, Automobile Parts Industrial Zone, International F-1 Racing Field, the new Anting town, a Quality Inspection Center of Shanghai Auto Group and Shanghai Second-hand Auto Transaction Market. The newly built Automobile College of Tongji University will also be established there.

The total development area of SHIAC will take 68 sq km. The market opportunities that foreign investors might enjoy are really promising.

Shanghai International Automobile City Development Corporation
79 Moyu Road,
Anting Town, Jiading District, Shanghai
P. R. China 201805
Tel: (86)(21) 59562324
Fax: (86)((21) 59563621

SHANGHAI CHEMICAL INDUSTRIAL PARK

Our Rating:	A
Year of Establishment:	2001
Location:	Jinshan District, Shanghai
Size:	23.4 sq km
Major Investors:	Sinochem Shanghai, Shanghai Huayi Group, Gaoqiao Petrochemica, Industrial Investment Group, Shanghai Jiushi, Bayer and British Petroleum
Total Foreign Direct Investment:	USD6 billion (estimated)
Major Industries Encouraged:	Chemical and petrochemical industry

On 6 January 2001, with registered capital of RME2.16 billion (USD262 million), Shanghai Chemical Industrial Park (SCIP) Development Corporation was jointly established by major Chinese enterprises such as Sinochem Shanghai Co. Ltd. (www.spc.com.cn), Shanghai Huayi Group (www.shhuayi.com), Shanghai Gaoqiao Petrochemical Co. Ltd. (www.sinogpc.com), Shanghai Industrial Investment Group Co. Ltd. and Shanghai Jiushi Co. Ltd.

With total development area of 23.4 sq km and first phase at 10 sq km, the total investment for SCIP will be RMB 150 billion (USD18.2 billion), which ranks the largest industrial project in Mainland China. It is located in Jinshan District in southern part of Shanghai Municipality, along the north bank of Hangzhou Bay.

Major MNCs such as Bayer, BASF and British Petroleum have joined SCIP. The total investment for the Bayer project will be USD3.1 billion; and a joint venture formed by Sinochem, Sinochem Shanghai and British Petroleum will cost USD2.748 billion. It is expected that by the end of 2005, 12 major projects will be completely established and start operation.

According to the master development plan of Shanghai Municipality, SCIP will be one of the four key industrial bases of Shanghai. The SCIP Development Corporation is in charge of the planning, development and coordination affairs of the park. It offers one-stop service to all qualified foreign investors.

The Development Corporation of Shanghai Chemical Industrial Park
10, Lane 18, Gaoan Road, Shanghai
P. R.China 200030
Tel: (86)(21) 64713298
Fax: (86)(21) 64713301
Email: webmaster@scip-cn.com
Website: www.scip-cn.com

SHANGHAI COMPREHENSIVE INDUSTRIAL DEVELOPMENT ZONE

Our Rating:	AA
Year of Establishment:	1995
Location:	Fengxian District, Shanghai
Size:	20.8 sq km
Major Investors:	GE, Pioneer Electronics, Matsushita Electric, SGL Carbon, Nu Skin, Bagardi, Greek Hitec Plastic, Fuji Electric, Leiyunshang Pharmaceuticals, Shuangling TCL Air Conditioner, Hangxing Cleaning Equipment, Nanqiao Transformer Group, Zhezhong Electric Equipment and Cixing Bearing Group.
Total Foreign Direct Investment:	N.A.
Major Industries Encouraged:	Electronics, plastics, Machinery, information technologies, new materials, green products and real estate

INTRODUCTION

Formerly named as Shanghai Fengpu Industrial Park that was founded in August 1995, Shanghai Comprehensive Industrial Development Zone (SCIDZ) is one of Shanghai's nine municipal-level industrial zones. On 5 April 2000, Shanghai Industrial Investment Group became an important shareholder of the newly established SCIDZ development Co. Ltd.

Located in Fengxian District, SCIDZ lies 30 km away from downtown Shanghai. It is 50 km from Pudong International Airport and 25 km from Shanghai Hongqiao International Airport.

INVESTMENT CLIMATE

SCIDZ has a total development area of 20.8 sq km with 10 sq km for the first phase. To create high-standard infrastructure, large amount of capital has been invested. The One-stop Investment Service Center provides convenience as for registering for all the investors with efficient and quality services.

According to the Administrative Committee of SCIDZ, major industries encouraged are information technology, new materials, high-tech industries, green products, real estate and tertiary industries. At the same time, Fengxian Professional School and Shanghai Commercial Professional College will provide ample human resources for enterprises in SCIDZ. The Development Corporation of SCIDZ is the organization in charge of the planning, development and coordination affairs of the Zone.

Subsidiary zones have been designed for investors from Europe, Japan and Singapore, as well as a special subzone for SMEs. By now, major MNCs have joined SCIDZ, such as GE, Pioneer Electronics, Matsushita Electric and SGL Carbono. Other foreign investors include Nu Skin, Bagardi, Greek Hitec Plastic, Fuji Electric and so on. At the same time, many domestic enterprises have established operations in SCIDZ, including Leiyurshang Pharmaceutical Company, Shuangling TCL Air Conditioner, Hangxing Cleaning Equipment, Nanqiao Transformer Group, Zhezhong Electric Equipment and Cixing Bearing Group.

SCIDZ Development Corporation
111 Fengpu Avenue
Fengxian District, Shanghai
P. R. China 201400
Tel: (86)(21) 67100345, 67100465
Fax: (86)(21) 67100123
Email: shfpres@public.sta.net.cn
Website: www.fengpu.com

JIADING INDUSTRIAL PARK

Our Rating:	A
Year of Establishment:	1992
Location:	Jiading District, Shanghai
Size:	24.8 sq km
Major Investors:	Koito Automobile Lamps, Fujitsu General, Aurora Office Equipment, Shanghai Global Control System, Shanghai Peggy Food, Carrier Transicoid Equipment, Tokan Ceramics, GEM Electronics, Shanghai Morgan Matroc Technical Ceramic and Sanei Electric
Total Foreign Direct Investment:	USD1.1 billion
Major Industries Encouraged:	Automobile related industries, electronics, food, metal processing, new materials, optical-mechanical-electrical integration technologies and communication equipments.

INTRODUCTION

With total development area of 24.8 sq km, Jiading Industrial Park (JDIP) was established in 1992 and was upgraded to be a municipal-level industrial park in 1994. It is located in Jiading District in northwest Shanghai, bordering Kunshan and Taicang in Jiangsu province.

In 1999, Jiading was listed as one of the best host cities by Taiwan Electrical Machinery and Electronic Association (TEEMA). As a component of the industrial park, a subsidiary high-tech zone is now being developed. In addition, the Pioneering Park for Returned Overseas Chinese Students in JDIP has become the hottest one among all same kind of parks in China. Every year, hundreds of overseas Chinese students start their own businesses in the park.

The park is about 25 km to Hongqiao International Airport and 75 km to Pudong International Airport. The nearest seaport, Zhanghuabang International Container Port is just 25 km away.

INVESTMENT CLIMATE

Jiading offers rich human resources to foreign investors. The Jiading campus of Shanghai University and a few research institutes of Chinese Academy of Sciences (CAS) are all located within the city. Overall, there are more than 6,000 R&D professionals.

Lots of multinational companies from the United States, Germany. Taiwan, Japan and other countries have established operation in JDIP, such as Shanghai Koito Automobile Lamps Co. Ltd., Shanghai Automobile Brake Systems Co. Ltd., Fujitsu General Co. Ltd., ZF Shanghai Steering Co. Ltd., Aurora Office Equipment, Shanghai Global Control System Co. Ltd., GEM Electronics, Shanghai Morgan Matroc Technical Ceramic Co. Ltd., Shanghai Peggy Food Co. Ltd., Shanghai Carrier Transicoid Equipment Co. Ltd., Shanghai Tokan Ceramics Co. Ltd. and many others.

Sixteen projects have investment over USD10 million. With investment commitment of USD93.1 million, Shanghai Koito Automotive Lamps Co. Ltd. is the largest Sino-foreign joint venture in JDIP. So far, a total number of 214 foreign enterprises have joined the Park.

The Administrative Committee of Jiading Industrial Park
555 Yecheng Road
Jiading District, Shanghai
P. R. China 201821
Tel: (85)(21) 59162708, 52162331
Fax: (86)(21) 59161486
Email: jdiz@jdiz.com
Website: www.jdiz.com

QINGPU INDUSTRIAL PARK

Our Rating:	A
Year of Establishment:	1995
Location:	Qingpu District, Shanghai
Size:	16.16 sq km
Major Investors:	Dupont, Hoechst A.G., BASF, Fuji Electric, Yingji DTF, Happy Goal Inc., UFI Group, ISEA LORENZI, TLS International, SUNNY and JENTECH
Total Foreign Direct Investment:	N.A.
Major Industries Encouraged:	Electronics, information technology, biomedicine, fine chemical engineering, new materials, precision instruments, greed food and packaging

With total development area of 16.16 sq km, Qingpu Industrial Park (QPIP) was established in 1995 as a municipal-level industrial park. It is located in Qingpu District in southwest Shanghai. It is 17 km to Hongqiao International Airport and 45 km to Shanghai Port.

Many international companies have established operation in QPIP, including Dupont and Suzuka International from the United States, Hoechst A.G., BASF and CeDo from Germany, Yongji DTF and TLS International from Singapore, UFI Group and ISEA LORENZI from Italy, Fuji Electric, SUNNY and JENTECH from Japan, Happy Goal Inc. and HCP International from Virgin Islands. The industries to be further promoted in the park are electronics, information technology, biomedicine, fine chemical engineering, new materials, precision instruments, green food and packaging.

Qingpu is an administrative district of Shanghai Municipality. Its further development will be tightly integrated with that of Shanghai and the Yangtze River Delta. The Development Corporation of Qingpu Industrial Park is in charge of the planning, development and coordination affairs of the park. It offers one-stop service to foreign investors.

The Development Corporation of Qingpu Industrial Park
5500 Waiqingsong Highway
Qingpu District, Shanghai
P. R. China 201700
Tel: (86)(21) 59724619
Fax: (86)(21) 59722856
Email: sqpiz@sqpiz.com
Website: www.greenin.com.cn

SONGJIANG INDUSTRIAL PARK

Our Rating:	A
Year of Establishment:	1992
Location:	Songjiang District, Shanghai
Size:	20.56 sq km
Major Investors:	Hitachi, Fujitsu, Mitsui Toatsu Chemicals, Minolta, Dow Chemical, Weyerhaerser, 3M, ICI, Nestle, ABB, Itochu, Sumitomo, Tomen, Marubeni, Nissho Iwai, Swire, Kenwood, Komatsu, Sunrise and Yeo's
Total Foreign Direct Investment:	USD1.6 billion (end 2000)
Major Industries Encouraged:	Electronics, machinery, food, textiles and chemicals

INTRODUCTION

Songjiang Industrial Park (SJIP) was established in 1992 as Shanghai's first municipal-level industrial park in its suburb districts. It is located in Songjiang District in southwest area of Shanghai, about 30 km from downtown area of Shanghai. The total development area is 20.56 sq km. It is about 22 km to Hongqiao International Airport, where daily flights are available to many major cities worldwide. Meanwhile, the park is 35 km and 50 km to Jinshan International Container Port and Wusong Port respectively.

INVESTMENT CLIMATE

By the end of 2000, 173 foreign enterprises with total investment of USD1.6 billion had joined the park. Major investors include Hitachi, Fujitsu, Mitsui Toatsu Chemicals, Minolta, Dow Chemical, Weyerhaerser, 3M, ICI, Nestle, ABB, Itochu, Sumitomo, Tomen, Marubeni, Nissho Iwai, Swire, Kenwood, Komatsu, Sunrise and Yeo's. Many small and medium sized enterprises also established subsidiaries here. Most of the enterprises in the park are specialized in electronics, machinery, food, textiles and chemicals.

Songjiang Industrial Park Administration Committee
81 East Rongle Road,
Songjiang District, Shanghai
P. R. China 201600
Tel: (86)(21) 57741102, 57743493
Fax: (86)(21) 57743188, 57741102
E-mail: sjiz@public.sta.net.cn

WAIGAOQIAO FREE TRADE ZONE

Year of Establishment:	June 1990
Location:	Pudong New District, Shanghai
Size:	10 sq km
Major Investors:	GE, Toshiba, IBM, Philips and Intel
Total Foreign Direct Investment:	USD6.56 billion
Major Industries Encouraged:	Free trade, export processing, logistics, warehousing and commodities exhibition

INTRODUCTION

Waigaoqiao Free Trade Zone (WGQFTZ) is China's earliest and biggest free trade zone. It was approved by the State Council in June 1990, and now covers 10 sq km. The population of professionals and specialists in the zone is over 50,000.

By the end of 2001, 5,022 projects had been set up in the zone, and the total investment was USD6.56 billion.

In 2000, the gross industrial output of all enterprises was RMB70.7 billion (USD8.57 billion) and the total sales was RMB62.35 billion (USD7.56 billion). Total export was USD7.62 billion, with import of USD5.64 billion. Total cargo and containers handled by Waigaoqiao Port was 9.64 million tons and 1.21 million TEUs, respectively.

Located in the northeast of Shanghai, WGQFTZ is at the entrance of Yangtze River where the so-called "golden waterway" meets the east coast of China.

It takes 40 minutes to drive to Hongqiao International Airport, 20 minutes to Pudong International Airport and 30 minutes to the People's Square and the City Hall.

INVESTMENT CLIMATE

The development focus of the zone is free trade, export processing, logistics, warehousing and commodities exhibition. Major MNCs such as GE, Toshiba, IBM, Philips and Intel have established subsidiaries in the park. Waigaoqiao Automobile Exchange Market is one key project. Another project is the biochemical and medical instruments market.

In 2000, 181 new foreign projects were approved and the total investment was USD547 million. Among the 181 projects, 53 are for export processing and 128 for warehousing and logistics.

Administrative Committee of WGQFTZ
Tel: (86)(21) 50461100
Fax: (86)(21) 50461441
Website: www.waigaoqiao.gov.cn

ZHANGJIANG HIGH-TECH PARK

Our Rating:	AA
Year of Establishment:	July 1992
Location:	Pudong New District, Shanghai
Size:	25 sq km
Major Investors:	Shanghai State Bio-tech and Pharmaceutical Base, National Information Technology Industrial Base, National Science and Technology Innovation Base, Pudong Software Development Park Co. Ltd., Pudong Java Application Research Center, Motorola, Baosteel High-tech Park Co. Ltd., Afataike, LG, SmithKlineBeecham, Roche, Rhodia and United Signals
Total Foreign Direct Investment:	USD6.6 billion
Major Industries Encouraged:	Information technology, bioengineering, biomedicine, education and real estate

INTRODUCTION

Zhangjiang High-tech Park (ZJHTP) is located in the central part of Pudong New District, Shanghai. It was approved by the State Council in July 1992 and will become one of the four great industrial bases of Shanghai. The other three are Shanghai International Automobile City, Shanghai Baosteel Base and Shanghai Chemical Industrial Park.

The park covers an area of 25 sq km. The north of the Park is the picturesque Tomson Golf Course with groups of villas, and the northwest lie the Pudong Central Park, the new Shanghai International Expo Center and the Government Administration Buildings. Longdong Expressway connects it with the downtown area of Shanghai and the Pudong International Airport. Overall, the park is well situated with convenient transportation and beautiful natural surroundings.

INVESTMENT CLIMATE

The development focus of ZJHTP includes information technologies, bio-engineering, medicine, and real estate. It now hosts the State Bio-tech and Pharmaceutical Base (Shanghai), National Information Technology Industrial Base, National Science and Technology Innovation Base, Pudong Software Development Park Co. Ltd., Pudong Java Application Research Center, Motorola, Baosteel High-tech Park Co. Ltd., Afataike, LG, SmithKlineBeecham, Roche, Rhodia and United Signals. At the end of June 2002, the total number of international and domestic enterprises was 457 and the total investment was USD6.6 billion.

There are six subsidiary districts in the park, including the Technology Innovation District, the Research & Education District, the High-tech Industrial District, the Entertainment District, the Traditional Industrial District and a commercial and residential district.

Integrated Circuit industry plays an important role in the development of information technology of the park. Several world-class IC manufacture companies have established in the park, such as SMIC Shanghai Co. Ltd. with investment of USD1.48 billion, Hongli Semiconductor Shanghai and Tailong Semiconductor Co. Ltd with investment of USD400 million .

Zhangjiang High-tech Park Administration Committee
200 Longdong Avenue
Pudong New District, Shanghai
P. R. China 201204
Tel: (86) (21) 50801818
Fax: (86) (21) 50800686
Email: zjhtp@public.sta.net.cn
Website: www.china-zj.com/index.htm

SONGJIANG EXPORT PROCESSING ZONE

Year of Establishment:	2000
Location:	Songjiang District
Size:	1.98 sq km
Major Investors:	N.A.
Total Foreign Direct Investment:	USD1 billion (estimated)
Major Industries Encouraged:	IT, bio-pharmaceuticals, new building materials, fine chemicals and light machinery

INTRODUCTION

Shanghai Songjiang Export Processing Zone (SJEPZ) was officially established by the State Council on 27 April 2000.

SJEPZ is located in southwest Shanghai, east of Songjiang urban area, and is within Songjiang Industrial Park, which is one of Shanghai's key industrial zones. It has a development area of 1.98 sq km. There are plans for about 100 tenant enterprises to locate within SJEPZ with an estimated total investment of USD1 billion after construction is completed. This will generate RMB18 billion (USD2.18 billion) of gross industrial output and create 15,000 jobs. It is 18 km away from downtown Shanghai, 20 km away from Hongqiao International Airport and 42 km away from Pudong International Airport.

INVESTMENT CLIMATE

Key industries encouraged by SJEPZ include information technology, bio-pharmaceuticals, new building materials, fine chemicals and light machinery.

Investors in the zone can enjoy special tax incentives. As services and institutions including customs, goods inspection, commercial transactions, taxation, banking, and foreign trade are readily available, investors can finish all export procedures within the zone.

SJEPZ is only 47 km from Shanghai Wusong Port. Shanghai New Railway Station is 40 km away from the zone and the railway line from Shanghai to Zhejiang and other southern provinces is very near. The light rail network from Songjiang to Shanghai's city area is being planned.

Shanghai-Hangzhou Expressway is situated at the north side of SJEPZ. Three other major highways are next to the zone and connect to expressways that lead to Hangzhou and Nanjing.

The Administrative Committee of Shanghai Songjiang Export Processing Zone
81 Rongle East Road
Songjiang, Shanghai
P. R. China 201613
Tel: (86)(21) 57741102, 57741859
Fax: (86)(21) 57743188
E-mail: sjiz@public.sta.net.cn
Wedsite: www.sjepz.com

SHANGHAI SOFTWARE DEVELOPMENT PARK

Year of Establishment:	1999
Location:	Shanghai
Size:	45 ha
Major Investors:	Wonders Information, Fudan Guanghua Information Industries, VSC, SJTU Withub Information Industries, Pudong Software Park Development Co., Baud Data Communications, Fudan Net-Info, Microsoft, HP, Huawei Technologies, Zhongxin, Kingstar Group and Shanghai Integra Info Tech.

INTRODUCTION

As a key element of Shanghai's IT industry, Shanghai Software Development Park (SHSDP) was established in 1999. It now consists of 3 subsidiary parks, Pudong Software Park (www.spsp.com.cn), Fudan Software Park and SJTU Caohejing Software Park. The government support fund has reached RMB3.7 billion (USD484.5 million).

INVESTMENT CLIMATE

Over 748 enterprises have registered in the park and 49 of them have formally joined and started operation. The domestic capital was RMB1.9 billion (USD230million) and foreign capital was around USD224 million. Some of the prestigious companies in the park include Wonders Information Co. Ltd., Fudan Guanghua Information Industries, VSC, SJTU Withub Information Industries, Pudong Software Park Development Corporation, Baud Data Communications, Shanghai Fudan Net-Info Co. Ltd., Kingstar Group, Integra Info Tech, Microsoft and HP.

China Electronics Corporation and Zhangjiang High-tech Park Development Corporation are the two major shareholders of Pudong Software Park Co. Ltd.

It is estimated that by 2005, the sales revenue of Shanghai's software industry will be at least RMB50 billion (USD6.06 billion)

and export will be more than USD400 million. The population of software professionals in Shanghai will then increase from 32,000 to 100,000.

The 50 universities and colleges, such as Fudan University, Tongji University, Shanghai Jiaotong University, Shanghai University, Donghua University, East China University of Science & Technology and East China Normal University, in Shanghai will provide the essential human resources. In particular, Fudan University, Tongji University, Shanghai Jiaotong University and East China Normal University have established software colleges to train more young professionals. Shanghai Super-computing Center is located at Zhangjiang High-tech Park, Pudong New District.

Shanghai Pudong Software
Development Park Co. Ltd.
Zhangjiang High-tech Park
Pudong New District, Shanghai
P. R. China 201203
Tel: (86)(21) 38954510
Email: spsp@public.sta.net.cn
Website: www.spsp.com.cn

SHANGHAI JIAOTONG UNIVERSITY SCIENCE PARK

Year of Establishment:	1999
Location:	Shanghai
Major Supporting Institutions:	Shanghai Jiaotong University
Major Investors:	SJTU Industrial Group, SJTU Industrial Investment Group
Major Industries Encouraged:	Information technology, new materials, new energy, biotechnologies, aviation engineering, mechanical engineering, advanced manufacturing technologies and micro-nanometer technologies

INTRODUCTION

Shanghai Jiaotong University Science Park (SJTUSP) was set up in 1999 and was authorized the status of National University Science Park in May 2001. Now, SJTUSP mainly consists of four subsidiary zones, the Withub Zone, Zhangjiang Zone in Pudong, Mingu Zone and Xinhua Zone. The Withub zone, which is the only one located at the core campus of SJTUSP, aims to become a high-tech zone mainly engaged in information technology, new materials, new energy and bio-technologies.

Enterprises joining SJTUSP enjoy advantages of resources and opportunities offered by SJTU as well as of Shanghai itself. The academic fields cover natural science, engineering, management, agriculture, humanities, social science, law and so on. At the university, there are 16 State Key Subjects, nine Municipality Key Subjects, nine State Key Laboratories, one State Technological Transfer Center and two State Engineering Research Center. Among the 1,900-personnel university faculty, there are eight CAS (Chinese Academy of Science) fellows, nine CAE (Chinese Academy of Engineering) fellows, 460 professors and around 700 associate professors. The number of students is 22,000, with 4,900 postgraduates pursuing master degree and 1,900 pursuing doctorate degree.

To date, the university has established cooperation agreements with more than 80 overseas universities, such as Columbia University, UC-Berkeley, Washington University, Cornell University, University of Michigan and University of Pennsylvania in the United States, University of British Columbia and University of Alberta in Canada, UNSW in Australia, University of Birmingham and Strathclyde University in UK, Institute National Polytechnique de Grenoble and Ecole Centrale de Paris in France, Technical University of Munich and Technical University of Berlin in Germany, Waseda University, Osaka University and Tokyo Institute of Technology in Japan. Alliances have also been established with more than 30 major MNCs.

INVESTMENT CLIMATE

Some SJTU majors are at world-class levels, such as electronic & telecommunication systems navigation engineering, materials science & processing, mechanical engineering & advanced manufacturing technologies and micro-nanometer technologies. Some other academic fields have achieved leading position in China, for instance, large-scale integrated circuits, computer science, optical-fiber technologies, automatic controlling, thermal energy composite materials, theoretical physics, bioengineering and system engineering. Particularly, some projects have brought attractive investment returns for companies in Shanghai and other Chinese cities such as high-definition digital TV system, MCFC fuel battery, micro machine with 1-mm motor, Santana piston production line, 6000-meter deep sea daggling observation system and super-speed optical wave communication network etc.

Now, under SJTU Industrial Group and SJTU Industrial Investment Group, there are 24 university-affiliated enterprises, such as SJTU Nanyang Group, SJTU Only Group, Shanghai Withub Information Industries and Shanghai GoFly Group.

The development of SJTU Only Group is quite impressive. From 1991 to 1999, its sales revenue increased from RMB0.4 million (USD48,485) to RMB840 million (USD101.8 million) and became a top player in China's healthcare product market.

Shanghai Jiaotong University Scientific Development and Cooperation Office
1954 Huashan Road,
202 Shanghai Jiaotong University
Haoran Scientific Building
Shanghai, P. R. China 200030
Tel: (86)(21) 62932047, 62932048
Fax (86)(21) 6293 2451
Website: www.kejichu.sjtu.edu.cn
E-mail: kaifa@mail.sjtu.edu.cn

FUDAN UNIVERSITY SCIENCE PARK

Year of Establishment:	2000
Location:	Shanghai
Major Supporting Institutions:	Fudan University
Major Investors:	Fudan University Science Park Development Corporation
Major Industries Encouraged:	Information technology, biomedicine, new materials, environmental protection, venture capital, pharmaceuticals, medical instruments and communication equipments.

INTRODUCTION

Since its establishment in 1905, Fudan University has developed into one of the best universities in China. After merging with Shanghai Medical University, Fudan University now consists of 17 colleges and 43 departments. The academic fields cover humanities, social science, economics, journalism, law, international relations, business administration, life science, natural science, engineering, information technologies, software development, medicine, pharmacy, public health and nursing. Among the 2,400 personnel teaching staffs, there are 19 CAS (Chinese Academy of Science) and CAE (Chinese Academy of Engineering) fellows 1,300 professors and associate professors.

R&D resources of the university are rich: it owns 45 State Key Subjects, 5 State Key Laboratories, 57 research institutes and 80 multi-disciplinary research centers.

Located in Shanghai, Fudan University Science Park (FDUSP) includes the state-level Fudan Software Development Center, Shanghai Yangpu Venture Incubation center, Fudan-SK Entrepreneurial Center, Guoquan Zone and Fenglin Zone.

INVESTMENT CLIMATE

Currently, Fudan University has 99 affiliate enterprises and their total sales revenue reached RMB1.16 billion (USD140.6 million) in 2000. Their industries cover fields such as information technology, biomedicine, new materials, environmental protection, chemical engineering, communications, medical instruments and investment fund.

With registered capital of RMB100 million (USD12.1 million), Fudan University Science Park Development Corporation is responsible for planning and development of the science park.

Fudan University Science Park Investment Service Center
139 Handan Road, Shanghai
P. R. China 200437
Tel: (86)(21) 65311017
Fax: (86)(21) 65448060
Email: xcqian@fudan.edu.cn

TIANJIN

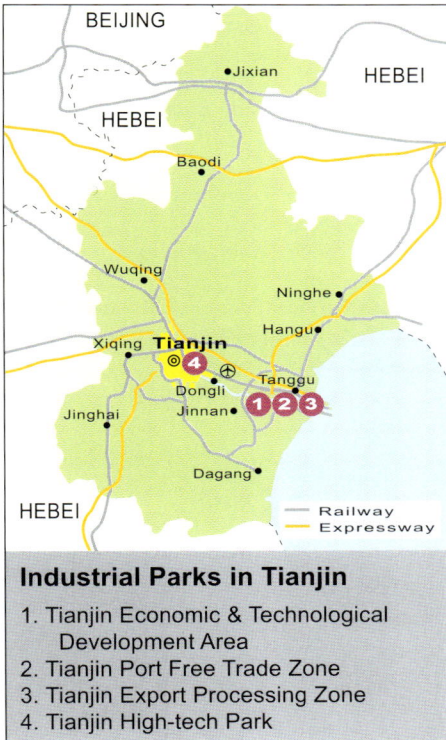

Industrial Parks in Tianjin

1. Tianjin Economic & Technological Development Area
2. Tianjin Port Free Trade Zone
3. Tianjin Export Processing Zone
4. Tianjin High-tech Park

INTRODUCTION

Tianjin was established in the Sui Dynasty when the Grand Canal was built. It became the second largest industrialized city and foreign trade port, next to Shanghai, in China and the biggest financial center in northern China in the 1860s. Due to its seaport location, Tianjin serves as the gateway to Beijing and the hinterland in North China.

GEOGRAPHY

Situated at the North China plains, Tianjin faces Bohai Bay in the east and borders Beijing and Hebei Province in the west. The land is mainly made up of plains (95%) and low hills. It covers 11,920 sq km. In the municipality, there are 13 urban and suburban districts and five counties.

The municipality has a temperate sub-humid monsoon climate with some continental characteristics and four seasons. The average temperature in January is -5°C and in July is 26°C. There will be about 80 days of ice period at the seaport per year. Annual precipitation is between 500 mm and 700 mm.

TRAVEL INFORMATION

Travelers may arrive in Tianjin by rail, expressway and air.

From Tianjin Airport to:

Guangzhou	2 hrs 50 mins
Shenzhen	2 hrs 40 mins
Xiamen	2 hrs 15 mins
Shantou	2 hrs 40 mins
Chengdu	3 hrs
Changsha	1 hr 55 mins
Pudong (Shanghai)	1 hr 45 mins
Nanjing	1 hr 40 mins
Xi'an	1 hr 30 mins
Hong Kong	3 hrs

CLIMATE OF FOREIGN INVESTMENT

In 2001, Tianjin's GDP increased by 12.0% to RMB182.7 billion (USD22.1 billion). It is the major industrial base in North China. The total industrial output in 2001 reached RMB285.2 billion (USD34.6 billion), which was mainly contributed by industries such as electronics, automobiles, metallurgical engineering, pharmaceuticals, textiles, chemicals and mechanicals. High-tech enterprises contributed a share of 31.3% in the total, up 19.3% from the previous year.

The infrastructure in Tianjin is well developed. Beijing-Shanghai and Beijing-

Fact Sheet	2001
Area (sq km)	11,920
Population (million)	10.04
GDP (RMB billion)	182.7
GDP Growth Rate	12.0%
Consumption Expenditure (RMB billion)	
• Government	27
• Household	83.2
Per capita annual	
• disposable income of urban residents (RMB '000)	8.96
• net income of rural households (RMB '000)	4.8
Contractual FDI (USD million)	4,630
Industrial Value Added (RMB bn)	80.7
Imports (USD million)	8,685
Exports (USD million)	9,502
Universities & Colleges	37

Harbin Railways intersect here and its expressways connect with national highway networks in the northeast, northwest and north China. Tianjin Port handled more than 113.7 million tons of cargo and 2.01 million TEUs in 2001. It has scheduled shipping routes to over 300 ports in the world. Tianjin International Airport will become the largest freight airport in north China with handling capacity of 120,000 tons each year.

In 2001, foreign investors showed renewed interest in Tianjin and signed 618 new projects with the municipality. Contractual and utilized FDI in 2001 recorded USD4.63 billion and USD3.22 billion respectively. By the end of 2001, investors from 110 countries and regions had established a presence in Tianjin, of which more than 200 are world famous MNCs, such as Motorola, GM, Exxon Mobil, Caltex, Shell, Caterpillar, Boeing, Coca Cola, Nestle, Siemens, Volkswagen, LG, Hyundai, Samsung, Sumitomo, Honda, Toyota, NEC, Mitsubishi, Canon, Sanyo and Matsushita etc.

To facilitate FDI, the municipality has designated a number of development zones to host FIEs, including Tianjin Economic Development Area (TEDA), Tianjin High-tech Park, Tianjin Export Processing Zone, Tianjin Port Free Trade Zone, and other sub-level industrial parks.

The Municipal Government of Tianjin
Website: www.tianjin.gov.cn
www.tianjin-window.com

Tianjin Foreign Economic Relations and Trade Commission
Website: www.tjfetc.gov.cn
www.tjfisc.gov.cn

Tianjin Foreign Investment Office
11th Floor, TEDA Building
256 South Jiefang Road
Hexi District, Tianjin
Tel: (86)(22) 87310501, 87310502
Fax: (86)(22) 87310589
Website: www.tjinvest.gov.cn

TIANJIN ECONOMIC AND TECHNOLOGICAL DEVELOPMENT AREA

Our Rating:	AAA
Year of Establishment:	1984
Location:	Tianjin
Size:	33 sq km
Major Investors:	Motorola, Nestle, SEW, Novo Nordisk, AT&T, Coca-Cola, Pepsi, Volkswagen, Shell, Yamaha, Samsung, Yazaki Auto etc.
Total Foreign Direct Investment:	USD16.9 billion (by May 2002)
Major Industries Encouraged:	Electronics & telecommunications, food, bio-engineering & pharmaceuticals, machinery, software development and new energies.

INTRODUCTION

Tianjin Economic and Technological Development Area (TEDA) was one of the first development areas to be established in China by the State Council on 6 December 1984.

TEDA, with a planned area of 33 sq km, is divided into 2 major estates (south and north) by the extension of the Beijing-Tianjin-Tanggu Expressway which cuts across TEDA and leads to the port. South of the expressway is the Financial-Trade-Residential Estate with a planned area of 8 sq km; to the north is the Industrial Estate with a planned area of 25 sq km.

TEDA, located in the Binhai New Area of Tianjin Municipality, is 140 km from Beijing and 45 km from downtown Tianjin. To the east lies Tianjin Xingang (New Harbor), the biggest port in North China, which has China's second largest container terminal and has the capacity to handle 100 million tons annually. Outside TEDA are three sub-level parks, namely Yat-Sen Scientific Industrial Park, Chemical Industrial Park and Microelectronics Industrial Park. In 2001, the GDP of TEDA reached USD3.759 billion; the total industrial output and export stood at USD10.42 billion and USD4.03 billion, respectively.

INVESTMENT CLIMATE

The daily supply of purified water is more than 100,000 tons. Electric power is mostly supplied from the Beijing-Tianjin-Tangshan Grid. Users are supplied with piped natural gas and LPG. A central heating system and decentralized heating are both available.

Foreign-invested enterprises

At present, 3,445 foreign-invested companies have located in TEDA, and total investment had exceeded USD16.9 billion by the end of May 2002. Motorola, Nestle, SEW and Novo Nordisk represent the four key pillar industries — manufacturing of telecommunication equipment, food processing, machinery and bio-pharmaceuticals. There are more than 200 transnational enterprises with over USD6 billion of investments. Many renowned enterprises have already set up their business here, including AT&T, Motorola, Coca-Cola, Pepsi, Volkswagen, Siemens, Kraft Food,

Ting Hsin, Great Wall, Nestle, Shell, Yamaha, Samsung, Yazaki Auto etc.

Regional advantage

Being at the center of the fertile and productive northern coastline, and serving as a major gateway to North China and the Northwest, Tianjin enjoys an advantageous location. It is the largest port in North China with links to over 300 ports in 170 countries and regions.

TEDA's location is more advan-tageous: it is close to both Tianjin and Beijing and on the docrstep of three Northeastern provinces. TEDA is in a highly populated, urbanized area with good transportation, developed commerce and market and huge purchasing potential.

Industrial base

Tianjin, the birthplace of China's modern industry, is one of the most important and comprehensive industrial bases. The secondary sector makes up over 50% of its GDP with over 10,000 enterprises, mainly electronics, automobile, metallurgy, machinery, steel chemicals, textiles and pharmaceuticals.

Tianjn has some advantage over other large industrial cities, because of its abundant natural resources, including petroleum, natural gas, metallic and nonmetallic minerals, geothermal energy and sea salt. The industrial production costs, including those of land, labor, and energy, within TEDA are relatively low.

ISO14001 certified

TEDA was awarded the ISO14001 certificaton on 10 May 2000. Each year the TEDA Administration spends more than 3% of its GDP equivalent on environmental protection.

Now, TEDA has launched the second phase of cevelopment to create an even better investment and living environment. Four other industries are encouraged: software development, bioengineering, new energies, and environmental protection technologies and products.

TEDA Administrative Committee
Economic Development Bureau
3F, AI Investment Service Center
19 Hongda Street, TEDA
Tianjin, P . R . China 300457
Tel: (86)(22) 25201906, 25201348
Fax: (86)(22) 25201412
Email: teda@teda.gov.cn
Website: www.teda.gov.cn

TIANJIN PORT FREE TRADE ZONE

Year of Establishment:	1991
Location:	Tianjin Municipality
Size:	7 sq km
Major Investors:	Caltex, Caterpillar, Omron, Ford, Toyota, Henkel
Total Foreign Direct Investment:	USD2.3 billion
Major Industries Encouraged:	Warehousing, processing industry, shipping, packaging, logistics, commerce and real estate

INTRODUCTION

Tianjin Port Free Trade Zone (TJFTZ) was approved by the State Council in May 1991. It is the biggest free trade zone in North China and a main gateway to the sea for several administrative regions in North China and the Republic of Mongolia.

Located in the central area of Bohai Sea Rim, TJFTZ covers 7 sq km. The development focus of TJFTZ is on warehousing, processing industry, shipping, packaging, logistics and real estate.

By the end of 2001, over 4,000 foreign enterprises had joined TJFTZ, including 33 Fortune 500 companies, and total contractual investment was USD5 billion. The amount of utilized foreign investment was USD2.3 billion which accounted for about 80% of total investment in the zone.

INVESTMENT CLIMATE

The investment for infrastructure development was about RMB1.62 billion.

TJFTZ is 55 km from downtown Tianjin and 170 km from Beijing. The Beijing-Tianjin-Tanggu Expressway heads directly to TJFTZ, providing TJFTZ easy access to the two largest cities in North China.

It takes 30 minutes to drive from TJFTZ to Tianjin Airport and 90 minutes to Beijing Capital International Airport.

The zone is one kilometer away from Tianjin New Port, which is the largest port and the largest container terminal in North China. Regular routes are available to many ports around the world.

Baotai Industrial Park is a key project of TJFTZ, and covers one sq km. It is a joint venture between TJFTZ and Tianjin Economic and Technological Development Zone (TEDA). The park is mainly devoted to the development of technology-intensive and energy-saving technologies and environmentally friendly projects.

The Administrative Committee Tianjin Port Free Trade Zone
Tel: (86)(22) 25761003, 25760424
Fax: (86)(22) 25761742, 25761022
Email: hgzhang@adm.tjftz.gov.cn
Website: www.tjftz.gov.cn

TIANJIN EXPORT PROCESSING ZONE

Year of Establishment:	2000
Location:	Tianjin Municipality
Size:	2.54 sq km
Major Investors:	N.A.
Total Foreign Direct Investment:	N.A.
Major Industries Encouraged:	Export processing, storage, warehousing and transportation

INTRODUCTION

Tianjin Export Processing Zone (TJEPZ) is one of the export processing zones approved to set up on 27 April 2000 by the State Council. It is a closed special area under the custody of the Customs, 24 hours a day. Characterized as "within the territory but out of tariff", TJEPZ is designed to host processing-oriented foreign companies while special policies and incentives are granted by the central government.

TJEPZ is located on the northwestern part of TEDA with a planned area of 2.54 sq km. One sq km of land will be developed for the first phase.

INVESTMENT CLIMATE

In 1999, the investment for the infrastructure construction, development and renovation amounted to RMB6 billion while an annual growth rate of 10% of investment is maintained. Proximity to a sophisticated sea-land-air transportation network has made it a strong surplus to improve the logistics efficiency of TJEPZ companies.

Being at the center of the Circum-Bohai Economic Rim, TJEPZ's strategic location offers time and cost savings for distributing products into and out of this area.

In addition to the fast growing consumer market, the business-to-business market is also quite developed. Tianjin's comprehensive industrial foundation provides a sophisticated network of supporting industries, which makes it possible for local procurement and sourcing. In most cases, manufacturers of various industries from machine tools to clothing, from electronics to enzymes may always find the majority of the raw material and components they need from a local source.

TJEPZ enterprises have direct and easy access to a pool of engineering and managerial talent. However, the strength of TJEPZ's work force is not just in high-end jobs. Tianjin has long been a major manufacturing center over the past century, thus the work force is ready and available at every level of production.

TJEPZ Administrative Commission
No. 19 Hongda Avenue, TEDA, Tianjin
P. R. China 300457
Tel: (86)(22) 25202249, 25201724
Fax: (86)(22) 25201012
E-mail: yougen@tdb.teda.tj.cn or
　　　　lili@tdb.teda.tj.cn
Wesite: www.teda.gov.cn/myfzj/ckjgq/

TIANJIN HIGH-TECH PARK

Our Rating:	A
Year of Establishment:	1991
Location:	Wuqing, Tianjin
Size:	24.8 sq km
Major Investors:	Magnequench, Danfoss Inc, Purno, Tomen Corporation, Marubeni, Mitsui, Sumitomo, Yamaha and Itochu Corporation
Total Foreign Direct Investment:	USD640 million
Major Industries Encouraged:	Electronics, information technology, new materials especially new construction materials, bio-engineering, magnetic materials, bio-pharmaceutical engineering and production of healthcare products

INTRODUCTION

Tianjin High-tech Park (TJHTP), also known as Wuqing High-tech Park, was approved by the State Council in 1991. It is located in Wuqing, the northwestern suburb of Tianjin municipality. The total planned area is 24.8 sq km. The development area for the first stage is 6.4 sq km, which is made up of three subsidiary districts: a 3 sq km new technology district, a 2 sq km economic development area and a 1.4 sq km residential district.

By April 2002, 390 enterprises from 30 countries and regions had established operations in TJHTP. The total investment amount was RMB7.2 billion (USD872 million). The amount of foreign direct investment was about USD640 million. Total sales revenue of park enterprises was RMB14.7 billion in 2001.

The main investment fields include electronics, information technology, new materials especially new construction materials, bio-engineering, magnetic materials, bio-pharmaceutical and manufacturing of healthcare products.

Foreign investors are mainly from US, Finland, Denmark and Japan. These foreign-invested enterprises include Magnequench, Danfoss Inc, Purno, Tomen, Marubeni, Mitsui, Sumitomo, Yamaha and Itochu.

INVESTMENT CLIMATE

TJHTP is located between Beijing and downtown Tianjin. The Jing-Jin-Tang Expressway runs through it. It is 70 km from Beijing and it takes 30 minutes to reach downtown Tianjin and Tianjin Airport.

There are several major railroads next to TJHTP, such as Jing-Hu (Beijing-Shanghai) Railway and Jing-Ha (Beijing-Harbin) Railway, Jing-Jiu (Beijing-Kowloon) Railway The Jing-Jin-Tang Expressway (Beijing-Tianjin-Tanggu Port) has an entrance as well as an exit near TJHTP.

Tianjin High-tech Park Administrative Committee
Tel: (86)(22) 82115688
E-mail: batman@tjuda.com
Website: www.tjuda.com

TIANJIN UNIVERSITY SCIENCE PARK

Year of Establishment:	1999
Location:	Tianjin Municipality
Major Supporting Institution:	Tianjin University
Major Investors:	TJUSP Science & Technologies Development Co
Major Industries Encouraged:	New materials under extreme conditions, bio-medicine, defense-related new materials, rare earth materials, e-business and Internet security software

Located in Tianjin municipality, the Tianjin University Science Park (TJUSP) comprises the 4-acre TJU Campus Zone, the 15-acre Campus Ring Zone and 30-acre Industrial Zone located at Tianjin Economic & Technological Development Area (TEDA).

An important feature of TJUSP is its cooperative relationship with TEDA. The two sides formed TJUSP Science & Technologies Development Corporation to manage and promote TJUSP. In the following 5-year period, TEDA will invest RMB150 million in TJUSP annually.

TJUSP aims to become the premier R & D base for new materials under extreme conditions, recyclable resources, advanced manufacturing technologies, biomedicine engineering, defense-related new materials, rare earth materials, e-business and development of Internet security software. According to the development plan of the park, high-tech industries will account for 60% of all enterprises in the park and the rest will be in finance, property development, commerce and other tertiary industries.

Established in 1895, Tianjin University started the history of modern advanced education in China. Now, the university has about 1,200 professors and associate professors, five CAS fellows and four CAE fellows. The number of students is about 22,000. At the university, there are 48 research institutes, five State Key Laboratories, one State Engineering Research Center, two State New Technology Popularization Centers and seven open laboratories at ministry and municipality level.

Tianjin University has formed sister-university relationships with 73 overseas universities, including the University of New South Wales and Macquarie University in Australia, McGill University and University of Waterloo in Canada, Rwth Aachen and Dresden University of Technology in Germany, Kobe University in Japan, Saint-Petersburg State University in Russia, University of London Queen Mary College in UK, University of Wisconsin-Madison and University of Iowa in the United States. Major MNCs such as Motorola (China), Tianjin OTIS Elevators, Emerson Electric, Honeywell, United Technologies, IBM, Caltex Petroleum, Cheil Industries and Siemens have conducted joint research projects with the university.

Tianjin University Science Park Administrative Committee
E-mail: ch-z@yeah.net
Website: www.tusp.org

TIANJIN HUAYUAN
SOFTWARE DEVELOPMENT PARK

Year of Establishment:	N.A.
Location:	Tianjin Municipality
Size:	N.A.
Major Investors:	Tianjin Tiancai, Tianjin Computing Center, Shinyun Software Technologies, Tianjin Research Institute of Computer Science Jinke Electronics and AIT Electronic Information

Tianjin Huayuan Software Development Park (TJSDP) is located at Huayuan Industrial Zone, a subsidiary zone of Tianjin High-tech Park, about 8 km to downtown Tianjin.

By the end of 2001, 31 software enterprises have become members of the park, such as Tianjin Tiancai Co. Ltd., Tianjin Computing Center, Shinsoft, Tianjin Research Institute of Computer Science and Jinke Electronics Co. Ltd. Other leading software companies in TJSDP include AIT Electronic Information Co. Ltd., Hyland Technologies and Hengyuan Technologies.

The International Entrepreneur Center in TJSDP provides a full range of services in banking, finance, law, information, customs procedures, networking and communications to TJSDP's enterprises.

In Tianjin, Nankai University and Tianjin University are among China's top 35 universities that have established software colleges.

Administrative Committee of Tianjin Huayuan Software Development Park
8 West Science Road
Nankai District, Tianjin
P. R. China 300192

GUANGXI

Industrial Parks in Guangxi

1. Nanning Economic & Technological Development Zone
2. Dongxing Border Economic Cooperation Zone
3. Pingxiang Border Economic Cooperation Zone
4. Nanning High-tech Park
5. Guilin High-tech Park

INTRODUCTION

Guangxi is the only western region in China with access to the sea. It is the most populous and developed among the five autonomous regions.

GEOGRAPHY

Guangxi Zhuang Autonomous Region lies on the southern end of China's meandering coastline and its southwest borders Vietnam. Guangxi has a total area of 236,660 sq km and administers nine municipalities and five sub-province level prefectures, with Nanning as the capital. Most of the territory is covered by mountains and hills, with only 15% being plains. Guilin is famous for its Karst caves, which are common in the region.

By the end of 2001, the population was 47.88 million, with one third from China's largest ethnic group – Zhuangs. There are altogether 47 minority groups living in Guangxi, which accounts for 38% of the total population. Their colorful traditions and diverse cultures added to Guangxi's attractiveness to visitors.

The region enjoys a subtropical humid monsoon climate, with average annual temperature ranging from 16°C to 23°C, and rainfall between 1,500-2,000 mm.

Fact Sheet	2001
Area (sq km)	236,660
Population (million)	47.88
GDP (RMB billion)	223.1
GDP Growth Rate	8.2%
Consumption Expenditure (RMB billion)	
• Government	28
• Household	93.6
Per capita annual	
• disposable income of urban residents (RMB '000)	6.6
• net income of rural households (RMB '000)	1.9
Contractual FDI (USD million)	587
Industrial Value Added (RMB bn)	67.1
Imports (USD million)	562
Exports (USD million)	1,236
Universities & Colleges	30

TRAVEL INFORMATION

The most convenient way to visit is by air.

From Nanning Airport to:
Beijing	3 hrs 15 mins
Shanghai Hongqiao	3 hrs
Chongqing	2 hrs 15 mins
Guangzhou	1 hr 5 mins
Bangkok	3 hrs
Hong Kong	1 hr 20 mins

From Guilin Airport to:
Beijing	2 hrs 45 mins
Shanghai Hongqiao	2 hrs 20 mins
Fukuoka	4 hrs
Guangzhou	50 mins
Seoul	3 hrs
Hong Kong	1 hr 30 mins

From Beihai Airport to:
Beijing	3 hrs
Shenzhen	55 mins
Guangzhou	50 mins
Hong Kong	1 hr 20 mins

From Liuzhou Airport to:
Beijing	3 hrs 15 mins
Shanghai Pudong	2 hrs 20 mins

INVESTMENT CLIMATE

Guangxi, with 39% of its territory covered by forest, is rich in natural resources including different kinds of nonferrous minerals, hydraulic power, and marine resources. With its natural reserves and 15 cultural and historic relics, Guangxi has tremendous potential for tourism related developments.

The transportation system in Guangxi has been greatly improved. Beihai and Fangchenggang are the two important harbours, and Nanning, Guilin, Beihai all have international airports.

In 2001, Guangxi's GDP reached USD27 billion, but the total foreign trade slid by 11.8% to USD1.8 billion, which was caused by the dramatic drop in export demand. FDI inflow also showed signs of slowdown. Contractual and utilized FDI declined by 17.3% and 26.8% respectively.

The local government encourages foreign investors to participate in developing the infrastructure, basic and high-tech industries, export oriented production, agriculture and technical upgrading of traditional enterprises in the province. ETDZs and high-tech parks had been set up in Nanning, Liuzhou, Guilin, and Qinzhou.

Guangxi Autonomous Region Government
Website: www.gxi.gov.cn

Guangxi Economic Information Center
Website: www.gx.cei.gov.cn

Guangxi Foreign Trade and Economic Cooperation Department
Xinghu Road, Nanning, Guangxi
P. R. China 530022
Tel: (86)(771) 5869622, 5854189

NANNING ECONOMIC AND TECHNOLOGICAL DEVELOPMENT ZONE

Our Rating:	BB
Year of Establishment:	1992
Location:	Nanning, Guangxi
Size:	10.8 sq km
Major Investors:	N.A.
Total Foreign Direct Investment:	USD180 million (2001)
Major Industries Encouraged:	Paper-making, biotechnology, fine chemical engineering, food processing

INTRODUCTION

Nanning Economic and Technological Development Zone (NNETDZ) was established in October 1992, and managed directly by the People Government of Nanning City. It was approved as a national ETDZ in May 2001.

The planned area is 10.80 sq km, with 7.68 sq km of land developed from the first phase of 9.46 sq km.

NNETDZ is situated in the southern part of Nanning City, the provincial capital of Guangxi Zhuang Autonomous Region.

It comprises three areas: the north, central and south. These three areas are connected, yet each has its own emphasis. The north area emphasizes foreign-invested enterprises and pollution-free, high value-added and high-tech projects; the central area is a base for processing and warehousing industries; the south area attracts mainly export oriented enterprises and all kinds of deep-processing projects, and has an industrial zone for small and medium sized enterprises and the largest privately-run industrial zone in the whole of Guangxi.

NNETDZ is five km from the city center. It is four to five km from Nanning Railway Cargo Station and Nanning City's largest warehouse base. It is 17 km from Nanning Airport, where there are direct flights to Hong Kong and Macau.

In 2001, the gross industrial output of NNETDZ was RMB1.6 billion, with GDP RMB540 million, industrial value added RMB480 million, and total foreign trade USD20 million. Contractual foreign investment was USD580 million while utilized foreign investment amounted to USD180 million.

INVESTMENT CLIMATE

After seven years of construction on barren land, 9.6 sq km has been leveled. Two water plants with a daily water supply of 100,000 tons have been built. There are one each of 220 kV and 110 kV substations as well as three 35 kV substations, a 55 km power line, 63 km of water pipes, and 60 km of drainage pipelines. A 61 km stretch of roads have been constructed within NNETDZ, a telecommunication center has been built and put in operation, enabling program-controlled telephones and mobile phones, domestic and international post, and telecommunication services.

By end 2001, there were 232 enterprises in the park; 62 were foreign enterprises - five with investment of over USD10 million, and one over USD30 million. There are three projects made by Fortune 500 corporations.

Key industries encouraged by NNETDZ include paper-making, bio-technology, chemical engineering and food processing.

Investing in NNETDZ will be capitalizing on the regional advantage of Nanning City as the central point of the Greater Southwest market – one-quarter of China's area and one-fifth of China's population.

The Administrative Committee of Nanning Economic & Technological Development Zone
76 Jiangnan Road
Nanning City, Guangxi
P. R. China 300457
Tel: (86)(771) 4516161/4516293
Fax: (86)(771) 4516162
E-mail: nndev.zo@163.net
Website: www.neda.gxi.gov.cn

DONGXING BORDER ECONOMIC COOPERATION ZONE

Year of Establishment:	1992
Location:	Dongxing city, Guangxi
Size:	4.07 sq km
Major Investors:	The Municipal Government
Total Foreign Direct Investment:	N.A.
Major Industries Encouraged:	Export-oriented trade, processing industry, sea products processing, Chinese traditional medicine manufacturing and tourism

INTRODUCTION

Dongxing Border Economic Cooperation Zone was authorized and established in 1992 by the State Council as a national border zone. It is located at the most southwest point of China's coastline and is also the most convenient border gateway to Southeast Asia. During the past few years, the zone was developed into the most active border trade cooperation area for the bilateral trade between China and Vietnam.

Dongxing is 170 km away from Nanning, the capital city of Guangxi and 60 km from Fangcheng Port.

INVESTMENT CLIMATE

Border trade cooperation has been developing well, especially in recent years. In 1998, the GDP of Dongxing was around RMB1.11 billion, the fiscal income was around RMB105.6 million.

Now each year, the value of border trade is above RMB500 million. More than 800,000 tourist visit or transfer at Dongxing.

Preferential policies have been carried out to attract foreign investment in the zone. According to the master plan, it will be developed with the focus on border trade and import/export trade, especially in export-oriented processing industry, real estate, financing and banking, insurance, storage, tourism and other services.

The Administrative Committee of Dongxing Border Economic Cooperation Zone
Dongxing city, Guangxi
P. R. China 538100
Tel: (86)(770) 7683572

PINGXIANG BORDER ECONOMIC COOPERATION ZONE

Year of Establishment:	1992
Location:	Pingxiang city, Guangxi
Size:	7.2 sq km
Major Investors:	The Municipal Government
Total Foreign Direct Investment:	N.A.
Major Industries Encouraged:	Export-oriented trade, processing industry etc.

INTRODUCTION

Pingxiang Border Economic Cooperation Zone was authorized and established in 1992 by the State Council as a national border zone. The zone is located at the border between China and Vietnam, which has been one of the main passages connecting southwest China to Vietnam and Southeast Asia. Transportation is convenient, with inter-national railroad as well as National Highway No. 322 running through the border zone. Within the border trade cooperation zone are Pingxiang Station, agencies of national first-grade port, and some other foreign affairs department offices. An area of 4.2 sq km has been well developed from the total planned area of 7.2 sq km.

INVESTMENT CLIMATE

The border trade cooperation has been developing well, especially during recent years. To date, the total investment commitment is around RMB400 million, and the zone has established a complete infrastructure system.

Preferential policies were implemented to attract foreign investment in the zone. According to the master plan, it will be developed with the focus on border trade and import-export trade.

The Administrative Committee of Pingxiang Border Economic Cooperation Zone
7 Nantian Road
Dongxing city, Guangxi
P. R. China 532600
Tel: (86)(771) 8523099

NANNING HIGH-TECH PARK

Our Rating:	B
Year of Establishment:	1992
Location:	Nanning city, Guangxi Autonomous Region
Size:	18 sq km
Major Investors:	N.A.
Total Foreign Direct Investment:	N.A.
Major Industries Encouraged:	Biological engineering, pharmaceuticals, electronics, information technologies, new materials and optical-electronic-mechanical integration technologies

INTRODUCTION

Nanning High-tech Park (NNHTP) is located in the suburban area of Nanning, the capital city of Guangxi Autonomous Region. It was approved by the State Council in 1992. The total area of the park is 18 sq km.

Key industries of the park include biological engineering, pharmaceuticals, electronics, information technology, new materials and optical-electronic-mechanical integration technologies.

Now, there are over 700 enterprises in the park. A total of 20 State Torch-program projects and other 280 new high-tech products have been developed. Moreover, the total annual sales of all enterprises in the park is RMB24.5 billion, the industrial output is RMB18 billion, and the export is USD80 million.

At the end of 1999, over 70 foreign enterprises have started operations in the park. The investors are mainly from Canada, France, Germany, Hong Kong, Malaysia, Taiwan and United States.

INVESTMENT CLIMATE

The park consists of a high-tech incubation center, a software development center, a scientific industrial zone, a central park and an agricultural and bio-engineering zone.

Nanning Yinhe Software Development Park was established in January 2001. It is only five km from Nanning Railway Station, five km from Nanning Port, and it takes 30 minutes to drive from the center to Nanning Airport. A few centers have been set up, such as the software R&D center, the software testing center, the software export center, the telecommunication and information center, the training center and several incubating centers for software firms. By the end of 1999, over 60 software companies joined the center with their professionals over 1,000. Over 110 software products, including system integration, e-business, advanced telecommunication technology, CAI program, ERP, CRM, IDC and GIS, have been initiated in the park.

The Administrative Committee of Nanning High-tech Park
10th Level, Chuanye Tower
Torch Road No. 1, Nannning
Guangxi, P. R. China 530003
Tel: (86)(771) 3836393
Fax: (86)(771) 3827201
Email: invest@gxi.gov.cn
Website: www.nnhitech.gov.cn

GUILIN HIGH-TECH PARK

Our Rating:	BBB
Year of Establishment:	May 1988
Location:	Guilin City, Guangxi Autonomous Region
Size:	83 sq km
Major Investors:	NEC, Marconi, Nokia, Pepsi, IngersollRand
Total Foreign Direct Investment:	USD83.3 million
Major Industries Encouraged:	Electronics information technologies, electronic-mechanical integration technology, bio-pharmaceuticals, new materials and environment protection technologies

INTRODUCTION

Guilin High-tech Park (GLHTP) is a state-level industrial park in Guilin city of Guangxi Autonomous Region. Guilin is one of the most beautiful cities in China. GLHTP was established in May 1988 and was approved by the State Council in March 1991. It's the first high-tech park in five Auto-nomous Regions. The total area is 83 sq km.

In 2000, the gross industrial output of all enterprises in the park was RMB5.92 billion, about USD717 million. Over 150 enterprises belong to high-tech industries. A total of 688 high-tech projects have been started in the park. Ten enterprises have annual sales over RMB100 million.

At the end of 2000, there were around 900 enterprises in the park, of which 200 were foreign enterprises. The key industries are electronics, information technology, electronic-mechanical inte-gration technology, bio-pharmaceuticals, new materials, environment protection technologies and office automation products.

Total investment of foreign enterprises amounted to USD83.3 million. They mainly come from United States, UK, Finland, Japan and Korea. Major MNCs like NEC, Marconi, Nokia, Pepsi and IngersollRand have established operations in the park.

INVESTMENT CLIMATE

There are 14 colleges and research institutes in GLHTP. It has 8 state-level and province-level product testing centers, with nine exhibition halls, conference and training centers.

GLHTP is located on the east of Lijiang River, a world-famous beautiful scenic site. The Guilin Liangjiang International Airport offers both domestic and international flights to many cities.

The city of Guilin has a total population of 4.76 million. Within the area of GLHTP, there are many historical and tourist sites — such as Seven-Star Rock, Moon Crescent Mountain and Yinzhen Rock etc.

The Administrative Committee of Guilin High-tech Park
High-tech Development Tower
Guilin, Guangxi, P. R. China 541004
Tel:(86)(773) 5812466, 5819972, 5819973
Fax: (86)(773) 5819185, 5814333
Email: tzfz@guilin-ctp.net.cn
Website: guilin-ctp.net.cn

INNER MONGOLIA

Industrial Parks in Inner Mongolia

1. Hohhot Economic & Technological Development Zone
2. Manzhouli Border Economic Cooperation Zone
3. Erenhot Border Economic Cooperation Zone
4. Baotou High-tech Park

INTRODUCTION

Inner Mongolia Autonomous Region was established in 1947, the earliest one of its kind in China. Mongolian people are proud of Genghis Khan, who became the first emperor of Yuan Dynasty in Chinese history.

The inland region, renowned as the "treasure basin", is rich in natural resources. It boasts wide forests in the east, iron in the west, grains in the south, and animal husbandry in the north. It has more than 30 types of minerals (such as rare earth and coal) which are listed among the top ten largest reserves in China.

GEOGRAPHY

Inner Mongolia is located in the southeast of the Mongolia Highland, with 50% of its area at 1,000 m above sea level. It takes up one eighth of China's total land area, and stretches over the northeast, north and northwest of China. Its border with eight chinese provinces. The international border line with Russia and Mongolia is 4,221 km long.

The topography is diverse, with numerous lakes, over 1,000 rivers, three major ranges of mountains, and four main plains.

The region has characteristics of a continental climate but the weather varies tremendously. In winter, the temperature drops from -10°C in the southwest to -26°C in the northeast. However, the average

Fact Sheet	2001
Area (sq km)	1,183,000
Population (million)	23.77
GDP (RMB billion)	154.5
GDP Growth Rate	9.6%
Consumption Expenditure (RMB billion)	
• Government	33.5
• Household	53.7
Per capita annual	
• disposable income of urban residents (RMB '000)	5.53
• net income of rural households (RMB '000)	1.95
Contractual FDI (USD million)	262
Industrial Value Added (RMB bn)	50.7
Imports (USD million)	140
Exports (USD million)	630
Universities & Colleges	21

temperature in July falls between 18°C and 24°C.

The population of Inner Mongolia is made up of Hans (74%), Mongolians (16%) and 47 minorities.

TRAVEL INFORMATION

Hohhot and Baotou are the two major airports in Inner Mongolia.

From Hohhot Airport to:
Beijing	1 hr 5 mins
Shanghai Pudong	2 hrs 55 mins
Wuhan	2 hrs 5 mins
Guangzhou	4 hrs 20 mins
Shenzhen	5 hrs

From Baotou Airport to:
Beijing	1 hr 5 mins
Shanghai Pudong	2 hrs 25 mins
Wuhan	2 hrs 10 mins
Guangzhou	4 hrs 40 mins

INVESTMENT CLIMATE

Inner Mongolia is an important national production base of steel, coal, edible oil, sugar, forestry and animal husbandry. The ratio of three sectors is 23.4:40.4:36.2. Light industry, mostly in agricultural and animal products processing, is growing fast.

Inner Mongolia's railway system has been greatly improved. The region now has 19 trunk and 12 branch lines, totaling 6,000 km. The highway network has a total length of 63,000 km and connects 95% of all the towns in Inner Mongolia. Over 20 air routes serve seven civil airports in Inner Mongolia.

In 2001, there are 81 new foreign invested projects signed with a total of USD262 million committed FDI, thus increasing the number of registered FIEs to 778. Investors are invited to engage in the deep processing and comprehensive development of agriculture and animal husbandry, infrastructure development, tourism, exploitation of mineral resources, petrochemical and sophisticated chemical industry, and industries that involve advances technology.

Inner Mongolia Foreign Trade and Economic Cooperation Department
138, West Zhongshan Road
Hohhot, Inner Mongolia
Tel: (86)(471) 6964301
Fax: (86)(471) 6962138
Email: nmgwjmt@public.hh.nm.cn,
        nmgftec@mail.ec.com.cn
Website: www.gov.nm.cninfo.net

HOHHOT ECONOMIC AND TECHNOLOGICAL DEVELOPMENT ZONE

Our Rating:	BB
Year of Establishment:	2000
Location:	Hohhot, Inner Mongolia
Size:	9.8 sq km
Major Investors:	N.A.
Total Foreign Direct Investment:	USD59.22 million
Major Industries Encouraged:	Information technology, biological engineering and pharmaceuticals, new materials and fine chemical engineering

INTRODUCTION

Hohhot Economic and Technological Development Zone (HTETDZ) in northwest China is located at the periphery of Hohhot City and was built in 1992. It was approved in 1995 by the Autonomous Region Government as a provincial-level development zone. In July 2000, HTETDZ was upgraded to a state-level development zone by the State Council. HTETDZ is demarcated into Ruyi District and Jinchuan District, with a total planned area of 9.8 sq km.

Traffic is smooth within HTETDZ, as it is next to 3 national highways and Jinglan Railway. The eastern area is near Hohhot Airport which has 40 domestic and two international flights (to Mongolia and Russia).

In 2001, the gross industrial output of HTETDZ was RMB3.76 billion, an increase of 61.78% over the previous year. The industrial value added was RMB1.39 billion, an increase of 64.73%.

INVESTMENT CLIMATE

There are rich natural resources around HTETDZ. Within a radius of 200 km, there are rich deposits of more than a hundred types of minerals such as coal, natural gas, kaolin, iron and wild medicinal herbs. There are also abundant underground water resources with excellent water quality.

By the end of 2001, infrastructure investment amounted to RMB1.73 billion. There are 37 km of completed roads and 913,000 sq m of greenery. HTETDZ is also capable of providing 23,500 kVA of daily power supply, 118 tons/hr of heat supply, 45,600 tons of daily water supply and dealing 6,000 tons waste water per day.

HTETDZ is Hohhot City's second communication hub. It has a developed communication network.

There are 811 domestic enterprises, with registered capital of RMB2.5 billion and total investment of RMB4.81 billion.

Investors from ten countries and regions of Southeast Asia, North America and Europe have invested in HTETDZ. There are 77 foreign invested projects with utilized investment of USD59.22 million. Eight projects have investment of more than USD10 million.

Five key industries such as information technology, biological engineering, pharmaceuticals, new materials and fine chemicals are stressed in the Zone.

HETDZ Administrative Committee
Huhhot Economic and Technological
Development Zone
2 Yiwei Road
Inner Mongolia
P. R. China 010010
Tel: (86)(471) 4696491/4696492/4696495
Fax: (86)(471) 4696492
Website: www.hetdz.com.cn

MANZHOULI BORDER ECONOMIC COOPERATION ZONE

Year of Establishment:	1992
Location:	Manzhouli city, Inner Mongolia Autonomous Region
Size:	6.4 sq km
Major Investors:	The Municipal Government
Total Foreign Direct Investment:	N.A.
Major Industries Encouraged:	Export-oriented trade, processing industry, etc.

Manzhouli Border Economic Cooperation Zone was authorized and established in 1992 by the State Council as the national border zone. The city is China's biggest trading center with Mongolia in the west and with Russia in the north. Among similar economic zones in Northeast Asia, it is the most important hub for border trading and a distribution center on the Euro-Asia Bridge. The handling capacity of railroad system is five million tons of cargo per year.

The zone has total development area of 6.4 sq km. It will include a few subsidiary parks for high-tech industries, processing industries, warehousing, commerce, entertainment and residential facilities.

The Administrative Committee of Manzhouli Border Economic Cooperation Zone
301 National Road East
Manzhouli city
Inner Mongolia
P. R. China 021400
Tel: (86)(470) 6225166
Fax: (86)(470) 6220366

ERENHOT BORDER ECONOMIC COOPERATION ZONE

Year of Establishment:	1993
Location:	Erenhot city, Inner Mongolia
Size:	3 km
Major Investors:	The Municipal Government
Total Foreign Direct Investment:	N.A.
Major Industries Encouraged:	Border trade, processing industry, entertainment, agriculture and husbandry infrastructure development

Erenhot Border Economic Cooperation Zone was authorized and established in 1992 by the State Council as the national border zone. It is located only one km away from the city of Erenhot and 2.5 km from international boundary. The zone is equipped with a good transportation system and multi-function service centers. In particular, the zone is part of the Erenhot Sino-Mongolia free-trade area and has been granted national preferential policies for further development.

In 2000, the GDP of Erenhot City was RMB301.5 million, an increase of 12.1% over 1999. Now, there are 43 border trade companies in the city. Total value of import was USD331.8 million (+32.2%) and export was USD72.1 million (+17.5%).

The Administrative Committee of Erenhot Border Economic Cooperation Zone
The Co-inspection Building
Youyi Street, Erenhot city
Inner Mongolia
P. R. China 011100
Tel: (86)(479) 7523512
Fax: (86)(479) 7521930

BAOTOU HIGH-TECH PARK

Our Rating:	B
Year of Establishment:	September 1990
Location:	Baotou, Inner Mongolia
Size:	49 sq km
Major Investors:	N.A.
Total Foreign Direct Investment:	N.A.
Major Industries Encouraged:	Rare earth products, information technologies, metalllurgical technologies, new materials, light industry and food processing

INTRODUCTION

Baotou High-tech Park (BTHTP) is located in Baotou, which is a key industrial city of Inner Mongolia Autonomous Region. The park was established in September 1990 and was approved by the State Council as a state-level high-tech park in November 1992. It is also called China's Rare Earth Valley as the reserve of rare earth in Baotou accounts for 97% of the national total, and 77% of the world's total.

The total land area of the park is 49 sq km. In the park, there is a university science park a science & technology zone and China's first incubation zone for rare earth enterprises. Cooperation has been established between the park and several universities and research institutes, such as Tsinghua University, Chinese Academy of Engineering and Inner Mongolia University.

In 2000, the total industrial output of all park enterprises was RMB3.65 billion with profit of RMB660 million, and the export value totaled USD72.95 million. It is estimated that by the end of 2005, the total industrial output of all park enterprises will reach RMB10.6 billion fo which RMB8.5 billion will come from high-tech enterprises, and the total export will be USD150 million.

A total of 840 enterprises have registered in the park. These include Inner Mongolia High-tech Holdings, Inner Mongolia Hefa Rare Earth Co. Ltd. (hefare.com) and Rare Earth High-tech Co. Ltd. (reht.com).

INVESTMENT CLIMATE

BTHTP focuses on industrial sectors like rare earth products, information technologies, metallurgical technologies, new materials, light industry and food processing.

There are over 100 research institutes in Baotou, including two state level ones, namely Baotou Rare Earth Institute and China Weaponry No. 52 Institute. Baotou University of Iron & Steel Technology (www.btu.edu.cn) is located in the city where over 100,000 technical professionals and more than 500,000 experienced workers are living.

Baotou is located in the midwest of Inner Mongolia, facing Yellow River. It is 700 km from Beijing and has an important position in transportation within Inner Mongolia as well as Ningxia. The high-tech park is six km from the railway station and 16 km from the civilian airport. Railways connect Baotou to Beijing, Shanghai, Tianjin, Ningbo, Yinchuan, Lanzhou, Taiyuan, Xi'an, Wuhan and other

Chinese cities. National Highway No. 110 and 210 run through the city.

Baotou has long been famous for its natural resources. Besides rare earth, the city is also rich in non-ferrous metals and inorganic nonmetal resources. The niobium resource of the city ranks second in the world. Overall, the city is the largest base for the rare earth industry, and an important base for the steel, mechanical, non-ferrous and textile industries.

The Administrative Committee of Baotou High-tech Park
Tel: (86)(472) 5118888
Fax: (86)(472) 5159784
Email: zsj@re-zone.gov.cn
Website:re-zone.gov.cn

Baotou High-tech Park Beijing Office
Room 1516, Digital Plaza A
2 Zhongguancun South Avenue
Haidian District, Beijing
Tel: (86)(10) 82515158
Fax: (86)(10) 82515168
Email: rebj@re-zone.gov.cn

Industrial Park in Ningxia

Yinchuan Economic & Technological Development Zone

INTRODUCTION

Ningxia lies in the plateau and the transitional belt between the Erdos tableland and the Mongolian Great Desert. In the Old Stone Age 30,000 years ago, Chinese ancestors lived along the Water Cave Ravine on the bank of Yellow River. Different ethnic groups of Han, Mongolian, Hui, Tibetan and Manchu harmoniously coexist, together with their respective cultures and customs.

GEOGRAPHY

Ningxia is located in northwest China on the upper reaches of the Yellow River. The Yellow River runs across the region from the west to the northeast for 397km, and its basin covers nearly 75% of Ningxia's total land area.

The climate of this inland area is continental cold desert. Annual average temperature ranges from 5°C to 9°C.

TRAVEL INFORMATION

Civilian airliners from Hedong Airport of Yinchuan can fly to more than ten major domestic cities. A new civil airport in Guyuan is under construction.

From Yinchuan Airport to:

Beijing	1hr 40 mins
Shanghai	3 hrs
Guangzhou	3 hrs 55 mins
Chengdu	2 hrs 40 mins

INVESTMENT CLIMATE

In 2001, the GDP of Ningxia was USD3.1 billion, with a growth rate of 10.1%. The major industries of Ningxia were coal, pharmaceuticals, electricity, metallurgy, chemical, textiles, paper making, food processing, machinery and building materials.

With the geographical advantages near the Yellow River, Ningxia has favorable conditions for developing agriculture. In 2001, the output value of agriculture was USD600 million, with a growth rate of 6.3%. The well-known specialties, such as fruits of Chinese wolfberry (called red treasure), licorice, lambskin, black moss, wool and its products, are Ningxia's traditional export commodities.

Ningxia's exports have grown by over 10% annually for the past five consecutive years. In 2001, Ningxia hit a record high foreign trade volume of USD536 million, an increase of 21% over 2000. Exports of electro-mechanical and high-tech products have accounted for 45.4% of the region's total. The region's commodities, such as Ningxia's special products like chrome, beryllium and

Fact Sheet	2001
Area (sq km)	66,400
Population (million)	5.6
GDP (RMB billion)	29.8
GDP Growth Rate	10.1%
Consumption Expenditure (RMB billion)	
• Government	6
• Household	13
Per capita annual	
• disposable income of urban residents (RMB '000)	5.5
• net income of rural households (RMB '000)	1.8
Utilized FDI (USD million)	16.8
Industrial Value Added (RMB bn)	10.2
Imports (USD million)	180
Exports (USD million)	356
Universities & Colleges	7

silica gel, are now exported to over 84 countries.

Ningxia has rich mineral reserves with nearly 54 mineral resources found in the territory of Ningxia. In addition, it enjoys superior energy and water sources, which provide favorable conditions for its economic development.

Over the past years, Ningxia has developed a transportation network of railway, highway and airway.

The Bao-Lan (Baotou-Lanzhou) and Bao-Zhong (Baoji-Zhongwei) Railways run across Ningxia's northwest area with connections to Jing-Bao and Long-Hai Railways respectively. They have become an important part of the New Asia-Europe Land Bridge linking Asia with Europe. The upcoming Zhongwei-Taiyuan Line will form a new route from northwest to northern China.

Several major highway projects under construction include Dandong-Lahsa, Yinchuan-Qingdao and Yinchuan-Wuhan expressways. After all these projects are completed, an express highway net will come into being, with Yinchuan as the center and connecting all the neighboring regions, cities and provinces.

Ningxia's civil aviation has also developed rapidly in recent years. Yinchuan Hedong Airport, 4D class main line airport, has regular scheduled flights flying directly to Beijing, Guangzhou, Shanghai, Xi'an, Wuhan, Chengdu, Chongqing, Kunming and other cities.

As for telecommunication, a fibre optical network supplemented by satellite system has been set up. At present, every administrative village has been reached by public road, electricity, telephone, broadcasting and television. The urban facilities such as power supply, water supply, drainage works, sewage treatment, central heating system, and gas supply have been rapidly improved.

At present, Ningxia has 56 scientific research institutes, employing 130,000 researchers and technicians. There are 7 universities and colleges, 26 polytechnic schools, 36 vocational training schools and 5,000 primary and middle schools with enrollment of a million students.

With its rich natural resources and improved infrastructure facilities, Ningxia is attracting an increasing number of foreign investors. In 2001, the region approved 43 foreign-funded projects, involving realized foreign investment of USD50.9 million respectively.

Ningxia Hui Autonomous Region Foreign Trade and Economic Cooperation
119 Jiefang West Road
Yinchuan, Ningxia
Tel: (86)(951) 5019122
Fax: (86)(951) 5019120
Email: nxdoftec@nxdoftec.gov.cn
Website: www.nxdoftec.gov.cn

YINCHUAN ECONOMIC AND TECHNOLOGICAL DEVELOPMENT ZONE

Our Rating:	B
Year of Establishment:	July 2001
Location:	Yinchuan, Ningxia
Size:	7.5 sq km
Major Investors:	Western E-business Corp., YCETDZ Investment Holdings, Ningxia Jadebird Broadcasting Network and Ningxia Comprehensive Investment Co.
Total Foreign Direct Investment:	RMB90 million (end 2000)
Major Industries Encouraged:	Biopharmaceuticals, gas, chemicals, innovation of traditional industries and information technologies.

INTRODUCTION

Yinchuan Economic and Technological Development Zone (YCETDZ) was approved and established by the State Council in July 2001.

YCETDZ is located in Ningxia Autonomous Region's provincial capital, Yinchuan City. It has a planned area of 7.5 sq km which is divided into two districts. District I, 3 km away from the city center, has an area of 2.26 sq km. District II is a new district with an area of 5.24 sq km, located in the southern part of the industrial zone.

YCETDZ is located at Helan Mountain's east; the central part of Yinchuan Plains. The annual average temperature is 9°C with an annual average precipitation of 181 mm, 3,000 sunlight hours, and 170 days of frost-free period.

There are three highways leading out of YCETDZ to Inner Mongolia, Gansu Province, Shaanxi Province and the rest of the country. YCETDZ is only 3 km away from Yinchuan Railway Station, 25 km away from Hedong Airport and 8 km from Helan Mountain Airport. Both the western and northern sides of YCETDZ are next to the railway tracks —

to provide easy access for large warehouses in the zone.

At the end of 2000, registered enterprises numbered 1,143, among which were 22 foreign enterprises. The total investment amounted to RMB250 million, with utilized foreign investment of RMB90 million. Total export volume was USD4.8 million.

INVESTMENT CLIMATE

The investment of infrastructure development in District II has reached RMB300 million. Daily supply of natural gas is 20,000 sq m. Water supply comes from a water plant in the northern part of Yinchuan with a daily production of 100,000 tons. The capacity of program controlled telephones is large enough to satisfy the requirements of investors. A broadband network and the sewage and rubbish treatment management solution is being built. YCETDZ is developing solar and wind-powered resources, too.

Set up in 1992, District I has preliminarily achieved unique industry advantage in special pharmaceuticals, integration of mechatronics and information technologies.

YCETDZ is the only state-level economic and technological development zone in Ningxia Autonomous Region. It is a new economic region with high-tech enterprises and a base for the opening of Western China.

At present, there are 169 research institutes and more than 76,000 professionals in Yinchuan.

Currently, YCETDZ is focusing on six high-tech industries and traditional industries that can be upgraded with advanced technology. They are information industries, special pharmaceuticals with focus in bio-engineering, natural gas-related industries with focus in advanced engineering technology, traditional industries upgraded with advanced technology, financial services, and supporting services.

YCETDZ Administrative Committee
Tel: (86)(951) 5050325
Fax: (86)(951) 5058658
Email: Ycda.office@ycda.gov.cn
Website: www.ycda.gov.cn

TIBET

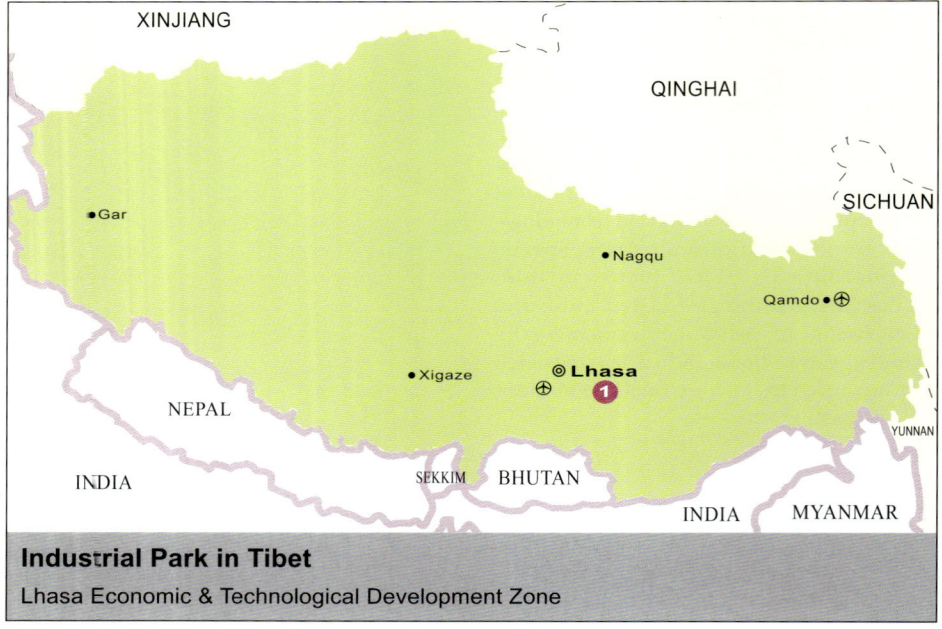

XINJIANG

QINGHAI

SICHUAN

• Gar

• Nagqu

Qamdo •⊕

• Xigaze   ⊕ ⊚ **Lhasa**
                    ❶

NEPAL

YUNNAN

INDIA   SEKKIM   BHUTAN

                    INDIA   MYANMAR

Industrial Park in Tibet
Lhasa Economic & Technological Development Zone

INTRODUCTION

Tibet is the second largest and least populous province-level region in China. The written history of Tibet dates back to the 7th century when the present Tibetan script was invented. It was in the Sakya period of the late 13th century that Tibet officially became an inseparable part of China.

GEOGRAPHY

Tibet lies at the main part of Qinghai-Tibet Plateau, reputed to be the "Roof of the World" averaging 4,000 m above sea level. There are more than 40 snow-capped mountain peaks above 7,000 m in the southwest of Tibet, including the world highest Mt. Everest. Kunlun, Himalaya, Gangdis and Henduan Mountains are also scraping the sky.

Though the climate in Tibet is of alpine type, the direction and altitude of the mountains distribute the climate and rainfall unevenly between south and north slopes, valleys and mountains. Normally, areas in the south slope receive more sunshine and more rainfall.

The 1.2 million sq km territory has a 4,000 km long border with Myanmar, Bhutan, Sikkim, Nepal, India, and Kashmir. The Government of Tibet Autonomous Region administers Lhasa and six prefectures including Linzhi, Qamdo, Xigaze, Nagqu and Ali.

Since the Chinese liberation in the 1950s, Tibet's population has grown rapidly. In 2001, it had 2.63 million residents, of which 92% are of Tibetan ethnic group.

Fact Sheet	2001
Area (sq km)	1,200,000
Population (million)	2.63
GDP (RMB billion)	13.86
GDP Growth Rate	12.6%
Consumption Expenditure (RMB billion)	
• Government	2
• Household	4.9
Per capita annual	
• disposable income of urban residents (RMB '000)	7.12
• net income of rural households (RMB '000)	1.40
Contractual FDI (USD million)	2.96
Industrial Value Added (RMB bn)	1.1
Imports (USD million)	12.4
Exports (USD million)	82.4
Universities & Colleges	3

TRAVEL INFORMATION

The Holy Snow Land is best reached by air.

From Lhasa Airport to:

Beijing	4 hrs 50 mins
Shanghai Hongqiao	6 hrs
Guangzhou	5 hrs 30 mins
Chongqing	2 hrs 5 mins
Kunming	2 hrs 40 mins
Xi'an	3 hrs 45 mins
Chengdu	1 hr 45 mins
Xining	2 hrs
Katmandu	1 hr 20 mins

CLIMATE OF FOREIGN INVESTMENT

In 2001, Tibet achieved a GDP growth rate of 12.6%, one of the highest in China. The GDP was USD168 million, to which only 0.25% was contributed by FIEs.

Qinghai-Tibet Highway, the artery for Tibet's access to the outside world, accounts for 85% of all cargo transports to this remote region. Highways to Sichuan, Xinjiang and Yunnan are also available. Railway to Lhasa is now under construction. However, passengers prefer to approach the capital by air. In 2001, Lhasa airport welcomed 600,000 visitors.

Still a virgin land for FDI, Tibet had only attracted 123 such projects by the end of 2001. In the same year, nine FIEs were newly set up in Tibet, with investment of USD2.96 million. To facilitate capital inflows, Tibet adopts a tax policy of "lenience and simplicity" toward foreign investors. Some categories of taxes are exempted, such as adjustment tax on fixed assets investment, consumption tax, tax on urban land usage, property tax, taxes for agriculture and animal husbandry etc. More investment funds are channeling into education, infrastructure, agriculture, animal husbandry and forestry, high-tech industries, Tibetan pharmaceuticals, and conservation of ecological environment.

Tibet Government Beijing Office
Tel: (86)(10) 64018822-3309
Fax: (86)(10) 64019831
Email: tg@tibetguide.com.cn
Website: www.tibetguide.com.cn

The Economy and Trade Department of Tibet Autonomous Region
15 Linkuo North Road, Lhasa, Tibet
Tel/Fax: (86)(891) 6322542

Department of Foreign trade and Economic Cooperation
184 Beijing Middle Road
Lhasa, Tibet
Tel/Fax: (86)(891) 6822438

China Tibet Information Center
Website: www.tibetinfor.com

Other useful links:
Website: www.tibet-tour.com
www.tibet-china.org

LHASA ECONOMIC AND TECHNOLOGICAL DEVELOPMENT ZONE

Our Rating:	C
Year of Establishment:	September 2000
Location:	Lhasa, Tibet
Size:	5.46 sq km
Major Investors:	N.A.
Total Foreign Direct Investment:	N.A.
Major Industries Encouraged:	Tibetan medicines, tourism, solar energy and processing of husbandry products and wood products

The State Council upgraded Lhasa Economic and Technological Development Zone (LAETDZ) to be a state-level development zone on 19 September 2000, on the basis that Tibet Economic and Technological Development Zone was established in 1992. LAETDZ is located at Dongga Town of Duilongdeqing County. The area for development is 5.46 sq km and it consists of 'A' and 'B' Districts, facing each other.

The Chinese government has announced that a massive railway project is underway to link the remote Western Region - Tibet. This 1,118 km railway project will start from Golmud City, Qinghai Province and go right across Tibet to end in Lhasa. Once completed, it will be the first railway to reach Tibet from other provinces. The development focus of LAETDZ includes Tibetan medicine, tourism, solar energy and processing of animal husbandry products.

XINJIANG

Industrial Parks in Xinjiang

1. Urumqi Economic & Technological Development Zone
2. Shihezi Economic & Technological Development Zone
3. Bole Border Trade Cooperation Zone
4. Yining Border Trade Cooperation Zone
5. Tacheng Border Trade Cooperation Zone
6. Urumqi High-tech Park

INTRODUCTION

Xinjiang Uygur Autonomous Region, located in the farmost northwestern China and the hinterland of Eurasia, is the largest administrative region of China. Urumqi is the capital city.

GEOGRAPHY

Xinjiang has an area of 1.66 million sq km and covers one sixth of China's national territory. Eight countries share the Xinjiang border and together they form a border line of more than 5,400 km, the longest in China. These countries are: the People's Republic of Mongolia, Russia, Kazakhstan, Kirghizstan,

Tajikistan, Afghanistan, Pakistan and India. Xinjiang has a typical sunny continental climate.

TRAVEL INFORMATION

Xinjiang ranks top in China's western provinces and autonomous regions in transportation facilities.

From Urumqi Airport to:

Beijing	3 hrs 25 mins
Moscow	5 hrs 45 mins
Hong Kong	4 hrs 55 mins
Guangzhou	4 hrs 20 mins
Shanghai	4 hrs 10 mins

Fact Sheet	2001
Area (sq km)	1,660,000
Population (million)	18.8
GDP (RMB billion)	148.5
GDP Growth Rate	8.1%
Consumption Expenditure (RMB billion)	
• Government	10.2
• Household	40.6
Per capita annual	
• disposable income of urban residents (RMB '000)	6.59
• net income of rural households (RMB '000)	1.71
Utilized FDI (USD million)	20.3
Industrial Value Added (RMB bn)	45
Imports (USD million)	1,103
Exports (USD million)	668
Universities & Colleges	22

INVESTMENT CLIMATE

Xinjiang s economy has made great progress in recent years. In 2001, Xinjiang's GDP amounted to USD18.0 billion, up 8.1% from the previous year. Total value added industrial output reached USD5.45 billion, an increase of 8.0% over 2000.

Heavy industries like oil, petrochemicals and coal production formed the fundamental part of Xinjiang's industrial development, accounting for 84% of the total industrial output in 2001. Xinjiang's light industries consist of textiles and garments (especially wool and cashmere), leather processing, papermaking, sugar refining and carpet weaving. They made up 15.8% of the total industrial output in 2001.

In 2001, the oasis agriculture of Xinjiang reached USD6.0 billion, which is 33.3% of the GDP. With an arable land of 33,400 sq km and reclaimable land of 66,700 sq km, Xinjiang offers a good basis for the production of livestock, fruit and melon, cotton and woollen textile. Xinjiang is the biggest cotton production base in the country.

Xinjiang is referred to as "A Plateful of Treasures" because there is an enormous amount of deposited natural resources with a total of 122 different kinds of minerals. It also has rich deposits of copper and nickel, which are rarely found elsewhere in the country.

In addition, Xinjiang's prospective reserves of oil and gas amount to 30 billion tons, making up 35% of the country's total prospective reserve, ranking it first in the country. The reserves of coal, with an amount of 27 billion tons, account for 40% of the country's total reserve.

In recent years, Xinjiang's investment environment has been significantly improved. There are highways radiating in all directions, reaching 35,600 km and covering over 99% of the counties and region.

The annual Urumqi Trade Fair is the biggest and the most comprehensive one in China's Northwest. It ranks with Guangzhou Fair, Shanghai Fair and Harbin Fair as one of China's 4 biggest international trade fairs.

In 2001, there were 53 new foreign funded projects being approved, down 8.6% from 2000. Total realized foreign investment was USD20.4 million.

At the end of 2001, the total investment in the region from 36 countries was USD400 million.

Xinjiang Autonomous Region Government
Website: www.xj.gov.cn

Xinjiang Urumqi Fair Office
Tel: (86)(991) 2850479,2879890
Fax: (86)(991) 2879890, 2860255
Email: urumqfair@mail.wl.xj.cn

Beijing Office of Xinjiang Government
Tel: (86)(10) 6833266

Shanghai Office of Xinjiang Government
Tel: (86)(21) 65532387

URUMQI ECONOMIC AND TECHNOLOGICAL DEVELOPMENT ZONE

Our Rating:	B
Year of Establishment:	1992
Location:	Urumqi, Xinjiang
Size:	4.34 sq km
Major Investors:	Kunlun Biotechnologies, Guanghui Industries, Markor Furnitures and Harmang Equipment Co.
Total Foreign Direct Investment:	USD145 million (Contractual)
Major Industries Encouraged:	Construction materials, furniture, home electronics, alcohol, chinese medicine, health food and bio-technology

INTRODUCTION

Urumqi Economic and Technological Development Zone (UETDZ) was established in 1992 and the zone was officially approved by the State Council on 25 August 1994. The first phase of UETDZ is 4.34 sq km.

Located in Diwobao District of the new city area of Urumqi City, UETDZ is two kilometers away from Urumqi International Airport, two kilometers to North Urumqi Cargo Terminal, 3.5 km to West Railway Station (a marshalling yard of the second Eurasia Land Bridge), and about ten kilometers to South Urumqi Railway Station for passengers. This recently operated railway provides additional land access between China, Kazakhstan and European countries, making it yet another strong lever in promoting economic cooperation and commodity flow between the two continents.

At present, infrastructure has been developed in the 3.5 sq km startup area, with supplies of water and power, a network capacity of 100,000 telephones, and convenient communication system. Green areas account for about 26.3% of the whole UETDZ.

INVESTMENT CLIMATE

Over 210 projects have been set up in UETDZ, and there are 65 foreign businesses currently operating in UETDZ. The contractual and utilized foreign investment were USD145.4 million and USD 68.8 million respectively.

UETDZ is also a window to the opening of Western China. This unique location provides special geographical advantages for UETDZ.

The Chinese government has extended its policies to the west of China in favor of regional developments. During the tenth Five-Year Plan period, the central government will provide RMB100 billion for the development of the oil, grain, and cotton resources in the region. As the provincial capital, Urumqi will certainly lead the trend.

The Administrative Committee of Urumqi ETDZ
Tel: (86)(991) 3716656
Fax: (86)(991) 3713116
E-mail: uetda@public.w1.xj.cn
Website: www.urumqi.gov.cn

SHIHEZI ECONOMIC AND TECHNOLOGICAL DEVELOPMENT ZONE

Our Rating:	B
Year of Establishment:	1992
Location:	Shihezi City, Xinjiang
Size:	20.67 sq km (first phase is 5.3 sq km)
Major Investors:	Xinjiang Kesai Biological Engineering Co., Dadao Xinxing Jiancai Co., Xintian Weimonte Irrigation Co. and Xinrun Qiliu Fang Co.
Total Foreign Direct Investment:	N.A.
Major Industries Encouraged:	Food, cotton weaving, construction materials, pharmaceuticals and fine chemical engineering

INTRODUCTION

SHZETDZ was established with the approval of the People's Government of Xinjiang Autonomous Region in 1992 and was further upgraded to a state-level development zone by the State Council on 24 April 2000. It has a planned area of 20.67 sq km.

Located in the eastern suburb of Shihezi City, SHZETDZ is 150 km distant to Urumqi city. The Shihezi Airport is only four km away from the zone, is partly operational and still under expansion phase.

At the end of 1999, there were 263 enterprises set up in the Zone, with total realized fixed asset investment of RMB1.1 billion and registered capital of RMB700 million. Total industrial output increases at an annual rate of 40%.

INVESTMENT CLIMATE

The first phase of 5.3 sq km was completed and equipped with water supply, drainage, power supply, heat supply, roads, tele-communications and leveled ground.

The zone is able to supply 43,000 tons of water daily and the water supply capacity will be increased by almost 40,000 tons.

There is a communication network capacity of 25,000 telephones with the Euroasia fiber optic cable in operation.

Foreign investors from US, Japan, Italy, Singapore, Hong Kong and Taiwan have so far invested in the zone.

Industries such as food, cotton weaving, construction materials, pharmaceuticals, fine chemical engineering etc. have been established in the zone.

Shihezi ETDZ Administrative Committee
No. 56, Sidong Road
Shihezi City, Xinjiang
P. R. China 832014
Tel: (86)(993) 2015928 / 2610328
Fax: (86)(993) 2611868 / 2611370
E-mail: kfqgwh@xjshz.com

BOLE BORDER ECONOMIC COOPERATION ZONE

Year of Establishment:	1992
Location:	Bole city, Xinjiang Autonomous Region
Size:	7.83 sq km
Major Investors:	N.A.
Total Foreign Direct Investment:	N.A.
Major Industries Encouraged:	Export-oriented trade, processing industry etc.

Bole Border Economic Cooperation Zone was authorized and established in 1992 by the State Council as a national border zone. The zone is in fact an integrate part of the development of Bole city, which has long been considered as the key city of Buoertala Mongolian Autonomous Prefecture. The zone has been developing fast, from the base of its old city. The total planned area of the zone is around 7.83 sq km. The industrial section within the zone covers an area of 4.85 sq km, which is around 61.9% of the total area. The development of the zone is greatly helped by the convenient transportation system. It has a fine railroad, and the Ala Mountain Highway, is an attraction for all investors. The major industries of Bole include cotton, sugar, edible oil and beverages.

The Administrative Committee of Bole Border Economic Cooperation Zone
Changcheng Road East
Bole City, Xinjiang
P. R. China 833400
Tel: (86)(909) 2223275

YINING BORDER ECONOMIC COOPERATION ZONE

Year of Establishment:	1992
Location:	Yining City, Xinjiang Autonomous Region
Size:	6.5 sq km
Major Investors:	Puyi plastics, Honey processing plant and SM Yining timber plant
Total Foreign Direct Investment:	N.A.
Major Industries Encouraged:	Export-oriented trade, textile, wine brewing, paper manufacturing, pharmaceuticals, construction materials, forestry and tourism

Yining Border Economic Cooperation Zone was established in 1992, and it was authorized by the State Council as a national border zone. It is located in Yining City.

The zone has attracted an investment commitment of over RMB110 million. Over 95 enterprises have been established in the zone, and most of them are engaged in export-oriented trade, textile, wine brewing, paper manufacturing, pharmaceuticals, construction materials, forestry and tourism. By the end of 2005, the industrial output of the zone is expected to reach RMB200 million (USD24.1 million), and the total export volume will be USD5.42 million.

The city of Yining lies in the central of Yili River Valley, against the Kegurqin Mountains and facing the Yili River in the south. The city has beautiful surroundings, and the suburban areas look like huge gardens — with poplar and apple trees everywhere.

The Administrative Committee of Yining Border Economic Cooperation Zone
Beijing Road
Yining City, Xinjiang
P. R. China 835000
Tel: (86)(999) 8133066
Fax: (86)(999) 8128184
Email: lfa_yn@mail.xj.cninfo.net
Website: www.ycatv.com.cn/kfa/

TACHENG BORDER ECONOMIC COOPERATION ZONE

Year of Establishment:	1992
Location:	Tacheng city, Xinjiang
Size:	6.5 sq km
Major Investors:	The City Government
Total Foreign Direct Investment:	N.A.
Major Industries Encouraged:	Export-oriented trade, processing industry and logistics

Tacheng Border Economic Cooperation Zone was authorized and established in 1992 by the State Council as a national border zone. Tacheng city is located in the northwest of Xinjiang Autonomous Region and is adjacent to Kazakhstan. The zone is located in the east part of the city. It is 12 km from the Baketu land port. It has a commercial center for domestic and foreign trade, a foreign trade processing section, a storage section and a port service department. The commercial center has reached an agreement with Yuhua Company from Guangdong province, and Yinyu Company from Hong Kong to jointly develop Tacheng International Trade Corridor. The first phase of this project has business area of 50,000 sq m.

The Administrative Committee of Tacheng Border Economic Cooperation Zone
Guangming Street
Tacheng city, Xinjiang
P. R. China 834700
Tel: (86)(901) 6226163

URUMQI HIGH-TECH PARK

Our Rating:	B
Year of Establishment:	1992
Location:	Urumqi, Xinjiang
Size:	18.7 sq km
Major Investors:	Xinjiang New Energy Holdings, Huashidan Pharmaceuticals, Huachun Co. and Western Co.
Total Foreign Direct Investment:	USD44.8 million
Major Industries Encouraged:	Information technology, new materials (especially new construction materials), bio-pharmaceuticals, magnetic materials and healthcare products

INTRODUCTION

Urumqi High-tech Park (UHTP) was approved by the State Council in 1992 and is the only state-level high-tech park in Xinjiang Autonomous Region. The park is located in the urban area of Urumqi, the capital city of Xinjiang. The total planned area is 18.7 sq km.

At the end of 2000, there are 143 high-tech enterprises out of a total 679 enterprises in the park. There are 51 foreign enterprises in the park with total investment of USD44.8 million. These investors are mainly from US, Canada, Germany, Singapore, Korea, Thailand, Russia, Japan, Hong Kong, Macau and Taiwan. The main investment fields are information technology, new materials (especially new construction materials), bio-pharmaceuticals, magnetic materials and healthcare products.

INVESTMENT CLIMATE

Baihuacun Software Development Park (www.xjbhesoftp.com) is a key subsidiary UHTP. The investment in this park is RMB270 million. With advanced office building, an exhibition center and a training center, the park has established cooperation with IBM, CISCO, SVN and major domestic software firms.

Besides Baihuacun Software Development Park, the area also contains a bio-pharmaceutical park, an entrepreneur park for overseas Chinese students and the Xinjiang University Science Park.

Urumqi is the economic, commercial and cultural center and is an important city along the Second Asia-Europe Continental Bridge. More than 51 minorities live in the city, making it among the regions with the most minorities in China.

The Administrative Committee of Urumqi High-tech Park
Diamond City
5 Beijing South Road
Urumqi, Xinjiang
P. R. China 830011
Tel: (860)(991) 3830834
Email: uctp@mail.xj.cninfo.net
Website: www.uctp.gov.cn

ANHUI

Railway
Expressway

HENAN

Huaibei
Suzhou

JIANGSU

Fuyang
Huainan
Bengbu

Chuzhou

Hefei ①⑥

Lu'an
Chaohu
Ma'anshan ④

Wuhu ②

Tongling ⑤
Chizhou
Xuancheng

HUBEI

Anqing ③

Huangshan

JIANGXI
ZHEJIANG

Industrial Parks in Anhui

1. Hefei Economic & Technological
   Development Zone
2. Wuhu Economic & Technological
   Development Zone
3. Anqing Economic & Technological
   Development Zone
4. MaanshanEconomic & Technological
   Development Zone
5. Tongling Economic & Technological
   Development Zone
6. Hefei High-tech Park

INTRODUCTION

Anhui is considered as the first region settled by Han Chinese, who moved southwards in the 3rd century B.C. Today the province is one of the most important agricultural provinces in China. Most of the inhabitants live on the plains near Huaihe River in northern Anhui. Major cities in the province include Hefei, Wuhu, Anqing, Ma'anshan, Tongling, Bengbu and Chaohu etc.

GEOGRAPHY

Anhui is located at the central part of Southeast China and at the downstream reaches of Yangtze River. It has a warm temperate and subtropical climate. With total land area of 140,000 sq km and a population of 59 million, Anhui is rich in land resources and aquatic products, with more than 100 valuable plants and animals. Its jurisdiction covers 6 districts, 19 cities and 59 counties, and the provincial capital city is Hefei. The area includes Huaibei Plain, Jianghuai Hill, Dabie mountainous land, Wanzhong Plain, and Wannan mountainous land. The famous mountains are Huangshan Mountain (Yellow Mountain) and Jiuhua Mountain. The main rivers running through the province are Yangtze River and Huaihe River. There are mainly two minority ethnic groups living in the province, namely Hui and She. Famous cultural and historical attractions of the province are Huangshan Mountain, Jiuhuashan Mountain and Tianzhu Mountain.

TRAVEL INFORMATION

From Hefei Airport to:
Hong Kong	1hr 20mins
Beijing	1hr 55mins
Guangzhou	10mins
Shanghai Hongqiao	1hr 5mins

INVESTMENT CLIMATE

Anhui has been one of China's largest producers of grain, edible oil and cotton. It is also famous for its abundant natural resources. However, from the national perspective, the economic development of Anhui is rather slow due to its large population. To date, there are 370,000 industrial enterprises in the province, producing mineral and agriculture raw

Fact Sheet	2001
Area (sq km)	140,000
Population (million)	59.8
GDP (RMB billion)	329
GDP Growth Rate	8.6%
Consumption Expenditure (RMB billion)	
• Government	40.1
• Household	114
Per capita annual	
• disposable income of urban residents (RMB '000)	5.67
• net income of rural households (RME '000)	2.02
Contractual FDI (USD million)	340
Industrial Value Added (RMB bn)	119.1
Imports (USD million)	1,340
Exports (USD million)	2,280
Universities & Colleges	55

materials. Major industrial products include raw coal, coke, iron, steel, nonferrous metals, crane, hydraulic machinery, tractor, diesel, water pump, fertilizer, and textiles. In 2001, Anhui's GDP reached RMB329 billion, an increase of 8.6% over the previous year. The ratio of primary, secondary and tertiary industry is 22.9:43:34.1. The total industrial output was RMB141 billion with emphasis and continuous effort in agricultural products such as edible oil, cotton and wheat.

In 2001, the retail sales of consumer goods was around RMB114 billion, an increase of 8.4%, excluding inflation. Foreign trade increased by 8.2% over the previous year, with exports being USD2,280 million and imports being USD1,340 million, increases of 5.1% and 13.9% respectively. The major trading partners of the province are African countries, European countries, Oceania countries and North American countries. The commodities include rice, sweet potato, soybeans, green tea and red tea, fruits, raw coal, steel, fertilizer and textiles.

Anhui has established a relatively complete transportation system that includes railway, highway and expressway linking the province to cities like Nanjing, Beijing, Shanghai, Hangzhou, Xuzhou and Jiujiang. The Zhujiaqiao harbor at Wuhu city can accommodate 5,000 to 10,000 tonnage capacity vessels, with regular routes to countries and regions worldwide such as Japan, Hong Kong, South Korea and South East Asia etc. With a modern telecommunication network, there were a total of 7.4 million users for fixed & mobile telephone lines.

The population with college or higher education level increases rapidly. In 2001, a total of 55 higher education institutions accomodates 252,000 university and college students.

In Anhui province, there are 52 universities, colleges and research institutions altogether. Besides the above mentioned, other important ones include Anhui Medical University (www.ahmu.edu.cn), Anhui Normal University (www.ahnu.edu.cn), Anhui University of Technology (www.ahut.edu.cn) etc.

Anhui Provincial Government
Website: www.ah.gov.cn

Anhui Provincial Department of Foreign Trade and Economic Cooperation
389-399 Jinzhai Road
ShenAn Square, Hefei
Anhui province
P. R. China 230000
Tel: (86)(551) 2831260, 2831286

Anhui FDI Promotion Center
Tel: (86) (55) 2817278
Fax: (860) (55) 2817768

HEFEI ECONOMIC AND TECHNOLOGICAL DEVELOPMENT ZONE

Our Rating:	BBB
Year of Establishment:	1993
Location:	Hefei, Anhui
Size:	39 sq km
Major Investors:	Coca-Cola and John Deere from the US; Hitachi Excavators and Mitsubishi Heavy Industries from Japan; Fuchs Lubricants from Germany; Chiatai Fodder from Thailand and GT Tires from Indonesia
Total Foreign Direct Investment:	USD1.11 billion (end 2001)
Major Industries Encouraged:	Electronics, equipment manufacturing, chemical engineering and food

INTRODUCTION

Hefei Economic and Technological Development Area (HFETDZ) is a State-level development zone established in April 1993.

Geographic location

HFETDZ is located nine km south of Hefei City. The east of HFETDZ borders Luogang Inter-national Airport and Lurong Expressway. It has a planned area of 39 sq km. The basic infrastructure of the start-up phase of 6 sq km has been completed.

HFETDZ connects to the national road network through more than ten main and trunk roads. The two major cities in East China, Nanjing and Shanghai, can be reached within two hours and five hours with the Hefei-Nanjing-Shanghai Expressway.

Key statistics

In 2001, HETA's gross industrial output is RMB4.3 billion; the GDP volume is RMB1.5 billion; gross import-export volume is RMB210 million and fiscal revenue is RMB207.5 million.

By the end of 2000, there are 230 domestic and foreign enterprises, with total investment of RMB14.14 billion. There are 89 foreign enterprises with total investment of USD1.12 billion from 18 countries and regions worldwide.

INVESTMENT CLIMATE

Domestic enterprises like Hai'er Industrial Park and Jiale Grease were established in HFETDZ. Large number of foreign enterprises have invested in the area, those famous enterprises include: Coca-Cola from the US, John Deere from the US, Mitsubishi Heavy Industries from Japan, Fuchs Lubricants from Germany, Hitachi Excavators from Japan, Chiatai Fodder from Thailand and GT Tires from Indonesia.

Major industries include electronics, equipment manufacturing, chemical engineering, foodstuff etc.

Nine sub-zones are being planned for HFETDZ. They are: Foreign Investors Industrial Zone, Modern Agricultural Technology Model Park, Civil Technology Park, Export Processing Zone, Lianhua

Community, Jinxiu Community, Haiheng Community, Fangxin Community and Zhaoxia Community.

Hefei is a historical city, a developing industrial city, a national "garden city" and one of the key scientific and educational bases of the country. Hefei has convenient transportation and is an important national railroad hub under construction. Luogang International Airport is in Hefei's suburbs and the IDD service has links with almost 200 countries and regions in the world.

Hefei is a Grade-A open city in China with more than 1,000 foreign enterprises. It has became sister cities with Kurume of Japan, Albory of Denmark and Columbus of the US.

Hefei is the center of economics, politics, culture and education of the province. There are 13 Universities and Colleges, University of Science & Technology of China, Anhui University, Hefei University of Technology,

200 research institutes such as Chinese Academy of Sciences (CAS) Hebei Branch, 160,000 tech professionals and 300,000 skilled industrial workers.

HFETDZ Administrative Committee
Mingzhu Plaza
South Suburbs, Hefei
Anhui, P. R. China 230601
Tel: (86)(551) 3812989, 3811070
Fax: (86)(551) 3812940, 3811889
Email: info@hetac.com
Website: www.hetac.com/eindex.html

WUHU ECONOMIC AND TECHNOLOGICAL DEVELOPMENT ZONE

Our Rating:	BB
Year of Establishment:	1993
Location:	Wuhu, Anhui
Size:	10 sq km
Major Investors:	Siemens, Knauf Plastic Co., Ltd and GEA Group, Hitachi, Chia Tai Group and Formosa Plastics
Total Foreign Direct Investment:	USD220 million
Major Industries Encouraged:	Automobiles and its components, electronics, electrical appliances and new construction materials

INTRODUCTION

Wuhu Economic and Technological Development Zone (WUETDZ) was established and approved by the State Council in April 1993 and has carried out preferential policies similar to coastal development zones.

Geographic location

WUETDZ is located at the north of Wuhu City, next to the foreign trade port, the railway station and Yangtze River Bridge. Its main trunk road connects with the city district and three expressways. It is 70 minutes away from Nanjing Lukou International Airport and Hefei Luogang Airport by car.

Three expressways (Wuhu-Hefei, Wuhu-Ningbo and Wuhu-Hangzhou) and five trunk railways (Wuhu-Ningbo, Wuhu-Tongling, Wuhu-Huainan, Xuanchen-Hangzhou and Anhui-Jiangxi) intersect at Wuhu City.

In 2001, WUETDZ's GDP was RMB4.12 billion, an increase of 23% over the previous year. Its total industrial output was RMB12.06 billion, up 42%from year 2000.

INVESTMENT CLIMATE

Infrastructure

By the end of 2001, ten sq km of land has been developed. Accumulated fixed assets investment was RMB1.2 billion. A broadband communication network has been built. A power station is under construction. The percentage of greenery is 32%. At present, around 36 km of roads and 1.3 million sq m of all infrastructure and utilities have been completed.

Wuhu Port has more than 70 berths and annual tonnage capacity of 23 million tons. Domestic listed enterprises such as Conch Group, Kelon, Midea, Start Computer, Guangdong Fenghua High-tech Group, Tonghua Jingma Pharmacy Group, Yingke New Materials Stock Co. Ltd etc. There are also well known domestic enterprises such as FAW Group, Yangzi Group, and Rongshida Group etc. have invested in WETDZ.

By the end of 2001, 131 enterprises have joined the zone with gross investment commitment of RMB8.51 billion. Contractual capital is USD504 million and utilized foreign capital is USD220 million. Major foreign enterprises with investment in WUETDZ include Siemens VDO Automotive Instruments, Knauf Plastic and GEA Group from Germany, Hitachi from Japan, Cha Tai Group from Thailand, Pacific Ocean Co., Ltd from Malaysia, Formosa Plastics Group Co., Ltd, etc.

Key industries in WUETDZ are new construction material, automobiles and its components, electronics and electrical appliances.

The High & New Technology Entrepreneur Service Center opened on 8 December 1999. Wuhu Software Park was also opened in December 2001. At present, about 50 high-tech enterprises have located in the park.

Regional advantage

WUETDZ is located at the west of Yangtze Delta. It is the hub of North and South China as well as East and West China due to its centralized geographic location in China. Because of its favorable location and convenient transportation, it is an excellent place for investors to build production bases, logistics centers for both the markets of East and Central China.

Administrative Committee of WUETDZ
Yinghu North Road
Wuhu, Anhui P. R. China 241009
Tel: (86)(553) 5841555, 5847780
Fax: (86)(553) 5841876
E-mail: wuetdz@mail.ahwhptt.net.cn
Website: www.wuetdz.gov.cn

ANQING ECONOMIC AND TECHNOLOGICAL DEVELOPMENT ZONE

Our Rating:	C
Year of Establishment:	1992
Location:	Anqing, Anhui
Size:	7.2 sq km
Major Investors:	Xinyuan Petrochemical Technology Development, Beche Precision Forging, Anling Chemical Industry, Huaan Electronic Technology, Wasco Artware, Tongfa Water Supply Equipement, Anqing Petrochemical Haida LPG and Jinlinmei Grain & Oil Food
Total Foreign Direct Investment:	N.A.
Major Industries Encouraged:	Electronics, new materials, laser tech & products, Optical-mechanical-electronic integration, genetic engineering & products, new energy and environmental protection technologies

Anqing Economic & Technological Development Zone (AQETDZ) was established in 1992. It has a total planned area of 7.2 sq km and 3.5 sq km for the first stage. The zone is located in northern Anqing, an important industrial and commercial city in Anhui province. The population of the urban area is around 600,000.

AQETDZ is just four km away from Anqing Airport and four km from the port. At the end of June 2000, around 232 projects have been registered in AQETDZ. Foreign enterprises have established more than 70 projects in the development zone; and their total contractual capital was around USD180 million.

Major investors in AQETDZ include Anhui Xinyuan Petrochemical Technology Development Co. Ltd, Anqing Beche Precision Forging Co. Ltd., Anling Chemical Industry Co. Ltd., Huaan Electronic Technology, Wasco Artware Co. Ltd., Tongfa Water Supply Equipement Co. Ltd., Anqing Petrochemical Haida LPG Co. Ltd. and Jinlinmei Grain & Oil Food Company.

Enterprises are most welcomed especially in IT products, new materials, laser tech & products, optical-mechanical-electric integration, genetic engineering & products, new energy and environmental protection technologies & products.

Administrative Committee of AQETDZ
Tel: (86)(556) 5314842, 5338456
Email: webmaster@china-anqing.com
Website: aqdz.china-anqing.org
china-anqing.org

MAANSHAN ECONOMIC AND TECHNOLOGICAL DEVELOPMENT ZONE

Our Rating:	B
Year of Establishment:	N.A.
Location:	Maanshan city, Anhui
Size:	6.8 sq km
Major Investors:	Huade Textile, Sinma Special Cars and Honda Metallurgical Equipments
Total Foreign Direct Investment:	N.A.
Major Industries Encouraged:	Infrastructure development, textile & clothing, automobile and machinery

With a total planned area of 6.8 sq km, Maanshan Economic & Technological Development Zone (MASETDZ) is located in south Maanshan city, Anhui Province. The city has an area of 1,684 sq km and a population of 1.16 million people.

Located in the eastern part of Anhui, MASETDZ has a convenient transportation system. It is just 28 km away from Lukou International Airport in Nanjing, the capital city of Jiangsu province, and has easy access to Shanghai and other major cities in Yangtze River Delta. The annual cargo volume of Maanshan port is over ten million tons. According to statistics from the Administrative Committee of MASETDZ, the GDP per capita of Maanshan city has continuously been ranked the top in Anhui province. With an annual output of four million tons, Maanshan Iron & Steel Group Co. Ltd. is one of China's largest industrial enterprises and is listed in the Hong Kong Exchange.

Domestic and foreign investors who have established operations in MASETDZ include Huade Textile Co. Ltd., Sinma Special Cars Co. Ltd. and Honda Metallurgical Equipments Co. Ltd. The major industries that are mostly welcomed include infrastructure development, textile & clothing, automobile, machinery etc.

The Administrative Committee of MASETDZ is in charge of the planning, development and coordination affairs of the park. It offers one-stop services to foreign investors.

Administrative Committee of MASETDZ
Tel: (86) (555) 2349128, 2361277
Fax: (86) (555) 2365133
Email: maskfab@masinvestment.com
Website: www.metd.gov.cn

TONGLING ECONOMIC AND TECHNOLOGICAL DEVELOPMENT ZONE

Our Rating:	C
Year of Establishment:	1993
Location:	Tongling, Anhui
Size:	13.2 sq km
Major Investors:	Jinda Copper Materials, Xinwa Insulating Material Xinda Chemcial Industry, Huarui Electronic Jinggong Special Enameled Wire, TLETDZ Group and Ginlong Copper Minerals
Total Foreign Direct Investment:	N.A.
Major Industries Encouraged:	Cooper products processing, chemicals, electronics, medicals, textile, garment processing, machinery, urban infrastructure development and environmental protection technologies

Tongling Economic & Technological Development Zone (TLETDZ) is located in Tongling city, Anhui. Conveniently located beside Yangtze River, Tongling has easy access to Shanghai, Nanjing and Suzhou. It aims to develop into a high-tech and export-oriented zone. The copper processing industry of Tongling enjoys a long history and plays an important role in China's copper industry.

The total area of the zone is 13.2 sq km, with 0.5 sq km as the development area for the first stage and 3 sq km for the second stage. Investors from the United States, Australia, Portugal, Italy, Germany, Hong Kong, Taiwan and Singapore have established around 43 industrial projects in fields like copper processing, electronics, chemistry, medicine, garment, furniture manufacturing.

Some domestic and foreign investors, such as Jinda Copper Materials Group, Xinwa Insulating Material, Xinda Chemcial Industry, Huarui Electronics, Jinggong Special Enameled Wire, TLETDZ Group Corporation and Ginlong Copper Minerals with investment of RMB2.4 billion, have operations in TLETDZ. The major industries that are mostly welcomed are copper products processing, chemicals, textile, garment processing, machinery, development of energy resources, urban infrastructure development and environmental protection technologies and equipment.

With total assets of RMB350 million, the Tongling Economic & Technical Development Zone Group Corporation has been established to manage the planning, development and coordination affairs of the park.

Tongling Economic & Technological Development Zone Group Corp
Tel: (86)(562) 2806585
Fax: (86)(562) 2819312
Email: zhaoshang@tetda.com
Website: www.tetda.com

HEFEI HIGH-TECH PARK

Our Rating:	A
Year of Establishment:	October 1990
Location:	Hefei, Anhui
Size:	40 sq km
Major Investors:	Maytag, Sanyo, Toyota. Mitsubishi, ABB, Hyundai and Philco
Total Foreign Direct Investment:	USD640 million
Major Industries Encouraged:	Bioengineering, information technology, optical-mechanical-electronic integration technology and real estate

INTRODUCTION

Hefei High-tech Park (HHTP) is located in the southeast of Hefei, the capital city of Anhui Province. It was established in October 1990 and was approved by the State Council as a national high-tech park in March 1991. In 1997, it became a high-tech park opened for member nations of Asia Pacific Economic Cooperation (APEC). The total area of the park is around 40 sq km.

The development focus of the park is bioengineering, information technology, optical-mechanical-electronic integration technologies and real estate. At the end of 2000, around 678 enterprises have joined in Hefei HTP and their total investment was RMB9.4 billion. The number of enterprises increased to 718 in May 2001 and the total investment amounts increased to RMB10.97 billion. The accumulated foreign investment reached USD640 million. Many famous MNCs have set up in the park, such as Maytag, Philco, Sanyo, Toyota, Mitsubishi, ABB and Hyundai.

INVESTMENT CLIMATE

Some well-known projects have been developed in Hefei HTP. Anhui Wanyan Electronics System Corporation surprised the world with the first VCD player. Maytag invested USD180 million to produce a series of AI household electrical appliances. Philco are producing 1.2 million air conditioners annually with an investment commitment of USD110 million.

Located within the area of HHTP is Hefei State University Science and Technology Park, which consists of Science Park of Anhui University, Hefei Biomedicine Industrial Park and Hefei Entrepreneurship Park for Overseas Chinese Students.

Now, 17,000 professionals are working in the park.

Administrative Committee of Hefei High-tech Park
669 Changjiang West Road
Hefei, Anhui P. R. China 230088
Tel: (86)(551) 5313264
Fax: (86)(551) 5312961
Email: hfgxq@mail.hf.ah.cn
Website: www.hfnhz.com.cn

HEFEI UNIVERSITY SCIENCE PARK

Year of Establishment:	1999
Location:	Hefei, Anhui
Size:	60 ha
Major Supporting Institutions:	University of Science & Technology of China, Anhui University and Hefei University of Technology
Major Investors:	Daqing Petroleum Administration, Sino Petrochem, Baoshan Steel, Legend and Hai'er
Total Foreign Direct Investment:	N.A.
Major Industries Encouraged:	Information Technology, microelectronics, software development, new materials and bio-engineering

Located in the southwest of Hefei, Hefei University Science Park (HFUSP) is jointly developed by University of Science & Technology of China (www.ustc.edu.cn), Anhui University (www.ahu.edu.cn) and Hefei University of Technology (www.hfut.edu.cn). In 2001, the park was awarded the status of National University Science Park.

The park is composed of seven subsidiary zones: USTC Zone, AHU Zone, HUT Zone, Software Zone, Biomedical Zone, New Materials Zone and Entrepreneur Zone.

Under the direct leadership of Chinese Academy of Sciences, University of Science & Technology of China (USTC) is one of the leading universities of China. Among the 1,800 personnel in the university, there are 15 fellows of CAS and CAE, 476 professors and 721 associate professors. The total number of students is around 13,000. Major international academic journals such as US-based Science and French-based Research have listed USTC as one of the most excellent Chinese universities.

The university has established cooperation with major Chinese enterprises such as Daqing Petroleum Administration,

Sino Petrochem, Baoshan Steel, Legend and Hai'er . More than 40 overseas universities have established academic links with USTC such as Purdue University, Tokyo University, Imperial College in UK, University of Rome, University of Stuggart, Moscow State University, Hong Kong University of Science & Technology etc.

At the end of 2000, over 102 enterprises joined University Science Park; and their industries cover information, micro-electronics, software development, new materials and bioengineering.

With registered capital of RMB15 million, HFUSP Development Corporation is in charge of the planning and development affairs of the science park.

Hefei University Science Park Development Corporation
669 Changjiang West Road
Hefei, Anhui Province
P. R. China 230000
Tel: (86)(551) 5315184
Fax: (86)(551) 5315250
Email: hfusp@163.net
Website: www.hfusp.com

FUJIAN

ZHEJIANG

JIANGXI

Nanping• Ningde•

Sanming•

Fuzhou⦿ ⊕
3 5 8
•Fuqing
Putian• **2**

Longyan•

•Quanzhou

Zhangzhou• ⊕
•Xiamen
4 6 7

GUANG
DONG

Dongshan•
1

—— Railway
—— Expressway

Industrial Parks in Fujian

1. Dongshan Economic & Technological Development Zone
2. Fuqing Rongqiao Economic & Technological Development Zone
3. Fuzhou Economic & Technological Development Zone
4. Xiamen Haicang Taiwan Investment Zone
5. Fuzhou Free Trade Zone
6. Xiamen Xiangyu Free Trade Zone
7. Xiamen Torch High-tech Park
8. Fuzhou High-tech Park

INTRODUCTION

Fujian Province is one of China's experimental zones for comprehensive reforms. The province has different windows opened to the outside world. This includes Special Economic Zones (SEZs), Economic and Technological Development Zones (ETDZs), coastal open cities and coastal open zones with the practice of special policies in their

economic activities with the outside world. Fujian is also a major hometown of overseas Chinese. Approximately 8 million overseas Chinese are of Fujian origin.

GEOGRAPHY

Fujian lies at the southeastern coast of China next to Guangdong with its provincial capital, Fuzhou, being in the first batch of coastal open cites in 1984. It has an area of 121,700 sq km, with a population of 34 million. The provincial government has a jurisdiction of nine administrative prefectures and municipalities, which are further divided into 64 counties. Fujian has minority ethnic groups of Hui, Miao, Manchu, Gaoshan and She. Major cities are Fuzhou and Xiamen. The main tourist attractions are Gulangyu Island and Mount Wuyishan. The mild, humid, subtropical climate is especially conducive to crop production, with its 1.24 million hectares of cultivated land, of which one million hectares are rice fields.

TRAVEL INFORMATION

From Fuzhou Airport to:

Kuala Lumpur	4hrs 30mins
Bangkok	5hrs
Hong Kong	1hr 30mins
Macau	1hr 40mins
Beijing	2hrs 40mins
Shanghai Hongqiao	1hr 15mins

From Xiamen Airport to:

Beijing	2hrs 40mins
Hong Kong	1hr
Shanghai Hongqiao	1hr 35mins
Shenzhen	55mins
Singapore	4hrs
Macau	1hr 10mins

Fact Sheet	2001
Area (sq km)	121,700
Population (million)	34.7
GDP (RMB billion)	425.8
GDP Growth Rate	9%
Consumption Expenditure (RMB billion)	
• Government	37.4
• Household	150
Per capita annual	
• disposable income of urban residents (RMB '000)	8.3
• net income of rural households (RMB '000)	3.4
Contractual FDI (USD million)	3,918
Industrial Value Added (RMB bn)	164.5
Imports (USD million)	8,704
Exports (USD million)	13,926
Universities & Colleges	33

INVESTMENT CLIMATE

Fujian, rich in biological resources, is one of the main forestry zones in South China. Its forest coverage ranks top in mainland China with 90% of the mountains and hills.

The economy has seen rapid development since China adopted the open reform policies. In 2001, Fujian's GDP reached RMB425.8 billion, an increase of 9% over the previous year. The ratio of primary, secondary and tertiary industries is 15.3:44.7:40. The total industrial output was RMB190.4 billion, with electronics and food processing being two largest sectors.

The market in retail sales was RMB150 billion, an increase of 11.8% – excluding the inflation factor.

Foreign trade increased by 6.6% over the previous year, with its exports at USD13,926 million and imports at USD8,704 million, an increase of 7.9% and 4.7% respectively. Fujian's major trading partners are the US, Hong Kong, Taiwan, Japan and Germany.

Fujian's foreign direct investment comes mainly from Hong Kong, Taiwan, the US and Japan, with Hong Kong being the largest. There is a total of 1,670 newly signed contracted investment projects, an increase of 14.1% over the year before, and also an increase of 3% in actual amounted to USD3,918 million.

Infrastructure in Fujian is well-developed, with numerous highways & expressways linking to Beijing, Kunming, Chengdu and Lanzhou. The harbors located along the coastal cities can accommodate 10,000 to 50,000-tonnage capacity vessels, and shipping routes go to the US, Japan, Hong Kong, Europe, etc.

Fujian Provincial Government
Website: www.fujian.gov.cn

Fujian Department of Foreign Trade and Economic Cooperation
92 ShiFa Building Level 13-17
North Road, Fuzhou
Fujian, P. R. China 350003
Tel: (86)(591) 7841917, 7590268
Fax: (86)(591) 7856133

DONGSHAN ECONOMIC AND TECHNOLOGICAL DEVELOPMENT ZONE

Our Rating:	BBB
Year of Establishment:	1993
Location:	Dongshan Fujian
Size:	10 sq km (first phase is 3.5 sq km)
Major Investors:	Dongshan Huanong Foodstuff, Oukai Metalwork and Haikui Aquatic Products Group
Total Foreign Direct Investment:	USD306.3 million
Major Industries Encouraged:	Electronics, foodstuff, light industries and new construction materials

INTRODUCTION

Dongshan Economic and Technological Development Zone (DSETDZ) was established in January 1993 with the approval of the State Council. It covers a total planned area of 10 sq km. DSETDZ is planned to be a com-prehensive development zone, having several functional areas for industry, residence and commerce. At present, the first phase of 3.5 sq km has been completed.

By the end of December 2001, 85 foreign-invested enterprises have been admitted into DEDZ with a contracted foreign capital of USD0.52384 billion and actual utilized foreign capital of USD306.3 million. Domestic investment projects add up to 121, amouting to RMB724.5 million. The major industries include electronics, foodstuff, light industries, and new types of construction materials.

Dongshan Island is located in the south of Fujian Province. It is 141 nautical miles from Kaohsiung on the east and 210 nautical miles from Hong Kong on the south. Dongshan Port is one of the nearest ports to Taiwan.

INVESTMENT CLIMATE

Dongshan Port is a state-level grade-A port organization. The port has one 5,000-tonnage dock and one 3,000-tonnage dock. A 25,000-tonnage is under construction. Scheduled voyages (two times per week) of loose cargo and container are available between Hong Kong and Dongshan Port.

The distance from DSETDZ to Shantou Airport is 90 km, and to Xiamen Airport is 100 km.

DSETDZ Committee Building,
Fujian Province P. R. China 363400
Tel: (86)(596) 5885867, 5885007
Fax: (86)(596) 5885790
E-mail: jfj@detdz.com
Website: www.detdz.com

FUQING RONGQIAO ECONOMIC AND TECHNOLOGICAL DEVELOPMENT ZONE

Our Rating:	AA
Year of Establishment:	1987
Location:	Fuqing, Fujian
Size:	28 sq km (first phase is 10 sq km)
Major Investors:	Salim Group, Siemens, Samsung
Total Foreign Direct Investment:	USD1.83 billion
Major Industries Encouraged:	Information Technology, electronics

INTRODUCTION

Fuqing Rongqiao Economic & Technological Development Zone (FRETDZ) was established in 1987 by the overseas Chinese of Fuqing, and was approved as a state-level development zone by the State Council on 21 October 1992. It has planned area of 28 sq km; to date an area of 10 sq km has been developed as the first phase.

Fuqing is located between the two major cities of Fujian Province, Fuzhou and Xiamen. It is only 45 km from Fuzhou Changle International Airport. It faces Taiwan Straits and is 80 nautical miles from Taiwan's Hsinchu City, thus becoming mainland China's nearest city to Taiwan.

Fubei Highway connects FRETDZ and Yuanhing Investment Zone. These trunk roads link the roads of towns and villages, forming a well-connected road network. The density of roads in the city is 49.5 km per 100 sq km, ranking it first in the province.

At present, there are 303 foreign-invested enterprises with total investment of USD1.83 billion and export value of USD5.75 billion.

INVESTMENT CLIMATE

Fuqing has many harbors and excellent conditions to develop ports. In 1995, Fuqing was approved as a Grade-A open port by the State Council. Xinghua Bay, Fuqing Bay, Songxia Port, Niutouwei Port and Jiangyinbi Port can provide more than 100 deepwater berths for development. A 300,000-tonnage deepwater berth can also be built. Two docks have been built: Yuanhong Dock, a 30,000-tonnage dock, and Rongqiao Dock, a 30,000-tonnage container dock.

Many international renowned enterprises have congregated at FRETDZ, such as Salim Group, Siemens, Samsung, etc.

FRETDZ Administrative Committee
Tel: (86)(591) 5377812, 5377819
Fax: (86)(591) 5377820
E-mail: fredz@publ.fz.fj.cn
Website: www.fqrq.doe2e.com/

FUZHOU ECONOMIC AND TECHNOLOGICAL DEVELOPMENT ZONE

Our Rating:	AA
Year of Establishment:	1985
Location:	Fuzhou, Fujian
Size:	16 sq km (first phase is 4.4 sq km)
Major Investors:	JVC, Epson, Mitsubishi, Hitachi
Total Foreign Direct Investment:	USD 1.1 billion
Major Industries Encouraged:	Electronics, electronical instruments, bio-pharmaceuticals, machinery, building materials, textile and other light industries

INTRODUCTION

Fuzhou Economic and Technological Development Zone (FZETDZ) was established in January 1985 with the approval from the State Council. FZETDZ has a total planned area of 16 sq km, with first phase development area of 4.4 sq km. It is China's only open development zone that combines a state-level development zone, a free trade zone, a Taiwanese investment zone and a high-tech park altogether.

FZETDZ is located in Mawei at the estuary of the Min River. Mawei is the gateway to Fuzhou, the provincial capital, and a transportation hub for Southeast Fujian.

By the end of 2000, 794 foreign-funded enterprises had located in the zone, with a total investment exceeding USD3.67 billion. Contractual foreign investment is more than USD 1.7 billion with actual utilized investment over USD 1.1 billion.

INVESTMENT CLIMATE

Mawei Port, known since ancient times as the gateway to Fuzhou by water, is the major cargo distribution center in Southeast Fujian and the Min River valley. With an annual handling capacity of 15 million tons of cargo, the port is equipped with thirteen 10,000-tonnage quay berths (including three container terminals and an international passenger terminal). National Highway No.104 from Beijing to Fuzhou cuts across the development zone.

Investors from over 30 countries and regions worldwide have invested in FETDZ. Some of them are well-known transnational corporations such as JVC, Epson, Mitsubishi, Hitachi etc.

Main industries in the zone include electronics, electrical instruments, bio-pharmaceuticals, machinery, metallurgy, building materials, textile and other light industries.

Economic Development Bureau of FZETDZ
Tel: (86)(591) 368289, 3681122
Fax: (86)(591) 3684146
E-mail: mwwlzx@public.fz.fj.cn
Website: www.fdz.com.cn

XIAMEN HAICANG TAIWAN INVESTMENT ZONE

Our Rating:	AA
Year of Establishment:	1989
Location:	Xiamen, Fujian
Size:	100 sq km
Major Investors:	Kodak, Yude
Total Foreign Direct Investment:	USD1.94 billion (end March 2002)
Major Industries Encouraged:	Light sensitization, chemical fibers and plastics

INTRODUCTION

In May 1989, as trade activities became more common between Mainland China and Taiwan, the State Council decided to set up a Taiwanese investment zone in the Xiamen Haicang areas. Haicang Taiwan Investment Zone (HCTIZ) was established with a planned area of 100 sq km as the largest Taiwanese investment zone in Mainland China.

Haicang is located at the periphery of the Xiamen-Zhangzhou-Quanzhou 'Golden Triangle' area, overlooking Xiamen Island. It is only 10km from Xiamen international Airport.

By the end of March 2002, 178 foreign-invested enterprises have joined HCTIZ with total investment of USD3.98 billion, among which contractual foreign capital is USD3.35 billion and utilized foreign capital is USD1.94 billion. Among the enterprises, 48 Taiwanese enterprises had total investment of USD1.698 billion, contracted investment of USD1.64 billion and utilized investment of USD1.076 billion. An average Taiwan-invested project has reached USD35 million.

INVESTMENT CLIMATE

The investment for infrastructure deveopment is RMB22.4 billion. In Haicang Port, four 35,000-tonnage coal wharves have been built, among which two 50,000-tonnage container terminals were built by an international container company in collaboration with Hong Kong's Hutchison-Whampoa Ltd. Container throughput has reached 270,130 TEUs. A 22-kilometer Haicang Railway which services the port has been completed and has been integrated into the national freight railway.

Major foreign-invested enterprises include Kodak, Yude, etc. Major industries include film, chemical fibers and plastics.

Xiamen Haicang Administrative Committee
Haicang New Town, Xiamen Fujian
P. R. China 361026
Tel: (86)(592) 6051028
Fax: (86)(592) 6051048
E-mail: bgs@haicang.com
Website: www.haicang.com

FUZHOU FREE TRADE ZONE

Year of Establishment:	1992
Location:	Fuzhou, Fujian
Size:	1.8 sq km
Major Investors:	N.A.
Total Foreign Direct Investment:	USD481.5 million
Major Industries Encouraged:	Warehousing, processing, shipping, packaging and real estate

INTRODUCTION

Fuzhou Free Trade Zone (FZFTZ) was approved by the State Council in November 1992, and has a planned area of 1.8 sq km. The major supporting industries of the zone are warehousing, processing, shipping, packaging and real estate.

By the end of 2000, over 600 projects had been set up in the zone and 368 were foreign-invested projects. The total investment was USD1.03 billion, including USD545.96 million of domestic investment and USD481.5 million of foreign investment.

INVESTMENT CLIMATE

Fuzhou FTZ is 149 nautical miles from Keelung Port, 492 km from Hong Kong and 433 km from Shanghai. Several expressways as well as highways run through Fuzhou FTZ and the railroad network connects Fuzhou FTZ with other major cities in Fujian province as well as other parts of China. Fuzhou FTZ is 15 km from the international airport, where flights are available to Guangzhou, Hong Kong, Beijing and Shanghai etc.

Mawei Qingzhou Port is in the lower reaches of Minjiang River, and is the key part of Fuzhou Port. Shipping lines are available to Japan, the Philippines, Singapore and Hong Kong. The international container terminal has collabrations with the Port of Singapore Authority (PSA).

Fuzhou Port is located in the pivotal experimental area for the cooperation between Mainland China and Taiwan. The ship named Minyuan No. 1 frequently goes between Fuzhou Port and Kaoshiung Port.

There are five subsidiary zones within FZFTZ, namely international trade zone, duty-free processing zone, duty-free storage zone, duty-free wharf zone and high-tech zone.

In the International Trade Zone, international commodities fairs can be held. The duty-free processing zone is a combination of free trade and manu-facturing. Official tariffs will be waived for machines and equipment imported for production.

The Administrative Committee of Fuzhou Free Trade Zone
East Luoxing Road
Fuzhou, Fujian Province
P. R. China
Tel: (86) (591) 3983940, 3682059
Fax: (86) (591) 3982681
E-mail: invest@fzftz.gov.cn
Website: www.fzftz.gov.cn

XIAMEN XIANGYU FREE TRADE ZONE

Year of Establishment:	1992
Location:	Xiamen, Fujian
Size:	2 sq km
Major Investors:	N.A.
Total Foreign Direct Investment:	USD15 million (first half of 2001)
Major Industries Encouraged:	International trade, trade with Taiwan, entrepot trade, bonded storage and export-oriented processing, as well as related business such as finance, insurance, commodities exhibition, wharf management, transportation and information service

INTRODUCTION

Xiamen Xiangyu Free Trade Zone (XMFTZ) was approved by the State Council in October 1992, and the development area is 2 sq km. Xiamen FTZ is located in the northwestern part of Xiamen, with Dongdu Port to the west, the Port Railway to the east, Xiamen Bridge to the north and the Xiangyu Docks to the south.

Xiamen FTZ has been encouraging international trade, trade with Taiwan, entrepot trade, bonded storage and export-oriented processing, as well as related business such as finance, insurance, commodities exhibition, wharf management, transportation and information service.

By the end of 2000, total investment in the zone was RMB1.16 billion. In the first six months of 2001, the import was around USD150 million and the export was USD18 million. The amount of foreign direct investment during the half year was around USD15 million.

INVESTMENT CLIMATE

Xiamen FTZ is directly accessible by National Highway No. 319 and No. 324. It is 6 km from Xiamen Railway Station. which connects to the national railway network via the Yinxia Railroad.

Xiamen FTZ is 2 km from Xiamen International Airport, where frequent flights are available to Singapore, Penang, Kuala Lumpur, Jakarta, Manila, Hong Kong and major cities in China.

Xiamen FTZ is located in the area of the deepwater Dongdu Port, which is an important container terminal in South China.

The Administrative Committee of
Xiamen Xiangyu Free Trade Zone
Tel: (86)(592) 6035831
Fax: (86)(592) 6035830
E-mail: xiangyug@public.xm.fj.cn
Website: www.shinyco.com

XIAMEN HIGH-TECH PARK

Our Rating:	AA
Year of Establishment:	1990
Location:	Xiamen, Fujian
Size:	10 sq km
Major Investors:	Dell, Panasonic, National, Fuji, ABB, Genius Optical, Motic, EUPA, Bourns, Yaxon and Epteck
Total Foreign Direct Investment:	N.A.
Major Industries Encouraged:	Electronics, information technologies, telecommunication equipments, bio-pharmaceuticals, biological techniques and software development

INTRODUCTION

Xiamen High-tech Park (XMHTP) is located in the suburbs of Xiamen City, Fujian Province. It was established in December 1990 and was awarded the state-level status in March 1991. The park has a total area of 10 sq km.

In 2000, the sales revenue of enterprises in XMHTP was RMB11 billion and exports were USD550 million. Fifteen enterprises have annual turnover of more than RMB100 million. Among all the enterprises in Xiamen HTP, around 52% are engaged in electronics and information technology.

By July 2001, 26 of the Fortune 500 companies had established operations in XMHTP, such as Dell, Panasonic, National, Fuji, ABB etc. Other investors engaged in high-tech operations include Genius Optical, Motic, EUPA, Bourns, Yaxon and Epteck.

INVESTMENT CLIMATE

Xiamen HTP is divided into five subsidiary parks, namely Luqiao High-tech Park, Torch High-tech Park, Overseas Chinese Students Entrepreneurship Park, Xiamen Biological Park and Xiamen Software Park.

High-tech Park is the center for electronics and information technology. Overseas Chinese Students Entre-preneurship Park is focused on business initiated by Chinese students who returned from overseas. The enterprises are mainly in electronics, information technology and telecommunication equipment.

The Biological Park will focus on areas of biopharmaceuticals and biological technologies.

The Administration Committee of Xiamen High-tech Park
5th Level, North Guangxia Tower
Xiamen High-tech Park
Xiamen, Fujian
P. R. China 361000
Tel: (86)(592) 6035175
Fax: (86)(592) 6035174
E-mail: Torch@public.xm.fj.cn
Website: www.xmhtic.xm.fj.cn

FUZHOU HIGH-TECH PARK

Our Rating:	A
Year of Establishment:	1988
Location:	Fuzhou, Fujian
Size:	5.6 sq km
Major Investors:	Chunghwa Picture Tube Co. Ltd., JVC, Epson and South Coast Biology Project Co. Ltd.
Total Foreign Direct Investment:	N.A.
Major Industries Encouraged:	Electronics, information technologies, semiconductors, biomedicine, bioengineering, chemical engineering, metallurgical machinery

INTRODUCTION

Fuzhou High-tech Park (FZHTP) is located in Fuzhou, the provincial capital of Fujian Province. It was established in 1988 and was approved state-level status by the State Council in 1991. The total land area of the park is 5.6 sq km. FZHTP is tightly integrated with Fuzhou Economic & Technological Development Zone, the Free Trade Zone and the Taiwan Investment Area, which are all located in the city.

The development focus of Fuzhou HTP includes electronics, information technology, semiconductors, development of software products, biomedicine, bioengineering, chemical engineering, metallurgical machinery. Major enterprises such as Chunghwa Picture Tube Co. Ltd., JVC, Epson and South Coast Biology Project Company have joined Fuzhou HTP.

Fuzhou is located in the lower reaches of Minjiang River. With a convenient and well-developed transportation network, Fuzhou is a busy and prosperous city. It has easy access to Beijing, Guangzhou, Hong Kong, Shanghai, Shenzhen, Xiamen and many other major cities.

The Administrative Committee of Fuzhou High-tech Park
Tel: 86-591-3973933
Fax: 86-591-3975668
Website: www.fdz.com.cn/fzkjq.asp

XIAMEN EXPORT PROCESSING ZONE

Year of Establishment:	2000
Location:	Xiamen, Fujian
Size:	2.24 sq km (first phase is 1.46 sq km)
Major Investors:	Amoisonic Electronics, Sanli Automotive Components, Baite Plastic Packaging
Total Foreign Direct Investment:	USD60 million (contracted)
Major Industries Encouraged:	Information technologies, biopharmaceuticals, fine chemical engineering and precise machinery

INTRODUCTION

Xiamen Export Processing Zone (XMEPZ), the former Xiamen Xingling Export Processing Zone, was established with the approval of the State Council on 27 April 2000. It was renamed "Xiamen Export Processing Zone" in November 2001. The total planned area of XEPZ is 2.244 sq km.

XMEPZ is located at the southern part of Xiamen Haicang Taiwan Investment Zone. It is 10 km from Gaoqi International Airport; 1.5 km from Haicang Port and 3 km from Haicang Railway Station.

INVESTMENT CLIMATE

After more than a year of construction and an investment of RMB150 million, XMEPZ has completed the first phase of infrastructure construction such as roads, water and power utilities and other complementary facilities.

XMEPZ encourages export-oriented high-tech industries such as IT, bio-pharmaceuticals, fine chemical engineering and precision machinery.

XMEPZ Administrative Committee
2F CCB Building
170 Canghong Road
Xiamen, Fujian
P. R. China 361021
Tel: (86)(592) 6586665
Fax: (86)(592) 6586664
E-mail: webmaster@xmckjgq.com
Website: www.xmckjgq.com

FUZHOU SOFTWARE DEVELOPMENT PARK

Year of Establishment:	2001
Location:	Fuzhou, Fujian province
Size:	76.5 ha
Major Investors:	Chase Science, New Continental Computers, Power Source Communications, Straits Tianyin Computers, Ruidi Software Co. Ltd., Star Information Technologies and Fujian Fujitsu Communication Software

Fuzhou Software Development Park is located in Fuzhou. With a total development area of 76.5 hectares, the park is demarcated into two areas, namely the 1.5-hectare Software Development Center and the 75-hectare Software Industrial Base. Now, more than 2,500 professionals are working in the park, including more than 200 with doctoral degrees and master degrees in software engineering and relevant majors. The park is 3 km from downtown Fuzhou.

Among the enterprises of FZSDP, the performance of Chase Science Co. Ltd., New Continental Computers, Power Source Communications, Straits Tianyin Computers, Ruidi Software Co. Ltd., Star Information Technologies and Fujian Fujitsu Communication Software Co. Ltd. are impressive. Their products include Chinese voice intelligence system, MRP system, sea defense automatic commanding system, fingerprint system, electricity management system and color vision transmission system. Other important software companies in Fuzhou include Fuzhou Strongsoft Development Co. and Fuzhou Teleware Electronics Co.

Over 33 universities and colleges in the province provide essential intellectual resources for the development of software industries. They include Xiamen Unviersity, Fujian Normal Univerity, Fuzhou University, Jimei University and Huaqiao University. Xiamen University has established a software college in the city of Xiamen.

Administrative Committee of
Fuzhou Software Development Park
Venture Plaza
548 North Industrial Road
Fuzhou, Fujian province
P. R. China 350002
Fax: (86)(591) 3722394
Website: www.fzsoftwarearea.com

GANSU

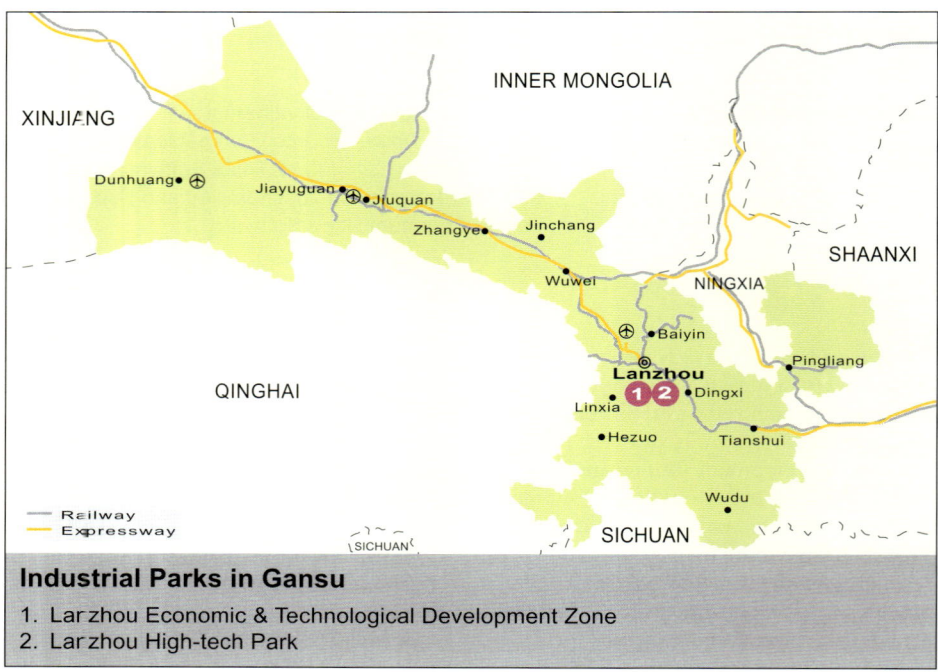

Industrial Parks in Gansu

1. Lanzhou Economic & Technological Development Zone
2. Lanzhou High-tech Park

INTRODUCTION

Gansu is known for various cultural relics such as the ancient "Silk Road" and Mongo Grottoes in Dunhuang. Gansu is a major agriculture base of Chinese medical herbs and together with the favorable conditions for developing animal husbandry. But she faces an adverse ecological environment with acute shortage of water resources, sparse vegetation and serious water and soil loss. In recent years, Gansu focuses on using biological methods, construction projects and technology measure to bring her soil erosion under control.

GEOGRAPHY

Gansu is surrounded by Qinghai-Tibet Plateau, Inner Mongolia Plateau and Huangtu Plateau. On the south is Sichuan, north is Inner Mongolia, Ningxia and Outer Mongolia and east is Shanxi. The provincial capital, Lanzhou, is a hub of transportation, communications and center of commerce and trade. Total land area of 390,000 sq km and population of 26 million, it is rich in minerals and in hydro-power because of the Bailong river, a branch of Yangtze River. It has large land resources too, but the percentage of utilizable land and cultivated land is low. Due to most of the areas are plateau and mountainous with an altitude 1,000 metres above sea level, temperature changes drastically during day and night.

Fact Sheet	2001
Area (sq km)	390,000
Population (million)	25.6
GDP (RMB billion)	107.3
GDP Growth Rate	9.4%
Consumption Expenditure (RMB billion)	
• Government	13
• Household	39.5
Per capita annual	
• disposable income of urban residents (RMB '000)	5.4
• net income of rural households (RMB '000)	1.5
Contractual FDI (USD million)	160
Industrial Value Added (RMB bn)	35.6
Imports (USD million)	303
Exports (USD million)	476
Universities & Colleges	25

TRAVEL INFORMATION

From Lanzhou Airport to:

Beijing	2hrs
Shenzhen	3hrs 15 mins
Guangzhou	2hrs 50mins
Shanghai Hongqiao	2hrs 25mins

INVESTMENT CLIMATE

Gansu is abundant in natural resources with 145 kinds of minerals, 659 species of wild animals, 441 species of birds and 951 species of Chinese medical plants. Though with her rich ecological environment, Gansu is also putting effort in readjusting its industrial structure and stepping up the static economic structure in order to increase government revenue problem and capital shortage. This is done to accelerate development of its resources based industries by implementing incentives to encourage foreign investment. Her oil refinery and petrochemical industry, two machinery manufacturing centers (Lanzhou and Tianshui), the industrial production of high speed cameras and tape making equipment, together contributed to the gross domestic product (GDP) and they formed the pillar of Gansu's economy. In year 2001, it has GDP of RMB107 billion, an increase of 9.4% over previous year. The proportional ratios of primary, secondary and tertiary industries are 19.3:44.8:35.9. The total industrial output was RMB48 billion.

The consumable market in retail sales was RMB39.5 billion, an increase of 9.02%. The foreign trade increased by 36.76% over year 2000 with its export at USD476 million and imports at USD303 million, which is an increase of 14.78% and 95.73% respectively. Her major trading partners are Hong Kong, US, Japan, Australia and Germany. The commodities include wheat, highland barley, millet, soybeans, wool, coal, petroleum, nickel, copper, sulphur and zinc. Actual foreign direct investment is USD160 million with major sources from Hong Kong, US, Philippines, UK and Taiwan.

In fact, Lanzhou is a major transportation hub in China with the intersection point of four trunk railway lines linking to Xinjiang, Qinghai, and crosses to Asia-Europe Continental Bridge. There were 3.8 million users for fixed & mobile telephone lines.

The population with college or higher education level increases rapidly. In 2001, a total of 25 higher education institutions recorded 111,000 persons received full time higher education and 45,000 new enrollments.

Gansu Provincial Government
Website: www.gansu.gov.cn

LANZHOU ECONOMIC AND TECHNOLOGICAL DEVELOPMENT ZONE

Our Rating:	BBB
Year of Establishment:	1993
Location:	Lanzhou, Gansu
Size:	9.42 sq km
Major Investors:	Gansu Langang Petrochemical, Weixin Pharmaceutical, Linkage System
Total Foreign Direct Investment:	N.A.
Major Industries Encouraged:	Fine chemical engineering, biotechnology & new pharmaceuticals, energy-saving & environmental protection technologies

INTRODUCTION

Lanzhou Economic & Technological Development Zone (LZETDZ) is established in early 1993. The planned area is 9.42 sq km.

LZETDZ is located at both banks of the Yellow River of Anning District and Qilihe District of the central part of Lanzhou City and includes both the north and south areas. It is demarcated into industrial, residential, commerce, high-tech, warehousing, free trade and integrated functional zones.

By June 1999, gross sales revenue of park enterprises was RMB1.43 billion, an increase of 40.3% over the same period a year before.

INVESTMENT CLIMATE

At present, developed land area is 1.59 sq km, completed construction area is 542,900 sq m, and investment for infrastructure is RMB1.83 billion.

Lanzhou is one of the hubs of China's 12 main transport backbones and is the integrated transport hub of the Greater Northwestern Railway, Expressway and air route. The West Freight Station is the largest freight station in the Western Regions and also a primary container transfer center on the New Euro-Asia Transcontinental Bridge.

Lanzhou is an integrated industrial base where the main industries are oil and chemical engineering, color metallurgy, mechatronics, light textiles. As part of the Yellow River Upstream Economic Zone and Longhai-Lanzhou-Xinjiang Economic Belt, Lanzhou plays the role of a key city in the Western regions.

Situated in the western part of China, most of Lanzhou's main productivity factors have a low cost advantage compared to coastal regions. The cost of power and water for industrial use is lower than coastal regions.

Lanzhou ETDZ Administrative Committee
324 Donggan West Road
Lanzhou, Gansu
P. R. China 730000
Tel: (86)(931) 8862469
Fax: (86)(931) 8882492

LANZHOU HIGH-TECH PARK

Our Rating:	BBB
Year of Establishment:	1998
Location:	Lanzhou, Gansu Province
Size:	29.18 sq km
Major Investors:	Three Star Petrochemical, Langang Petro-chemical, Weixin Pharmaceutical, Wan Wei Multimedia and Chee Zheng Tibetan Medicines
Total Foreign Direct Investment:	N.A.
Major Industries Encouraged:	Fine chemical engineering, bio-technology and new pharmaceutical, energy-saving and environment friendly technologies and information technologies

INTRODUCTION

Lanzhou High-tech Park (LZHTP) is located in the suburbs of Lanzhou, the capital city of Gansu Province. It was approved by the State Council in March 1992 and is the only such park in the province. It in the suburb area of Lanzhou, and has a total planned area of 29.18 sq km.

Over 500 enterprises have registered and moved into the park; 253 of them belong to high-tech industries and 237 are private enterprises. Among them, 29 enterprises have annual sales of over RMB10 million and five enterprises have annual sales of over RMB100 million.

Over RMB1.83 billion has been invested for infrastructure development in the newly built area of the park. The Lanzhou Yintan Yellow River Bridge has been built with total investment of RMB171 million. Another key infrastructure project is the Lanzhou No. 2 Telecommunication Network Pivot Project, with total investment of RMB568 million.

INVESTMENT CLIMATE

With increasingly improved investment climate in the park, many enterprises have chosen Lanzhou HTP. The major investors are Three Star Petrochemical Co Ltd (threestar.com.cn), Langang Petrochemical Co Ltd, Weixin Pharmaceutical Co Ltd, Wan Wei Multimedia Co Ltd and Chee Zheng Tibetan Medicines Co. Ltd. (chee-zheng.com.cn).

Lanzhou has rich human resources. The park enjoys an extensive cooperation with various high education institutes such as Lanzhou University (lzu.edu.cn), Gansu University of Technology (gsut.edu.cn), Northwest Normal University (nwnu.edu.cn) and Gansu Agricultural University.

The Administrative Committee of Lanzhou High-tech Park
Email: smc@gansu.gov.cn

GUANGDONG

Industrial Parks in Guangdong

1. Daya Bay Economic & Technological Development Zone
2. Guangzhou Development Zones
3. Nansha Economic & Technological Development Zone
4. Zhanjiang Economic & Technological Development Zone
5. Huizhou Huitai Industrial Park
6. Qingyuan Economic Development Experimental Zone
7. Shantou Free Trade Zone
8. Shenzhen Free Trade Zones
9. Shenzhen Grand Industrial Zone
10. Shenzhen Export Processing Zone
11. Shenzhen High-tech Park
12. Foshan High-tech Park
13. Zhongshan Torch High-tech Park
14. Huizhou Zhongkai High-tech Park
15. Zhuhai Free Trade Zone
16. Zhuhai High-tech Park

INTRODUCTION

Guangdong has played a pioneering role in China's economic reforms ever since the national opening policies carried out in the late 1970s. China's three SEZs (Special Economic Zones), namely, Shenzhen, Zhuhai and Shantou, are located in its coastal areas. The largest SEZ, Hainan, used to be a part of Guangdong before 1988. With Hong Kong and Macau at each side of the Pearl River estuary, the province has become one of China's most important economic engines, with its GDP exceeding a trillion RMB in 2001, leading all other domestic counterparts.

GEOGRAPHY

Guangdong is located at the south end of the Chinese mainland, with a coastline of about 3,368 km and many islets scattered around South China Sea. The Pearl River within its territory is the third largest river in China. It forms a delta region economically

Fact Sheet	2001
Area (sq km)	177,901
Population (million)	77.83
GDP (RMB billion)	1,055.6
GDP Growth Rate	9.5%
Consumption Expenditure (RMB billion)	
• Government	158
• Household	451.5
Per capita annual	
• disposable income of urban residents (RMB '000)	10.42
• net income of rural households (RMB '000)	3.77
Contractual FDI (USD million)	13,435
Industrial Value Added (RMB bn)	471.9
Imports (USD million)	81,070
Exports (USD million)	95,420
Universities & Colleges	71

comparable to the Yangtze Delta in eastern China led by Shanghai.

With the third largest population in China, Guangdong is administratively divided into 21 municipalities, 31 county level cities and 45 counties. Overseas Chinese with Guangdong origin now number 22 million all over the world.

TRAVEL INFORMATION

From Guangzhou Airport to:

Beijing	2 hrs 45 mins
Shanghai Hongqiao	2 hrs
Xi'an	2 hrs 15 mins
Shenyang	3 hrs 15 mins
Hong Kong	1 hr
Tokyo	3 hrs 55 mins
Sydney	11 hrs 15 mins
Singapore	3 hrs 55 mins
Los Angeles	13 hrs

From Shenzhen Airport to:

Beijing	2 hrs 40 mins
Shanghai Hongqiao	1 hr 50 mins

INVESTMENT CLIMATE

In 2001, Guangdong's per capita GDP reached RMB13,612, about 12 times of that in 1978. It has been ranked top among all Chinese regions in terms of foreign trade, with exports accounting for more than one third in the national total. High-tech industries account for 23% in both total industrial value-added and total exports. Electronics and telecommunication products have become Guangdong's strengths, being ranked first in China for 11 consecutive years.

In 2001, another 5,317 new foreign projects were signed in the province. Among the Fortune 500 MNCs, 250 have already set up their operations.

The province has established many industrial parks, especially in Guangzhou and Shenzhen. They include 4 state-level ETDZs, 6 FTZs, 2 EPZs, 10 high-tech parks at state or provincial level, and 50 development zones. High-tech, electromechanical and petrochemical industries are the future directions.

Guangdong Provincial Government
Website: www.gd.gov.cn
Guangdong Provincial Development Commission
Website: www.invest.gd.gov.cn
Foreign Investment Promotion Center
Guangdong Provincial Department of Foreign Trade and Economic Cooperation
Room 418 DOFTEC Building
351 Tianhe Road, Guangzhou
Guangdong
P. R. China 510620
Tel: (86)(20) 38819398, 38819399
Fax: (86)(20) 38819393
Email: tousu@gddoftec.gov.cn
cujin@gddoftec.gov.cn
Website: www.gddoftec.gov.cn

DAYA BAY ECONOMIC AND
TECHNOLOGICAL DEVELOPMENT ZONE

Our Rating:	BBB
Year of Establishment:	1993
Location:	Huizhou, Guangdong
Size:	150 sq km
Major Investors:	CNOOC - Shell Petrochemicals
Total Foreign Direct Investment:	USD29.37 million
Major Industries Encouraged:	Petrochemical engineering, electronics and information technology

INTRODUCTION

Daya Bay Economic & Technological Development Zone (DYBETDZ) in Huizhou City was established by the State Council in May 1993. As for Daya Bay, it occupies 268 sq km of land area and 488 sq km of sea area. Its coastline is 51 km long.

DYBETDZ is situated in the south of Huizhou, Guangdong province, and borders Shanwei in the east and Shenzhen in the west. It is 60 km from Hong Kong by land, and 47 nautical miles from Hong Kong's central harbor by sea.

INVESTMENT CLIMATE

Shenzhen Airport, 70 km away from Daya Bay ETDZ, has been built as an international airport. Huizhou Airport, 36 km away from Daya Bay, has opened more than 20 domestic airlines for both passenger and cargo transportation.

The investment of CNOOC-Shell petrochemical project (formally called Nanhai Petrochemical project) totals USD4.05 billion. The foreign partner of the JV project is Shell (Nanhai) Private Co., Ltd under the British-Netherlands Shell Group, having 50% shareholding; the Chinese partners of the JV comprise two companies: CNOOC and Guangdong Investment & Development Co.,

Ltd. with 45% and 5% shareholdings respectively. The two Chinese partners merged to become Zhonghai Petrochemical Investment Co., Ltd to establish a JV with the foreign partner. The JV and local contracts were signed respectively in Beijing and Huizhou in end October 2000. In December of the same year, the JV named CNOOC-Shell Petrochemicals Co., Ltd was established in Huizhou. The project is scheduled to be completed and put into operation at the end of 2005.

The annual handling capacity of Huizhou Port reaches 14 million tons, while the storage capacity in warehouse area is 800,000 sq m. When the port is developed to its fullscale, the handling capacity can exceed 100 million tons.

Huizhou Daya Bay ETDZ
  Administrative Committee
Huizhou City
Guangdong 516081
Tel: (86)(752) 5579462, 5577773
Fax: (86)(752) 5573622
E-mail: hzdybzsj@pub.huizhou.gd.cn
Website: www.gddayawan.gov.cn

GUANGZHOU DEVELOPMENT ZONES

Our Rating:	AA
Year of Establishment:	1984 (GETDD), 1991 (GHIDZ), GFTZ (1992), 2000 (GEPZ)
Location:	Huangpu-Tianhe, Guangzhou
Size:	30 sq km (GETDD), 47.44 sq km (GHIDZ), 1.4 sq km (GFTZ) 3.05 sq km (GEPZ)
Major Investors:	P&G, Allied Signal, Pepsico, Baxter World Trade, Kellogg's, Warner-Lambert, Pfizer Owens-Corning, Amway Pacific, Colgate, Kimberly-Clark, Delphi, Mitsubishi Electric, Mitsui & Co., Nippon Steel, Matsushita, Sankyo, Itochu, Asahi Glass, Sumitomo, Casio, Showa, Yamaha, Tomen, Yakult, Schering AG, Linde AG, Bosch, Siemens, Lohmann Haas Pharmaceutical, IKA, TotalFinaElf, Carrefour, BHP, ICI Omicron, ABB, Nestle, Want Want, Dow Chemical, Hutchison, Swire Duro, Inchcape, Jardine M&E, Ting-Xin, President, Novo, Ericsson, LG etc.
Total Foreign Direct Investment:	USD1.3 billion (GETDD), USD115.2 million (GHIDZ), USD196 million (GFTZ)
Major Industries Encouraged:	Fine chemicals, food and beverage, electronics and electrical devices, raw material, machinery, and packaging materials manufacturing; bioengineering, information technology, optical-mechanical-electronic integration, and industries involving high and new technologies, high value added services

INTRODUCTION

Guangzhou Development Zones comprise of four state-level industrial parks: Guangzhou Economic and Technological Development District (GETDD), Guangzhou High-tech Industrial Development Zone (GHIDZ), Guangzhou Free Trade Zone (GFTZ) and Guangzhou Export Processing Zone (GEPZ). The area is the only one in China that contains four kinds of industrial parks under a single administrative committee.

GETDD is among the first batch of state-level ETDZ approved by the State Council in 1984. It has a total planned area of 30 sq km, and is divided into three parts of West Section, East Section and Yonghe Taiwanese Investment Zone.

GHIDZ is also one of the earliest state-level high-tech parks approved by the State Council in March 1991. It is made up of five sub-parks, namely, Guangzhou Science Park (GSP), Tianhe, Huanghuagang, and Civil Science and Technology Park, and Nansha Information Park. The total planned area is 47.44 sq km, of which GSP occupies 37.47 sq km. For a more efficient and pro-business management, the administrations of GETDD and GHIDZ were merged in December 1998.

GFTZ, approved by the State Council on 13 May 1992, lies to the north of GETDD. The total 1.4 sq km planned area is to be developed in two phases. The first phase of 1 sq km is to be developed for trade, warehousing, processing and wharf construction. The second phase, started in 1997, is targeted to be an IT base with a computer industrial city planned. In August 2001, the government of Guangzhou decided that GFTZ merge into GETDD. And on 7 June 2002, it formally became an integrated part of the development zone.

GEPZ is the latest member of the grand Guangzhou Development Zones. It was approved in April 2000 by the State Council with other 14 counterparts across China. Located in the East Section of GETDD, the 3.05 sq km area is solely dedicated to export processing and related logistics. A starting phase of 90 ha has been put into operation under 24-hour Customs supervision.

GEOGRAPHY

Guangzhou Development Zones are located in the center of the Pearl River Delta, the most developed area of South China. GETDD lies 30 km to the east of downtown Guangzhou, 120 km away from Shenzhen and 65 nautical miles from Hong Kong by waterway. GSP of GHIDZ is 15 km east to the city of Guangzhou.

The zones boast of easy and convenient land and water transportation. Running across GETDD and GHIDZ is a network of highways and expressways in all directions, including Guangzhou-Shenzhen First-class National Highway, Guangzhou-Shantou Highway, Guangzhou-Shenzhen-Zhuhai Expressway, and Guangzhou-Huizhou Expressway.

Guangzhou-Shenzhen Railway runs through the East Section of GETDD. Huangpu Newport, situated in the West Section of GETDD, is connected to Xiayuan

Marshalling Station by a branch line of freight transport railway. It is the largest container port in South China, with 12 deepwater berths over 20,000-tonnage. Together with special wharves for coal and petroleum, the total annual handling capacity exceeds 60 million tons.

Ferries between Guangzhou and Hong Kong are also available in West Section of GETDD. The journey takes one hour and 50 minutes.

Baiyun Airport, one of China's top three international airports, is 41 km away or a 35-minute ride from GETDD via expressway. Air routes link to all major domestic cities in China and international destinations, such as Manila, New York, Osaka, Bangkok, Singapore, Sydney, Melbourne and Los Angeles.

Key statistics

The key statistics of GETDD, GHIDZ and GFTZ of 2001 are shown in the following table:

Industrial Park	GETDD	GHIDZ	GFTZ
GDP (RMB billion)	17.34	-	2.99
Total industrial output (RMB billion)	43.4	15.83	-
Total fiscal revenue (RMB million)	5,630	-	111
Contractual FDI (USD million)	1,296	115.2	196
Utilized FDI (USD million)	500.1	61.73	128
Export (USD million)	251.5	77.31	168

INVESTMENT CLIMATE

Infrastructure

Water supply in the industrial parks can satisfy all enterprises' daily industrial and sanitary needs. For instance, the water plant in West Section is designed to supply 80,000 tons of water per day. There is also a sewage treatment plant with a handling capacity of 30,000 cu m of per day.

Power supply is sufficient as it is supported by the Guangdong Grand Power Network. Specific heat supply center, installed with two sets of 10 tons/hr boilers and two sets of 4 tons/hr boilers, has been set up in GETDD.

A program-controlled digital microwave telephone system of 16,000 lines is available in GETDD, providing DDD, IDD calls, telex, electronic data transmission, facsimile services. Cable TV system is also available in the parks.

For the convenience and better living of expatriates and staff of the enterprises, well-equipped hospitals, health centers, banks, hotels, recreational centers, gyms, educational institutions including kindergartens, primary and high schools have been set up in GETDD.

Foreign-invested enterprises

GETDD and GHIDZ have approved more than 1,100 foreign-invested projects, among which 386 industrial enterprises have already been put into operation. Fifty-five MNCs of "Fortune Global 500" have set up their enterprises there with investors from 33 countries and regions worldwide. Major investors include P&G, Allied Signal, Pepsico, Baxter, Kellogg's, Warner-Lambert, Pfizer, Owens-Corning, Amway, Colgate, Kimberly-Clark, Delphi from the US, Mitsubishi Electric, Mitsui & Co., Nippon Steel, Matsushita, Sankyo, Itochu, Asahi Glass, Sumitomo, Casio, Showa, Yamaha, Tomen, Yakult from Japan, Reckitt & Colman, Watcombe, Fosroc, Thorn Lighting from UK, Schering, Linde, Siemens, IKA, Ibg and Bosch from Germany, Coates Larillux, TotalFinaElf, Schneider, Atofina, SAT Telecom from France, ICI, Avery Dennison, Akzo Nobel from the Netherlands, Want Want, Elec & Elteck Huangpu from Singapore, Ting-Xin and President from Taiwan, and Hutchinson, Swire Duro, HK & China Gas from Hong Kong, etc.

Currently, fine chemical manufacturing, food and beverage, electronics and electrical devices, raw material, machinery and packaging materials manufacturing form the mainstay of industries in the development zones. The administration aims to build up an open economy led by high-tech industries in its second phase of advancement. Importantly, it will accelerate the constructions of GSP and GEPZ. By 2005, the whole area, supported by modernized industries and high value-added tertiary sector, is expected to account for one fifth of Guangzhou's economy.

Economic Development Bureau /
Investment Promotion Bureau
Guangzhou Economic and
Technological Development District
Guangzhou High-tech Industrial
Development Zone
Guangzhou Export Processing Zone
Guangzhou Free Trade Zone
703, Block A, Administrative Building
Guangzhou Economic and
Technological Development District
Guangzhou, P. R. China 510730
Tel: (86)(20) 82212159, 82224517,
82212192, 82224516
Fax: (86)(20) 82224515, 82212136
Email: invest@getdd.com.cn
Website: http://www.getdd.com.cn

NANSHA ECONOMIC AND TECHNOLOGICAL DEVELOPMENT ZONE

Our Rating:	A
Year of Establishment:	1993
Location:	Guangzhou, Guangdong
Size:	54 sq km
Major Investors:	GE, BAsF
Total Foreign Direct Investment:	N.A.
Major Industries Encouraged:	Electronics, information, new materials etc.

INTRODUCTION

On 12 May 1993, the State Council approved the establishment of Guangzhou Nansha Economic and Technological Development Zone (NSETDZ). Since then, Nansha has shed its former identity as a sleepy border town to join the ranks of China's state-level development zones.

On 23 July 1996, NSETDZ was approved by the State Council as a Class-A open port in China In the same year, Nansha ETDZ was ranked among "China's Top 50 Development Zones with Excellent Environments for Investment".

NSETDZ is near Hong Kong and Macau, and has the geographical advantages of being in the heart of the Pearl River Delta area as well as being the hub of transportation. The sea route distances from Nansha to Hong Kong and to Macau are 38 and 41 nautical miles respectively, and the overland distance between Nansha and downtown Guangzhou is 54 km. The area of Nansha ETDZ is about 54 sq km, approximately three times that of Macau.

INVESTMENT CLIMATE

Presently, 206 foreign-invested enterprises have been established in Nansha ETDZ by investors from 18 countries and regions worldwide, such as world-renowned multi-national companies like GE from the US, BASF from Germany etc. Nansha is now playing an increasingly important role as a pivotal point to boost the economic development in the Pearl River Delta area. Prominent foreign-invested enterprises in Nansha ETDZ include: GE Plastics (China) Co Ltd with total investment of USD120 million, the Chinese-Japanese Baogan & Jinchang Steel Ordering & Processing Co Ltd.

Within a radius of 60.5 km with Nansha at its center, there are seven airports, 200 km of freeways and about 27,000 km of highways. This radius encompasses 14 major cities, 420 towns and districts. All this reflects clearly the important role of Nansha as a hub of transportation both in maritime and overland traffic.

Nansha ETDZ Administration Committee
Butterfly Garden Nansha Harbor-Entrance Broadway Panyu City, Guangdong Province
P. R. China 511458
Tel: (86)(20) 84688120, 84688220
Fax: (86)(20) 84688119, 84687763
Website: www.nansha.gov.cn/e/index.htm

ZHANJIANG ECONOMIC AND TECHNOLOGICAL DEVELOPMENT ZONE

Our Rating:	A
Year of Establishment:	1984
Location:	Zhanjiang, Guangdong
Size:	9.2 sq km
Major Investors:	Canon, Gestetner, Schaan
Total Foreign Direct Investment:	USD480 million (end 1998)
Major Industries Encouraged:	biopharmaceuticals, chemical engineering materials, mechatronics communications, office supplies, agricultural by-products and foodstuff

Zhanjiang Economic and Technological Development Zone (ZJETDZ) was established on 29 November 1984 with the approval of the State Council. It has a planned area of 9.2 sq km, demarcated into a 1.2 sq km administrative district, a 3.2 sq km industrial district and a 1.4 sq km business and residential district.

It takes 20 minutes to drive from the ZJETDZ to the airport, railway station and port.

Zhanjiang Port, one of China's eight major ports, is a natural deepwater harbor. It has 24 above 10,000-tonnage berths, including a 50,000-tonnage oil wharf. It has an annual throughput of 17.86 million tons.

Presently, there are scheduled flights from Zhanjiang Airport to places like Beijing, Guangzhou, Hong Kong, Changsha, Shanghai, Shenzhen, Kunming, Zhengzhou, Xiamen, Guiyang, Chongqing, Zhuhai, Wuhan, Shantou, Haikou and Sanya etc.

ZJETDZ has attracted over 300 foreign investors from countries and regions such as Japan, the US, France, Liechtenstein, Hong Kong, Singapore, Taiwan, etc. By the end of 1998, there were 354 approved foreign-invested projects with USD480 million of utilized foreign capital, among which 17 project with investment total of more than USD10 million.

The main industries in the zone include biopharmaceuticals, chemical engineering materials, mechatronics communications, office supplies, agricultural by-products and foodstuff.

HUIZHOU HUITAI INDUSTRIAL PARK

Our Rating:	A
Year of Establishment:	1992
Location:	Huizhou, Guangdong
Size:	6.7 sq km
Major Investors:	Sony, SPG, Kenwood, Shinwa Industries, ATI Electronics, Urmet, Clipsal, Turbocomm and CoolerMaster
Major Industries Encouraged:	Information technology, electronics, mechanical-electronic integration, new materials, food and beverage

Huizhou Huitai Industrial Park is located at the southern part of Huizhou, Guangdong province. It is near Huizhou Customs Authority, Huizhou Airport and West Lake Tourism Resorts. Huizhou is about 80 km to Hong Kong and 130 km to Guangzhou.

Established in 1992, the initial start-up area of the industrial park is 1.78 sq km and it will be expanded to 6.7 sq km in the near future. By now, more than 30 foreign enterprises have joined the park, such as Sony, SPG, Kenwood, Shinwa Industries, ATI Electronics, Urmet, Clipsal, Turbocomm, CoolerMaster etc. The investors mainly come from Japan, the US, Italy, Australia, Taiwan and Hong Kong. They are engaged in industries such as information technology, electronics, mechanical-electronic integration, new materials, food and beverage production.

Encouraged industries include electronics, CNOOC-Shell supporting projects, tourism, forestry, food & beverages, chemical industry, railway, highway and hotels.

Administrative Committee of Huizhou Huitai Industrial Park
18 Huitai Road
Huitai Industrial Park
Huizhou, Guangdong
P. R. China 516006
Tel: (86)(752) 2600555
Fax: (86)(752) 2609880
E-mail: huitai@huitai.net
Website: www.huitai.net

QINGYUAN ECONOMIC DEVELOPMENT EXPERIMENTAL ZONE

Our Rating:	BB
Year of Establishment:	1991
Location:	Qingyuan, Guangdong
Size:	9.6 sq km
Major Investors:	Sina Mars Group, Yuejiang Auto Manufacturing, Rowa Electronics, Nanyuan Yinfong Chemical, Agile Manufacturing Chemical, Qingyuan Medical Rubber Products Factory, Qingke Chocolate Food, Jingtai Chemcial Fiber, and Fulong Polishing Material Factory
Major Industries Encouraged:	Automobile manufacturing, textile, chemical fiber, construction materials, electronics, food, chemical engineering and clothing

Total Foreign Direct Investment: USD112 million

Qingyuan Economic Development Experimental Zone (QYEDEZ) is located at Qingyuan city, Guangdong province. It is about 150 km to Hong Kong and 53 km to Guangzhou, the provincial capital. The experimental zone is 60 km to Guangzhou Baiyun International Airport and 34 km to the newly built international airport. The railway station and port are both just 10 km away.

Established in 1991, the initial start-up area of the industrial park is 4.9 sq km and the total planned area is around 9.6 sq km. By the end of 2001, 215 enterprises had established operations in the zone, such as Sina Mars Group, Yuejiang Auto Manufacturing, Rowa Electronics, Nanyuan Yinfong Chemical Co. Ltd., Agile Manufacturing Chemical Co. Ltd., Qingyuan Medical Rubber Products Factory Qingke Chocolate Food Co. Ltd., Jingtai Chemcial Fiber Co. Ltd., Qingyuan Fulong Polishing Material Factory, etc. Total investment of 65 foreign enterprises in the zone is around USD112 million. As an important part of its China business, Sina Mars APP had invested an amount of USD60 million for the joint venture. The investment commitment of Rowa Electronics and Yuejiang Auto Manufacturing are both above USD10 million.

As an essential part of the experimental zone, a Taiwan Investment Park has been established. It aims to develop into an export processing zone and free trade zone.

Administrative Committee of QEZDEZ
Tel: (86)(763) 3383848
Fax: (86)(763) 3483278
Website: www.qyedta.com

SHANTOU FREE TRADE ZONE

Year of Establishment:	1993
Location:	Dahao District, Shantou, Guangdong
Size:	2.34 sq km
Major Investors:	Goworld Lamination, Zhongwang Fabrics, Zhongxin Edible Oil, Huayi Biotech, Vastco
Total Foreign Direct Investment:	N.A.
Major Industries Encouraged:	Export processing, foreign trade, warehousing and transport, finance and information

INTRODUCTION

Shantou Free Trade Zone (SFTZ) is located in Dahao District of Shantou SEZ. It was approved by State Council in early January 1993, and has a planned area of 2.34 sq km. In December 1993, SFTZ passed the inspection by General Customs Administration and started hailing for foreign investment especially after 1996.

INVESTMENT CLIMATE

Situated at the midpoint of Hong Kong (179 nautical miles southwest) and Taiwan's Kaohsiung (180 nautical miles northeast), Shantou enjoys unique locational advantage in regional transit transportation. It has a long history of foreign trade and is among China's first four Special Economic Zones. Besides, 12 million ethnic Chao-Shan overseas Chinese – three times the current population in the area – including the famous Hong Kong tycoon Li Ka-shin, gives the city additional merit in attracting overseas funds. SFTZ is connected to Guangzhou and Shenzhen by expressways. At the same time, National Highway No. 324 links it to Xiamen in Fujian Province. Shantou is also the east terminal of Guangzhou-Meixian-Shantou Railway, which joins Beijing-Kowloon Railway at Longchuan. Flights are scheduled from Shantou to Hong Kong, Beijing, Guangzhou, Shanghai and other major domestic cities.

SFTZ has easy and direct access to seaports where shipping lines are available to 160 ports in over 40 countries and regions. A port for its exclusive use is just 500m away, where 30,000-dwt ships can call at directly. FTZ boasts low costs and factory rentals. Land for industrial projects is transferred at RMB240 per sq m or 50% of its original price, and factories and warehouses are leased out at RMB8-15 per sq m, allegedly one tenth and one fifth of that in Shanghai, respectively. As SFTZ eagerly welcomes foreign capital, the administrative committee provides "one-stop" service for all investment related documentation and formalities.

Administrative Committee of Shantou Free Trade Zone
Dahao, Administrative Building
Shantou, Guangdong
P. R. China 515071
Tel: (86)(754) 7590271, 7590990, 7590278
Fax: (86)(754) 7590127, 7590224
Email: ftzst@pub.shantou.gd.cn
Website: www.stftz.gov.cn

金海灣大酒店

GOLDEN GULF HOTEL

★ ★ ★ ★ ★

Member of China Famous Hotels Corporation
One of the 50 best star-rated Hotels of China
Member of International Golden Keys Organization

Add:96 Jinsha Road,Shantou,Guangdong,China

P.C.:515041

TEL:+86-754-8263263

FAX:+86-754-8265163

Toll Free Reservation:800—810—5198

HongKong Office:+852-23014138

E-mail:stgghotl@pub.shantou.gd.cn

URL:www.goldengulfhotel.com

Free Trade Zones
in Shenzhen

Shenzhen – the first Special Economic Zone (SEZ) of China, a dynamic and booming garden city – hails enterprises and talents from everywhere. Given unique location and distinctive incentives, the three Free Trade Zones (FTZs) – Futian, Shatoujiao and Yantian Port, become ideal places for foreign investors to access the enormous China market.

FTZs enjoy the most preferential policies in China. As a bonded system with EDI Customs clearance is adopted here, personnel, goods and currencies can get in and out at ease. High-tech industries, modern logistics and international trade form the core part of our FTZs' development.

Up to now, lured by unparalleled geographical advantage and perfect investment climate, 1,089 enterprises from 25 countries or regions worldwide have settled down with us. World famous brands and multinationals, such as Wal-mart, IBM, SGS-Thomson, ECS, LEO, Panasonic, Sumitomo, Itochu, Nippon Express, are full of confidence in their investments made with us.

The Administration is constantly seeking the best solutions to serve our investors and enterprises inside the zones – just to make sure you can maximize benefits out of your commitments.

深圳之保税区

SHATOUJIAO FREE TRADE ZONE

Year of Establishment:	1991
Location:	Shatoujiao, Yantian, Shenzhen
Size:	0.27 sq km
Major Investors:	ECS, LEO Group, Preview Technology, Spectrum Industrial, Chow Tai Fook Jewellery, TSL
Total Foreign Direct Investment:	USD350 million
Major Industries Encouraged:	Advanced export-oriented industries

INTRODUCTION

Shatoujiao Free Trade Zone (SFTZ) was formerly established by Shenzhen Municipal Government in 1987, the earliest of its kind in China. It was formally endorsed by the State Council on 28 May 1991. Although the small FTZ occupies only an industrial land area of 0.27 sq km and a residential area of 0.15 sq km, it is the predecessor to the other two FTZs later established in Shenzhen.

SFTZ is situated in the east of Shenzhen SEZ, one kilometer from Yantian Port and 2 km from the checkpoint to Hong Kong in the south. It is connected with the city by Wutongshan Tunnel to its west.

INVESTMENT CLIMATE

As the oldest FTZ in China, SFTZ had attracted many export processing enterprises at the beginning. There are 76 export-oriented enterprises in the zone, most of which are invested by investors from Hong Kong, Taiwan, Japan and the US. Their products are mainly computer mother-boards, monitors, intelligent toys, gold jewelry, textiles and garment and plastic products. In particular, a Gold and Jewelry Mansion has just been put into use for jewelry processing, exhibition and trading, having attracted jewelry dealers from Hong Kong like Chow Tai Fook and TSL. Two computer motherboard makers, ECS and Amertek, both funded by Taiwanese investors, ranked among the top exporters in China. Preview Technology and Spectrum Industrial are also doing well in SFTZ.

The rental of office space and plant building in SFTZ is about HKD35-45 and HKD19-36 per sq m per month, respectively.

Shenzhen Administrative Bureau of Free Trade Zones
No. 1, Guihua Road
Futian Free Trade Zone
Shenzhen, Guangdong
P. R. China 518038
Tel: (86)(755) 83590143
Fax: (86)(755) 83590154
Website: www.szftz.gov.cn

Investment Consulting Shatoujiao Free Trade Zone Service Center
Tel: (86)(755) 25260333

FUTIAN FREE TRADE ZONE

Year of Establishment:	1991
Location:	Futian, Shenzhen
Size:	1.35 sq km
Major Investors:	IBM, SGS-Thomson, JDS Uniphase, Nippon Express, Wal-mart, Great Wall Computer, Shenzhen SEG
Total Foreign Direct Investment:	USD1.569 billion
Major Industries Encouraged:	High-tech and modern logistics industries, warehousing. trading and exhibition

INTRODUCTION

Futian Free Trade Zone (FFTZ) was approved by the State Council on 28 May 1991. After the Customs' inspection on its enclosed territory on 18 February 1993, it was put into operation. With an area of 1.35 sq km and additional 0.33 sq km for residential purpose, FFTZ is located in the southern area of Shenzhen and directly links Hong Kong via Lok Ma Chau Bridge.

FFTZ remains the only FTZ in China that has direct access to non-Mainland territory. Hong Kong container trailers owned by FFTZ enterprises can get in or out of the zone freely. Approved private cars may also enter FFTZ from Hong Kong and be allowed to drive in Shenzhen SEZ.

INVESTMENT CLIMATE

FFTZ has been encouraging developments of high-tech and modern logistics industries as well as international and domestic trading in the zone. To date, over 763 enterprises from 22 countries or regions worldwide have set up their operations in FFTZ, mainly engaged in micro-electronics, computer and accessories, optical fiber communication components, bioengineering and pharmaceuticals. SGS-Thomson, together with its Chinese partner, Shenzhen SEG, has committed a total investment of USD220 million in super-large IC encapsulation testing and designing.

Next to Huanggang Customs checkpoint and the future Huanggang Subway Terminal to the east and Guangzhou-Shenzhen Express to the north, FFTZ enjoys unique locational advantages. The rental of office space and plant building in the zone averages HKD55 and HKD30-45 per sq m per month.

Shenzhen Administrative Bureau of Free Trade Zones
No. 1, Guihua Road
Futian Free Trade Zone
Shenzhen, Guangdong
P. R. China 518038
Tel: (86)(755) 83590143
Fax: (86)(755) 83590154
Website: www.szftz.gov.cn

Investment Consulting
Futian Free Trade Zone Service Center
Tel: (86)(755) 83590915

YANTIAN PORT FREE TRADE ZONE

Year of Establishment:	1996
Location:	Yantian Port, Shenzhen
Size:	0.85 sq km
Major Investors:	Liyou Industrial, Nippon Express Cargo Service
Total Foreign Direct Investment:	USD32 million
Major Industries Encouraged:	Warehousing, modern logistics, entrepot trade, bonded commodities exchange and exhibition, high-tech industries

INTRODUCTION

Yantian Port Free Trade Zone (YPFTZ) was approved by the State Council on 27 September 1996 and started operation on 8 January 1999. The initial phase of planned area is 0.85 sq km which is separated by Yantian Port Boulevard into the north (0.65 sq km) and the south (0.17 sq km) part. The two parts are to be linked by an insulated viaduct.

Located within Yantian Port, the fourth largest container terminal in China with 2.75 million TEUs handled in 2001, YPFTZ has direct access to the wharves. Through a local specialized railway, it also connects with Beijing-Guangzhou and Beijing-Kowloon Railway. With adjacent expressways, YPFTZ has a highly-developed land-sea transportation network.

INVESTMENT CLIMATE

Given the advantages of adjoining the port, YPFTZ encourages warehousing, logistics, entrepot trade, bonded commodities exchange and exhibition, especially in the south part of the zone that aims to be a regional logistics hub.

High-tech industries such as information technology, new materials, bioengineering, electronic-mechanical integration and software development, and industries related to the port will be introduced in the north part of YPFTZ.

Established enterprises in the zone include Liyou, Nippon Express and Yanping Man Fai Cargo Service, all providing warehousing and logistic services for trade leaders such as TOYS' RUS and Nike.

The rental of warehouse in YPFTZ ranges from HKD50 to 60 per sq m per month.

Shenzhen Administrative Bureau of Free Trade Zones
No. 1, Guihua Road
Futian Free Trade Zone
Shenzhen, Guangdong
P. R. China 518038
Tel: (86)(755) 83590143
Fax: (86)(755) 83590154
Website: www.szftz.gov.cn

Investment Consulting Yantian Port Free Trade Zone Service Center
Tel: (86)(755) 25354471

SHENZHEN GRAND INDUSTRIAL ZONE

Our Rating:	AA
Year of Establishment:	1994
Location:	Pingshan and Kengzi, Longgang District, Shenzhen
Size:	174.4 sq km
Major Investors:	N.A.
Total Foreign Direct Investment:	USD610 million (June, 2001)
Major Industries Encouraged:	Electronics and IT; and industries with advanced technology; financial, real estate, trade and other tertiary services

INTRODUCTION

Shenzhen Grand Industrial Zone (SGIZ), formerly known as Shenzhen Longgang Grand Industrial Zone, was established by the Shenzhen Municipal Government in July 1994. This large scale industrial area is intended to be the key industrial base for Shenzhen's future economic growth. Some special rules announced by the Municipal Government in December 2000 further showed the local authority's decision to expedite its development.

Covering a total area of 174.4 sq km outside the developed Shenzhen Special Economic Zone, SGIZ rides over two towns of Longgang Distric – Pingshan and Kengzi – where such a large parcel of land can be offered. Altogether, 109 sq km is suitable for development and construction, among which 31 sq km has been allocated for urban land use. Currently, the detailed control plan of 38 sq km central area has been completed, which includes a 3-sq km Shenzhen Export Processing Zone.

INVESTMENT CLIMATE

Infrastructure

Three longitudinal and three latitudinal highways, with widths varying from 30 to 80 meters, form the main frame of SGIZ's road system, radiating to Shenzhen-Guangzhou, Shenzhen-Huizhou, Shenzhen-Shantou Expressways. It is only 20 km from Yantian Port, 25 km from railway station, 40 km from Shenzhen-Hong Kong checkpoints, and 60 km from China's fourth largest international airport in Bao'an.

There are five water supply factories nearby with total capacity of up to 144,000 tons per day. The annual water supply may be increased ten times after Songzikeng Reservoir is connected to Xizhijiang Water Diversion Works.

The altitude of SEPZ ranges between 45-50 meters. A flood drainage and interception system guarantees SGIZ is flood-free. Sewage is channeled through various branch pipelines to trunk pipes for treatment at a water treatment factory.

The total load of power in the initial phase is 309,000 kW. There are three 110kV transformers, with a capacity of 50,000 kVA each, providing electricity for SGIZ. As Daya Bay Nuclear Power Station lies to the east and Shenzhen LP Gas Reception Station to the south of SGIZ, power and gas supplies are abundant.

At present, an equipped capacity of 3,000 programmed phone switching system is available for SGIZ. This will be expanded to 60,000. As underground piping has already been completed, an optical fiber and broadband network will make SGIZ more accessible in a world of information.

Two residential cum commercial districts will be developed in SGIZ, totaling three sq km. A complete range of facilities for living and leisure will soon be set up.

Key preferential policies

- SGIZ offers land at competitive prices to investors and exempts them from urban facilities fee at the initial stage of development. Prices of public utilities are under strict control. Low cost housing is also provided for key personnel of enterprises in SGIZ.
- Enterprise income tax is levied at 15%, which is equivalent to that in SEZs.
- Enterprises with operational terms not less than ten years are eligible for "two-year exemption and three-year half reduction" in income tax from the first profit-making year.
- High-tech enterprises may enjoy "two-year exemption and eight-year half reduction" in income tax and other preferential treatments.
- Infrastructural construction projects may enjoy "five-year exemption and five-year half reduction" in income tax.
- Products for export by foreign-funded enterprises shall be exempted from value-added tax (VAT) and consumption tax except otherwise stipulated by the State.

The Management Committee of Shenzhen Grand Industrial Zone and Shenzhen Export Processing Zone
Business Invitation Office (SEPZ)
No. 1 Lanzhu Road
Pingshan Town, Longgang District
Shenzhen, Guangdong
P. R. China 518118
Tel: (86)(755) 84622218, 84622220
Fax: (86)(755) 84622226

Business Invitation Office (Shenzhen City)
Floor 10, Commercial Bank Building
Shennan Avenue Central
Shenzhen, Guangdong
P. R. China 518031
Tel: (86)(755) 25879777, 25899833
Fax: (86)(755) 25879822
Website: http://www.szgiz.gov.cn

SHENZHEN EXPORT PROCESSING ZONE

Year of Establishment:	2000
Location:	Pingshan, Longgang District, Shenzhen
Size:	3 sq km
Major Investors:	N.A.
Total Foreign Direct Investment:	USD342.77 million
Major Industries Encouraged:	Export processing

INTRODUCTION

Shenzhen Export Processing Zone (SEPZ), one of the 15 Export Processing Zones (EPZs), was approved by the State Council in April 2000 and was put into operation on 31 March 2001.

SEPZ is an integrated part of Shenzhen Grand Industrial Zone (SGIZ). Located in Pingshang, Longgang District, it has an area of 3 sq km.

Surrounded by mountains and litchi trees, SEPZ is convenient in transportation: 60 km from Shenzhen Huangtian International Airport, 20 km from Yantian International Container Terminal, about 25 km from Pinghunan Railway Scheduling Station, about 40 km from Wenjindu, Luohu, and Huanggang checkpoints. Shenzhen-Shantou expressway is just next to SEPZ and a national first-grade highway runs through the zone.

INVESTMENT CLIMATE

SEPZ is set up with Customs seclusion and supervision facilities according to the requirements of the General Customs Administration. There is a 9.1 km long steel barrier with gates, checkpoints, closed circuit TV monitoring systems equipped. Wide roads crisscross SEPZ. Water plumbing and electricity supply are available. And the optical fiber and broadband transmission network are ready for use. It is an intelligent information industrial zone with superior infrastructure.

The Customs office stationed at SEPZ provides 24-hour services for the enterprises in the EPZ. An E-customs networking management system ensures efficient and hassle-free declaration, document review and customs clearance at one time. All the formalities required by Customs and other administrative organizations can be completed via a "one-stop" procedure in the EPZ.

**The Management Committee of
  Shenzhen Grand Industrial Zone and
  Shenzhen Export Processing Zone
Business Invitation Office (SEPZ)**
No. 1 Lanzhu Road, Pingshan Town
Longgang District, Shenzhen
Guangdong, P. R. China 518118
Tel: (86)(755) 84622218, 84622220
Fax: (86)(755) 84622226

Business Invitation Office (Shenzhen City)
Floor 10, Commercial Bank Building
Shennan Avenue Central, Shenzhen
Guangdong, P. R. China 518031
Tel: (86)(755) 25879777, 25899833
Fax: (86)(755) 25879822
Website: http://www.szgiz.gov.cn

SHENZHEN HIGH-TECH PARK

Our Rating:	AA
Year of Establishment:	1996
Location:	Shenzhen, Guangdong
Size:	11.5 sq km
Major Investors:	Legend, Huawei Technologies, Zhongxin Telecommunications, Kexing Biotech, Kangtai, Lucent Technologies, Philips, Perkin Elmer, Alcatel and Compaq
Total Foreign Direct Investment:	N.A.
Major Industries Encouraged:	Electronics, information technology, bioengineering, new materials and optical-mechanical-electronic integration technologies

INTRODUCTION

Shenzhen High-tech Park (SZHTP) is located in western Shenzhen. It was awarded state-level status in September 1996. The total development area is 11.5 sq km.

In 2000, total industrial output of park enterprises was RMB45.6 billion, and high-tech products accounted for RMB44.8 billion; total exports were USD1.8 billion; total investment for infrastructure development was RMB1.5 billion; total industrial output and exports of Shenzhen HTP reached RMB83.8 billion and USD4.58 billion.

INVESTMENT CLIMATE

The development focus of the park includes electronics, information technology, bioengineering, new materials and optical-mechanical-electronic integration technologies and products.

In Shenzhen HTP, a large number of top domestic enterprises such as Legend Group, Huawei Technologies, Zhongxin Telecommunications, Kexing Biotech and Kangtai have established operations. Major foreign investors that have invested in Shenzhen HTP include Lucent Technologies, Philips, Perkin Elmer, Alcatel and Compaq etc. As China's economy has grown, an increasing number of foreign investors have been attracted to Shenzhen HTP, such as IBM, Epson, Olympus.

Shenzhen HTP has established close relationships with many prestigious Chinese universities such as Tsinghua University, Peking University, People's University of China, Harbin Institute of Technology, Nankai University, and Hong Kong University of Science & Technology. Shenzhen Virtual University Park (SZVUP) now accommodates 40 Chinese and foreign universities.

Administrative Committee of SZHTP
Shennan Avenue
Shenzhen, Guangdong
P. R. China 518057
Tel: (86)(755) 6551512
Fax: (86)(755) 6551526
E-mail: webmaster@szhtp.com
Website: www.shipgov.net

FOSHAN HIGH-TECH PARK

Our Rating:	A
Year of Establishment:	1992
Location:	Foshan, Guangdong
Size:	7.55 sq km
Major Investors:	N.A.
Total Foreign Direct Investment:	N.A.
Major Industries Encouraged:	Electronics, information technology, bioengineering, optical-electronic-mechanical integration and new materials

INTRODUCTION

Foshan High-tech Park (FSHTP) is located in Foshan City, Guangdong. It was approved by the State Council in December 1992. The total development area of Foshan HTP is 10 sq km. Foshan city is located southwest of Guangzhou. About 500,000 residents are living in the urban area of Foshan.

In 2001, the total industrial output of Foshan HTP was around RMB18.6 billion. To date, around 70 enterprises have established operations in the park. Investors come mainly from the US, Japan, Canada, Sweden, Italy, Hong Kong and Taiwan.

INVESTMENT CLIMATE

A total of RMB3.1 billion has been invested in infrastructure development. The development of the park is fast, especially in the areas of electronics, information technology, bioengineering, optical-electronic-mechanical integration and new materials.

Foshan HTP has a well developed transportation system. Guangzhou, Hong Kong, Macao, Jiangmen and other cities in South China can be easily accessed by expressways.

Currently, there are 30,000 industrial enterprises in Foshan City. Among them, 12 companies have annual sales of over RMB1 billion and 276 have sales of over RMB100 million. Successful local enterprises include Foshan Ceramics, Kelon, Midea Group and Nanhai Sanlun. In 2001, total import-export of Foshan was USD6.36 billion; the accumulated FDI. At the end of 2001, there were 5,305 foreign enterprises in Foshan. Major MNCs such as GE, DuPont, Siemens, Thomson, Sanyo, Toshiba, Matsushita, Puhang and Nortel have established subsidiaries there.

FSHTP Administrative Committee
3rd Level, Building No. 10
Foshan Government
Dafu Road, Foshan
Guangdong Province
P. R. China 528000
Tel: (86)(757) 3386093
Fax: (86)(757) 3355686
E-mail: hitech@fs-hitech.gov.cn
Website: www.foshan.gov.cn/
   investment/kaifa.htm

ZHONGSHAN TORCH HIGH-TECH PARK

Our Rating:	A
Year of Establishment:	1990
Location:	Zhongshan, Guangdong
Size:	15.1 sq km
Major Investors:	Changhong Group, TCL Group and China National Offshore Oil Corp.
Total Foreign Direct Investment:	N.A.
Major Industries Encouraged:	Computer components, computer injection machinery, hydro-nickel battery, fine-chemical engineering, medical testing liquid, superior audio machinery, packaging and printing

INTRODUCTION

Zhongshan High-tech Park (ZSHTP) is located in the eastern part of Zhongshan. It was awarded state-level status in 1991. The park covers 15.1 sq km.

ZSHTP has 8 major industries, electronics, information technology, new energy, new materials, biopharmaceuticals, packaging and printing industry, electronic-mechanical integration and textile industry. Zhongshan is China's largest packaging and printing producing base. In 1994, healthcare technology R&D center was established.

INVESTMENT CLIMATE

In 2000, the total industrial output of park enterprises was RMB18.9 billion and the GDP was RMB4.39 billion. There are 5 major companies, namely Torch High-tech Group, Torch High-tech Shareholding Ltd, Zhongshan Port Industrial Group, Zhanjiabian Enterprise Group, Zhongshan High-tech Park Real Estate Co. Ltd.

To date, there are over 200 industrial enterprises in Zhongshan HTP, including 124 foreign-invested ones. Over 300 kinds of high-tech products have been developed in the park, mainly in computer components, computer injection machinery, hydro-nickel battery, fine welding pipe, fine-chemical engineering, medical testing liquid, superior audio machinery, color TV sets, packaging and printing.

As the hometown of Mr. Sun Yat-Sen, the pioneer of China's democratic movement, Zhongshan is 86 kilometers away from Guangzhou and 65 kilometers to Macau. The total population of the city is 2.36 million.

In 2001, the GDP of Zhongshan reached RMB35.94 billion (USD4.35 billion). The total foreign trade was USD6.09 billion and the utilized FDI was USD566 million. Weili Group and Robust Group are two of the most successful local enterprises. Changhong Group, TCL Group and China National Offshore Oil Corp. have established subsidiaries there.

Administrative Committee of Zhongshan Torch High-tech Park
Kangle Avenue, Zhongshan Port
Zhongshan, Guangdong
P. R. China 528400
Tel: (86)(760) 5597902, 5597906
Fax: (86)(760) 5592917
E-mail: info@zstorch.gov.cn
Website: www.zstorch.gov.cn

HUIZHOU ZHONGKAI HIGH-TECH PARK

Our Rating:	A
Year of Establishment:	1992
Location:	Huizhou, Guangdong
Size	8.8 sq km
Major Investors:	TCL Group, Macat Group, Fushen Garment Industries, Qiaoxing Telecommunications, Huizhou Petrochemical, Guanghui Group, Huizhou South Rare Earth Metal Materials, Huizhou Huaxing Telecommunications, Huizhou Aviation Technologies LG Electronics and Hong Kong Great Wall Electronics
Total Foreign Direct Investment:	N.A.
Major Industries Encouraged:	Electronics, information technology, optical-mechanical-electronic integration technologies and products

INTRODUCTION

Huizhou Zhongkai High-tech Park (HZHTP) is located in southwestern area of Huizhou City, in the southeastern Guangdong. With total area of 8.8 sq km, the park was awarded state-level status by the State Council in November 1992. It is 7 kilometers from downtown Huizhou, 68 km from Shenzhen and 90 km from Hong Kong.

By the end of 2000, 87 enterprises, among which 15 are high-tech enterprises, have joined HZHTP. The total industrial output of park enterprises was RMB13.6 billion, and the industrial output and export of high-tech enterprises was RMB11.69 billion and USD57 million respectively.

INVESTMENT CLIMATE

To date, over RMB340 million has been invested in infrastructure development. The development of the park is fast, especially in industries such as electronics, information technology, optical-mechanical-electronic integration technologies and products.

Successful local enterprises include TCL Group, Macat Group, Fushen Garment Industries, Qiaoxing Telecommunications, Huizhou Petrochemical Corporation, Guanghui Group, Huizhou South Rare Earth Metal Materials Co. Ltd., Huizhou Huaxing Telecommunications Co. Ltd and Huizhou Aviation Technologies. Increasing numbers of foreign investors such as LG Electronics and Hong Kong Great Wall Electronics have been attracted to HZHTP.

HZHTP is located near Hui-Shen (Huizhou-Shenzhen) Expressway and Jing-Jiu (Beijing-Kowloon) Railway, and has a well-developed transportation network. Huizhou University is the major local university.

The Administrative Committee of Huizhou Zhongkai High-tech Park
Tel: (86)(752) 2600059, 2603402
Fax: (86)(752) 2600059
E-mail: hzzk@pub.huizhou.gov.cn
Website: www.hzzk.org

ZHUHAI FREE TRADE ZONE

Year of Establishment:	1996
Location:	Hongwan, Zhuhai
Size:	3 sq km
Major Investors:	Siemens, MTU, Zhongfu, Livzon
Total Foreign Direct Investment:	N.A.
Major Industries Encouraged:	International trade, bonded warehousing, logistics, export-oriented manufacturing and processing, bonded goods display, financial and insurance services.

INTRODUCTION

Zhuhai Free Trade Zone (ZFTZ) was approved by the State Council on 3 November 1996. It was put into operation only after 28 October 1999 when a Customs branch was set up. With an initial start-up area of 3 sq km, it aims to expand to 6 sq km finally.

ZFTZ is located in the south part of Zhuhai SEZ and has direct access to Macau SAR via Hengqing Bridge and Lotus Bridge. It is 15 km distance to the city proper, 18 km and 45 km far from Jiuzhou Container Port and Zhuhai Habor, respectively. Zhuhai Airport lies 30 km in its southeast and Macau International Airports is just 8 km away.

INVESTMENT CLIMATE

So far, there are 81 enterprises registered in ZFTZ, of which the investors come from the US, Germany, Australia, Japan, Taiwan, and the two SARs of Hong Kong and Macau, covering industries of aviation, electronics, optical fiber, biopharmaceuticals, digital technology, audio equipment, packaging, furniture, and warehousing and logistics. Twenty enterprises are already in operation with a similar number under construction. Among others, the total investment of Siemens was USD45 million. Another Germany-based enterprise, MTU, also established a joint venture with China Southern Airline in aviation generator maintenance and the investment was about USD180 million.

Land cost in ZFTZ is relatively lower than in other places around Pearl River Delta. Subsidized by local government, land price is maintained at an affordable level of RMB166 per sq m approximately for 50-year use. The salary for a normal worker hired in ZFTZ ranges from RMB600-800 per month.

In 2001, the total industrial product sales and the value of warehoused and exported goods of ZFTZ enterprises both reached RMB500 million. FDI in ZFTZ shows accelerated growing trend this year, thanks to China's entry into WTO in December 2001.

The Administrative Committee of Zhuhai Free Trade Zone
Hongwan, Zhuhai
Guangdong, P. R. China 519030
Tel: (86)(756) 8824345, 8825123
Fax: (86)(756) 8824166
E-mail: zhftz@pub.zhuhai.gd.cn
Website: www.zhfreetradezone.org

ZHUHAI HIGH-TECH PARK

Our Rating:	AA
Year of Establishment:	1993
Location:	Zhuhai, Guangdong
Size:	9.8 sq km
Major Investors:	Dell, Flextronics, MEKTEC, Tomita Electronics, Hong Kong United Laboratories, Korea HANARO, Hong Kong Qingmu Electronics, Hong Kong United Laboratories and Yangtze Group
Total Foreign Direct Investment:	USD6.62 billion
Major Industries Encouraged:	Electronics, information technology, aerospace technology, environment protection technology and products, pharmaceuticals and new materials

INTRODUCTION

Zhuhai High-tech Park (ZHHTP) is located in the western part of Zhuhai City. It was awarded state-level high-tech park status by the central government in March 1993. It has a combined development area of 9.8 sq km.

INVESTMENT CLIMATE

Up to now, about 2,600 Foreign-invested enterprises, including 20 Fortune Global 500 corporations, have invested in ZHHTP. The major foreign investors include Dell, Flextronics, MEKTEC Manufacturing Corporation, Japan Tomita Electronics, Hong Kong United Laboratories, Korea HANARO, Hong Kong Qingmu Electronics, Hong Kong United Laboratories and China Yangtze Group etc. The accumulated foreign investment is USD6.62 billion.

The park consists of four subsidiary zones, namely Nanping High-tech Zone, Sanzao High-tech Zone, Xinqing High-tech Zone and Baijia High-tech Zone. In addition, there are some other specialized sub-areas within ZHHTP, such as Aerospace Technological Park, Entrepreneurship Park for Returned Overseas Chinese Students, Taiwanese Electronics Park, United Nation TIPS Development Zone and Zhuhai Software Park of Harbin Institute of Technology.

Several international banks such as Citibank, Standard Chartered Bank, Bank of East Asia and Great Atlantic Ocean Bank have established operations in ZHHTP.

The Administrative Committee of Zhuhai High-tech Park
230 Redhill Road, Zhuhai
Guangdong Province
P. R. China 519001
Tel: (86)(756) 2616399, 2616299
Fax: (86)(756) 2616099
E-mail: zhhitech@pub.zhuhai.gd.cn
Website: www.zhuhai-hitech.com

GUANGZHOU SOFTWARE DEVELOPMENT PARK

Year of Establishment: 1999

Location: Guangzhou, Guangdong

Size: 90 ha

Major Investors: Digital China, First International Computers, Sunwah Group, China Weal Business Machinery, Suntek Tech, Sigma Datas, FENet Royalstone, Excellence Network and Bonson Technologies

Guangzhou Software Development Park (GZSDP) was established in August 1999 as a software industry base under the State Torch Program. With a total development area of 2 sq km, the park comprises three subsidiary parks, namely Tianhe Software Park, Guangdong Software Park and Nansha Information Technology Park.

According to the development plan of GZSDP, its annual growth rate will be at least 30% and the total sales revenue of member enterprises will soon reach RMB13 billion. It is estimated that four or five companies will have annual sales of over RMB1 billion.

More than 629 enterprises have entered the park and started operation. Most of the member enterprises are specialized in software development and system integration with more than 16,000 employees. The enterprises of GZSDP account for about 80% of software companies in Guangzhou City. In 2000, the total sales revenue of GZSDP enterprises was RMB2.57 billion. Among these enterprises, 30 are key software enterprises of Guangdong Province; 14 have sales revenue of over RMB100 million in 2000, and four have been awarded the ISO9000 certificates. By the end of 2000, 51 foreign software enterprises established in GZSDP and the total registered capital was USD63 million.

Representative enterprises of the park include Digital China Guangzhou, First International Computers, Sunwah Guangzhou, Huanan Information System, China Weal Business Machinery Co. Ltd., Guangzhou Suntek Tech Co. Ltd., Sigma Datas Co. Ltd., FENet Royalstone, Excellence Network and Bonson Technologies. Overall, the total sales of software enterprises in Guangzhou Software Development Park accounted for about 10% of China's software market.

Guangzhou Software Development Park
11F, 888 Tianhe North Road
Guangzhou, Guangdong
P. R. China 510635
Tel: (86)(20) 87548833
Fax: (86)(20) 87548120
E-mail: info@thstp.com
Website: www.thstp.com

SOUTH CHINA UNIVERSITY
OF TECHNOLOGY SCIENCE PARK

Year of Establishment:	2000
Location:	Guangzhou, Guangdong
Major Supporting Institutions:	South China University of Technology
Major Investors:	South China Information Technologies, SCUT Computer Network Engineering, SCUT Software Research Center, Wanfu Biopharmaceuticals, Huajing Metallurgical Materials Industries and SCUT Computer Application Research Institute
Major Industries Encouraged:	Electronics, new materials, bioengineering, environmental protection and mechanical-optical-magnetic integration

South China University of Technology Science Park (SCUTSP) is the only national university science park in South China (Fujian, Guangdong and Guangxi). The 12-hectare main zone is located at the north campus of South China University of Technology in Guangzhou.

The total investment for infrastructure of SCUTSP will be around RMB300 million. According to the master plan, the industrial focus is on electronics, information technology, new materials, bioengineering, environmental protection and mechanical-optical-magnetic integration.

South China University of Technology can offer strong R&D support to SCUTSP enterprises. More than 5,000 students are pursuing degrees at master and doctoral levels. South China University of Technology has established links with many overseas universities, such as Tokyo Institute of Technology, University of Queensland, University of New South Wales, Georgia Institute of Technology, Texas Tech University, McGill University, University of Birmingham and University of Liverpool and the University of Hong Kong. With registered capital of RMB30 million and 22 member enterprises, Guangzhou Huagongda Group is the core enterprise of SCUT's affiliated industries.

At the same time, potential investors could take full advantages of other resources that Guangzhou can provide. It is the largest city in south China and is adjacent to Hong Kong. In Guangzhou, there are several prestigious institutions such as Sun Yat Sen University, South China Normal University, Guangzhou University, South China Agricultural University and First Military Medical University.

SCUTSP Development Corporation is in charge of the development affairs of the university science park. Preferential tax policy and other attractive incentives will be offered to enterprises in the park.

South China University of Technology Science Park Corporation
1st Level, Building Three
Wusan Road, Tianhe District
Guangzhou, Guangdong
P. R. China 510640
Tel: (86)(20) 87111098, 87111298
Fax: (86)(20) 87112133
Website: www2.scut.edu.cn/scientific/

Book, Newsletter, ...cument,
Research Report, ...nnual Report,
Newpaper Ar... ...nnual Report,
Initial Public Offer(IPO)Prospectus,
Training Manual, Handbook Review,
Professional Manual(engineering/IT),
Marketing Materials(catalog/brochure etc),
...pywriting, Branding, etc...

PROFESSIONAL TRANSLATION

Translation Process

Compliance with international standards with comprehensive quality assurance procedures on the translation.

Document Translation Service Scope

Translation of various business, legal, scientific and technological materials.

Source Languages

Traditional Chinese, Simplified Chinese, English.

Target Languages

Traditional Chinese, Simplified Chinese and English.

Domain Specialties

Business Management, Legal, Information Technology, Mechanics, Automobile, Electronics, Computer, Telecommunication, Medicine, Chemical, Petroleum and Natural Gas, Energy, Environment Protection, and Construction. Other domain specialties are available upon request.

Website: www.chinaknowledge-press.com E-mail: info@chinaknowledge.com

CHINA MARKET RESEARCH

China Knowledge Press (CKP) provides independent insight, analysis, and in-depth research reports to investors worldwide. Our founding principle is "the investor's right to know"- providing the most up-to-date, accurate and reliable research and information on China

CKP has more than fifty experienced China specialists from diverse industries which include international investment banking, market research, publishing, press and rating agencies. In addition, CKP also collaborate with top Chinese universities and other market specialists to fulfill our clients' specific needs.

With experience and expertise, as well as our extensive research network in China, CKP has developed a series of unique products – China Market Research Report (CMRR). We achieve high-quality research reports by utilizing experienced professionals, tailored methodologies and rigorous standards of quality control.

Let CKP's unique China Market Research Reports assist you in making strategic market decisions and managing risks in China's growing market.

ADVERTISING

CHINA MARKET RESEARCH

ADVERTISING INDUSTRY

Advertising

Market Analysis
& Outlook

China Knowledge Press

APPAREL

CHINA MARKET RESEARCH

SPORTS APPARELS MARKET

Apparel

Market Analysis
& Outlook

China Knowledge Press

ADVERTISING

CHINA MARKET RESEARCH

ADVERTISING INDUSTRY

Advertising

Market Analysis
& Outlook

China Knowledge Press

BANKING & FINANCE

CHINA MARKET RESEARCH

INVESTMENT BANKING INDUSTRY

Banking & Finance

Market Analysis
& Outlook

China Knowledge Press

Co-published by
Genetick Capital

CHINA MARKET RESEARCH

FUND MANAGEMENT INDUSTRY

Banking & Finance

Market Analysis
& Outlook

China Knowledge Press

Co-published by
Genetick Capital

CHINA MARKET RESEARCH

VENTURE CAPITAL & PRIVATE EQUITY FIRMS

Banking & Finance

Market Analysis
& Outlook

China Knowledge Press

Co-published by
Genetick Capital

AUTOMOTIVE

CHINA MARKET RESEARCH

AUTOMOBILE INDUSTRY IN CHINA
(Volume I)

Automotive

Market Analysis
& Outlook

China Knowledge Press

CHINA MARKET RESEARCH

AUTOMOBILE INDUSTRY IN CHINA
(Volume II)

Automotive

Market Analysis
& Outlook

China Knowledge Press

CONSTRUCTION

CHINA MARKET RESEARCH

CONSTRUCTION MATERIALS MARKET

Construction

Market Analysis
& Outlook

China Knowledge Press

ENERGY

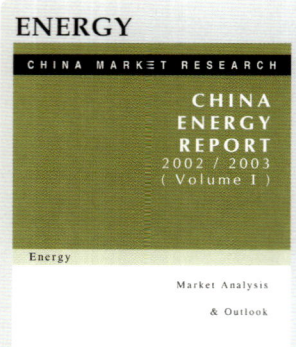

CHINA MARKET RESEARCH

**CHINA
ENERGY
REPORT**
2002 / 2003
(Volume I)

Energy

Market Analysis
& Outlook

China Knowledge Press

CHINA MARKET RESEARCH

**CHINA
ENERGY
REPORT**
2002 / 2003
(Volume II)

Energy

Market Analysis
& Outlook

China Knowledge Press

FOOD & BEVERAGE

CHINA MARKET RESEARCH

**FAST FOOD
RESTAURANTS
IN SHANGHAI**

Food & Beverage

Market Analysis
& Outlook

China Knowledge Press

HEALTHCARE

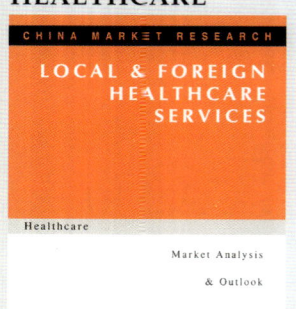

CHINA MARKET RESEARCH

**LOCAL & FOREIGN
HEALTHCARE
SERVICES**

Healthcare

Market Analysis
& Outlook

China Knowledge Press

IT TELECOMMUNICATION

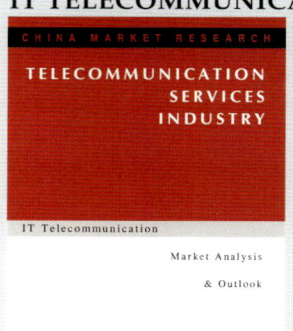

CHINA MARKET RESEARCH

**TELECOMMUNICATION
SERVICES
INDUSTRY**

IT Telecommunication

Market Analysis
& Outlook

China Knowledge Press

CHINA MARKET RESEARCH

**SOFTWARE
INDUSTRY**

IT Telecommunication

Market Analysis
& Outlook

China Knowledge Press

PROFESSIONAL SERVICES

CHINA MARKET RESEARCH

**ACCOUNTING
SERVICE
MARKET**

Professional Services

Market Analysis
& Outlook

China Knowledge Press

CHINA MARKET RESEARCH

**LEGAL SERVICE
MARKET**

Professional Services

Market Analysis
& Outlook

China Knowledge Press

PUBLISHING

CHINA MARKET RESEARCH

**PUBLISHING
IN CHINA**
A Special Report
& Industry Outlook

Publishing

Market Analysis
& Outlook

China Knowledge Press

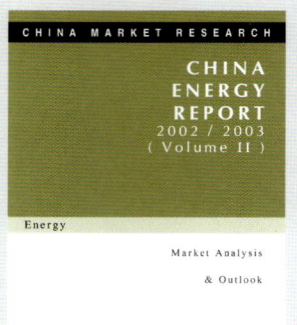

PETROCHEMICAL

CHINA MARKET RESEARCH

PETROCHEMICAL INDUSTRY IN CHINA
2002 / 2003
(Volume I)

Petrochemical

Market Analysis

& Outlook

China Knowledge Press

CHINA MARKET RESEARCH

PETROCHEMICAL INDUSTRY IN CHINA
2002 / 2003
(Volume II)

Petrochemical

Market Analysis

& Outlook

China Knowledge Press

CHINA MARKET RESEARCH

PETROCHEMICAL INDUSTRY IN CHINA
2002 / 2003
(Volume III)

Petrochemical

Market Analysis

& Outlook

China Knowledge Press

LOGISTICS

CHINA MARKET RESEARCH

LOGISTICS & SHIPPING INDUSTRY

Logistics & Shipping

Market Analysis

& Outlook

China Knowledge Press

REAL ESTATES

CHINA MARKET RESEARCH

REAL ESTATES MARKET IN SHANGHAI

Real Estates

Market Analysis

& Outlook

China Knowledge Press

CHINA MARKET RESEARCH

REAL ESTATES MARKET IN BEIJING

Real Estates

Market Analysis

& Outlook

China Knowledge Press

PULP & PAPER

CHINA MARKET RESEARCH

PAPER PRODUCTION & CONSUMPTION
YEARBOOK 2001 / 2002

Pulp & Paper

China Knowledge Press

RETAIL & WHOLESALE

CHINA MARKET RESEARCH

RETAIL SECTOR IN SHANGHAI

Retail & Wholesale

Market Analysis

& Outlook

China Knowledge Press

TEXTILE

CHINA MARKET RESEARCH

TEXTILE IMPORT & EXPORT
YEARBOOK 2001

Polyester Market

Market Analysis

& Outlook

China Knowledge Press

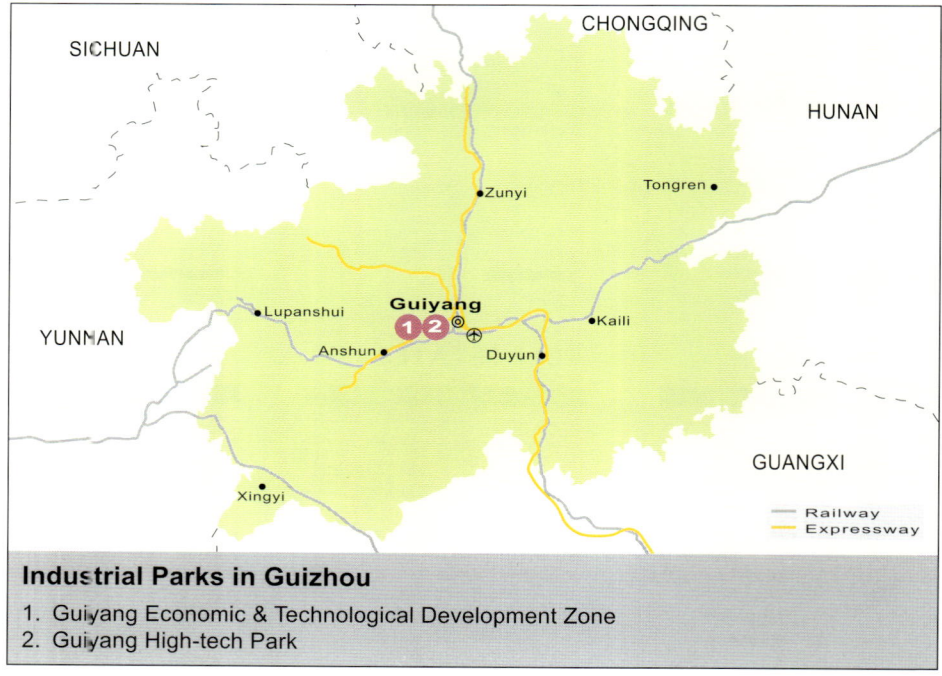

Industrial Parks in Guizhou

1. Guiyang Economic & Technological Development Zone
2. Guiyang High-tech Park

INTRODUCTION

Guizhou is one of the cradles for the ancient civilization of China. The province is rich in forest resources and boasts rich deposits of minerals, water resources and wildlife. It has particularly rich reserves of coal, phosphorus and mercury etc. Out of its 120 kinds of minerals, 21 kinds rank in the top three in China. There are over 3,800 species of wild animals and more than 3,700 kinds of medical herbs found in the province.

GEOGRAPHY

Guizhou is located in the mountainous regions of the Yunnan-Guizhou Plateau in Southwest China. These mountainous areas spread throughout 87% of the total land areas. The complex landscape varies in different waves and sizes of the mountain region. With most areas above 1,000 m in latitude, the province has three neighboring provinces: Hunan, Sichuan and Yunnan. The provincial Capital is Guiyang, which has been approved by the State Council of China as an inland open city. Other important cities include the province are Anshun and Zunyi. The provincial government had a jurisdiction of 9 prefectures and as many as 86 counties. The total land area is 174,000 sq km and the population is 35 million. There are various limestone sites and unique natural landscape in the province, which has a typical sub-tropical plateau climate but with high precipitation in the central and southwestern regions. Many minority ethnic groups are living in Guizhou, such as Miao, Buyi, Dong,

Fact Sheet	2001
Area (sq km)	174,000
Population (million)	35.2
GDP (RMB billion)	108.2
GDP Growth Rate	8.8%
Consumption Expenditure (RMB billion)	
• Government	18
• Household	60
Per capita annual	
• disposable income of urban residents (RMB '000)	5.1
• net income of rural households (RMB '000)	1.4
Contractual FDI (USD million)	28
Industrial Value Added (RMB bn)	33.5
Imports (USD million)	228
Exports (USD million)	422
Universities & Colleges	20

billion, an increase of 10% over the previous years. Exports amounted to USD422 million and imports to USD228 million.

Guizhou has a well connected transportation network in air, railway, expressway and highway. There are railways to provinces of Guangxi, Sichuan, Yunnan and Hunan. The new Yuhuai Railway is under construction and will be completed in 2006. There are a total of five state highways linking to cities like Shanghai, Kunming, Wanding, Nanning and Beihai. The utilized foreign direct investment in 2001 was around USD28 million, mainly in raw materials, plant equipment, non-ferrous and chemicals.

Guizhou Provincial Government
Website: www.gzgov.gov.cn

Yi, Shui, Hui, Gelo etc. Famous attractions of Guizhou are Huangguoshu Waterfall, limestone caves and many others.

TRAVEL INFORMATION

From Guiyang Airport to:
Hong Kong	1hr 25mins
Beijing	2hrs 30mins
Shenzhen	1hr 20mins
Shanghai Pudong	2hrs 10mins

INVESTMENT CLIMATE

Guizhou's rich reserves of minerals rank among the top in China. In 2001, the total production output of coal and phosphorus reached 37 million tons and 6.6 million tons respectively. In 2001, the GDP of Guizhou was around RMB108 billion, an increase of 8.8% over the previous year. The ratio of primary, secondary and tertiary industry was 1.1:11.4:12.1, and the total industrial output was RMB39 billion. In 2001, the retail sales of consumer goods, was about RMB37.8

GUIYANG ECONOMIC AND TECHNOLOGICAL DEVELOPMENT ZONE

Our Rating:	BB
Year of Establishment:	1993
Location:	Guiyang Guizhou
Size:	63.13 sq km
Major Investors:	N.A.
Total Foreign Direct Investment:	USD62.92 million (2001)
Major Industries Encouraged:	Mechanical engineering, power mechanics, machine tools, airplane components, automobiles and motorcycle components

INTRODUCTION

Guiyang Economic and Technological Development Zone (GYETDZ) was initially built in March 1993 and being authorized as a state-level Development Zone by the State Council in Feb 2002. The zone has a total area of 63.13 sq km with the first phase of 9.55 sq km.

GYETDZ is located in the southern part of Guiyang City, the provincial capital of Guizhou Province.

In 2001, the GDP volume of the zone was RMB1.21 billion, gross industrial output was RMB2.2 billion and total gross fiscal revenue was RMB130 million. There were 490 projects registered in the zone, with total investment of RMB8.3 billion and utilized foreign capital of USD62.92 million. The export totaled more than USD90 million.

INVESTMENT CLIMATE

There are more than 400 industrial enterprises in GYETDZ, among which 23 are medium to large state-owned enterprises and 25 are foreign-invested enterprises. Together, they have fixed assets of more than RMB4 billion.

Major industries including mechanical engineering, power mechanics, machine tools, airplane components, automobiles, motorcycle components, are promoted in the zone. There are more than 60,000 employees and 7,000 technical professionals.

Administrative Committee of GYETDZ
443, Huanghe Road,
Guiyang, Guizhou
P. R. China 550006
Tel: (86)(851) 3833531, 3830813
E-mail: geta@cnuninet.com
Website: www.geta.gov.cn

GUIYANG HIGH-TECH PARK

Our Rating:	B
Year of Establishment:	October 1992
Location:	Guiyang, Guizhou
Size:	11.3 sq km
Major Investors:	Zhenghua Group, Yungao Corp, Wanjiang, Xintian, Tian'an, Southern Jiangtong
Total Foreign Direct Investment:	N.A.
Major Industries Encouraged:	phosphorus chemical engineering, aluminum chemical engineering, mechanical engineering, measuring instrument and grinding machinery

INTRODUCTION

Guiyang High-tech Park (GYHTP) is located in the northeast part of Guiyang. It is a state-level park awarded by the State Council in October 1992. The total area of the park is 11.3 sq km. In 1998, GYHTP was divided into three sub-zones according to the new development plan, namely the Golden Sun Technological Park, the New Sky Industrial Park and the Magic Technologies Street.

The major industries of the park include phosphorus chemical engineering, aluminum chemical engineering, mechanical engineering, measuring instrument, fine optical instruments and pharmaceuticals.

INVESTMENT CLIMATE

To date, over RMB1 billion has been invested for the infrastructure development. GYHTP is 6.5 km away from the downtown area of the city, 25 km from Longdongbao International Airport and 12 km from the railway station. Air routes are available to Hong Kong, Guangzhou, Shanghai, Shenzhen and other major Chinese cities.

As the capital city of Guizhou province, Guiyang is the economic and cultural center of the province. The city is famous for its rich natural resources. It is called China's Tennessee because of the rich hydrolic and power resources. Additionally, it has rich resources like coal, phosphorus and aluminum.

Guiyang High-tech Park
Administrative Committee
Guiyang, Guizhou
P. R. China 550022
Tel: (86)(851) 4720441
Fax: (86)(851) 4720443
Website: www.guz.cei.cn/kfc/
home.htm

New Sky Industrial Park
New Sky Avenue, Guiyang
Guizhou Province
P. R. China 550018
Tel: (86)(851) 6460673

HAINAN

Industrial Parks in Hainan

1. Yangpu Economic Development Zone
2. Haikou Free Trade Zone
3. Haikou High-tech Park

INTRODUCTION

Hainan was separated out from Guangdong Province by the central government in September 1987. In April 1988, it was designated as the fifth Special Economic Zone (SEZ) in China, the last but largest one following Shenzhen, Xiamen, Zhuhai and Shantou. Since then, the transformation has exerted profound impact on its independent pursuit of economic development.

GEOGRAPHY

Located in the southernmost part of Chinese administrative map, Hainan, the second largest island next to Taiwan, was mostly known as an tropical tourist heaven. It is the only province in China that lies entirely south to the Tropic of Cancer. Rainfall descends from the east coast to the southwest, ranging between 2,400 mm and 900 mm.

The territory consists of two major cities at municipality level, including Haikou and Sanya, and 17 counties or county-level cities. Among the 7.96 million population, 17.3% are of minorities. Li, taking a share of 16%, forms the largest group besides Han people.

TRAVEL INFORMATION

There are two international airports located in Haikou and Sanya.

From Haikou Airport to:

Fact Sheet	2001
Area (sq km)	34,000
Population (million)	7.96
GDP (RMB billion)	56.61
GDP Growth Rate	8.9%
Consumption Expenditure (RMB billion)	
• Government	5
• Household	18.7
Per capita annual	
• disposable income of urban residents (RMB '000)	5.8
• net income of rural households (RMB '000)	3.0
Contractual FDI (USD million)	467
Industrial Value Added (RMB bn)	9.11
Imports (USD million)	961
Exports (USD million)	801
Universities & Colleges	9

Beijing	3 hrs 30 mins
Shanghai Pudong	2 hrs 30 mins
Guangzhou	1 hr
Nanchang	1 hr 45 mins
Chengdu	2 hrs 15 mins
Sanya	30 mins
Hong Kong	1 hr

INVESTMENT CLIMATE

Since its inception of SEZ in 1988, Hainan has greatly developed its infrastructure, in particular the island-wide road system, seaport and airport facilities, to lure visitors as well as foreign investors. The local economy has maintained a moderate growth vis-à-vis the other four SEZs. In 2001, the province's GDP stood at USD6.86, with an annual increase of 8.9%. However, FDI inflow and exports both showed signs of decline.

Abundant agricultural resources and beautiful landscapes are the two main attractions of Hainan that may become future growth engines for the island's economy. Seabed oilfields in the continental shelf around Spratly Islands may well offer promising opportunities for further exploration.

The province government is also making efforts to boost its lagged industrial capabilities. A few development zones have been nominated and foundations are being laid. Yangpu Economic and Technological Development Zone, comprising an allocated area of free trade zone, tops the list. It sits on the west coast of the island and aims at being a modern industrial port city

Hainan Provincial Government
Website: www.hainan.gov.cn

Foreign Investment Administration Office
Hainan Department of Foreign Trade and Economic Cooperation
Tel: (86)(898) 65342064, 65343636
Fax: (86)(898) 65338762
Website: www.doftec.hainan.gov.cn

YANGPU ECONOMIC DEVELOPMENT ZONE

Our Rating:	B
Year of Establishment:	1992
Location:	Yangpu, Hainan
Size:	31 sq km
Major Investors:	N.A.
Total Foreign Direct Investment:	USD 82.75 million
Major Industries Encouraged:	Parquet flooring, rubber processing, paper pulp, flour processing, automobile engine assembling and electric machine iron core manufacturing

INTRODUCTION

Yangpu Economic Development Zone (YEDZ, a State-level Economic and Development Zone approved by the State Council, was established in March 1992 with land area of 31 sq km. YEDZ is located in Yangpu Peninsula in northwest Hainan Province, surrounded by the sea on three sides, with a 24 km long coastline. YEDZ enjoys the preferential policies of a special economic zone.

INVESTMENT CLIMATE

In 2001, gross import and export of YEDZ was USD176million. More than RMB5 billion has been invested into YEDZ for infrastructure development, the GDP is RMB 325.6 million. By the end of 2001, 24 foreign investment projects had been set up in the park with contractual investment of USD 82.75 million and utilized investment of USD 24.31 million. The investment of domestic enterprises is RMB 733 million. Haikou Meilan International Airport is 145 km away from Yangpu.

YEDZ Administrative Committee
Tel: (86)(898) 28829017, 28829058
Fax: (86)(898) 28829028, 28829059
E-mail: info@ypeda.com, ypttr@163.net
Website: www.yangpu.hainan.gov.cn

HAIKOU FREE TRADE ZONE

Year of Establishment: October 1992

Location: Haikou, Hainan Province

Size: 1.93 sq km

Major Investors: N.A.

Total Foreign Direct Investment: N.A.

Major Industries Encouraged: export-oriented manufacturing, duty-free storage, international trade, commodities exhibition, financial and insurance

Haikou Free Trade Zone (HFTZ) was approved by the State Council in October 1992, with development area of 1.93 sq km. It has been encouraging export-oriented manufacturing, duty-free storage, international trade, commodities exhibition, financial and insurance.

HFTZ is located to the south of the downtown Haikou, the capital city of Hainan Province.

By the end of 1997, over RMB408 million has been invested in the development of infrastructure. A total of 310 enterprises have entered the HFTZ, and 77 are foreign enterprises. The registered capital commitment was USD197.58 million, while the contractual investment was USD438.64 million.

HFTZ has a well-developed transportation network. It is around 3.5 km from the downtown district of Haikou Meilan Airport and Haikou Port. The Port is roughly 324 nautical miles from Hong Kong and 360 km from Guangzhou.

It is one of the ten largest airports in China with flights available to Singapore, Bangkok, Kuala Lumpur, Hong Kong, Beijing, Shanghai and many Chinese cities.

The Administrative Committee of Haikou Free Trade Zone
Email: invest@hkftz.gov.cn
Website: www.hkftz.gov.cn

HAIKOU HIGH-TECH PARK

Our Rating:	BB
Year of Establishment:	1992
Location:	Haikou, Hainan
Size:	18 sq km
Major Investors:	N.A.
Total Foreign Direct Investment:	USD27 million
Major Industries Encouraged:	Electronics, bio-medicine, new materials, energy saving technologies and products and advanced tropical agriculture

INTRODUCTION

Haikou High-tech Park (HHTP) is located in Haikou, the provincial city of Hainan. It was awarded the status of state-level high-tech park by the State Council in 1992. The total land area of the park is 18 sq km.

Haikou is the capital city of Hainan Province, and it is a beautiful city. The city enjoys a typical tropical climate. It has a coastal line of 54 km and has long been famous for its sea beaches, long hours of sunshine, clean air and comfortable temperature. There are several historical sites in the city, such as Hai'rui Cemetery and Wugong Temple.

INVESTMENT CLIMATE

In 2001, the total sales income of all enterprises in the park was RMB4.23 billion. Several high-tech enterprises in industries such as bio-pharmaceuticals, electronics and information technologies joined Haikou HTP in 2001 and together with other investors, the total investment capital had increased to RMB216 million (USD27 million)

According to the development plan of the park, the major industries to be promoted include electronics, bio-medicine, new materials, energy saving technology and products and advanced tropical agriculture.

Currently, rubber manufacturing, textile, production of food & beverages, and pharmaceuticals are the pillar industries of Haikou city. In Haikou, there are 5 Universities and colleges, such as Hainan University, Hainan medical College and Hainan Normal College.

The Administrative Committee of Haikou High-tech Park
Yuke Plaza, Science Avenue
Haikou, Hainan
P. R. China 570208
Tel: (86)(898) 8664518
Website: www.haikou.gov.cn/
hkarchive/hktz/

Industrial Parks in Hebei

1. Qinghuangdao Economic & Technological Development Zone
2. Tangshan Economic & Technological Development Zone
3. Yanjiao Economic & Technological Development Zone
4. Baoding High-tech Park
5. Shijiazhuang High-tech Park

INTRODUCTION

Hebei is one of China's major agricultural base as well as a major producer of iron and steel. The province ranks 14th in terms of land resources, but the resource per capita is still poor due to the large population. There are over 1000 utilizable species. At the same time, Hebei also has rich marine resources and there are many tourist attractions. The provincial capital city of Hebei province is Shijiazhuang. After expansion of the designed coastal open economic zones since

1985, many cities and regions in Hebei have been chosen to be open to foreign investors, and enjoy preferential economic policies.

GEOGRAPHY

Hebei is located in the northern part of the North China Plain, encircling Beijing and Tianjin, and lies on the coast of the Bohai Bay. It is to the north of the lower Yellow River and to the west of Bohai Sea with a coastline of around 500 km. It is bordering Liaoning, Inner Mongolia, Shanxi, Henan and Shandong provinces.

TRAVEL INFORMATION

From Shijiazhuang Airport to:
Hong Kong	2hrs 40mins
Shenzhen	2hrs 40mins
Beijing	30 mins
Shanghai Pudong	1hr 40mins

From Qinghuangdao Airport to:
Guangzhou	2hrs 25mins

INVESTMENT CLIMATE

The economic development of Hebei is fast, and the major fields of foreign investments have been concentrated in pharmaceutical industry, logistics and tourism. Two major economic development belts have been developed in the province, namely the Jing-Jin-Ji (Beijing-Tiangjin-Hebei) Economic Rim and the Bohai Bay Belt.

In 2001, its agricultural and animal husbandry output ranked the fourth and the second respectively in China. In addition, the province is also famous for its fruit and milk production. At the same time, Hebei is the major producer of iron and steel in China. The output of iron and steel has been ranking among the top of China. Meanwhile, the province has rich resources such as marble,

Fact Sheet	2001
Area (sq km)	190,000
Population (million)	67.4
GDP (RMB billion)	557.55
GDP Growth Rate	8.7%
Consumption Expenditure (RMB billion)	
• Government	51.1
• Household	177.8
Per capita annual	
• disposable income of urban residents (RMB '000)	5.98
• net income of rural households (RMB '000)	2.6
Contractual FDI (USD million)	940
Industrial Value Added (RMB bn)	241.54
Imports (USD million)	1,780
Exports (USD million)	3,960
Universities & Colleges	68

University, Heibei University of Science & Technology and Heibei Medical University.

According to the master plan of Hebei, it will be equipped with China's largest and most advanced provincial optical network upon the agreement between Hebei Telecom and Nortel Networks Inc, to install a 10 gigabits-per-second (Gbps) optical network to link up the 11 major cities of the province.

Hebei Provincial Government
www.hebnet.gov.cn
www.hebei.net.cn

potassium sand shale, natural oilstone, titanium, dolomite and vermiculite.

Major export products include crude oil, cotton, yarn and fabrics, iron and steel, antibiotics and food. At the same time, major import products include fertilizer, chemical raw materials, machinery and electronic products. Investors from many countries and regions worldwide have started cooperation with Hebei, such as the EU, Japan, the United States, Singapore, the Republic of Korea, Hong Kong and Taiwan.

Since Beijing has been granted the authority to host the Olympics in 2008, Chinese government has decided to invest over RMB100 billion to improve the infrastructure around the Jing-Jin-Tang (Beijing-Tianjin-Tangshan) area, from which Hebei will definitely benefit a lot.

The major cities of heibei province include Shijiazhuang, Tangshan, Baoding, Handan, Qinghuangdao and Xingtai. Together, there are 68 Universities and Colleges in the province such as Heibei University, Yanshan

QINHUANGDAO ECONOMIC AND TECHNOLOGICAL DEVELOPMENT ZONE

Our Rating:	BBB
Year of Establishment:	1984
Location:	Qinghuangdao, Hebei
Size:	28.39 sq km
Major Investors:	Itochu, Fujitsu, LG, Chia Tai, Mannesmann and TI Group
Total Foreign Direct Investment:	USD3.18 billion (end 2000)
Major Industries Encouraged:	Metallurgy, machinery, electronics, light textile, refined chemical industry, building materials and garments

INTRODUCTION

Qinhuangdao Economic & Technological Development Zone (QDETDZ) was established in October 1984 with the approval of the State Council. It is demarcated into East and West districts, covering development area of 28.39 sq km (10 sq km for the West and 18.39 sq km for the East).

The West district of QDETDZ, lies in the west of Qinhuangdao City. It is 281 kilometers away from Beijing and 245 kilometers away from Tianjin, it has an excellent geographic location.

The East district of QDETDZ, is located in the southeastern coast of Qinhuangdao City. It borders Liaoning Province on the east and faces Bohai Sea on the south.

INVESTMENT CLIMATE

After more than a decade of development, about 8 sq km of land has been ready. Qinhuangdao Port is also an important commercial port for Northeast China, North China and Bohai Economic Circle, with great amount of bulk grain, wood, minerals, chemical fertilizer, cement and containers entering and exiting the port. In 2000, the cargo volume of Qinhuangdao Port exceeded 90 million tons, ranking 4th among the continental ports.

It takes approximately two hours from Beijing to Qinhuangdao by express train. QDETDZ has easy access. Shanhaiguan Port and Shanhaiguan Cargo Station.

At present, investors from United States, Germany, Japan, Australia, Korea, Singapore, etc. have invested in QDETDZ. Some transnational companies, for instance, Fujitsu, LG, Chia Tai, Mannesmann, TI Group, Itochu Corporation, are the major investors.

By the end of 2000, the number of all investment projects was 2,509. There were 525 foreign investments projects with total investment of USD3.18 billion.

The industries to be promoted include metallurgy, machinery, electronics, light textile, refined chemical industry, building materials and garments.

QETDZ Administrative Committee
Tel: (86)(335) 8059045, 8052614, 8051872
Fax: (86)(335) 8051519
E-mail: business@mx.qetdz.com,
business3@mx.qetdz.com
Website: www.qetdz.com.cn

沈阳
Shenyang

承德
Chengde

锦州
Jinzhou

营口
Yingkou

辽东半岛

丹东
Dandong

平壤
Pyongyang

北京
Beijing

廊坊
Langfang

秦皇岛
Qinhuangdao

唐山
Tangshan

天津
Tianjin

大连
Dalian

渤海
BoHai

沧州
Cangzhou

黄骅
Huanghua

环渤海经济圈

东营
Dongying

烟台
Yantai

威海
Weihai

德州
Dezhou

济南
Ji'nan

泰安
Tai'an

Tangshan, an industrial city with its glorious past in modern times of China, is now a strategic par of the Beijing-Tianjin-Tangshan economic triangle. Located at the center of Bohai Sea Economic Rim of North China, Tangshan welcomes international businessmen to visit and explore the enormous opportunities in China.

Tangshan New & High-tech Development / Economic & Technological Development Zone (TSDZ) offers such opportunities and genuine partnership to all investors – no matter you are an MNC or currently a small and medium enterprise. With just an hour's ride away from Beijing and significant savings in expenses, we provide cost-effective solutions to investors who are seeking places for expansion or relocation of existing businesses.

With candic, considerate and a "can do" attitude, our management will provide you truly efficient and helpful services - for we understand that our achievement is only based on your success

唐山高新技术开发区
Tangshan New & High-Tech Development Zone

TANGSHAN NEW & HIGH-TECH DEVELOPMENT ZONE

Our Rating:	AA
Year of Establishment:	1992
Location:	Tangshan, Hebei
Size:	13 sq km
Major Investors:	Matsushita, Itochu, Rockwell, BOC Group, Conch Sunstone Medicals.
Major Industries Encouraged:	mechanical-electronic integration technologies, electronics, energy saving technologies, medicals, new materials, construction materials and fine chemicals

INTRODUCTION

Initially established in 1992, Tangshan New & High-tech Development Zone (TSDZ) was upgraded to be a key provincial-level economic and technological development zone (ETDZ) cum high-tech park of Hebei in 1998. The total development area of the zone is around 13 sq km and 3.22 sq km of the first stage has already been built.

By the end of April 2001, 585 projects, including 50 high-tech enterprises and 64 foreign companies, had joined TSDZ. Their industries cover financial service, insurance, mechanical-electrical manufacturing, construction materials, bioengineering, wholesale, information technologies, transportation, real estate, environmental protection facilities, energy supply, printing, social and medical service.

TSDZ is located at the northern part of Tangshan city. It is only 180 km to Beijing and 120 km to Tianjin. With population of 1.63 million living in the urban area, Tangshan is among China's 35 largest cities.

INVESTMENT CLIMATE

The total investment and total foreign investment in TSDZ was approximately RMB2.5 billion and USD216 million

respectively. Nine enterprises have invested more than USD10 million. Major foreign investors come from Japan, US, Germany, Canada, Korea, Hong Kong and Taiwan. Famous investors include Matsushita Electric, NGK Insulator, Marmon Group, Itochu, Rockwell and Conch.

The Administrative Committee of Tangshan New & High-tech Development Zone
Business Promoting Bureau
The Torch Building, Jianshebei Road
Tangshan, Hebei
P. R. China 063020
Tel: (86)(315) 3179735, 3178029
Fax: (86)(315) 3178031
Email: yanny@tsdz.net
Website: www.tsdz.net

Singapore:
Tel: (65) 63108737
Fax: (65) 63108738
Email: info@chinaknowledge.com

YANJIAO ECONOMIC AND TECHNOLOGICAL DEVELOPMENT ZONE

Our Rating:	BBB
Year of Establishment:	1992
Location:	Sanhe, Hebei
Size:	15 sq km
Major Investors:	Jiexi Medicals, Xiehe Medicals, Fangda Medicals, Yongguang Pharmaceutical, Taiyi Healthcare Products, Suzhong Pollen, Tianhao Pharmaceutical, Tongji Hospital, Shengwei Medicals, Shenglong Medicals
Total Foreign Direct Investment:	N.A.
Major Industries Encouraged:	Information technologies, electronics, biomedicine, new materials, green food and tourism

Established in 1992, Yanjiao Economic & Technological Development Zone (YJETDZ) consists of Yanjiao IT Industrial Park and Yanjiao Biomedical Park. The 50-hectare IT Industrial Park now has around 14 IT projects that are mainly established by the research institutes of the Chinese Ministry of Information Industry. Particularly, Jitong Communications has invested RMB870 million to establish a state-level network-controlling center. Foreign investment mainly come from the US, Japan, Canada, Singapore, Malaysia, Korea and Hong Kong.

The Biomedical Park has attracted many companies in the medical industry, such as Jiexi Medicals Co. Ltd., Xiehe Medicals Co. Ltd., and Fangda Medicals Co. Ltd. The investment of a large part of the enterprises is above USD5 million.

YJETDZ is located at Sanhe city, Hebei province. It is 30 km to downtown Beijing and 120 km to Tianjin. The Capital International airport in Beijing is just 25 km away.By the end of 2001, over 300 projects had been set up.

YJETDZ Administrative Committee
2 North Yingbin Road
Yanjiao, East Beijing
P. R. China 101601
Tel: (86)(10) 61590856
Fax: (86)(10) 61594131
Email: info@yjkfq.com
Website: www.yjkfq.com

BAODING HIGH-TECH PARK

Our Rating:	BB
Year of Establishment:	September 1992
Location:	Baoding, Hebei
Size:	14 sq km
Major Investors:	Hebei Gunner Group, Baoding JFF Storage Battery, Lucky Film Group, Hebei Tainwei Group and Sanmiguel
Total Foreign Direct Investment:	N.A.
Major Industries Encouraged:	Electronics, information technology, biological engineering, new materials, light industry and food

INTRODUCTION

Baoding High-tech Park (BDHTP) is located in Baoding city of Hebei Province. It gained the status of state-level high-tech park in September 1992. The total development area of the park is 14 sq km.

Frequently cited as the southern gateway of Beijing, Baoding covers land area of 22,100 sq km and has population of 10.5 million. It enjoys history of more than 2,000 years.

At the end of 2001, the number of registered enterprises in BDHTP was 981, among which 171 were foreign enterprises and 124 were high-tech enterprises. The total industrial output of enterprises was RMB29.12 billion, among which RMB22.32 billion was achieved by high-tech enterprises.

The development focus of the park is electronics, information technology, biological engineering, new materials, light industry, food industry, and optical electronic-mechanical integration technologies and products. Major investors include Hebei Gunner Group (www.gunner.com.cn), Baoding JFF Storage Battery (www.jinfeng-fan.com.cn), Lucky Film Group and Tainwei Group (www.btw.com.cn).

INVESTMENT CLIMATE

BDHTP consists of three subsidiary parks, namely the Central Science Park, North China Industrial Zone (the east park) and Bada Industrial Zone (the west park).

The North China Industrial Zone is designed to become a science and education center. Hebei No.2 Foreign Language College has moved into the park; Hebei University will also establish a branch campus here.

The Bada Industrial Zone is specialized in food and other light industries. With total investment of RMB1.27 billion(USD150 million) Sanmiguel is the largest investor in the zone.

BDHTP is located in the golden delta of Beijing, Tianjin and Shijiazhuang (the capital of Hebei Province). The city is 137 km to Beijing, 145 km to Tianjin and 120 km to Shijiazhuang.

BDHTP Administration Committee
118 Huaxian Road,
Baoding, Hebei Province
P. R. China 071051
Tel: (86)(312) 3108886
Fax: (86)(312) 3108830
Email: zhaoshang1@bd-ctp.net.cn
        maxuelu@bd-ctp.net.cn
Website: www.bd-ctp.net.cn

SHIJIAZHUANG HIGH-TECH PARK

Our Rating:	A
Year of Establishment:	1991
Location:	Shijiazhuang, Hebei
Size:	18 sq km
Major Investors:	Itochu, NEC, Nichimen, Nisshoiwai, NTT, Fujitsu, Hoechst, Monsanto, Seghers and Golden Lion Group
Total Foreign Direct Investment:	USD817 million
Major Industries Encouraged:	automobile components, electronic instruments, hydraulic technologies, new materials, pharmaceuticals, environment protection technologies and fine optical instruments

Shijiazhuang High-tech Park (SJZHTP) is mainly composed of three subsidiary zones, namely East Zone, West Zone and Liancun Zone. Shijiazhuang HTP is located in northeast part of Shijiazhuang. It gained the status of state-level high-tech park in 1991. The total development area of the park is 18 sq km.

The major development fields are production of automobile components, production of electronic instruments, hydraulic technologies, new materials, pharmaceutical, environment protection technologies and production of fine optical instruments.

The total investment of 1,347 enterprises was RMB22 billion. Together, 110 foreign enterprises have established subsidiaries in the park and their total investment was USD817 million. Major investors include Itochu, NEC, Nichimen, Nisshoiwai, NTT, Fujitsu, TMD Friction from the United Kingdom, Monsanto from the United States, Hoechst from Germany, Seghers from Belgium and Golden Lion Group from Malaysia.

The East Zone has an area of 9.8 sq km. To date, over 360 enterprises are operating in the area, including 42 foreign enterprises. Major investors include Weisheng Pharmaceuticals and Shijiazhuang Fiber Co. Ltd. In fact, the investment of Weisheng Pharmaceuticals is over USD46 million and the investment of Fiber Co. is RMB3.57 billion, about USD432 million.

The Liangcun Zone is mainly engaged in bio-pharmaceutical engineering, chemical engineering, and food industry. Over 165 enterprises have entered the zone and the total investment was about RMB5.66 billion. The Sino-Germany joint venture, Huayao-HST Pharmaceuticals, had an investment of DM138 million; and Sino-American, Huasheng Pharmaceuticals, committed investment of USD32.4 million.

Shijiazhuang High-tech Park Administrative Committee
151 Yellow River Avenue
Shijiazhuang, Hebei Province
P. R. China 050035
Tel: (86)(311) 5961924
Fax: (86)(311) 5963266
Email: public@shidz.com
Website: www.shidz.com.cn

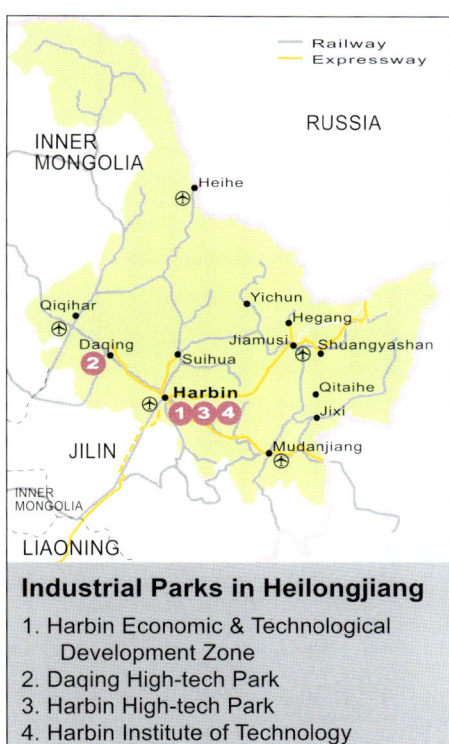

Industrial Parks in Heilongjiang

1. Harbin Economic & Technological Development Zone
2. Daqing High-tech Park
3. Harbin High-tech Park
4. Harbin Institute of Technology Science Park

INTRODUCTION

Heilongjiang boasts vast cultivated and fertile land, and ample timber reserves. It has high quality water resources for agriculture, industrial uses and human consumption. Daqing oil field, is one of the few large oil fields in China. The province's mineral resources in gold, coal and graphite also hold important roles in China's trade and investment.

GEOGRAPHY

Heilongjiang is the northernmost province in China, bordering Russia, Jilin and Inner Mongolia. Its provincial capital is Harbin. The provincial government has jurisdiction over 14 cities and prefectures, and 68 counties. The total land area is 469,000 sq km, and it has a population of 37 million. Among its beautiful and famous scenic places are Five Grand Lakes, Songhua River, and a variety of waterfalls and caves. Its climate is drastic as temperature can fall to -45°C in winter. The minority ethnic groups are Hui, Man, Korean, Mongolian, Daur, Oroqen, Hezhen, Kirgiz etc. Harbin, Mudanjiang and Jiamusi are the province's major cities.

TRAVEL INFORMATION

From Harbin Airport to:

Niigata	2hrs 10mins
Seoul	2hrs 20mins
Hong Kong	4hrs 40mins
Beijing	1hr 40mins
Shanghai Pudong	3hrs 30mins

INVESTMENT CLIMATE

Heilongjiang, with her rich natural resources, is an important base of agriculture and industry materials such as grain, wood, coal and oil etc. The good harvest in 2001 saw a total production of 26.5 million tons, including 8.2 million tons of corn, 938,000 tons of wheat and 5 million tons of soybeans. The industrial production of coal, crude oil and timber are 51 million tons, 52 million tons and 6.4 million cu m respectively. The same year saw a GDP of RMB356 billion, an increase of 9.3% over the previous year. The ratio of primary, secondary and tertiary industry is 11.5:56.1:32.4. The total industrial output was RMB199.8 billion.

The consumable market in retail sales was RMB119.8 billion, an increase of 9.6% over the previous year.

Fact Sheet	2001
Area (sq km)	469,000
Population (million)	37.5
GDP (RMB billion)	356.1
GDP Growth Rate	9.3%
Consumption Expenditure (RMB billion)	
• Government	51.3
• Household	119.9
Per capita annual	
• disposable income of urban residents (RMB '000)	5.5
• net income of rural households (RMB '000)	2.3
Contractual FDI (USD million)	1,190
Industrial Value Added (RMB bn)	176.8
Imports (USD million)	1,770
Exports (USD million)	1,610
Universities & Colleges	47

Foreign trade increased by 13.3%, with exports at USD1,610 million and imports at USD1,770 million, increase of 11.1% and 15.4% respectively. Major trading partners with Heilongjiang are Hong Kong, Japan, Russia, South Korea and Taiwan. Commodities include light industrial products, textiles and electronic products. Contractual foreign direct investment reached USD1,190 million, with investors from Hong Kong, the US, Taiwan and UK.

The harbor at Harbin is the largest inland transportation hub on Songhua River. There are 22 state level harbors in Heilongjiang. The province has also developed a good network of railway, expressway and highway. Together, there are 47 Universities and Colleges in Heilongjiang, such as Northeastern Agricultural University, Harbin Institute of Technology, Heilongjiang University, Daqing Petroleum College and Northeastern Forestry University.

Heilongjiang Provincial Government
www.hlj.gov.cn

Heilongjiang Provincial Department of
Foreign Trade and Economic
Cooperation
173 Heping Road
Nangang District
Harbin City
P. R. China 150040
Tel : (86)(451) 2621704/2621064

HARBIN ECONOMIC AND TECHNOLOGICAL DEVELOPMENT ZONE

Our Rating:	BBB
Year of Establishment:	1991
Location:	Harbin, Heilongjiang
Size:	14 sq km
Major Investors:	Hafei Automobile Manufacturing, Dongan Generator Company, Coca-Cola, Tung Yee Industries, Yi Da Pharmaceuticals
Total Foreign Direct Investment:	N.A.
Major Industries Encouraged:	Automobile manufacturing, food processing, pharmaceuticals, electronics, business services and real estate development

INTRODUCTION

Harbin Economic and Technological Development Zone (Harbin ETDZ) was established on June 1991 and was approved to be a State development zone in April 1993.

There is a planned development area of 14 sq km, separated into an administrative services zone and a general industrial zone, where Russia Export Processing Zone, High-Technology Incubation Center, Environmental Industrial Zone are included.

At the end of 2001, there were 383 foreign-invested enterprises with investors from 32 countries and regions. 1,366 domestic have also enterprises invested in the zone.

INVESTMENT CLIMATE

Utilities such as water supply, drainage, heat supply, power supply, communications, roads, railways have been developed in Harbin ETDZ.

There are six key industries: automobile manufacturing (e.g. Hafei Automobile Manufacturing Pte Ltd, Harbin Dongan Generator Company, food processing (e.g. Harbin Coca-Cola, Harbin Tung Yee Industries), pharmaceuticals (e.g. Yi Da Pharmaceuticals), electronics, business services and real estate development.

Harbin ETDZ Administrative Committee
368 Changjiang Road
Nangang District, Harbin
Heilongjiang Province
P. R. China 150090
Tel: (86)(451) 2281107
Fax: (86)(451) 2310931
E-mail: hetdz@mail.irb.com.cn
Website: http://etdz.harbin.gov.cn

DAQING HIGH-TECH PARK

Our Rating:	BBB
Year of Establishment:	1992
Location:	Daqing, Heilongjiang
Size:	47.33 sq km
Major Investors:	Tontru Co. Ltd.,Huake Co. Ltd., Control Development Technology Co. Ltd., Dahwa ITE and Zhengfa Group
Total Foreign Direct Investment:	N.A.
Major Industries Encouraged:	processing of petrochemical products, processing of agricultural products, construction materials, pharmaceuticals, electronics, information technologies, mechanical engineering, new materials, electromechanical engineering and bio-engineering

INTRODUCTION

Daqing High-tech Park (DQHTP) is located in the east of Daqing, a key industrial city of Heilongjiang Province. It was awarded state-level status in 1992. The total land area of the park is 47.33 sq km.

At the end of 2001, 726 enterprises (including 127 foreign enterprises) had established operations in the park, with total investment commitment of RMB800 million. The major investment fields are processing of petrochemical products, processing of agricultural products, construction materials, pharmaceuticals, electronics, information technologies, mechanical engineering, new materials, electromechanical engineering and bioengineering.

INVESTMENT CLIMATE

Daqing is the world's 11th largest oil field, and China's most important petroleum industry base. Its GDP ranked 12th among major Chinese cities. In 1999, the city's GDP was RMB71.41 billion (USD8.65 billion), and its population was 2.42 million.

The park's major enterprises include Daqing Tontru Co. Ltd. (www.dqtontru.com), Daqing Huake Co. Ltd. (www.huake.com), Control Development Technology Co. Ltd. (www.controltech.com.cn), Dahwa ITE (www.dhichina.com) and Zhengfa Group (www.zhengfa.com).

Inside the park, there are three sub-zones, namely the 9.8 sq km Hongwei Chemical Industrial Zone, the 5.1 sq km Xinghua Chemical Industrial Zone, and the 1.78 sq km Linyuan Chemical Industrial Zone.

Two provincial highways connect the Park to the downtown district; National Highway 301 also runs through the Park. Ha-Da (Harbin-Daqing) Expressway runs by the north of the Park.

The Administrative Committee of Daqing High-tech Park
Email: jkj@dhp.gov.cn
Website: www.dhp.gov.cn

HARBIN HIGH-TECH PARK

Our Rating:	A
Year of Establishment:	March 1991
Location:	Harbin, Heilongjiang
Size:	23.9 sq km
Major Investors:	N.A.
Total Foreign Direct Investment:	N.A.
Major Industries Encouraged:	electronics, optical-electromechanical integration technologies, new materials, bio-engineering and new energy

Harbin High-tech Park (HRHTP) is located in Harbin, the capital city of Heilongjiang Province. Together with Daqing High-tech Park, it was awarded the status of state-level high-tech park in March 1991. The total development area of the park is 23.9 sq km.

By the end of 1996, over 964 enterprises had entered the Park, including 125 foreign-invested ones.Sales of enterprises was RMB6.84 billion, the tax revenue was RMB850 million, and the export was USD190 million. Over 15 enterprises had annual sales exceeding RMB100 million. The main industries are electronics, optical-electromechanical integration technologies, new materials, biological engineering and new energy. As China's economy has grown, increasing numbers of foreign investors have been attracted to HRHTP.

The park consists of four subsidiary zones: Nangang Zone, Pingfang Zone, Yingbin Zone and University Science Park.

The Department of Foreign Trade and Economic Cooperation of Heilongjiang
Email: doftec@451.com
Website: www.hl-doftec.gov.cn

HARBIN INSTITUTE OF TECHNOLOGY SCIENCE PARK

Year of Establishment:	1993
Location:	Harbin, Heilongjian Province
Size:	N.A.
Major Supporting Institutions:	Harbin Institute of Technology
Major Investors:	HIT Banner Group, Huike Industries, HIT Heite Computers
Major Industries Encouraged:	Automation System, Electronics, Information Technology and Software Development

Harbin Institute of Technology Science Park (HITSP) was given the status of National University Science Park in May 2001 by Chinese Ministry of Education and Ministry of Science & Technology.

So far, the Park has attracted over 24 enterprises, including HIT Banner Group, Shanghai Huike Industries, HIT Heite Computers, HIT Sandi Automation System, HIT Xinghe Industries, HIT Jixing Electronics etc. The industrial fields of these enterprises cover automation system, electronics, information technology, software development etc.

Harbin Institute of Technology (www.hit.edu.cn) is a top Chinese university in engineering and technology. The fields of University research cover a wide range of areas, including space engineering, electronic science and engineering, material science and engineering, energy science and engineering, electrical engineering and automation, mathematics, physics, chemistry, management, humanities and social sciences, civil engineering, environmental engineering, architecture, transportation science and engineering, computer science and engineering and automobile engineering.

The university has established international cooperation with 80 overseas universities, such as Wisconsin-Madison, UC-Berkeley, University of Toronto, University of Virginia and Imperial College in London etc. At the same time, HIT has developed cooperation with major MNCs such as IBM, Motorola, HP, Microsoft, Emerson, CISCO, Rockwell, Volkswagen, Siemens, National, NTT, Canon, Omron and SMC. The major domestic partners include Huawei, Haier, Hisense, Baosteel, Anshan Steel, First Auto Group, Daqing Petroleum Administration and Zhongxin Telecommunications etc.

According to the master plan of HITSP, the member enterprises will be mainly engaged in industries such as computer science, electrical engineering, electronics, automation engineering and digital-controlling instruments. In the near future, the park is planned to own seven zones and two districts with specific functions.

HIT Science Park Co. Ltd.
434, Postal Street
Harbin, Heilongjiang Province
Email: astrodragon@263.net
Website: www.hit.edu.cn/gong
daxw/kejiyuan

SUIFENHE BORDER ECONOMIC COOPERATION ZONE

Year of Establishment: 1992

Location: Suifenhe city, Heilongjiang

Major Industries Encouraged: export-oriented trade, high-tech industry and processing industry

Suifenhe Border Economic Cooperation Zone was established in 1992, and authorized by the State Council as a national border zone. It borders the most developed seaside frontier with the richest resources in Far East Russia. One busy railway and two highways connect the zone with Russia, which makes the transportation network a busy and convenient one.

The Administrative Committee of Suifenhe Border Economic Cooperation Zone
Governmental Mansion
Suifenhe city
Heilongjiang
P. R. China 157300
Tel: (86) (453) 3924494
Fax: (86) (453) 3922560

HEIHE BORDER TRADE COOPERATION ZONE

Year of Establishment:	1992
Location:	Heihe city, Heilongjiang
Major Industries Encouraged:	Export-oriented trade, high-tech industry and processing industry

Heihe Border Economic Cooperation Zone was established in 1992, and was authorized by the State Council as a national border zone. It is located in Heihe city, and is across the river from Blagoveshchensk, the third largest city in Far East Russia. Heihe city stands in a key position to carry on foreign trade and economic cooperation with Russia. Within the zone, on in other areas of the city, there are abundant natural resources. Heihe itself is also a famous tourist attraction.

**The Administrative Committee of
Heihe Border Trade Cooperation Zone**
8 Tongjiang Road
Heihe city, Heilongjiang
P. R. China 164300
Tel: (86) (456) 8225705
Fax: (86) (456) 8223391

HENAN

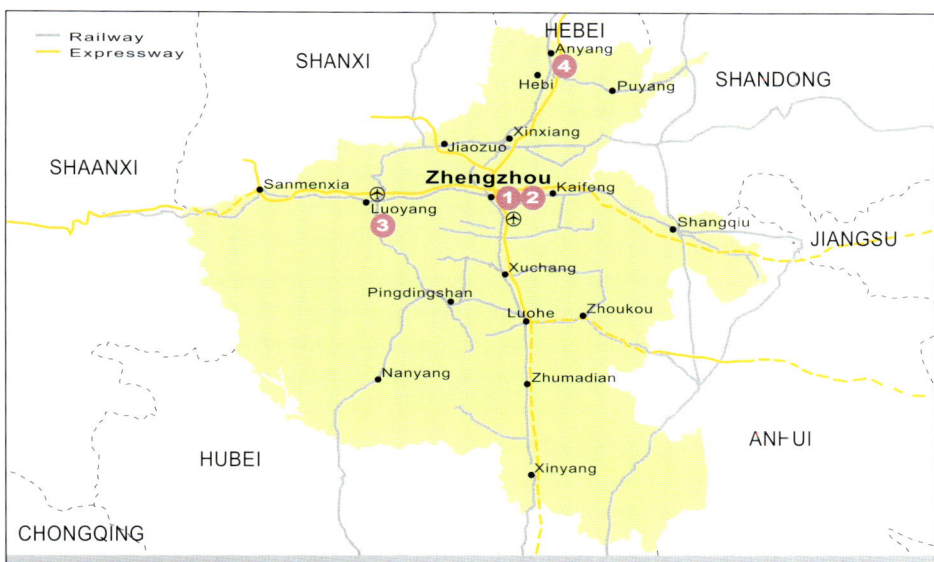

Industrial Parks in Henan

1. Zhengzhou Economic & Technological Development Zone
2. Zhengzhou High-tech Park
3. Luoyang High-tech Park
4. Anyang Economic & Technological Development Zone

INTRODUCTION

Henan is located in the central plains of China and it has been considered as one of the cradles for Chinese civilization. The province has a temperate climate with heavy rainfall in summer. In the province, there are rich reserves of water and hydraulic resources. Running through the province are four rivers, namely Yellow River, Hanshui River, Huaihe River and Weihe River. The provincial capital is Zhengzhou, and other major cities include Kaifeng, Luoyang, Xinxiang and Nanyang. Due to the mild weather and fertile land, Henan is one of China's major grain producers. The grain output of Henan ranked second in 1999, and other major agricultural products include wheat, beans, ramie, oil and cotton. In fact, Henan is China's important cotton producer, and a specialized market for cotton has been established in Zhengzhou.

TRAVEL INFORMATION

From Zhengzhou Airport to:

Hong Kong	2hrs 40mins
Shanghai Hongqiao	1hr 15mins
Beijing	1hr 10mins
Guangzhou	2hr

Fact Sheet	2001
Area (sq km)	167,000
Population (million)	95.5
GDP (RMB billion)	564.5
GDP Growth Rate	9.1%
Consumption Expenditure (RMB billion)	
• Government	67
• Household	197.9
Per capita annual	
• disposable income of urban residents (RMB '000)	5.267
• net income of rural households (RMB '000)	2.098
Contractual FDI (USD million)	864
Industrial Value Added (RMB bn)	228.8
Imports (USD million)	1,078
Exports (USD million)	1,715
Universities & Colleges	65

INVESTMENT CLIMATE

There are rich natural resources in Henan. The reserves of molybdenum, marble, asbestos, aluminum, natural gas, bauxite, coal and refractory clay are among the largest in China. Additionally, Zhongyuan Oilfield in Henan is one of the largest ones in China. At present, half of aluminum oxide output of the country is from Henan.

The key industries of Henan are food processing, coal, metallurgy, machinery, chemicals, petroleum refining, construction materials, textiles and electronics. The province has several top brands producers such as Xinfei electronic appliance, Lotus Flower gourmet powder, Chundu and Shuanghui ham sausage etc. A list of famous products of the province, also includes glass shells of color TV tubes, large tractors, heavy tyres, grinding wheels, bearings, aluminum, type fabrics, machine-made paper, paper boards etc.

Major exports of Henan include agricultural products and processed agricultural products, textiles, ceramics, machinery, metals and coal. Main export markets are in the US, Japan, the EU, Hong Kong, Russia, South Korea etc. Major imports include electronic components, chemicals, salt and copper etc, which are mainly the US, Australia, Hong Kong, Japan and Netherlands etc.

Foreign investment in the province has been growing well, especially from the US, Malaysia, Singapore and Taiwan. A large part of foreign investment focuses on fields like agriculture, electronics, petrochemicals, machinery, construction materials and infrastructure etc. Several famous international companies have set up operations in Henan, such as Mitsui, Sumitomo, Itoh, GE Renault etc. The invested enterprises are mainly engaged in energy, telecommu-nications, machine building, agriculture and real estate.

In Henan, there are 65 Universities and Colleges, such as Henan University, Zhengzhou University and Henan University of Science & Technology.

Henan Provincial Government
Website: www.henan.gov.cn

ZHENGZHOU ECONOMIC AND TECHNOLOGICAL DEVELOPMENT ZONE

Our Rating:	BBB
Year of Establishment:	April 1993
Location:	ZhengZhou, Henan
Size:	12.49 sq km (first phase is 5 sq km)
Major Investors:	LG-Philips, Pepsico, TNT, Jinwei, Tung Yee
Total Foreign Direct Investment:	USD24.8 million
Major Industries Encouraged:	Electronics, information technology, electric power equipment, printing & packaging and food processing

INTRODUCTION

Zhengzhou Economic and Technological Development Zone (ZZETDZ) was established on April 1993 with a total planned area of 12.49 sq km. It was approved as a State-level Development Zone by the State Council on 13 February 2000, and is Henan Province's only state-level ETDZ. ZZETDZ is seven kilometers away from the city center. In 2001, the GDP of ZZETDZ was RMB1.12 billion, up 35.7% over the previous year, among which industrial value-added was RMB680 million, up 35%.

INVESTMENT CLIMATE

Xinzheng International Airport is 22 kilometers to the south of ZZETDZ. National Highway No.107 and Zhengzou-Xuchang Expressway pass the area on the west side.

In the Zone, there are 90 domestic enterprises with registered capital of RMB620 million and fixed assets of RMB2.8 billion.

There are 46 foreign enterprises with total investment of USD98.04 million and utilized FDI of USD24.8 million. Seven projects have investments of more than USD10 million each and 3 projects more than USD30 million each. Three projects are undertaken by Fortune 500 companies.

Major foreign invested enterprises include LG-Philips, Pepsico, TNT, Jinwei and Tung Yee. Major industries in ZZETDZ include electronics, information technology, electric power equipment, printing & packaging and food processing.

ZZETDZ Administrative Committee
Hanghai East Road, Zhengzhou Henan
P. R. China 450047
Tel: (86)(371) 6782001, 6781981, 6781252
Fax: (86)(371) 6781248, 6782001
E-mail: zhaoshj@public2.zz.ha.cn
Website: www.zz-economy.gov.cn

ZHENGZHOU HIGH-TECH PARK

Our Rating:	BBB
Year of Establishment:	March 1991
Location:	Zhengzhou, Henan
Size:	18.6 sq km
Major Investors:	N.A.
Total Foreign Direct Investment:	N.A.
Major Industries Encouraged:	Software engineering, information technology, ultra-hard materials, bio-pharmaceuticals, electronics, new materials,optical-electronic-mechanical integration technologies & products and environment technologies

INTRODUCTION

Zhengzhou High-tech Park (ZZHTP) is located in the northwestern suburbs of Zhengzhou, the provincial capital of Henan. It was authorized by the State Council as a State High-tech park in March 1991. Total development area of the park is 18.6 sq km. It is 13 kilometers away from down-town area.

At the end of 2000, 959 enterprises had joined ZZHTP and the total investment commitment was RMB11.43 billion. The development focus of ZZHTP includes software engineering, information technology, ultra-hard materials and bio-pharmaceuticals.

INVESTMENT CLIMATE

ZZHTP consists of the Entrepreneurship Center, Central Software Zone, Optical-Electronic-Mechanical Industrial Zone, Bio-pharmaceutical Industrial Zone, New Materials Industrial Zone, University Science Park and an Incubation Center of CAS (Chinese Academy of Science) Henan Branch.

Established in May 1995, the Entrepreneurship Center plays a key role in the innovation system of ZZHTP.

Central Software Zone was set up in September 1999. Enterprises in the zone focus on software R&D, software testing and services etc. Bio-pharmaceutical Industrial Zone was established in January 2000. It supports the development of genetic pharmaceuticals, biological products, agricultural bioengineering and Chinese medicine.

A number of research institutes and colleges lie to the north of the high-tech park and many large and medium-sized enterprises are located in the west area.

Zhengzhou High-tech Park
Administrative Committee
Tel: (86)(371) 7983654
Fax: (86)(371) 7981424
Website: www.zzgx.gov.cn

LUOYANG HIGH-TECH PARK

Our Rating:	BB
Year of Establishment:	1992
Location:	Luoyang, Henan
Size:	30 sq km
Major Investors:	Hussmann, North Glass Co. Ltd, Sino-American Biotechnology Co. Ltd., Luoyang Aviation Electrical Factory and Jiaxing Venture Capital
Total Foreign Direct Investment:	N.A.
Major Industries Encouraged:	Electronics, information, bio-technology and new materials

INTRODUCTION

Luoyang High-tech Park (LYHTP) is located in Luoyang city of Henan Province, about eight kilometers from the downtown area. It was authorized by the State Council as a State high-tech park in 1992. The total development area of the park is around 30 sq km. LYHTP consists of Zhongya Commercial Area, Zhoushan Electronics Industrial Zone and Sanshan Technical Industrial Zone.

A large number of well-known enterprises have joined LYHTP. Important investors include Luoyang Hussmann, North Glass Co. Ltd, Sino-American Biotechnology Co. Ltd., Luoyang Aviation Electrical Factory and Jaxing Venture Capital etc.

INVESTMENT CLIMATE

Luoyang has many research institutes and technology development organizations, among which 14 are at ministry level and 18 are at province level. Among the over 500 senior researchers in the city, there are 2 fellows of CAS (Chinese Academy of Sciences) and 2 fellows of CAE (Chinese Academy of Engineering). The city also has 6 state-level engineering and technology centers as well as 6 state-level product testing centers.

Luoyang is a major industrial city in Henan Province. Two important railways, namely Longhai (from Lianyungang to Lanzhou) and Jiaozhi (from Jiaozhuo to Zhicheng), run across the city. It is also a key station of the 2nd Euro-Asia Continental Bridge (Lianyungang-Rotterdam), through which goods can be transported directly to Middle Asia, East Europe, West Europe and other regions of the world. The city connects to has Kaifeng-Zhengzhou-Luoyang Expressway and Luoyang-Sanmenxia Expressway.

LYHTP is 15 kilometers away from Luoyang Airport.

Luoyang High-tech Park
Administrative Committee
Room 911, Peony Hotel
2 Nanchang Road
Luoyang, Henan Province
P. R. China 471003
Tel: (86)(379) 4902653, 4902740
Fax: (86)(379) 4902448
E-mail: dwjmj@lhdz.gov.cn
Website: www.lhdz.gov.cn

ANYANG ECONOMIC AND TECHNOLOGICAL DEVELOPMENT ZONE

Our Rating:	B
Year of Establishment:	1992
Location:	Anyang, Henan
Size:	2.6 sq km
Major Investors:	Sino-Italy Prast Glass Steel, Shenghua Plant Protein.
Total Foreign Direct Investment:	N.A.
Major Industries Encouraged:	Iron and steel, electronics, mechanical instruments, chemical engineering and food

Anyang Economic & Technological Development Zone (AYETDZ) is located in the southeast part of Anyang city, Henan province. With over 3,000 years' history, Anyang city is recognized as one of China's seven famous ancient capital cities. Conveniently located in northern Henan province, Anyang borders three provinces, namely Shanxi, Hebei and Shandong, and is about 500 kilometers from Beijing. Xinzheng International Airport is about 160 kilometers away. The total population of Anyang is five million.

The key industries in AYETDZ as well as in the city include iron & steel, electronics, mechanical instruments, medicals, chemical engineering and food. Anyang Steel Corporation and Anyang Color TV Tube Glass Co. Ltd are recognized among China's 500 largest industrial enterprises. With total sales of RMB4.5 billion and profit of RMB740 million, Anyang Steel Corporation is the largest steel corporation in Henan province. Anyang Color TV Tube Glass Co. Ltd is the largest Sino-foreign joint venture in the province and the products have 40% domestic market share. Other important local enterprises include Anyang Chemicals, Flying Eagle Group, Panda Electronics, Yellow River Tyres Co. Ltd and Anyang Tobacco Factory.

Established in 1992 and upgraded to be a province-level development zone in 1995, AYETDZ will develop 2.6 sq km in the initial stage. By the end of 1998, 113 projects, including 22 high-tech ones, were approved to join AYETDZ and the total investment commitment was around RMB1.25 billion.

Administrative Commities of AYETDZ
Tel: (86)(372) 2969893, 2997518
Fax: (86) (372) 2961067
E-mail: ahnidz@public.ayptt.ha.cn
Website: www.anyang.gov.cn/bgxq

HUBEI

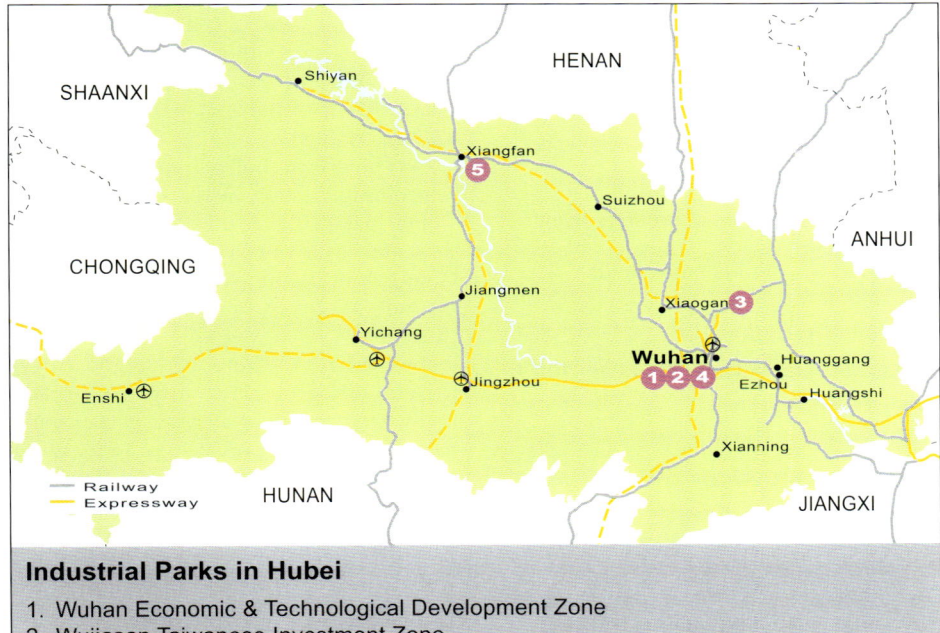

SHAANXI

HENAN

Shiyan

Xiangfan
5

Suizhou

ANHUI

CHONGQING

Jiangmen

Xiaogan 3

Yichang
⊕

Wuhan ⊕
1 2 4

Huanggang

Jingzhou

Ezhou
Huangshi

Enshi ⊕

Xianning

Railway
Expressway

HUNAN

JIANGXI

Industrial Parks in Hubei
1. Wuhan Economic & Technological Development Zone
2. Wujiasan Taiwanese Investment Zone
3. Xiaogan Economic & Technological Development Zone
4. Wuhan East Lake High-tech Park
5. Xiangfan High-tech Park

INTRODUCTION

Located in the central part of China, Hubei province is the cradle of Chu culture and renowned for its long history and outstanding celebrities. The capital city is Wuhan.

GEOGRAPHY

Hubei is located at the middle part of Yangtze River, and got its name from its location to the north of Dongting Lake (Hu means Lake and Bei means North). The province covers a total area of 185,900 sq km and has a population of 60 million. It boasts abundant natural resources such as animals, plants, minerals and especially water resources. The exploitable capacity of hydraulic power is 33.57 million kW, ranked 4th in the country. Some hydropower stations have been constructed, such as Gezhouba Dam, GeheYan Dam. The Three Gorges Dam Project with an installed capacity of 18.20 million kW is still under construction.

Hubei has four distinct seasons. The average temperature is 2°-4°C in January and 26°-29°C in July.

Fact Sheet	2001
Area (sq km)	185,900
Population (million)	60
GDP (RMB billion)	466.2
GDP Growth Rate	9.1%
Consumption Expenditure (RMB billion)	
• Government	47.6
• Household	197.5
Per capita annual	
• disposable income of urban residents (RMB '000)	5.85
• net income of rural households (RMB '000)	2.35
Utilized FDI (USD million)	1,561
Industrial Value Added (RMB bn)	109.7
Imports (USD million)	1,780
Exports (USD million)	1,800
Universities & Colleges	60

TRAVEL INFORMATION

There are seven airports in Hubei. The largest is Wuhan Tianhe International Airport.

From Wuhan Airport to:
Beijing	1hr 50mins
Shenzhen	1hr 25mins
Shanghai	1hr 25mins
Hong Kong	1hr 50mins

INVESTMENT CLIMATE

With favorable geographic position and convenient transportation, Hubei plays an important role in the country's economic development. In 2001, the province's GDP reached RMB466.2 billion, an increase of 9.1% over 2000. The ratio of primary, secondary and tertiary sectors is 14.9: 49.6: 35.5.

The pillar industries include automobile, iron and steel, mechanical and electrical equipment, textile, chemical industry and building materials. In 2001, the total value added of heavy industry is RMB69.2 billion, while that of light industry is RMB40.4

billion. The proportion of heavy and light industries is 1.71: 1.

Total exports and imports in 2001 reached USD3.58 billion, increasing by 11.5% over 2000, with exports of USD1.80 billion and imports USD1.78 billion.

The utilized foreign investment in 2001 was USD1.56 billion, a sharp increase of 47.5% over 2000.

As Hubei is the hub of transportation and telecommunication in the central part of China, major cities of the country are linked with Hubei via railways, including Beijing-Guangzhou, Beijing-Kowloon, Shanghai-Wuhan, Wuhan-Chengdu and Jiaozuo-Zhicheng.

In addition, there are eight inter-provincial and 118 intra-provincial highways, connecting all cities, counties and most villages in the province. As for the water route, Wuhan and Huangshi are the major harbors along Yangtze River and they can accommodate vessels up to 3,000-5,000 tons.

Hubei's high-tech industries have developed rapidly with China Optics Valley as its focus, which is among the top in the world in optics communication and laser technology.

Hubei Provincial Government
Tel: (86)(27) 87235544
Fax: (86)(27) 87235552
Website: www.hubei.gov.cn

Hubei Provincial Foreign Trade and
Economic Cooperation Department
Tel: (86)(27) 85774070
Fax: (86)(27) 85773668
Email: hitic@public.wh.hb.cn
Website: www.hubei.gov.cn

Hubei FDI Service Center
Tel: (86)(27) 85807372

WUHAN ECONOMIC AND TECHNOLOGICAL DEVELOPMENT ZONE

Our Rating:	A
Year of Establishment:	1991
Location:	Wuhan, Hubei
Size:	31 sq km (first phase 14 sq km)
Major Investors:	Citroen, Dongfeng Automobile
Total Foreign Direct Investment:	N.A.
Major Industries Encouraged:	Automobiles & automotive components, bioengineering & new pharmaceuticals; electronics, mechanical-electronics integration; new materials and advance agriculture

Wuhan Economic and Technological Development Zone (WHETDZ) was established in May 1991 and was approved as a state development zone in April 1993. It covers of 31 sq km and 14 sq km has been developed. When fully occupied, the zone can be further expanded to an area of 90 sq km.

WHETDZ is located in the southwest of Wuhan City, between the Middle Ring Road and the Outer Ring Road of the city area. It is only 15 km from the downtown area.

In 2000, the GDP of WHETDZ was RMB5.56 billion and the gross industrial output was RMB15.17 billion.

Major industries in WEDZ include: automobiles & automotive components, bioengineering & new pharmaceuticals; electronics, mechanical-electronics integration, new materials and advanced agriculture.

It was among the top 10 state-level ETDZs in 1998, in terms of economic achievement. WHETDZ has convenient access to Beijing, Zhuhai, Shanghai and Lhasa via highways or expressways, and is connected to Beijing-kowloon and Beijing-Guangzhou Railways, the two important national transportation arteries in China.

WETDZ Administrative Committee
Dunyang Plaza, Wuhan
Hubei P. R. China 430056
Tel: (86)(27) 84891441
Fax: (86)(27) 84891934
E-mail: wetdz@public.wh.hb.cn
Website: www.wedz.com.cn

WUHAN WUJIASAN
TAIWANESE INVESTMENT ZONE

Our Rating:	BBB
Year of Establishment:	1992
Location:	Wuhan, Hubei
Size:	20 sq km
Major Investors:	N.A.
Total Foreign Direct Investment:	N.A.
Major Industries Encouraged:	Food, restructuring of existing enterprises, high-tech agriculture, software development, microelectronics, bio-engineering, information technologies, shopping malls and other services

Wuhan Wujiasan Taiwanese Investment Zone is located at the western part of Wuhan, which is the capital city of Hubei province. It is 12 km to the downtown area, 18 km to Wuhan Tianhe International Airport and 7 km to Hankou Railway Station.

The major industries encouraged in the investment zone include food, restructuring of existing enterprises, high-tech agriculture, software development, microelectronics, bio-engineering, information technology, shopping malls and other services.

The Administrative Committee of Wuhan Wujiasan Taiwanese Investment Zone is the government agency in charge of the planning, development and administration of the development zone.

Administrative Committee of Wuhan Wujiasan Taiwanese Investment Zone
4 Wunan Road
Wujiasan, East Lake District
Wuhan, Hubei
P. R. China 430000
Tel: (86)(27) 83891127
Fax: (86)(27) 83390012

XIAOGAN ECONOMIC AND TECHNOLOGICAL DEVELOPMENT ZONE

Our Rating:	B
Year of Establishment:	1989
Location:	Xiaogan, Hubei
Size:	15.5 sq km
Major Investors:	Hanguang Electrical Engineering Factory, Hua Zhong Precision Instruments Factory, Sino-French Sanjiang Renault Automobile, Sino-Germany Epcos Electronics, Sanhuan Wall Materials, Sanjiang Walite Special Cars and Jian Bird Aluminum
Major Industries Encouraged:	Aviation technologies, new materials, bio-technology, automobile technology, high-tech agriculture, medical instruments and environment protection technologies

Xiaogan Economic & Technological Development Zone (XGETDZ) is located at the eastern part of Xiaogan, an important industrial city of Hubei province. It is 32 km to Wuhan Tianhe International Airport and 49 km to Hankou Railway Station in Wuhan.

Major investors in XGETDZ include Hanguang Electrical Engineering Factory, Hua Zhong Precision Instruments Factory, Sino-French Sanjiang Renault Automobile Co. Ltd., Sino-Germany Epcos Electronics Co. Ltd., Sanhuan Wall Materials Co. Ltd, Sanjiang Walite Special Car Company and Jian Bird Aluminum Corporation.

According to the master plan, XGETDZ will be divided into the 6 sq km High-tech Industrial Park and 6.8 sq km High-tech Agricultural Park. The major industries to be encouraged in the industrial park include aviation industry, new materials, bio-technology, automobile technology, medical instruments and environmental protection technologies. Advanced agriculture and farming of aquatics will be promoted in the agricultural park.

Administrative Committee of XGETDZ
Tel: (86)(712) 2327073
Fax: (86)(712) 2330128
Email: xgkfqzsj@xg.hb.cninfo.net

WUHAN EAST LAKE HIGH-TECH PARK

Our Rating:	AA
Year of Establishment:	1991
Location:	Wuhan, Hubei
Size:	N.A.
Major Investors:	Changfei Fiber-optical Cables, NEC, Mitsui, Siemens, Xerox, Lixing Power Source, Kernel Biological Pesticide, RHK Group Wuhan Jianming Pharmaceutical and Lishizheng
Total Foreign Direct Investment:	N.A.
Major Industries Encouraged:	Fiber-optical technologies and products, bio-engineering, electronics, new materials, software development and laser technologies

INTRODUCTION

Wuhan East Lake High-tech Park (WHHTP) is located in the suburbs of Wuhan. It was authorized as a State high-tech park in 1991 and is dubbed China Optics Valley (www.chinaov.org).

The major industries include fiber-optical technologies and products, biological engineering, electronics, new materials, software development, laser technologies and other advanced technologies.

Wuhan HTP is China's largest production base of fiber-optical cables with key players such as Changfei Fiber-optical Cables Co Ltd, Wuhan Research Institute of Post and Telecommunications, Wuhan Lixing Power Source Co Ltd., Kernel Biological Pesticide Co Ltd and RHK Group. The IT industry is also developing well with the support of Intel, IDG and HSBC.

INVESTMENT CLIMATE

Key software products developed in the park include operating system software, education software, CAD software, satellite communication and GIS software. Key players include Wuhan University Sino-software Company, Kaimu Company, Dameng Company, Shipu Company, Tianyu Software Company and Huazhong University of Science and Technology Image Company.

Large venture capitalists in the park provide important capital support for enterprises with high growth potential. More than ten enterprises have been listed in the two Chinese exchanges — such as Wuhan East Lake High-tech Group, HUST Technology and Yangtze Telecommunication.

Wuhan is a center for advanced education. Institutions such as Wuhan University, Huazhong University of Science and Technology, Wuhan Biological Product Research Center, Hubei Pharmacy Industrial Research Institute are all located in the park.

Administrative Committee WHHTP
Tel: (86)(27) 87804115, 87806529
Fax: (86)(27) 87802764
Email: dhgx@public.wh.hb.cn

XIANGFAN HIGH-TECH PARK

Our Rating:	BBB
Year of Establishment:	November 1992
Location:	Xiangfan, Hubei
Size:	7.5 sq km
Major Investors:	ACTOR
Total Foreign Direct Investment:	USD450 million
Major Industries Encouraged:	fine chemicals and new materials automobile-related products

INTRODUCTION

Xiangfan High-tech Park (XFHTP) is located in the northern part of Xiangfan, an important industries city in northwestern Hubei. It was approved by the State Council in November 1992. The total development area is 7.5 sq km.

Currently, the park has nearly 300 high-tech enterprises. For the first quarter of 2001, the total capital investment reached RMB52.97 million, and the investment for industrial projects was RMB31 million. The development focuses on aviation technologies, electromechanical integration, information technologies, and new materials.

Among all the enterprises in the park, 36 are foreign invested companies. The total foreign investment was USD450 million.

INVESTMENT CLIMATE

Key products in the park include the additive production base for lead-acid battery and the production base of computer chips. The first base is the result of cooperation between XFHTP and Japanese investors. The second one is a joint venture between the high-tech park and ACTOR from Silicon Valley, California.

Xiangfan has a well-developed transportation system. National Highway No. 316 and No. 207 run across the city and intersect at XFHTP. The park has easy access to Xiangfan Railway Station and Xiangfan Civil Airport.

Located in northwest area of Hubei Province, Xiangfan city has a long history. Old city walls have been kept well in the city, telling tourists that it had been prosperous thousands of years ago. The Old Long-Zhong, the original home for the legendary politician Zhuge Liang in the Three Kingdoms (220-265), is in the suburban area of the city.

The Administration Committee of Xiangfan High-tech Park
Torch Tower, 2 Chuangye West Road
Xiangfan, Hubei Province
P. R. China 441002
Tel: (86)(710) 3228418
Fax: (86)(710) 3220246
Email: xfhdz@263.net
Website: www.xfhdz.org.cn

WUHAN EAST LAKE
UNIVERSITY SCIENCE PARK

Year of Establishment:	2000
Location:	Wuhan, Hubei
Major Supporting Institutions:	Wuhan University, Huazhong University of Science & Technology
Major Investors:	WHU Hoyo, WHU Hongyi, WHU Organic Silicon, WHU Taitong GPS Technologies and WHU Luojia Electronic Information Technologies and Yangpu Sunshine Industries
Major Industries Encouraged:	Optical-mechanical-electrical integration, optical storage, optical-electrical measurement instruments, GPS/GIS/RS, ITS and intelligent architecture system

Wuhan East Lake University Science Park (WHUSP) is composed of several subsidiary parks attached to Wuhan University, Huazhong University of Science & Technology, Wuhan University of Technology, Central China Normal University, Wuhan Branch of CAS and Greatwall Science Park. The total area to be developed is around 14 sq km.

According to the master plan of WHUSP, the major industries to be developed include optical-mechanical-electrical integration, optical storage, optical - electrical measurement instruments, GPS/GIS/RS, ITS and intelligent architecture system. Member enterprises enjoy efficient research and development support from the institutions. The university science park has two subsidiary parks, namely Wuhan University Science Park and Huazhong University of Science & Technology Science Park (HZUSTSP).

Managed by WHUSP Development Corporation, WHUSP is located in Wuhan Science-tech New Town and covers 60 hectares. The major developers include Wuhan University and Wuhan High-tech

Holdings, whose total assets is around RMB10 billion and controls 43 subsidiaries in Wuhan China Optical Valley.

The current Wuhan University is a merge of former Wuhan University, Wuhan Hydropower & Electricity University, Wuhan University of Mapping Technology and Hubei Medical University in 2000.

Member enterprises in HZUSTSP are mainly engaged in digital-controlling system, information technology, laser engineering, electronics and integration technologies.

Wuhan University Science Park
Tel: (86)(27) 87923865
Fax: (86)(27) 87923868
Email: webmaster@wusp.com.cn
Website: www.wusp.com.cn

Huazhong University of Science & Technology Science Park Development
Tel: (86)(27) 87922852
Fax: (86)(27) 87922851

HUBEI SOFTWARE DEVELOPMENT BASE

Year of Establishment:	N.A.
Location:	Wuhan, Hubei
Size:	100 hectares
Major Investors:	Chinasoft Wuhan, Wuhan Tianyu Info Tech, Wuhan East Lake Software Industries
Major Industries Encouraged:	N.A.

The 100-hectare Hubei Software Development Base is located with in Wuhan East Lake High-tech Park.

Together, member enterprises of the base employ more than 1,000 professionals. Key organizations include Wuhan Chinasoft Co. Ltd., Wuhan Tianyu Information Technologies and Wuhan East Lake Software Industries. Other important software companies in Wuhan city include Tianyuan Software Co. Ltd. (www.tianyuansoft.com), Argosoft Co. Ltd. (www.argosoft.com), Kingdee International Software Wuhan Corporation (www.kingdee.com) and JoinEasy Software Engineering Co. Ltd. (www.join-easy.com).

In Hubei province, there are 60 universities and colleges. Among them, Wuhan University and Huazhong University of Science & Technology have established software colleges offering bachelor and master degrees in software development and engineering.

The Administrative Committee of Hubei Software Development Base
52 Nanyuan Village, Fruit Lake
Wuchang, Wuhan
Hubei Province
P. R. China 430071
Fax: (86)(27) 87881792

HUNAN

HUBEI

Zhangjiajie
Changde
Yueyang

CHONG
QING

Yiyang
Jishou
Ningxing **Changsha**
Loudi
Xiangtan
Zhuzhou
Huaihua
Shaoyang
JIANGXI

GUIZHOU

Hengyang
Yongzhou

Chenzhou

GUANGXI

Railway
Expressway
GUANGDONG

Industrial Parks in Hunan

1. Changsha Economic & Technological Development Zone
2. Changsha High-tech Park
3. Zhuzhou High-tech Park
4. Huaihua Economic Development Zone
5. Ningxiang Economic & Technological Development Zone
6. Hunan Powerise Software Development Park
7. Yuelu Mountains University Science Park

INTRODUCTION

Hunan, called "Xiang" for short, is located to the south of the Yangtze River's middle reaches The capital city of Hunan is Changsha.

GEOGRAPHY

Hunan was named after its location to the south of Dongting Lake. It covers a total area of 212,000 sq km and has population of 64.4 million. Hunan is a place full of rich natural resources. The province possesses 134 kinds of minerals. Its reserves of antimony and tungsten are among the largest in the world. The export volume of antimony accounts for more than half of the nation's total. The deposits of other 20-odd minerals rank among China's top three places. It also abounds in forest resources, with reserves of 245 million cubic meters of timber. There are more than 100 scenic spots in Hunan. The most attractive of them is the Wulingyuan Scenic Area with Zhangjiajie State Forest Park as its center, inscribed by UNESCO on the World Heritage List.

Hunan has four distinctive seasons. The average temperature is 3°-8°C in January and 27°-30°C in July.

TRAVEL INFORMATION

From Changsha Airport to:

Beijing	1hrs 40mins
Shenzhen	55mins
Shanghai Pudong	1hr 35mins
Hong Kong	1hr 15mins

INVESTMENT CLIMATE

As a transportation hub in South China, Hunan has formed a complete transportation network consisting of railways, national or provincial highways, inland waterways and air routes.

The trunk railways in Hunan include Beijing-Guangzhou, Hunan-Guizhou, Hunan-Guangxi, Zhicheng-Liuzhou and Zhejiang-jiangxi, running in all directions through Hunan, and the Luoyang-Zhanjiang railway line runs through six cities from north to south of Hunan. Seven national highways extend to every part of the province with a total length of 60,000 km, ranked 4th in China.

Fact Sheet	2001
Area (sq km)	212,000
Population (million)	64.4
GDP (RMB billion)	398.3
GDP Growth Rate	9.0%
Consumption Expenditure (RMB billion)	
• Government	68
• Household	151
Per capita annual	
• disposable income of urban residents (RMB '000)	6.78
• net income of rural households (RMB '000)	2.26
Contractual FDI (USD million)	1,331
Industrial Value Added (RMB bn)	131
Imports (USD million)	1,004
Exports (USD million)	1,754
Universities & Colleges	61

The province has built modern telecommunication networks. International and domestic direct dialing telephone service is available in all of Hunan's cities and counties. Hunan has been rated as one of China's most advanced provinces in terms of telecommunications.

In 2001, Hunan's GDP achieved RMB398.3 billion, an increase of 9.0% over 2000. The proportion of primary, secondary and tertiary sectors is 20.7: 39.4: 39.9. The industrial output totaled RMB157 billion, up 10.5% from the previous year. Pillar industries at Hunan are metallurgy, machinery (including electric locomotives, tractors, heavy machine tools and high-precision electronic equipment) and electronics, foodstuffs, chemicals, textiles, energy and building materials.

Hunan's foreign trade also witnessed rapid growth in recent years. In 2001, the approved foreign projects totaled 350, with contractual foreign investment of USD1.33 billion, up 21.7% from the previous year.

Actual realized investment amounted to USD1.19 billion, an increase of 7.1% over 2000. Major investors are from Hong Kong, USA, Taiwan, and UK. Cities attracting most foreign investment in the province are Changsha, Hengyang and Zhuzhou. Other important cities in the province include Yueyang, Huaihua and Changde. In the past 20 years, more than 23,000 scientific and technical achievements have been made in Hunan including two-line breeding of hybrid rice, Galaxy super computer, research in magnet suspension train and genetic engineering.

Hunan Provincial Government
Website: www.hunan.gov.cn

Hunan Department of Foreign Trade and Economic Cooperation
80 Wuyi Road (C), Changsha, Hunan, P. R. China 410000
Tel: (86)(731) 2288189, 2287190
Website: www3.hunan.gov.cn/wjt

CHANGSHA ECONOMIC AND TECHNOLOGICAL DEVELOPMENT ZONE

Our Rating:	BBB
Year of Establishment:	1992
Location:	Changsha, Hunan
Size:	20 sq km
Major Investors:	N.A.
Total Foreign Direct Investment:	N.A.
Major Industries Encouraged:	Microelectronics, new materials, bioengineering, information technologies, communications and new energy

INTRODUCTION

Changsha Economic and Technological Development Zone (CSETDZ) was established in August 1992 with development area of 20 sq km and a first phase of 14 sq km.

CSETDZ is located in Xingsha Town, an eastern suburb of Changsha City, the provincial capital of Hunan. It is also at the crossing point of State Highway No.319, No.107 and Beijing-Zhuhai Expressway. It is eight kilometers from the city area, railway station and Huanghua International Airport. CSETDZ has signed 307 investment projects with both domestic and foreign investors.

INVESTMENT CLIMATE

CSETDZ is divided into eight sections: New Industrial Area, Trade and Finance Area, Tourist and Villa Area, Culture and Education Area, Administration Area, Residential Area, Xingsha Grand Market and Science & Technology Park.

Presently, RMB850 million has been invested in infrastructure development – 28 main roads with total length of 60 kilometers have been built; a 21-floor telecom building provides 100,000 digital program-controlled telephones; 100,000 tons of water and 2.4 million kWh of electricity are supplied daily. Major industries to be promoted in the zone include microelectronics, new materials, bioengineering, IT, communications and new energy.

Administrative Committee of CSETDZ
Tel: (86)(730) 4011108
Website: www.chinafdi.gov.cn/hunan/
english/kfq-e/xs-ehost.htm

CHANGSHA HIGH-TECH PARK

Our Rating:	A
Year of Establishment:	March 1991
Location:	Changsha, Hunan
Size:	18.6 sq km
Major Investors:	LG, ICI, Broad Air-con Group, Hunan Computers, Powerise Group, Sany Corporation and Haili Chemicals etc.
Total Foreign Direct Investment:	N.A.
Major Industries Encouraged:	Electronics, information technologies, biol-engineering, new materials, fine chemicals, advanced agriculture, optical-electronic-mechanical integration technologies and other advanced manufacturing technologies

INTRODUCTION

Changsha High-tech Park (CHTP) is located in the central area of Changsha, the capital city of Hunan. It gained state-level status in March 1991 and is now one of the two such high-tech parks in the province. The total development area of the park is 18.6 km.

At the end of 2000, there were 616 high-tech enterprises in the park, over 200 being foreign-invested ones. Over 645 high-tech projects have been carried out in the park, with over 200 among state-level and province-level key projects. In the same year, the high-tech industrial output was RMB20.3 billion. Over 39 enterprises had annual sales of over RMB100 million each.

The core industries in the park are electronics, information technologies, biological engineering, new materials, fine chemical engineering, advanced agriculture, optical-electronic-mechanical integration technologies and products, and other advanced manufacturing technologies.

INVESTMENT CLIMATE

Foreign investors in the park mainly come from the United States, the United Kingdom, Germany, Italy, Canada, Sweden, Thailand, Korea, Japan, Taiwan, Hong Kong and Macau. Major foreign companies here include LG and ICI. Some good examples of successful local companies are Broad Air-conditioning Group, Hunan Computers, Powerise Group, Sany Corporation and Hunan Haili Chemicals.

In Changsha, there are several famous universities and colleges such as Central South University, Hunan University, National Defense University of Technology, Hunan Normal University, Hunan Agricultural University, and Changsha University.

Administrative Committee of CHTP
Tongzipo, Hexi District
Changsha, Hunan
P. R. China
Tel: (86)(731) 8806521
Fax: (86)(731) 8806540
Email: cshtz@cshtz.com
Website: www.cshtz.gov.cn

ZHUZHOU HIGH-TECH PARK

Our Rating:	BB
Year of Establishment:	November 1992
Location:	Zhuzhou, Hunan
Size:	35 sq km
Major Investors:	Hongyuan Group, Hunan Torch, Guoguang
Total Foreign Direct Investment:	USD109.9 million (2001 done)
Major Industries Encouraged:	Non-ferrous metallurgical industry, mechanical equipments, chemical engineering, electronic engineering, electronics, non-ferrous metal and construction materials

INTRODUCTION

Zhuzhou High-tech Park (ZHTP) is located at Zhuzhou, an other important industrial city of Hunan Province. It gained state-level status in November 1992. The total development area of the park is 35 sq km.

Zhuzhou is located in the east part of Hunan Province and the middle reaches of Xiangjiang River. To the north is Changsha, the capital city of Hunan Province, and Wuhan, the capital city of Hubei Province; and to the south is Guangzhou, the capital city of Guangdong Province. The city is one key point of Hunan's Changsha-Zhuzhou-Xiangtan Economic Triangle. Among the total population of 3.68 million, 680,000 are living in the urban area.

The development focus of the park is non-ferrous metallurgical industry, mechanical equipments, chemical engineering, electronic engineering, electronics, non-ferrous metal and construction materials.

In 2001, the Park attracted 78 new projects with investment at RMB2.39 billion. The number of new foreign enterprises was 12 with total investment of USD109.9 million.

INVESTMENT CLIMATE

The park consists of three subsidiary industrial zones, namely the industrial science park, the agricultural science park and the civil science park.

Three major railways, which include the Jing-Guang (Beijing-Guangzhou) Railway, Zhe-Gan (Zhejiang-Jiangxi) Railway and Xiang-Qian (Hunan-Guizhou) Railway meet in Zhuzhou. National Highway No. 107 (Beijing-Guangzhou) and No. 320 (Shanghai-Kunming) are running through the city. The city is 60 km away from Changsha Huanghua International Airport.

With over 2,000 industrial enterprises, Zhuzhou is an important industrial base of Hunan Province. It is famous for the non-ferrous metallurgical industry, mechanical manufacturing, chemical engineering and construction materials. Over 40 research institutes and 80,000 R&D professionals are working in the city. In Zhuzhou, there are three colleges, including Zhuzhou Institute of Technology.

Administrative Committee of ZZHTP
Torch Tower, Hexi District
Zhuzhou, Hunan
P. R. China 412007
Tel: (86)(773) 8818549
Fax: (86)(773) 8827230
Email: zhaoshangju@zzhitech.com
Website: www.zzhitech.com/zzj.asp

HUAIHUA ECONOMIC DEVELOPMENT ZONE

Our Rating:	B
Year of Establishment:	1992
Location:	Huaihua, Hunan
Size:	19 sq km
Major Investors:	Baoqing Group
Total Foreign Direct Investment:	N.A.
Major Industries Encouraged:	Pharmaceuticals, new construction materials, food, textile, mechanical manufacturing, electronics, chemical engineering, commerce and logistics

INTRODUCTION

Located in Huahuai, the most important industrial and commercial city in western Hunan, Huaihua Economic Development Zone is divided into Hutian Development Zone and Hexi New District. The total development area is to be 19 sq km.

With land area of 27,600 sq km, Huaihua city is the largest administrative region in Hunan province and has abundant resources of forests, agricultural products, minerals and hydropower. The city contains 12 county-level units with a 4.8 million people, of which one third are minorities. There are also many historic and tourism resorts in the city.

With well-developed railway network, the city is conveniently linked to many major cities such as Beijing, Shanghai, Guangzhou, Chongqing, Zhengzhou, Hangzhou, Wuhan, Kuming and Chengdu. Zhijiang Airport is near to the city, too, which is currently under redevelopment.

INVESTMENT CLIMATE

Besides the two subsidiary development zones, Huaihua itself is developing very fast. The major industries to be promoted include pharmaceuticals, new construction materials, food production, textile, timber processing, mechanical manufacturing, electronics, chemical engineering, commerce, logistics etc.

Huaihua municipal government has a list of projects for potential investors, covering energy development, transportation, tourism, agriculture, forestry, food, beverages, light industries, infrastructure development, pharmaceuticals and chemical engineering.

In addition, located in the bordering region of three southwestern provinces of Hunan, Guizhou and Guangxi, Huaihua will probably become a premier growth pole of a vast region with a total area of 90,000 sq km and a population of 15 million people.

The Foreign Investment and Economic Cooperation Burean of Huaihua
29 Yingfeng Road
Huaihua, Hunan
P. R. China 418000
Tel: (86)(745) 2234508
Fax: (86)(745) 2236641
Website: www.huaihua.gov.cn/second/ zsyz/zsyz.asp

NINGXIANG ECONOMIC AND TECHNOLOGICAL DEVELOPMENT ZONE

Our Rating:	B
Year of Establishment:	1998
Location:	Ningxiang, Hunan
Size:	10 sq km
Major Investors:	Sichuan Top Group, Dalian Mincheng High-tech Corporation and Changsha Xianghui Corporation
Major Industries Encouraged:	Electronics, new materials, fine chemical engineering, metallurgical industry, medical industry, textile and food production

INTRODUCTION

Established in 1998, Ningxiang Economic and Technological Development Zone (NXETDZ) is located at Ningxiang County, an administrative region of Changsha city. It is 40 km to downtown Changsha and 60 km to Huanghua International Airport.

Ningxiang is the hometown of former Chinese President Liu Shaoqi. The county now has population of 1.3 million and is often cited as the No.1 agricultural county of Hunan province. It encourages industries such as construction materials, mechanical manufacturing, chemical engineering, mineral production, food, clothing and so on. In particular, Yinhai Petrochemicals Co. Ltd. is China's largest base of citrate production.

INVESTMENT CLIMATE

The total development area of NXETDZ is 10 sq km, with two sq km at the start-up stage. The major industries to be promoted in the development zone include electronics, new materials, fine chemical engineering, metallurgical industry, medical industry, textile, food production and so on.

Sichuan Top Group, which is China's major software developer, has invested RMB230 million here to establish Hunan Software Development Park and Top Information Technologies College, which will accommodate 1,500 students. At the same time, the investment commitment from Dalian Mincheng High-tech Corporation is about RMB174 million. A hot spring resort and a golf course will be established soon with RMB300 million investment commitment from Changsha Xianghua Co. Ltd.

In 2001, the gross industrial output of all enterprises in NXETDZ was RMB385 million, a 48% growth over the previous year.

The Administrative Committee of NXETDZ is the agency in charge of the planning, development and administration of the whole zone.

Administrative Committee OF NXETDZ
Tel: (86)(731) 7800096
Fax: (86)(731) 7800159
Email: nxgyy@public.cs.hn.cn
Website: www.nxgyy.com

HUNAN POWERISE SOFTWARE DEVELOPMENT PARK

Year of Establishment:	1994
Location:	Changsha, Hunan
Size:	35 ha
Major Investors:	Powerise Software Development, Powerise Computers, Hunan Delison System Integration, Hunan Powerise Communications, Longsea Info Tech, HCC Info Software, Hunan Post Science, Hunan Forescape, Supertech System and Heaman Info Industries
Total Foreign Direct Investment:	N.A.
Major Industries Encouraged:	Software projects and related services

INTRODUCTION

The Powerise Software Development Park plays an important role for the software industry of China. To date, the government support fund for the park has reached RMB800 million.

INVESTMENT CLIMATE

There are 31 key enterprises operating in the park, such as Powerise Software Development Co. Ltd., Hunan Powerise Computers Co. Ltd., Hunan Delison System Integration Co. Ltd., Hunan Powerise Communications Co. Ltd., Longsea Info Tech, HCC Info Software Co. Ltd., Hunan Post Science, Hunan Forescape, Supertech System Hunan Co. Ltd. and Hunan Heaman Info Industries. These enterprises mainly provide products and services in fields like system integration, software application, and technological support for major enterprises and government agencies in many major other parts of China.

Since its establishment in 1994, Hunan Powerise Group has established subsidiaries in more than 100 cities across China. It has also established an R&D Center in the Silicon Valley and marketing companies in Japan and Hong Kong. The major cooperative partners of Powerise Group include Motorola, IBM, HP, Oracle and CISCO.

At the end of 2000, the total sales revenue of all member enterprises was RMB3.2 billion, with profit of RMB680 million. Around 6,000 software professionals are closely working with these enterprises.

The development of Powerise Park is strongly supported by the R&D resources in Changsha, include Central South University, Hunan University and University of National Defense Technology. The achievements of UNDT researchers on Yinhe Supercomputer series are at leading positions in China. In addition, Hunan University and University of National Defense Technology have established software colleges.

Powerise Software Development Park
Changsha, Hunan
P. R. China 410013
Tel: (86)(731) 8909000
Fax: (86)(731) 8909260
Email: powerise@public.cs.hn.cn
Website: www.powerise.com.cn

YUELU MOUNTAINS UNIVERSITY SCIENCE PARK

Year of Establishment:	1999
Location:	Changsha, Hunan
Size:	N.A,
Major Investors:	Hunan provincial government, YLMUSP Development Corporation
Major Industries Encouraged:	Electronics, computer science, chemical engineering, materials science, mechanical manufacturing, auto engineering, environmental engineering.

INTRODUCTION

Yuelu Mountains University Science Park (YLMUSP) is located in Changsha, the hometown of many Chinese leaders such as Mr. Mao Zedong and Mr. Zhu Rongji.

The university science park is jointly initiated and supported by Central South University, Hunan University, University of National Defense Science & Technology, Hunan Normal University, Changsha Research Institute of Ore Smelting, Changsha Mine Research Institute and Changsha Research Institute of Construction Machinery.

By mid-2001, around 74 enterprises had entered the park. According to the master plan of the YLMUSP, the capital support from Hunan provincial government will be RMB50 million. YLMUSP Development Corporation will be responsible for the management affairs of the park.

HUMAN RESOURCES

The history of Hunan University could be traced back to the Yuelu School established in 976 A.D. of Song Dynasty. It gained the present name in 1926 and is often referred to as a 1,000-year old college. The current Hunan University is composed of the former Hunan University and Hunan College of Finance & Economy. Top majors of Hunan University include architecture, chemical engineering, materials science, mechanical manufacturing, autoengineering, computer science, environmental engineering, mechanical-electronic integration and auto controlling.

Central South University is another prestigious university in Changsha. Merged with former Central South University of Technology, Hunan Medical University and Changsha Railway College, the university has 27 schools and colleges, with majors covering engineering, science, medical science, literature, law, economics, business administration, philosophy, education, etc. The university has established international exchange relationship with more than 100 overseas universities and institutions, such as Chulalongkon University, Aachen University of Technology, Technical University of Berlin, Nagoya University and Tokyo University, University of Melbourne, Pusan National University, Toronto University, Glasgow University, University of Minnesota, University of Utah and Texas A&M University.

JIANGSU

Industrial Parks in Jiangsu

1. China-Singapore Suzhou Industrial Park
2. Lianyungang Economic and Technological Development Zone
3. Kunshan Economic and Technological Development Zone
4. Nanjing Economic and Technological Development Zone
5. Nantong Economic and Technological Development Zone
6. Changzhou New District
7. Nanjing High-tech Park
8. Suzhou New District
9. Wuxi New District
10. Zhangjiagang Economic and Technological Development Zone
11. Taichang Economic Development Zone

INTRODUCTION

In terms of total GDP, Jiangsu is the second largest economy in China. It was one of the cradles of Chinese modern industry. Contrary to Zhejiang's success in private economy, Jiangsu is known for its "Su Nan (or Southern Jiangsu) Model" which is demonstrated by booming collective or township enterprises in the 1980s and 1990s.

Recently, the province's economy has been increasingly driven by the influx of FDI. Among others, China-Singapore Suzhou Industrial Park, a high-profile bilateral cooperative project between China and Singapore, has attracted much attention besides investment from foreign investors.

Fact Sheet	2001
Area (sq km)	102,600
Population (million)	73.55
GDP (RMB billion)	951.5
GDP Growth Rate	10.2%
Consumption Expenditure (RMB billion)	
• Government	77
• Household	287
Per capita annual	
• disposable income of urban residents (RMB '000)	7.38
• net income of rural households (RMB '000)	3.78
Contractual FDI (USD million)	15,110
Industrial Value Added (RMB bn)	426.9
Imports (USD million)	22,470
Exports (USD million)	28,880
Universities & Colleges	78

GEOGRAPHY

Jiangsu is located in the upper middle part of China's east coast. With an area of 1.1% of the national total, the province has the fourth largest population in China.

Jiangsu is also called "water land" for its widespread lakes, rivers and canals which account for 17% of its total area. The part of South Jiangsu is closer to Shanghai and thus has enjoyed the spillover effects of Shanghai's development. Spanning over subtropical and temperate monsoon climate zones, Jiangsu has four distinct seasons. Temperature only occasionally falls below 0°C in a year.

The provincial government administers 13 prefecture level cities and 64 county level units. Nanjing, one of China's 7 ancient capitals, is the provincial center of culture and politics. However, Suzhou, Wuxi and Changzhou, or the Su-Xi-Chang Area, which is adjacent to Shanghai, contributes the biggest share to Jiangsu's economy.

TRAVEL INFORMATION

From Nanjing Airport to:

Beijing	1 hr 15 mins
Guangzhou	2 hrs
Chongqing	2 hrs
Xi'an	2 hrs
Hong Kong	2 hrs 15 mins

INVESTMENT CLIMATE

Jiangsu has a convenient transportation system. Nanjing is the largest inland port in Asia. Lianyungang and Nantong are the two important ports among the first batch of 14 coastal open cities in China.

The province has also established a comprehensive industrial structure, led by mechanical, electronics, chemical, automobile, textile, metallurgical, construction materials and food industries. High-tech enterprises have also grown robustly.

New approved FIE projects in 2001 rose to 3,581 with total contractual investment of USD15.1 billion, 42.2% increase from the previous year. There were 549 projects with investment of above USD10 million each, 13 of them with investment of more than USD100 million.

Jiangsu has set up 80 state or province level development zones. In 2001, those industrial parks accounted for 40% of the provincial exports and received 82% of the total FDI in Jiangsu. They are mostly located in Suzhou, Wuxi, Changzhou and Nanjing. There are 78 university & colleges in Jiangsu, including Nanjing University and Southeast University.

Jiangsu Provincial Government
Website: www.jiangsu.gov.cn

Jiangsu Department of Foreign Trade and Economic Cooperation
29 East Beijing Road, Jiangsu
P. R. China 210008
Tel: (86)(25) 7712600

CHINA-SINGAPORE SUZHOU INDUSTRIAL PARK

Our Rating:	AAA
Year of Establishment:	1994
Location:	Suzhou, Jiangsu
Size:	70 sq km (Phase I is 8 sq km)
Major Investors:	Samsung, AMD, Hitachi Semiconductor, Sumitomo Bakelite, Nokia, GlaxoWellcome, Littlefuse, Lilly, Eisai, Eka, Emerson Electric, Grundfos Pumps, MTU Engineering, Singapore Technologies, Wing Tai, Comfort, Isola Laminate Systems, Vesuvius Advanced Ceramics, Beautycos and Nabisco.
Total Foreign Direct Investment:	USD4.65 billion
Major Industries Encouraged:	Electronics, pharmaceuticals, chemicals, precision engineering, new materials and light industry

INTRODUCTION

China-Singapore Suzhou Industrial Park (SIP) is a high-profile bilateral cooperative project between the Chinese and Singapore governments. On 26 February 1994, Chinese Vice Premier Mr Li Lanqing and Singapore Senior Minister Mr Lee Kuan Yew signed the Agreement on the Joint Development of Suzhou Industrial Park in Beijing.

The 70 sq km SIP will be developed in three phases. The Master Plan has adopted the advanced urban development experience of Singapore and other countries in the world.

Suzhou Industrial Park (SIP) is only one hour's ride to airports in Shanghai and two hours' ride to Nanjing, the provincial capital of Jiangsu, via Shanghai-Nanjing Expressway.

In 2001, SIP's GDP was RMB18 billion, fiscal revenue was RMB2.4 billion and total import-export was USD3.7 billion, of which exports amounted to USD1.6 billion.

INVESTMENT CLIMATE

The infrastructure and utilities projects have been developed to world-class standard. China-Singapore Suzhou Industrial Park Development Co. Ltd., or CSSD, a joint venture between a Chinese consortium and a Singaporean consortium, is the organization that takes charge of the development of overall township.

The infrastructure development, costing about RMB8.9 billion by the end of 2001, has laid down superior conditions for investment. The so-called Nine Utilities and Land-filling Project, namely road, power, water, gas, steam, communications, sewage treatment, drainage, cable TV and land leveling, has been accomplished within the Phase I area.

Foreign enterprises

Approved foreign enterprises numbered 725 with an accumulated contractual investment of USD12.4 billion and utilized foreign capital of USD4.65 billion. Forty-one Fortune

500 corporations have invested in 47 projects in SIP. There are three projects with a total investment of more than USD1 billion, 26 projects with a total investment of more than USD0.1 billion, and 60 projects with more than USD30 million. Major MNCs in SIP include Samsung, Hitachi, AMD, Sumitomo, Nokia, Glaxowellcome, Lilly, Eisai, Emerson Electric, Wing Tai and Nabisco etc.

Major industrial clusters in SIP include electric and electronics, pharmaceuticals and chemicals, precision engineering and new materials.

SIP has also been adopting as well as adapting Singapore's experience in economic development and public administration. New regulations of urban construction and environmental protection, the concept of Central Provident Fund (CPF), and recruitment approach of civil servants have been brought into effect in SIP.

With a population of 5.8 million, Suzhou offers a rich pool of talents. It produces about 20,000 graduates annually from universities, polytechnics, specialized secondary schools and vocational training schools.

Suzhou has a one-million-strong industrial workforce, generally well educated and hard working. To better meet investors' needs for senior skilled workers, Suzhou Industrial Park has set up its own training center-Institute of Vocational Technology (IVT). It fully adopts Singapore's Nanyang Polytechnic's experience in vocational training and software management. Its graduates, trained in the areas of industrial electronics, modern communications, mechatronics and precision engineering, are even recruited by the SIP investors before graduation.

The Park has become one of the youngest yet most vigorous development zones in China. When fully developed, it will accommodate 600,000 people and provide 360,000 job opportunities. SIP is expected to become one of the most competitive industrial parks in China.

China-Singapore Suzhou Industrial Park Development Co. Ltd.
Suzhou Head Office
12F International Building
2 Suhua Road
Tel: (86) (512) 62882828
Fax: (86) (512) 62881297

Singapore Branch
9 Temasek Boulevard #22-01
Suntec Tower 2
Singapore 038989
Tel: (65) 63320650
Fax: (65) 63376610
Website: www.cssd.com.sg

Suzhou Industrial Park Administrative Committee (SIPAC)
International Building
2 Suhua Road
Suzhou Industrial Park,
Suzhou, Jiangsu Province
P. R. China 215021
Tel: (86)(512) 2881710, 2881708, 2881735
Fax: (86)(512) 2881765
Email: etdb@sipac.gov.cn
Website: www.sipac.gov.cn

中国农业银行苏州分行
AGRICULTURAL BANK OF CHINA SUZHOU BRANCH

Agricultural Bank of China, Suzhou Branch (ABC Suzhou) is one of the largest state-owned banks in Suzhou, famous for its financial strength, an extensive network and a spectrum of services provided. Today, the bank has built a network of nine sub-branches and over 300 service outlets throughout the municipality of Suzhou.

In recent years, ABC Suzhou has sped up its pace of transforming into a stated-owned commercial bank, based on 'Market to be Guide, Client to be God, Benefit to be Goal'. The bank has effectively increased market shares to realize its healthy development. In 2001, its profit amounted to RMB600 million. By the end of June 2002, its deposits reached RMB50.8 billion with a market share of 23.4%, and loans rose to RMB30 billion with a market share of 22%, ranking the first among all local financial institutions. The bank also boasts of high quality services such as e-Banking and Funds Transfer, which increasingly make it the preferred choice for local clients.

ABC Suzhou is the principal bank authorized to handle foreign business related transactions in this area. Facing a growing globalized economy, the bank sets the goal to promote its international operations. In 2001, international businesses totaled USD8 billion with a market share of 33%, leading all local counterparts. More than half of the new loans have been injected into those state-level development zones, such as Suzhou Industrial Park and free trade zones. Currently, most foreign invested enterprises in Suzhou have become the bank's proud clientele.

ABC Suzhou believes in equality, cooperativeness and mutual benefit. It will cater to clients' diversified and sophisticated needs by leveraging on its strong financial resources and its integrated global network.

21-23 Shishan Road, Suzhou New
District, Suzhou, Jiangsu, China
Tel: 86-512-67775580,
        68242294
Fax: 86-512-67775800,
        68240501

SUZHOU NEW DISTRICT

Our Rating:	AAA
Year of Establishment:	1990
Location:	Suzhou, Jiangsu
Size:	52 sq km
Major Investors:	Motorola, P&G, Harman, Solutia, Dupont, Coastal, Siemens, Phillips, Logitech, Schindler, Freudenberg, Schott, Moeller, Fujitsu, Matsushita, Canon, Seiko, Epson, NGK, Fukuda Metal, Mitsui Sumitomo, Mitsui Chemicals, NDK, Itochu, Mitsubishi, Inax, Yokogawa, NSG, Shimadzu, Fuji Chemicals and Benq
Total Foreign Direct Investment:	N.A.
Major Industries Encouraged:	Electronics, information technologies, precision machinery and fine chemicals

INTRODUCTION

Suzhou New District (SND) is located in the western part of Suzhou, Jiangsu Province. Similar to China-Singapore Suzhou Industrial Park, SND is also one of the eight administrative districts of Suzhou City. It was approved as a state high-tech park in 1992. The total development area of the district is 52 sq km. SND is designated as an industrial park open to Asia Pacific Economic Cooperation (APEC) members in 1997. In the next year, it became China's first ISO14000 certified Area.

Suzhou is located in the Yangtze River Delta, together with other cities such as Shanghai, Nanjing, Wuxi and Changzhou. It is adjacent to Shanghai, about an hour's drive via Shanghai-Nanjing Expressway.

The major industries of the park are electronics, information technology, precision machinery and fine chemicals. About 36% of the investors come from Europe and the US, 31% from Taiwan, 27% from Japan and 6% from other regions.

The total import and export volume of SND reached USD5.9 billion, which makes up 1% of the national total in China. Its GDP and total industrial output were RMB16 billion and RMB40.1 billion respectively in 2001.

INVESTMENT CLIMATE

Many international enterprises have joined SND, such as Motorola, PPG, P&G, Upjohn, Harman, Solutia, Dupont and Coastal from the US, Siemens, Phillips, Akzo Nobel, Logitech, Schindler, Freudenberg, Schott, StoraEnso, Ondeo, Alstom, Moeller and Filtronics from Europe, Sony Chemicals, Fujitsu, Fuji Film, Matsushita, Panasonic, Canon, Sumitomo Electrical, Seiko Epson, NGK, Fukuda Metal, Mitsui Sumitomo Bank, Mitsui Chemicals, NDK, Itochu, Mitsubishi, Inax, Yokogawa, NSG, Shimadzu and Fuji Chemicals from Japan, and Benq, Asus, Yageo, Chunghwa, Umax, Sampo, Evergreen, Chinpoon, Gold Circuits, CMS and Grand Pacific from Taiwan, etc.

SND is 80 kilometers away from Shanghai Hongqiao International Airport, 120 kilometers away from Shanghai Pudong International Airport, 200 kilometers away from Nanjing International Airport and 40 kilometers away from the smaller airports in Suzhou, namely Shuofang Airport and Guangfu Airport, respectively.

In addition, some important ports such as Shanghai Port, Zhangjiagang Port, Taicang Port and Changshu Port are all located around Suzhou. Three national highways, namely, No. 202 National Highway (from Yantai to Shanghai), No. 312 National Highway (from Shanghai to Xinjiang) and No. 318 National Highway (from Shanghai to Tibet) all run across SND. A well-developed expressway system, which consists of Shanghai-Nanjing Expressway, Airport Expressway and Suzhou-Jiaxing-Hangzhou Expressway, provides easy access to other cities in East China. Beijing-Shanghai Railway runs through Suzhou. China's first express railway between Beijing and Shanghai is now also under construction.

SND consists of three subsidiary areas, namely the central business district, the residential area and the industrial area. The development area in the first stage is 25 sq km and the 2nd stage of 11 sq km in the northern part of SND was started in August 2001.

Suzhou New District Administrative Committee
8 Yunhe Road, Suzhou New District
Suzhou, Jiangsu Province
P. R. China 215011
Tel: (86)(512) 68251888
Fax: (86)(512) 68251579
Email: director@cs-snd.com.cn
Website: www.cs-snd.com.cn

LIANYUNGANG ECONOMIC AND TECHNOLOGICAL DEVELOPMENT ZONE

Our Rating:	BBB
Year of Establishment:	1984
Location:	Lianyungang, Jiangsu
Size:	45 sq km
Major Investors:	Zhongshan Anlun, Hengrui Group, Jianghe Group, Lianzhong Group and Ruyi Group
Total Foreign Direct Investment:	N.A.
Major Industries Encouraged:	Pharmaceuticals, textile, chemical and electronics.

INTRODUCTION

Approved by the State Council in 1984 as one of the state development zones, Lianyungang Economic and Technological Development Zone (LYGETDZ) covers an area of 45 sq km, of which six sq km has been developed.

LYGETDZ is located in the eastern part of Lianyungang City. It is 22 kilometers from downtown and five kilometers from the new area of the Lianyungang Port.

INVESTMENT CLIMATE

Lianyungang Port is one of the eight biggest ports in China. There are 55 container liners setting off from the port every month. Cargo can be transported to some 600 ports around the world. Its annual handling capacity is 22.2 million tons. The actual handling volume was 20.17 million tons in 1999 and 27.0 million tons in 2000.

Lianyungang is the eastern terminal of China's most important latitudinal railway, Longhai Railway. It is a transportation artery connecting East and West China and called the New Eurasia Continental Bridge as it goes westward through central Asian countries to Rotterdam, the Netherlands, totaling 10,900 kilometers.

LYGETDZ has been attracting investors from some 35 countries and regions, such as

Japan, Korea, the US and Australia. Some 300 foreign funded enterprises have been set up in LYGETDZ.

Four major industries have been developed in the park namely medicine, textile, chemical industry and electronics. Zhongshan Anlun, Hengrui Group, Jianghe Group, Lianzhong Group, Ruyi Group are some successful enterprises.

Lianyungang has abundant mineral resources, of which 40 industrial minerals have been found, including phosphorite and serpentine which rank the first in northern China. Its neighbor, Donghai, has the largest crystal deposit in China. Surrounded by a 162-kilometer long coastline and bordering Haizhou Bay (one of China's eight biggest fishing bases), Lianyungang has rich ocean resources. China has listed Haizhou Bay as one of the three Ocean Special Development Zones.

Administrative Committee of LYGETDZ
Huangjiunian, Lianyungang
Jiangsu Province
P. R. China 222047
Tel: (86)(518) 2396838
Fax: (86)(518) 2341573
Email: jiangwd@lygetdz.gov.cn
Website: www.lygetdz.gov.cn

KUNSHAN ECONOMIC AND TECHNOLOGICAL DEVELOPMENT ZONE

Our Rating:	AAA
Year of Establishment:	1985
Location:	Kunshan, Jiangsu
Size:	28 sq km (6.18 sq km)
Major Investors:	Nan Ya Plastics, Compaq Computer, Guangzhi Electronics, Makita Corporation, Giant Bicycle
Total Foreign Direct Investment:	USD5.1 billion (end 2001)
Major Industries Encouraged:	electronics, precision engineering and fine chemicals

INTRODUCTION

Kunshan Economic and Technological Development Zone (KSETDZ) was established in 1985 and later approved as a state-level development zone in 1992. KSETDZ covers a land area totaling 28 sq km. At present, a Microelectronics Industrial Park, an Export Processing Zone and a Business Incubator Park for Overseas Chinese Scholars have been set up in KSETDZ.

KSETDZ is situated to the east of Kunshan City, 50 kilometers to the west of Shanghai and 37 kilometers east of Suzhou.

In 2001, KSETDZ achieved RMB10.3 billion in GDP, RMB31.2 billion in total industrial output, and RMB8.1 billion in industrial value-added, up 20% over the previous year. Total import-export was around USD3.12 billion.

INVESTMENT CLIMATE

The park has invested more than RMB3 billion on infrastructure development such as transport, communications, water supply, energy and greenery etc.

Shanghai Hongqiao International Airport is 45 km away from KSETDZ, and Shanghai Pudong International Airport is 100 km away.

KSETDZ can export directly from Shanghai Port, Zhangjiagang Port, and Taicang Port. There is an extensive highway network in the zone, with Shanghai-Nanjing Expressway and State Highway 312, both running through KSETDZ.

By the end of 2001, foreign investors from more than 36 countries and regions such as the US, Japan, South Korea, EU, Taiwan etc. had invested in 650 projects, with contracted foreign investment of USD4.8 billion, of which Taiwanese capital accounted for 65%. There are 150 projects with a total investment of more than USD10 million each. Fortune 500 corporations have committed 22 investment projects. KSETDZ now features 3 key industries, namely electronics, precision engineering and fine chemicals.

Investment Promotion Bureau of KSETDZ
2nd Floor, International Plaza
167 Qianjing Middle Road
Kunshan, Jiangsu
P. R. China 215300
Tel: (86)(520) 7303999
Fax: (86)(520) 7313888
E-mail: ketd@ketd.gov.cn
Website: www.ketd.gov.cn

NANJING ECONOMIC AND TECHNOLOGICAL DEVELOPMENT ZONE

Our Rating:	AA
Year of Establishment:	1992
Location:	Nanjing, Jiangsu
Size:	13.37 sq km
Major Investors:	Sharp, SAES Getters, Philips Magnetic Materials, Fujikura, AO Smith, LG, Cuccess Pharmaceutical, Meirui Pharmaceutical, ADC Telecom, Arrow Glassware, Xingang Hi-tech, Xingang Electric Power etc.
Total Foreign Direct Investment:	USD1 billion (end 2001)
Major Industries Encouraged:	Electronics, information, biomedicine, light machinery, fine chemical engineering, logistics and warehousing

INTRODUCTION

Nanjing Economic and Technological Development Zone (NJETDZ) was established on 18 September 1992. It was approved as a State-level Development Zone by the State Council on 15 March 2002. The development area covers 13.37 sq km.

NJETDZ is located in the northeast suburbs of Nanjing. It is 15 kilometers away from downtown Nanjing.

In 2001, the GDP of NJETDZ was RMB6 billion and export was USD390 million. More than 900 enterprises had joined the zone, among which foreign invested enterprises invested a total of USD1.02 billion with USD420 million utilized.

INVESTMENT CLIMATE

More than RMB2 billion has been invested in infrastructure development.

Major industries include electronics, information technology, biomedicine, light machinery, precision chemical engineering, logistics and warehousing, etc.

Administrative Committee of NJETDZ
100 Xingang Avenue
Foreign Trade Port District
Nanjing, Jiangsu
P. R. China 210038
Tel: (86)(25) 5800800
Fax: (86)(25) 5800900
E-mail:gwh@njxg.com
Website: www.njxg.com

NANTONG ECONOMIC AND TECHNOLOGICAL DEVELOPMENT AREA

Our Rating:	A
Year of Establishment:	1984
Location:	Nantong, Jiangsu
Size:	20 sq km
Major Investors:	Itochu, Marubeni, Toray, Teijin, Zeneca, ITT, Reilly, Air Liquide, San Teh and Synthetic Rubber
Total Foreign Direct Investment:	USD1 billion
Major Industries Encouraged:	N.A.

INTRODUCTION

Nantong Economic and Technological Development Zone (NTETDZ), one of the first 14 development zones in China, was approved by the state government on 19 December 1984.

NTETDZ lies in the center of China's golden coastline and the north side of the Yangtze River Delta. NTETDZ is well recognized as the gateway to the Yangtze. It is well linked by Shanghai-Nanjing Expressway to the south and connected with Nanjing-Nantong Expressway to the north. The planned Su-Tong Yangtze Bridge will strengthen Nantong's position as a hub for south-north coastal highway transportation and establish direct access to Shanghai.

INVESTMENT CLIMATE

Nantong Port provides direct international container service to Hong Kong, Japan, Korea and 28 other destinations worldwide every day. NTETDA port facilities are capable of handling containers, bulk cargo, chemical products, petroleum and LPG. Currently, Nantong handles 23.99 million tons of cargo and 160,000 TEUs of containers per year.

NTETDZ is 100 kilometers away from Shanghai Hongqiao International Airport, 150 kilometers from Pudong International Airport, 240 kilometers from Nanjing Lukou Airport. Nantong Airport, 16 kilometers away, offers domestic flights to Beijing, Dalian, Guangzhou, Shenzhen, Qingdao and Xiamen.

Investors from 22 countries and regions operate over 200 foreign-invested enterprises in NTETDA. They have committed a total of USD2 billion with over USD1 billion already paid-up. Those companies include Itochu, Marubeni, Toray and Teijin of Japan, Zeneca of UK, ITT and Reilly of USA, Air Liquide of France, San Teh of Singapore, and Synthetic Rubber of Taiwan.

Administrative Committee of NTETDZ
Fumin Port, Nantong
Jiangsu, China 226009
Tel: (86)(513) 3596030
Fax: (86)(513) 3596033
E-mail: info@netda.com
Website: www.netda.com

CHANGZHOU NEW DISTRICT

Our Rating:	AA
Year of Establishment:	1995
Location:	Changzhou, Jiangsu
Size:	116 sq km
Major Investors:	GE, IMETAL, Mannesmann, Anglia, DISA, George Fischer, Flextronics, Amphend, Iveco, Matther & Toledo, Leoni, Fujitsu, OKI, Marubeni, Bridgestone, Hitachi, Komatsu, Robin, Itochu, Kymco and Sunball
Total Foreign Direct Investment:	N.A.
Major Industries Encouraged:	Motorcycles, electronics, computer components, engineering-use plastics, environment protection technology, pharmaceuticals and sanitary materials

INTRODUCTION

Changzhou New District (CZND) is located in the north area of Changzhou City, Jiangsu Province. It was approved with the status of state-level high-tech park in May 1995. The total area of CZND is 116 sq km, comprising Changzhou High-tech Zone (30 sq km), Xinlong Zone and New Port Zone (38 sq km). Bordering Shanghai-Nanjing Railway in the south and the Yangtze River in the north, CZND is 160 kilometers away from Shanghai and 120 kilometers away from Nanjing. Flights are available from Changzhou to Beijing, Dalian, Chongqing, Chengdu, Guangzhou and Xi'an.

The core industries of CZND are motorcycles, electronics, computer components, plastic engineering, environment protection technology, bio-chemical, pharmaceuticals and sanitary materials.

INVESTMENT CLIMATE

CZND is only kilometer away from Shanghai-Nanjing Expressway. It is on the midpoint of Shanghai-Nanjing Railway. Changzhou Airport is about 20 kilometers from CZND and its air flights connect to major cities of China.

Over RMB2.56 billion has been invested for infrastructure development. Many investors have established operations in the district. General Electric, IMETAL, Mannesmann, Anglia, DISA, George Fischer, Flextronics, Amphend, Caltex, Ashland Chemicals, Iveco, Matther & Toledo, Leoni, Fujitsu, OKI, Marubeni, Bridgestone, Hitachi, Komatsu, Robin, Itochu, Kymco and Sunball are the major MNCs that have invested in the district.

There are some important subsidiary zones within CZND, namely Electronics Industrial Park, Software Park, Riverside Industrial Zone and International Environment Protection Industrial Park.

The 8.92 sq km Electronics Industrial Park is located in the central part of CZND. Jointly designed by consultants from Taiwan and Shanghai-based Tongji University, the park followed the development model of Taiwan

Hsinchu Science Industrial Park. Investors from the US and Taiwan have invested heavily in the park.

Software Park was established in 1999, and the development area for the first stage was around 1.5 sq km. It comprises an incubation zone and an industrial zone. Near the park, there are several universities and colleges such as Hohai University and Changzhou Institute of Technology.

Riverside Industry Area has an area of 37 sq km, and is specialized in heavy chemical industry and raw material industry. Over ten projects from famous companies have established operations in the park.

Located in the north part of CZND, International Environment Protection Industrial Park covers eight sq km. It comprises a core industrial park, Scientific Research Park, Exhibition Center of Environment Protection Products and Consultation Center. The main technologies and products developed in the park are related to water saving, water treatment, air pollution control, environment monitoring, waste treatment, energy saving, green energy and comprehensive utilization of resources.

Foreign Investment Bureau
Administrative Committee of CZND
Tel: (86)(519) 5108600, 5108229
E-mail: cndfi@public.cz.js.cn
Website: www.cznd.org.cn

NANJING HIGH-TECH PARK

Our Rating:	AA
Year of Establishment:	1991
Location:	Nanjing, Jiangsu
Size:	16.5 sq km
Major Investors:	Nanjing Organon Pharmaceutial, Zhengzhong Bioengineering, Rally Biochemical, East Medicine Factory and Sanneng
Total Foreign Direct Investment:	N.A.
Major Industries Encouraged:	Electronics, information technology, bioengineering, new materials, petrochemicals, software development and aviation technology

INTRODUCTION

Nanjing High-tech Park (NJHTP) is a state-level high-tech park in Nanjing. It was approved as a state-level high-tech park in March 1991. The total development area is 16.5 sq km.

Over 1,000 enterprises have established in NJHTP, among which over 100 enterprises are foreign-invested enterprises. In 2001, the total industrial output was RMB33.5 billion. There are around 150 high-tech enterprises in the park.

NJHTP focuses industries such as electronics, information technology, bioengineering, new materials, petrochemicals, software development and aviation technology.

INVESTMENT CLIMATE

Nanjing HTP comprises several subsidiary parks, namely Software Park, Bio-pharmaceutical Park and Chemical Industrial Park.

Located in the southern area of NJHTP, Bio-pharmaceutical Park aims to become a quality innovation center for the bioengineering industry. Currently, there are a number of enterprises such as Nanjing Organon Pharmaceutial Co. Ltd., Zheng-zhong Bio-engineering Co. Ltd., Nanjing Rally Biochemical Co. Ltd., East Medicine Factory, and the Biological Reaction Engineering Center of Nanjing University of Chemical Engineering.

Chemical Industrial Park is located in the northern area of Nanjing, and it is 30 kilometers from downtown area. The park has an area of 41 sq km and is focused on petrochemical industry, such as organic chemical industrial materials, meticulous chemical engineering, high polymer materials and new chemical materials.

Administrative Committee of NJHTP

P.O. Box 3209, Pukou District
Nanjing, Jiangsu
P. R. China 210061
Tel: (86)(25) 8843 666
Fax: (86)(25) 8843 843
Email: njhnza@public1.ptt.js.cn
Website: www.njnhz.com.cn

WUXI NEW DISTRICT

Our Rating:	AAA
Year of Establishment:	1993
Location:	Wuxi, Jiangsu
Size:	83 sq km
Major Investors:	Kodak, Seagate, GE, Maxell, Sharp, Hitachi, Nittobo, Toshiba, Matsushita, Siemens, Bosch, Bayer, Astra, Volvo Penta, Auchan, Valmet, President Group and Roche
Total Foreign Direct Investment:	USD2.67 billion
Major Industries Encouraged:	Electronics, information technology, electromechanical engineering, bioengineering, new materials and fine chemicals

INTRODUCTION

Wuxi New District (WND) is located in the southeastern part of Wuxi city, Jiangsu Province. As a high-tech industrial park, it gained state-level endorsement in 1992. Currently, the total development area of the new district is 83 sq km. Its development is mainly based on Wuxi High-tech Park and Wuxi Singapore Industrial Park. WND is six kilometers from the downtown area. In 2000, WND became an ISO14000 certified National Exemplary Area.

The major industries at WND include electronics, information technology, electromechanical engineering, bioengineering, new materials, and fine chemical engineering.

INVESTMENT CLIMATE

WND is located beside the beautiful Taihu Lake. Shanghai-Nanjing Expressway, National Highway No. 312, Beijing-Shanghai Railway and Beijing-Hangzhou Grand Canal all run through Wuxi City.

WND is 130 kilometers away from Shanghai Port and 40 kilometers from Zhangjiagang Port. It only takes 70 minutes to drive to Shanghai Hongqiao Airport via the expressway. Flights are available from the local airport in Wuxi to Beijing, Guangzhou, Shenzhen and some other cities.

Wuxi will become an advantageous location for the coming Beijing-Shanghai Express Railway.

By the end of 2001, WND accommodated over 469 foreign invested enterprises whose total investment was around USD5 billion. 141 enterprises had investments of more than USD10 million and 25 companies had investments of above USD100 million. Thirty Fortune 500 MNCs have established subsidiaries in the district. These include Kodak, Seagate, GE and Maxell from the US, Sharp, Hitachi, Nittobo, Toshiba and Matsushita from Japan, Siemens, Bosch and Bayer from Germany, Astra and Volvo Penta from Sweden, Auchan from France, Valmet from Finland and President Group from Taiwan and Roche from Switzerland.

According to the administrative committee of WND, the high-tech park has established cooperation with some international counterparts, such as Newland Science Park in the United Kingdom and the

Triangle Research Park in North Carolina, USA.

WND consists of three key subsidiary parks, namely Wuxi Singapore Industrial Park, National Agricultural High-tech Park and Entrepreneurship Park for Overseas Chinese Scholars.

The industrial focus of Wuxi Singapore Industrial Park is electronics, optical technology, information technology, telecommunication equipment, medical and healthcare products, automotive and aerospace components. The development of Agriculture High-tech Park is well-supported by Nanjing Agricultural University.

Wuxi Entrepreneurship Park for Overseas Chinese Scholars is designed as a national incubation center for Chinese students returning from overseas studies to pursue advanced R & D and establish new ventures. Wuxi Evermore Software, Zhongxing Light-Electronic Technology Co Ltd and Baitai Research Institute at Wuxi University of Light Industry are among such successful start-up ventures.

The Investment Board of Wuxi New District
3rd Level, Administration Building
5 Tianshan Road, Wuxi New District
Wuxi, Jiangsu Province
P. R. China 214028
Tel: (86)(510) 5219388, 5217777
Fax: (86)(510) 5215876
Email: wnd@wnd.gov.cn
Website: www.wnd.gov.cn

ZHANGJIAGANG ECONOMIC AND TECHNOLOGICAL DEVELOPMENT ZONE

Our Rating:	AA
Year of Establishment:	1993
Location:	Zhangjiagang, Jiangsu
Size:	6.2 sq km
Major Investors:	East Ocean Oils & Grains Okamoto Hosiery Making, Huafeng Machinery, Dow Chemical, Asahi Chemical and Chevron
Total Foreign Direct Investment:	USD380 million
Major Industries Encouraged:	Machinery, petrochemical and chemicals

INTRODUCTION

Zhangjiagang Economic & Technological Development Zone (ZJGETDZ) is located at the center of Zhangjiagang city which is under the jurisdiction of Suzhou. The city boasts 30 wharves with more than 10,000 tonnages. In June 2002, there are over 33 foreign enterprises in ZJGETDZ with total utilized foreign investment of USD500 million.

With total development area of 6.2 sq km, ZJGETDZ was established in November 1993. It is 15 kilometers from both Zhangjiagang International Port and Zhangjiagang Free Trade Zone. It takes two hours to drive to Shanghai Hongqiao International Airport or Nanjing Lukou Airport. Since its establishment, RMB1.2 billion has been invested to develop infrastructure facilities.

INVESTMENT CLIMATE

By the end of 2000, around 200 projects including 31 FIEs were established in the park. The total contractual foreign investment was USD380 million. Overseas investors include Okamoto Hosiery Making Co. Ltd., Huafeng Machinery Co. Ltd., Dow Chemical, Asahi Chemical, and Chevron.

The subsidiaries of Dow Chemical, Asahi Chemical and Chevron are mainly located in Jiangsu Yangtze River International Chemical Industrial Park. Companies like East Sea Grains & Oils Co. Ltd., Oriental Unocal Energy Co. Ltd., Dow-Asahi Chemical Industrial Base and Chevron Chemical Industrial Base all have investment commitments of USD55 million to USD400 million.

Administrative Committee of ZJGETDZ
Yuefeng Mansion
Zhangyang Road
Zhangjiagang, Jiangsu
P. R. China 215600
Tel: (86)(520) 8673996
Fax: (86)(520) 8673996
E-mail: uuzjgedz@public1.sz.js.cn
Website: www.zjgedz.com

TAICANG ECONOMIC DEVELOPMENT ZONE

Our Rating:	A
Year of Establishment:	1991
Location:	Taicang city, Jiangsu Province
Size:	25 sq km (Phase I 7.1 sq km)
Major Investors:	Wall's, Nike, Trane Air Conditioner, C&H Toys, Tiger Drylac, Keerya Knitting, Jinyuan Travelling Products, Kern-Liebers Springs, Tox-Pressotechnik, Wegoma Machineary, Shimei Electronics, KOA Electronics, Taitrok, German Enterprise Technician Train Center and Yokohoma.
Total Foreign Direct Investment:	USD900 million
Major Industries Encouraged:	Precision instruments, biomedicine, electronics, information technology, food processing, real estate and tourism

INTRODUCTION

Taicang Economic Development Zone (TCEDZ) is located at the eastern part of Taicang city. With total development area of 12 sq km, the zone was established in January 1991 and was upgraded to be a province-level zone in 1993. It is 40 kilometers to Shanghai Hongqiao International Airport and 18 kilometers to Taicang Port. Taicang is under the administration of Suzhou and is adjacent to Jiading District.

INVESTMENT CLIMATE

By the end of 2001, with total investment of RMB10 billion, over 400 projects joined TCEDZ. The total number of FIEs was around 150 and total investment was USD900 million. Twelve projects had investments of above USD10 million. About 20 Japanese enterprises have established subsidiaries and they are mainly specialized in fields like electronics, information technology and garment manufacturing. Most of the 18 German enterprises in TCEDA are specialized in the fields of designing and manufacturing of precision instruments.

The FIEs in TCEDA include Wall's China Co. Ltd. (Taicang), Nike (Suzhou) Sports Co. Ltd., Trane Air Conditioner Co. Ltd., C&H Toys Co. Ltd., Tiger Drylac Co. Ltd., Keerya Knitting Co. Ltd., Jinyuan Travelling Products Co. Ltd., Kern-Liebers Springs Co. Ltd., Tox-Pressotechnik Ltd., Wegoma Machineary Equipment Co. Ltd., Shimei Electronics, KOA Electronics Co. Ltd., Taitrok Co. Ltd., German Enterprise Technician Train Center and Yokohoma Tape Co. Ltd. Their industries cover precision instruments, biomedicine, electronics, information technology, food processing, real estate and tourism.

The Development Corporation of Taicang Economic Development Zone
Taicang, Jiangsu
P. R. China 215000
Tel: (86)(520) 3571888, 3576084, 3578569
E-mail: infoport@tcip.net.cn
Website: www.jstced.com

NANJING SOFTWARE DEVELOPMENT PARK

Year of Establishment:	1999
Location:	Nanjing, Jiangsu
Size:	1 sq km (Phase I is 40 ha)
Major Investors:	Jiangsu Nandasoft, Lian Chuang Technologies, Tonmac Software, Nanjing Microne Electronics, Mobilesoft Nanjing and Golden Eagle Software Systems
Total Foreign Direct Investment:	N.A.
Major Industries Encouraged:	Software development

INTRODUCTION

Nanjing Software Development Park (NJSDP) is planned to become the center of high-tech industries in Nanjing City as well as Jiangsu province. It is part of Nanjing High-tech Park. The initial start-up area of the park was 40 ha and will be expanded to the whole planned area of one sq km in 2005.

INVESTMENT CLIMATE

The first 12,000 sq m of office space has already been occupied. Around 66 software companies have joined the park; about 2,500 software professionals are working with these enterprises. Major organizations include Jiangsu Nandasoft Co. Ltd., Lian Chuang Technologies, Tonmac Software Co. Ltd., Nanjing Microne Electronics Co. Ltd., Mobilesoft Nanjing Co. Ltd. and Golden Eagle Software Systems Co. Ltd. Another 30 enterprises will join by the end of 2002. Their products and services cover communication, network, management information system, network security and so on. In 2000, the total sales revenue of these enterprises was RMB800 million.

The start-up area of the park is around 40 hectares and by 2005 another area of 60 hectares will be developed in Jiangning Economic & Technological Zone near Nanjing. At that time, it will accommodate around 600 software companies, of which five will have annual sales over RMB1 billion. The total sales of all enterprises by then are expected to be around RMB20 billion.

Human resources

In Nanjing, there are many universities, colleges and research institutions, such as Nanjing University, Southeast University, Hohai University, China Pharmaceutical University, Nanjing Normal University, Nanjing University of Technology, Nanjing University of Posts & Telecommuncations and other universities and colleges. That provides essential intellectual resources to the software industry of Nanjing.

Administrative Committee of NJSDP
Website: www.njnhz.com.cn/software/
index_soft.htm

XUZHOU ECONOMIC AND TECHNOLOGICAL DEVELOPMENT ZONE

Our Rating:	A
Year of Establishment:	1992
Location:	Xuzhou, Jiangsu
Size:	19.8 sq km
Major Investors:	Caterpillar, Liebherr, Chia Tai and Xuzhou Construction Machinery Group
Total Foreign Direct Investment:	N.A.
Major Industries Encouraged:	Environmental protection products & technologies, machinery and new materials

INTRODUCTION

With total development area of 19.8 sq km, Xuzhou Economic & Technological Development Zone (XZETDZ) was establis-hed in 1992. It is located in Xuzhou city in the northern part of Jiangsu Province. The zone is 6.8 kilometers from downtown Xuzhou and 1.8 kilometers to the Railway Station.

According to the master plan, XZETDZ is divided into six sub-zones, namely, Taiwan Industrial Park, Environmental Industries Park, Mechanical Industry Park, New Materials Industry Park, Education Technologies Park and the residential area.

INVESTMENT CLIMATE

By the end of 2000, more than 1,000 enterprises had registered in XZETDZ, including over 200 from overseas. Many major MNCs have established their agencies and offices in XZETDZ, such as Caterpillar, Liebherr and Chia Tai Group. The state-level R&D Center of Xuzhou Construction Machinery Group is also located in XZETDZ.

Administrative Committee of XZETDZ
Tel: (86)(516) 7793400, 7791145
E-mail: zsj@xedz.com
Website: www.xedz.com

TAIZHOU ECONOMIC DEVELOPMENT ZONE

Our Rating:	BBB
Year of Establishment:	1996
Location:	Taizhou, Jiangsu
Size:	25.6 sq km
Major Investors:	Chunlan Group, Yangtze Medicals Group, Linghai Motors, Taixing Reducer Group and Jiangsu Airship Gear.
Total Foreign Direct Investment:	N.A.
Major Industries Encouraged:	Information technology, electronics, chemical engineering, pharmaceuticals, petrochemicals, construction materials and garment manufacturing

INTRODUCTION

With total development area of 25.6 sq km, Taizhou Economic Development Zone (TZEDZ) was established in 1996. It is divided into three subsidiary parks, namely Riverside Industrial Park, High-tech Park and Chunlan Industrial Park.

The development of Riverside Industrial Park is closely related with that of the Taizhou Port. For example, logistics and chemical engineering; while in the high-tech park, enterprises specialized in information technology, microelectronics, mechanical-electric integration and biomedicine are most welcomed: investors from Germany, South Korea, Singapore and Hong Kong have invested over RMB300 million in Chunlan Industrial Park.

Taizhou is an important agricultural production base of China. The population of Taizhou is around 5 million and the land area is about 5,793 sq km. It is 260 kilometers from Shanghai Hongqiao International Airport, 180 kilometers from Nanjing Lukou Airport and 90 kilometers to Changzhou Airport.

INVESTMENT CLIMATE

Many local enterprises have grown to be top Chinese company groups. Representative ones include Chunlan Group, Yangtze Pharmaceuticals, Linghai Motors, Taixing Reducers Group, Yangtze Pharmaceuticals Group and Jiangsu Airship Gear Co. Ltd. Among these successful enterprises in TZEDZ, the performance of Chunlan Group is most impressive. Now, it has more than 20 affiliated companies, include overseas subsidiaries in the US, Italy, Japan, Singapore and Hong Kong.

Administrative Committee of TZEDZ
18 Qingnian South Road
Taizhou, Jiangsu
P. R. China 225300
Tel: (86)(523) 6881660
Fax: (86)(523) 6881660
E-mail: kfqtz@pub.tz.jsinfo.net
Website: www.tzdz.com

SOUTHEAST UNIVERSITY SCIENCE PARK

Year of Establishment:	1992
Location:	Nanjing, Jiangsu
Size:	60 ha
Major Supporting Institutions:	Southeast University
Major Investors:	SEUSP Holdings Corporation
Total Foreign Direct Investment:	N.A.
Major Industries Encouraged:	Advanced technologies in electronics, computer science, telecommunication equipments and software development

INTRODUCTION

Southeast University Science Park (SEUSP) is located in Nanjing. SEUSP comprises of two subsidiary zones, namely the Entrepreneur Zone and the Industrial Zone. Entrepreneur Zone is near the state-level Nanjing High-tech Park; and it is the development center for advanced technologies in electronics, computers, telecommunication and software. Currently more than 40 high-tech enterprises have joined the zone. The 60-hectare industrial zone is located within Jiangning Economic & Technological Development Zone. The enterprises that have entered the Industrial Zone enjoy relevant preferential policies given by ETDZs.

INVESTMENT CLIMATE

With registered capital of RMB100 million, SEUSP Holdings Corporation is in charge of the planning and development of the park.

As the result of a merger of former Southeast University, Nanjing Railway Medical College, Nanjing Transportation College and Nanjing Geological School, Southeast University (SEU) enjoys a history of over 100 years. Some of its majors are among the best in China, such as architecture, civil engineering, electronic information, mechanical engineering, power & energy and transportation research. Among the 2,600 strong university faculty, there are 370 professors and 1,000 associate professors.

SEU has established exchange relationships with many overseas universities, such as University of Pennsylvania, Ohio State University and Syracuse University in the US, Royal Melbourne Institute of Technology in Australia, The Swiss Federal Institute of Technology in Switzerland, Warwick University in the UK, L'University de Rennes in France and Hong Kong University. Some MNCs such as Motorola, Sun Microsystems, Philips and Nokia have conducted cooperative projects with the university.

Southeast University Science Park Holdings Corporation
6 Changjiang Hou Street
Xuanwu District,
Nanjing, Jiangsu
P. R. China 210000
Tel: (86)(25) 4500023, 3600111
Fax: (86)(25) 3600859
Email: yudh@seu.edu.cn

NANJING GULOU UNIVERSITY SCIENCE PARK

Year of Establishment:	2000
Location:	Nanjing, Jiangsu
Size:	N.A.
Major Supporting Institutions:	Nanjing University, Hehai University, China Pharmaceutical University, Nanjing Normal University, Nanjing University of Technology, Nanjing University of Posts & Telecommunications, Nanjing Medical University and Nanjing Chinese Medicine University
Major Investors:	Jiangsu Nandasoft, Nanjing Fujitsu Nanda Software Corporation, Nanda Pharmaceuticals
Major Industries Encouraged:	Computer software, electronic information, biomedicine, fine chemical engineering, new materials, mechanical-electronic integration, therapy and health care, scientific information consulting.

INTRODUCTION

Nanjing Gulou University Science Park (NGUSP) is jointly initiated by Nanjing University (NJU) and the government of Gulou District of Najing. It is also supported by other seven universities nearby, including Hehai University, China Pharmaceutical University, Nanjing Normal University, Nanjing University of Technology, Nanjing University of Posts & Telecommuncations, Nanjing Medical University and Nanjing Chinese Medicine University. NGUSP was approved with the status of National University Science Park in May 2001. Consequently, in September 2001, NGUSP Holdings Corporation, with registered capital of RMB118 million, was established by a few organizations, such as Nanjing University, Shanghai Tianwei Investment, Nanjing Central Mall Holdings, Jiangsu Xingsheng Investment, Nanjing Nanzi Investment, Tianyuan Investment and Gulou State Assets Management Center.

The development focus of NGUSP is in high-tech industries such as computer software, electronic information, pharmaceutical, fine chemical engineering, new materials, mechanical-electronic integration, therapy and health care, scientific informa-tion consulting and evaluation services. According to the master plan, NGUSP will set up an Entrepreneurship development center, the testing base and industrial bases at Nanjing High-tech Park and Nanjing Economic & Technological Development Zone.

INVESTMENT CLIMATE

By the end of 1999, the park has around 68 NJU affiliated enterprises and joint ventures. They are mainly engaged in four kinds of industries, namely pharmaceutical manufac-turing, electronics, information technology, new materials and new energy. Among them, the development of Jiangsu Nandasoft is most impressive, which was established in

1998 by Nanjing University and Jiangsu Provincial IT Industrial Investment Company. Jiangsu Nandasoft has a registered capital of RMB70 million. In 2000, it achieved sales revenues of RMB160 million, and the profit was around RMB7.4 million. The company is mainly specialized in software development for network security and Internet solutions. In 2001, it was successfully listed in Hong Kong.

Other representative organizations include Nanjing Fujitsu Nanda Software Corporation and Nanda Pharmacy. NGUSP Administrative Committee and NGUSP Holdings Corporation are responsible for handling the major affairs of NGUSP. A one-stop Service Center has been established to provide quality service for entrepreneurs and incubation projects. Towards the end of 2004, NGUSP aims to incubate 30 high-tech ventures and the total sales revenue of enterprises will reach RMB3 billion, with a profit of more than RMB300 million. NGUSP will contribute significantly to the economy of Nanjing city as well as Jiangsu province.

As one of China's top universities, NJU offers strong intellectual resources to Nanjing as well as to other parts of China. Among the 2000-strong university faculty, there are 564 professors, 21 CAS (Chinese Academy of Science) fellows, and two CAE (Chinese Academy of Engineering) fellows. The academic fields cover humanities, social sciences, natural sciences, advanced engineering and technologies, life sciences and management. The total number of students is around 27,000, among which 5,874 are pursuing advanced study at master or doctoral levels. During the period of 1992-1998, the number of articles by NJU scholars that was cited by SCI ranked the top among all Chinese universities. With impressive achievements in various fields, NJU has received more than 40 premier honors such as National Natural Science Award, National Science & Technology Advancement Award and National Invention Award. At the same time, NJU owns 28 State Key Subjects, 10 State Key Laboratories, 94 research institutes, 62 multi-disciplinary research centers and so on.

Nanjing University has extensive international links with overseas universities and research institutions. Now, it has established cooperative relationships with more than 100 overseas universities. The Johns Hopkins-Nanjing University Center for Chinese and American Studies, Gottingen-NJU Economic Law Institute and Sino-Dutch International Business Center are all located at the NJU campus.

Nanjing Gulou University Science Park Holdings Ltd
22 Hankou Road, Nanjing University
Nanjing, Jiangsu
P. R. China 210093
Tel: (86)(25) 3593317
Fax: (86)(25) 3592918
Email: ndcy@netra.nju.edu.cn
Website: www.nju.edu.cn/njuc/service/
          chye/kejiyuan/index.htm

KUNSHAN EXPORT PROCESSING ZONE

Year of Establishment:	1998
Location:	Kunshan, Jiangsu
Size:	2.86 sq km
Total Foreign Direct Investment:	USD420 million
Major Industries Encouraged:	electronics, export processing related industries, precision instruments

Kunshan Export Processing Zone (KSEPZ) was set up in April 1998. On 27 April 2000, KSEPZ was approved by the State Council to be one of the first 15 EPZs in China.

KEPZ is located within the Kunshan Economic and Technological Development Zone. It is divided into the East district and the West district. The East district is one sq km and the West district is 1.86 , sq km. They are formally closed on October 2000.

At present, KSEPZ has 12 foreign-invested enterprises with total investment of USD420 million.

KSEPZ is close to the Shanghai-Nanjing Expressway, Shanghai Port, and Zhangjiagang Port. National Highway No. 312 and Shanghai-Nanjing Railway run across the entire EPZ. It is only half an hour's drive to Shanghai Hongqiao International Airport.

The sum of more than RMB100 million has been invested in infrastructure, customs inspection facilities and greenery, etc.

KSEPZ plans to attract high-tech export processing MNCs focusing on electronics, export processing and precision instruments.

CHINA-SINGAPORE SUZHOU INDUSTRIAL PARK EXPORT PROCESSING ZONE

Year of Establishment: 2000

Location: Suzhou, Jiangsu

Size: 2.9 sq km (41 hectares for Phase One)

Major Investors: N.A.

Total Foreign Direct Investment: USD570 million

Major Industries Encouraged: N.A.

China-Singapore Suzhou Industrial Park Export Processing Zone (SIPEPZ) was established on 27 April 2000. It is one of 15 experimental export-processing zones that enjoy the convenience and privileges of "operating within the border yet without customs declaration".

CS-SIPEPZ covers an area of 2.9 sq km to be developed in three phases. Development of the first phase of 41 hectares has been completed and 15,000 sq m space of ready built factory has been occupied ever since it was finished in April 2001. The circling of the zone with iron fence has been completed and the first batch of ready-built factories will be put into use by the end of 2002. More than 15 foreign investors are ready to move in with a total investment of USD570 million.

At present, various utilities of infrastructure development have been completed in the first phase. An inspection area, supervision warehouses and Customs offices have also been built.

ZHANGJIAGANG FREE TRADE ZONE

Our Rating:	To be rated
Year of Establishment:	1992
Location:	Zhangjiangang, Jiangsu
Size:	3.1 sq km (phase I)
Major Investors:	Shuan Der Industry, President Nisshin Food, Chevron Chemical Industry, Oriental Unocal Energy, Optrex Electronics, Nankang Rubber Industrial, Hexin Chemical Industrial
Total Foreign Direct Investment:	N.A.
Major Industries Encouraged:	Mechanical engineering, information technology, electronics, wool spinning, cotton spinning, knitting, fashion manufacturing, and storage of chemical products

INTRODUCTION

Zhangjiagang Free Trade Zone (ZJGFTZ) was established on 20 December 1992. It is the only inner waterway free trade zone in China. With the first phase of 3.1 sq km located at the Yangtze River bank of Zhangjiagang city. In 2001, the GDP of Zhangjiagang was RMB30.68 billion.

Within the area of Zhangjiagang FTZ, there are 10 warehousing enterprises, and the warehouse area was 80,000 sq m.

ZJGFTZ is located at the low reaches of the Yangtze River, and has easy access to major cities including Shanghai, Nanjing, Suzhou, Wuxi and Changzhou. It is 120 kms from Shanghai, 220 kms from Nanjing, 100 kilometers from Suzhou, 58 kms from Wuxi, 55 kms from Changzhou and 62 kms from Nantong. Zhangjiagang Port is a key entry port of wood, botanic oil, steel and chemical products. Along the Yangtze River, it is easy to reach Wuhan and Chongqing in the upper reaches of the river.

INVESTMENT CLIMATE

ZJGFTZ consists of Electro-mechanical Industrial Park, Knitting Industrial Park, Products Storage Area and Chemical Industrial Park.

The main focus of the first park is mechanical engineering, information technology and electronics. The development of the second park will focus on wool spinning, cotton spinning, knitting and fashion manufacturing. The products storage area will be specialized in the storage of chemical products. Development of chemical engineering will be the main focus of the chemical industrial park.

By the end of 2001, a total of RMB1.07 billion had been invested into the development of infrastructure in Zhangjiagang FTZ. By the end of May 2002, there were 2,700 registered companies in Zhangjiagang FTZ with annual total foreign trade of USD600 million.

Administrative Committee of ZJGFTZ
Zhangjiagang, Jiangsu Province
P. R. China 215634
Tel: (86)(512) 58320702
Fax: (86)(512) 53830295
Email: wangpei@ftz.js.cn
Website: www.zjgftz.gov.cn

JIANGXI

Industrial Parks in Jiangxi

1. Nanchang Economic & Technological Development Zone
2. Nanchang High-tech Park
3. Jinlu Software Development Park

INTRODUCTION

Jiangxi Province is called "Gan" in short. The provincial capital is Nanchang, while Jiujiang and Jingdezhen are inland open cities authorized by the State Council to enjoy preferential investment policies similar to coastal open cities.

GEOGRAPHY

Jiangxi Province lies in southeast China and along the south bank of the Yangtze River. Jiangxi has four distinct seasons. The average temperature is 4°-9°C in January and 28°-30°C in July.

TRAVEL INFORMATION

From Nanchang Airport to:
Beijing	2hrs
Shenzhen	1hr 10mins
Shanghai Pundong	55mins
Hong Kong	1hr 20mins

INVESTMENT CLIMATE

With population of 42 million and an area of 166,900 sq km, Jiangxi has rich resources in soil, water, forest and mineral resources. Jiangxi has seen its economy develop enormously. In 2001, Jiangxi's GDP amounted to RMB216 billion. Agriculture output reached RMB79 billion, an increase of 3.0% over 2000, while the industrial output was RMB141 billion. Fiscal revenue reached RMB13.2 billion, up 18.3% over 2000. Jiangxi's major industries are energy, mining, raw materials, machinery, automobile, airplane and chemicals etc.

Jiangxi's foreign trade and have been expanding vigorously. In 2001, Jiangxi's total trading volume amounted to USD1,530 million, with imports of USD492 million and exports of USD1,039 million.

Jiangxi province has a well developed transportation system. There are seven major trunk railways (Beijing-Kowloon, Zhejiang-Jiangxi, Yingtan-Xiamen, Nanjing-Nanchang, Xiangtan-Jiujiang, Wuhan-Jiujiang, Xiangtan-Ji'an) as well as ten branch railways passing through the province. Beijing-Kowloon railway starts from Beijing in the north and ends at Kowloon in the south, with 700 km going through Jiangxi province.

Jiangxi's highway system is composed of six national highways.

Jiangxi also has a good inland waterway system, which totals more than 5,537 km.

Fact Sheet	2001
Area (sq km)	166,900
Population (million)	42
GDP (RMB billion)	216
GDP Growth Rate	8.8%
Consumption Expenditure (RMB billion)	
• Government	28
• Household	76.2
Per capita annual	
• disposable income of urban residents (RMB '000)	5.5
• net income of rural households (RMB '000)	2.2
Utilized FDI (USD million)	396
Industrial Value Added (RMB bn)	28.6
Imports (USD million)	492
Exports (USD million)	1,040
Universities & Colleges	47

Foreign Investment Office of Jiangxi Provincial Government
2F, 200 Zhanqian Road
Zhanqian
P. R. China 330001
Tel: (86)(719) 6246244, 6246242
Fax: (86)(719) 6246239

Jiangxi Provincial Economic Government
Website: www.jiangxi.gov.cn

Guan River converges into Poyang Lake and then to the Yangtze River. Water routes run to every port along the Yangtze River, connecting up to Wuhan, Chongqing, Nanjing, Shanghai, and to Japan, Southeast Asia and other countries.

With a rapidly improved infrastructure environment, Jiangxi attracts an ever-increasing amount of foreign investment. In 2001, the utilized foreign direct investment was USD396 million, of which USD53 million was from Taiwan is .

Major important cities in Jiangxi include Nanchang, Jinjiang, Jingdeshen, Yingtan, Fuzhou, Ji'an and Ganzhou. There are 47 universities and colleges in Jiangxi, which include Nanchang University, East China Jiaotong University, jiangxi Agricultural University, Jiangxi University of Finance & Economy and Nanchang College of Aviation Engineering.

NANCHANG ECONOMIC AND TECHNOLOGICAL DEVELOPMENT ZONE

Our Rating:	BB
Year of Establishment:	1992
Location:	Nanchang, Jiangxi
Size:	9.8 sq km
Major Investors:	Qinghua High-tech Park, Electronic Power Science Park
Total Foreign Direct Investment:	N.A.
Major Industries Encouraged:	Home electronics, machinery, construction materials, food and auto parts

INTRODUCTION

Nanchang Economic and Technological Development Zone (NCETDZ) was established in spring 1992. It has development area of 9.8 sq km.

The zone is located at Changbei New Town of Nanchang City, across the river from the old downtown area.

INVESTMENT CLIMATE

By the end of 2001, around 220 domestic enterprises and 70 foreign-invested enterprises have set up in NCETDZ, with total investment of RMB4.2 billion. The GDP volume of the zone was RMB1.5 billion and gross industrial output was RMB3.5 billion.

The railway and road network is well developed. There are three national highways and three trunk railways to Beijing, Shanghai, Kunming and Kowloon. Along the Beijing-Kowloon Railroad in Nanchang ETDZ, there are Changbei Passenger Station and Changbei Freight Station. The new Nanchang Changbei airport is only 10 km from NCETDZ. Flights are available to Beijing, Hong Kong and Shanghai.

Administrative Committee of NCETDZ
Fenglin Avenue, Changbei,
Nanchang City, Jiangxi
P. R. China 330013
Tel: (86)(791) 3805606
Fax: (86)(791) 3805611

NANCHANG HIGH-TECH PARK

Our Rating:	BB
Year of Establishment:	1991
Location:	Nanchang, Jiangxi
Size:	19.5 sq km
Major Investors:	Keguang, Nanchang Aland Electromagnetic Locker, Nanchang Star, Jiangxi Hengda High-tech and CN Show Information Industries
Total Foreign Direct Investment:	N.A.
Major Industries Encouraged:	Electronics, software development, optical-electronic-mechanical integration, bio-pharmaceuticals, mechanical instruments and new materials

INTRODUCTION

Nanchang High-tech Park (NCHTP) gained state-level status in November 1992 and now is the only national high-tech park in the province. Total development area of the park is 19.5 sq km, and the central district is about 6.8 sq km.

The park is three km away from the downtown Nanchang, three km to Nanchang Railway Station, the largest station along Beijing-Kowloon Railway and 26 km to Nanchang Changbei International Airport.

INVESTMENT CLIMATE

NCHTP has attracted enterprises such as Keguang Co. Ltd. (www.keguang.net), Nanchang Aland Electromagnetic Locker Co. Ltd. (www.china-aland.com), Nanchang Star Co. Ltd. (www.ncstar.-com.cn), Jiangxi Hengda High-tech Co. Ltd. (www.hengda.com) and CN Show Information Industries Co. Ltd. (www.cnshow.-com) to be located in the park.

Jinlu Software Park is at the east of Nanchang HTP. It aims to become an intellectual and ecological garden as well as environmentally friendly industrial zone.

Chinese students from abroad who completed their studies had set up ventures in fields like electronics, software development, optical-electronic-mechanical integration, bio-pharmaceuticals and new materials.

In Nanchang city, there are 136 research institutes and technology development institutes, as well as 12 universities and colleges.

Nanchang is the capital city of Jiangxi Province and it is the only provincial capital along Beijing-Kowloon Railway.

Administrative Committee of NCHTP
Torch Street, Gaoxin Road
Nanchang, Jiangxi Province
P. R. China 330029
Tel: (86)(791) 8103024
Fax: (86)(791) 8104528
Email: office@nchdz.com
         edd@nchdz.com
Website: www.nchdz.net

JINLU SOFTWARE DEVELOPMENT PARK

Year of Establishment: 1998

Location: Nanchang, Jiangxi

Size: 50 ha

Major Investors: Shenghua Kehuan Computer Technologies, Tsinghua University Science Park Co. Ltd., Nanchang University Computer Engineering Co. Ltd., Shebao Computers, CNShow Info Industries, Strong IT Industries, Nanchang Star Electronics, American FutureNet Tech and Founder Electronics

INTRODUCTION

Located beside the beautiful Aixi Lake of Nanchang High-tech Park, the Jinlu Software Development Park (JLSPP) has an area of 50 hectares. The total investment commitment is about RMB280 million. According to specialized functions, the park is divided into three sub-zones, namely the Industrial Zone, the Service Zone and the Residential Zone. An important feature of the software development park is that the administrative committee aims to develop it into an important garden-type software development base for Nanchang as well as for Jiangxi province.

INVESTMENT CLIMATE

Major corporations have joined JLSDP, such as Jiangxi Shenghua Kehuan Computer Technologies, Tsinghua University Science Park Co. Ltd. Nanchang Subsidiary, Nanchang CN Show Info Industries (www.cnshow.com), Jiangxi Strong IT Industries (www.strongit.com.cn), Nanchang Start Electronics (www.ncstar.-com), American FutureNet Tech Nanchang Company (www.futurenet-tech.com), Nanchang University Computer Engineering Corporation, Jiangxi Shebao Computers and the Nanchang subsidiary of Founder Electronics, etc.

Forty-seven universities and colleges are located in Jiangxi province. They include Nanchang University (ncu.edu.cn), East China Jiaotong University (www.ecjtu.jx.cn), Jiangxi Normal University (www.jxnu.edu.cn) and Jiangxi University of Finance & Economics (www.jxufe.edu.cn).

Administrative Committee of JLSDP
Torch Street, Qingshan Lake Avenue
Nanchang, Jiangxi
P. R. China 330029
Tel: (86)(791) 8103326
Fax: (86)(791) 8104528
Email: info@jinlusoft.com
Website: www.jinlusoft.com

JILIN

Industrial Parks in Jilin

1. Changchun Economic & Technological Development Zone
2. Jilin Economic & Technological Development Zone
3. Jilin High-tech Park
4. Changchun High-tech Park

INTRODUCTION

Known for its "three treasures" in northeast China - ginseng, marten fur and pilose antlers, Jilin also boasts great stretches of fertile black soil, rich resources of minerals, traditional Chinese medicines, and one of the six major forest regions in China. The province has long been an important base for the nation's heavy industries since liberation in 1949. Automobile, railway carriage, iron alloy, tractor, carbon products, timber and plywood from Jilin are all among the top in China.

GEOGRAPHY

With an area of 137,400 sq km, Jilin Province is located in the northeast of China, bordering Russia on the east and separated from North Korea by Tumen River and Yalu River in its southeast. With a continental monsoon climate, Jilin has four distinct seasons and abundant rainfalls. However, winter is freezingly cold and long here, with average temperature as low as -16°C in January.

With total population of 26.9 million, Jilin is a multi-ethnic province with 43 ethnic groups including the Han, Man, Korean, Mongolian and Xibo. Administratively, the province is divided into eight municipalities and an autonomous prefecture.

Fact Sheet	2001
Area (sq km)	187,400
Population (million)	26.91
GDP (RMB billion)	203.2
GDP Growth Rate	9.3%
Consumption Expenditure (RMB billion)	
• Government	32.6
• Household	90.6
Per capita annual	
• disposable income of urban residents (RMB '000)	5.34
• net income of rural households (RMB '000)	2.18
Utilized FDI (USD million)	338
Industrial Value Added (RMB bn)	55.7
Imports (USD million)	1,670
Exports (USD million)	1,463
Universities & Colleges	39

foreign trade volume also increases. Import and export reached USD1.67 billion and USD1.46 billion, respectively. In 2001, both increases by a two-digit margin from last year.

Important cities in Jilin include Changchua, Jilin, Yanji, Tonghua and Siping. In Jilin, there are 39 universities and colleges, which include Jilin University, Northeast Normal University, Yanbian University, Northern University and Changchun University.

Jilin Provincial Government
www.jilin.gov.cn

Jilin Department of Foreign Trade and Economic Cooperation
Tel: (86)(431) 5623443

TRAVEL INFORMATION

From Changchun Airport to:

Beijing	1 hr 30 mins
Shanghai Pudong	2 hrs 30 mins
Dalian	1 hr 5 mins
Xi'an	3 hrs
Xiamen	3 hrs
Shenzhen	4 hrs

INVESTMENT CLIMATE

For its heavy concentration on mechanical, petrochemical, metallurgical and forest industries, Jilin has one of China's most intensive railway networks. However, those "pillar industries" are still largely taken by state-owned enterprises that account for a significant part of the provincial economy.

In 2001, the utilized FDI of Jilin province amonted to USD338 million. The province also attracted 842 domestic investment projects with total investment of RMB64.4 billion. As the province is opening up, the

CHANGCHUN ECONOMIC AND TECHNOLOGICAL DEVELOPMENT ZONE

Our Rating:	A
Year of Establishment:	1992
Location:	Changchun, Jilin
Size:	20 sq km
Major Investors:	Pepsico, Coca-Cola, Johnson, Unicom and Delphi Packard
Total Foreign Direct Investment:	USD2.346 billion (end 2001)
Major Industries Encouraged:	Automotive parts, optoelectronics communications, deep processing of agricultural Products, biopharmaceuticals and new construction materials.

INTRODUCTION

Changchun Economic and Technological Development Zone (CCETDZ) was established in July 1992 and was approved as a state-level development zone in April 1993 by the State Council. The area of the zone totals 20 sq km.

CCETDZ is situated in the southeastern part of Changchun City. It is five kilometers from the city center of Changchun, 7.8 kilometers from the railway station and 14.8 kilometers from Changchun airport.

In 2001, CCETDZ's GDP was RMB39.96 billion, fiscal revenue was RMB5.06 billion, and total import and export was USD1.02 billion. By end 2001, there are 2,968 domestic and foreign enterprises in CCETDZ. A total of 391 foreign-invested enterprises had invested USD2.3 billion.

INVESTMENT CLIMATE

CCETDZ has put in RMB3.48 billion for infrastructure development. By the end of 2001, 33 transnational corporations from 25 countries and regions had joined in CCETDZ. Ten Fortune 500 corporations such as

Pepsico, Coca-Cola, Johnson and Delphi Packard have set up operations in CCETDZ.

There are five major industries in CCETDZ: automotive parts manufacturing, opto-electronics communications, deep processing agricultural products, biopharmaceuticals and new construction materials.

In Changchun, there are Jilin University, Northeast Teachers University, Changchun Optical Fine Mechanics and Physics Institute, Changchun Applied Chemistry Institute, Changchun Institute of Geography and Changchun Satellite Observation Station.

It is comparatively close to Mongolia, Russia and South Korea, etc.

Administrative Committee of CCETDZ
118, Ziyou Road, Changchun
Jilin, P. R. China 130031
Tel: (86)(431) 4630011
Fax: (86)(431) 4644215
E-mail: cetdz@mail.cetdz.com.cn
Website: www.cetdz.com.cn

JILIN ECONOMIC AND TECHNOLOGICAL DEVELOPMENT ZONE

Our Rating:	BBB
Year of Establishment:	N.A.
Location:	Jilin city, Jilin
Size:	43.5 sq km
Major Investors:	Jilin Chemical Fiber Group, Tianhe Agricultural Products, Jilin Ferroalloys Group, Jilin Paper Mill, Jidong Cement, Wahaha Group and Yili Group
Major Industries Encouraged:	chemical engineering, metallurgical industry, chemical fiber, processing of agricultural products, food, bioengineering, pharmaceuticals and healthcare products.

INTRODUCTION

Jilin Economic & Technological Development Zone (JLETDZ) is located at the northwestern part of Jilin city, which is about 90 km to Changchun, the capital city of Jilin province and five km to the Jilin Airport, and eight km to Jilin Railway Station.

The total development area of JLETDZ will be 43.5 sq km. Now, major enterprises include Jilin Chemical Fiber Group, Jilin Tianhe Agricultural Products Co. Ltd., Jilin Ferroalloys Group, Jilin Paper Mill Jidong Cement, Wahaha Group and Yili Group. Industries welcomed by the JLETDZ are chemical engineering, metallurgical industry, chemical fiber, processing of agricultural products, food, bio-engineering, pharmaceuticals and healthcare products.

INVESTMENT CLIMATE

According to the master plan, JLETDZ is divided into 4 parts, namely, the Chemical Industrial Park, the Food Industrial Park and the Textile Industrial Park. The Medical Industrial Park is specialized in the development of traditional Chinese pharmaceuticals, mini-molecule medicine, biopharmaceuticals and health products. The 270 hectare Food Industrial Park is specialized in production of milk products, drinks such as fruit juice, vegetable juice and tea drinks, and advanced processing of corn. The 200 hectare Textile Industrial Park is specialized in production of textile materials, chemical fiber and leather products. It is estimated that by 2010, the GDP of JLETDZ will reach RMB10 billion.

With population of 4.35 million and 1.7 million in the urban area, Jilin is one of China's 32 largest cities.

Administrative Committee of JLETDZ
1 Gongnong Road, Jiuzhan Street
Jilin City, Jilin
P. R. China 132101
Tel: (86)(432) 3055138
Fax: (86)(432) 3055138
Email: jeda@public.jl.jl.cn
Website: www.jeda.gov.cn

JILIN HIGH-TECH PARK

Our Rating:	BBB
Year of Establishment:	November 1992
Location:	Jilin City, Jilin Province
Size:	11.18 sq km
Major Investors:	N.A.
Total Foreign Direct Investment:	N.A.
Major Industries Encouraged:	Chemical Engineering, Mechanical engineering and Pharmaceuticals

INTRODUCTION

Jilin High-tech Park (JLHTP) is located in Jilin City of Jilin Province, which connects the Changbai Mountain Region and Songliao Plains. With history of more than 300 years, Jilin City owns a few wonderful resorts such as Songhua Lake and Jilin Meteorite area.

JLHTP gained state-level status in November 1992. The total development area of the park is 11.18 sq km.

The high-tech park consists of four subsidiary zones, namely Jiangnan Zone, Jiangbei Fine Chemical Engineering Zone, Jiuzhan Industrial Zone and Fengman Industrial Zone. The pillar industries of the park include fine chemical engineering, new materials, mechinery and bio-pharmaceutical engineering.

INVESTMENT CLIMATE

At the end of 1999, 72 enterprises in the park had sales of over RMB10 million and 21 enterprises had sales of more than RMB100 million. By the end of 2000, the numbers increased to 92 and 30 respectively.

In 2000, a total of 12 foreign projects with an investment of USD11.26 million were established in the park. The amount of domestic investment was around RMB2.07 billion. The total industrial output of all park enterprises was RMB21.5 billion. JLHTP

hosts several large-sized industrial enterprises including Jilin Chemical Group, Jilin Fiber Group, Huaxin Group and Jiangbei Mechanical Factory.

The city of Jilin has more than 30 research institutes, a few colleges and polytechnic schools.

Administrative Committee of JLHTP
Torch Tower, 6 Shenzhen Street
Jilin City, Jilin, P. R. China
Tel: (86)(432) 4798186
Fax: (86)(432) 4798000
Email: webmaster@jlhitech.com
Website: www.jlhitech.com.cn

CHANGCHUN HIGH-TECH PARK

Our Rating:	A
Year of Establishment:	March 1991
Location:	Changchun, Jilin
Size:	49 sq km
Major Investors:	General Motors, Ford, Daimler Chrysler, Siemens, Itochu and Marubeni
Total Foreign Direct Investment:	N.A.
Major Industries Encouraged:	Automobile engineering, new materials, bioengineering, optical electromechanical integration, electronics and information engineering

INTRODUCTION

Changchun High-tech Park (CCHTP) is located in the southern suburban area of Changchun. It gained state level status in March 1991. The total development area of the park is 49 sq km.

The development of the park focuses on automobile engineering, new materials, bio-engineering, optical electromechanical integration technologies, electronics and information technology.

INVESTMENT CLIMATE

In 2000, the realized foreign investment was USD82.75 million and the total output of high-tech enterprises was RMB11 billion.

In the first half year of 2001, the total industrial output of park enterprises was RMB9.96 billion, the total foreign investment was USD57 million, and the domestic investment was RMB625 million.

At the end of 2000, CCHTP attracted 247 foreign enterprises. MNCs such as General Motors, Ford, Daimler Chrysler, Siemens, Itochu and Marubeni have established subsidiaries in the park.

The transportation system of the park is quite developed. Changchun-Dalian Expressway runs through the zone. The Park is 2.5 km from the Railway Station and 10 km from Changchun Airport.

Currently, there are 18 universities and colleges in Changchun, including Jilin University, and 39 research institutes and laboratories.

Administrative Committee of CCHTP
4000 Guigu Avenue
Changchun, Jilin
P. R. China 130012
Tel: (86)(431) 5538062, 5171617, 5171619
Fax: (86)(431) 5538063-8200
Email: invest@chida.gov.cn
         zsj@infowindows.net
Website: www.chida.gov.cn

HUNCHUN BORDER ECONOMIC COOPERATION ZONE

Year of Establishment:	1992
Location:	Hunchun, Jilin
Size:	24 sq km
Major Industries Encouraged:	Export-oriented trade, high-tech industries, and processing industry, especially in textile, metal, and food processing and new construction materials

INTRODUCTION

Hunchun Border Economic Cooperation Zone was authorized and established in 1992 by the State Council. It was one of the national border zones. The zone located in Hunchun, adjacent to Russia and is along the coast. The lower stream of the Tumen River passes through the zone.

The zone is four km from the downtown area of Hunchun city, 41 km from the Russian Posyet port and 63 km from Zarubino port. Mahalino is connected to the zone by the railway system.

INVESTMENT CLIMATE

The zone is mainly engaged in the development of export oriented processing trade, high-tech industry, textile, new construction materials, metal processing and food processing industry. In addition, efforts has been taken to develop tourism, real estate, banking and finance and entertainment facilities etc.

Over RMB200 million has been pumped into the development. By the end of 2001, 180 projects had been approved in the park, with total contractual investment of RMB3.2 billion, among which contractual FDI was USD130 million.

Administrative Committee of Hunchun Border Trade
Cooperation Zone
1 Xin'an Street, Hunchun, Jilin
P. R. China 133300
Tel: (86)(440) 7611567
Fax: (86)(440) 7611543
Email: jjfzj@hcbecz.com
website: www.hcbecz.com

LIAONING

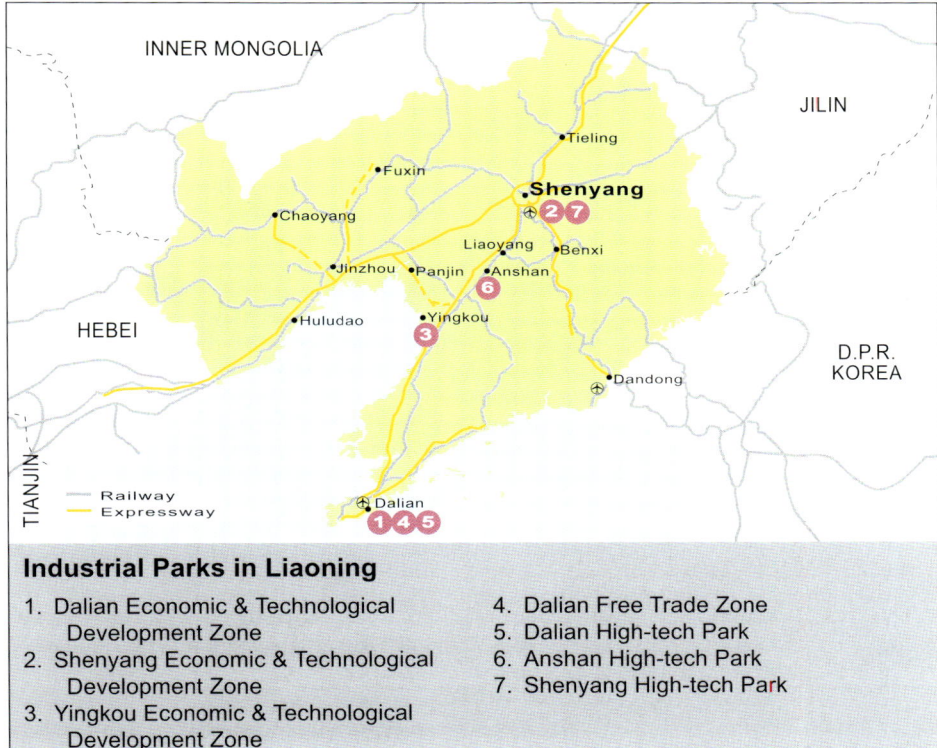

INNER MONGOLIA

JILIN

- Tieling
- Fuxin
- **Shenyang** ⊕ ②⑦
- Chaoyang
- Liaoyang
- Benxi
- Jinzhou •Panjin •Anshan ⑥
- Huludao
- Yingkou ③
- HEBEI

D.P.R.
KOREA

⊕ Dandong

TIANJIN

- Railway
- Expressway

⊕ Dalian ①④⑤

Industrial Parks in Liaoning

1. Dalian Economic & Technological
   Development Zone
2. Shenyang Economic & Technological
   Development Zone
3. Yingkou Economic & Technological
   Development Zone
4. Dalian Free Trade Zone
5. Dalian High-tech Park
6. Anshan High-tech Park
7. Shenyang High-tech Park

INTRODUCTION

Liaoning, is the only coastal province in northeastern China. With abundant natural resources and aggressive opening strategies, the province has grown into a dynamic economy of the Bohai Sea Economic Rim.

GEOGRAPHY

Situated at the crossroads between northern and northeastern China and surrounded by Bohai Sea and Yellow Sea, Liaoning covers total land area of 145,900 sq km, of which 60% is mountainous. It borders Jilin, Inner Mongolia and Hebei in China, and North Korea in the southeast. With Liaodong

Peninsula protruding to the south, the province has a coastline as long as 2,178 kms.

Liaoning's climate belongs to the monsoon type. The temperature in January drops from -5°C to -15°C, and averages 24°C in summer.

There are 14 prefecture level cities under the jurisdiction of the province, together with 44 county level cities and counties. Shenyang, located in the central part of the province, is the provincial capital. Other important cities include Dalian, Anshan, Dandong, Yingkou, Benxi and Jinzhou.

Fact Sheet	2001
Area (sq km)	145,900
Population (million)	41.94
GDP (RMB billion)	503.3
GDP Growth Rate	9%
Consumption Expenditure (RMB billion)	
• Government	62
• Household	375
Per capita annual	
• disposable income of urban residents (RMB '000)	5.80
• net income of rural households (RMB '000)	2.56
Utilized FDI (USD million)	3,110
Industrial Value Added (RMB bn)	244.4
Imports (USD million)	8,800
Exports (USD million)	11,110
Universities & Colleges	67

TRAVEL INFORMATION

From Shenyang Airport to:

Beijing	1 hr 10 mins
Shanghai Pudong	2 hrs
Hong Kong	4 hrs 15 mins
Tokyo	2 hrs 50 mins
Seoul	1 hr 40 mins
Bangkok	5 hrs 30 mins

From Dalian Airport to:

Beijing	1 hr 10 mins
Shanghai Pudong	1 hr 35 mins
Guangzhou	3 hrs 15 mins
Hong Kong	3 hrs 30 mins
Tokyo	2 hrs 40 mins
Nagoya	2 hrs 15 mins

INVESTMENT CLIMATE

Although Liaoning is one of the traditional heavy industrial bases of oil, steel and coal for the nation, it has benefited much from the early economic reforms. Petrochemicals, metallurgy, electronics and mechanic have now become four pillar industries in the province. The secondary sector accounts for half of Liaoning's economy, among which state-owned enterprises play a pivotal role, making up almost two thirds of total industrial output.

Compared with other northern provinces, Liaoning has made tremendous progress in foreign economic cooperation. Total foreign trade was USD19.9 billion in 2001, 31% contributed by FIEs established in the province. By the end of 2001, the number of FIEs had grown to 13,158, including MNCs and big coporations such as Pfizer, Du Pont, Goodyear, Michelin, Swiss Liebherr, BASF, Mitsubishi, Panasonic, Toshiba, Sanyo, Mitsui, Hyundai Electron, Cheungkong, New World, and Singapore's PSA etc.

There are all kinds of industrial parks located in Shenyang, Dalian, Benxi, Fushuan at varied levels, and border trade cooperation zones in Dandong. The province hosts 67 universities and colleges, such as Northeaster University, Dalian University of Technology, Liaoning University and China Medical University.

Liaoning Provincial Government
Website: www.ln.gov.cn

Liaoning International Investment Promotion Center
Tel: (86)(24) 86895802
Fax: (86)(24) 86895582

Liaoning Department of Foreign Trade and Economic Cooperation
Tel: (86)(24) 86892225
Fax: (86)(24) 86893858
Website: www.china-liaoning.org

DALIAN ECONOMIC AND TECHNOLOGICAL DEVELOPMENT ZONE

Our Rating:	AA
Year of Establishment:	1984
Location:	Dalian, Liaoning
Size:	28 sq km
Major Investors:	Total Fina Elf, Toshiba, Canon, Pfizer, Mitsubishi, Sanyo, Pohang Steel, LG, Thyssen-Krupp, Marubeni, Daewoo, Konica, YKK, Omron, TDK, Nisshin and Mabuchi
Total Foreign Direct Investment:	USD3.55 billion (utilized value, end 2001)
Major Industries Encouraged:	Microelectronics, new materials, bioengineering, information technology, oceanic development, energy saving and environment protection, recycling, infrastructure development, commerce, tourism and restructuring state-owned enterprises

INTRODUCTION

Dalian Economic and Technical Development Zone, or called Dalian Development Area (DDA) locally, was among the first such zones to be authorized by the State Council of China in 1984. After 17 years of development, Dalian Development Area (DDA) has a population of more than 200,000 and a developed area of 36 sq km.

In 2001, the GDP of DDA reached RMB20.14 billion and total industrial output was RMB42.1 billion. Exports grew 13.9% to USD2.7 billion, which were 88.9% contributed by foreign enterprises in the zone.

INVESTMENT CLIMATE

Since 1984, DDA has spent over USD1 billion on infrastructure and public utilities, to provide all the amenities of a modern urban center. It has its own power and thermal supplies, telecommunications, waste water treatment facilities and cable TV, all of which can be easily and efficiently connected to factory premises.

By the end of 2001, 1,384 foreign investment projects had been established in the zone. Accumulated contractual and utilized FDI amounted to USD7.79 billion and USD3.55 billion respectively. There are 287 projects with investment of over USD10 million. In 2001, 66 new FIE projects were registered, with USD600 million in contractual foreign investment.

North American and European investors made up 28% of the total investment. To date, the largest investor in the zone is the French-based multinational corporation, Total Fina Elf, which has invested USD 300 million in a petrochemical joint venture.

Dalian has 11 universities and colleges, such as Dalian University of Technology, Dalian Marine Universiy, Dalian university, Dalian Medical University and over 40 research institutes and laboratories. DDA management team is working closely with local institutes to upgrade training in the DDA, to prepare more workers for new technological challenges.

Dalian is a conduit to two major regions for resources and markets – Northeastern China and the Bohai Rim. The three northeastern provinces, Liaoning, Jilin and Heilongjiang, and Inner Mongolia have combined population of over 125 million people, contributing 13% of China's total GDP.

The so-called Bohai Economic Rim includes the provinces of Liaoning, Hebei, and Shandong, and two municipalities of Beijing and Tianjin. With 21% of China's total population, it is one of China's fastest developing consumer markets. The presence of China's top universities and research facilities in this region has enhanced the development of high-tech industries.

Port Authority of Singapore (PSA) is a joint-venture partner in the development of Dalian's Dayaowan Container Terminal. Dalian is now China's third largest port in cargo throughput, and the fifth largest in terms of container handling.

DDA is committed to environment-friendly sustainable development, and it was the first Zone in China to be awarded the ISO 14001 certificate in recognition of its achievements in such area.

In 2001 Dalian, was elected to the prestigious United Nations Environment Program's Global 500 Roll of Honor for its outstanding contributions to the protection of the environment.

Foreign Investment Service Center of DLETDZ
P. R. China
Tel: (86)(411) 7612005, 7612011, 7611995

Economic Development Bureau
Tel: (86)(411) 7613959

SHENYANG ECONOMIC AND TECHNOLOGICAL DEVELOPMENT ZONE

Our Rating:	AA
Year of Establishment:	1988
Location:	Shenyang, Liaoning
Size:	32 sq km
Major Investors:	Coca-Cola, Alcatel, Denmark Noel, Bridgestone, Nissan Motor, President Enterprise, Mitsui, Furukawa Electric, Matsushita, ABB, Mitsubishi, Jiali Beverage, Michelin, Tingyi Food, Yamanouchi Pharmaceutical
Total Foreign Direct Investment:	USD2.6 billion
Major Industries Encouraged:	Modern industries led by high-tech advancement, comprehensive development of secondary and tertiary industries

INTRODUCTION

Founded in June 1988, Shenyang Economic and Technological Development Zone (SYETDZ) was designated as a State-level development zone in April 1993 by the State Council.

SYETDZ covers 32 sq km. The first phase area on the eastern side is 4.48 sq km, the second phase on the western side is 7.7 sq km and the third phase will take up 19.82 sq km.

INVESTMENT CLIMATE

Major foreign-invested enterprises in SYETDZ include Coca-Cola, Alcatel, Denmark Noel, Bridgestone, Nissan Motor, President Enterprise, Mitsui, Furukawa Electric, Matsushita, ABB, Mitsubishi, Hong Kong Jiali Beverage, Michelin, Tingyi Food and Yamanouchi Pharmaceutical etc. Their combined contractual Investment was more than USD2.6 billion.

Within a sphere of 150 kilometers, seven large industrial bases can be found, i.e. iron in Anshan, coal in Fushun, chemical fiber in Liaoyang, coal and steel in Benxi, petroleum in Panjin, grain and coal in Tieling, power supply in Fuxin — marked by close economic ties, huge market capacity and great prospects. The bases are not only the source of abundant minerals but also a market with great potential.

With population of 6.8 million in Shenyang and nearby cities, an industrial system containing metallurgy, chemical and medical products, light textile, electronics, automobile, aviation, construction materials and manufacturing of machinery as its mainstay has been firmly established.

Shenyang is the largest commercial and economic center and commodities distribution center in Northeast China.

Administrative Committee of SYETDZ
Tel: (86)(24) 25810324
Fax: (86)(24) 25812748
E-mail: sydz@sydz.gov.cn
Website: www.sydz.gov.cn

YINGKOU ECONOMIC AND TECHNOLOGICAL DEVELOPMENT ZONE

Our Rating:	BBB
Year of Establishment:	1992
Location:	Yingkou, Liaoning
Size:	16 sq km
Major Investors:	Bohai Oil and Grains, Kerry, Itokin
Total Foreign Direct Investment:	USD1.08 billion
Major Industries Encouraged:	Aquaculture, construction,service industries, minerals processing, processing of agricultural products, timber

INTRODUCTION

Yingkou Economic and Technological Development Zone (YKETDZ) was established in 1992.

Yingkou's GDP increased 11.6% to RMB19.23 billion in 2001. The city has total population of 2.27 million while 890,000 are living in urban areas. By the end of 2001, 484 foreign investment projects had been set up in YKETDZ, with contractual investment of USD1.08 billion and utilized FDI of USD310 million. Major enterprises in the zone include Bohai Oil and Grains, Kerry, Itokin and Orion. At present, foreign investors in the zone come from 24 countries and regions.

YKETDZ is located in the south of Yingkou City, Liaoning Province. It is in the middle of Liaodong Peninsula on the east bank of Bohai Bay.

INVESTMENT CLIMATE

Since the establishment of the zone, the investment for infrastructure development has reached RMB2.97 billion.

Yingkou New Port is a national key project built in 1982. The present through put is 25 million tons a year. At present, regular container routes have been opened to Hong Kong, Japan (Kobe, Yokohama and Nagoya) and South Korea (Pusan).

It takes only an hour and a half to arrive at Dalian Airport and two hours to Shenyang Airport.

Yingkou encourages foreign investment in the following areas:
- Agricultural projects such as crop breeding, aquatics farming, shore exploitation, greenhouse flowers and plants, economic crops, aquatic products, and processing of farm products.
- Chemical industry, machinery and electronics by use of advanced technologies.
- Service sectors such as tourism, catering, real estate etc.
- Infrastructure development.
- Deep processing of resources such as food processing, wood products, leather products; and labor-intensive industries such as garment and textile, etc.

Investment Bureau of YKETDZ
8 Qiantangjiang Road
Tel: (86)(417) 6244372, 6244373, 6251223
Fax: (86)(417) 6244371
E-mail: invest@ykdz.gov.cn
Website: www.ykdz.gov.cn

DALIAN FREE TRADE ZONE

Year of Establishment:	May 1992
Location:	Dalian, Liaoning
Size:	N.A.
Major Investors:	Nippon Express, Mitsubishi Corporation, Itochu and Kind Resources
Total Foreign Direct Investment:	USD810 million
Major Industries Encouraged:	Export-oriented processing industry, international trade, duty-free storage, products exhibition and related services

INTRODUCTION

Dalian Free Trade Zone (DLFTZ) was approved by the State Council in May 1992. The development focus of the zone includes processing, storage and international trade. Inside the zone, there are petrochemical products market and e-business centers. DLFTZ has been growing fast, especially in export oriented processing industry, international trade, duty-free storage, products exhibition and related services.

In 2000, the GDP of DFTZ was RMB2.24 billion and the total industrial output was RMB2.01 billion. The actual utilized foreign investment was USD810 million and the number of foreign enterprises was more than 900.

INVESTMENT CLIMATE

DLFTZ is located between Dalian Economic and Technological Development Zone (DDA) and Dayaowan International Port.

It is 24 kilometers from Dalian International Airport, where flights are available to Hong Kong, Macau, Tokyo, Osaka, Fukuoka, Sendai, Seoul, Beijing, Guangzhou, Shanghai and many other Chinese cities.

The railway within DLFTZ is connected with Jinyao Railway as well as other major railways running through northeast China. The highway in DLFTZ directly goes to Shenyang-Dalian Expressway.

By the end of 2000, nearly 1,000 enterprises coming from over 30 countries and regions worldwide such as Nippon Express, Mitsubishi Corporation, Itochu and Kind Resources, had joined DLFTZ.

Investment Promotion Bureau of DLFTZ
Tel: (84)(411) 7308570, 7308569
Fax: (86)(411) 67318017
E-mail: huiminli@online.ln.cn,
         dlftzjp@online.ln.cn
Website: www.dlftz.gov.cn

DALIAN HIGH-TECH PARK

Our Rating:	AA
Year of Establishment:	1991
Location:	Dalian, Liaoning Province
Size:	35.6 sq km
Major Investors:	N.A.
Total Foreign Direct Investment:	USD290 millon
Major Industries Encouraged:	Electronics, new material, bio- pharmaceuticals, energy saving and environment protection

INTRODUCTION

Dalian High-tech Park (DLHTP) is located in the southwest part of Dalian city. It was authorized as a state-level high-tech park in March 1991. The total development area is 35.6 sq km.

In 2001, the city of Dalian gained the honor of Global 500 under the United Nations Environment Program. The city boasts beautiful coastal scenery, numerous parks and surrounding hills.

After five years of development, 1,700 enterprises, which include 400 high-tech enterprises and 500 foreign enterprises, had established subsidiaries in the park. The total accumulated investment was over RMB3 billion, of which contractual FDI was USD290 million

Major industries encouraged in the park include electronics, new materials, bio-pharmaceuticals, energy saving and environment protection.

INVESTMENT CLIMATE

By the end of 2000, over 2.5 billion RMB had been invested in infrastructure development. DLHTP includes Qixian Hill Incubation Center, Dalian Software Development Park, Dalian Overseas Chinese Entrepreneurship Center and Huanghe Tech City.

Dalian High-tech Park is only 5 km from Dalian International Airport, 7 kms from Dalian Port, 4.5 km from Dalian Railway Station and 15 km from the entrance of Shenyang-Dalian Expressway. The Port Authority of Singapore (PSA) was jointly established Dalian Container Terminal with its partners in July 1996 to handle the container business for the port.

Around the park, there are two universities and seven vocational training institutes. Dalian is home to some universities such as North-east University of Finance and Economics, Dalian Foreign Language University and Dalian University of Technology.

Administrative Committee of DLHTP
Tel: (86)(411) 36980000
Fax: (86)(411) 3686426
E-mail: zhuren@www.ddport.com
website: www.ddport.com

ANSHAN HIGH-TECH PARK

Our Rating:	BB
Year of Establishment:	1991
Location:	Anshan, Liaoning
Size:	27.1 sq km
Major Investors:	Haier, Top Group, China resources
Total Foreign Direct Investment:	N.A.
Major Industries Encouraged:	Information technology, automation, new materials and new energy

INTRODUCTION

Anshan High-tech Park (ASHTP) is located in the eastern part of Anshan city. It was authorized as a state-level park in 1991. The total development area of the park is 7.9 sq km.

Major industries in the Park include electronics, information technology, optical electromechanical integration technologies and products, new materials, and environment protection equipment.

By the end of 2001, 1,062 enterprises had entered the park. The main fields of foreign investment include machinery, metallurgy, electronics and telecommunication, petrochemical engineering and bio-pharmaceuticals.

INVESTMENT CLIMATE

To date, over 100 million RMB has been invested infrastructure development.

ASHTP encourages developments in liquid crystal display (LCD), program-controlled telephone equipment, digital program-controlled exchanger, satellite communication receiving project and television transmitters. It also welcomes automation related technologies, new materials, new energy, energy-saving technologies and environmental protection technologies.

As an important industrial city in Northeast China, Anshan is known as a "City of Steel" in China. It has easy access to Shenyang and Dalian.

ASHTP is 3.5 kilometers from the downtown area of the city, 13 kilometers from Qianshan Mountain Tourism Resort, 80 kilometers from Shenyang Taoxian Airport and 15 kilometers from Anshan Tengao Airport. It is also linked to the Shenyang-Dalian Expressway. Yingkou Bayu port is 125 kilometers away, about one and a half hours' drive.

Administrative Committee of ASHTP
Wangjiayu, Jiubao District
Anshan, Liaoning
P. R. China
Tel: (86)(412) 5211018, 5211028
Fax: (86)(412) 5211058
Website: www.asht-zone.gov.cn

SHENYANG HIGH-TECH PARK

Our Rating:	A
Year of Establishment:	1998
Location:	Shenyang, Liaoning
Size:	34.2 sq km
Major Investors:	Legend, Huawei Technologies, Toshiba, Digital China, Founders Computer, Stone.
Total Foreign Direct Investment:	N.A.
Major Industries Encouraged:	Electronics, information technology, bio-pharmaceuticals, new energy, new materials and software development

INTRODUCTION

Shenyang High-tech Park (SYHTP) is located in the southern part of Shenyang city, the capital of Liaoning Province. It was established in 1988 and authorized as a state-level high-tech park in 1991. The total development area of the park is 34 sq km.

The main fields of foreign investment include electronics, information technology, bio-pharmaceuticals, new energy, new materials and software development.

Major investors in the park include Legend, Huawei Technologies, Toshiba, Digital China, Founders Computer and Stone.

INVESTMENT CLIMATE

In 2001, the GDP of SYHTP was RMB5.8 million, an increase of 30% over 2000. The sales revenue for high-tech products was RMB16 billion.

A large pool of talent is available. Around the park, there are 12 universities and colleges, such as Northeast University, China Medical University and Shenyang Pharmaceutical University. In addition, there are 28 research institutes, 8 engineering center and 220 large-scale laboratories.

According to the master development plan, SYHTP consists of 8 subsidiary industrial parks, which include a sofware industrial park, an electronics industrial park, a biopharmaceutical industrial park, a new materials industrial park, a new energy industrial park, an agri-tech park, a Straits Science Park and a university science park.

Administrative Committee of SYHTP
Tel: (86)(24) 23787807
fax: (86)(24) 23706894
E-mail: 111@sygx.gov.cn
Website: www.sygx.gov.cn

NORTHEASTERN UNIVERSITY SCIENCE PARK

Year of Establishment:	1992
Location:	Shenyang, Liaoning
Major Supporting Institutions:	Northeastern University
Major Investors:	NEU Alpine Software Group
Major Industries Encouraged:	Software development, information technology

The idea of establishing Northeastern University Science Park (NEUSP) started in the late 1980s, and it was in 1992 that the core strategy of focusing on information technology and software development was confirmed. A very important member enterprise of NEUSP, NEU Alpine Corporation emerged as China's first software company to be listed on the stock market. NEUSP now aims to be a leading national university science park, particularly in the fields of software development and information technology.

Northeastern University (NEU) was established in 1923. It now has eight colleges in Shenyang, the provincial capital of Liaoning province, and a branch campus in Qinhuang-dao, an important industrial city in Hebei province. Among the 1,800-strong university faculty, there are 264 professors and 642 associate professors. The major research fields include humanities, social sciences, business administration, natural science, civil engineering, material science, mechanical engineering and information technology etc.

In 1995, the NEU Software Center was named as a State Engineering Research Center for computer software development (the only one at that moment); in 1997, the NEU Automation Center was authorized with the status of State Automation Engineering Technology Research Center. With support from Eastern Software Corporation, the State Digital Medical Instruments Engineering and Technology Research Center was established at Northeastern University in 1999.

The university has established international exchange links with 73 overseas universities in 18 nations.

Northeastern University Science Park
Shenyang, Liaoning
P. R. China
Website: www.neu.edu.cn

DANDONG BORDER ECONOMIC COOPERATION ZONE

Year of Establishment:	1992
Location:	Dandong, Liaoning
Size:	12.3 sq km
Major Investors:	Dandong City Government, Inchon Government of South Korea and ENFEI Garments
Major Industries Encouraged:	Microelectronics, bioengineering, information and telecommunication, environmental protection

INTRODUCTION

Dandong Border Economic Cooperation Zone (DDBECZ) was established in July 1992, and was authorized as a state-level development zone by the State Council of China. The zone has development area of 12.3 sq km, and is located in Dandong, the largest border city of China.

In 1999, the import-export volume totaled USD179.15 million, and the export volume was USD141.1 million.

INVESTMENT CLIMATE

DDBECZ is consists of three sub-zones, namely Business and Tourism Section, Port Trade Area, Gold Spring Industrial Section and Dadong Port Bonded Warehousing & Processing Area.

Over 1,200 investors from 18 countries and regions worldwide have started their businesses in DDBECZ. One famous example is the "Inchon Industrial Park of South Korea in Dandong", which was jointly invested and constructed by Dandong Government and Inchon Government of South Korea. The park is located in the Gold Spring Industrial Section.

After an initial stage development and construction, manufacturing enterprises like ENFEI Garments of South Korea have invested here one after another, and have been put into production. The master plan of the zone indicates another high-tech industrial park and an 8-kilometer long develop-ment belt from the Yalu River Bridge to Jiangwan Industrial Area in Langtou town.

Administrative Committee of DDBECZ
No. 3 Building, Cooperation Zone
Dandong, Liaoning
P. R. China 118000
Tel: (86)(415) 3122384, 3142077
E-mail: dbecz@mail.ddptt.ln.cn
Website: dbecz.ddptt.ln.cn/dbecz

DALIAN SOFTWARE DEVELOPMENT PARK

Year of Establishment: 1998

Location: Dalian, Liaoning

Size: 3 sq km

Major Investors: China Netcom, NEUSOFT, NEUSOFT Training Institute, NEUSOFT-Bitco Software, NEU Nokia, Langchao China Software

Dalian Software Development Park (DLSDP) is part of the state-level Dalian High-tech Park, and it has a first-phase development area of 3 sq km. The park is located in southwest Dalian city, a major industrial and commercial center in Northeastern China. It is 9 kilometers to Dalian International Airport, 12 kilometers to Dalian Port and 10 kilometers to the Railway Station.

The total government fund reached RMB1.3 billion. The first-phase projects include the 11,000sq m Venture Center, the 7,000 sq m residential apartments for software professionals, the 8,000 sq m NEUSOFT Building, the 19,700 sq m NEUSOFT Training Center and major infrastructure work of roads, telecommunication, power and water supply facilities.

According to the park's master plan, the total sales revenue of member enterprises will reach RMB2 billion at the end of 2005. By now, more than 70 companies have joined the park, for example, the Northeastern Data Center of China Netcom with investment of RMB200 million, Dalian NEU-Bitco Software Co. Ltd, Dalian Modern High-tech, NEU Nokia Communications, China Software Dalian Company the NEUSOFT Training Institute which can accommodate 2,000 students. In particular, NEUSOFT has established six subsidiaries in Dalian city; the sales revenue of a major subsidiary, NEU Daian Company, exceeded RMB100 million in 2000. More than 2,000 software professionals are working in the park.

Dalian Software Development Park is adjacent to Dalian University of Technology, Northeastern University of Finance and Economics, and Dalian Maritime University. Other universities and colleges in the city include Dalian University and Dalian University of Foreign Learning. Dalian University of Technology is one of the first 35 Chinese universities that have established software colleges.

Administrative Committee of DLSDP
Tel: (86)(411) 4760030
E-mail: dlrjy@mbox.dl.cei.gov.cn
Website: www.ddport.com/introduce/
software/software.htm

DALIAN EXPORT PROCESSING ZONE

Year of Establishment:	2000
Location:	Dalian, Liaoning
Size:	7.16 sq km
Major Investors:	Haier, Dow Corning Silicon, Guangyang Bearing, Genben Chemistry, Yamaguchi, Chiyoda Air-con etc.
Total Foreign Direct Investment:	USD135 million (end April 2001)
Major Industries Encouraged:	Export processing and its related warehousing and transportation

INTRODUCTION

Dalian Export Processing Zone (DLEPZ) is one of the 15 Export Processing Zones approved by the State Council in April 2000. It is one of the three Pilot Zones among the 15 and is the only EPZ in Northeast China.

The 7.16 sq km DLEPZ consists of District A of 1.5 sq km, District B of 1.45 sq km and District C of 4.21 sq km. It was formally put into operation on 16 July 2001.

DLEPZ is located in the new city center of Dalian. It borders Dalian Economic and Technological Development Zone (DDA) to the west and is just opposite Dalian Free Trade Zone.

INVESTMENT CLIMATE

Located nearby, DLEPZ and Dalian Free Trade Zone share the same management committee. The 1.5 sq km District A of DLEPZ has been completed and occupied. Dalian Haier Industrial Park (DLHIP), covering an area of 30 ha, is situated in DLEPZ. With an area of one sq km, District B, south of District A, becomes DLEPZ's focus of further development.

By the end April of 2001, about 20 foreign investments such as Haier, Dow Corning Silicon, Guangyang Bearing, Genben Chemistry, Yamaguchi and Chiyoda Air-con had invested in DLEPZ with total investment of USD135 million.

Administration Committee of DLEPZ
Investment Promotion Bureau
Tel: (86)(411) 7312440, 7308566, 7312442
E-mail: huiminli@online.ln.cn
Website: www.dlftz.gov.cn

QINGHAI

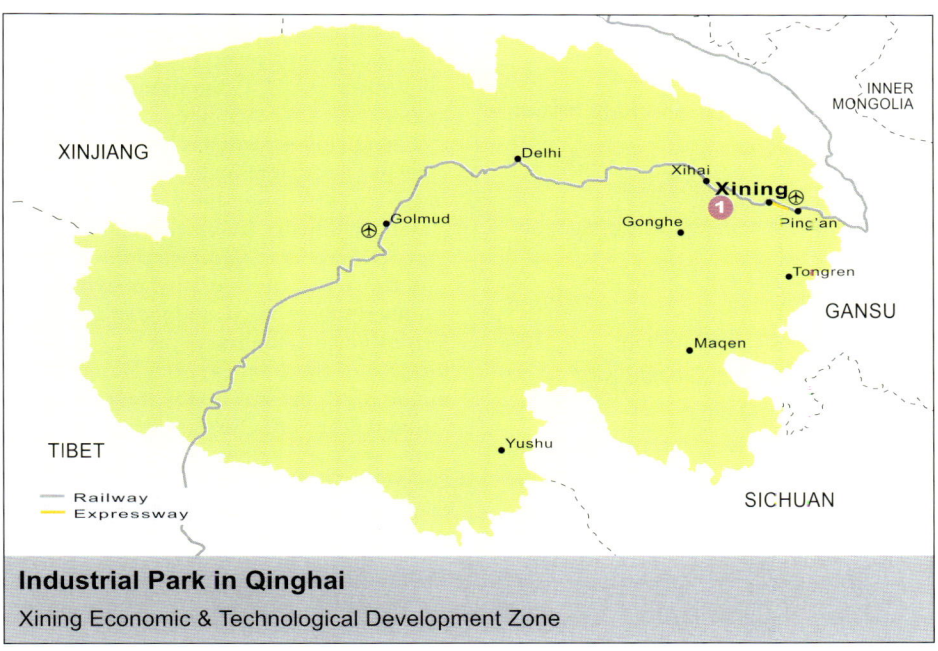

XINJIANG

INNER MONGOLIA

Delhi

Xihai
Xining
Golmud   Gonghe   Ping'an

Tongren

GANSU

Maqen

TIBET   Yushu

— Railway   SICHUAN
— Expressway

Industrial Park in Qinghai
Xining Economic & Technological Development Zone

INTRODUCTION

Qinghai, a large province in the western part of China, has the largest inland salt-water lake in the country, Qinghai Lake. The total salt reserve of Qinghai is estimated at 70 billion tons and hydraulic power of the province is said to be around 21.65 million kW. Many minority natio-nalities are living in the area, and make up to as much as 43% of the province's popu-lation. Major groups include Tibetan, Hui (Muslim), Tu, Salar, Mongolian and Kazak. The capital city of the province is Xining, which was approved by the State Council in 1992 to be an inland open city.

GEOGRAPHY

Qinghai is situated at the northeast of Qinghai-Tibet Plateau. As much as 85% of the province area has an average altitude of 3,000 m above the sea level. It is also located in the upstream of the Yangtze River as well as the Yellow River. To its northeast lies Gansu province, and Xinjiang is located to the north of Qinghai while Tibet is to the south. The province administers Xining, one prefecture, six autonomous prefectures, and 39 counties and county-level cities.

TRAVEL INFORMATION

From Xining Airport to:
Chongqing	1hr 40mins
Shenzhen	3hrs 50mins
Nanjing	2hrs
Xi'an	1hr 10mins

Fact Sheet	2001
Area (sq km)	720,000
Population (million)	5.23
GDP (RMB billion)	30.1
GDP Growth Rate	12%
Consumption Expenditure (RMB billion)	
• Government	10
• Household	9
Per capita annual	
• disposable income of urban residents (RMB '000)	5.8
• net income of rural households (RMB '000)	1.6
Contractual FDI (USD million)	198
Industrial Value Added (RMB bn)	8.92
Imports (USD million)	56
Exports (USD million)	149
Universities & Colleges	11

INVESTMENT CLIMATE

The province has rich reserves of oil and natural gas at the Qandam Basin. Qinghai Oil Field is one of China's four largest natural gas fields. In 1999, the crude oil output reached 1.9 million tons. The province is also rich in many mineral resources such as non-ferrous metals, rare metals, salt, potassium chloride, magnesium chloride, lithium, boron and lead, among which the reserve of potassium accounts for as much as 97% of China's total. Qinghai is China's major livestock husbandry base with husbandry areas as large as 90% of the province size. Major breeding animals include cattle, donkey, yak, sheep camel and horses. Xining wool is famous at home as well as abroad.

Major industries of the province include petrochemicals, electricity, chemical salts, non-ferrous metals, metallurgy, machinery, electronics, foodstuffs, leather and textiles. Industrial enterprises are mainly located in Xining, Golmud and Qaidam Basin. The large salt lake in the Qaidam Basin, with its huge reserves of potassium, magnesium, lithium, natural gas and crude oil, provides the raw materials for the heavy industries of the province.

In 2001, Qinghai government approved 47 new investment project with contractual investment of USD198 million. The utilized amount was USD 99 million.

Foreign investment has been encouraged in fields like exploration of resources, energy industry, salt chemistry industry, raw materials industry, livestock husbandry and process industry of livestock products.

Export products of the province are mainly resource based, and the share of non-ferrous metal and mineral products account for 55% of the total export volume. Other major products are honey, textile, metal silicone etc. In Qinghai, there are 11 universities and colleges, including Qinghai University, Qinghai Normal University and Qinghai Medical College.

Qinghai Provincial Government
Website: www.qh.gov.cn

Foreign Investment Bureau
Qinghai Department of Foreign Trade and Economic Cooperation
25 Shulin Lane, Xining, Qinghai
P. R. China 810007
Tel: (86)(971) 8174514, 8138513
Fax: (86)(971) 8176805, 8176805
Website: www.qhwjmt.gov.cn

XINING ECONOMIC AND TECHNOLOGICAL DEVELOPMENT ZONE

Our Rating:	B
Year of Establishment:	2000
Location:	Xining, Qinghai
Size:	12.79 sq km
Major Investors:	N.A.
Total Foreign Direct Investment:	RMB1.1 billion
Major Industries Encouraged:	Saline chemistry, petrochemicals, Chinese and Tibetan herbs, food, biochemistry, environmental protection, technologies, finance, real estate, brokerage, and trading services.

INTRODUCTION

Xining Economic and Technological Development Zone (XNETDZ) was established with the approval of the State Council on 3 July 2000 and is the only one of its kind in Qinghai Province. It has a total development area of 12.79 sq km with a first phase development area of 4.4 sq km.

XNETDZ is located at the East Gate of Xining City, the provincial capital of Qinghai Province. It is five kilometers from the city center, three kilometers from the railway station and 30 kilometers away from the airport.

XNETDZ will be focusing on four major industrial clusters. They include saline chemistry and petrochemical industry; Chinese and Tibetan herbs, food and biochemistry; environmental protection and high-tech industries; and logistics, finance, real estate, brokerage, and trading services.

INVESTMENT CLIMATE

In 2001, XNETDZ invested RMB117 million in infrastructure development. In 2001, there were 16 cooperation agreements signed with contractual investment of RMB1.1 billion. By February 2002, 36 enterprises were approved to set up in XNETDZ and 11 enterprises had started operations. Among the approved enterprises, four were Sino-foreign joint ventures.

Administrative Committee of XNETDZ
36, Bayi West Road
Xining, Qinghai
P. R. China 810007
Tel: (86)(971) 8125306
Fax: (86)(971) 8125196
E-mail: xnjfj@163.com
Website: www.xnkfq.com

SHAANXI

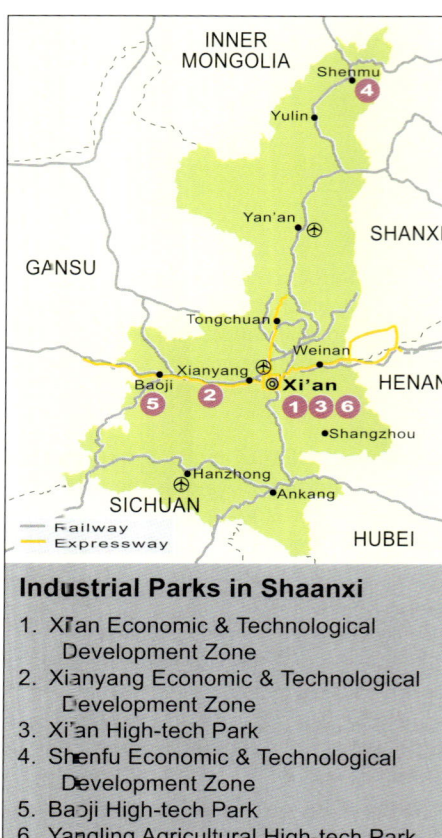

Industrial Parks in Shaanxi

1. Xi'an Economic & Technological Development Zone
2. Xianyang Economic & Technological Development Zone
3. Xi'an High-tech Park
4. Shenfu Economic & Technological Development Zone
5. Baoji High-tech Park
6. Yangling Agricultural High-tech Park

INTRODUCTION

Shaanxi distinguishes itself as one of the cradles of Chinese civilization and revolution. The provincial capital, Xi'an, has been the capital city for 14 feudal dynasties with history of more than 3,000 years, including the Zhou, Qin, Han, Sui and Tang dynasties. It had been the most prosperous region in the world for around one thousand years ever since the first Chinese emperor, Qinshihuang of the Qin Dynasty, who established his kingdom there around 2,200 years ago. Xi'an is the biggest business and commercial center in northwest China, and is one of China's seven famous ancient capital cities. It used to be China's political, economic and cultural center and is the starting point of the legendary Silk Road. Many historical sites make the city full of wonder, such as the Huaqing Pool which was already famous in the Western Zhou Dynasty over 3,000 years ago; the matriarchal clan community at Banpo village; the first Qin Emperor's Terra-Cotta Warriors and Horses, known as the world's eighth wonder; the imperial mausoleums of the Han and Tang Dynasties; the Great Mosque with unique features; the Big Wild Goose Pagoda and the Small Wild Goose Pagoda built in the Tang Dynasty; the Bell Tower and the Drum Tower of the Ming Dynasty; and the Forest of Stone Tablets.

GEOGRAPHY

Shaanxi is situated in the center of China geographically. The hinterland province extends from the Northern Shaanxi Plateau, Guanzhong Plain, to the mountain ranges in the south. The southern border of the province forms a part of the divisional line that divides China into the north and the south. The Yellow River runs in the east and parts Shaanxi from Shanxi Province.

Shaanxi covers three climate zones with temperate and subtropical characteristics. Its annual temperature averages between 8°C-16°C and annual precipitation ranges from 300 to 700 mm. The province administers one prefecture, 9 prefecture-level cities and 87 countries and country-level cities.

Fact Sheet	2001
Area (sq km)	205,600
Population (million)	36.59
GDP (RMB billion)	184.1
GDP Growth Rate	9.1%
Consumption Expenditure (RMB billion)	
• Government	23
• Household	66.5
Per capita annual	
• disposable income of urban residents (RMB '000)	5.48
• net income of rural households (RMB '000)	1.52
Contractual FDI (USD million)	730
Industrial Value Added (RMB bn)	45.5
Imports (USD million)	954
Exports (USD million)	1,110
Universities & Colleges	47

TRAVEL INFORMATION

Xi'an has the fourth largest airport in China.

From Xi'an Airport to:

Beijing	1 hr 30 mins
Shanghai Hongqiao	1 hr 55 mins
Nanjing	1 hr 10 mins
Hong Kong	2 hrs 30 mins
Tokyo	4 hrs
Seoul	2 hrs 30 mins

INVESTMENT CLIMATE

As the northwestern transportation hub in China, the province has easy connection to the vast hinterland in the northwest China. Xi'an is in the center of the railway, highway and airway network in northwest China.

Local industries are led by the production of energy, machinery and textile. As an important destination for tourists, tourism in Shaanxi has generated spillovers for the service sector.

Having lagged behind Chinese coastal region for two decades, Shaanxi is now vigorously promoting its strategic location and natural resources to attract foreign investors. The province has identified ten major development zones, half of which are located in Xi'an. In 2001, contractual FDI increased by 46.2% to reach USD730 million and utilized FDI rising by a 22% margin to USD352 million. Important cities in Shaanxi province include Xi'an, Xianyang, Baoji, Hanzhong and Yan'an.

As a prestigious province abundant in historical sites and cultural relics, Shaanxi is catching up its economic strength, especially at a time China enters WTO and calls for grand development in the western regions. In Shaanxi, there are 47 universities and colleges, such as Xi'an Jiaotong University, Chang'an University, Xi'an University of Electronic Science & Tech, North Western University and North Western Polytechnic University.

Shaanxi Provincial Government
Website: www.shaanxi.gov.cn

Information Net of Shaanix Foreign trade and Economy
Website: www.sx-trade.com

Shaanxi Chamber of International Commerce
Website: ccpit.shaanxi.gov.cn

XI'AN ECONOMIC AND TECHNOLOGICAL DEVELOPMENT ZONE

Cur Rating:	A
Year of Establishment:	1993
Location:	Xi'an, Shaanxi
Size:	23.5 sq km
Major Investors:	Coca-Cola, GM, HP, Mitsubishi Electric ABB, Rolls Royce, Taikoo Group, Siemens and Ting Hsin
Total Foreign Direct Investment:	USD408 million (end 1999)
Major Industries Encouraged:	Electronic-mechanical integration, medicines, bioengineering, foodstuff and new materials

INTRODUCTION

Xi'an Economic and Technological Development Zone (XAETDZ) was established in October 1993 and was approved as a state-level development zone by the State Council in February 2000. It covers 23.5 sqkm. XAETDZ is located outside the North Gate of Xi'an City and is about 5.5 km from the downtown. It is 30 km away from Xi'an Airport.

By the end of 1999, 193 projects had entered Xi'an ETDZ with total investment of RMB11.55 billion and contracted foreign investment of USD720 million. Utilized investment was more than RMB6.5 billion, among which foreign investment was USD410 million.

INVESTMENT CLIMATE

The zone now includes Yanliang Industrial Park, Jinhe Industrial Park, Lantian Industrial park, Fengjin Industrial Park and Weiyang Industrial Park. Longhai Railway is next to the periphery of XAETDZ. A passenger transport station and freight station are both five km away from Xi'an ETDZ.

Many world famous corporations such as Coca-Cola, GM, HP ABB, Mitsubishi Electric, Rolls Royce, Taikoo Group, Siemens, Ting Hsin International Group have set up enterprises in Xi'an ETDZ.

Administrative Committee of XAETDZ
Investment Promotion Department
Tel: (86)(29) 6515975, 6524692
Fax: (86)(29) 6517874
E-mail: xetdz@xetdz.com.cn
Website: www.xetdz.com.cn

XIANYANG ECONOMIC AND TECHNOLOGICAL DEVELOPMENT ZONE

Our Rating:	B
Year of Establishment:	1992
Location:	Xianyang, Shaanxi
Size:	15.9 sq km
Major Investors:	Rainbow Group, Xianyang Pianzhuan Group, Huaxing Electronic Industries,Huadian Materials, Golden Hill Electronics Group, Xianyang Mechanical Designing, Buchang Pharmaceuticals, Momeide Pharmaceuticals and Kanghui Pharmaceuticals
Total Foreign Direct Investment:	N.A.
Major Industries Encouraged:	Electronics, information technology, pharmaceuticals, bio-technology and new materials

INTRODUCTION

Established in 1992, Xianyang Economic & Technological Development Zone (XYETDZ) is located at Xianyang, an important industrial and commercial city of Shaanxi. The city is about 24 km from Xi'an, 10 km from the Xianyang International Airport and 5 km from Xianyang Railway Station. Xianyang is a famous ancient city. Emperor Qinshihuang established his kingdom, the Qin Dynasty, here in B.C. 221. With total population of 4.7 million, there is a large pool of R&D professionals in Xianyang.

INVESTMENT CLIMATE

With a total development area of 15.9 sq km, more than 200 enterprises have joined in the XYETDZ by the end of 2000. The total industrial output of member enterprises was RMB14.3 billion in 1999. The major industries encouraged are pharmaceuticals, bio-technology and new materials.

The performance of Xianyang's electronic industry was particularly impressive. Several famous enterprises are located in Xianyang city, such as Rainbow Group, Pianzhuan Group (www.pian-zhuan.com.cn), Huaxing Electronic Industries (www.hx795.com), Huadian Materials Co. Ltd. (www.huadian.org), Golden Hill Electronic Group, Xianyang Mechanical Designing, Hongshun Airport Facilities Development, Shaanxi Buchang Pharmacy (www.buchang.com.cn), Shaanxi Momeide Pharmacy and Xianyang Kanghui Pharmacy.

Administrative Committee of XYETDZ
1 Gaoxin Road
Xianyang, Shaanxi
P. R. China 712021
Tel: (86)(910) 3313823
Fax: (86)(910) 3337281
Email: xygxq@263.net
Website: www.xygxq.com

XI'AN HIGH-TECH PARK

Cur Rating:	AA
Year of Establishment:	March 1991
Location:	Xi'an, Shaanxi
Size:	29.15 sq km
Major Investors:	Bosch, Brothers, Daikin, NEC, Fujitsu, Microsoft, Datang Telecom, Haixing Technologies, Dongsheng Pharmaceuticals and Buchang Pharmaceuticals
Total Foreign Direct Investment:	USD840 million
Major Industries Encouraged:	Electronics, information technologies, optical-electronic-mechanical engineering, bio-pharmaceuticals and software development.

INTRODUCTION

Xi'an High-tech Park (XAHTP) is located in Xi'an. It was authorized as a national high-tech park in March 1991, and became a special high-tech park opening for APEC member nations.

The total development area of the park is around 29.15 sq km. It is 7 km away from the downtown, 11 km from the railway station and 35 km from the airport. The development focus is on electronics, information technologies, optical- electronic-mechanical engineering, biopharmaceuticals and software develop-ment.

By the end of 2001, over 4,100 enterprises had joined the park, including 703 high-tech enterprises and 488 foreign enterprises. The total contractual investment commitment was USD840 million.

In 2001, the total sales revenue and total industrial output of all member enterprises was RMB35.72 billion and RMB25.26 billion respectively. The GDP of the park was around RMB10.46 billion.

INVESTMENT CLIMATE

In 2001, the park has 3 enterprises with annual sales of over RMB2 billion, 9 enterprises with sales of over RMB1 billion and 61 enterprises with sales of over RMB100 million. Major MNCs who had established affiliates in the park include Bosch, Brothers, Daikin, NEC, Fujitsu and Microsoft.

XAHTP consists of 9 subsidiary parks, namely the Electronic Industrial Park, Chang'an Technology Park, Xi'an Software Park, Hi-tech Export Processing Base, Xi'an Jiaotong University Science Park, Northwest Polytechnic University Science Park, Bio-pharmaceutical Park and Advanced Material Science Park. Since its establishment in May 1998, the Entrepreneurship Park for Overseas Chinese Students has attracted over 400 overseas students to start their businesses in the Park.

Investment Bureau of XAHTP
Tel: (86)(29) 8211744
Fax: (86)(29) 8244367
Email: xdz-zsj@xdz.gov.cn
Website: www.xdz.gov.cn

SHENFU ECONOMIC AND TECHNOLOGICAL DEVELOPMENT ZONE

Our Rating:	B
Year of Establishment:	1993
Location:	Shenmu, Shaanxi
Size:	N.A.
Major Investors:	YSQ Electricity, Shenmu Electricity, Shenmu Dianhua, SeaBay Mining Industries, SFETDZ Leaf Amylun and SFETDZ Coal Industries
Total Foreign Direct Investment:	N.A.
Major Industries Encouraged:	Electricity, Coal Chemical Engineering, metallurgical industry, construction materials and high energy-consumption industries

INTRODUCTION

Established in 1993 and upgraded to the province level, Shenfu Economic & Technological Development Zone (SFETDZ) is located at Shenmu County in the northernmost part of Shaanxi province. Nearby, the Shenhua Group (www.shenhuagroup.com.cn) manages the Shenfu Dongshen Coal Mine. With total investment of RMB45 billion in the first stage, the Shenfu Dongshen Mine produces 40 million tons of coal every year. The annual production capacity will be increased to 60 million tons in 2005.

INVESTMENT CLIMATE

At the end of 2000, 12 projects had been undertaken in SFETDZ with total investment commitment of RMB1.9 billion. The investment in infrastructure develop-ment was RMB180 million. Major industries encouraged in the SFETDZ include electricity, coal chemical engineering, metallurgical industry, construction materials and high energy consumption industries etc. Their development will be integrated with the development of the abundant energy resources in the region. The major

investors include Sheng-hua YSQ Electricity Co. Ltd. (www.ghepc.-com), Shenmu Electricity Co. Ltd., Shenmu Dianhua Co. Ltd., Sea Bay Mining Industries Co. Ltd., SFETDZ Leaf Amylum Co. Ltd. and SFETDZ Coal Industries Co. Ltd.

The Administrative Committee of SFETDZ is the government agency in charge of the planning, development and administration of the development zone.

The Administrative Committee of SFETDZ
Dongxin Street
Shenmu, Shaanxi Province
P. R. China 719300
Tel: (86)(912) 8338198, 8334088
Fax: (86)(912) 8334088
Email: gwhxmb@sina.com
Website: www.sfkfq.com.cn

BAOJI HIGH-TECH PARK

Our Rating:	BB
Year of Establishment:	1992
Location:	Baoji, Shaanxi
Size:	5.77 sq km
Major Investors:	Top Group, Mincheng High-tech and Xianghui Corporation
Total Foreign Direct Investment:	N.A.
Major Industries Encouraged:	Microelectronics, aviation technologies, life science, bio-engineering and new materials

INTRODUCTION

Baoji High-tech Park (BHTP) is located in Baoji city. It was authorized as a state high-tech park in November 1992. The total development area of the park is 5.77 sq km.

The development focus of the park includes microelectronics, aviation technologies, life science, bioengineering and new materials.

INVESTMENT CLIMATE

In the park, an incubation service center has been set up to encourage the commercialization of scientific achievements. At the same time, the park enjoys rich human resources in the city as well as in nearly cities in the province. The total population of Baoji is 3.68 million, with 610,000 living in the urban area. Among them, there are 150,000 experience workers and more than 10,000 technical professionals.

There are many large state-owned enterprises in Baoji. Their major strengths are in machinery, electronics, light industry and non-ferrous metallurgicals.

Located in the west part of Shaanxi, Baoji is an important industrial city along the Eurasian Continental Bridge. Three major railways, namely Longhai (Qinhuangdao-Lanzhou), Baocheng (Baoji-chengdu) and

Baozhong (Baoji-zhongwei), meet in the city. The high-tech park is 100 km away from Xianyang International Airport.

Currently, there are 500 enterprises in the park, including 100 high-tech firms and 2 projects of Fortune Global 500.

Baoji is a famous cultural city with long history. It is an important stop for the legendary Silk Route and the "Hometown of Bronze". The cities hosts many historical sites including Tiantai Mountain, Famen Temple, Jinhe Taoist Temple and Temple of Zhuge Liang. It is also exciting to explore Taibai State Forest Park and Tiantai Mountain Forest Park.

Administrative Committee of BHTP
19 Torch Road
Baoji High-tech Park
Baoji, Shaanxi Province
P. R. China 7271106
Tel: (86)(917) 3319896, 3316986
Fax: (86)(917) 3319818
Email: bjgxq@public.xn.sn.cn
Website: www.bj-hightech.com

YANGLING AGRICULTURAL HIGH-TECH PARK

Our Rating:	B
Year of Establishment:	1997
Location:	Yangling, west Xi'an, Shaanxi
Size:	N.A.
Major Investors:	Yangling Modern Agriculture Development, Hengtai Botanic Nutrition, WoLing Resin-reducing International, Qinchuan Water Equipment Engineering, Fulushou Health Food, Zhongfu Biological Engineering and Banchuan Titanium Development
Total Foreign Direct Investment:	N.A.
Major Industries Encouraged:	Pesticide, agricultural engineering, bio-pharmaceuticals, healthcare products, environment friendly technologies and husbandry

INTRODUCTION

Yangling Agricultural High-tech Park (YLAHTP) is located at Yangling, which is a west suburb of Xi'an in Shaanxi Province. It was authorized as a state-level high-tech park in 1997, and was the only such park specialized in agricultural R&D, which covers forestry and husbandry, and related experimental production. The park is 82 km away from the downtown Xi'an.

Since its establishment, YLAHTP is growing fast. In 1997, there are only 17 enterprises in the park and the number increased to 348 in 2001.

INVESTMENT CLIMATE

By the end of 2001, the total investment in fixed assets reached RMB1.08 billion, including RMB768 million in infrastructure development. Over 4,000 professionals and specialists are now working in the park.

Northwest University of Agriculture Science & Technology (former Northwest Farming and Forestry School) was esta-blished in Yangling in 1934. The university plays an important role for the research and development of China's agriculture.

Longhai Railway (from Qinhuangdao to Lanzhou) and Xibao Expressway (from Xi'an to Baoji) run through the city. The park is 70 km away from Xi'an Xianyang International Airport and it takes 40 minutes by car to arrive there.

Administrative Committee of YLAHTP
8 Yangling Road, Yangling
Shaanxi
P. R. China 712100
Tel: (86)(29) 7011355
Fax: (86)(29) 7011353
Website: www.ylagri.gov.cn

XI'AN SOFTWARE DEVELOPMENT PARK

Year of Establishment:	1997
Location:	Xi'an, Shaanxi
Size:	60 ha
Major Investors:	IBM, HP, Philips, NEC and Fujitsu
Total Foreign Direct Investment:	N.A.
Major Industries Encouraged:	N.A.

Located within the area of Xi'an High-tech Park, the Xi'an Software Development Park is divided into a 2.5 hectare Incubation Zone and a 12 hectare Industrial Zone. In the Industrial Zone, there are international conference center, a training center, a software-testing center, high-standard offices, residential apartments, sports & entertainment centers.

The total government investment for the park is more than RMB700 million. More than 400 software enterprises have joined the park, which account for 90% of all software enterprises in Xi'an, with 40,000 personnel professionals working in the park. Prominent ones include Xi'an Seastar Group (www.seastar.com.cn), Xi'an SynchroSoft Co. Ltd. (www.synchro-soft.com), Xi'an Future Software Co. Ltd. (www.future-software.com.cn), Xi'an Bit Service Computer Software Co. Ltd. (bit-service.com) and Xi'an Golden Leaf NWPU Software Co. Ltd. The major products of these companies are widely applied in fields like telecommunication, Internet, operating system, info security, CAD/CAM, database application, GIS and CTI.

Major international corporations have joined the park such as IBM, HP, Philips, NEC and Fujitsu. In particular, Fujitsu aims to develop its largest global R&D base here and employ more than 1,000 professionals.

It is expected that by 2005, there will be around 1,000 software enterprises and 60,000 professionals in the park. The total sales revenue of products and services will be RMB20 billion, with profit of RMB2.5 billion.

In Shaanxi province, there are 47 universities and colleges, such as Xi'an Jiaotong University (www.xjtu.edu.cn), Northwestern University (www.nwu.edu.cn), Northwestern Polytechnic University (www.nwpu.edu.cn), Xi'an University of Electronic Science & Technology (www.xidian.edu.cn) and Changan University (www.xahu.edu.cn). Professional software colleges have been established at Xi'an Jiaotong University, Northwestern Polytechnic University and Xi'an University of Electronic Science & Technology.

Administrative Division of Xi'an Software Development Park
9 Gaoxin Third Road
Xi'an, Shaanxi
P. R. China 710075
Tel: (86)(29) 8227287
Fax: (86)(29) 8236554
Email: softpark@pub.xaonline.com
Website: www.xasoftpark.com

XI'AN JIAOTONG UNIVERSITY SCIENCE PARK

Year of Establishment:	2000
Location:	Xi'an, Shaanxi
Size:	68 ha
Major Supporting Institutions:	Xi'an Jiaotong University
Major Investors:	Create Group
Total Foreign Direct Investment:	N.A.
Major Industries Encouraged:	Information technology, biomedicine, new energy, environmental protection technologies

Xi'an Jiaotong University (www.xjtu.-edu.cn) enjoys a history of more than 100 years. Widely recognized as one of China's top five universities in science & technology, the university now has 641 professors, five CAS fellows and four CAE fellows. At the university, there are 11 State Key Subjects, five State Key Laboratories, four State Professional Key Laboratories and one State Engineering Research Center.

After the merger with Xi'an Medical University and Shaanxi University of Finance & Economics in 2000, the academic majors of XJTU now cover natural science, engineering, medicine, economics, management, humanities, social science, law and so on. Till now, the university has established cooperation relationship with more than 100 overseas universities.

At the end of 2000, the total assets of 38 XJTU affiliated enterprises were about RMB1 billion. Their products include intelligent home electronics, laser express molding machine, circumvolve auto compressor, high-quality color kinescope and so on. Among the affiliated enterprises, the development of Create Group (www.create-group.com.cn) is most impressive.

The total planning area of Xi'an Jiaotong University Science Park (XJTUSP) is about 68 hectares. The development focus is information technology, biomedicine, new energy and environmental protection technologies. According to the master plan of XJTUSP, there will be investment commitment of RMB500 million for infrastructure development and RMB2.2 billion for project investment in 2002. In the near future, there will be a Management Building, a Creative Incubation Plaza, a Technology Plaza, an Education Plaza and a Digital Residential Zone. Overall, XJTUSP aims to become a leader among the 22 national university science parks.

Xi'an Jiaotong University Science Park Development Corporation
4th Level, Entrepreneurship Park
Jiaotong University Campus
Xinqing South Road
Xi'an, Shaanxi
P. R. China 710049
Tel: (86)(29) 2666995
Fax: (86)(29) 2668008
Email: service@xjtusp.com
Website: www.xjtusp.com

NORTHWEST SCI-TECH UNIVERSITY OF AGRICULTURE AND FORESTRY SCIENCE PARK

Year of Establishment:	2001
Location:	Yangling, Shaanxi
Size:	20 ha
Major Supporting Institutions:	Northwest Science-Tech Univ. of Agriculture & Forestry
Major Investors:	The Government of Yangling
Total Foreign Direct Investment:	N.A.
Major Industries Encouraged:	Agricultural products, forestry products, irrigation technologies, bio-engineering, agricultural chemicals, medicine, agriculture mechanics, environmental protection technologies and comprehensive utilization of resources

INTRODUCTION

The unique feature that distinguishes Northwest Science & Technological University of Agriculture and Forestry Science Park (NWSTUAFSP) from other national university science parks is its specialization in agriculture and forestry. The 20 hectare park is an essential part of Yanglin Agricultural High-tech Park (www.ylagri.-gov.cn), which is the only such zone in China. It enjoys preferential policies applied to China's state high-tech parks as well as university science park.

INVESTMENT CLIMATE

Merged with former Northwest Agricultural University whose history could be traced back to 1934, Northwestern Forestry College, and five other major research institutes such as Shaanxi Provincial Academy of Agriculture and Shaanxi Provincial Academy of Forestry, the university is now the largest agricultural university in China. The university is committed to promoting sustainable development of agriculture in the vast lands of western China. The university now has about 300 professors and more than 500 associate professors. During the recent years, more than 600 programs have been awarded National Science & Technology Advance Award and other honors.

As a part of Yangling Agricultural High-tech Park, NWSTUAFSP relies on the development of the state high-tech park and support from the university. By the end of March 2002, 430 enterprises, among which 14 are foreign enterprises, had joined the high-tech park, with total capital of RMB1.5 billion. Major projects, such as the a hectare International Life Science Industrial Zone are to be undertaken with total investment of RMB2 billion.

NWSTUAFSP Development Corporation
Yanglin, Shaanxi Province
P. R. China 712100
Tel: (86)(29) 7082809
Website: www.nwsuaf.edu.cn

NORTHWESTERN POLYTECHNIC UNIVERSITY SCIENCE PARK

Year of Establishment:	2000
Location:	Xi'an, Shaanxi
Size:	N.A.
Major Supporting Institutions:	Northwestern Polytechnic University and Xi'an High-tech Park
Major Investors:	NWPUSP Development Corporation
Major Industries Encouraged:	New materials, software development, biology, mechanics and electronics

INTRODUCTION

Jointly developed by Xi'an High-tech Park (www.xdz.com.cn) and Northwestern Polytechnic University (www.nwpu.edu.cn), Northwestern Polytechnic University Science Park (NWPUSP) became one of China's 22 National University Science Parks in May 2001.

INVESTMENT CLIMATE

With start-up capital of RMB60 million, the NWPUSP Development Corporation was established at the end of March 2000. Its main shareholders are Northwestern Polytechnic University (66.7%) and Xi'an High-tech Park (33.3%). Since then, international organizations such as United Nations Industrial Development Organi-zation, Japan International Technology Association and Japan International Architecture Association have visited and assessed the park. In 2001, 19 enterprises joined the park. Their operations cover new materials, software development, biology, mechanics and electronics etc.

Located in Xi'an, the 45-year old Northwestern Polytechnic University is a top Chinese university specialized in aviation, aeronautics and navigation. Currently, the university has 10 State Key Subjects, 10 State Key Laboratories, 11 fellows of CAS and CAE, and over 1,200 professors and associate professors. As a milestone in the history of the university, on 22 January 2002, agreement was signed among State Defense Science & Technology Commission, Ministry of Education, Shaanxi Province and Xi'an city to invest RMB900 million to develop Northwestern Polytechnic University into a world-class university.

NWPUSP Development Corporation is now in charge of the planning and management affairs of the university science park. For potential investors, the park could be considered as a qualified incubation base for high-tech projects.

NWPUSP Development Corporation
127 Friendship West Road
Xi'an, Shaanxi
P. R. China 710072
Tel: (86)(29) 8311550
Fax: (86)(29) 8491000
Email: market@npustp.com
 Business@npustp.com
Website: www.npustp.com

Industrial Parks in Shandong

1. Qingdao Economic & Technological Development Zone
2. Weihai Economic & Technological Development Zone
3. Jinan Economic & Technological Development Zone
4. Weihai Export Processing Zone
5. Yantai Economic & Technological Development Zone
6. Jinan High-tech Park
7. Qingdao High-tech Park
8. Weihai High-tech Park
9. Weifang High-tech Park
10. Zibo High-tech Park

INTRODUCTION

The history of Shandong province can be traced back to the Spring-Autumn and Warring States period 2,700 years ago. It was the birthplace of two revered Chinese philosophers, Confucius and Mencius, and the famous military strategist, Sun Tzu.

Shandong is China's top producer of a range of agricultural products such as wheat, corn, peanuts, meat, seafood and fruits. Two decades of economic reforms have changed the industrial landscape of the province. In terms of GDP, it is now the third largest in China.

GEOGRAPHY

The peninsula-shaped province enjoys a strategic location in China's east coast, separating Bohai Sea and Yellow Sea. The meandering coastline allows Shandong to have as many as 26 seaports, such as Qingdao, Yantai and Rizhao.

The territory has a temperate monsoon climate, with windy and dry spring, hot and rainy summer, sunny autumn and cold dry winter. The annual rainfall in the province is about 550-950 mm.

Shandong comprises 17 prefecture-level cities, with Jinan being the provincial capital.

Fact Sheet	2001
Area (sq km)	156,700
Population (million)	90.41
GDP (RMB billion)	943.8
GDP Growth Rate	10.1%
Consumption Expenditure (RMB billion)	
• Government	75.3
• Household	283
Per capita annual	
• disposable income of urban residents (RMB '000)	7.10
• net income of rural households (RMB '000)	2.80
Contractual FDI (USD million)	6,720
Industrial Value Added (RMB bn)	290.8
Imports (USD million)	10,830
Exports (USD million)	18,130
Universities & Colleges	67

Other important cities in the province include Qingdao, Yantai, Weihai, Weifang and Zibo etc. The population and its density are ranked second largest in China.

TRAVEL INFORMATION

From Jinan Airport to:
Beijing	55 mins
Shanghai Hongqiao	1 hr 20 mins
Shenzhen	2 hrs 15 mins
Hong Kong	2 hrs 40 mins

From Qingdao Airport to:
Beijing	1 hr 10 mins
Shanghai Pudong	1 hr 5 mins
Hong Kong	3 hrs 5 mins
Seoul	1 hr 20 mins

From Yantai Airport to:
Beijing	1 hr 10 mins
Shanghai Pudong	1 hr 25 mins
Hong Kong	3 hrs 10 mins
Seoul	1 hr

INVESTMENT CLIMATE

Shandong is rich in mineral resources and crude oil. Shengli Oil Field is a famous oil field as its crude oil output accounted for around 17% of China's total. The deposits of over 59 minerals such as sulphur, diamond, graphite, coal, iron, magnetite etc. in the province ranks among the top in the country.

In 2001, Shandong achieved GDP of RMB944 billion, contributed by the primary, secondary and tertiary sectors by ratios of 14.4:49.3:36.6. The economy of the province used to be largely driven by the development of heavy industries and state-owned enterprises. But in recent years, Shandong has become a hot place for foreign investment.

The leading industries in Shandong include energy, chemicals, metallurgy, building materials, machinery, electronics, textiles and food. The main products of the province include coal, crude oil, concrete, fertilizers, wine and beer. Shandong has successfully promoted many famous brand names such as Hai'er Electronics, Hisense Electronics, Zhangyu Wine, Tsingdao Beer and Qingqi Motorcycle.

With 26 ports, 8 airports, 2,002 kilometers of expressways and 2,930 kilometers of highways within its territory, Shandong boasts a well-developed infrastructure.

Major export products of the province are machinery, electronics, chemicals, textiles, garments etc. Major import products are steel, machinery, wool, chemicals, raw materials, computers, complete sets of equipment and technology and fertilizers.

Shandong has recently put substantial effort into attracting FDI to boost an open economy. As a member of the Northeast Asian Economic Rim as well as having historical ties with Germany and Japan, the province has drawn foreign investment from Korea, Japan, Germany and the traditional sources of Hong Kong, Taiwan and Singapore. In 2001, 3,058 new FIEs were approved with total contractual foreign capital of USD7.16 billion. Total contractual foreign direct investment was USD6.72 billion; the utilized mount was USD3.62 billion.

Shandong Provincial Government
Website: www.sd-china.com

Shandong Investment Net
Website: www.sdinvest.com

Shandong Economic Information Network
Website: www.sd.cei.gov.cn

QINGDAO ECONOMIC AND TECHNOLOGICAL DEVELOPMENT ZONE

Our Rating:	AA
Year of Establishment:	1984
Location:	Qingdao, Shandong
Size:	N.A.
Major Investors:	Matsushita, Hai'er and Hisense
Total Foreign Direct Investment:	USD1.7 billion (Nov 2001)
Major Industries Encouraged:	N.A.

INTRODUCTION

Qingdao Economic and Technological Development Zone (QDETDZ), also known as Qingdao Development Area, was established in October 1984. It was among the first group of state-level development zones.

Situated on the western coast of Jiaozhou Bay and facing Qingdao City across the sea, QDETDZ is only 2.26 nautical miles from Qingdao at the narrowest point. It is 53 kilometers away from Qingdao International Airport, about 50 minutes' ride by car.

The zone has been growing fast, especially during recent years. By the end of 2000, achieved GDP of QDETDZ was RMB8.5 billion; achieved local fiscal revenue was RMB600 million; achieved gross industrial output was RMB21.8 billion and gross exports were USD610 million.

INVESTMENT CLIMATE

By the end of 2001, there were 1,231 foreign projects in QDETDZ, with USD3.21 billion in contractual investment and USD1.7 billion in utilized investment. There were 118 projects with individual investments above USD10 million, and 3 projects exceeding USD100 million.

The major industries to be promoted in QDETDZ include consumer electronics, building materials, petrochemicals, machinery, pharmaceuticals and tourism.

Qingdao, located at the southwestern end of Shandong Peninsula, is a famous open coastal city characterized by port trade, light chemical industry, financial service, tourism and oceanographic research. As one of the top five foreign trade ports in China, Qingdao is also a famous historical and cultural city and a famous summer resort.

Foreign Trade Bureau of QDETDZ
0620 Room, Zerun Mansion
369, Changjiang Middle Road
Qingdao, Shandong
P. R. China 266555
Tel: (86)(532) 6092801
Fax: (86)(532) 6988629
E-mail: propro@bestinvest.org
Website: www.bestinvest.org

WEIHAI ECONOMIC AND TECHNOLOGICAL DEVELOPMENT ZONE

Our Rating:	A
Year of Establishment:	1992
Location:	Weihai, Shandong
Size:	36 sq km
Major Investors:	Daiwoo
Total Foreign Direct Investment:	USD1.2 billion
Major Industries Encouraged:	Automobiles, electronics, foodstuff, textiles, pharmaceuticals, chemical engineering, construction materials and machinery

INTRODUCTION

Weihai Economic and Technological Development Zone (WETDZ) was established as a state-level development zone with the approval from the State Council in 1992 It covers 36 sq km.

The zone is located in Weihai City, which is at the most eastern of Shandong Peninsula. It is only 20 kilometers from Weihai Airport.

In 2001, the GDP of WETDZ was RMB2.5 billion, up 24.9% over the previous year; the gross industrial output was RMB4.9 billion, up 30%; total industrial value-added was RMB1.752 billion, up 24.4%. Together, 345 foreign investment projects have been established in the zone with investment of USD1.2 billion. 23 projects have investment of over USD10 million.

INVESTMENT CLIMATE

Major industries to be promoted in the park include automobiles, electronics, foodstuff, textiles, pharmaceuticals, chemical engineering, construction materials and machinery.

Economic Development Bureau of WETDZ
Tel: (86)(631) 5980066, 5980600
Website: www.eweihai.net.cn

JINAN ECONOMIC AND TECHNOLOGICAL DEVELOPMENT ZONE

Our Rating:	A
Year of Establishment:	N.A.
Location:	Jinan, Shandong
Size:	N.A.
Major Investors:	Jinan Jingheng, Jinan New Century Electronics, Luneng Finemores Logistics Co. Ltd., Luneng Fuji GIS Co. Ltd., Shandong Luneng Plastic Metalwork Co. Ltd., Luneng Electronics and Shandong Dema Construction Materials Co. Ltd.
Major Industries Encouraged:	New materials, microelectronics, information technology, communication, food, printing and entertainment facilities

Jinan Economic and Technological Development Zone (JNETDZ) is located in Jinan, the provincial capital of Shandong province.

JNETDZ is located in the southwestern part of Jinan city and adjacent to Changqing County and Huaiyin District. It comprises 5 subsidiary high-tech parks, namely Luneng Industrial Park, Taiwanese Investment Park, Food Industrial Park, Microelectronics Park and a Testing Base. Major industries encouraged in JNETDZ include new materials, microelectronics, information technology, communication, food, printing and entertainment facilities.

By the end of 2001, 45 enterprises had joined JNETDZ, including 13 foreign companies from Germany, the US, Japan, South Korea, Australia, Sweden, Singapore, New Zealand, Taiwan, Hong Kong etc. Among the 45 enterprises, about 10 have investment of more than RMB100 million (USD12 million). Major enterprises include Jingheng Co. Ltd., Jinan New Century Electronics, Luneng Finemores Logistics, Luneng Fuji Electrical Co. Ltd., Luneng Plastic Metalwork Co. Ltd. and Luneng Electronics.

Administrative Committee of JNETDZ
Lingyan Middle Road, Changqing
Jinan, Shandong
P. R. China
Tel: (86)(531) 7227668
Fax: (86)(573) 2208570
E-mail: jnedz@public.jn.sd.cn
Website: www.jnedz.gov.cn

WEIHAI EXPORT PROCESSING ZONE

Year of Establishment:	2000
Location:	Weihai, Shandong
Size:	2.6 sq km
Major Investors:	N.A.
Total Foreign Direct Investment:	N.A.
Major Industries Encouraged:	Export processing, warehousing and transportation

INTRODUCTION

Weihai Export Processing Zone (WEPZ) was set up with the approval of the State Council on 27 April 2000 as one of China's 15 Export Processing Zones. It is located in the southeast area of Weihai Economic and Technological Development Zone .The zone covers 2.6 sq km and is divided into two development phases, with the first phase being 1.34 sq km and the second phase 1.26 sq km. It is 30 kilometers to Weihai Airport and three kilometers to Weihai Railway Station.

INVESTMENT CLIMATE

Necessary utilities such as power supply, water supply, heat supply, roads, sewage treatment, communications, and ventilation have been completed.

Enterprises in WEPZ are mainly engaged in export processing, warehousing and transportation serving the enterprises inside the zone.

Weihai New Port is only 6 kilometers away. At present, there are regular cargo shipping lines to South Korea, Hong Kong and Japan.

Administrative Committee of WEPZ
Eastern Qilu Road
Weihai, Shandong
P. R. China 264205
Tel: (86)(631) 5981671, 5981672
Fax: (86)(631) 5981632
E-mail: whbsq@whpublic.sd.cninfo.net
Website: http://whckjgq.51.net

YANTAI EXPORT PROCESSING ZONE

Year of Establishment:	2000
Location:	Yantai, Shandong
Size:	4.17 sq km
Major Investors:	N.A.
Total Foreign Direct Investment:	N.A.
Major Industries Encouraged:	Export processing, storage and transportation

Yantai Export Processing Zone (YTEPZ) is one of China's first 15 export processing zones approved by the State Council on 27 April 2000. The total construction area of YTEPZ is 4.17 sq km, in which the initial zone covers 3 sq km.

YTEPZ lies in the northern part of Yantai City, and faces Japan and Korea across the Bohai sea. It is only 17 kilometers away from YTEPZ to Yantai Airport, and one kilometer from Yantai Railway Station. YTEPZ is very near to Yantai Port that has two container berths of 15,000-tonnage and 30,000-tonnage capacities and two bulk cargo berths of 15,000-tonnage and 20,000-tonnage.

Infrastructure development has been completed. Standard workshops of 120,000 sq m and bonded warehouses of 40,000 sq m are also built. YTEPZ has attracted investors from countries and regions such as Japan, Korea, Singapore, Hong Kong, Taiwan, Sweden, the United States and Canada etc.

Administrative Committee of WHEPZ
Tel: (86)(0535) 6800043
Fax: (86)(0535) 6840880
E-mail: ytftzac@public.ytpt.sd.cn
Website: www.yantaiepz.gov.cn

JINAN HIGH-TECH PARK

Our Rating:	A
Year of Establishment:	March 1991
Location:	Jinan, Shandong
Size:	9.26 sq km
Major Investors:	Little Duck Group, Langchao Group, Qingqi Motorcycles, Zhongchuang Group, Qilu Pharmaceuticals
Total Foreign Direct Investment:	N.A.
Major Industries Encouraged:	Electronics, information technology bio-engineering, chemical engineering, electrical engineering, new materials and software

INTRODUCTION

Jinan High-tech Park (JNHTP) is located in the east part of Jinan city. It was authorized by the State Council as a state-level high-tech park in March 1991.

JNHTP's total development area is 9.26 sq km. Within the zone, there are special parks in the east: Qilu Software Park, a university science park, an electronics industrial park and Chemical Fiber Park.

INVESTMENT CLIMATE

Over 1 billion RMB has been invested in infrastructure development.

JHTP focuses on high-tech industries such as electronics, information technology, biological engineering, chemical engineering, electrical engineering, new materials and software development. Over 60 enterprises are located in JNHTP, such as Little Duck Group, Langchao Group, Qingqi Group, Zhongchuang Group and Qilu Pharmaceuticals Group.

Qilu Software Park was established in November 1995. It now contains over 100 enterprises including five large IT enterprises, like Zhongchuang Software Engineering Co. Ltd., Langchao Group and Shandong Computing Center. Extensive cooperation has be established between the software park and many international companies including Microsoft, Intel, Sybase, HP, IBM and Oracle.

The university science park is another key project of JNHTP. It is the result of the cooperation between JNHTP and Shandong University.

In Jinan, there are 11 universities and colleges, such as Shandong University and Shandong Normal University. Some important research institutes such as Shandong Academy of Sciences and Shandong Agriculture Academy of Science are also located in the city.

Administrative Committee of JNHTP
Tel: (86)(531) 8871618
Fax: (86)(531) 8871574
E-mail: zsj@jctp.gov.cn
Website: www.jctp.gov.cn

QINGDAO HIGH-TECH PARK

Our Rating:	AA
Year of Establishment:	1992
Location:	Qingdao, Shandong
Size:	67 sq km
Major Investors:	Lucent Technologies, HP, Coca-Cola, Mitsubishi, Daewoo, Haier, Hisense, Double-star Group, Aucma Group, Shandong Textiles Import & Export Corporation, Shandong Arts & Crafts Imp & Exp Co. and Tsingdao Beer Group
Total Foreign Direct Investment:	USD720 million
Major Industries Encouraged:	Consumer electronics, information technology, bioengineering, communication technology, new materials and other advanced technologies

INTRODUCTION

Qingdao High-tech Park (QDHTP) was authorized by the State Council as a state-level high-tech park in 1992. The total development area is 57 sq km. It is close to the old downtown area of the city.

INVESTMENT CLIMATE

Qingdao is the biggest industrial city in Shandong Province. QDHTP focuses on consumer electronics, information technology, bioengineering, communication technology, new materials and other advanced technologies. In 2001, the GDP of QDHTP was RMB6.9 billion.

Major domestic corporations have joined QDHTP, such as Haier Group, Hisense Group, Double-star Group, Aucma Group, Shandong Textiles Import & Export Corporation, Liangmu Corporation, Shandong Arts & Crafts Imp & Exp Co Ltd and Tsingdao Beer Group.

QDHTP has successfully attracted some prominent foreign investors, such as Lucent Technologies, HP, Coca-Cola, Mitsubishi and Daewoo. By the end of 1999, 621 foreign enterprises had set up subsidiaries in the park; among them 74 had investments of over USD10 million. The total contractual investment was USD1.69 billion and the utilized investment was USD720 million.

There are three subsidiary zones in QDHTP, namely Electronic Information Zone, New Materials Zone and Bioengineering Zone. Surrounding QDHTP are some universities and colleges, such as Qingdao University and Qingdao Maritime University.

The zone is 17 kilometers from Qingdao International Airport, where flights are available to Seoul, Pusan, Hong Kong, Tokyo, Beijing, Shanghai, Guangzhou, Shenzhen and other major cities.

Administrative Committee of QDHTP
E-mail: info@hi-tech.chinaqingdao.net
info@laoshan.net
Website: www.hi-tech.chinaqingdao.net

WEIHAI HIGH-TECH PARK

Our Rating:	A
Year of Establishment:	1991
Location:	Weihai, Shandong
Size:	39.8 sq km
Major Investors:	Samsung Electronics, Beiyang Electrical Co. Ltd.
Total Foreign Direct Investment:	N.A.
Major Industries Encouraged:	Electronics, electrical engineering, new materials and bio-pharmaceuticals

INTRODUCTION

Weihai High-tech Park (WEHTP) is located in the west area of Weihai city. The total development area of the park is 39.8 sq km. WEHTP has a coastline of 12.5 kilometers.

The total investment of the 1,271 projects in the park was RMB15.5 billion. Over 561 projects belong to high-tech industries and the total investment for these enterprises was RMB5.5 billion. In 2000, the value-added of high-tech enterprises accounted for 47% of the total. The export of high-tech products was USD150 million. Major investors include Samsung Electronics and Beiyang Electrical Co. Ltd.

INVESTMENT CLIMATE

Over RMB1.1 billion has been spent for infrastructure development. Foreign investors come mainly from the US, Germany, South Korea, Japan, Hong Kong and Taiwan.

The development focus of WEHTP includes electronics, electrical engineering, new materials and biopharmaceuticals. The sector of electronics and information technology accounted for about 51% of the total high-tech enterprises, and it specializes in the production of fax machines, bubblejet printers and laser printers. The incubation center has attracted more than 30 high-tech enterprises.

The new materials sector accounts for 30% of the high-tech enterprises in the park and the development emphasizes on is the production of carbon fiber textiles and fiberglass fishing boats.

Approximately 7% of the high-tech enterprises belong to the biopharmaceuticals sector, particularly in high polymer materials and genetic engineering pharmaceuticals.

WEHTP is 3 kilometers away from downtown area of the city, 4 kilometers away from Weihai Port, 10 kilometers from the railway station, 35 kilometers from Weihai Airport and 80 kilometers from Yantai International Airport.

WEHTP has been conferred the ISO14001 Certification in recognition of its performance in environment protection. It is the second Chinese high-tech park to be awarded such honor after Suzhou New District.

Administrative Committee of WEHTP
Torch Tower, 198 Culture West Road
Weihai, Shandong
P. R. China 264209
Tel: (86)(631) 5629193
E-mail: webmaster@whtdz.com.cn
Website: www.whtdz.com.cn

WEIFANG HIGH-TECH PARK

Our Rating:	BBB
Year of Establishment:	1991
Location:	Weifang city, Shandong
Size:	16.1 sq km
Major Investors:	N.A.
Total Foreign Direct Investment:	USD364 million
Major Industries Encouraged:	Nanometer technology, chemical engineering, new materials, electronics, information technology, real estate development and optical-electronic-mechanical integration technologies

INTRODUCTION

Weifang High-tech Park (WFHTP) is located in Weifang City. The total development area is 16.1 sq km.

The core industries of WFHTP include nanometer technology, chemical engineering, new materials, electronics, information technology, real estate development and optical-electromechanical integration and products.

WFHTP consists of four sub-zones, namely Software Development Park, University Industrial Park, Private Enterprise Park and Taiwanese Investment Park. By the end of 2001, total contractual investment was USD364 million.

INVESTMENT CLIMATE

To date, over RMB4.6 billion has been invested for infrastructure development.

Jiaoji Expressway and Jiqing Expressway run through WFHTP. It takes 1.5 hours to drive to Qingdao in the east, and 1.5 hours to Jinan in the west. The park is 5 kilometers from Weifang Railway Station and 10 kilometers from Weifang Airport.

Administrative Committee of WFHTP
E-mail: tjxx@public.wfptt.sd.cn
Website: www.wfgx.gov.cn

ZIBO HIGH-TECH PARK

Our Rating:	BBB
Year of Establishment:	November 1992
Location:	Zibo, Shandong
Size:	77.2 sq km
Major Investors:	Xianxing Electronics, Qilu Petrochemcial, Dongda Group, Xinhua Pharmaceuticals and New Torch Information Industries
Total Foreign Direct Investment:	N.A.
Major Industries Encouraged:	CAD/CAE/CAM technologies and products, software development, system integration technology, network equipment, microelectronics and semiconductors

INTRODUCTION

Zibo High-tech Park (ZBHTP) is located in the northern part of Zibo City. It was awarded the state-level status in November 1992. The total develop-ment area is 77.2 sq km.

The main industries of the park include CAD/CAE/CAM technologies and pro-ducts, software development, system integration technology, network equipment, microelectronics and semicon-ductors.

INVESTMENT CLIMATE

By the end of 2001, RMB4.2 billion has been invested in infrastructural development.

Within ZBHTP, there are a few subsidiary zones; a Pharmaceutical industrial zone, a comprehensive zone for science, engineering and trade, and an export-oriented industrial zone.

Major enterprises in the park include Xianxing Electronics, Qilu Petrochemcial, Dongda Group, Xinhua Pharmaceuticals Group and New Torch Information Industries.

Located in the central of Shandong Peninsula. Zibo enjoys long history, famous for being the capital city of the Qi Kingdom more than 2000 years ago. It has rich natural resources and has enjoyed rapid economic growth during the past decade.

ZBHTP is 60 kilometers away from Jinan International Airport. Jiaoji Railway, Xintai Railway, Zidong Railway, National Highway No. 309 and No. 205 intersect in the park.

The Administrative Committee of ZBHTP
Tel: (86)(533) 3582819
Fax: (86)(533) 3580065
E-mail: webmaster@china-zibo.com
Website: www.china-zibo.com

SHANDONG UNIVERSITY SCIENCE PARK

Year of Establishment:	2000
Location:	Jinan, Shandong
Major Supporting Institutions:	Shandong University and Jinan Economic & Technological Development Zone
Major Investors:	Shandong Keyuan Company, Shandong OMA Information Industries, Shandong Lianrun Technologies
Major Industries Encouraged:	Optical-electrics, electric and electrical engineering, new materials, biotechnology, new medicine, new energy, environmental protection technologies and information technology

Shandong University Science Park (SDUSP), one of China's first 22 national university science parks, is located in Jinan. It comprises an Entrepreneurs Zone and an Industrial Zone. The Entrepreneur Zone is located just beside the campus of Shandong University while the 22 hectare Industrial Zone is located in the Jinan Economic & Technological Development Zone. The latter is divided into six functional areas: a 2-hectare Optical-Electronics sub-zone, a 4-hectare Electric and Electrical Engineering sub-zone, a 2-hectare New Materials sub-zone, a 5-hectare Biotechnology cum New Medicine sub-zone, a 2.5-hectare New Energy and Environmental Protection Technologies sub-zone, and the 6-hectare Information Technologies sub-zone.

Shandong University provides important intellectual backup for the enterprises at SDUSP. it was established in 1901, and now the university is a merger of the former Shandong University, Shandong Medical University and Shandong University of Technology.

The number of students in the university is around 32,000, among which 5,000 are postgraduates pursuing master or doctorate degrees. The university has developed leading advantage in fields such as new materials, advanced manufacturing technology, chemistry and chemical engineering, life science, pharmaceutical research, computer and communication technology. Extensive international cooperation has been established between Shandong University and more than 50 overseas institutions.

SDUSP Development Corporation is in charge of the development and operation of the University Science Park. Major enterprises in SDUSP include Shandong Keyuan, Shandong OMA Industries and Shandong Lianrun Technologies and others. The performance of Shandong OMA Industries is impressive. With more than 300 employees and sales offices in many cities all around China, it is now the largest OMR producer in Asia Pacific.

SDUSP Development Corporation
Room 500, C Zone
Tel: (86)(531) 2922730, 2955081-8588
Fax: (86)(531) 2922731
Email: sdusp@sdu.edu.cn
Website: www.sdusp.sdu.edu.cn

QILU SOFTWARE DEVELOPMENT PARK

Year of Establishment:	N.A.
Location:	Jinan, Shandong
Size:	38 hectares
Major Investors:	ChinaCreate Engineering, GenerSoft Company of Langchao Group, Qilu Software, The Integrated Electronic System Research Institute, Shandong Provincial Computing Center and Shandong Luneng Software

Qilu Software Development Park (QLSDP) is located in the eastern part of Jinan High-tech Park, and it covers 38 hectares. The administrative committee of QLSDP has planned to expand the total area to 120 hectares and aims to become the largest and most comprehensive software development base in China.

Currently, 51 software enterprises have joined the park. The prominent ones include Shandong ChinaCreate Engineering Co. Ltd., Shandong GenerSoft Company of Langchao Group, Qilu Software Co. Ltd., the Integrated Electronic System Research Institute, Shandong Provincial Computing Center and Shandong Luneng Software Co. Ltd etc.

In 2000, the total sales revenue of park enterprises was RMB2.03 billion, a 79% increase over 1999. The profit was RMB110 million, up 28%. It is estimated that by 2005, there will be 400 software enterprises operating in QLSDP with total sales of RMB8 billion.

Overall, in Shandong province, there are about 540 software enterprises that employ 30,000 software professionals. With a total investment of RMB500 million, Qilu Software College was established in July 2001 at Shandong University to further promote the software industry of the province.

Administrative Committee of QLSDP
40 Garden Road
Jinan, Shandong
P. R. China
Tel: (86)(531) 8915952
Fax: (86)(531) 8915592
E-mail: jnioz@public.jn.sd.cn

SHANXI

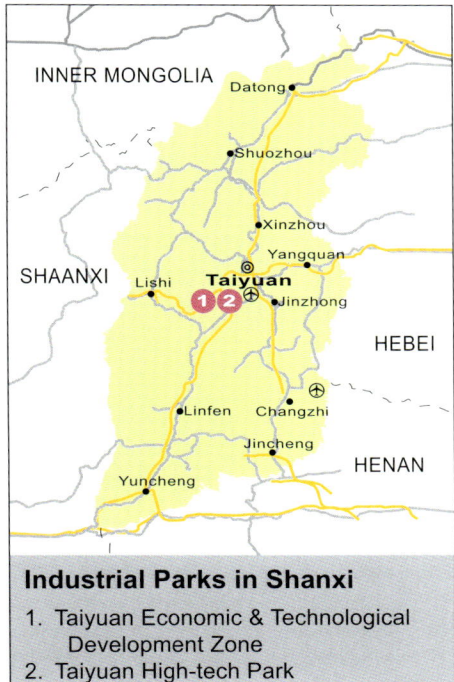

Industrial Parks in Shanxi

1. Taiyuan Economic & Technological Development Zone
2. Taiyuan High-tech Park

INTRODUCTION

Facing the Yellow River in the west and the Taihang Mountains in the east. Shanxi province is a landlocked area. The capital city is Taiyuan. Other major cities include Datong, Yangquan, Changzhi and Jincheng.

GEOGRAPHY

Shanxi province is located on the east part of North China's Loess Plateau. Mountains and hills occupy 69% of its territory, with the rest shared by basins and terraces. Apart from Taihang, famous mountains include Hengshan (or the North Great Mountain in China), Wutai (the peak of North China), Zhongtiao and Luliang mountains.

The province has a temperate monsoon climate with continental characteristics. Winters are dry and cold with temperature ranging from -12°C to -2°C; summers are warm with an average temperature at 26°C. Annual precipitation ranges between 400-500 mm.

TRAVEL INFORMATION

From Taiyuan Airport to:

Hong Kong	2hrs 40mins
Shanghai Hongqiao	1hr 50mins
Beijing	50mins
Guangzhou	2hrs 40mins
Shenzhen	2hrs 45mins
Chongqing	2hrs

INVESTMENT CLIMATE

Shanxi is famous for its heavy industry, particularly in energy and chemicals. Heavy industry accounts for over 80% of the province's total industrial output.

The province's coal fields are among China's largest ones, covering a total area of 64,800 sq km. Major coalfields are located near Taiyuan and Datong. The coal output of Shanxi province ranked the top in China, and nearly accounts for one-fourth of the country's total. In addition, Taiyuan Iron and Steel Works is China's largest base for special steel. The annual output capacity is around 2.7 million tons of steel. Aluminum industry has also become one of the local pillar industries.

The province has been encouraging industries of machinery and electronics. Recently, several large and medium-sized enterprises have become famous for their brands in China, such as Taiyuan Heavy Machinery Group Company, Taiyuan Mining Machinery Plant, Yuci Hydraulic Component Plant, etc. Other main industries include

Fact Sheet	2001
Area (sq km)	156,000
Population (million)	32.7
GDP (RMB billion)	177.46
GDP Growth Rate	8.3%
Consumption Expenditure (RMB billion)	
• Government	29
• Household	68
Per capita annual	
• disposable income of urban residents (RMB '000)	5.39
• net income of rural households (RMB '000)	1.956
Contractual FDI (USD million)	590
Industrial Value Added (RMB bn)	77.4
Imports (USD million)	471
Exports (USD million)	1464
Universities & Colleges	39

Shanxi Agricultural University and Shanxi Medical University.

Shanxi Provincial Government
Website: www.shanxi.gov.cn

Shanxi Foreign Trade & Economic
Department
Tel: (86)(351) 4042185

Shanxi Foreign Enterprises Association
Tel: (86)(351) 4040123

coke, mining equipment, machine tools, automobiles, metallurgy, chemical fertilizer, printing, papermaking, food, textile, etc

One key export product is cokecoal, which accounts for around 60% of the province's total export. Other major export products are textiles, metals, minerals and chemicals etc. The main markets for exporting are the USA, Japan, Korea and Germany. Major import products are iron grind, machinery, electronic equipment and chemicals. As for the foreign investments, they are mainly engaged in infrastructure construction, light industry, food processing, metal producing, machinery and electronics.

The government has been encouraging foreign investment commitment in fields like telecommunication, transportation, electricity, energy raw materials, infra-structures construction and water control projects.

Together, there are 39 universities and colleges in Shanxi, including Shanxi University, Taiyuan Polytechnic University,

TAIYUAN ECONOMIC AND TECHNOLOGICAL DEVELOPMENT ZONE

Our Rating:	B
Year of Establishment:	1992
Location:	Taiyuan, Shanxi
Size:	9.6 sq km
Major Investors:	CAS Coal Research Institute, Hengkang Milk
Total Foreign Direct Investment:	USD10 million
Major Industries Encouraged:	Electronics & mechatronics, bio-pharmaceuticals, coal-chemical-new materials, high-tech planting & aquatic breeding and food

INTRODUCTION

Taiyuan Economic and Technological Development Zone (TYETDZ) was established in 1992. In June 2001, it was approved as a state-level development zone. Covering 9.6 sq km, TYETDZ is located at the southern part of Taiyuan City.

INVESTMENT CLIMATE

In 2001, The GDP of TYETDZ was RMB188 million, increased 225% over the previous year; industrial value-added was RMB6.23 million; gross industrial output was RMB140 million, up 40%.

By the end of 2001, about 66 ha of land was developed. The investment infrastructure development was RMB210 million.

Dayun Highway crosses Shanxi Province from North to South and National Highway No 208 passes the zone. On the left of TYETDZ is the State 307 Highway and Grade-A Taiyu Highway. The entrance of Taiyuan-Shijiazhuang-Beijing Expressway is just two km away.

By railway, people can reach major domestic cities such as Beijing, Shanghai, Qingdao, Tianjin, Xi'an, Chengdu and Hangzhou etc.

Taiyuan Airport is only two km from TYETDZ.

Major industries to be promoted include electronics and mechatronics, bio-pharmaceuticals, coal-chemical new materials, aquatic breeding and innovative food processing.

Administrative Committee of TYETDZ
Chuangye Street, 128 Subzone
Taiyuan, Shanxi
P. R. China 030032
Tel: (86)(351) 7098055, 7093269
Fax: (86)(351) 7098043

TAIYUAN HIGH-TECH PARK

Our Rating:	B
Year of Establishment:	1991
Location:	Taiyuan, Shanxi
Size:	8.8 sq km
Major Investors:	N.A.
Total Foreign Direct Investment:	N.A.
Major Industries Encouraged:	Electronics, information technologies, biological engineering, optical-electromechanical integration technologies and products, new materials, new energy, energy-saving technologies and pharmaceuticals

INTRODUCTION

Taiyuan High-tech Park (TYHTP) is located in the south part of Taiyuan. It was the only high-tech zone in the province and was authorized the status of state-level high-tech park in November 1992. The total development area of the park is 8.8 sq km.

The core industries of the park include electronics, information technologies, biological engineering, optical-electro-mechanical integration technologies and products, new materials, new energy, energy-saving technologies and pharmaceuticals.

By the end of 2001, 526 enter-prises had joined the park. In 1998, the total sales of the park's member enterprises were RMB3.5 billion.

INVESTMENT CLIMATE

TYHTP is seven km from Taiyuan Railway Station and six km from Taiyuan Airport. It is located at the entrance of Taiyuan-Shijiazhuang Expressway which links the capital cities of the two provinces (Shanxi and Hebei). National Highway No. 108 and No. 208 are running through the area.

Taiyuan is a beautiful city, with many historical sites in the city, such as Jinci Temple, Shengmu (Saint Mother) Hall, Congshan Temple, Double Tower temple and Dafo (Big Buddha) Temple.

Administrative Committee of TYHTP
Tel: (86)(351) 7024897
Fax: (86)(351) 7024897
Website: www.tyctp.com.cn

SICHUAN

Industrial Parks in Sichuan

1. Chengdu Economic & Technological Development Zone
2. Western Software Development Park
3. Chengdu High-tech Park
4. Mianyang High-tech Park

INTRODUCTION

Sichuan Province is known as the Land of Abundance. The provincial capital is Chengdu. Sichuan is also one of the major industrial bases in Western China. In addition to heavy industries such as coal, energy, iron and steel, Sichuan has established a light manufacturing sector comprising construction materials, wood processing, food and silk processing etc. Chengdu and Mianyang are the manufacturing bases for textiles and electronics. Deyang, Panzhihua and Yibin are the industrial bases for machinery, metallurgy industry and wine, respectively. Remarkably, the wine production of Sichuan accounts for around 21.9% of the country's total.

GEOGRAPHY

Located in the southwest China, Sichuan borders several provinces and regions like Guizhou, Yunan, Tibet, Qinghai, Gansu and Shaanxi. The typography of the province forms one of the four biggest basins in China-Sichuan Basin. Plains only account for 5% of the province's total area of 485,000 sq km. Climate in Sichuan is very diversified, ranging from subtropical monsoon type to plateau type. Temperature in January can vary from 6°C to -10°C, while summer in the southeast will be extremely hot.

Fact Sheet	2001
Area (sq km)	488,000
Population (million)	86.4
GDP (RMB billion)	442.2
GDP Growth Rate	9.2%
Consumption Expenditure (RMB billion)	
• Government	56
• Household	168
Per capita annual	
• disposable income of urban residents (RMB '000)	6.36
• net income of rural households (RMB '000)	1.98
Contractual FDI (USD million)	1,100
Industrial Value Added (RMB bn)	140.8
Imports (USD million)	1,520
Exports (USD million)	1,580
Universities & Colleges	57

TRAVEL INFORMATION

From Chengdu Airport to:

Tokyo	4hrs 30mins
Osaka	4hrs
Seoul	3hrs 15mins
Bangkok	2hrs 45mins
Hong Kong	2hrs 10mins
Beijing	2hrs 10mins
Shanghai Hongqiao	2hrs 10mins

INVESTMENT CLIMATE

Sichuan is one of China's major agricultural production bases. Grain, including rice and wheat, ranks first in China. Major economic crops include rapeseed, citrus fruit, peach, sugar cane and sweet potato. Sichuan also has the largest pork output and the second largest silkworm cocoon output in China. Moreover, the province is well-known for its abundance in mineral resources. It has over 132 types of proven underground mineral resources, among which over 11 types are the largest reserves in China, such as vanadium, titanium and lithium. Panxi region alone accounts for 13.3% of iron reserves, 93% of titanium, 68% of vanadium and 83% of cobalt of the whole country.

Sichuan encourages investment in fields like electronics and information technology, machinery and metallurgy (including automobiles), hydropower, pharmaceutical, food and beverage industries.

Major exports of Sichuan include chemical and industrial raw materials, steel products, garments and textiles, silk and fabrics, electronics and power generation equipment. On the other hand, major imports include aviation equipment, electronic components, electronic appliances, automobile spare parts, chemical raw materials, steel products, non-ferrous metals, electronics and machinery and so on.

Sichuan boasts rich human resources. With as many as 57 universities and colleges, the province holds a leading position in research fields like molecular chemistry, leather, nuclear technology, aerospace and aviation technology, generic engineering and optical fiber communication. Xichang is the national high-tech research center for rocket launching. Sichuan is also famous for its contribution in chinese traditional medicine.

Tourism is highlighted in the province's 10th five-year plan (2001-2005). To attract new investment resources and management skills, the provincial government has announced its plan to transfer the management of 10 scenic spots, such as Jiuzhaigou and Huanglong Temple, to private operators. Investment in hotels, tourism manpower training is encouraged.

Sichuan Provincial Government
Website: www.sichuan.gov.cn

Sichuan Provincial Investment Bureau
Tel: (86)(28) 6604434, 6606633
Fax: (86)(28) 6604238, 6606600

CHENGDU ECONOMIC AND TECHNOLOGICAL DEVELOPMENT ZONE

Our Rating:	A
Year of Establishment:	1990
Location:	Chengdu, Sichuan
Size:	26 sq km
Major Investors:	N.A.
Total Foreign Direct Investment:	USD198 million
Major Industries Encouraged:	machinery, electronics, new construction materials, pharmaceuticals and food processing

INTRODUCTION

Chengdu Economic and Technological Development Zone (CDETDZ) was established in July 1990 and was approved as Sichuan Province's only State-level development zone on February 2000. The zone covers 26 sq km.

CDETDZ is located at Longquanyi District, east of Chengdu City. It is 13.6 kilometers from the downtown, and 30 kilometers from Chengdu International Airport.

In 2001, the GDP of CDETDZ was RMB3.07 billion, up 46.2% over the previous year; industrial value-added was RMB970 million, up 42.6%.

INVESTMENT CLIMATE

After more than 10 years of development, 10.25 sq km of land has been developed. Total fixed assets investment is RMB5.05 billion, among which investment on infrastructure development was RMB1.23 billion.

At present, 406 projects have been set up in CDETDZ by domestic and foreign investors, among which are 87 foreign-projects with combined contractual investment of USD198 million and utilized foreign investment of USD67.4 million. Foreign investment comes from more than 10 countries and regions worldwide, such as the USA, Canada, Japan, Hong Kong, Macau, Taiwan etc.

Major industries to be promoted in the zone include machinery, electronics, new construction materials, pharmaceuticals and food processing.

Administrative Committee of CDETDZ
3, Longdu South Road
Chengdu, Sichuan
PR. China
Tel: (86)(28) 4853233
Fax: (86)(28) 4872887
E-mail: cdetdz@mail.sc.cninfo.net
Website: www.cdetdz.com

WESTERN SOFTWARE DEVELOPMENT PARK

Year of Establishment:	1997
Location:	Chengdu, Sichuan
Size:	60 ha
Major Investors:	Top Group, Western Software Park Co.
Total Foreign Direct Investment:	N.A.
Major Industries Encouraged:	Software development

Established in 1997, the development of Western Software Development Park (WSDP) has close relations with and also relies on Sichuan Top Group. With registered capital of RMB100 million, Chengdu Western Software Park Co. Ltd was established in 1998. Top Group and the Software Institute of Chinese Academy of Sciences were the two major shareholders. In October 1999, the park was awarded the ISO 9001 certification.

Enterprises in WSDP mainly specialize in the development of professional application software, education software, entertainment software and office software, such as information management system of taxation, automatic taxation system, computerised magnetic card, industrial administration system, expressway charging system etc. In 2000, there were about 3,000 software professionals working in the park. The total sales revenue was RMB680 million. It is estimated that in 2005, the sales revenue of about 500 domestic and foreign companies in the park will be RMB10 billion. The export will be USD200 million.

Chengdu, has a few prestigious universities like Sichuan University, University of Electronic Science & Technology of China and Southwest Jiaotong University. Every year, about 10,000 students graduate with bachelor's degree in computer science, electronics and other IT-related majors. Sichuan University and University of Electronic Science & Technology both have established software colleges.

WSDP has established successful relationships with many international IT companies, including Hughes Network System, Microsoft Corporation, HP, Intel, IBM, Cisco and NEC.

Western Software Park Co. Ltd.
Hongguang Industry District
Chengdu, Sichuan
P. R. China 611700
Tel: (86)(28) 7986215, 7986312
Fax: (86)(28) 7955211, 7986300
E-mail: westsoft@topgroup.com.cn
Website: www.westsoft.com.cn

CHENGDU HIGH-TECH PARK

Our Rating:	A
Year of Establishment:	1991
Location:	Chengdu, Sichuan
Size:	47 sq km
Major Investors:	N.A.
Total Foreign Direct Investment:	USD330 million
Major Industries Encouraged:	Software, Chinese traditional medicines

INTRODUCTION

Chengdu High-tech Park (CDHTP) is located in the southern part of Chengdu, the provincial capital of Sichuan. It was authorized as a state high-tech park by the State Council in March 1991. The total development area of the park is 47 sq km.

In 2000, the GDP of CDHTP was RMB10 billion and the total industrial output was RMB20 billion.

INVESTMENT CLIMATE

CDHTP comprises the original Industrial Park, Processing and Trade Development Zone, Western Software Park, Straits Science Park, National Industrial Base for Chinese Traditional Medicines and an Incubation Center. Within CDHTP, there are several key universities and research institutes, such as Sichuan University and Sichuan Academy of Sciences.

As the provincial capital, Chengdu enjoys a well-developed transportation network. CDHTP is 4.5 kilometers away from the downtown and 5 kilometers from Chengdu Shuangliu International Airport. Chengdu Southern Railway Station is located at the park.

Administrative Committee of CDHTP
Tel: (86)(28) 5184155
Website: www.cdgxq.gov.cn

MIANYANG HIGH-TECH PARK

Our Rating:	B
Year of Establishment:	1992
Location:	Mianyang, Sichuan
Size:	14.1 sq km
Major Investors:	Changhong Group
Total Foreign Direct Investment:	N.A.
Major Industries Encouraged:	Electronics, fine chemical engineering, information technology and new materials

INTRODUCTION

Mianyang High-tech Park (MYHTP) is located in Mianyang, an important industrial city of Sichuan Province. It was authorized as a state-level high-tech park by the State Council in 1992, and is one of the two state-level high-tech parks in the province. The total development area of MYHTP is 14.1 sq km.

The main industrial fields of MYHTP include electronics, information technology, bio-engineering, optical-electromechanical integration technology, fine chemical engineering, new materials and new energies.

INVESTMENT CLIMATE

About 931 enterprises have joined the park. In 1999, the total industrial output was RMB16.4 billion; the GDP of MYHTP was RMB4.5 billion. In the same year, 101 new projects were set up and the total investment was RMB866 million.

The development focus of MYHTP is on electric appliances, fine chemical engineering, information technology and new materials. Changhong Group, one of China's largest manufacturers of home electronics, is located in Mianyang.

Several key research institutes, such as Physics Research Institute of China Academy of Sciences and China Aerodynamics Research are located in the city. 170,000 professionals, including 18 CAS fellows, work in the park.

CHENGDU EXPORT PROCESSING ZONE

Year of Establishment:	2000
Location:	Chengdu, Sichuan
Size:	3 sq km
Major Investors:	Convac Scientific & Technical Co., Ltd., Sichuan Gaolong Machinery Ltd.
Total Foreign Direct Investment:	N.A.
Major Industries Encouraged:	Optical recording equipment, aircraft parts

INTRODUCTION

Chengdu Export Processing Zone (CDEPZ) was established on 27 April 2000 with the approval of the State Council. It is one of the first batch of EPZs and the only State-level EPZ in Western China. CDEPZ has a planned area of 3 sq km.

CDEPZ is situated inside the Dayuan block of the Chengdu High-tech Park. It is located about 11.4 kilometers from Tianfu Square which is Chengdu's downtown area, 16.4 kilometers from Shuangliu International Airport and 5.4 kilometers from Southern Railway Station.

INVESTMENT CLIMATE

Foreign invested enterprises in the zone are developing well. One famous example is Convac Scientific & Technical (Chengdu) Co., Ltd. It has foreign investment of USD10 millions. The main products are optical recording equipment.

Another example is Sichuan Gaolong Machinery Ltd. It is recognized as the most successful joint venture in the zone.

Located in one of the most important electronic industry bases in China, Chengdu, the zone has special advantages in technology and human resources supply. The Optical-electrics Research Institute of China Science Academy, Chengdu Branch and Chengdu Electronic Sciences Technology University are all located there. Sichuan Ermei Semiconductor Material Factory can produce 1,000 tons of polycrystalline silicon per year.

Administrative Committee of CDZPZ
18 Chuangye Road, Gaoxin Avenue,
Chengdu, Sichuan
P.R. China 610041
Tel: (86)(28) 85328899
Fax: (86)(28) 85321788
E-mail: info@scepz.gov.cn
Website: www.scepz.gov.cn

UNIVERSITY OF ELECTRONIC SCIENCE AND TECHNOLOGY SCIENCE PARK

Year of Establishment:	2000
Location:	Chengdu, Sichuan
Major Supporting Institutions:	University of Electronic Science & Technology
Major Investors:	Gold Disk UESTC Multimedia, UESTC Pioneer Technologies, UESTC Comsys Information Industries and Coreland
Major Industries Encouraged:	Information technologies such as microwave communication, e - banking, electronic materials, software, system integration, automatic controlling, integrated circuits.

The total area of University of Electronic Science & Technology of China Science Park (UESTCSP) is 120 hectares, including the 50-hectare on-campus zone and the 70-hectare off-campus zone. By the end of 2000, about 50 high-tech enterprises had joined the park. Their products are related to information technologies such as microwave communication, electronic banking, electronic materials, software development, system integration, automatic controlling, integrated circuits, internet technology etc. Among them, the developments of Gold Disk UESTC Multimedia, UESTC Pioneer Technologies, UESTC Comsys Information Industries and Coreland are most impressive.

University of Electronic Science & Technology of China is located in Chengdu. Now, the university has 4 CAS (Chinese Academy of Science) fellows, 6 State Key Subjects, 4 State Key Laboratories and 27 other Key Laboratories.

In addition, the university has established joint R & D centers with Epson, HP, Motorola, IBM, Intel, Samsung, Texas Instruments and other international electronic giants. It also maintains links with major domestic groups like Zhongxin Telecommunication, China Aeronautical Science & Technology, TCL, Konka, China Eastcom, Datang Telecom, Shenzhen R&D Technologies etc.

Meanwhile, the university has developed exchange programs with many overseas universities, such as UC-Berkeley, Stanford University and Massachusetts Institute of Technology (MIT) in the US, University of Leeds and Imperial College in the UK, Technical University of Munich in Germany, and Kyoto University in Japan.

According to the master plan of UESTCSP, it will become a part of the Chengdu-Deyang-Mianyang Information Corridor, which aims to become China's western "Silicon Valley".

UESTC Industrial Development Division
Chengdu, Sichuan
P. R. China
Tel: (86)(28) 3343343
Website: www.id.uestc.edu.cn

SICHUAN UNIVERSITY SCIENCE PARK

Year of Establishment: 2000

Location: Chengdu, Sichuan

Major Supporting Institutions: Sichuan University

Major Investors: SCUSP Group, Zhisheng Software, Nengshi Internet Security Company, Luneng Science & Technologies Development Corporation and SCUSP Mianyang Corporation

Major Industries Encouraged: Electronics information technology, biomedicine, environmental engineering, new materials, fine chemical engineering, software and internet security technologies.

Located in Chengdu, Sichuan University Science Park (SCUSP) is developed by Sichuan University and a few enterprise groups. It includes a 120-hectare Sichuan University-Shandong Luneng Science & Technology Zone at Chengdu High-tech Park and a 15-hectare SCU Mianyang Science Park at Mianyang City. Other corporate partners include Sichuan Dikang Group, Sichuan Guangyao Group and Sichuan Quanxin Group etc.

According to the master plan of SCUSP, the park comprises three subsidiary zones, namely the Incubation Zone of Research Achievements, the Incubation Zone and the High-tech Industrial Zone. In the High-tech Industrial Zone there will be five subsidiary villages, including an electronic & information technology village, a biotechnology and products village, the village of new materials and fine chemical engineering, the village of environmental protection technologies and engineering, and the village of mechanical-electronic integration.

The resources that SCUSP and enterprises can draw from the university are plentiful.

After the merger with former Sichuan University, Chengdu University of Science & Technology and Western China Medical University in 2000, Sichuan University is now the largest university in western China. Now, the university has 15 State Key Subjects and 41 key laboratories at state, ministry and province levels. 900 professors and 2, 400 associate professors are working at the university. The number of students is about 34,000, including more than 27, 000 undergraduates and 7,000 postgraduates.

Sichuan University Science Park
Development Corporation
Chengdu, Sichuan Province
P. R. China
Tel: (86)(28) 5407336
Website: www.scu.edu.cn

YUNNAN

Industrial Parks in Yunnan

1. Kunming Economic & Technological Development Zone
2. Kunming High-tech Park
3. Hekou Border Ecomomic Cooperation Zone
4. Ruili Border Economic Cooperation Zone
5. Wanting Border Economic Cooperation Zone

INTRODUCTION

Yunnan is located in the southwestern part of China, and as much as 94% of the province's areas are mountains and highlands. About 34% of the population is ethnic minorities, including Yi, Bai, Hani, Zhuang, Dai and Miao. In the province, there are several major cities that enjoy national preferential policies, such as Kunming, Ruili, Wanting and Hekou. The province is a major forest zone, where the forest area accounts for 24% of the total of the country. It is also one important base for aromatic plants and flora with more than 300 varieties of essential oil-bearing plants and over 2,500 kinds of ornamental plants and flowers.

GEOGRAPHY

Yunnan borders Myanmar, Laos and Vietnam. It is surrounded by four provinces and regions namely Guizhou, Guangxi, Sichuan and Tibet. Generally, it is a highland province with topographical feature stretching from the northwest to the southeast, resulting in a diversity of elevations and climates. Most area of the province falls in subtropical humid monsoon climate zone. The central plateau of Yunnan is long famous for its 'Spring all year round' mild weather.

Fact Sheet	2001
Area (sq km)	380,000
Population (million)	42.9
GDP (RMB billion)	108.2
GDP Growth Rate	8.8%
Consumption Expenditure (RMB billion)	
• Government	50.5
• Household	37.8
Per capita annual	
• disposable income of urban residents (RMB '000)	6.8
• net income of rural households (RMB '000)	1.53
Vitalisedl FDI (USD million)	64.6
Industrial Value Added (RMB bn)	72.2
Imports (USD million)	750
Exports (USD million)	1,240
Universities & Colleges	29

TRAVEL INFORMATION

From Kunming Airport to:

Bangkok	2hrs
Singapore	3hrs 40mins
Seoul	4hrs 30mins
Hong Kong	1hr 55mins
Shanghai Pudong	2hrs 50mins
Beijing	3hrs

INVESTMENT CLIMATE

Yunnan is famous for being China's major producer of copper, lead, zinc, tin and aluminum. Gejiu city is known as the Kingdom of Zinc, where the reserve of zinc ranks the top in China. It also enjoys rich natural resources like germanium, indium, zirconium, platinum, rock salt, nickel, phosphate, arsenic and blue asbestos.

Food processing industry plays an important role. Pu'er Tea is originated in Yunnan. Tobacco and cigarettes of the province are important source of revenue.

Yuxi is one of China's most important tobacco bases, where locates the country's largest cigarette manufacturer, Hongta Group. In addition, Yunnan is China's major coffee growing and processing base. By May 2001, Pu'er had become China's largest coffee plantation base.

Major export products of the province include phosphates, jade ornaments, garments, kidney beans, tobacco, tea, tin and machine tools. Major imports include agricultural products, machinery for tobacco and raw materials.

Major foreign investors come from Hong Kong, the Virgin Islands, the United States, Japan, Germany, Singapore and Taiwan. The border trade in three border economic cooperation zones in Hekou, Ruili and Wanting has been growing fast. For foreign investment, the main fields highlighted are metallurgy, machinery, electronics, textiles, light industry, printing, agriculture, animal husbandry and the tertiary industries such as tourism, transportation, post and telecommunication and real estate.

Yunnan aims to become the largest flower producer and export base. Currently, Yunnan has 3 big flower producing areas including Kunming, Xishuangbanna and Diqing. The annual output is 1.1 billion bunches and the capacity is still growing. Kunming successfully hosted the 14th International Horticulture Expo in 2000.

Yunnan Provincial Government
Website: www.yn.gov.cn
Yunnan Foreign Trade and Economic Cooperation
119, Taoyuan Street, Kunming Yunnan
P. R. China 650011
Tel: (86)(871) 3185012
Fax: (86)(871)3149574
Website: www.bottec.gov.cn

KUNMING ECONOMIC AND TECHNOLOGICAL DEVELOPMENT ZONE

Cur Rating:	BBB
Year of Establishment:	1992
Location:	Kunming Yunnan
Size:	13.5 sq km
Major Investors:	Top Group, Zhongguancun Technologies, Kunlene Film, Maxyee and Yunnan Aerospace
Total Foreign Direct Investment:	USD 164 million
Major Industries Encouraged:	Tobbcao related industries, bio-pharmaceuticals and optical-mechanical-electric integration technologies

Kunming Economic and Technological Development Zone (KMETDZ) is a state-level Zone established in 1992. It is the only such zone in Yunnan Province. The zone has a development area of 13.5 sq km, and over 4 sq km has been well developed. The administrative committee has invested over RMB409 million for infrastructure development. The zone is located in the east part of Kunming and is 5 km from the downtown.

By the end of 2001, KMETDZ total fixed assets investment commitment was RMB3.52 billion. Over 44 foreign investment projects have been undertaken in the zone with contractual foreign investment of USD164 million and utilized investment of USD84.33 million. Seven projects have investment of over USD10 million. There are 117 domestic enterprises and 10 high-tech ones.

In 2001, the GDP of the zone was RMB1.494 billion and industrial output was RMB2.598 billion.

The main industries of KMETDZ include optical electromechanical integration, biological pharmaceutical industry and tobacco related industry.

Major enterprises in the zone include Top Group, Zhongguancun Technologies, Kunlene Film Industries, Maxyee and Yunnan Aerospace Industries.

The zone is 1.8 km from Kunming International Airport and 3 km from Kunming Railway Station, where several main railroads are connecting the Kunming to Guizhou, Guangxi and Vietnam.

Administrativve Committee of KMETDZ
Changhong Road
Kunming, Yunnan
P. R. China 650217
Tel: (86)(871) 7275011, 7275008
Fax: (86)(871) 7275005
Website: www.ketdz.gov.cn

KUNMING HIGH-TECH PARK

Our Rating:	BB
Year of Establishment:	1992
Location:	Kunming, Yunnan
Size:	11.5 sq km
Major Investors:	Baiyao Pharmaceuticals, spirin, Yongkang Pharmaceuticals, Baker Norton, Kunming Pharmaceuticals, Dianhong Pharmaceuticals Yunnan Tin Group and Yunnan Copper Group
Total Foreign Direct Investment:	N.A.
Major Industries Encouraged:	bio-pharmaceuticals, electronics, new materials and environment protection technologies

INTRODUCTION

Kuming High-tech Park (KMHTP) is located in the northwest part of Kunming. It was authorized as state-level high-tech park by the State Council in 1992, and is the only state high-tech park in the province. The total development area of the park is 11.5 sq km. The park consists of the New District and Jinding Science Park.

By the end of 2001, 878 enterprises, including 121 high-tech ones, had joined KMHTP. The number of foreign enterprises totaled 51.

INVESTMENT CLIMATE

The development focus includes bio-pharmaceuticals, electronics, new materials and environment technologies. Major enterprises include Baiyao Pharmaceuticals, Spirin, Yongkang Pharmaceuticals, Kunming Baker Norton, Kunming Pharmaceuticals, Dianhong Pharmaceuticals, Yunnan Tin Group and Yunnan Copper.

The park consists of Yunnan Software Park, Yunnan University Science Park and Yunnan Modern Pharmaceuticals Park. There are 107 software enterprises and over 1,400 software professionals in the park. The University Science Park was established in 1999 and has extensive cooperation with local universities, colleges and other research institutes. There are six biopharmaceutical enterprises in the Pharmaceutical Park, which include Biological Institute of Chinese Academy of Medical Science, Kunming Pharmaceutical Group and Yunnan Baiyao Pharmaceutical. Coorperation has been establised with Kunming medical college, Yunnan Pharmaceuticals, Yunnan Drug Control Institute, Yunnan Bio-Industry Research Institute, Yunnan Minority Medicine Research Institute and Yunnan Spice Research Institute.

The Administrative Committee of KMHTP

Kunming, Yunnan
P.R. China 650000
Tel: (86)(871) 8320385, 8311306
Fax: (86)(871) 8318435
Email: kmgx@kmhnz.gov.cn
Website: www.kmhnz.gov.cn

HEKOU BORDER ECONOMIC COOPERATION ZONE

Year of Establishment:	early 1990s
Location:	Hekou, Yunnan province
Size:	N.A.
Major Investors:	N.A.
Total Foreign Direct Investment:	N.A.
Major Industries Encouraged:	Sino-Vietnam border trade cooperation

INTRODUCTION

Hekou Border Economic Cooperation Zone is a State-level Border (HKBECZ) Zone in Yunnan Province that was approved by the State Council in early 1990s. It is one of the three similar zones in the province where main border trade is Sino-Vietnam business.

The Zone is separated from Vietnam only by a bridge and is linked with Ho Chi Minh City and Hanoi by Yunnan-Vietnam Railway, Kunming-Hanoi highway and the Red River.

INVESTMENT CLIMATE

Business between Chinese and Vietnamese is growing fast, especially during recent years. In 1999, the total foreign trade of the Sino-Vietnam business was USD72.21 million and the border trade was USD45.94 million. The main export products include clothing, cotton yarn, ceresin wax, mechanical equipments, batteries, fruits, rice seeds and tobacco.

In fact, Vietnam government also encourages the Sino-Vietnam border trade as well. With effect from 15 January 1999, the import and export products have been catalogued in accordance with international tax rate and three kinds of products, namely rubber, coal and marine, are exported with zero rate tax. From March 1999, the government encourages more trade channels and more types of products to be traded.

Investment Promotion Department of HKBECZ
Hekou, Honghe, Yunnan
P. R. China 661300
Tel: (86)(873) 2124543, 2123084
Fax: (86)(873) 2123466
Email: hhjx@hhzs.net
Website: www.hhzs.net
www.hh.gov.cn

RUILI BORDER ECONOMIC COOPERATION ZONE

Year of Establishment:	1992
Location:	Ruili, Yunnan province
Size:	N.A.
Major Investors:	N.A.
Total Foreign Direct Investment:	N.A.
Major Industries Encouraged:	Sino-Myanmar border trade cooperation

INTRODUCTION

Ruili Border Economic Cooperation Zone (RLBECZ) is a State-level Border Zone approved by the State Council in 1992. It is one of the three such zones in Yunnan Province with border trade between China and Myanmar business.

The Zone adjoins to Ruili city in the north and Man Wing city of Myanmar in the south. It is the national checkpoint to Myanmar, and an entrepot for Burmese. The import and export, processing industry, local agriculture and biological resource within the area are very promising.

INVESTMENT CLIMATE

The Sino-Myanmar business is growing fast. Myanmar is now one of Yunnan's biggest foreign trade partners. In 1999, the Sino-Myanmar trade accounted for 77.44% of Yunnan's foreign trade. In the same year, the export for electromechanical equipments was USD55.28 million.

The main exports include fiber cloth, cotton yarn, ceresin wax, mechanical equipments, fruits, rice seeds, fiber yarn and tobacco.

Investment Promotion Department of RLBECZ
South suburb, Ruili
Yunnan,
P. R. China 678600
Tel: (86)(692) 4148655
Fax: (86)(692) 4148059

WANTING BORDER ECONOMIC COOPERATION ZONE

Year of Establishment:	1992
Location:	Wanting, Yunnan
Size:	5 sq km
Major Investors:	N.A.
Total Foreign Direct Investment:	N.A.
Major Industries Encouraged:	Sino-Laos border trade, tourism and commerce

Wanting Border Economic Cooperation Zone is a State-level Border (WTBECZ) Zone that was approved by the State Council in 1992. It is one of the three similar zones in Yunnan Province. It is for the border trade between China and Myanmar, too.

It is located at the Sino-Myanmar border, and the terminal of No.320 National Road with 28.64 km frontier line. The zone covers 5 sq km. It focuses on the development of trading, processing, agriculture resources and tourism.

Investment Promotion Department of WTBECZ
Economic & Trade Sub-bureau
118 Minzhu Road
Wanting
Yunnan P. R. China 678500
Tel: (86)(692) 5151404

YUNNAN PROVINCE
UNIVERSITY SCIENCE PARK

Year of Establishment: 1999

Location: Kunming, Yunnan

Major Supporting Institutions: Yunnan University, Kunming University of Science & Technology and Yunnan Normal University

Major Investors: YNU Science & Technology, YNU Biology CORP.

Major Industries Encouraged: bio-pharmaceuticals, life science

Yunnan Province University Science Park (YNPUSP) was established as an experimental site of university science park in 1999 and was awarded the status of National University Science Park in May 2001. The park is effectively supported by Yunnan University (www.ynu.edu.cn), Kunming University of Science & Technology (www.kmust.edu.cn) and Yunnan Normal University (www.ynnu.edu.cn).

Established in 1922, Yunnan University (YNU) is now recognized as a key university, thanks to the Western Development Strategy. It is located in Kunming, the capital city of Yunnan province. The university now has 15 colleges, covering a wide range of fields such as economics, executive education, arts & social science, life science, chemistry, information technology, development research, technical training, law, public administration, business, tourism management, foreign languages, design, pharmaceuticals and international culture. The university also owns three State Teaching & Research Talents Development Bases. Besides, two State Key Subjects and 16 Provincial Key Subjects are now being undertaken at the university. In addition, the university is equipped with one State New Medicine R&D Center and a Education Ministry Key Laboratory of the Ministry of Education.

The development of YNU affiliated enterprises is very impressive. Over the past ten years, the YNU Science & Technology has grown into a public company with total assets of more than RMB1 billion from the humble start of less than RMB100, 000. On top of that, YNU Biology Corporation has become a leading Chinese corporation in single-clone antibody research.

**Yunnan Province University
Science Park**
Kunming, Yunnan Province
P. R. China 650000
Website: www.ynu.edu.cn

KUNMING SOFTWARE DEVELOPMENT PARK

Year of Establishment:	1998
Location:	Kunming, Yunnan
Size:	N.A.
Major Investors:	Nantian Information Industries, Mingxing Computers, Tsinghua Tongfang Group, Spring Valley Technologies and American Wangson International Group

INTRODUCTION

Kunming Software Development Park (KMSDP) was established in December 1998. Closely linked with most of the Yunnan's software enterprises and IT organizations, it is an important part of Kunming High-tech Park. Prominent member enterprises include Kunming Subsidiary of Nantian Information Industries Group (www.nantian.com.cn) Kunming Mingxing Computers, the Yunnan subsidiary of Tsinghua Tongfang Group, Kunming Spring Valley Technologies and subsidiary of American Wangson International Group (www.wangson.com.cn). In 1998, their total sales revenue was RMB115 million.

INVESTMENT CLIMATE

The major products and services of enterprises in the park include research & development of application software, management information system, network engineering, system integration technologies, office automation, communication management and manufacturing automation process.

Kuming Software Development Park has close relations with universities, colleges and research institutions in Yunnan province. In fact, there are 29 such institution, including Yunnan University (www.ynu.edu.cn) and Yunnan Normal University (www.ynnu.edu.sg). Yunnan University has established a software college.

Administrative Committee of KMSDP
Kunming, Yunnan
P. R. China 650000
Tel: (86) (871) 8188795
Email: 1m@mail.khtz.gov.cn
Website: www.swp.khtz.gov.cn

ZHEJIANG

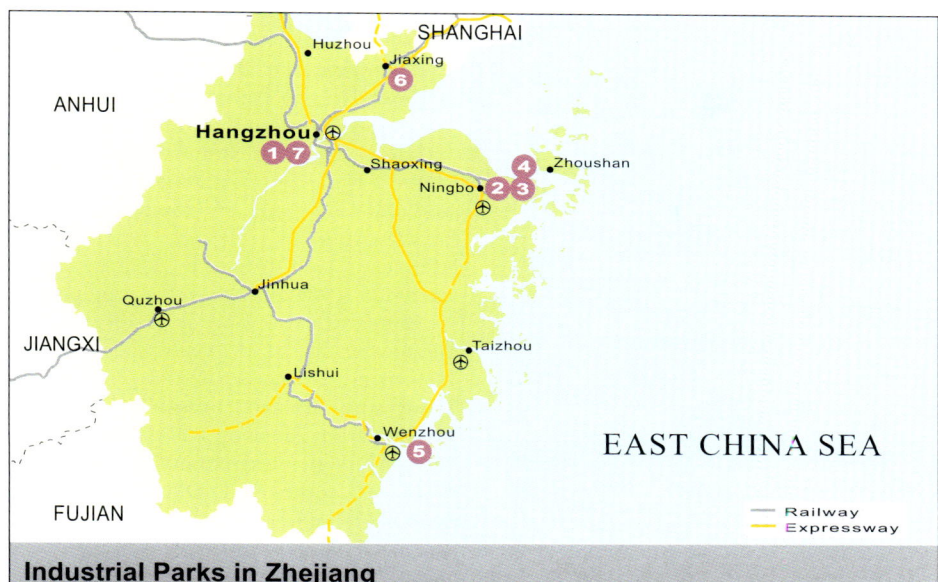

ANHUI

SHANGHAI

Huzhou

Jiaxing **6**

Hangzhou ⊕

1 **7**

Shaoxing

4 Zhoushan

Ningbo **2** **3**
⊕

Jinhua

Quzhou
⊕

JIANGXI

Lishui

Taizhou ⊕

Wenzhou
⊕ **5**

EAST CHINA SEA

FUJIAN

— Railway
— Expressway

Industrial Parks in Zhejiang

1. Hangzhou Economic & Technological
   Development Zone
2. Ningbo Economic & Technological
   Development Zone
3. Ningbo Free Trade Zone
4. Ningbo Daxie Development Zone
5. Wenzhou Economic & Technological
   Development Zone
6. Jiaxing Economic & Technological
   Development Zone
7. Hangzhou High-tech Park

INTRODUCTION

A place well known for its deep-rooted cultural heritage and self-reliance, Zhejiang has achieved a remarkable annual average GDP growth of 13.2%. With the 11ᵗʰ largest population, it is ranked fourth in total GDP among all mainland administrative regions. Apart from economic advancement, the beauty of Zhejiang also lies in its natural attractions, cultural and historical relics, and pro-business atmosphere.

GEOGRAPHY

Zhejiang is located in the east coast of China. Bordering Jiangsu and Shanghai in the north, they together form the Yangtze River Delta,

the most developed area in China. Although Zhejiang accounts for only 1.1% of the national total land area, of which only one third are plains, it supports 4.4% of China's total population. With more than 2,000 islets scattered in East China Sea, the province boasts the nation's biggest fishery.

It administers 11 municipalities, including Hangzhou, Ningbo, Wenzhou, Jiaxing, Jinhua, Shaoxing, Zhoushan and others.

Zhejiang enjoys a mild subtropical humid monsoon climate with four distinct seasons. The average temperature is 3°C-8°C for January and 28°C for July. The annual rainfall is 1,500 mm.

Fact Sheet	2001
Area (sq km)	101,800
Population (million)	46.1
GDP (RMB billion)	670
GDP Growth Rate	10.5%
Consumption Expenditure (RMB billion)	
• Government	87
• Household	255
Per capita annual	
• disposable income of urban residents (RMB '000)	10.5
• net income of rural households (RMB '000)	4.6
Contractual FDI (USD million)	5,020
Industrial Value Added (RMB bn)	310.5
Imports (USD million)	9,820
Exports (USD million)	22,980
Universities & Colleges	58

TRAVEL INFORMATION

Hangzhou, Ningbo and Wenzhou have three large airports.

From Hangzhou Airport to:
Beijing	2 hrs 10 mins
Guangzhou	2 hrs
Xiamen	1 hr
Hong Kong	1 hr 55 mins
Bangkok	4 hrs 50 mins

From Ningbo Airport to:
Beijing	2 hrs
Shanghai Pudong	40 mins
Guangzhou	1 hr 50 mins
Hong Kong	2 hrs 5 mins

From Wenzhou Airport to:
Beijing	2 hrs 20 mins
Shanghai Hongqiao	1 hr
Chongqing	2 hrs 10 mins
Guangzhou	1 hr 50 mins
Hong Kong	1 hr 35 mins

INVESTMENT CLIMATE

Thanks to its advantageous location, Zhejiang has five major ports in Ningbo, Zhoushan, Zhapu, Haimen and Wenzhou with 34 harbors. The total annual throughput is 270 million tons. Blessed with deepwater harbors, Ningbo Beilun and Zhoushan are the largest iron ore and oil transshipment bases in China, respectively. Railways connect Hangzhou with Shanghai, Ningbo and cities in Jiangxi, and are now extended to Wenzhou. Expressways will be 1,000 kilometers long in total by 2002. There are currently seven airports in the province.

Zhejiang's economy is visibly characterized by the rapid development in non-state owned enterprises and surges in foreign trade and inward foreign investment. Exports from Zhejiang have registered the highest growth rates in China ever since 1999.

In 2001, contractual FDI inflows doubled with a total of USD5.0 billion which ranked it 6th in China. The utilized FDI was USD4.52 billion. Development zones benefited the most as they absorbed 65.9% of the amount.

Zhejiang Provincial Government
Website: www.zj.gov.cn
www.zhejiangchina.com

Zhejiang Foreign Trade and Economic Cooperation Department
Tel: (86)(571) 87706099
Fax: (86)(571) 87706029
Website: www.zftec.gov.cn

HANGZHOU ECONOMIC AND TECHNOLOGICAL DEVELOPMENT ZONE

Our Rating:	AA
Year of Establishment:	1990
Location:	Hangzhou, Zhejiang
Size:	104.7 sq km
Major Investors:	Motorola, Coca-Cola, Siemens, Matsushita, Mitsubishi, Sumitomo, Toshiba, Asahi, LG
Total Foreign Direct Investment:	USD920 million (Utilized)
Major Industries Encouraged:	Research and manufacturing in fields like mobile communication, integrated circuits (IC), information equipment, multi-layer circuit board, electronics

INTRODUCTION

Hangzhou Economic and Technological Development Zone (HETDZ) is a state-level ETDZ approved by the State Council in April 1993. The zone is located in the east part of Hangzhou and covers 104.7 sq km.

HETDZ has been encouraging research and manufacturing in fields such as mobile communication, integrated circuits (IC), information technology, multi-layer circuit board and home electronics.

INVESTMENT CLIMATE

By the end of 2001, over RMB11.37 billion has been invested for fixed asset investment, and investment for infrastructure was RMB2.15 billion. Over 195 foreign development enterprises have entered HETDZ. Contractual foreign investment was USD2.05 billion, and actual foreign investment was USD920 million. There are 72 projects with investment of over USD10 million, and 11 projects over USD30 million.In fact, 13 Fortune 500 companies, such as Motorola, Coca-Cola, Siemens, Matsushita, Mitsubishi, Sumitomo, Toshiba, Asahi, LG and others

have established 22 projects in HETDZ. By the end of 2001, 1,084 enterprises have joined HETDZ. Registered capital was RMB2.35 billion, and the total investment was RMB7.53 billion.

In 2001, the GDP of HETDZ was RMB5.75 billion, and industrial output was RMB27.89 billion. Import volume was USD860 million and export volume was USD490 million.

Hangzhou is a beautiful city. It is famous for its clean air, blue sky, nice building and well-protected environ-ment. West Lake, which ranks among the best tourist attractions in China, is located in the city.

The Administrative Committee of HETDZ
Yindu Mansion, Xiasha
Hangzhou, Zhejiang
P. R. China 310018
Tel: (86)(571) 86910312, 86911468
Fax: (86)(571) 86911467, 86911473
E-mail: hetz@mail.hz.zj.cn
Website: www.hetz.gov.cn

NINGBO ECONOMIC AND TECHNOLOGICAL DEVELOPMENT ZONE

Our Rating:	AA
Year of Establishment:	1984
Location:	Ningbo, Zhejiang
Size:	29.6 sq km
Major Investors:	Exxon, Samsonite, DOW Chemical, Abbott, BP, Hoechst, Mannesmann, Esselte, Itochu, Mitsubishi, Marubeni, Samsung, APP
Total Foreign Direct Investment:	USD1.68 billion (Utilized)
Major Industries Encouraged:	Electronics, bio-pharmaceuticals, precision machinery semiconductors

INTRODUCTION

Ningbo Economic and Technological Development Zone (NBETDZ) is a state-level zone approved by the State Council in October 1984. It is located in northeastern Ningbo, 27 kilometers from the downtown, and has covers 29.6 sq km. It is next to Beilun Port, one of China's top deepwater ports.

The five supporting industries of the zone include petrochemical, steel, food, textiles and automotive manufacturing.

INVESTMENT CLIMATE

In 2001, the GDP of NBETDZ was RMB8.7 billion, and industrial output was RMB27.2 billion. Total foreign trade was USD1.48 billion, of which import were USD940 million. To date, over RMB15 billion has been invested for infrastructure development.

By the end of 2001, 603 foreign projects have set up in NBETDZ. Total investment was USD5.87 billion and utilized foreign investment was USD1.68 billion. Among the projects, 112 have investment of over USD10 million. To date, 22 Fortune 500 companies such as Exxon, Samsonite, DOW Chemical, Abbott, BP, Hoechst, Mannesmann, Esselte, Itochu, Mitsubishi, Marubeni, Samsung, APP,

and many Taiwanese companies have also established operations in NBETDZ.

NBETDZ can easily access Beilun Port where regular shipping lines are available to over 500 ports worldwide. It claims to be the largest deepwater port in China and is currently ranked second in cargo handling.

The Adminstration Committee of NBETDZ
477 West Mingzhou Road
Chuangye Building, Beilun
Ningbo, Zhejiang
P. R. China 315800
Tel: (86)(574) 86850220, 86850225
Fax: (86)(574) 86885325
Website: www.netd.com.cn

NINGBO FREE TRADE ZONE

Year of Establishment:	1992
Location:	Beilun, Ningbo, Zhejiang Province
Size:	2.3 sq km
Major Investors:	Exxon, Mannesmann, Xerox, DOW, Sony, DuPont, Hoechst, Itochu, Mitsubishi, Sanyo, Carrefour, Unic, Marubeni, Samsung, LG, C.T. Group.
Total Foreign Direct Investment:	USD2.52 billion
Major Industries Encouraged:	Electronics and information, semiconductor and photoelectric industries, software development, precision machinery, distribution and logistics.

INTRODUCTION

Ningbo Free Trade Zone (NFTZ), approved by the State Council in 1992, has grown to be one of the most developed areas in the mainland of China. Situated at Beilun seaport area of Ningbo, NFTZ enjoyed rapid growth over the last decade.

The major economic indicators of NFTZ in 2001 are as follows:

Indicator	Amount	increase
GDP	RMB2.55 billion	21.1%
Contractual FDI	USD330 million	29.8%
Foreign Trade	USD700 million	28.4%
Fiscal Revenue	RMB600 million	65.7%

INVESTMENT CLIMATE

Locational advantage

Adjacent to Shanghai and endowed with natural deepwater seaports, Ningbo, a city famous for its historical heritage of business culture and acumen, is fast gaining its economic impetus since the 1990s. Beilun Port is currently the second largest port in China, after Shanghai, with cargo handled exceeding 120 million tons per year. It has 24 berths above 10,000-tonnage and direct voyage to 520 ports worldwide. Container handling capacity has surpassed 1 million TEUs and keeps increasing by a margin of 45% annually.

NFTZ is also at the east terminal of Shanghai-Hangzhou-Ningbo Expressway and Railway. It is a 1.5-hour ride to Hangzhou, the capital of Zhejiang Province, or three hours' drive to Shanghai. With Ningbo-Shanghai Cross-sea Bridge completed, the journey to Shanghai will be shortened to 1.5 hours.

There are four international airports located in distances within 0.5 to 3 hours' ride from Ningbo, namely, Shanghai Hongqiao and Pudong Airports, Hangzhou Xiaoshan Airport and the local Ningbo Lishe Airport. International couriers like EMS, UPS, TNT, DHL, FedEx all have set up their representative offices in NFTZ.

Infrastructure

NFTZ boasts complete infrastructural developments in its garden-style industrial estates.

- Two power stations with total capacity of 4 million kW supply sufficient electricity to NFTZ. Enterprises can access uninterruptible double-loop power supply.
- Daily water supply reaches 350,000 tons.

- Heat supply at 100 tons per hour is provided by a plant six km away.
- Program-controlled telephony and optical fiber broadband network are both available in NFTZ.
- Industrial gas supply is provided by Messer Sunshine Gas and Esso to the zone.
- Sewage treatment for rainfall and waste water is separately processed at a daily capacity of 180,000 tons.

Foreign-invested enterprises

By the end of 2001, more than 3,700 foreign invested enterprises had been incorporated in NFTZ, with investors from 35 countries and regions and a total investment of USD2.52 billion. Many MNCs, including Exxon, Mannesmann, Xerox, DOW, Sony, DuPont, Hoechst, Itochu, Mitsubishi, Sanyo, Carrefour, Unic, Marubeni, Samsung, LG, C.T. Group, all have made a presence in NFTZ.

Although as an FTZ, international trade, export processing and bonded warehousing are the basic functions to develop, NFTZ has in addition designated a few special sub-parks to encourage high-tech developments. These are Electronics and Information Industrial Park, Semiconductor and Photoelectric Industrial Park, Ningbo International Software Park, Precision Machinery Industrial Park, Overseas Chinese Scholars Pioneering Park, and a Distripark to provide logistics.

With most preferential policies and an efficient one-stop service provided by the local administration, NFTZ will be an ideal place for foreign investors to land their projects in the Greater Shanghai Area.

The Administrative Committee of Ningbo Free Trade Zone
NFTZ Mansion, Beilun
Ningbo, Zhejinag
P. R. China 315800
Tel: (86)(574) 86880139, 86820207, 86820209
Fax: (86)(574) 86896543, 86883518
Email: nftz@nftz.gov.cn
Website: www.nftz.gov.cn
www.nftz.com

Foreign Investment Service Center
Tel: (86)(574) 86820208

Economic and Trade Service Center
Tel: (86)(574) 86870412

NINGBO DAXIE DEVELOPMENT ZONE

Our Rating:	BBB
Year of Establishment:	1993
Location:	Daxie Island, Ningbo, Zhejiang
Size:	35.8 sq km
Major Investors:	BP-Amoco, CITIC
Total Foreign Direct Investment:	USD190 million (Utilised)
Major Industries Encouraged:	Oil storage and transshipment, petrochemical, environmental engineering, marine industries, wood processing, high-tech industries, etc.

INTRODUCTION

Ningbo Daxie Development Zone (DXDZ) was initiated by CITIC (China International Trust and Investment Corporation) and co-developed by the Ningbo government in 1992. It was approved as a state-level ETDZ by the State Council on 5 March 1993.

DXDZ is located in the Daxie Island of Ningbo, east of Beilun Port and about 40 kilometers to the city of Ningbo. DXDZ covers 35.8 sq km and has a coastline of 26 kilometers including 10.7 kilometers of deepwater coastline.

INVESTMENT CLIMATE

In 2001, the contractual foreign investment commitment was USD500 million, and the utilized foreign investment commitment was USD190 million. The GDP of the year was over RMB3 billion.

Daxie Island is less than 500 meters off the mainland and is situated in the midpoint of China's coastal line. It is 100 kilometers south of Shanghai

With RMB450 million invested, the sea-spanning bridge between Daxie Island and the mainland has been completed. It links Daxie with the national highway network. A pan-island road system has also been formed within Daxie.

The Liquefied Petroleum Gas (LPG) Terminals Project is co-invested by BP-Amoco and Chinese partners, with total investment over USD96.5 million.

The Administrative Committee of DXDZ

Daxie, Ningbo, Zhejiang
P. R. China 315812
Tel: (86)(574) 86768552, 86768227
Fax: (86)(574) 86768433, 86767850
E-mail: citicdx@mail.nbptt.zj.cn
Website: www.citic-daxie.com

WENZHOU ECONOMIC AND TECHNOLOGICAL DEVELOPMENT ZONE

Cur Rating:	BBB
Year of Establishment:	1992
Location:	Wenzhou, Zhejiang
Size:	5.11 sq km
Major Investors:	Jodoll Garment, Shengshida, Fangyun Garments, Tiancheng Finery, Chaoqun Shoes, Gold Emperor Shoes, Baideli Leather, Hehe Zipper, Pearlescent Pigments
Total Foreign Direct Investment:	USD68.5 million (Utilised)
Major Industries Encouraged:	Electromechanical equipment, chemical and pharmaceutical,construction materials, textiles, real estate development, and urban infrastructure development

INTRODUCTION

Wenzhou Economic and Technological Development Zone (WZETDZ) was approved as a state-level ETDZ by the State Council in March 1992. It is the only ETDZ in the southern Zhejiang. The main supporting industries of WZETDZ include textile and garment, leather products, bio-pharmaceuticals and enviroment protection technologies.

INVESTMENT CLIMATE

In 2001, the GDP of WETDZ was RMB3.04 billion, the industrial output was RMB7.53 billion and the export volume was USD185 million. By the end of 2001, investment for infrastructure development was RMB1.54 billion.

793 projects have been carried out in the zone, which had total investment of RMB9.318 billion. Among those projects, 161 are foreign investment projects, which had total investment of USD380 million. The contractual and utilized foreign investment stood at USD180 million and USD68.5 million respectively. Among the projects, 12 projects had investment of over USD10 million.

Wenzhou, the place of origin of the "Wenzhou Model", was equivalent to the private economy in China. Its diligent and pragmatic people, with their sharp business acumen doing business everywhere in China and abroad, are known for their "Wenzhou Spirit". WZETDZ is 11 kilometers away from Wenzhou Airport.

The Administrative Commission of WZETDZ

12th Floor, Development Zone Mansion
Tangjiaqiao South Road
Wenzhou, Zhejiang
P. R. China 325011
Tel: (86)(577) 8910102, 8910103, 8910212
 Fax: (86)(577) 8910130, 88910803
E-mail: wetdz@wetdz.gov.en
Website: www.wetdz.gov.cn

JIAXING ECONOMIC AND TECHNOLOGICAL DEVELOPMENT ZONE

Our Rating:	A
Year of Establishment:	1992
Location:	Jiaxing, Zhejiang
Size:	18.73 sq km
Major Investors:	Hankook Tyre, Eastern Steel Cord, Tongmin Enterprise, Jasmi Silk Products, Idea Silk, Huafei Stainless Steel, Expro, Showa, Dongfeng Power Machinery, Top QPC Handicrafts, Tiandi Furniture, and Dae Kwang Mold.
Total Foreign Direct Investment:	USD400 million
Major Industries Encouraged:	Electronics, information technology, food, textile, machinery and chemical industry

INTRODUCTION

Jiaxing Economic and Technological Development Zone (JXETDZ) is located in the northwestern part of Jiaxing, a 1,000-year-old ancient city, in the northern Zhejiang. It is 90 kilometers away from Shanghai and Hangzhou, the provincial capital. Expressways and railways connect Jiaxing to major cities in eastern China. By the end of 2001, 93 foreign enterprises from Hong Kong, Taiwan, the US, Japan, Singapore and South Korea have set up in JXETDZ.

INVESTMENT CLIMATE

It is about 3 kilometers from the downtown. The total land size is 18.73 sq km. According to the master plan, it is divided into four sub-level industrial parks, namely, electronics and information technology, food processing, light industry and textile, machinery and chemicals.

By the end of 2001, JXETDZ has attracted 188 industrial enterprises, including 93 foreign enterprise engaged in industries such as electronics, machinery, metal products, light industry, textile and chemicals. The total contractual and utilized FDI stood at USD650 million and USD400 million, respectively.

The Administrative Committee of JXETDZ
1 Dongsheng West Road
Jiaxing, Zhejiang
P. R. China 314001
Tel: (86)(573) 2208501, 2208502
Fax: (86)(573) 2208570
E-mail: jedz@mail.jxptt.zj.cn
Website: www.jxedz.com

HANGZHOU HIGH-TECH PARK

Our Rating:	AA
Year of Establishment:	1990
Location:	Hangzhou, Zhejiang
Size:	N.A.
Major Investors:	Motorola, Bosch, Nokia, UTstar.com
Total Foreign Direct Investment:	N.A.
Major Industries Encouraged:	Micro-electronic information technology, biopharmaceutical engineering, new materials, optical electromechanical integration technologies, and computer engineering

INTRODUCTION

Hangzhou High-tech Park (HZHTP) was started in March 1990 and was accorded state-level status in 1991. The main part of HHTP is adjacent to the beautiful West Lake.

The park has been focusing on five major high-tech industries, namely micro-electronics, biopharmaceutical engineering, new materials, optical-electromechanical integration technologies, and computer engineering.

By 2001, HZHTP's total contractual and utilized FDI reached USD103.8 million and USD52.8 million respectively.

INVESTMENT CLIMATE

HHTP comprises three separate parts, the Main Park, Xiasha Industrial Park and Zhijiang Industrial Park. The Main Park contains 16 universities and colleges, and nine state-level laboratories.

Xiasha Industrial Park is located at the northern bank of Qiantang River next to Hangzhou ETDZ.

Zhijiang Park is five kilometers away from downtown and is situated at the southern bank of Qiantang River. Inside the Zhijiang Park, sub-level parks with special characteristics also exist.

These include Software Development Park, MNC High-tech Park, and Entrepreneurship Park for Chinese Students Back from Overseas. The MNC High-tech Park is devoted to international MNCs that might establish R & D centers in China.

HZHTP has easy access to Hangzhou Xiaoshan International Airport, where flights are available to Bangkok, Macau, Hong Kong, Beijing and Guangzhou. Hangzhou is also at the midpoint of Shanghai and Ningbo Port, with an expressway which conveniently extends to the two cities.

The Administrative Committee of HZHTP
199 Wenshan Road
Hangzhou, Zhejiang
P. R. China
Tel: (86)(571) 88060686
Fax: (86)(571) 88060686
E-mail: gwh@hhtz.com
Website: www.hhtz.com

ZHEJIANG UNIVERSITY SCIENCE PARK

Year of Establishment:	1999
Location:	Hangzhou, Zhejiang
Size:	113 ha
Major Supporting Institutions:	Zhejiang University
Major Investors:	ZJUSP Development Corp. ,Nandu Properties etc.
Major Industries Encouraged:	Genetic engineering, micro-system, life science, hydraulic-pressure engineering, digital communications, pharmaceuticals, Chinese medicine, new materials, softwaremedical technology, automation, investment management, environmental engineering and nanometer technologies.

INTRODUCTION

Zhejiang University Science Park (ZJUSP) is located in Hangzhou, facing the world-renowned West Lake. Having been accorded the status of National University Science Park on 2 December 1999, the park includes some 100 ha core district and subsidiary parks in other cities, such as Ningbo, Jiaxing, Wenzhou and Shaoxin. The start-up zone will be put into full use in 2004.

With registered capital of RMB100 million, ZJUSP Construction Holdings Corporation was established in September 2001. The major shareholders include ZJUSP Development Corporation (40%), Nandu Properties (30%), with total assets of RMB3 billion, and Shanghai Shihe Internet Technologies (30%).

INVESTMENT CLIMATE

By the end of 2001, there were more than 134 high-tech enterprises, with registered capital of RMB457 million. Among those enterprises, around 88 are new ventures established in 2001. Their industries cover gene engineering, micro-system, life sciences, hydraulic-pressure engineering, digital communications, pharmaceuticals, Chinese medicine research, new materials, software, medical technology, automation, investment management, environmental engineering and nanometer technologies. ZJUSP is strongly supported by resources provided by Zhejiang University. The prestigious 105-year old University, was merged by former Zhejiang University, Hangzhou University, Zhejiang Agricultural University and Zhejiang Medical University in 1998. The research strength of the university is strong as it has 1,000 professors and 2,400 associate professors on campus.

ZJUSP Development Co Ltd
Hangzhou, Zhejiang
P. R. China
Tel: (86)(571) 87951088, 7952493
Fax: (86)(571) 87952499
E-mail: zusp@sun.zju.edu.cn
Website: www.zju.edu.cn

HANGZHOU EXPORT PROCESSING ZONE

Year of Establishment:	2000
Location:	Hangzhou, Zhejiang
Size:	2.92 sq km
Major Investors:	Matsushita, Yazaki, Toshiba
Total Foreign Direct Investment:	USD80 million (end April 2002)
Major Industries Encouraged:	Export-related industries

INTRODUCTION

Hangzhou Export Processing Zone (HZEPZ) was approved by the State Council in April 2000 It is located within the area of Hangzhou Economic and Technological Development Zone and forms an important part in the ETDZ. It covers 2.92 sq km with 2 sq km as the phase I area.

INVESTMENT CLIMATE

In the first four months of year 2002, the zone approved seven new FIEs with contractual FDI of USD47.82 million, among the top three of all 17 Chinese EPZs. So far, eight renowned MNCs have invested in HZEPZ, including Matsushita and Yazaki, of which five have already been in operation with expected exports worth USD50 million. In May 2002, Toshiba announced its USD57 million plan to develop an global IT base in HZEPZ with investment of USD 96 million. The main products will be Toshiba note books with annual ouput of 750,000 and 2.4 million in 2004. Although being an inland EPZ, HZEPZ enjoys a well-developed transportation network. The newly built Shanghai-Hangzhou-Ningbo Expressway runs through HZEPZ. It now takes 90 minutes' drive to get to Shanghai and Ningbo Port by expressway. Hangzhou Xiaoshan International Airport is 10 kilometers away.

The Administrative Committee of HZEPZ
Tel: (86)(571) 86912771, 86910670.
Fax: (86)(571) 86911747
E-mail: hepz@hetz.gov.cn
Website: www.hetz.gov.cn

HONG KONG

SHENZHEN

NEW TERRITORIES

Yuen Long   Tai Po

KOWLOON
Kwai Chung
Kowloon Tong
Tseung Kwan O
Lantau Island   Cyberport
HONGKONG

HONG KONG SAR

S O U T H   C H I N A
S E A

■ Hong Kong Science &
Technology Parks

Industrial Parks in Hong Kong

Hong Kong Science & Technology Parks
The Cyberport

INTRODUCTION

Once the richest British colony, Hong Kong returned to the mainland of China on 1 July 1997, ending the centuries old humiliation of the Chinese nation since the Opium War in the 18th century. The smooth transfer of administration is a great tribute to the success of the late Deng Xiaoping's "One Country, Two Systems" framework. It is enshrined in the "Basic Law", the de facto constitution governing the first Special Administrative Region after 1997.

GEOGRAPHY

The annual average temperature ranges from 15.8°C in January to 28.8°C in July. Total rainfall is about 1,300 to 3,000 mm, varying in different locations.

By the end of 2001, there were 6.73 million residents, most being of the Cantonese dialect group. However, English is also widely used as a working language.

ECONOMIC DEVELOPMENT

Thanks to its laissez-faire philosophy, Hong Kong now boasts a sound and affluent economy and a small government with the world's fourth largest foreign exchange reserves holding.

Hong Kong's economy has undergone a remarkable transformation in the past two decades, from a labor-intensive manufacturing base to a service economy with 86% of GDP generated by the tertiary sector. Serving as an entrepot to the mainland, Hong Kong increases trading activities, mainly in electronics products and textiles, tremendously. The re-export volume is now more than the SAR's GDP in 2001.

However, the local economy deteriorated in 2001, due largely to the global weakened market after the 11 September 2001 terrorist attacks in the US. Real GDP in 2001 slid 0.7%, compared to an increase of 9.5% just a year before. The unemployment rate soared to 7.1% in April 2002, depicting a rather melancholy picture for the second-term SAR government. But recovery signs were shown after the SAR chief executive announced a package of initiatives to boost the economy. The latest forecasts of the territory's growth in 2002, while maintained or re-adjusted by a number of private sector analysts, range from 0% to 2.7%, averaging at 1.5%.

INFRASTRUCTURE

The high profile Hong Kong International Airport (HKIA) at Chek Lap Kok was opened in July 1998. It has a current throughput capacity of 45 million passengers and three million tons of cargo per year.

Fact Sheet	2001
Total Land Area	1,098.5 sq km
Population ('000)	6,732
Currency	Hong Kong Dollar (HKD), HKD7.8= USD1
GDP	HKD1,262.6 billion or USD161.9 billion
GDP per capita	USD24,070
Domestic Exports (f.o.b.)	USD19.7 billion
Re-exports (f.o.b.)	USD170.2 billion
Imports (c.i.f.)	USD201.1 billion
FDI Stock	USD455.3 billion (2000)
FD Inflow	USD61.82 billion (2000)
Employed Population	3.44 million
Unemployment Rate	6.1%
Visitors	13.725 million

There are some 66 international airlines providing about 3,600 scheduled flights each week between the SAR and 130 destinations worldwide. The ultimate design will enhance its capacity to handle up to 87 million passengers and nine million tons of cargo annually.

Hong Kong is one of the major ports of the world. In 2001, a total of 37,350 vessels called at the port and 17.7 million passengers passed through its terminals. The Kwai Chung container port, which has 18 berths and eight existing terminals, alone handled 11.3 million TEUs in 2001. With another 6.5 million TEUs handled in midstream and other wharves, Hong Kong Port maintained its status of the world's busiest container port in 2001.

Highways, subways and railway network in the SAR are among the most heavily used in the world and link up to the mainland's traffic system via Shenzhen. Hong Kong also boasts one of the world's most sophisticated and successful telecommunication markets. Connected to nine submarine cable systems and powered by 40 satellite earth station antennas, local external fixed telecom network services (FTNS) are provided by 21 licensees as at September 2001.

FOREIGN INVESTMENT OPPORTUNITIES

At the end of 2000, the stock of FDI in Hong Kong amounted to USD455.3 billion, of which 44% come from three offshore tax havens, i.e. British Virgin Islands, Bermuda and Cayman Island. Apart from that, mainland China provided the largest source of FDI, accounting for 31.3% of the total stock. The Netherlands and the US are the distant second and third investors. Manufacturing received only two percent of the total. The bulk of FDI is in investment holdings, real estate, financial services, commerce and trade.

The FDI inflow in 2000 surged to USD61.8 billion, 2.5 times that in 1999. However, outflow FDI from Hong Kong was also substantial, registering USD59.3 billion in 2000.

Being an international hub and the gateway to China, having sound infrastructure, abundant supporting services, and most importantly, the freest economy, Hong Kong embraces globalization of trade and services in all sectors. Visibly, various industrial parks, including the much controversial Cyberport, have been inaugurated to encourage high-tech industries and to help Hong Kong respond quickly to future changes in the global economy. The SAR is also studying the feasibility of a Chinese Medicine Port in the future.

The Government of Hong Kong SAR
Website: www.gov.hk
www.investhk.gov.hk
www.firstchoicehongkong.gov.hk

HONG KONG SCIENCE AND TECHNOLOGY PARKS

Our Rating:	AA
Year of Establishment:	2001
Location:	Tai Po, Kowloon Tong, Tseung Kwan O, Yuen Long
Size:	Varied
Major Investors:	Solomon Systech, SAE Magnetics, Kinetana, RCL, Pico, Nissin, Nikko, Nestle, Oracle, TUV, Lattice, Silicon, Graphics, Motorola, Philips, ABB, Bridgestone, Yakult and Carlsberg, etc.
Total Foreign Direct Investment:	NA
Major Industries Encouraged:	High-tech preferred but companies of all sizes and stages are welcome.

INTRODUCTION

The Hong Kong Science and Technology Parks Corporation (HKSTP), an SAR government statutory body, was officially incorporated on 7 May 2001, following a merger among three companies that were managing five individual industrial estates. These are:

- Science Park, Tai Po, New Territories;
- Tech Centre at Kowloon Tong;
- Tai Po Industrial Estate, New Territories;
- Yuen Long Industrial Estate at Yuen Long, New Territories;
- Tseung Kwan O Industrial Estate at Tseung Kwan O, Kowloon.

INVESTMENT ENVIRONMENT

The five sub-level parks are distributed in Kowloon and New Territories, but are easily accessible by public transportation.

Facing Tolo Habor, the Science Park can be reached by railway or highway and conveniently connects to mainland China as well as the HKIA. It offers essential support facilities and is in the vicinity of Chinese University of Hong Kong and industrial facilities. The total area is about 22 ha when all three phases are completed. As at April 2002, it has signed with 16 tenants who formed four technology clusters: IT and telecommunications, electronics, bio-technology and precision engineering.

The Tech Centre is actually a grade-A office building located next to the City University of Hong Kong. It has some 20 tenants to date. The other three industrial estates are all accessible by highway and have given residence to over 90 companies from Asia, the US and Europe.

Gateway Office
19/F, Tower 6, The Gateway
9 Canton Road, Kowloon, Hong Kong
Tel: (852)26291818
Fax: (853)26291833

Tech Centre Office
1/F, Tech Centre, 72 Tat Chee Ave.
Kowloon Tong, Hong Kong
Email: enquiry@hkstp.org
Website: www.hkstp.org

THE CYBERPORT

Our Rating:	A
Year of Establishment:	2000
Location:	Telegraph Bay, Pokfulam, Hong Kong Island
Size:	24 ha
Major Investors:	GE, Sonnera, PCCW, and (prospective) Cisco, CMGI, Hewlett- Packard, Hikari Tsushin, Hua Wei, IBM, Legend, Microsoft, Oracle, Portal, Silicon Graphics, Softbank, Sybase, Yahoo!.
Total Foreign Direct Investment:	NA
Major Industries Encouraged:	IT, information services, multimedia content creation and related sectors.

INTRODUCTION

The Cyberport project is the SAR's flagship information infrastructure project aimed to create a strategic cluster of the world's leading IT enterprises and top-notch IT talents in Hong Kong. The concept is to consolidate Hong Kong's position as a hub on the global IT map. In the long term, the Cyberport may enhance the competitiveness of other sectors and provide a new tourist attraction in Hong Kong.

The project was endorsed by the government on 17 May 2000 and is now being built on a piece of reclaimed land occupying 24 ha in the Southern District of Hong Kong Island, near the University of Hong Kong and not far from Central district. The USD1.92 billion Cyberport has been carried out by Pacific Century CyberWorks (PCCW, a subsidiary of Pacific Century Group led by Richard Li, son of Hong Kong's tycoon Li Ka-shing. However, the ownership and management rights belong to Hong Kong SAR government. Upon completion, it will be handed back to Hong Kong Cyberport Management Co. Ltd., a private company wholly owned by the Financial Secretary Inc. of the government.

The Cyberport will accommodate over 100 IT and IT-related companies. The Phase I building was near completion in April 2002, and the rest will be finished by the end of 2003.

INVESTMENT ENVIRONMENT

Although companies of varying sizes and at different stages of development are all welcome, priority will be given to companies which

* introduce or use leading-edge IT applications;
* provide services to enhance traditional services delivery (e.g. distance learning, securities trading and multimedia film production);
* provide essential services in support of global or regional business (e.g. software development);
* utilize the Cyberport as a hub of the global information infrastructure (e.g. corporate information network or customer service network).

Cyberport is scheduled to be opened in three phases. It will comprise highly intelligent offices with 335,275 sq m of office space, an educational, entertainment and retail complex called Cybercenter with 82,300 sq m space, and a 176-room hotel. The residential portion of the project, nearly 3,000 luxury apartments on the site in the Pokfulam district, will be developed after the inception of the Cyberport and completed by 2007.

The monthly rental of the office space is now set at USD1.4-1.7 per sq ft lettable. By April 2001, 290 companies had expressed their interest in taking up tenancy, and 15 have already signed letters of intent to become anchor tenants, most of them being internationally renowned MNCs.

The Secretariat
The Committee on Admission of
  Cyberport Office Tenants (CACOT)
Information Technology and
  Broadcasting Bureau (ITBB),
The Government of the Hong Kong
  Special Administrative Region
1/F Murray Building,
Garden Road,
Central, Hong Kong
Tel: (852) 2189 2306, 21892296
Fax: (852) 28270119

Cyberport Division, ITBB
Tel: (852) 21892284
Fax: (852) 28276646
Email: cyp-itbb@itbb.gov.hk

Websites:
Information Technology and
Broadcasting Bureau
Website: www.digital21.gov.hk
        www.info.gov.hk/itbb

The Cyberport
Website: www.cyberport.com.hk
        www.info.gov.hk/itbb/cyberport
        www.cyberport-management.com
        www.cyberport-project.com.hk

MACAU

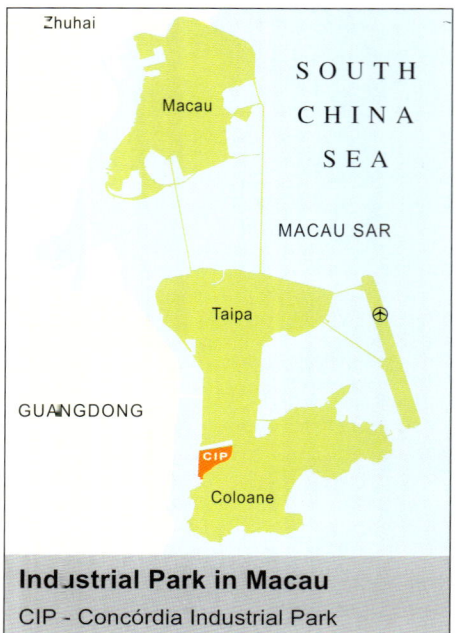

Zhuhai

SOUTH CHINA SEA

Macau

MACAU SAR

Taipa

GUANGDONG

CIP

Coloane

Industrial Park in Macau

CIP - Concórdia Industrial Park

Fact Sheet	2001
Total Land Area	25.4 sq km
Population	437,900
Currency	Pataca (MOP), MOP1.03= HKD1
GDP	MOP49.80 billion or USD6.20 billion
GDP per capita	USD14,281
Exports	USD2.39 billion
Imports	USD2.30 billion
Total FDI	USD390.3 million (net book value)
Employed Population	207,000
Unemployment Rate	6.5%
Visitors	10.28 million

INTRODUCTION

When China resumed sovereignty over Macau at midnight on 20 December 1999, the former Portuguese colony which was the first European settlement in the Far East since the 16th century, became the second Special Administrative Region (SAR) of China. In accordance with the principle of "One Country, Two Systems", Macau's capitalist system will remain unchanged for 50 years. Governed by the Basic Law, the SAR enjoys a high degree of autonomy and executive, legislative and independent judicial power.

GEOGRAPHY

Macau is a small city situated on the west bank of Pearl River on the southeast coast of China. The SAR borders Zhuhai SEZ, and is only 60 km from Hong Kong and 145 km from Guangzhou.

The total land area of Macau has been progressively expanded through reclamation from the sea, from a mere 2.78 sq km in 1840 to 25.4 sq km today. The territory of Macau consists of the peninsula of Macau and the two islands of Taipa and Coloane.

Macau has a monsoon climate with hot wet summers, mild autumns and cool dry winters. Annual average temperature is about 22.6°C and typhoons from the South Pacific Ocean often occur during the summer.

There are 437,900 people living in Macau, making it one of the most densely populated areas in the world. Over 96% of the SAR's population speaks Chinese, but Cantonese is predominantly spoken as a dialect. Two percent of the local population speaks Portuguese. Although Portuguese and Chinese are the two official languages in Macau, English and Chinese are most frequently used in business.

ECONOMIC DEVELOPMENT

Macau is a small but highly open economy. The liberal free market principles, with no import tariff or exchange restriction on capital and profit repatriation, have ensured the city's prosperity for decades. Though affected by the Asian financial crisis, the economy has recently shown signs of recovery. In 2001, its GDP stood at around USD6.20 billion or USD14,281 per capita, increasing by 2.1% year on year.

Famous for casinos and a massive annual inflow of more than nine million visitors, Macau has successfully shifted from being a manufacturing-based economy to a service economy. Since 1992, the tourism sector and related services alone employ 30% of the local workforce, generating 40% of the territory's total revenue, surpassing that from exports. This is mainly contributed to by the 40-year-old gambling industry. It now accounts for almost half the local economy.

The financial industries have also grown rapidly in tandem with the boom in casinos. There are a total of 22 banks, with half being foreign, and 24 insurance companies operating in Macau. The tertiary sector contributed 90.7% of GDP.

As a result of cheap labor being offered in neighboring regions, manufacturing, which previously had a heavy emphasis on textiles, has been withering. The local government is now trying to introduce advanced technology to stay competitive, and is dedicated to finding new markets for local top quality products.

INFRASTRUCTURE

The SAR's three parts are linked up by two long bridges between Macau Peninsula and Taipa Island, and a six-lane highway between the latter and Coloane Island. Another bridge is erected between Taipa and Montanha Island before linking to the Zhuhai-Guangzhou expressway.

Macau International Airport is located on Taipa Island. The around-the-clock operation is designed to handle six million people yearly. The airport now has more than a dozen airlines flying to and from important cities in mainland and Southeast Asia. Helicopter service is also available between Macau and Hong Kong.

Built to process an annual average of 30 million passengers, a new ferry terminal has greatly enhanced Macau's capacity to handle tourists from Hong Kong and the mainland, as jetfoils are the most popular choice of incoming visitors. In addition, a container and fuel terminal at Ka Ho Port on Coloane Island has bolstered the SAR's role as a trading hub between the Chinese hinterland and other regions.

FOREIGN INVESTMENT OPPORTUNITIES

Macau is an independent tariff region and a free port. It is a member of the WTO and an associate member of the Economic and Social Commission for Asia and the Pacific. It is also a beneficiary of the EU's General Scheme of Preferences and WTO's Agreement on Textiles and Clothing. On the other hand, it serves as a gateway to the Chinese mainland as well as a bridge to the Portuguese-speaking and Cantonese-speaking communities worldwide.

The financial system in Macau is sound and stable, largely because the local currency is pegged to the USD through the HKD.

Taxation is fairly low in the SAR with complementary (profits) tax ranges from 2% to 15%, and a 50% off profit tax for industry.

The Government of Macau SAR
Website: www.macau.gov.mo

Macau Trade and Investment
   Promotion Institute
Website: www.ipim.gov.mo

CONCÓRDIA INDUSTRIAL PARK

Cur Rating:	BBB
Year of Establishment:	1993
Location:	Coloane Island, Macau SAR
Size:	117,272 sq m
Major Investors:	Nittobo Mei Cheong Glass Weaving, Liu's Commerce & Industry, Chin Ip Electrical Appliance, Seng San Enterprise, Casix Optronic, Efacec Oriente, Durffee, Ashford Lab.
Total Foreign Direct Investment:	USD80.4 million
Major Industries Encouraged:	New and advanced technologies or products; investments in equipment and machinery directly connected with production processes; export-oriented, high value-added, vocational and professional training courses; energy-saving, etc.

INTRODUCTION

Concórdia Industrial Park was set up on a reclaimed part of Coloane Island in 1993, amid the SAR government's commitment to stimulate FDI and to enhance industrial diversification. It is managed by Concórdia Industrial Park, Ltd. (SPIC), co-invested by SAR government and Macau Trade and Investment Promotion Institute (IPIM), to accommodate non-pollutive industries based on the guidelines and strategies formulated by the SAR government.

To date, eight companies have been set up in the park by investors from Japan, China, Portugal, Hong Kong and Macau itself, with a total commitment of over USD80 million.

INVESTMENT ENVIRONMENT

The park is four kilometers from the airport, an equal distance from Ka Ho Container Port, and within a 20-minute ride from the border with mainland China.

Besides general fiscal and financial incentives offered in Macau, park tenants enjoy low land prices, rentals and compensation fees, exemption of property transfer tax and stamp duty, mortgage of land, etc.

SPIC has submitted a proposal to the SAR government to expand its territory to satisfy the future demands for industrial land from potential investors. It has also formed a joint venture to promote mainland industrial parks to foreign investors and eventually tap the spillover effect on Macau.

Concórdia Industrial Park, Ltd.
Av. da Amizade 918, World Trade Centre,
13th Floor A&B, Macau
Tel: (853) 786636
Fax: (853) 785374
Email: spic@macau.ctm.net
Website: www.concordia-park.com

Business Directory

When making a call to China from abroad, dial 86 (China's country code) + area code (e.g. 10 for Beijing) + fixed phone number. But when making a call within China, 0 should be added before Area code, that is, 0 + Area code (e.g. 010 for Beijing) + fixed phone number. When calling a mobile phone, no area code is needed.

Telephone Codes

Municipalities	Area	Code
Beijing	Beijing	10
Shanghai	Shanghai	21
Tianjin	Tianjin	22
Chongqing	Chongqing	23

Autonomous Reg.	Area	Code
Guangxi	Nanning	771
	Pingxiang	771
	Sanjiang	772
	Liuzhou	772
	Yangshuo	773
	Wuzhou	774
	Guilin	773
	Wuzhou	774
	Guigang	775
	Yulin	775
	Baise	776
	Tianyang	776
	Qinzhou	777
	Hechi	778
	Beihai	779
Inner Mongolia	Haila'er	470
	Hohhot	471
	Baotou	472
	Huolinguole	475
	Erenhot	479
	Wulanhaote	482
Ningxia	Helan	951
	Yinchuan	951
	Shizuishan	952
	Wuzhong	953

	Area	Code
	Guyuan	954
Tibet	Lhasa	891
	Xigaze	892
	Nyingchi	894
	Qamdu	895
Xinjiang	Karamay	990
	Hami	902
	Aletai	906
	Urumqi	991
	Aksu	997
	Kashi	998
	Shihezi	993
	Huocheng	999
	Xinyuan	999
	Yining	999

Provinces	Area	Code
Anhui	Hefei	551
	Chuzhou	550
	Bengbu	552
	Wuhu	553
	Huainan	554
	Ma'anshan	555
	Anqing	556
	Suzhou	557
	Fuyang	558
	Haozhou	558
	Lixin	558
	Taihe	558
	Guoyang	558
	Yingshan	558
	Huangshan	559
	Huaibei	561
	Tongling	562
	Xuancheng	563
	Liu'an	564
	Huoqiu	564
Fujian	Fuzhou	591
	Changle	591
	Fuqing	591
	Lianjiang	591
	Xiamen	592
	Ningde	593
	Putian	594
	Anxi	595
	Hui'an	595
	Jinjiang	595

	Quanzhou	595		Foshan	757
	Shishi	595		Nanhai	757
	Yongchun	595		Deqing	758
	Zhangzhou	596		Zhaoqing	758
	Liancheng	597		Zhanjiang	759
	Sanming	598		Xuwen	759
	Nanping	599		Shanwei	660
	Wuyishan	599		Zhongshan	760
Gansu	Lanzhou	931		Heyuan	762
	Linxia	930		Lianzhou	763
	Dingxi	932		Qingyuan	763
	Minxian	932		Shunde	765
	Jinchang	935		Yunfu	766
	Wuwei	935		Chaozhou	768
	Zhangye	936		Dongguan	769
	Anxi	937	**Hainan**	Haikou	898
	Dunhuang	937		Baisha	890
	Jiayuguan	937		Dongfang	890
	Jiuquan	937		Sanya	899
	Tianshui	938	**Hebei**	Haikou	898
	Chengxian	939		Handan	310
	Wudu	939		Weixian	310
	Maqu	941		Laiyuan	312
Guizhou	Guiyang	851		Baoding	312
	Zunyi	852		Xuanhua	313
	Anshun	853		Zhangjiakou	313
	Zhenning	853		Chengde	314
	Duyun	854		Fengning	314
	Kaili	855		Fengrun	315
	Tongren	856		Tangshan	315
	Bijie	857		Langfang	316
	Liupanshui	858		Cangzhou	317
	Xingyi	859		Hengshui	318
Guangdong	Guangzhou	20		Xintai	319
	Conghua	20		Qinhuangdao	335
	Panyu	20	**Heilongjiang**	Harbin	451
	Huadu	20		Acheng	451
	Zengcheng	20		Bayan	451
	Chaoyang	661		Binxian	451
	Yangjiang	662		Qiqiha'er	452
	Jieyang	663		Mudanjiang	453
	Shaoguan	751		Suifenhe	453
	Huizhou	752		Qitaihe	453
	Meizhou	753		Fujin	454
	Shantou	754		Hegang	454
	Shenzhen	755		Huanan	454
	Zhuhai	756		Jiamusi	454

	Zigong	813
	Mianyang	816
	Nanchong	817
	Dachuan	818
	Suining	825
	Guang'an	826
	Bazhong	827
	Luzhou	830
	Yibin	831
	Neijiang	832
	Ziyang	832
	Leshan	833
	Meishan	833
	Xichang	834
	Ya'an	835
	Ganzi	836
	Kangding	836
	Litang	836
	Barkam	837
	Songpan	837
	Deyang	838
	Guangyuan	839
Yunnan	Kunming	871
	Jinghong	691
	Luxi	692
	Wanding	692
	Dali	872
	Gejiu	873
	Qujing	874
	Baoshan	875
	Wenshan	876
	Yuxi	877
	Chuxiong	878
	Mojiang	879
	Simao	879
	Dongchuan	881
	Lincang	883
	Lushui	886
	Zhongdian	887
	Lijiang	888
Zhejiang	Hangzhou	571
	Quzhou	570
	Jiaxing	573
	Shangyu	575
	Ningbo	574
	Shaoxing	575
	Taizhou	576

Wenzhou	577
Lishui	578
Jinhua	579
Zhoushan	580

Advertising & Public Relations Firms

Beijing

B&B (Bauquis & Boyd) Int'l Ltd
☎ (86)(10) 85261228
Bates China
☎ (86)(10) 65973999
BBDO CNUAC
☎ (86)(10) 65263961
Bejing Asiaray Advertising
☎ (86)(10) 64283689
Bejing Dentsu
☎ (86)(10) 65541439
Beijing Guo'an Advertising Corp.
☎ (86)(10) 65050028
Ringier Pacific Ltd. Beijing Representatives
☎ (86)(10) 65281841
Burson Marsteller
☎ (86)(10) 65056363
China Global Public Relations Co.
☎ (86)(10) 63072690
Carat Media Service
☎ (86)(10) 67081537
China Int'l Advertising
☎ (86)(10) 65061172
Creasia Advertising
☎ (86)(10) 68038070
D'arcy Masius Benton & Bowles
☎ (86)(10) 84584177
DDB Beijing
☎ (86)(10) 85192486
Dentsu Beijing
☎ (86)(10) 65541439
Dentsu Yong & Rubicam Brand Communications
☎ (86)(10) 65059922
Euro RSCG Partnership
☎ (86)(10) 65975180
FCB China
☎ (86)(10) 83915088

Field Force Euro RSCG
☎ (86)(10) 65975180
Grey Worldwide
☎ (86)(10) 85181988
Huawen-Asatsu Int'l Advertising
☎ (86)(10) 64640088
J. Walter Thompson
☎ (36)(10) 65815050
Leo Burnett Shanghai Advertising
☎ (86)(10) 65058838
Logistix Integrated Communication
☎ (86)(10) 84049602
Lowe Lintas & Partners
☎ (86)(10) 65260801
McCann-Erickson Guangming
☎ (83)(10) 65683300
Mediacom Beijing
☎ (86)(10) 85181988
Megacom Advertising
☎ (86)(10) 65978768
Mindshare China
☎ (86)(10) 64440646
Motivator Beijing
☎ (86)(10) 65975180
Ogilvy & Mather
☎ (86)(10) 64436488
Optimum Media Direction
☎ (86)(10) 65612198
PMG Beijing
☎ (86)(10) 65925231
Publicis Ad-Link
☎ (86)(10) 65610293
Saatchi & Saatchi
☎ (86)(10) 65102255
Shanghai Hakuhodo Advertising
☎ (86)(10) 64630650
Sino Media Group
☎ (86)(10) 65816186
Starcom Worldwide
☎ (86)(10) 65058828
TBWA Leadavis China
☎ (86)(10) 85299111
The Media Edge
☎ (86)(10) 65059922
Universal McCann
☎ (86)(10) 65683300

Vision & Value
☎ (86)(10) 68314881
Zenith Media
☎ (86)(10) 65102277

Guangdong

Guangzhou
Bates China
☎ (86)(20) 83847756
BBDO CNUAC
☎ (86)(20) 86015087
Burson Marsteller
☎ (86)(20) 83220656 / 83220042
Carat Media Service
☎ (86)(20) 83313022
Creasia Advertising
☎ (86)(20) 87300558
D'arcy Masius Benton & Bowles
☎ (86)(20) 87321148
DDB Guangzhou
☎ (86)(20) 87520333
Dentsu Gangzhou
☎ (86)(20) 83511998
Dentsu Yong & Rubicam Brand
Communications
☎ (86)(20) 87554328
Euro RSCG Partnership
☎ (86)(20) 87521628
FCB China
☎ (86)(20) 87321214
Field Force Euro RSCG
☎ (86)(20) 81351250
Grey Worldwide
☎ (86)(20) 87321828
Guangxu Asatsu Advertising
☎ (86)(20) 87655611-7
Guangzhou Syspower Media
☎ (86)(20) 87373977
Guangzhou YC Press Advertising
☎ (86)(20) 87615321
Guangzhou Asiaray Wiseford Advertising
☎ (86)(20) 83193333
Hainan White Horse Advertising
☎ (86)(20) 83869288
J. Walter Thompson
☎ (86)(20) 38771810

L&L Advertising
☎ (86)(20) 87310183
Leo Burnett Shanghai Advertising
☎ (86)(20) 87553068
McCann–Erickson Guangming
☎ (86)(20) 83395461
Mediacom Guangzhou
☎ (86)(20) 87321828
Megacom Advertising
☎ (86)(20) 87320940
Mindshare China
☎ (86)(20) 87521997
Ogilvy & Mather
☎ (86)(20) 38771888
Publicis Ad-Link
☎ (86)(20) 83634166
Saatchi & Saatchi
☎ (86)(20) 38791228
Senses Filmpower
☎ (86)(20) 38820475
Starcom Worldwide
☎ (86)(20) 38770588
TBWA Leedavis China
☎ (86)(20) 87520966
The Media Edge
☎ (86)(20) 87554328
Universal McCann
☎ (86)(20) 83395461
Vision & Value
☎ (86)(20) 83563929
Vision Communications
☎ (86)(20) 83571216
Zenith Media
☎ (86)(20) 38791218
Zigma Advertising Associates
☎ (86)(20) 87574422

Shenzhen
Duo Doctor Advertisement Design Co., Ltd.
☎ (86)(755) 82096942
Haitian Advertising Design Corporation
☎ (86)(755) 83359817
Haitian Publication Design Corporation
☎ (86)(755) 83223927
Jiuchao Advertising Design
☎ (86)(755) 83941330

Q.F. Advertising Co., Ltd.
☎ (86)(755) 82290818
Shenzhen A-Flag Advertising Co.,Ltd.
☎ (86)(755) 83201995
Sino Media Group
☎ (86)(755) 83242823

Hong Kong
Bates China
☎ (852) 21036333
BBDO CNUAC
☎ (852) 28201888
Burson Marsteller
☎ (852) 28800229
Convey Advertising
☎ (852) 27393806
D'arcy Masius Benton & Bowles
☎ (852) 25905888
DDB Worldwide
☎ (852) 28280328
Dentsu
☎ (852) 21023333
Euro RSCG Partnership
☎ (852) 25901800
Grey Worldwide
☎ (852) 25106888
HCF Creative
☎ (852) 27979882
J. Walter Thompson
☎ (852) 22803333
Leo Burnett Shanghai Advertising
☎ (852) 25674333
Lowe & Partners Worldwide
☎ (852) 28950669
Ogilvy & Mather
☎ (852) 25680161
Optimum Media Direction
☎ (852) 29111668
Publicis Ad-Link
☎ (852) 28310091
Saatchi & Saatchi
☎ (852) 25823333
TBWA Leedavis China
☎ (852) 28332033
Zenith Media
☎ (852) 21036111

Hubei
Wuhan
Creasia
☎ (86)(27) 85713001

Shanghai
Asatsu Advertising
☎ (86)(21) 64674118
Asiaray Advertising
☎ (86)(21) 64031999
B&B (Bauquis & Boyd) Int'l Ltd.
☎ (86)(21) 28903121
Bates Shanghai
☎ (86)(21) 63582908
BBDO CNUAC
☎ (86)(21) 64679699
Burson Marsteller
☎ (86)(10) 62491640
Carat Media Service
☎ (86)(21) 52984280
Creasia Advertising
☎ (86)(21) 63509156
D'arcy Masius Benton & Bowles
☎ (86)(21) 52984333
DDB Shanghai
☎ (86)(21) 63509180
Dentsu Advertising
☎ (86)(21) 63501660
Dentsu Yong & Rubicam Brand
Communications
☎ (86)(21) 63867770
Eastern Draftworldwide
☎ (86)(21) 65975180
Euro RSCG Partnership
☎ (86)(21) 53965666
FCB China
☎ (86)(21) 63915252
Field Force Euro RSCG
☎ (86)(21) 63917766
Golden Horse Advertising
☎ (86)(21) 64380260
Grey Worldwide
☎ (86)(21) 63508660
Guangdong YC Press Advertising
☎ (86)(21) 62520515
J. Walter Thompson
☎ (86)(21) 52985598

Leo Burnett Shanghai Advertising
☎ (86)(21) 84049602
Lowe Lintas & Partners Worldwide
☎ (86)(21) 52984428
McCann-Erickson Guangming
☎ (86)(21) 65683300
Medai Partners Int'l
☎ (86)(21) 64401568
Mediacom
☎ (86)(21) 63508660
Megacom Advertising
☎ (86)(21) 63916262
Metro Ads Advertising
☎ (86)(21) 64748058
Mindshare China
☎ (86)(21) 52986388
Mission Advertising
☎ (86)(21) 62772771
Motivator Shanghai
☎ (86)(21) 53965666
Ogilvy & Mather
☎ (86)(21) 62183009
Optimum Media Direction
☎ (86)(21) 63758885
Publicis Ad-Link
☎ (86)(21) 63503678
Saatchi & Saatchi
☎ (86)(21) 62138822
Senses Filmpower
☎ (86)(21) 63278603
Shanghai Hakuhodo Advertising
☎ (86)(21) 64156776
Sino Media Group
☎ (86)(21) 62792541
Starcom Worldwide
☎ (86)(21) 62172248
TBWA Leedavis China
☎ (86)(21) 63906798
The Media Edge
☎ (86)(21) 63867770
Universal McCann
☎ (86)(21) 52400008
Vision & Value
☎ (86)(21) 62462000
Zenith Media
☎ (86)(21) 62133232

Zigma Advertising Associates
☎ (86)(21) 62791234

Sichuan
Chengdu
Field Force Euro RSCG
☎ (86)(28) 6719648

Tianjin
Tian Ya / Asiaray Advertising
☎ (86)(22) 25266881

Banks

Foreign Firms
Beijing
ABN AMRO Bank
☎ (86)(10) 65017766
Alahli Bank of Kuwait (KSC)
☎ (86)(10) 64963189
American Express Int'l Inc.
☎ (86)(10) 65052888
Arab Bank Private Limited Company
☎ (86)(10) 65182858
Asahi Bank Limited
☎ (86)(10) 65051337
Australia & New Zealand Banking Group
☎ (86)(10) 65102929
Banca Commerciale Italiana
☎ (86)(10) 64660088
Banca Di Roma
☎ (86)(10) 65003716
Banco Sabadell
☎ (86)(10) 64182366
Banca Nazionale del Lavoro
☎ (86)(10) 65002255
Banco Central Hispano
☎ (86)(10) 64638059
Banco Exterior de Espana S.A.
☎ (86)(10) 65122288
Banco Santander
☎ (86)(10) 65068020/1
Bangkok Bank
☎ (86)(10) 65055526/7

Bank Austria Creditanstalt
☎ (86)(10) 65900546
Bank of America
☎ (86)(10) 65053508
Bank of East Asia
☎ (86)(10) 65543101
Bank of Montreal
☎ (86)(10) 65102233
Bank of Nova Scotia
☎ (86)(10) 88091106
Bank of Tokyo Mitsubishi
☎ (86)(10) 65908888
Bank of Yokohama Limited
☎ (86)(10) 65051157
Banque Francaise de Commerce Exterieur
☎ (86)(10) 65002647
Banque Indosuez
☎ (86)(10) 65003574
Banque Nationale de Paris
☎ (86)(10) 65053685/7
Banque Paribas
☎ (86)(10) 65133990/2
Barclays Bank PLC
☎ (86)(10) 65122288
Bayerische Vereinsbank
☎ (86)(10) 65012105/6
Bear Stearns & Company
☎ (86)(10) 65055101
BNP Paribas
☎ (86)(10) 6505888
Chase Manhattan Bank
☎ (86)(10) 65881039
China International Capital Corp. Ltd
☎ (86)(10) 65051166
Chuo Mitsu Trust and Banking Co. Ltd.
☎ (86)(10) 65139851
Citibank N.A.
☎ (86)(10) 65102933
Commerzbank AG
☎ (86)(10) 65056680
Commonwealth Bank of Australia
☎ (86)(10) 65055350-2
Compagnie Financiere De CIcEtDe L'union Europeenne
☎ (86)(10) 65102167
Credit Agricole Indosuez
☎ (86)(10) 65003574

Credit Commercial De France
☎ (86)(10) 65263990
Credit Lyonnais
☎ (86)(10) 65004562
Credit Suisse First Boston
☎ (86)(10) 64671199
Credito Italiano
☎ (36)(10) 65126968
Daiwa Bank Limited
☎ (86)(10) 65908500
Dao Heng Bank Limited
☎ (86)(10) 88091328
Den Norske Bank
☎ (86)(10) 65918475
Deutsche Bank
☎ (86)(10) 65052305
Development Bank of Singapore
☎ (86)(10) 65051216
DG Bank
☎ (86)(10) 65006332
Dresdner Bank AG
☎ (83)(10) 85275688
Expo-t-Import Bank of Korea
☎ (83)(10) 64653371
First National Bank of Boston
☎ (86)(10) 65931850
First National Bank of Chicago
☎ (86)(10) 65003281
First Union Bank
☎ (86)(10) 65183853
Fleet National Bank
☎ (86)(10) 65931850
Fuji Bank
☎ (86)(10) 65002255
Generale Belgian Bank
☎ (86)(10) 65133310
Goldman Sachs (China) L.L.C.
☎ (86)(10) 65056888
Hang Seng bank
☎ (86)(10) 65260833
Hong Kong & Shanghai Banking Corp.
☎ (86)(10) 65260668
Hypovereinsbank
☎ (86)(10) 64651923
Industrial Bank of Japan
☎ (86)(10) 65139026

ING Bank
☎ (86)(10) 65900952
J.P Morgan & Co.
☎ (86)(10) 85296333
Korea Exchange Bank
☎ (86)(10) 65183101
Korea First Bank
☎ (86)(10) 65050256
LandesBank Baden-Wurttemberg
☎ (86)(10) 65900166
Lehman Brothers Incorporated
☎ (86)(10) 65050301
MayBank
☎ (86)(10) 65054983
Merrill Lynch International
☎ (86)(10) 65050290
Mitsubishi Bank Ltd.
☎ (86)(10) 65003345
Mitsubishi Trust & Banking Corp.
☎ (86)(10) 65139016/7
Mizuho Corporate Bank
☎ (86)(10) 65139026
Nanyang Commercial Bank
☎ (86)(10) 65954728
Natexis Banque
☎ (86)(10) 65055086
National Australian Bank
☎ (86)(10) 6565003581
National Bank of Canada
☎ (86)(10) 65978836
Nedcor Bank
☎ (86)(10) 64637939
Nordbanken AG
☎ (86)(10) 65909070
Royal Bank of Canada
☎ (86)(10) 65050358
Sanwa Bank
☎ (86)(10) 65182780
Schroders PLC
☎ (86)(10) 65907792
SOCIETE   ALE
☎ (86)(10) 65123650
Standard Chartered Bank
☎ (86)(10) 65669888
Sumitomo Mitsui Bank
☎ (86)(10) 65973351

Svenska Handelsbanken
☎ (86)(10) 65004691
Swiss Bank Corp.
☎ (86)(10) 65052213-5
Union Bank of Finland
☎ (86)(10) 65012181
Unicredito Italiano
☎ (86)(10) 65126968
Union Bank of Switzerland (UBS)
☎ (86)(10) 65052213
UBS Warburg Asia
☎ (86)(10) 65052283
UniBank
☎ (86)(10) 659009004
Union Bank of Finland
☎ (86)(10) 65012181
United Overseas Bank
☎ (86)(10) 65051863
UFJ Bank
☎ (86)(10) 65182780
Westdeutsche Landesbank
☎ (86)(10) 64651936
Westpac Banking Corp.
☎ (86)(10) 65123465
World Bank Resident Mission in China
☎ (86)(10) 65023361
Zurcher Kantonal Bank
☎ (86)(10) 65672539

Chongqing
Bank of East Asia
☎ (86)(23) 63730386
Bank of Nova Scotia
☎ (86)(23) 63733500
Hong Kong & Shanghai Banking Corp.
☎ (86)(23) 63740784
Sumitomo Bank Limited
☎ (86)(23) 62803394

Fujian
Fuzhou
Asahi Bank Limited
☎ (86)(591) 7839888
Bank of East Asia
☎ (86)(591) 7503581
DBS-Daoheng Bank
☎ (86)(591) 7544080

Hong Kong Jiyou Bank
☎ (86)(591) 7845908
Overseas Chinese Commercial Bank
☎ (86)(591) 7839788

Xiamen
Bank of East Asia
☎ (86)(592) 5072512
Bank of Orient
☎ (86)(592) 6025778
Bangkok Bank
☎ (86)(592) 5118833
Citibank N.A..
☎ (86)(592) 2023333
Credit Lyonnais
☎ (86)(592) 2396168
Hong Kong & Shanghai Banking Corp.
☎ (86)(592) 2397799
ING Bank
☎ (86)(592) 5113338
Mizuho Corporate Bank
☎ (86)(592) 2021111
The Overseas Chinese Bank
☎ (86)(592) 2022653
The Standard Chartered Bank
☎ (86)(592) 5052899
United Overseas Bank
☎ (86)(592) 5081601
Xiamen International Bank
☎ (86)(592) 5310686

Guangdong
Guangzhou
ABN AMRO Bank
☎ (86)(20) 83311886
American Express International Inc.
☎ (86)(20) 83311771
Australia & New Zealand Banking Group
☎ (86)(20) 83311490
Bank of America
☎ (86)(20) 81300888
Bank of East Asia
☎ (86)(20) 87511138
Bank of Montreal
☎ (86)(20) 86695148
Bank of Nova Scotia
☎ (86)(20) 83312862

Bank of Tokyo Mitsubishi
☎ (86)(20) 83316670
Banque Indosuez
☎ (86)(20) 86693303
Banque Nationale de Paris
☎ (86)(20) 86695822
Barque Paribas
☎ (86)(20) 86663388
Citibank N.A..
☎ (36)(20) 83771333
Credit Lyonnnais
☎ (36)(20) 86677166
Deutsche Bank AG
☎ (86)(20) 83312998
Hang Seng Bank
☎ (86)(20) 87520008
Hong Kong & Shanghai Banking Corp.
☎ (86)(20) 81363888
SOCIETE GENERALE
☎ (86)(20) 83878282
Standard Chartered Bank
☎ (83)(20) 87788813
Sumitomo Mitsui Bank
☎ (86)(20) 87520168
UFJ Bank
☎ (86)(20) 86677731

Shantou
Bangkok Bank
☎ (86)(754) 8166180
Overseas Chinese Commercial Bank
☎ (86)(754) 8260005

Shenzhen
Bank of East Asia
☎ (86)(755) 82282345
Bank of Tokyo Mitsubishi
☎ (86)(755) 82223060-2
Banque Indosuez
☎ (86)(755) 82228930/1
Banque Nationale de Paris
☎ (86)(755) 82238031
BNP Paribas
☎ (86)(755) 82325687
Citibank N A
☎ (86)(755) 82232338

Credit Lyonnais
☎ (86)(755) 82461265
Dao Heng Bank
☎ (86)(755) 82289000
Dresdner Bank AG
☎ (86)(755) 825592347
First Pacific Bank
☎ (86)(755) 82286744
Fuji Bank
☎ (86)(755) 82221918
Hang Seng Bank
☎ (86)(755) 82350388
Hong Kong & Shanghai Bank Corp.
☎ (86)(755) 82238016
ING Bank
☎ (86)(755) 82299775
Krediet Bank N.V
☎ (86)(755) 82461188
Mizuho Corporate Bank
☎ (86)(755) 82221918
Nanyang Commercial Bank
☎ (86)(755) 8222890-3
Po Sang Bank
☎ (86)(755) 83358270
SOCIETE GENERALE
☎ (86)(755) 82338930
Standard Chartered Bank
☎ (86)(755) 82461688
UFJ Bank
☎ (86)(755) 82202202
United Overseas Bank
☎ (86)(755) 82322755
Union Bank of Hong Kong Limited
☎ (86)(755) 82269111
Zhuhai
Bank of East Asia
☎ (86)(756) 28875549
Standard Chartered Bank
☎ (86)(756) 83333993

Hainan
Sumitomo Mitsui Bank
☎ (86)(890) 8822701

Hong Kong
ABN AMRO Bank N.V.
☎ (852) 27003000

American Express Bank
☎ (852) 28440688
Australia & New Zealand Banking Group
☎ (852) 28437111
Baden-Wurttembergische Bank
Aktiengesellschaft
☎ (852) 28499666
Banca di Roma S.p.A.
☎ (852) 25212221
Banca Monte dei Paschi di Siena, S.p.A.
☎ (852) 22952800
Banca Nazionale del Lavoro S.p.A.
☎ (852) 21010700
Banco Bilbao Vizcaya Argentaria, S.A.
☎ (852) 25823111
Bangkok Bank
☎ (852) 28016688
Bank Brussels Lambert S.A.
☎ (852) 29731300
Bank Melli Iran
☎ (852) 25211127
Bank of America (Asia)
☎ (852) 25972888
Bank of India
☎ (852) 25240186
Bank of Montreal
☎ (852) 25224182
Bank of New York
☎ (852) 28409888
Bank of Nova Scotia
☎ (852) 25295511
Bank of Scotland
☎ (852) 25212155
Bank of Taiwan
☎ (852) 25210567
Bank of Tokyo Mitsubishi
☎ (852) 28627888
Bank One
☎ (852) 28449222
Barclays Bank Plc.
☎ (852) 29032000
Bayerische Hypo- und Vereinsbank AG
☎ (852) 25334000
Bayerische Landesbank Girozentrale
☎ (852) 29788333
BNP Paribas
☎ (852) 29098888

Canadian Imperial Bank of Commerce
☎ (852) 28416111
Chang Hwa Commercial Bank
☎ (852) 29561212
Chiba Bank Ltd.
☎ (852) 28401222
Chinatrust Commercial Bank
☎ (852) 29161888
Chugoku Bank
☎ (852) 25230312
Citibank, N.A.
☎ (852) 28688888
Commerzbank AG
☎ (852) 28429666
Commonwealth Bank of Australia
☎ (852) 28447500
Coutts Bank (Schweiz) AG
☎ (852) 25256898
Credit Agricole Indosuez
☎ (852) 28489000
Credit Lyonnais
☎ (852) 28267333
Credit Suisse
☎ (852) 28414888
Daiwa Bank
☎ (852) 25216433
Deutsche Bank AG
☎ (852) 22038888
Development Bank of Singapore
☎ (852) 28683386
Dresdner Bank AG
☎ (852) 22388888
EFG Private Bank S.A.
☎ (852) 22983000
Equitable PCI Bank, Inc.
☎ (852) 28680323
First Commercial Bank
☎ (852) 28689008
Fleet National Bank
☎ (852) 25264361
Fortis Bank
☎ (852) 28230456
Hachijuni Bank
☎ (852) 28454188
Hamburgische Landesbank Girozentrale
☎ (852) 28432688

Hong Kong & Shanghai Banking Corp.
☎ (852) 28223059
Hua Nan Commercial Bank
☎ (852) 28240288
Indian Overseas Bank
☎ (852) 25227157
ING Bank
☎ (852) 28488488
JP Morgan Chase Bank
☎ (852) 26855111
Juroku Bank
☎ (352) 25265716
KBC Bank N.V.
☎ (852) 28793388
Korea Exchange Bank
☎ (852) 25201221
May Bank
☎ (852) 25227141
Mevas Bank
☎ (852) 29232800
Mizuho Corporate Bank
☎ (852) 21033000
Natexis Banques Populaires
☎ (852) 28280999
National Australia Bank
☎ (852) 28268111
National Bank of Canada
☎ (852) 28017555
National Bank of Pakistan
☎ (852) 25217321-3
The Ogaki Kyoritsu Bank
☎ (852) 25232058
Oversea-Chinese Banking Corporation
☎ (852) 28682086
Philippine National Bank
☎ (852) 25431066
PT. Bank Negara Indonesia (Persero) Tbk.
☎ (852) 28618600
Royal Bank of Scotland plc
☎ (852) 29662800
Sanpaolo Imi S.p.A.
☎ (852) 28479800
Seoul Bank
☎ (852) 25266754-5
Shiga Bank
☎ (852) 28456548

Shinkin Central Bank
☎ (852) 25373777
Shizuoka Bank
☎ (852) 25216547
SOCIETE GENERALE
☎ (852) 28445388
Standard Chartered Bank
☎ (852) 28203333
State Bank of India
☎ (852) 25233166
State Street Bank and Trust Company
☎ (852) 28405388
Sumitomo Mitsui Bank
☎ (852) 22062000
Svenska Handelsbanken AB (publ)
☎ (852) 28682131
Taipei Bank, Co.
☎ (852) 28104828
Taiwan Business Bank
☎ (852) 29710111
Toronto-Dominion Bank
☎ (852) 28464111
UBS AG
☎ (852) 29718888
UCO Bank
☎ (852) 25249240
UFJ Bank
☎ (852) 28433888
UniCredito Italiano Societa per Azioni
☎ (852) 28207688
United Overseas Bank
☎ (852) 28425666
United World Chinese Commercial Bank
☎ (852) 28775488
Wells Fargo Bank, N.A.
☎ (852) 23159500
Westdeutsche Landesbank Girozentrale
☎ (852) 28420288
Westpac Banking Corporation
☎ (852) 28429888
Yamaguchi Bank
☎ (852) 25217194

Hubei

Wuhan
ABN AMRO Bank
☎ (86)(27) 85845286

Bank of East Asia
☎ (86)(27) 83807777
Dai-Ichi Kangyo Bank
☎ (86)(27) 83796021
Hong Kong & Shanghai Banking Corp.
☎ (86)(27) 85720942
Industrial Bank of Japan Limited
☎ (86)(27) 5821155
Mizuho Bank
☎ (86)(27) 85821155

Jiangsu
Nanjing
Belgian United Bank
☎ (86)(25) 4705780
Standard Chartered Bank
☎ (86)(25) 4701432
Mizuho Bank
☎ (86)(25) 3329379

Suzhou
Sumitomo Mitsui Bank
☎ (86)(512) 8258205

Liaoning
Dalian
Bank of East Asia
☎ (86)(411) 2652873
Bank of Tokyo - Mitsubishi
☎ (86)(411) 3606000
Hong Kong & Shanghai Banking Corp.
☎ (86)(411) 2808196
Japan Shanyin Contract Bank
☎ (86)(411) 3696747
Korea Foreign Exchange Bank
☎ (86)(411) 2816153
Kyogyou Bank
☎ (86)(411) 3692712
Mizuho Bank
☎ (86)(411) 3602543
Nanyang Commercial Bank
☎ (86)(411) 2823636
Paris Bas Bank
☎ (86)(411) 2634776
Sanwa Bank
☎ (86)(411) 3603111

Standard Chartered Bank
☎ (86)(411) 2824585
Sumitomo Mitsui Bank
☎ (86)(411) 3637611
UFJ Bank
☎ (86)(411) 3603111
Western Japan Bank
☎ (86)(411) 2645569
Yamaguchi Bank
☎ (86)(411) 2630774

Shenyang
Sumitomo Mitsui Bank
☎ (86)(24) 22528310

Macau
Bank of America
☎ (853) 568821
Bank of East Asia
☎ (853) 335511
Commercial De Macau Bank
☎ (853) 791000
Commercial Portuguese Bank
☎ (853) 786769
Citibank NA
☎ (853) 378188
Delta Asia Bank
☎ (853) 559898
Espirito Santo Do Oriente Bank
☎ (853) 785222
Finibank
☎ (853) 322678
Hong Kong & Shanghai Banking Corp.
☎ (853) 553669
National Ultramarino Bank
☎ (853) 355111
National Paris Bank
☎ (853) 562777
Overseas Trust Bank
☎ (853) 329338
Seng Heng Bank
☎ (853) 555222
Standard Chartered Bank
☎ (853) 786111
Tai Fung Bank
☎ (853) 322323

Taipei Business Bank
☎ (853) 715175
Totta & Acores Bank
☎ (853) 573299
Weng Hang Bank
☎ (853) 335678

Shandong

Qingdao
Asahi Bank
☎ (36)(532) 3871239
Bank of East Asia
☎ (86)(532) 2877700
Hong Kong & Shanghai Banking Corp.
☎ (86)(532) 3871099

Shanghai
ABN AMRO Bank
☎ (86)(21) 63299303/50499303
American Express
☎ (86)(21) 64729390
America Boston No. 1 National Bank
☎ (86)(21) 63203772
ANZ Bank
☎ (86)(21) 68410111
Asia Commercial Bank
☎ (86)(21) 63236181
Australia & New Zealand Banking Group
☎ (86)(21) 68410111
Banca Commerciale Italiana
☎ (86)(21) 58799930
Banca Di Roma
☎ (86)(21) 63559010
Banca Intesa Spa
☎ (86)(21) 63513204
Banca Monte Deipaschi Di Siena Spa
☎ (86)(21) 63740661
Banca Nazionale del Lavoro
☎ (86)(21) 62490462
Banco Espirito Santo
☎ (86)(21) 58870016
Bangkok Bank
☎ (86)(21) 63233788
Bank of America NT & SA
☎ (86)(21) 68818686
Bank of East Asia
☎ (86)(21) 63297338

Bank of Nagoya
☎ (86)(21) 62754207
Bank of New York
☎ (86)(21) 58796622
Bank of Tokyo Mitsubishi
☎ (86)(21) 68411515
Banque Indosuez
☎ (86)(21) 63292228
Banque Nationale de Paris
☎ (86)(21) 64728762
Bayerische Landesbank
☎ (86)(21) 64651071
Chase Manhattan Bank
☎ (86)(21) 68411828
Chiba Bank
☎ (86)(21) 62780482
China International Capital Corporation
☎ (86)(21) 58796226
Citibank NA.
☎ (86)(21) 58791200
Commerzbank AG
☎ (86)(21) 5836666
Commonwealth Bank of Australia
☎ (86)(21) 63553939
Credit Gricole Indosuez
☎ (86)(21) 58795559
Credit Lyonnais
☎ (86)(21) 58870770
Credit Suisse First Boston
☎ (86)(21) 68818418
Czech Savings Bank
☎ (86)(21) 53060749
Daiwa Bank
☎ (86)(21) 62755198
Deutsche Bank AG
☎ (86)(21) 68410808
DBS
☎ (86)(21) 58767698
Dresdner Bank AG
☎ (86)(21) 50495588
Fleet National Bank
☎ (86)(21) 62798090
First Union Bank
☎ (86)(21) 58795418
Fortis Bank
☎ (86)(21) 68412233

Generale Bank
☎ (86)(21) 62486600
Goldman Sachs LLC
☎ (86)(21) 62797261
Hana Bank
☎ (86)(21) 68763938
Hang Seng Bank
☎ (86)(21) 58821338
Hanil Bank
☎ (86)(21) 62190606
Hong Kong & Shanghai Banking Corp.
☎ (86)(21) 68411888
Hypo-Bank
☎ (86)(21) 62780120
ING Bank N.V.
☎ (86)(21) 68413355
Joyo Bank
☎ (86)(21) 62090258
KBC Bank N.V.
☎ (86)(21) 58791599
Kookmin Bank (Korea)
☎ (86)(21) 62701616
Korea Development Bank
☎ (86)(21) 68751234
Mees & Pierso N.V.
☎ (86)(21) 68412233
Metrobank Shanghai
☎ (86)(21) 62192020
Merrill Lynch International
☎ (86)(21) 62797032
Mizuho Bank
☎ (86)(21) 68410001
National Westminster Bank
☎ (86)(21) 62798804
Natexis Banque
☎ (86)(21) 58875775
National Bank of Canada
☎ (86)(21) 62482316
NatWest Bank
☎ (86)(21) 62798820
Overseas Chinese Banking Corp.
☎ (86)(21) 58200200
Overseas Union Bank
☎ (86)(21) 50473688
Parisbas
☎ (86)(21) 58795640

Po Sang Bank
☎ (86)(21) 5308888
Rabo Bank
☎ (86)(21) 58889888
Royal Bank of Canada
☎ (86)(21) 63202823
Sanpolo Imi Bank
☎ (86)(21) 62496517
Sanwa Bank
☎ (86)(21) 58793818
Shinwa Bank
☎ (86)(21) 62701982
SOCIETE GENERALE
☎ (86)(21) 62497500
Standard Chartered Bank
☎ (86)(21) 58871230
State Bank of India
☎ (86)(21) 63852770
Sumitomo Bank
☎ (86)(21) 68415000
TM Int'l Bank
☎ (86)(21) 58886688
UBS AG
☎ (86)(21) 62199208
UBS Warburg
☎ (86)(21) 62199208
UFJ Bank
☎ (86)(21) 58793818
Unicredito Italiano
☎ (86)(21) 68412555
Union Bank of Hong Knog
☎ (86)(21) 58793628
Union Bank of Switzerland
☎ (86)(21) 63291438
Westdeutsche Landesbank
☎ (86)(21) 68413399

Tianjin

Bank of East Asia
☎ (86)(22) 23321662
Chohung Bank
☎ (86)(22) 23394043
Francaise Lyonnaise Credit Bank
☎ (86)(22) 23393010
Hong Kong & Shanghai Banking Corp.
☎ (86)(22) 24207888

Korea Foreign Exchange Bank
☎ (86)(22) 32124244
Mizuho Corporate Bank
☎ (86)(22) 23305448
Oriental Cherry Bank
☎ (86)(22) 23303994
Sakura Bank
☎ (86)(22) 23305996
Standard Chartered Bank
☎ (86)(22) 23314049
Sumitomo Mitsui Bank
☎ (86)(22) 23303334
Tokyo Mitsubishi Bank
☎ (86)(22) 23110088
UFJ Bank
☎ (86)(22) 23304852

Zhejiang
Ningbo
Standard Chartered Bank
☎ (86)(574) 7311167

DOMESTIC BANKS

Anhui
Hefei
Agricultural Bank of China
☎ (86)(551) 2843475
Bank of China
☎ (86)(551) 2658688
Bank of Communications
☎ (86)(551) 2637006
China Everbright Bank
☎ (86)(551) 2869527
China Construction Bank
☎ (86)(551) 2624321
Industrial & Commercial Bank of China
☎ (86)(551) 2642722

Wuhu
Agricultural Bank of China
☎ (86)(553) 3839340
Bank of China
☎ (86)(553) 3837183
Bank of Communications
☎ (86)(553) 3839500
China Construction Bank
☎ (86)(553) 3833011

Industrial Si Commercial Bank of China
☎ (86)(553) 3117919

Beijing
Agricultural Bank of China
☎ (86)(10) 68358266
Bank of China
☎ (86)(10) 66596688
Bank of Communications
☎ (86)(10) 88086132
Beijing City Commercial Bank
☎ (86)(10) 96169
China Construction Bank
☎ (86)(10) 63603664
China Everbright Bank
☎ (86)(10) 68560469
China Merchants Bank
☎ (86)(10) 66426917
China Minsheng Bank
☎ (86)(10) 68579321
Fujian Industrial Bank
☎ (86)(10) 88392537
Huaxia Bank
☎ (86)(10) 66150172
Industrial Si Commercial Bank
☎ (86)(10) 66410055
ShenZhen Development Bank
☎ (86)(10) 66421666
Shanghai Pudong Development Bank
☎ (86)(10) 68343849

Chongqing
Agricultural Bank of China
☎ (86)(23) 63854986
Bank of China
☎ (86)(23) 63889284
Bank of Communications
☎ (86)(23) 63639888
China Construction Bank
☎ (86)(23) 95533
China Everbright Bank
☎ (86)(23) 63792771
China Merchants Bank
☎ (86)(23) 63786768
China Minsheng Bank
☎ (86)(23) 69098388

Chongqing Commercial Bank
☎ (86)(23) 63836229
CITIC Industrial Bank
☎ (86)(23) 63868999
Fujian Industrial Bank
☎ (86)(23) 63650571
Huaxia Bank
☎ (86)(23) 63870999
Industrial & Commercial Bank of China
☎ (86)(23) 63788179
Shanghai Pudong Development Bank
☎ (86)(23) 63639788
Shenzhen Development Bank
☎ (86)(23) 63651611

Fujian
Fuzhou
Agricultural Bank of China
☎ (86)(591) 7837360
Bank of China
☎ (86)(591) 7090999
China Bank of Communications
☎ (86)(591) 3312417
China Construction Bank
☎ (86)(591) 7821770
China Everbright Bank
☎ (86)(591) 7835833
China Merchants Bank
☎ (86)(591) 7611212
China Minsheng Bank
☎ (86)(591) 7619124
CITIC Industrial Bank
☎ (86)(591) 7538066
Fujian Industrial Bank
☎ (86)(591) 7839338
Industrial & Commercial Bank of China
☎ (86)(591) 3321521
Xiamen International Bank
☎ (86)(591) 7534581

Xiamen
Agricultural Bank of China
☎ (86)(592) 6032476
Bank of China
☎ (86)(592) 5066466
China Construction Bank
☎ (86)(592) 2036262

China Bank of Communications
☎ (86)(592) 2046956
China Everbright Bank
☎ (86)(592) 2216299
Fujian Industrial Bank
☎ (86)(592) 5312577
Industrial Si Commercial Bank of China
☎ (86)(592) 5058800
Xiemen International Bank
☎ (86)(592) 5310686

Gansu
Lanzhou
Agricultural Bank of China
☎ (86)(931) 8895236
Bank of China
☎ (86)(931) 8417597
Bank of Communications
☎ (86)(931) 8820387
China Construction Bank
☎ (86)(931) 8418277
China Merchants Bank
☎ (86)(931) 8838148
Industrial & Commercial Bank of China
☎ (86)(931) 8773655

Guangdong
Guangzhou
Agricultural Bank of China
☎ (86)(20) 83558688
Bank of China
☎ (86)(20) 83338080
Bank of Communications
☎ (86)(20) 83557079
China Construction Bank
☎ (86)(20) 81300700
China Everbright Bank
☎ (86)(20) 38730926
CITIC Industrial Bank
☎ (86)(20) 83968068
China Merchants Bank
☎ (86)(20) 95555
China Minsheng Bank
☎ (86)(20) 87556761
Fujian Industrial Bank
☎ (86)(20) 37600821

Huaxia Bank
☎ (86)(20) 87384019
Industrial & Commercial Bank of China
☎ (86)(20) 87779888
Mizuho Corporate Bank
☎ (86)(20) 83858000
Shanghai Pudong Development Bank
☎ (86)(20) 87621919
Shengzhen Development Bank
☎ (86)(20) 87601008

Foshan
Agricultural Bank of China
☎ (86)(757) 222 2038
Bank of China
☎ (86)(757) 2225876
Bank of Communication
☎ (86)(757) 3335120
China Construction Bank
☎ (86)(757) 2225303
Guangdong Development Bank
☎ (86)(757) 2232388
Industrial & Commercial Bank of China
☎ (86)(757) 3331188

Shantou
Agricultural Bank of China
☎ (86)(754) 8459314
Bank of Communications
☎ (86)(754) 8625533
Bank of China
☎ (86)(754) 8520722
China Construction Bank
☎ (86)(754) 8451769
China Minsheng Bank
☎ (86)(754) 83261828
Industrial & Commercial Bank of China
☎ (86)(754) 8263945

Shenzhen
Agricultural Bank of China
☎ (86)(755) 82232355
Bank of Communications
☎ (86)(755) 83236000
China Construction Bank
☎ (86)(755) 82246142

China Everbright Bank
☎ (86)(755) 83286432
China Minsheng Bank
☎ (86)(755) 83262888
CITIC Industrial Bank
☎ (86)(755) 82137113
Fujian Industrial Bank
☎ (86)(755) 82136871
Guangdong Development Bank
☎ (86)(755) 82380013
Huaxia Bank
☎ (86)(755) 82275342
Industrial & Commercial Bank of China
☎ (86)(755) 82271164
Shanghai Pudong Development Bank
☎ (86)(755) 82093055
Shenzhen Development Bank
☎ (86)(755) 82088888-8120

Zhanjiang
Agricultural Bank of China
☎ (86)(755) 3333501
Bank of China
☎ (86)(755) 3380237
China Construction Bank
☎ (86)(755) 3153080
Guangdong Development Bank
☎ (86)(755) 3311904
Industrial & Commercial Bank of China
☎ (86)(755) 3336421

Zhongshan
Agricultural Bank of China
☎ (86)(755) 2603168
Bank of China
☎ (86)(755) 8306800
China Bank of Communications
☎ (86)(755) 3326369
China Construction Bank
☎ (86)(755) 5598258
Industrial & Commercial Bank of China
☎ (86)(755) 8813445
Zhuhai
Agricultural Bank of China
☎ (86)(756) 3333423
Bank of China
☎ (86)(756) 8883333

Bank of Communications
☎ (86)(756) 3338822
China Everbright Bank
☎ (86)(756) 3369138
Guangdong Development Bank
☎ (86)(756) 2113148
Industrial & Commercial Bank of China
☎ (86)(756) 3328666
Shenzhen Development Bank
☎ (86)(756) 2123888-8988
Xiemen International Bank
☎ (86)(756) 3335154
Zhuhai Commercial Bank
☎ (86)(756) 8121100

Guangxi
Guilin
Agricultural Bank of China
☎ (86)(773) 2826546
Bank of China
☎ (86)(773) 2835146
Bank of Communications
☎ (86)(773) 2829898
China Construction Bank
☎ (86)(773) 2805669
Industrial & Commercial Bank of China
☎ (86)(773) 2857038

Nanning
Agricultural Bank of China
☎ (86)(771) 2806241
Bank of China
☎ (86)(771) 5852717
Bank of Communications
☎ (86)(771) 2835133
China Construction Bank
☎ (86)(771) 5311691
China Everbright Bank
☎ (86)(771) 5840018
Industrial & Commercial Bank of China
☎ (86)(771) 5316617

Guizhou
Guiyang
Agricultural Bank of China
☎ (86)(851) 5966508

Bank of China
☎ (86)(851) 5815261
Bank of Communications
☎ (86)(851) 5861460
China Construction Bank
☎ (86)(851) 65976550
Industrial & Commercial Bank of China
☎ (86)(851) 5817092

Hainan
Haikou
Agricultural Bank of China
☎ (86)(898) 66772087
Bank of China
☎ (86)(898) 6778011
Bank of Communication
☎ (86)(898) 8532661
China Construction Bank
☎ (86)(898) 6720461
China Everbright Bank
☎ (86)(898) 68520710
Industrial & Commercial Bank of China
☎ (86)(898) 66772087
Shenzhen Development Bank
☎ (86)(898) 68511155

Hebei
Baoding
Agricultural Bank of China
☎ (86)(312) 3036123
Bank of China
☎ (86)(312) 3098601
China Construction Bank
☎ (86)(312) 3031022
Industrial & Commercial Bank of China
☎ (86)(312) 3120147

Shijiazhuang
Agricultural Bank of China
☎ (86)(311) 77026132
Bank of China
☎ (86)(311) 7036017
China Bank of Communications
☎ (86)(311) 7026358
China Construction Bank
☎ (86)(311) 7888866

China Everbright Bank
☎ (86)(311) 6672649
China Minsheng Banking Corp.
☎ (36)(311) 6033332
Huaxia Bank
☎ (36)(311) 8614572

Tangshan
Agricultural Bank of China
☎ (86)(315) 2321819
Bank of China
☎ (86)(315) 2335641
Bank of Communications
☎ (86)(315) 2826188
China Construction Bank
☎ (86)(315) 2817324
Industrial & Commercial Bank of China
☎ (86)(315) 2839888

Heilongjiang
Harbin
Agricultural Bank of China
☎ (86)(451) 6208846
Bank of China
☎ (86)(451) 3633518
Bank of Communications
☎ (86)(451) 2644828
China Everbright Bank
☎ (86)(451) 3618665
Harbin Commercial Bank
☎ (86)(451) 4612814
Industrial & Commercial Bank of China
☎ (86)(451) 4838024

Henan
Zhengzhou
Agricultural Bank of China
☎ (86)(371) 5952553
Bank of China
☎ (86)(371) 5728288
Industrial & Commercial Bank of China
☎ (86)(371) 5832124
Shanghai Pudong Development Bank
☎ (86)(371) 5743451
China Construction Bank
☎ (86)(371) 3943451

Bank of Communication
☎ (86)(371) 6965097

Luoyang
Industrial & Commercial Bank of China
☎ (86)(379) 3948361
Bank of Communication
☎ (86)(379) 3948361

Hubei
Wuhan
CITIC Industrial Bank
☎ (86)(27) 85496209
Huaxia Bank
☎ (86)(27) 85491630
China Merchants Bank
☎ (86)(27) 85495555
Bank of China
☎ (86)(27) 82813723
Agricultural Bank of China
☎ (86)(27) 87326666-2202
Bank of Communications
☎ (86)(27) 85487110
China Mingsheng Bank
☎ (86)(27) 82808355
China Everbright Bank
☎ (86)(27) 82210198

Hunan
Changsha
Agricultural Bank of China
☎ (86)(731) 4300265
Bank of China
☎ (86)(731) 4119033
Bank of Communications
☎ (86)(731) 4447400
China Construction Bank
☎ (86)(731) 4447044
China Merchants Bank
☎ (86)(731) 4302957
Industrial & Commercial Bank of China
☎ (86)(731) 4443049
Fujian Industrial Bank
☎ (86)(731) 4424945
China Everbright Bank
☎ (86)(731) 5555857

Zhuzhou
China Merchants Bank
☎ (86)(731) 4302957
China Everbright Bank
☎ (86)(731) 6762920

Inner Mongolia
Hohhot
China Construction Bank
☎ (86)(471) 6961866
Agricultural Bank of China
☎ (86)(471) 6903388
Bank of China
☎ (86)(471) 4690020
Industrial & Commercial Bank of China
☎ (86)(471) 6929472

Jiangsu
Changzhou
Industrial & Commercial Bank of China
☎ (86)(519) 8102627
Bank of Communications
☎ (86)(519) 66072196

Nanjing
Agricultural Bank of China
☎ (86)(25) 4205843
Bank of China
☎ (86)(25) 4207888
Bank of Communications
☎ (86)(25) 6639888
China Construction Bank
☎ (86)(25) 4200188
China Everbright Bank
☎ (86)(25) 3312086
CITIC Industrial Bank
☎ (86)(25) 3799181
Guangdong Development Bank
☎ (86)(25) 3305888
Huaxia Bank
☎ (86)(25) 4700088
Industrial & Commercial Bank of China
☎ (86)(25) 4705260
Fujian Industrial Bank
☎ (86)(25) 3193803
China Merchants bank
☎ (86)(25) 4780200

Shanghai Pudong Development Bank
☎ (86)(25) 459117
Shenzhen Development Bank
☎ (86)(25) 3328888
China Minsheng Bank
☎ (86)(25) 3279000

Suzhou

**Agricultural Bank of China,
Suzhou Branch**
21-23 Shishan Road, Suzhou New District
Suzhou, Jiangsu, China
☎ (86)(512) 67775580, 68242294
🖨 (86)(512) 67775800, 68240501

Bank of Communications
☎ (86)(512) 5239666
China Construction Bank
☎ (86)(512) 69623792
Huaxia Bank
☎ (86)(512) 67231727
China Merchants Bank
☎ (86)(512) 68651772
China Everbright bank
☎ (86)(512) 68668766
CITIC Industrial Bank
☎ (86)(512) 67201302
Shanghai Pudong Development Bank
☎ (86)(512) 67208070

Wuxi
Agricultural Bank of China
☎ (86)(510) 2753825
Bank of China
☎ (86)(510) 5803302
Bank of Communications
☎ (86)(510) 2708125
CITIC Industrial Bank
☎ (86)(510) 2766860
China Construction Bank
☎ (86)(510) 2702914
Huaxia Bank
☎ (86)(510) 2758388
Industrial & Commercial Bank of China
☎ (86)(510) 2709657

China Merchants Bank
☎ (86)(510) 2750777

Kunshan
Industrial & Commercial Bank of China
☎ (36)(520) 7611460

Jiangxi
Jiujiang
Agricultural Bank of China
☎ (86)(792) 8220274
Bank of China
☎ (83)(792) 8582342
China Bank of Communications
☎ (86)(792) 8231117
China Construction Bank
☎ (86)(792) 8226808
Industrial & Commercial Bank of China
☎ (86)(792) 8223104

Nanchang
Agricultural Bank of China
☎ (86)(791) 6693775
Bank of China
☎ (86)(791) 6471513
China Bank of Communications
☎ (86)(791) 6281014
China Construction Bank
☎ (86)(791) 6848165
Industrial & Commercial Bank of China
☎ (86)(791) 6695116

Jilin
Changchun
Agricultural Bank of China
☎ (86)(431) 2700686
Bank of China
☎ (86)(431) 5668847
Bank of Communications
☎ (86)(431) 8928485
China Construction Bank
☎ (86)(431) 8983529
China Everbright Bank
☎ (86)(431) 8400099
Industrial & Commercial Bank of China
☎ (86)(431) 8965669

Jilin
Agricultural Bank of China
☎ (86)(432) 4844693
Bank of China
☎ (86)(432) 4843717
China Bank of Communications
☎ (86)(432) 2454151
China Construction Bank
☎ (86)(432) 4808905
Industrial & Commercial Bank of China
☎ (86)(432) 2554016

Liaoning
Dalian
Agricultural Bank of China
☎ (86)(411) 2510800
Bank of China
☎ (86)(411) 2803300
China Bank of Communications
☎ (86)(411) 2639911
China Construction Bank
☎ (86)(411) 2818818
China Everbright Bank
☎ (86)(411) 2650538
China Merchants Bank
☎ (86)(411) 2715811
CITIC Industrial Bank
☎ (86)(411) 2821868
China Minsheng Banking
☎ (86)(411) 2580088
Huaxia Bank
☎ (86)(411) 2643158
Shenzhen Development Bank
☎ (86)(411) 2656666
Shanghai Pudong Development Bank
☎ (86)(411) 2553331

Shenyang
Agricultural Bank of China
☎ (86)(24) 22727847
China Merchants Bank
☎ (86)(24) 22895555
China Construction Bank
☎ (86)(24) 23216666
CITIC Industrial Bank
☎ (86)(24) 22842205

Industrial & Commercial Bank of China
☎ (86)(24) 23874286
Bank of China
☎ (86)(24) 2803300
Bank of Communications
☎ (86)(24) 22719497
Huaxia Bank
☎ (86)(24) 22879759
China Everbright Bank
☎ (86)(24) 23283723

Ningxia
Yinchuan
Agricultural Bank of China
☎ (86)(951) 6027614
Bank of China
☎ (86)(951) 5044671
China Construction Bank
☎ (86)(951) 4104666
Yinchuan Commercial Bank
☎ (86)(951) 6025431

Qinghai
Xining
Agricultural Bank of China
☎ (86)(971) 6145160
Bank of China
☎ (86)(971) 8180192
China Construction Bank
☎ (86)(971) 82681100
Industrial & Commercial Bank of China
☎ (86)(971) 6100814

Shaanxi
Xi'an
Agricultural Bank of China
☎ (86)(29) 7802646
Bank of Communications
☎ (86)(29) 7259535
Industrial & Commercial Bank of China
☎ (86)(29) 7272371
China Minsheng Bank
☎ (86)(29) 5240694
Shanghai Pudong Development Bank
☎ (86)(29) 7257008
China Merchants Bank
☎ (86)(29) 7234588

China Construction bank
☎ (86)(29) 7617515
Bank of China
☎ (86)(29) 7264646
China Everbright Bank
☎ (86)(29) 7254770

Shandong
Jinan
Agricultural Bank of China
☎ (86)(531) 6057113
Bank of China
☎ (86)(531) 6995099
Bank of Communications
☎ (86)(531) 7930978
China Construction Bank
☎ (86)(531) 6912621
Huaxia Bank
☎ (86)(531) 2024940
China Merchants Bank
☎ (86)(531) 6116666
Industrial & Commercial Bank of China
☎ (86)(531) 7925688
China Minsheng Bank
☎ (86)(531) 6121680
Shenzhen Development Bank
☎ (86)(531) 2661818
Shanghai Pudong Development Bank
☎ (86)(531) 6556866

Qingdao
Agricultural Bank of China
☎ (86)(532) 5826767
Bank of China
☎ (86)(532) 5818851
Bank of Communications
☎ (86)(532) 2967888
China Construction Bank
☎ (86)(532) 2651888
Industrial & Commercial Bank of China
☎ (86)(532) 5815513
Shenzhen Development Bank
☎ (86)(532) 83892895
China Merchants Bank
☎ (86)(532) 3899327
Huaxia Bank
☎ (86)(532) 5016367

CIT C Industrial Bank
☎ (36)(532) 5022889
China Everbright Bank
☎ (86)(532) 3893856

Yantai
Agricultural Bank of China
☎ (86)(535) 6241768
Bank of China
☎ (86)(535) 6238888
Bank of Communications
☎ (86)(535) 6677088
China Construction Bank
☎ (86)(535) 6603999
CITIC Industrial Bank
☎ (86)(535) 6611030
Industrial & Commercial Bank of China
☎ (86)(535) 6268888
Huaxia bank
☎ (86)(535) 6666220
China Everbright Bank
☎ (86)(535) 6656959

Weihai
Agricultural Bank of China
☎ (86)(631) 5323030
Bank of China
☎ (86)(631) 5326988
Bank of Communications
☎ (86)(631) 5226210
China Construction Bank
☎ (86)(631) 5219842
China Everbright Bank
☎ (86)(631) 5239645
CITIC Industrial Bank
☎ (86)(631) 5314680
Industria & Commercial Bank of China
☎ (86)(631) 5680800

Shanghai
Agricultural Bank of China
☎ (86)(21) 53961773
Bank of China
☎ (86)(21) 63291979
Bank of Shanghai
☎ (86)(21) 63370888

China Bank of Communications
☎ (86)(21) 63111000
China Construction Bank
☎ (86)(21) 63181818
China Merchants Bank
☎ (86)(21) 58791428
China Minsheng Bank
☎ (86)(21) 53857700
China Everbright Bank
☎ (86)(21) 63606551
CITIC Industrial Bank
☎ (86)(21) 63236323
Guangdong Development Bank
☎ (86)(21) 63022233
Shanghai Pudong Development Bank
☎ (86)(21) 63291188
Huaxia Bank
☎ (86)(21) 62257087
Industrial & Commercial Bank of China
☎ (86)(21) 58895588
Shenzhen Development Bank
☎ (86)(21) 58877777
Fujian Industrial Bank
☎ (86)(21) 62677771

Shanxi
Taiyuan
Agricultural Bank of China
☎ (86)(351) 4956830
Bank of China
☎ (86)(351) 4048556
China Construction Bank
☎ (86)(351) 6040226
Bank of Communications
☎ (86)(351) 4070094
Huaxia Bank
☎ (86)(351) 4080818
Industrial & Commercial Bank of China
☎ (86)(351) 3532002
China Minsheng Bank
☎ (86)(351) 4137483
China Everbright Bank
☎ (86)(351) 3531310

Sichuan
Chengdu

Agricultural Bank of China
☎ (86)(28) 6760700
Bank of China
☎ (86)(28) 6403252
Bank of Communications
☎ (86)(28) 6525666
Shanghai Pudong Development Bank
☎ (86)(28) 4396671
China Merchants Bank
☎ (86)(28) 6746688
CITIC Industrial Bank
☎ (86)(28) 5258888
China Everbright Bank
☎ (86)(28) 6654359
Industrial & Commercial Bank of China
☎ (86)(28) 6744876
Shenzhen Development Bank
☎ (86)(28) 86520989

Tianjin
Agricultural Bank of China
☎ (86)(22) 23309493
Bank of China
☎ (86)(22) 27102301
China Construction Bank
☎ (86)(22) 23300130
Industrial & Commercial Bank of China
☎ (86)(22) 24125588
Merchants Bank
☎ (86)(22) 83280810
Bank of Communications
☎ (86)(22) 23302004
CITIC Industrial Bank
☎ (86)(22) 23148855
Shenzhen Development Bank
☎ (86)(22) 28010300
Shanghai Pudong Development Bank
☎ (86)(22) 28208023
China Everbright Bank
☎ (86)(22) 23300180

Tibet
Lhasa
Agricultural Bank of China
☎ (86)(891) 6333750
Bank of China
☎ (86)(891) 6835078

China Construction Bank
☎ (86)(891) 6832565

Xinjiang
Urumqi
Bank of China
☎ (86)(991) 2615202
Bank of Communications
☎ (86)(991) 2831668
Agricultural Bank of China
☎ (86)(991) 2815295
Industrial & Commercial Bank of China
☎ (86)(991) 2651100
China Construction Bank
☎ (86)(991) 2848666
China Merchants Bank
☎ (86)(991) 95555

Yunnan
Kunming
Agricultural Bank of China
☎ (86)(871) 3179758
Bank of China
☎ (86)(871) 3175556
China Construction Bank
☎ (86)(871) 3120712
China Everbright Bank
☎ (86)(871) 3111068
Bank of Communication
☎ (86)(871) 3105250
Huaxia Bank
☎ (86)(871) 3153258
Industrial & Commercial Bank of China
☎ (86)(871) 95588
Guangdong Development Bank
☎ (86)(871) 4108955
China Merchants Bank
☎ (86)(871) 3182142
Shanghai Pudong Development Bank
☎ (86)(871) 5391774

Zhejiang
Hangzhou
Agricultural Bank of China
☎ (86)(571) 7226175
Bank of Communications
☎ (86)(571) 7082330

China Mingsheng Bank
☎ (86)(571) 87922222
Shenzhen Development Bank
☎ (86)(571) 87218321
CITIC Industrial Park
☎ (86)(571) 87032888
Huaxia Bank
☎ (86)(571) 87220709
China Merchants Bank
☎ (86)(571) 85789099
Bank of China
☎ (86)(571) 4207888
China Construction Bank
☎ (86)(571) 5313032
Industrial & Commercial Bank of China
☎ (86)(571) 87227000

Ningbo
Agricultural Bank of China
☎ (86)(574) 87315179
Bank of China
☎ (86)(574) 7196666
China Construction Bank
☎ (86)(574) 7313888
Guangdong Development Bank
☎ (86)(574) 7289888
Industrial & Commercial Bank of China
☎ (86)(574) 87361890
Bank of Communications
☎ (86)(574) 7285688
Shenzhen Development Bank
☎ (86)(574) 87720124
China Merchants Bank
☎ (86)(574) 87363181
Shanghi Pudong Development Bank
☎ (86)(574) 87275858
Fujian Industrial Bank
☎ (86)(574) 87730616
China Everbright Bank
☎ (86)(574) 87322903

Wenzhou
Agricultural Bank of China
☎ (86)(577) 88245678
Bank of China
☎ (86)(577) 8229321
Bank of Communications

☎ (86)(577) 8252225
China Construction Bank
☎ (86)(577) 8223557
China Merchants Bank
☎ (86)(577) 8288372
Guangdong Development Bank
☎ (86)(577) 8229896
Huaxia Bank
☎ (86)(577) 88398730
Industrial & Commercial Bank of China
☎ (86)(577) 88825941
Shenzhen Development Bank
☎ (86)(577) 8810862
China Merchants Bank
☎ (86)(577) 8288372

Business Schools

Beijing
Peking University Guanghua Management
School
☎ (86)(10) 62751665
🖷 (86)(10) 62757754
People's University of China Business School
☎ (86)(10) 62511342
🖷 (86)(10) 62511439
Tsinghua University School of Economics &
Management
☎ (86)(10) 62785535
🖷 (86) (10) 62785876
Northern Jiaotong University College of
Economics & Management
☎ (86)(10) 63240359
🖷 (86) (10) 63240359
Beijing Institute of Technology Management
School
☎ (86)(10) 68912481
🖷 (86) (10) 68912483
Beijing University of Aviation & Aerospace
Management School
☎ (86)(10) 82317836
🖷 (86) (10) 82828037
Beijing University of Posts & Telecommunication Management School
☎ (86)(10) 62282069
🖷 (86) (10) 62282069

Beijing University of Science & Technology
Management School
☎(86)(10) 62332745
🖶 (86) (10) 62327283
University of International Business &
Economics Graduate School
☎(86)(10) 64492151
🖶 (86)(10) 64493890
China Mines University Department of
Economics & Management
☎ (86)(10) 62331376
🖶 (86)(10) 62311667

Tianjin
Nankai University MBA Education Center
☎ (86)(22) 23508269
🖶 (86)(22) 23501039
Tianjin University MBA Education Center
☎ (86)(22) 27404047
🖶 (86)(22) 27401164
Tianjin College of Finance & Economics MBA
Education Center
☎ (86)(22) 28171151
🖶 (86)(22) 28171151
Hebei Technological University Management
School
☎ (86)(22) 26564102
🖶 (86)(22) 26564102

Shanghai
China Europe International Business School
☎ (86)(21) 28905890
🖶 (86)(21) 28905678
Fudan University Management School
☎ (86)(21) 65643935
🖶 (86)(21) 65646065
Shanghai Jiaotong University Management
School
☎ (86)(21) 62933213
🖶 (86)(21) 62825427
Tongji University College of Economics &
Management
☎ (86)(21) 65983280
🖶 (86)(21) 65983280
Shanghai University of Finance & Economics
Hengtong Business School
☎ (86)(21) 65366000-2260

🖶 (86)(21) 65421748
Donghua University Management School
☎ (86)(21) 62373535
🖶 (86)(21) 62708697
East China University of Sci & Tech
School of Economics & Management
☎ (86)(21) 64252634
🖶 (86)(21) 64251324
Shanghai Marine College Management
School
☎ (86)(21) 58855200-2405
🖶 (86)(21) 58854751

Heilongjiang
Harbin Institute of Technology Management
School
☎ (86)(451) 6414016
🖶 (86)(451) 6414024
Harbin Engineering University Management
School
☎ (86)(451) 2519205
🖶 (86)(451) 2533090

Jilin
Jilin University Business School
☎ (86)(431) 5166123
🖶 (86)(431) 5166257

Liaoning
Dalian Institute of Technology Management
School
☎ (86)(411) 4707704
🖶 (86)(411) 4708948
Liaoning University MBA Education Center
☎ (86)(24) 86864314
🖶 (86)(24) 86862411
Northeastern University College of Business
Administration
☎ (86)(24) 23893000-7685
🖶 (86)(24) 23891289

Jiangsu
Nanjing University International Business
School
☎ (86)(25) 3593515
🖶 (86)(25) 3592216

Southeast University College of Business Administration
☎ (86)(25) 3793776
🖳 (86)(25) 7712719
Nanjing Technological University College of Business Administration
☎ (86)(25) 4315665
🖳 (86)(25) 4315620
China Mines University College of Business Administration
☎ (86)(516) 3885209
🖳 (86)(516) 3884917

Anhui
University of Science & Technology of China MBA Education Center
☎ (86)(551) 3492258
🖳 (86)(551) 3492252

Zhejiang
Zhejiang University MBA Education Center
☎ (86)(571) 87951218
🖳 (86)(571) 87951358

Jiangxi
Jiangxi University of Finance & Economics Graduate School
☎ (86)(791) 3816085
🖳 (86)(791) 3816441

Fujian
Xiamen University College of Business Administration
☎ (86)(592) 2182873
🖳 (86)(592) 2182869

Hubei
Wuhan University Management School
☎ (86)(27) 87682891
🖳 (86)(27) 87870791
Huazhong University of Sci & Tech College of Business Administration
☎ (86)(27) 87542254
🖳 (86)(27) 87542154
Central South University of Finance & Economics MBA Education Center
☎ (86)(27) 88047866

Wuhan Technological University College of Business Administration
☎ (86)(27) 87859059
🖳 (86)(27) 87859011

Hunan
Hunan University College of Business Administration
☎ (86)(731) 8822216
🖳 (86)(731) 8823670
Central South University College of Business Administration
☎ (86)(731) 8830317
🖳 (86)(731) 8827784

Guangdong
Jinan University MBA Education Center
☎ (86)(20) 85220050
South China University of Technology College of Business Administration
☎ (86)(20) 87114693
🖳 (86)(20) 87114693
Zhongshan University Lingnan College
☎ (86)(20) 84039361
🖳 (86)(20) 84111918

Chongqing
Chongqing University College of Business Administration
☎ (86)(23) 65106388
🖳 (86)(23) 65105836

Sichuan
Southwest University of Finance & Economics Graduate School
☎ (86)(28) 73010707-2244
🖳 (86)(28) 7301887
University of Electronic Science & Technology Management School
☎ (86)(28) 3202681
🖳 (86)(28) 3334131
Southwest Jiaotong University College of Economics & Management
☎ (86)(28) 7600828
🖳 (86)(28) 7600826
Sichuan University Management School
☎ (86)(28) 5411434

Shaanxi

Xi'an Jiaotong University Management School
☎ (86)(29) 2668840
🖷 (86)(29) 2668840
Northwestern University MBA Education Center
☎ (86)(29) 8303502
🖷 (86)(29) 8303374
Northwestern Polytechnic University Management School
☎ (86)(29) 8493557
🖷 (86)(29) 5250199
Xi'an Polytechnic University College of Business Administration
☎ (86)(29) 3239700-2618
🖷 (86)(29) 3235545

Gansu

Lanzhou University School of Economics & Management
☎ (86)(931) 8912450
🖷 (86)(931) 8912622

Shanxi

Shanxi University of Finance & Economics MBA Education Centers
☎ (86)(351) 7231452
🖷 (86)(351) 7231452

Inner Mongolia

Inner Mongolia University MBA Education Center
☎ (86)(471) 4990702
🖷 (86)(471) 4969071

Yunnan

Yunnan University College of Business Administration
☎ (86)(871) 5034545
🖷 (86)(871) 5169337

Guangxi

Guangxi University Business School
☎ (86)(771) 3236994
🖷 (86)(771) 3237110

Henan

Zhengzhou University Graduate School
☎ (86)(371) 7763030-8001

Guizhou

Guizhou Technological University College of Economics & Management
☎ (86)(851) 5952217
🖷 (86)(991) 5952707

Xinjiang

Xinjiang College of Finance & Economics MBA Education Center
☎ (86)(991) 3716811-2327
🖷 (86)(991) 3716811-2327

Chinese Airlines Offices Abroad

Air China

Bangkok
☎ (66)(2) 6310728
☎ Airport (66)(2) 5354661
Berlin
☎ (49)(30) 2360810
Copenhagen
☎ (45)(3) 3149222
☎ Airport (45)(3) 2528816
Daegu
☎ (82)(53) 2536668
Frankfurt
☎ (49)(69) 233038
Fukuoka
☎ (81)(92) 2825611
Hiroshima
☎ (81)(82) 5448888
Hong Kong
☎ (852) 28610322
Istanbul
☎ (90)(212) 2327111/2
☎ Airport (90)(212) 5746040
Jakarta
☎ (62)(21) 5206467
☎ Airport (62)(21) 5506827

Karachi
☎ (92)(21) 5656881
Kuwait
☎ (96)(5) 2438568
London
☎ (44)(20) 76300919
Los Angeles
☎ (1)(310) 3350088
Melbourne
☎ (61)(3) 96421555
☎ Airport (61)(3) 96420235
Milan
☎ (39)(02) 8051666
Moscow
☎ (7)(95) 2925440
Nagoya
☎ (81)(52) 2201122
New York
☎ (1)(800) 9828802
Osaka
☎ (81)(6) 69461702
Paris
☎ (33)(1) 42666688
Pusan
☎ (82)(51) 4636888
Rome
☎ (39)(06) 8552249
San Francisco
☎ (1)(800) 9861985
Sendai
☎ (81)(22) 2212025
Seoul
☎ (82)(2) 7746686
Singapore
☎ (65) 62252177
☎ Airport (65) 65428292
Stockholm
☎ (46)(8) 216146
Sydney
☎ (61)(2) 92327277
Tokyo
☎ (81)(3) 52510711
☎ Airport (81)(476) 343941
Toronto
☎ (1)(416) 5818833
Vancouver
☎ (1)(604) 6850921

Vienna
☎ (43)(1) 5868008
Zurich
☎ (41)(1) 2136080

China Eastern Airlines

Bangkok
☎ (66)(2) 6366978
Brussels
☎ (32)(2) 5028270
Chicago
☎ (1)(312) 3378008
Fukuoka
☎ (81)(92) 4777818
Hong Kong
☎ (852) 28610288
Los Angeles
☎ (1)(626) 5831500
Madrid
☎ (34)(1) 3192056
Munich
☎ (49)(89) 2103860
Nagasaki
☎ (81)(958) 281510
Nagoya
☎ (81)(52) 2040668
Okayama
☎ (81)(86) 2335288
Osaka
☎ (81)(6) 4485161
Paris
☎ (33)(1) 44860300
San Francisco
☎ (1)(415) 9825515
Seattle
☎ (1)(206) 3435582
Seoul
☎ (82)(2) 5180330
Singapore
☎ (65) 63232632
Sydney
☎ (61)(2) 92901148
Tokyo
☎ (81)(3) 35061166

China Northern Airlines

Pyongyang

☎ (8)(502) 817351/659

Seoul

☎ (82)(2) 7759070

China Northwest Airlines

Fukuoka

☎ (81)(92) 4718831

Nagoya

☎ (81)(52) 5863121

Nigiita

☎ (81)(25) 2485701

Hiroshima

☎ (82)(82) 2456623

Hong Kong

☎ (852) 28277233

Seoul

☎ (82)(2) 7766699

China Southern Airlines

Amsterdam

☎ (31)(20) 4123120

Bangkok

☎ (66)(2) 2665688

Fukuoka

☎ (81)(92) 4818181

Hanoi

☎ (84)(4) 7716616

Hochiminh

☎ (84)(8) 8235588

Hong Kong

☎ (852) 28661331

Jakarta

☎ (62)(21) 5762088

Kuala Lumpur

☎ (60)(3) 2444432

Los Angeles

☎ (1)(323) 6538088

Manila

☎ (63)(2) 5513333

Melbourne

☎ (61)(3) 96709991

Osaka

☎ (81)(6) 64486655

Penang

☎ (60)(4) 2278878

Phnom Penh

☎ (855) 23424082

Seoul

☎ (82)(2) 34551600

Singapore

☎ (65) 62233233

☎ Airport (65) 65420338

Surabaya

☎ (62)(31) 5326319

Sydney

☎ (61)(2) 92311988

China Southwest Airlines

Kathmandu

☎ (411)(302) 411302

Singapore

☎ (65) 63339956

Bangkok

☎ (66)(2) 6621940

Hong Kong

☎ (852) 28610288

Nagoya

☎ (81)(52) 2202058

Xinjiang Airlines

Alma-Ata

☎ (7)(3272) 509485

Islamabad

☎ (9)(251)-851816

Moscow

☎ (7)(95) 9717916

Tashkent

☎ (7)(312) 210825

Yunnan Airlines

Bangkok

☎ (66)(2) 2163888

Seoul

☎ (82)(2) 7778666

Singapore

☎ (65) 63240188

Vientiane

☎ (856)(21) 252888

Hainan Airlines
Seoul
☎ (82)(2) 34449912

Chinese Domestic Airlines Offices

Anhui
Hefei HFE
Airport: Luogang Airport
☎ (86)(551) 3401197
China Eastern Airlines
☎ (86)(551) 2822357
China Southern Airlines
☎ (86)(551) 2838818
Hainan Air
☎ (86)(551) 4679999

Beijing
Beijing PEK
Airport: Capital International Airport
Air China
☎ (86)(10) 66016667 *International*
☎ (86)(10) 66013366 *Domestic*
China Eastern Airlines
☎ (86)(10) 64681166
China Southern Airlines
☎ (86)(10) 65072203
China Southwest Airlines
☎ (86)(10) 66017579
China Northwest Airlines
☎ (86)(10) 66017755
Shenzhen Air
☎ (86)(10) 66017755-2155
Shanghai Airlines
☎ (86)(10) 66017755-2147
Yunnan Airlines
☎ (86)(10) 84017871
China United Airline
☎ (86)(10) 65053300-32
Hainan Air
☎ (86)(10) 68526588

Chongqing
Chongqing CKG
Airport: Jiangbei Airport

☎ (86)(23) 67810868
China Southern Airlines
☎ (86)(23) 63510115
China Southwest Airlines
☎ (86)(23) 67878538
Hainan Air
☎ (86)(23) 63873080
Shanghai Airlines
☎ (86)(23) 63628000

Fujian
Fuzhou FOC
Airport: Changle Int'l Airport
Air China
☎ (86)(591) 7604862
Hainan Air
☎ (86)(591) 7570005
China United Air
☎ (86)(591) 7817028
Shanghai Airlines
☎ (86)(591) 7503166

Xiamen
Airport: Gaoqi Airport
China Easern Airlines
☎ (86)(592) 2028936
China Southern Airlines
☎ (86)(592) 5117777
China Southwest Airlines
☎ (86)(592) 5086515
Hainan Air
☎ (86)(592) 5151386
Shanghai Airlines
☎ (86)(592) 2210600

Gansu
Lanzhou ZGC
Airport: Zhongchuan Airport
China Northwest Airlines
☎ (86)(931) 8821964
Hainan Air
☎ (86)(931) 8620778

Guangdong
Guangzhou CAN
Airport: Baiyun International Airport

China South Airline
☎ (86)(20) 86682000
Air China
☎ (86)(20) 83637527
China Eastern Airlines
☎ (86)(20) 81350075
China Southwest Airlines
☎ (86)(20) 86620156
China Northwest Airlines
☎ (86)(20) 83321688
China United Air
☎ (86)(20) 83808287
Yunnan Air
☎ (86)(20) 86636328
Shanghai Airlines
☎ (86)(20) 87717888
Hainan Air
☎ (86)(20) 83270939

Shenzhen SZX
Airport: Huangtian Airport
China Southern Airlines
☎ (86)(755) 82333188 *Domestic*
☎ (86)(755) 26666447 *International*
Air China
☎ (86)(755) 83241441
China Eastern Airlines
☎ (86)(755) 83227740
China Southwest Airlines
☎ (86)(755) 83222279
Shenzhen Air
☎ (86)(755) 83668777
China Northwest Airlines
☎ (86)(755) 82243391
Hainan Air
☎ (86)(755) 83660561
China United Air
☎ (86)(755) 82238291
Shanghai Airlines
☎ (86)(755) 83243549
Yunnan Air
☎ (86)(755) 83690789

Shantou SWA
Airport: Shantou Chaoshan Airport
China Southern Airlines
☎ (86)(768) 2271929

Zhuhai
China Southern Airlines
☎ (86)(756) 3342000
China Northwest Airlines
☎ (86)(756) 7771871
China United Air
☎ (86)(756) 3352272

Guangxi
Nanning NNG
Airport: Wuxu Airport
☎ (86)(771) 64563604 *Inquiry*
☎ (86)(771) 66017755 *Ticket Office*
China Southern Airlines
☎ (86)(751) 5888592
Hainan Air
☎ (86)(751) 5880923

Guilin
Shanghai Airlines
☎ (86)(773) 2827046
China Southern Airlines
☎ (86)(773) 3808311
Hainan Air
☎ (86)(773) 3856677
China United Air
☎ (86)(773) 3832152

Guizhou
Guiyang KWE
Airport: Leizhuang Airport
China Southern Airlines
☎ (86)(451) 6819264
China Southwest Airlines
☎ (86)(451) 5958555
Hainan Air
☎ (86)(451) 2637953

Hainan
Haikou HAK
Airport: Meilan Airport
☎ (86)(898) 6780740
China Southern Airlines
☎ (86)(898) 66700792
China Southwest Airlines
☎ (86)(898) 6777854

China Northwest Airlines
☎ (86)(898) 6718438
Shanghai Airlines
☎ (86)(898) 66791927
Hainan Air
☎ (86)(898) 89999
Shenzhen Air
☎ (36)(898) 6714321

Sanya SYX
Airport: Sanya Phoenix Int'l Airport
☎ (86)(898) 88289128

Hebei
Shijiazhuang SJW
Airport: Zhengding Airport
☎ (86)(311) 5054084

Heilongjiang
Harbin HRB
Airport: Taiping Int'l Airport
Air China
☎ (86)(451) 2336161
Hainan Air
☎ (86)(451) 2230238
Shanghai Airlines
☎ (86)(451) 2637953

Henan
Zhengzhou CGO
Airport: Zhengzhou Xinzheng Airport
China Southern Airlines
☎ (86)(371) 5752030
Hainan Air
☎ (86)(371) 593439

Hubei
Wuhan WUH
Airport: Tianhe Airport
China Southern Airlines
☎ (86)(27) 83622000
China Southwest Airlines
☎ (86)(27) 83619392
Hainan Air
☎ (86)(27) 83617201

Shenzhen Air
☎ (86)(27) 83790455
Shanghai Airlines
☎ (86)(27) 82241008

Hunan
Changsha HHA
Airport:Huanghua Airport
China Southern Airlines
☎ (86)(731) 2241374
China Southwest Airlines
☎ (86)(731) 2253356
China Northwest Airlines
☎ (86)(731) 4465765
Hainan Air
☎ (86)(731) 5360640

Inner Mongolia
Hohbot
Air China
☎ (86)(471) 6964103
Hainan Air
☎ (86)(471) 6931612

Jilin
Changchun CGQ
Airport: Dafangshen Airport

Jiangsu
Nanjing NKG
Airport: Lukou Int'l Airport
Air China
☎ (86)(25) 4718600
China Eastern Airlines
☎ (86)(25) 9869986
China Southern Airlines
☎ (86)(25) 4492727
China Northwest Airlines
☎ (86)(25) 4528188
Hainan Air
☎ (86)(25) 4602888
Shenzhen Air
☎ (86)(25) 4490524
China United Airlines
☎ (86)(25) 3368586

Shanghai Airlines
☎ (86)(25) 4499757

Jiangxi
Nanchang KHN
Airport: Xiangtang Airport
Domestic: (86)(791) 6278223
China Eastern Airlines
☎ (86)(791) 8514195
China Southern Airlines
☎ (86)(791) 6256015
Hainan Air
☎ (86)(791) 6291117
Shanghai Airlines
☎ (86)(791) 6278246

Liaoning
Dalian DLC
Airport: Dalian Zhoushuizi Int'l Airport
Air China
☎ (86)(411) 4801161
China Southern Airlines
☎ (86)(411) 6645710
Hainan Air
☎ (86)(411) 3671635
Shanghai Airlines
☎ (86)(411) 3637480

Shenyang SHE
Airport Taoxian International Airport
China Southern Airlines
☎ (86)(24) 22526737
Shanghai Airlines
☎ (86)(24) 23235858

Ningxia
Yinchuan INC
Airport: Yinchuan Hedong Airport
China united Airlines
☎ (86)(951) 5066098
Shanghai Airlines
☎ (86)(951) 6022085

Qinghai
Xining XNN
Airport: Caojiapu Airport

Shandong
Jinan TNA
Airport: Yaoqiang Airport
China Eastern Airlines
☎ (86)(531) 7964445
China Southern Airlines
☎ (86)(531) 6911082
China United Airlines
☎ (86)(531) 6923359
Shanghai Airlines
☎ (86)(531) 6047146

Qingdao
Air China
☎ (86)(532) 3883650
China Eastern Airlines
☎ (86)(532) 2876174
China Southern Airlines
☎ (86)(532) 3873348
Hainan Air
☎ (86)(532) 5714190
Shanghai Airlines
☎ (86)(532) 5778653

Shaanxi
Xi'an XIY
Airport: Xianyang Airport
Air China
☎ (86)(29) 4296767
China Southern Airlines
☎ (86)(29) 8377070
Hainan Air
☎ (86)(29) 6291117
Shanghai Airlines
☎ (86)(29) 4261630

Shanxi
Taiyuan TYN
Airport: Wusu Airport
China Southern Airlines
☎ (86)(351) 4291088
Hainan Air
☎ (86)(351) 7286472

Shanghai
Shanghai SHA

Airport: Hongqiao International Airport

China Eastern Airlines

☎ (86)(21) 62475953 *Domestic*

☎ (86)(21) 62472255 *International*

Air China

☎ (86)(21) 62692999

China Southern Airlines

☎ (86)(21) 62262299

China Southwest Airlines

☎ (86)(21) 64333355

China Northwest Airlines

☎ (86)(21) 62794818

Shanghai Airlines

☎ (86)(21) 62551551, 62558888

SHANGHAI AIRLINES BUSINESS JET OPERATION DEPARTMENT

☎ (86)(21) 62555000

🖨 (86)(21) 62555333

Web: www.shanghai-air.com

Hainan Air

☎ (86)(21) 65608777

Shenzhen Air

☎ (86)(21) 62823274

Yunnan Airlines

☎ (86)(21) 62516966

Pudong PVG

Airport: Pudong Int'l Airport

Distance: 30 km from city

☎ (86)(21) 38484500

Sichuan

Chengdu CTU

Airport: Shuangliu Int'l Airport

☎ (86)(28) 5586440 *Inquiry*

☎ (86)(28) 2298169 *Domestic*

Air China

☎ (86)(28) 85572231

China Southern Airlines

☎ (86)(28) 86663618

China Southwest Airlines

☎ (86)(28) 86668080

Hainan Air

☎ (86)(28) 86669085

Shenzhen Air

☎ (86)(28) 86780948

Shanghai Airlines

☎ (86)(28) 86127000

Yunnan Air

☎ (86)(28) 86712833

Tianjin

Airport: Zhangguizhuang Airport

Air China

☎ (86)(22) 23301546

Hainan Air

☎ (86)(22) 23281998

Tibet

Lhasa LXA

Airport: Konggar Airport

☎ (86)(891) 6182220 *Domestic*

☎ (86)(891) 6838609 *International*

Xinjiang

Urumqi URC

Airport: Diwopu Airport

China Southern Airlines

☎ (86)(991) 4516865

China Northwest Airlines

☎ (86)(991) 4512748

Yunnan

Kunming KMG

Airport: Wujiaba Airport

China Southwest Airlines

☎ (86)(871) 3539702

China Southern Airlines

☎ (86)(871) 3101831

Air China

☎ (86)(871) 3159171

Hainan Air

☎ (86)(871) 3190790

Shanghai Airlines

☎ (86)(871) 3138502

Zhejiang

Hangzhou HGH

Airport: Jianqiao Airport

China Southern Airlines

☎ (86)(571) 87960000

China Eastern Airlines

☎ (86)(571) 7016688
Hainan Air
☎ (86)(571) 87290496
China United Airlines
☎ (86)(571) 85152600
Shanghai Airlines
☎ (86)(571) 5119928

Chinese Embassies & Consulates Abroad

ASIA

P. R. C Embassy in Pakistan
☎ (92)(51) 2824786

P. R. C Embassy in Republic of Korea
☎ (82)(2) 7381038
Website: www.chinaemb.or.kr
Pusan Consulate
☎ (82) (51) 7424991

P. R. C Embassy in Philippines
☎ (63)(2) 8443148

P. R. C Embassy in Malaysia
☎ (60) (3) 21428495

P. R. C Embassy in Japan
☎ (81)(3) 34033388
Website: www.china-embassy.or.jp
Osaka Consulate
☎ (81)(6) 64459481
Fukuoka Consulate
☎ (81)(92) 7131121
Sapporo Consulate
☎ (81)(11) 5635563
Nagasaki Consulate
☎ (81) (958) 493311

P. R. C Embassy in Thailand
☎ (66)(2) 2457044

P. R. C Embassy in Brunei
☎ (673) 334163

P. R. C Embassy in Singapore
☎ (65) 67351716

P. R. C Embassy in Qatar
☎ (974) 4884202

P. R. C Embassy in Kuwait
☎ (965) 5333340

P. R. C Embassy in United Emirates
☎ (9710(2) 434276
Dubai Consulate
☎ (971)(4) 3984357

P. R. C Embassy in Oman
☎ (968) 696698

P. R. C Embassy in Bahrain
☎ (973) 723800

P. R. C Embassy in Saudi Arabia
☎ (966)(1) 2812083

P. R. C Embassy in Turkey
☎ (90)(312) 4360328
Website: www.chinaembassy.org.tr
Istanbul Consulate
☎ (90)(212) 2992188

P. R. C Embassy in India
☎ (91)(11) 6871585
Mumbai Consulate
☎ (91)(22) 4915863

P. R. C Embassy in Indonesia
☎ (62)(21) 5761047

P. R. C Embassy in Viet Nam
☎ (84)(4) 8453736

P. R. C Embassy in Israel
☎ (972)(3) 5467277

AFRICA

P. R. C Embassy in Egypt
☎ (20)(2) 7261219
Website: www.chinaembassy.org.sg

P. R. C Embassy in South Africa
☎ (27)(12) 3424194

Durban Consulate
☎ (27)(31) 2080540
Cape Town Consulate
☎ (27)(21) 6740579
Johannesburg Consulate
☎ (27)(82) 6603680

EUROPE

P. R. C Embassy in Poland
☎ (48)(22) 8313836

P. R. C Embassy in Russia
☎ (7)(95) 2307524
Website: www.chinaembassy.ru
St. Petersburg Consulate
☎ (7)(812) 1147670

P. R. C Embassy in Romania
☎ (40)(21) 2329673

P. R. C Embassy in Hungary
☎ (36)(10) 4132420

P. R. C Embassy in Ireland
☎ (353) (1) 2691707

P. R. C Embassy in Spain
☎ (34)(91) 5194242
Barcelona Consulate
☎ (34)(3) 4556060

P. R. C Embassy in Austria
☎ (43)(1) 714314923

P. R. C Embassy in Belgium
☎ (32)(2) 7711309

P. R. C Embassy in Ireland
☎ (354) 5526322

P. R. C Embassy in UK
☎ (44)(20) 72994049
Website: www.chinese-embassy.org.uk
Manchester Consulate
☎ (44)(161) 224872
Edinburgh Consulate
☎ (44)(131) 3164789

P. R. C Embassy in Denmark
☎ (45) 39610081
Website: www.chinaembassy.dk

P. R. C Embassy in Germany
☎ (49)(30) 4723118
Website: www.china.botschaft.de
Hamburg Consulate
☎ (49) (40) 8227600
Munich Consulate
☎ (49) (89) 99738270

P. R. C Embassy in France
☎ (33)(1) 47233677
Website: www.amb-chine.fr
Marseille Consulate
☎ (33) (491) 320000

P. R. C Embassy in Finland
☎ (358)(9) 6848416
Website: www.chinaembassy-fi.org

P. R. C Embassy in Netherlands
☎ (31)(70) 3065061

P. R. C Embassy in Luxembourg
☎ (352) 436991
P. R. C Embassy in Malta
☎ (356)(21) 384889

P. R. C Embassy in Norway
☎ (47)(22) 449638
Website: www.chinese-embassy.no

P. R.C Embassy in Portugal
☎ (351)(1) 3928440
Website: www.embaxadachina.pt

P. R. C Embassy in Sweden
☎ (46)(8) 57936437
Website: www.chinaembassy.se
Gothenburg Consulate
☎ (46)(31) 842340

P. R. C Embassy in Switzerland
☎ (41)(31) 3527333
Website: www.china-embassy.ch

Zurich Consulate
☎ (41)(1) 2011073

P. R.C Embassy in Greece
☎ (30)(10) 6723282

P. R. C Embassy in Italy
☎ (39)(06) 8413458
Florence Consulate
☎ (39) (55) 5058188
Milan Consulate
☎ (39) (2) 5693960

OCEANIA
P. R. C Embassy in Australia
☎ (61)(2) 62734780
Website: www.chinaembassy.org.au
Melbourne Consulate
☎ (61)(3) 98220604
Perth Consulate
☎ (61)(8) 93218193
Sydney Consulate
☎ (61)(2) 93190678

P. R. C Embassy in New Zealand
☎ (64)(4) 4721382
Website: www.chinaembassy.org.nz
Auckland Consulate
☎ (64)(9) 5251588

NORTH AMERICA
P. R. C Embassy in Canada
☎ (1) (613) 7893434
Website: www.chinaembassycanada.org
Calgary Consulate
☎ (1)(403) 2643322
Toronto Consulate
☎ (1) (416) 9647260
Vancouver Consulate
☎ (1)(604) 7347492

P. R. C Embassy in USA
☎ (1)(202) 3282500
Website: www.china-embassy.org
Chicago Consulate
☎ (1)(312) 8080098

Houston Consulate
☎ (1)(713) 5244311
Los Angeles Consulate
☎ (1) (213) 8078088
New York Consulate
☎ (1)(212) 8687752
San Francisco Consulate
☎ (1) (415) 6742900

LATIN AMERICA
P. R. C Embassy in Mexico
☎ (52)(55) 56160609

P. R. C Embassy in Argentine
☎ (54)(11) 45438862

P. R. C Embassy in Brazil
☎ (55)(61) 3464436
Website: www.embchina.org.br
Rio De Janeiro Consulate
☎ (55)(21) 25514578
Sao Paulo Consulate
☎ (55)(11) 30829877

P. R. C Embassy in Peru
☎ (511) 2220841
Website: www.embajadachina.org.pe

P. R. C Embassy in Venezuela
☎ (58)(212) 9774949

Courier Services Agencies
Anhui
Hefei
China Post EMS
☎ (86)(551) 185
DHL-Sinotrans
☎ (86)(551) 3647179

Beijing
China Post EMS
☎ (86)(10) 185
DHL-Sinotrans
☎ (86)(10) 64662211
FedEx
☎ (86)(10) 64348999

TNT Skypack-Sinotrans Ltd
☎ (86)(10) 64677877
United Parcel Service (UPS)
☎ (86)(10) 65055005

Chongqing
China Post EMS
☎ (86)(23) 185
DHL-Sinotrans
☎ (86)(23) 67525559

Fujian
Fuzhou
China Post EMS
☎ (86)(591) 185
DHL-Sinotrans
☎ (86)(591) 7321111

Xiamen
China Post EMS
☎ (86)(592) 185
DHL-Sinotrans
☎ (86)(592) 6010503-6

Gansu
Lanzhou
China Post EMS
☎ (86)(931) 185
DHL-Sinotrans
☎ (86)(931) 8659666

Guangdong
Dongguan
China Post EMS
☎ (86)(569) 185
DHL-Sinotrans
☎ (86)(569) 2315150

Guangzhou
China Post EMS
☎ (86)(20) 185
DHL-Sinotrans
☎ (86)(20) 86646868
FedEx
☎ (86)(20) 85579225
TNT Skypak-Sinotrans
☎ (86)(20) 87532101

UPS
☎ (86)(20) 83486789

Huizhou
China Post EMS
☎ (86)(752) 185
DHL-Sinotrans
☎ (86)(752) 2310928

Jiangmen
China Post EMS
☎ (86)(750) 185
DHL-Sinotrans
☎ (86)(750) 3110000

Shenzhen
China Post EMS
☎ (86)(755) 185
DHL-Sinotrans
☎ (86)(755) 3152388
FedEx
☎ (86)(755) 27758686
TNT Skypak-Sinotrans Ltd
☎ (86)(755) 83401872

Zhanjiang
China Post EMS
☎ (86)(759) 185
DHL-Sinotrans
☎ (86)(759) 3393903

Zhongshan
China Post EMS
☎ (86)(760) 185
DHL-Sinotrans
☎ (86)(760) 3338186

Zhuhai
China Post EMS
☎ (86)(756) 185
DHL-Sinotrans
☎ (86)(756) 8280000

Hebei
Shijiazhuang
China Post EMS
☎ (86)(311) 185

DHL-Sinotrans
☎ (86)(311) 7756688

Heilongjiang

Harbin
China Post EMS
☎ (86)(451) 185
DHL-Sinotrans
☎ (86)(451) 2328433

Hong Kong

Antax Express International
☎ (852) 23364833
Atlas Express Worldwide Ltd.
☎ (852) 25299123
Bilter Courier Service Co.
☎ (852) 23955281
China-Trans Courier Service
☎ (852) 27985787
China Aviation Express (HK) Ltd.
☎ (852) 22517555
China Courier Services Ltd.
☎ (852) 25166213
China Oriental Express Co Ltd.
☎ (852) 27579053
China Travel Service (Cargo) Ltd.
☎ (852) 25349292
City Courier Services Co.
☎ (852) 23890161
Comax Express Ltd.
☎ (852) 27070246
DHL International Ltd.
☎ (852) 2765 8111
Dimerco Air Forwarders Ltd.
☎ (852) 27963671
DPE International
☎ (852) 27959268
Emery Worldwide
☎ (852) 27963883
Evergreen Delivery Courier Service Co.
☎ (852) 23903307
Express - Mail Transportation Int'l Co., Ltd.
☎ (852) 29540200
Fast Services Co.
☎ (852) 27430298
Federal Express Corp.
☎ (852) 28653302 HK Island

☎ (852) 23071060 Kowloon
☎ (852) 22616666 N. T.
Flying Asia Express Co.
☎ (852) 23969911
Glory Int'l Express Co.
☎ (852) 27822661
Great Ocean Int'l Express Co.
☎ (852) 23666789
Guangzhou Courier Service (HK) Co. Ltd.
☎ (852) 27079431
Kintetsu World Express
☎ (852) 27963298
Kwikmail Ltd.
☎ (852) 27955725
Macau Express Ltd.
☎ (852) 23118863
Morning Express Courier Co.
☎ (852) 23708222
Prompt Express Co.
☎ (852) 27875220
Rainbow Express
☎ (852) 23881315
Reliance Delivery Services Ltd
☎ (852) 27705433
Sinotrans (Hong Kong) Express Co., Ltd.
☎ (852) 27578660
Sky Way Courier Services Ltd.
☎ (852) 28930886
Skyhorse Express Co.
☎ (852) 27259992
Speedpost (Hong Kong Post)
☎ (852) 29212288
TNT Express
☎ (852) 23312663
United Professional Courier Co.
☎ (852) 27861393
UPS Parcel Delivery Service Ltd.
☎ (852) 27353535
Wholesale Express HK Co. Ltd.
☎ (852) 27952395
World Courier Hong Kong Ltd.
☎ (852) 28335775

Hubei

Wuhan
China Post EMS
☎ (86)(27) 185

DHL-Sinotrans
☎ (36)(27) 85755909

Hunan
Changsha
China Post EMS
☎ (86)(731) 185
DHL-Sinotrans
☎ (86)(731) 5217888

Jiangsu
Nanjing
China Post EMS
☎ (86)(25) 185
DHL-Sinotrans
☎ (86)(25) 6507050

Nantong
China Post EMS
☎ (86)(513) 185
DHL-Sinotrans
☎ (86)(513) 5222333

Suzhou
China Post EMS
☎ (86)(512) 185
DHL-Sinotrans
☎ (86)(512) 62566288

Wuxi
China Post EMS
☎ (86)(510) 185
DHL-Sinotrans
☎ (86)(510) 5227770

Yangzhou
China Post EMS
☎ (86)(514) 185
DHL-Sinotrans
☎ (86)(514) 7884000

Jilin
Changchun
China Post EMS
☎ (86)(431) 185

DHL-Sinotrans
☎ (86)(431) 4913888

Liaoning
Dalian
China Post EMS
☎ (86)(411) 185
DHL-Sinotrans
☎ (86)(411) 2725882
TNT Skypak-Sinotrans
☎ (86)(411) 2800519

Shenyang
China Post EMS
☎ (86)(24) 185
DHL-Sinotrans
☎ (86)(24) 23903652/39

Shandong
Qingdao
China Post EMS
☎ (86)(532) 185
DHL-Sinotrans
☎ (86)(532) 5723100

Shanghai
China Post EMS
☎ (86)(21) 185
DHL-Sinotrans
☎ (86)(21) 65362900
FedEx
☎ (86)(21) 62750808 Customer Service
☎ (86)(21) 54118333 Puxi Station
☎ (86)(21) 50320909 Pudong Station
Skypack-Sinotrans Ltd.
☎ (86)(21) 64211111
UPS
☎ (86)(21) 63115599
UPS-Sinotrans
☎ (86)(21) 62486060

Shanxi
Xi'an
China Post EMS
☎ (86)(29) 185

DHL-Sinotrans
☎ (86)(29) 7318311/13

Sichuan
China Post EMS
☎ (86)(28) 185
Chengdu
DHL-Sinotrans
☎ (86)(28) 85151100

Tianjin
China Post EMS
☎ (86)(22) 185
DHL-Sinotrans
☎ (86)(22) 2430 3388
TNT Skypak-Sinotrans
☎ (86)(22) 83830680

Zhejiang
Hangzhou
China Post EMS
☎ (86)(571) 185
DHL-Sinotrans
☎ (86)(571) 86077888
TNT Skypak-Sinotrans
☎ (86)(571) 85194672

Jiaxing
China Post EMS
☎ (86)(573) 185
DHL-Sinotrans
☎ (86)(573) 2223456

Jinhua
China Post EMS
☎ (86)(24) 185
DHL-Sinotrans
☎ (86)(579) 2361111

Ningbo
China Post EMS
☎ (86)(574) 185
DHL-Sinotrans
☎ (86)(574) 87123111

Wenzhou
China Post EMS
☎ (86)(577) 185
DHL-Sinotrans
☎ (86)(577) 88636789

Government Directory

Anhui
Anhui Provincial Government
☎ (86)(551) 2601114
Anhui Foreign Trade & Economic Co-op.
☎ (86)(551) 2831268
Hefei City Government
☎ (86)(551) 2674334
Hefei Customs
☎ (86)(551) 5321116
Hefei Foreign Trade & Economic Co-op.
☎ (86)(551) 2672306

Beijing
Ministry of Agriculture
☎ (86)(10) 64191114
Ministry of Civil Affairs
☎ (86)(10) 65235511
Ministry of Communications
☎ (86)(10) 65292030
Ministry of Construction
☎ (86)(10) 68394114
Ministry of Culture
☎ (86)(10) 65551114
Ministry of Education
☎ (86)(10) 66096114
Ministry of Finance
☎ (86)(10) 68551114
Ministry of Foreign Affairs
☎ (86)(10) 65961100
Ministry of Foreign Trade & Economic Co-op.
☎ (86)(10) 65198114
Ministry of Information Industry
☎ (86)(10) 66014249
Ministry of Justice
☎ (86)(10) 65205114

Ministry of Labor & Social Security
☎ (86)(10) 84201114
Ministry of National Security
☎ (36)(10) 65244702
Ministry of Public Health
☎ (86)(10) 68792114
Ministry of Public Security
☎ (86)(10) 65202114
Ministry of Railway
☎ (86)(10) 63240114
Ministry of Science & Technology
☎ (83)(10) 68515544
Ministry of State Land Resources
☎ (86)(10) 66127001
Ministry of Supervision
☎ (86)(10) 64014567
Ministry of Water Conservancy
☎ (86)(10) 63202114
People's Bank of China
☎ (86)(10) 66194114
State Economics & Trade Commission
☎ (86)(10) 63192334
State Copyright Administration of China
☎ (86)(10) 65127869
State Forestry Administration
☎ (86)(10) 84238619
State Security Regulation Committee
☎ (86)(10) 88061700
State Foreign Exchange Administration
☎ (86)(10) 68402107
State Council Hong Kong & Macau Affairs
☎ (86)(10) 68579977
State Council Overseas Chinese Affairs
☎ (86)(10) 68329955
State Council Taiwan Affairs Office
☎ (86)(10) 68328320
China Civil Aviation Administration
☎ (86)(10) 64091114
General Administration of Press and Publishing
☎ (86)(10) 65124433
General Administration of Customs
☎ (86)(10) 65194114
China Petroleums Chemical Industry Associate
☎ (86)(10) 84885058

China Machinery Industry Association
☎ (86)(10) 68510199
China Textile Industry Association
☎ (86)(10) 85229424
China Coal Industry Association
☎ (86)(10) 64202177
China Supply and Marketing
☎ (86)(10) 88086752
China Light Industry Association
☎ (86)(10) 68396113
National Association of Industry and commerce
☎ (86)(10) 65136677-2312
State Broadcasting & TV Bureau
☎ (86)(10) 86092707
State Bureau of Statistics
☎ (86)(10) 68580964
State Administration Industry and Commerce
☎ (86)(10) 68032233
National Medicines & Chemical Reagents Supervisory Administration
☎ (86)(10) 68313344
National Power Corp.
☎ (86)(10) 66054131
National Tourism Bureau
☎ (86)(10) 65201114
State Council Development Research Center
☎ (86)(10) 65596851
State Tax General Administration
☎ (86)(10) 63417114
Xinhua News Agency
☎ (86)(10) 63071114
Beijing Municipal Government
☎ (86)(10) 65192233
Beijing Customs
☎ (86)(10) 65194567
Beijing Foreign Economy & Trade Co-op
☎ (86)(10) 65236688
State Administration of Quality Supervision
☎ (86)(10) 65994600
State Drug Administration
☎ (86)(10) 88371540
China Council For the promotion of International trade
☎ (86)(10) 68013344

China Customs Administration
☎ (86)(10) 65194114
China Tobacco Administration
☎ (86)(10) 63605805

Chongqing

Chongqing Municipal Government
☎ (86)(23) 63852702
Chongqing Customs
☎ (86)(23) 67709114
Foreign Trade & Economy Co-op
☎ (86)(23) 67523525

Fujian

Fuzhou
Fujian Provincial People's Government
☎ (86)(591) 7021333
Foreign Trade & Econ. Co-op
☎ (86)(591) 7590268

Gansu

Lanzhou
Gansu Provincial Government
☎ (86)(931) 8465941
Gansu Foreign Trade & Economic Co-op
☎ (86)(931) 8616321
Lanzhou Foreign Economic & Trade Co-op
☎ (86)(931) 8460431

Guangdong

Guangzhou
Guangdong Provincial Government
☎ (86)(20) 83138114
Guangzhou Foreign Trade & Econ. Co-op
☎ (86)(20) 81080870
Guangdong Foreign Economy & Trade Co-op
☎ (86)(20) 38806659

Guangxi

Nanning
Guangxi People's Government
☎ (86)(771) 2618242
Guangxi Foreign Trade & Econ. Co-op
☎ (86)(771) 5311810

Nanning Econ. & Trade Bureau
☎ (86)(771) 3133562
Nanning City Government
☎ (86)(771) 5869813
Nanning Customs, PRC
☎ (86)(771) 5398355
Nanning Foreign Trade & Econ. Co-op
☎ (86)(771) 4810101

Guizhou

Guizhou Provincial Government
☎ (86)(851) 6822054
Guizhou Foreign Econ. & Trace Dept.
☎ (86)(851) 6822341
Guizhou Foreign Econ. Co-op
☎ (86)(851) 6823613
Guiyang City Government
☎ (86)(851) 5825818
Guiyang Customs
☎ (86)(851) 5786000

Hainan

Hainan Provincial Government
☎ (86)(898) 5342691
Hainan Foreign, Trade & Econ. Co-op
☎ (86)(898) 5342896
Haikou City Government Office
☎ (86)(898) 6798291
Haikou Foreign Trade & Econ. Co-op
☎ (86)(898) 6797781
Haikou Industrial & Commerce Admin.
☎ (86)(898) 6774376

Hebei

Hebei Provincial Government
☎ (86)(311) 7092680
Hebei Foreign Trade & Econ. Co-op
☎ (86)(311) 7044842
Shijiazhuang City Government
☎ (86)(311) 6045798
Shijiazhuang Trade Bureau
☎ (86)(311) 6032146
Shijiazhuang Customs
☎ (86)(311) 3033164

Heilongjiang

Heilongjiang Provincial Government
☎ (86)(451) 2622095
Heilongjiang Foreign Trade & Econ. Co-op
☎ (86)(451) 2621704
Harbin Customs
☎ (86)(451) 2381888

Henan

Henan Provincial Government
☎ (86)(371) 5954622
Henan Foreign Trade & Econ. Co-op
☎ (86)(371) 3943388
Zhengzhou City Government
☎ (86)(371) 7447715
Zhengzhou PRC Customs
☎ (86)(371) 5727563
Zhengzhou Foreign Trade & Econ. Co-op
☎ (86)(371) 6222422

Hong Kong

Central Policy Unit
☎ (852) 28102338
Financial Dept.
☎ (852) 28102589
Civil Service Bureau
☎ (852) 28103156
Commerce and Industry Bureau
☎ (852) 29187500
Education and Manpower Bureau
☎ (852) 28102631
Finance Bureau
☎ (852) 28103824
Home Affairs Bureau
☎ (852) 28352056
Information Technology and Broadcasting Bureau
☎ (852) 21892222
Planning and Lands Bureau
☎ (852) 29482035
Audit Commission
☎ (852) 23294210
Census and Statistics Department
☎ (852) 25824807
Civil Aviation Department
☎ (852) 28674332

Companies Registry
☎ (852) 22349933
Customs and Excise Department
☎ (852) 28521411
Immigration Department
☎ (852) 28246111
Information Technology Services Department
☎ (852) 29618102
Land Registry
☎ (852) 28678080
Radio Television Administration
☎ (852) 23396300
Office of the Telecommunications Authority
☎ (852) 29616333
Trade and Industry Department
☎ (852) 23922922
Treasury Dept.
☎ (852) 28295124
Hong Kong Tourism Board
☎ (852) 28076543
Hong Kong Science and Technology Parks Corporation
☎ (852) 26291818
Hong Kong Trade Development Council
☎ (852) 21830668
Mandatory Provident Fund Schemes Authority
☎ (852) 29180102

Hubei

Hubei Provincial Government
☎ (86)(27) 87816655
Hubei Foreign Trade & Econ. Co-op
☎ (86)(27) 87554233
Wuhan People's Government
☎ (86)(27) 82826114
Wuhan Foreign Econ. & Trade Co-op
☎ (86)(27) 85795417
Wuhan Foreign Investment Bureau
☎ (86)(27) 82848951

Hunan

Hunan Provincial Government
☎ (86)(731) 2212111
Hunan Foreign Econ. & Trade Committee
☎ (86)(731) 4449177

Changsha City Government
☎ (86)(731) 2220781
Changsha Customs
☎ (86)(731) 4449388

Inner Mongolia

Inner Mongolia People's Government
☎ (86)(471) 6946031
Inner Mongolia Foreign Trade & Economy Co-op
☎ (86)(471) 6964301
Hohhot City Government
☎ (86)(471) 6288065

Jiangsu

Jiangsu Provincial Government General
☎ (86)(25) 3396603
Jaingsu Foreign Trade & Econ. Co-op
☎ (86)(25) 7712600
Nanjing Customs
☎ (86)(25) 4422114

Jiangxi

Jiangxi Provincial Government Admin. Office
☎ (86)(791) 6224166
Jiangxi Foreign Trade & Econ. Co-op
☎ (86)(791) 6246332
Nanchang City Government
☎ (86)(791) 6771806
Nanchang Customs
☎ (86)(791) 6416318
Nanchang Foreign Trade Econ. Co-op
☎ (86)(791) 6408274

Jilin

Jilin Provincial Government
☎ (86)(431) 8912321
Jilin Foreign Trade & Cooperation Dept.
☎ (86)(431) 5627011
Changchun People's Government
☎ (86)(431) 8967000
Changchun Foreign Trade & Econ. Bureau
☎ (86)(431) 2710867
Changchun Customs
☎ (86)(431) 4630403

Liaoning

Liaoning Provincial Government
☎ (86)(24) 86893149
Liaoning Foreign Econ. & Trade Co-op
☎ (86)(24) 86892225
Shenyang City Government
☎ (86)(24) 22721824
Shenyang Customs
☎ (86)(24) 22828275
Shenyang Foreign Econ. & Trade Co-op
☎ (86)(24) 22828050

Macau

Government of Macau SAR
☎ (853) 726886
Econ. & Trade Secretary Office
☎ (853) 726886
Economic Affairs
☎ (853) 386937
Finance Dept.
☎ (853) 571600
Labor & Employment Services
☎ (853) 564109
Monetary Authority
☎ (853) 325416
Public Works & Transport
☎ (853) 722488
Statistics Dept.
☎ (853) 728188
Telecommunications & Information Tech.
☎ (853) 356328
Tourism Dept.
☎ (853) 315566

Ningxia

Ningxia People's Government
☎ (86)(951) 5016831
Ningxia Foreign Trade & Econ. Co-op
☎ (86)(951) 5055146
Yinchuan City Government
☎ (86)(951) 6029770
Yinchuan Customs
☎ (86)(951) 5030188

Qinghai

Qinghai People's Government
☎ (36)(971) 8244554
Qinghai Foreign Trade & Econ. Co-op
☎ (86)(971) 8176805
Xining City Government
☎ (86)(971) 8230419
Xining Foreign Trade & Econ. Co-op
☎ (83)(971) 6142130

Shaanxi

Shaanxi Provincial Government
☎ (86)(29)
Xi'an Foreign Econ. & Trade Co-op
☎ (86_(29) 7284865
Xi'an Foreign Econ. & Trade Commission
☎ (86)(29) 7285422
Xi'an Customs
☎ (86)(29) 5262332

Shandong

Shandong People's Government
☎ (86)(531) 6912828
Shandong Foreign Econ. & Trade Co-op
☎ (86)(531)
Jinan People's Government
☎ (86)(531) 6056888
Jinan Foreign Investment Enterprises
Admin. Bureau
☎ (86)(531) 6056909
Jinan Customs
☎ (86)(531) 2066611
Jinan Foreign Econ. & Trade Comission
☎ (86)(531) 6911387

Shanghai

Shanghai Government
☎ (86)(21) 33212810
Shanghai Municipal Customs
☎ (86)(21) 63232410
Shanghai Foreign Trade & Econ. Co-op
☎ (86)(21) 62752200
Shanghai Foreign Investment Committee
☎ (86)(21) 62752200

Shanxi

Shanxi Provincial Government
☎ (86)(351) 3044451
Shanxi Foreign Trade & Econ. Co-op
☎ (86)(351) 4041722
Taiyuan City Government
☎ (86)(351) 4227229
Taiyuan Customs
☎ (86)(351) 4061611
Taiyuan Foreign Trade & Econ. Co-op
☎ (86)(351) 4222073

Sichuan

Sichuan Provincial Government
☎ (86)(351) 6663798
Sichuan Foreign trade & Econ. Co-op
☎ (86)(351) 3334812
Chengdu City Government
☎ (86)(351) 6633706
Chengdu Customs
☎ (86)(351) 6401687
Chengdu Foreign Trade & Econ. Co-op
☎ (86)(351) 6634764

Tianjin

Tianjin Municipal Government
☎ (86)(22) 23305555
Tianjin Foreign Econ. Liaison Bureau
☎ (86)(22) 23312378
Tianjin Foreign Trade Bureau
☎ (86)(22) 23191251
Tianjing Customs
☎ (86)(22) 24201114

Tibet

People's Government of Tibet
☎ (86)(891) 6325889
Tibet Foreign Trade & Econ. Co-op
☎ (86)(891) 6832491
Lhasa Customs
☎ (86)(891) 6836663
Lhasa City Government
☎ (86)(891) 6323467
Lhasa Foreign Trade & Econ. Co-op
☎ (86)(891) 6815459

Xinjiang

Xinjiang People's Government
☎ (86)(991) 2330213
Xinjiang Foreign Trade & Econ. Co-op
☎ (86)(991) 2865720
Urumqi City Government
☎ (86)(991) 2819184
Urumqi Customs
☎ (86)(991) 3835181

Yunnan

Yunnan Provincial Government
☎ (86)(871) 3619773
Yunnan Customs
☎ (86)(871) 3016999
Kunming Foreign Trade & Econ. Co-op
☎ (86)(871) 3161839

Zejiang

Zhejiang Provincial Government
☎ (86)(571)
Zhejiang Foreign Investment Admin.
☎ (86)(571) 5153650
Hangzhou Customs
☎ (86)(571) 8076314
Hangzhou Foreign Trade & Econ. Co-op
☎ (86)(571) 5156707

Event Organizers

Beijing

Beijing Global Plan Limited Company
☎ (86)(10) 68596938
Beijing Designet Exhibition
☎ (86)(10) 62234411
Beijing Evergreen Conference & Exhibition
Solutions Ltd.
☎ (86)(10) 68728289
China International Exhibition Corporation
☎ (86)(10) 64671704
DMG World Media Ltd.
☎ (86)(10) 659366 11
E.J. Krause & Associates, Inc.
☎ (86)(10) 84511832

Great Wall International Exhibition Co., Ltd.
☎ (86)(10) 68748314
Hannover Fairs Asia Pte. Ltd.
☎ (86)(10) 65056210
Jingmu Int'l Exhibition Co. Ltd.
☎ (86)(10) 64663279
Pico Exhibition Services Co. Ltd.
☎ (86)(10) 64850999
Reed Exhibition
☎ (86)(10) 65260941

Chongqing

Chongqing International Technology
Exhibition Center (CITEC)
☎ (86)(23) 68633394

Fujian

Fuzhou

Fuzhou Int'l Conference & Exhibition Center
☎ (86)(591) 7801115

Xiamen

Xiamen Chinese Xingye Exhibition Co. Ltd.
☎ (86)(592) 5168881
Xiamen Intop Exhibition Company
☎ (86)(592) 2392333

Guangdong

Guangzhou

Guangdong Convention & Exhibition
Promotion (GDEXPO)
☎ (86)(20) 86565265
Pico Exhibition Services
☎ (86) (20) 87322990
Guangzhou Int'l Exhibition Co.
☎ (86)(20) 83504417

Shenzhen

Shenzhen Int'l Exhibition Center
☎ (86)(755) 25874391
Shenzhen High & New Tech. Trading &
Exhibition Center
☎ (86)(755) 82526030

Hong Kong

Adsale Exhibition Services Ltd.
☎ (352) 28118897
AKI Productions Ltd.
☎ (852) 26971221
Business & Industrial Trade Fairs Ltd.
☎ (852) 28652633
CIEC Exhibition Co. (HK) Ltd.
☎ (852) 28275078
China Promotion Ltd.
☎ (852) 25117427
CMP Media
☎ (852) 28276211
Elton Event Management Co. Ltd.
☎ (852) 23617257
E.J. Krause & Associates, Inc.
☎ (852) 25773343
Hannover Fairs Asia Pte Ltd.
☎ (852) 25265481
HKTDC Hong Kong
☎ (852) 25844333
Hong Kong Exhibition Co. Ltd.
☎ (852) 2804 1500
Messe Frankfurt (H.K.) Ltd.
☎ (852) 28027728
Munich Trade Fairs Consultancy
☎ (852) 25115199
Pico Exhibition Services
☎ (852) 26650990
Reed Exhibition
☎ (852) 28240330

Shanghai
Adsale Exhibition Services Ltd.
☎ (86)(21) 62781867
CMP Media
☎ (86)(21) 64371178
Hong Kong Exhibition Services
☎ (86)(21) 32095209
Munich Trade Fairs Consultancy
☎ (86)(21) 68863366
Pico Exhibition Services
☎ (86)(21) 39108330
Shanghai Int'l Exhibition
☎ (86)(21) 63872828
Shanghai Modern Int'l Exhibition Corp.
☎ (86)(21) 63217522

Shanghai Pudong Int'l Exhibition
☎ (86)(21) 62723462
Shanghai Union Int'l Exhibition
☎ (86)(21) 62997648
Shanghai World Trade Mart Co., Ltd.
☎ (86)(21) 62360208

Exercuitve Search Firms

Anhui
Wuhu Human Resource Market
☎ (86)(553) 3835331

Beijing
Alliance Consulting Ltd.
☎ (86)(10) 65007994
Atoz Consulting
☎ (86)(10) 65816776
Atoz headhunting Consulting
☎ (86)(10) 65816776, 65815779
Better Choice HR Co. Ltd.
☎ (86)(10) 85288787
Bo Le Associates, Ltd.
☎ (86)(10) 65676678
Buildhunter
☎ (86)(10) 82657419
Beijing Changzhi HR Management
Consulant Service Co.,Ltd.
☎ (86)(10) 66185833
Beijing Talent Consulting Agency
☎ (86)(10) 82755922
China Int'l Intellectech Corp.
☎ (86)(10) 65613920
CIASE Management Consultation
☎ (86)(10) 64926210, 65266307
COSCO Manning Cooperation Inc.
☎ (86)(10) 64984091
Demon Information Consulting Co. Ltd.
☎ (86)(10) 84512853
CyberOrient Headhunting Services.
☎ (86)(10) 62161485
CyberOrient Service Co Ltd
☎ (86)(10) 62161485
DoWelljoin Co. Ltd
☎ (86)(10) 661631741, 66163171,

Friendly Service Co Ltd
☎ (86)(10) 62032848, 82076709, 13801034963
Jinsong Zhuyou Information Ltd. Co.
☎ (86)(10) 62234411
Management Personnel Consulting
☎ (86)(10) 82071328
Orient Huibo HR Consulting
☎ (86)(10) 65062376
Perfect Public Relation Consulting Service
☎ (86)(21) 84470249
Qeewoo Consulting Company
☎ (86)(10) 87780532
Shuanggao HR Center
☎ (86)(10) 62140630
IT Consultancy & Services Pte. Ltd.
☎ (86)(10) 68580801
Talent Consulting Corporation
☎ (86)(10) 68319134
Top Job Way Headhunting Co.
☎ (86)(10) 84652510

Fujian
Fuzhou
Services & Technical Corp
☎ (86)(591) 7823208, 7382338, 7823226

Quanzhou
Job Training & Development Center
☎ (86)(595) 2633577

Guangdong
Dongguan
Humen HR Market
☎ (86)(769) 5500688

Guangzhou
Time Elite Enterprise Management
☎ (86)(20) 38868753, 38869755
Wise Eyes HR
☎ (86)(20) 83575022, 83584468
Bo Le Associates, Ltd.
☎ (86)(20) 83848386
China Star Corporation
☎ (86)(20) 38771293
Dian HR Service Co. Ltd.
☎ (86)(20) 81351833

Bridge Consultants Ltd.
☎ (86)(20) 38861434
EMDS Guangzhou Office
☎ (86)(20) 83831636
Friendship Foreign Service Corporation
☎ (86)(20) 87771148
Guangdong Talent & Intelligence Market
☎ (86)(20) 87593219
Guangzhou TimeElite Enterprise
Management Consulting Co., Ltd
☎ (86)(20) 38868753
Huanpu District Labor Service Co. Ltd.
☎ (86)(20) 82090848
Wise Eyes Information Co. Ltd.
☎ (86)(20) 83575022
Topper HR Consultant
☎ (86)(20) 83312086
United Resources Consulting
☎ (86)(20) 87766778

Shenzhen
China Star Corporation
☎ (86)(755) 83699840
Shenzhen Longgang Gongqingtuan Human Resources Exchange Center
☎ (86)(755) 28833637
Ineyes Information Co. Ltd.
☎ (86)(755) 83324731, 83206684
Shenzhen Unique Consulting
☎ (86)(755) 83926200
Aliba Headhunting Information Consulting
☎ (86)(755) 82475036
ZDL Headhunting
☎ (86)(755) 25188486, 25188768

Hong Kong
Bo Le Associates, Ltd.
☎ (852) 25254339
EMDS Consulting (HK) Ltd.
☎ (852) 2905 9007
TMP Worldwide eResourcing
☎ (852) 25751112
United Resources Consulting
☎ (852) 21392133
Wang & Li Asia Resources Online
☎ (852) 25881247

Hubei

Wuhan
Hubei Foreign Service Corporation
☎ (86)(27) 85773941
Niche Consulting
☎ (86)(27) 85757373
Wuhan Human Resource Market
☎ (86)(27) 82788579
Fords Consulting
☎ (86)(27) 82706609

Jiangsu

Nanjing
Jiangsu Foreign Enterprise Service Center
☎ (86)(25) 3601221
Nanjing Human Resource Market
☎ (86)(25) 3282630
Zhuoer Management and Consulting
☎ (86)(25) 6289797

Liaoning

Dalian
Dalian gloss occupation service Co, Ltd.
☎ (86)(411) 3677463
Dalian Universal HR Consultant Co, Ltd.
☎ (86)(411) 2818282

Shenyang
Foreign Enterprise Service Corporation
☎ (86)(24) 86081174
Int'l Econ. & Tech. Cooperation
☎ (86)(24) 23243298

Shaanxi

Xi'an
BH&H (Bohao HR Services Co. Ltd.
☎ (86)(29) 5222018
HRC Consulting Co.
☎ (86)(29) 8318451
Xi'an Human Resource Market
☎ (86)(29) 5215995
Xi'an High-tech Park HR
☎ (86)(29) 8314614

Shandong
China Labor Net

☎ (86)(538) 6232519

Shanghai
Andersen Consulting
☎ (86)(21) 63915588
Bo Le Associates Ltd.
☎ (86)(21) 53966686
Cai Fortune High-tech Executive Searching
☎ (86)(21) 65299403, 65306495
Director & Manager Resources Co.
☎ (86)(21) 62338413
EMDS Shanghai Office
☎ (86)(21) 52574104
Eve Business Consulting
☎ (86)(21) 68766568
Hewitt Consultancy Co. Ltd.
☎ (86)(21) 64515230
Join-Link Consulting Ltd.
☎ (86)(21) 63223767
LEK Consulting LLC
☎ (86)(21) 62728200
Oasis Executive Searching Group
☎ (86)(21) 62861992
Pudong Human Resource
☎ (86)(21) 68541246
Shanghai China Human Resources Market
☎ (86)(21) 58876116
Shanghai Foreign Service Co. Ltd.
☎ (86)(21) 63854052
Shanghai Fortune Consultant
☎ (86)(21) 62402111
Shanghai Ineyes Information Co. Ltd.
☎ (86)(21) 52573253
Shanghai Int'l Multisearch Co.
☎ (86)(21) 52120010
Shanghai Trade Union Overseas
Employment Services Company
☎ (86)(21) 62191398
Shanghai Zhiying Commercial Consultation
☎ (86)(21) 54043205
Shencai Net
☎ (86)(21) 62578582
TMP Worldwide eResourcing
☎ (86)(21) 28903230
Wang & Li Asia Resources Online
☎ (86)(21) 62175626

Witbright Information Consulting
☎ (86)(21) 64389536

Tianjing

Foreign Enterprise Service
☎ (86)(22) 83280090
TEDA
☎ (86)(22) 82118374
Tianjin Dagang Human Resource
☎ (86)(22) 63237863
Tianjing Tuoxin Lobor Service Center
☎ (86)(22) 88262147

Sichuan

Chengdu
Vastsea Consultants Co. Ltd.
☎ (86)(28) 2933648, 2933649

Zhejiang

Ningbo
People 258.com
☎ (86)(574) 87664857

Foreign Airlines

Beijing

Aeroflot Russian Int'l (SU)
☎ (86)(10) 6500 2980
Air France (AF)
☎ (86)(10) 65881388
Korean Air (KE)
☎ (86)(10) 65050088
Air Macau (NX)
☎ (86)(10) 65159398, 65158988
Air Ukraine
☎ (86)(10) 65010255
Alitalia (AL)
☎ (86)(10) 65056657
All Nippon Airways (NA)
☎ (86)(10) 65909191
Asiana Airlines (OZ)
☎ (86)(10) 65061118
Austrian Airlines (OS)
☎ (86)(10) 64622161
British Airways (BA)
☎ (86)(10) 65124070

Canadian Airlines (CP)
☎ (86)(10) 64637907
Cathy Pacific
☎ (86)(10) 65182533
Dragon Air (KA)
☎ (86)(10) 65182533
El Al Israel Airline Ltd.(LY)
☎ (86)(10) 65974512, 65974515
Finnair (AY)
☎ (86)(10) 65127180
Garuda Indonesia (GA)
☎ (86)(10) 65053168, 65052901
Iran Air (IR)
☎ (86)(10) 65124940
Israeli Airlines (LY)
☎ (86)(10) 65974512
Japan Airlines (JL)
☎ (86)(10) 65130888
LOT Polish Airlines (LO)
☎ (86)(10) 65007668
Lufthansa Airlines (LH)
☎ (86)(10) 64654488
Malaysia Airlines (MH)
☎ (86)(10) 65052681
MIAT Mongolian Airlines (OM)
☎ (86)(10) 65079297
Northwest Airlines (NW)
☎ (86)(10) 65053505
Pakistan Airlines (PK)
☎ (86)(10) 65051681
Qantas Airway (QF)
☎ (86)(10) 64673337
Royal Brunei (BI)
☎ (86)(10) 65055071
Scandinarian Airlines (SK)
☎ (86)(10) 85276100
Singapore Airlines (SQ)
☎ (86)(10) 65052233
Tarom-Romanian Air Transport (RO)
☎ (86)(10) 65002233
Thai Airways (TG)
☎ (86)(10) 64608899
United Airlines (UA)
☎ (86)(10) 64631111
Uzbekistan Airways(HY)
☎ (86)(10) 65006442

Vietnam Airlines
☎ (86)(10) 84541196

Chongqing
Asiana Airlines (OZ)
☎ (86)(23) 63836638
Dragon Air (KA)
☎ (86)(23) 62817434

Fujian
Fuzhou
Dragon Air (KA)
☎ (86)(591) 17821929

Xiamen
Air Macau (NX)
☎ (86)(592) 5114246
All Nippon Airways (NH)
☎ (86)(592) 22051888
Dragor Air (KA)
☎ (86)(592) 25117702
Malaysia Airlines (MH)
☎ (86)(592) 22108388

Guangxi
Guilin
Air Macau (NX)
☎ (86)(773) 3806175
Asiana Airlines (OZ)
☎ (86)(773) 32858985
Dragon Air (KA)
☎ (86)(773) 32823950

Guangzhou
Asiana Airlines (OZ)
☎ (86)(20) 87609037
Garuda Indonesia (GA)
☎ (86)(20) 83325424
Lufthansa German Airlines (LH)
☎ (86)(20) 86666965
Malaysia Airlines (MH)
☎ (86)(20) 83358828
Singapore Airlines (SQ)
☎ (86)(20) 87320600
Thai Airways Int'l (TG)
☎ (86)(20) 83338989

Vietnam Airlines (VN)
☎ (86)(20) 83867093

Hainan
Haikou
Air Macau (NX)
☎ (86)(898) 68533269
Dragon Air (KA)
☎ (86)(898) 68550312

Heilongjiang
Harbin
Aeroflot Russian Int'l (SU)
☎ (86)(451) 3633190
Asiana Airlines (OZ)
☎ (86)(451) 2344000

Hong Kong
Aeroflot Russian Int'l (SU)
☎ (852) 25372611
Air France (AF)
☎ (852) 25248145
Alitalia (AZ)
☎ (852) 25008488
All Nippon Airways (NH)
☎ (852) 28107100
Asiana Airlines (OZ)
☎ (852) 25238585
Austrian Airlines (OS)
☎ (852) 25255221
British Airways (BA)
☎ (852) 28229938
Canadian Airlines Int'l (CP)
☎ (852) 28678111
Cathay Pacific
☎ (852) 27471888
China Airlines
☎ (852) 28682299
Dragon Air (KA)
☎ (852) 28686777
El Al Israel Airline (LY)
☎ (852) 29730720
Emirates Airline (EK)
☎ (852) 25267171
Garuda Indonesia (GA)
☎ (852) 25229140

Japan Airlines (JL)
☎ (852) 25230081
Royal Dutch Airlines (KLM)
☎ (852) 28082118
Korean Air (KE)
☎ (852) 23686221
Lufthansa German Airlines (LH)
☎ (852) 25451033
Malaysia Airlines (MH)
☎ (852) 25218181
Qantas Airways (QF)
☎ (852) 28229000
Scandinarian Airlines (SK)
☎ (852) 28651370
Singapore Airlines (SQ)
☎ (852) 25296821
South African Airways (SA)
☎ (852) 27225768
Thai Airways Int'l (TG)
☎ (852) 28766222
United Airlines (UA)
☎ (852) 29651700
Uzbekistan Airways (HY)
☎ (852) 29651700
Vietnam Airlines (VN)
☎ (852) 28106680
Virgin Atlantic (VS)
☎ (852) 25326060

Hubei
Wuhan
Dragon Air (KA)
☎ (86)(27) 85806868

Hunan
Changsha
Dragon Air (KA)
☎ (86)(731) 5218888

Jiangsu
Nanjing
Air Macau (NX)
☎ (86)(25) 6799127
Asiana Airlines (OZ)
☎ (86)(25) 52480886

Jilin
Changchun
Asiana Airlines (OZ)
☎ (86)(431) 8948948

Liaoning
Dalian
All Nippon Airways (NH)
☎ (86)(41) 13605511
Dragon Air (KA)
☎ (86)(411) 12718855
Japan Airlines (JL)
☎ (86)(411) 13692525

Shenyang
Aeroflot Russian International (SU)
☎ (86)(24) 6809888
All Nippon Airways (NH)
☎ (86)(24) 2341811
Korean Air (KE)
☎ (86)(24) 22870088

Macau
Air Koryo
☎ (853) 356635
Air Macau
☎ (853) 396688
Eva Airways (BR)
☎ (86)(853) 726866
Singapore Airlines (SQ)
☎ (853) 711728/9

Shandong
Yantai
Asiana Airlines (OZ)
☎ (86)(535) 6628000

Qingdao
All Nippon Airways (NH)
☎ (86)(535) 23869725
Dragon Air (KA)
☎ (86)(535) 25776110
Japan Airlines (JL)
☎ (86)(535) 5710088

Shanghai

Aeroflot Russian International (SU)
☎ (86)(21) 64156700
Air France (AF)
☎ (86)(21) 63606688
Air Macau (NX)
☎ (86)(21) 62481110
Alitalia (AZ)
☎ (83)(21) 62683845
All Nippon Airlines (NH)
☎ (83)(21) 62797000
Asiana Airlines (OZ)
☎ (86)(21) 62194000
Austrian Airlines (OS)
☎ (86)(21) 63759051
British Airways (BA)
☎ (86)(21) 637578899
Canadain Airlines International (CP)
☎ (86)(21) 63758899
Dragon Air (KA)
☎ (86)(21) 63756375
Japan Airlines (JL)
☎ (86)(21) 64723000
Korean Air (KE)
☎ (86)(21) 62756000
Lufthansa German Airlines (LH)
☎ (86)(21) 58304400
Malaysia Airlines (MH)
☎ (86)(21) 62682900, 62798607
Northwest Airlines (NW)
☎ (86)(21) 62798088
Quantas Airways (QF)
☎ (86)(21) 62798660
Royal Dutch Airlines (KLM)
☎ (86) 21) 62798088
Singapore Airlines (SQ)
☎ (86)(21) 62891000
Thai Airways International (TG)
☎ (86)(21) 62484153
United Airlines (UA)
☎ (86)(21) 62798009, 62483333
Virgin Atlantic (VS)
☎ (86)(21) 53534600

Sichuan
Chengdu

Asiana Airlines (OZ)
☎ (86)(28) 86767666
Dragon Air (KA)
☎ (86)(28) 86725555

Tianjin

Air Ukraine (GU)
☎ (86)(22) 28137440
All Nippon Airways (NH)
☎ (86)(22) 23396688
Dragon Air (KA)
☎ (86)(22) 23110191
Japan Airlines (JL)
☎ (86)(22) 23139766
Korean Air (KE)
☎ (86)(22) 23190088

Yunnan
Kunming

Air Macau (NX)
☎ (86)(871) 7167378
Dragon Air (KA)
☎ (86)(871) 13561208
Korean Air (KE)
☎ (86)(871) 3158299
Thai Airways Int'l (TG)
☎ (86)(871) 13131163
Vietnam Airlines (VN)
☎ (86)(871) 13157179

Zhejiang
Hangzhou

Dragon Air (KA)
☎ (86)(571) 85068388

Ningbo

Dragon Air (KA)
☎ (86)(571) 87373188

Foreign-China Business Associations

Beijing

American Chamber of Commerce
☎ (86)(10) 85191920

British Chamber of Commerce
☎ (86)(10) 65126120
Canada China Business Council
☎ (86)(10) 65126120
China-Australia Chamber of Commerce
☎ (86)(10) 65905566
China-Britain Business Council
☎ (86)(10) 65936611
China-Italy Chamber Of Commerce
☎ (86)(10) 65973025
Danish Chamber of Commerce
☎ (86)(10) 64663388
European Union Chamber of Commerce
☎ (86)(10) 64622065
French Chamber of Commerce and Industry
☎ (86)(10) 84512071
German Industry and Commerce
☎ (86)(10) 65900326
Hong Kong Trade Development Council
☎ (86)(10) 65101700
Japan-China Economic Association
☎ (86)(10) 65139880
Japan-China Investment Promotion
Organization
☎ (86)(10) 65139890
Spanish Chamber of Commerce
☎ (86)(10) 65085238
Swedish Chamber of Commerce
☎ (86)(10) 64663388
US-China Business Council
☎ (86)(10) 65920727

Hong Kong

American Chamber of Commerce
☎ (852) 25260165
The Australian Chamber of Commerce
☎ (852) 25260165
The Hong Kong Australian Association
☎ (852) 28452257
Belgium-Luxembourg Chamber of
Commerce
☎ (852) 28230426
Canadian Chamber of Commerce
☎ (852) 25263207
Danish Business Association
☎ (852) 28278101

European Chamber of Commerce
☎ (852) 25123316
Finnish Business Council
☎ (852) 25123316
French Chamber of Commerce and Industry
☎ (852) 25236818
German Chamber of Commerce
☎ (852) 25265481
German Industry and Commerce
☎ (852) 25265481
The Dutch Business Association
☎ (852) 28152801
The Indian Chamber of Commerce
☎ (852) 25233877
Israeli Chamber of Commerce
☎ (852) 23121111
Italian Chamber of Commerce
☎ (852) 25218837
The Korean Chamber of Commerce
☎ (852) 25441713
New Zealand Hong Kong Business
Association
☎ (852) 25364469
Norwegian Chamber of Commerce
☎ (852) 25879953
The Singapore Chamber of Commerce
☎ (852) 28383733
Spanish Business Association
☎ (852) 27636236
Spanish Chamber of Commerce
☎ (852) 27636236
Swedish Chamber of Commerce
☎ (852) 25250349
Swiss Business Council
☎ (852) 25240590
British Chamber of Commerce
☎ (852) 28242211
US-China Business Council
☎ (852) 25275397

Shanghai

American Chamber of Commerce
☎ (86)(21) 62797119
Belgium Business Association
☎ (86)(21) 58791599
British Chamber of Commerce
☎ (86)(21) 62185022

Canada China Business Council
☎ (86)(21) 63598908
China-Australia Chamber of Commerce
☎ (86)(21) 62488310
China-Britain Business Council
☎ (86)(21) 62185183
French Trade Commission in Shanghai
☎ (86)(21) 53061100
French Chamber of Commerce and Industry
☎ (86)(21) 62813618
German Industry and Commerce
☎ (86)(21) 50812266
Hong Kong Trade Development Council
☎ (86)(21) 63528488
Japanese Chamber of Commerce
☎ (86)(21) 62752001
Liverpool Chamber of Commerce & Industry
☎ (86)(21) 63237703
Russian Federation Chamber of Commerce
☎ (86)(21) 62281304
Swedish Chamber of Commerce
☎ (86)(21) 64743533
US-China Business Council
☎ (86)(21) 62582582

Shandong
Singapore-Shandong Business Council
☎ (86)(531) 6929574

Foreign Embassies & Consulates

Beijing
Afghanistan
☎ (86)(10) 65321582
Albania
☎ (86)(10) 65321120
Algeria
☎ (86)(10) 65321231
Angola
☎ (86)(10) 65326968
Antigua and Barbuda
☎ (86)(10) 64606841
Argentine
☎ (86)(10) 65321406

Armenia
☎ (86)(10) 65325677
Australia
☎ (86)(10) 65322331
Austria
☎ (86)(10) 65322061
Azerbaijan
☎ (86)(10) 65324614
Bahrain
☎ (86)(10) 64635385
Bangladesh
☎ (86)(10) 65322521
Belarus
☎ (86)(10) 65326505
Belgium
☎ (86)(10) 65321736
Benin
☎ (86)(10) 65322741
Bolivia
☎ (86)(10) 65323074
Bosnia and Herzegovina
☎ (86)(10) 65326587
Botswana
☎ (86)(10) 65391616
Brazil
☎ (86)(10) 65322881
Brunei Darussalam
☎ (86)(10) 65324094
Bulgaria
☎ (86)(10) 65321946
Burkina Faso
☎ (86)(10) 65322550
Burundi
☎ (86)(10) 65322328
Cambodia
☎ (86)(10) 65321889
Cameroon
☎ (86)(10) 65321828
Canada
☎ (86)(10) 65323536
Central African Republic
☎ (86)(10) 65321789
Chile
☎ (86)(10) 65321591
Colombia
☎ (86)(10) 65323377

Cambodia
☎ (86)(10) 65321889
Congo(Republic)
☎ (86)(10) 65321658
Congo (Democratic)
☎ (86)(10) 65321363
Cote d'Ivoire
☎ (86)(10) 65321482
Croatia
☎ (86)(10) 65326241
Cuba
☎ (86)(10) 65326568
Cyprus
☎ (86)(10) 65325057
Czech
☎ (86)(10) 65326902
Denmark
☎ (86)(10) 65322431
Ecuador
☎ (86)(10) 65323849
Egypt
☎ (86)(10) 65321825
Equatorial Guinea
☎ (86)(10) 65323679
Eritrea
☎ (86)(10) 65326534
Estonia
☎ (86)(10) 64637913
Ethiopia
☎ (86)(10) 65321721
European Union Delegation of the
European Commission
☎ (86)(10) 65324443
Finland
☎ (86)(10) 65321817
France
☎ (86)(10) 65321331
Gabon
☎ (86)(10) 65322810
Germany
☎ (86)(10) 65322161
Ghana
☎ (86)(10) 65321319
Greece
☎ (86)(10) 65321317
Guinea
☎ (86)(10) 65323649

Guyana
☎ (86)(10) 65321337
Hungary
☎ (86)(10) 65321431
Iceland
☎ (86)(10) 65907795
India
☎ (86)(10) 65321856
Indonesia
☎ (86)(10) 65325488
Iran
☎ (86)(10) 65322040
Iraq
☎ (86)(10) 65323385
Ireland
☎ (86)(10) 65322691
Israel
☎ (86)(10) 65052970
Italy
☎ (86)(10) 65322131
Japan
☎ (86)(10) 65322361
Jordan
☎ (86)(10) 65323906
Kazakhstan
☎ (86)(10) 65326182
Kenya
☎ (86)(10) 65323381
Korea (DPR)
☎ (86)(10) 65321186
Korea
☎ (86)(10) 65320290
Kuwait
☎ (86)(10) 65322216
Kyrgyz
☎ (86)(10) 65326458
Latvia
☎ (86)(10) 65320106
League of Arab States
☎ (86)(10) 65324083
Lesotho
☎ (86)(10) 65326842
Luxembourg
☎ (86)(10) 65135937
Laos
☎ (86)(10) 65321224

Lebanon
☎ (86)(10) 65321560
Lesotho
☎ (86)(10) 65326842
Libya
☎ (86)(10) 65323666
Lithuania
☎ (86)(10) 64681150
Luxembourg
☎ (86)(10) 65135937
Macedonia
☎ (86)(10) 65326282
Madagascar
☎ (86)(10) 65321353
Malaysia
☎ (86)(10) 65322531
Mali
☎ (86)(10) 65321704
Malta
☎ (86)(10) 65323114
Marshall Islands
☎ (86)(10) 65325819
Mauritania
☎ (86)(10) 65321346
Mauritius
☎ (86)(10) 65325695
Mexico
☎ (86)(10) 65322574
Moldova
☎ (86)(10) 65325494
Mongolia
☎ (86)(10) 65321203
Morocco
☎ (86)(10) 65321796
Mozambique
☎ (86)(10) 65323664
Myanmar
☎ (86)(10) 65321425
Namibia
☎ (86)(10) 65324810
Nepal
☎ (86)(10) 65321795
Netherlands
☎ (86)(10) 65321131
New Zealand
☎ (86)(10) 65322731

Nicaragua
☎ (86)(10) 65323014
Niger
☎ (86)(10) 65324279
Nigeria
☎ (86)(10) 65323631
Norway
☎ (86)(10) 65322261
Oman
☎ (86)(10) 65323692
Pakistan
☎ (86)(10) 65322504
Palestine
☎ (86)(10) 65321361
Papua New Guinea
☎ (86)(10) 65324312
Peru
☎ (86)(10) 65323719
Philippines
☎ (86)(10) 65321872
Poland
☎ (86)(10) 65321235
Portugal
☎ (86)(10) 65323497
Qatar
☎ (86)(10) 65322231
Romania
☎ (86)(10) 65323442
Russia
☎ (86)(10) 65322051
Rwanda
☎ (86)(10) 65322193
Saudi Arabia
☎ (86)(10) 65324825
Senegal
☎ (86)(10) 65322593
Sierra Leone
☎ (86)(10) 65321222
Singapore
☎ (86)(10)85296256
Slovak
☎ (86)(10) 65321531
Slovenia
☎ (86)(10) 64681030
Somali
☎ (86)(10) 65321752

South Africa
☎ (86)(10) 65320171
Spain
☎ (86)(10) 65321986
Sri Lanka
☎ (86)(10) 65321861
Sudan
☎ (86)(10) 65323715
Suriname
☎ (86)(10) 65322939
Sweden
☎ (86)(10) 65323331
Switzerland
☎ (86)(10) 65322736
Syria Arab
☎ (86)(10) 65321372
Tajikistan
☎ (86)(10) 65322598
Tanzania
☎ (86)(10) 65321491
Thailand
☎ (86)(10) 65322151
Togo
☎ (86)(10) 65322202
Tunisia
☎ (86)(10) 65322435
Turkey
☎ (86)(10) 65322650
Turkmenistan
☎ (86)(10) 65326975
Uganda
☎ (86)(10) 65321708
Ukraine
☎ (86)(10) 65326359
United Arab Emirates
☎ (86)(10) 65326532
United Kingdom
☎ (86)(10) 65321961
United States of America
☎ (86)(10) 65323431
Uruguay
☎ (86)(10) 65324445
Uzbekistan
☎ (86)(10) 65326305
Venezuela
☎ (86)(10) 65321295

Vietnam
☎ (86)(10) 65321155
Yemen
☎ (86)(10) 65321558
Yugoslavia
☎ (86)(10) 65323516
Zambia
☎ (86)(10) 65321554
Zimbabwe
☎ (86)(10) 65323795

Chongqing
Canada
☎ (86)(23) 63738007
Japan
☎ (86)(23) 63733585
United Kingdom
☎ (86)(23) 63810321

Guangdong
Guangzhou
Australia
☎ (86)(20) 83350909
Cambodia
☎ (86)(20) 83338999
Canada
☎ (86)(20) 86660569
Denmark
☎ (86)(20) 86660353
France
☎ (86)(20) 83333405
Germany
☎ (86)(20) 81922566
Japan
☎ (86)(20) 83338999
Korea
☎ (86)(20) 38870555
Malaysia
☎ (86)(20) 87395660
Netherlands
☎ (86)(20) 83302067
Philippine
☎ (86)(20) 81886968
Polan
☎ (86)(20) 88862872

Thailand
☎ (86)(20) 81886968
United Kingdom
☎ (86)(20) 83336520
United States of America
☎ (86)(20) 81218000
Vietnam
☎ (86)(20) 86474899

Hong Kong
Australia
☎ (852) 28278881
Britain
☎ (852) 29013000
France
☎ (852) 31966100
Myanmar
☎ (852) 28277929
USA
☎ (852) 31966100
Canada
☎ (852) 28104321
Italy
☎ (852) 25220033
Argentne
☎ (852) 25233208
Namibia
☎ (852) 25861339
Czech
☎ (852) 28022212

Liaoning
Dalian
Japan
☎ (86)(411) 2712005-7

Shenyang
Japan
☎ (86)(24) 3227490
Korea
☎ (86)(24) 23857820
United States of America
☎ (86)(24) 23221198

Shandong
Qingdao

Korea
☎ (86)(532) 2888900

Shanghai
Australia
☎ (86)(21) 64334604
Austria
☎ (86)(21) 64740268
Belgium
☎ (86)(21) 64376579
Brazil
☎ (86)(21) 64370110
British
☎ (86)(21) 62797651
Canada
☎ (86)(21) 62798400
Chile
☎ (86)(21) 62498000
Cuba
☎ (86)(21) 62753078
Czech
☎ (86)(21) 64712420
Denmark
☎ (86)(21) 62090500
Finland
☎ (86)(21) 64740068
France
☎ (86)(21) 64377414
Germany
☎ (86)(21) 64336953
India
☎ (86)(21) 62758885
Iran
☎ (86)(21) 62814666
Israel
☎ (86)(21) 62098008
Italy
☎ (86)(21) 64716980
Japan
☎ (86)(21) 62780788
Korea
☎ (86)(21) 62196417
Mashaoer Islands
☎ (86)(21) 64371399
Mexico
☎ (86)(21) 64379585

Netherlands
☎ (86)(21) 62099076
New Zealand
☎ (86)(21) 64711108
Norway
☎ (86)(21) 63239988
Poland
☎ (86)(21) 64339288
Russia
☎ (86)(21) 63242682
Singapore
☎ (86)(21) 64370776
Sweden
☎ (86)(21) 6474 1311
Switzerland
☎ (86)(21) 62700519
Thailand
☎ (86)(21) 63234095
Turkey
☎ (86)(21) 64746838
United States of America
☎ (86)(21) 64336880
Yugoslavia
☎ (86)(21) 62081388

Sichuan
Chendu
United States of America
☎ (86)(28) 85583992

Freight & Shipping Agents

Anhui
Hefei
APL Co. Pte. Ltd.
☎ (86)(551) 3645527
Int'l Container Cargo Transport Company
☎ (86)(551) 4655643
Int'l Transportation Company
☎ (86)(551) 2622487
Ocean Transportation Company
☎ (86)(551) 2887983
OOCL (China) Ltd.
☎ (86)(551) 2821777
Sinotrans
☎ (86)(10) 65001144

Beijing
APL Company Pte. Ltd.
☎ (86)(10) 65913178
Bax Global
☎ (86)(10) 64365553
Cargo Services Far East Ltd
☎ (86)(10) 87310427
China Marine Shipping Agency
☎ (86)(10) 62295712
Chinese-Polish Joint Stock Shipping Co.
☎ (86)(10) 65321922
Compagnie Maritime D'ffretement (CMA)
☎ (86)(10) 64671938
COSCO Group
☎ (86)(10) 66493388
Danzas Z.F. Freight Agency Co. Ltd.
☎ (86)(10) 65915511
Fritz Logistics Service
☎ (86)(10) 64678877
Global Silverhawk Beijing
☎ (86)(10) 67675566
Golden Eagle International Forwarding
☎ (86)(10) 64651834
Hanjin Shipping
☎ (86)(10) 85191591/2
Hapag-Lloyd (China) Shipping Ltd.
☎ (86)(10) 65101599
Hyundai Merchant Marine Co. Ltd.
☎ (86)(10) 65900992
Jardine Shipping Agencies (HK) Ltd.
☎ (86)(10) 65933081
Kuehne & Nagel
☎ (86)(10) 64379633
Maersk (China) Shipping Co. Ltd.
☎ (86)(10) 67623090
Mitsui O.S.K. Lines (Asia) Ltd.
☎ (86)(10) 8529912
NYK Line
☎ (86)(10) 65052546
OOCL (China) Ltd.
☎ (86)(10) 85183456
P&O Nedlloyd
☎ (86)(10) 65671938
Pacific Int'l Lines (China) Ltd.
☎ (86)(10) 65542157
Panalpina China Ltd.
☎ (86)(10) 64623781

Penavico (China Ocean Shipping Agency)
☎ (86)(10) 64169988
Schenker (HK) Ltd.
☎ (86)(10) 64296520
Sinotrans
☎ (86)(10) 68405601
Transoceanic Shipping
☎ (86)(10) 64651080
Zhongji International Freight Forwarding
☎ (86)(10) 63906471

Chongqing

Ensign Freight Ltd.
☎ (86)(23) 67875405
Maersk Sealand
☎ (86)(23) 63829360
OOCL (China) Ltd.
☎ (86)(23) 63801767
P&O Nedlloyd Ltd.
☎ (86)(23) 67515405
Penavico
☎ (86)(23) 67875256

Fujian

Fuzhou
Cargo Services Far East Ltd.
☎ (86)(591) 7828363
Evergreen
☎ (86)(591) 7538112
Hang Tai Maritime (Int'l) Ltd.
☎ (86)(591) 7835499/79
Fritz Logistics Service
☎ (86)(591) 7548066
Maersk Sealand
☎ (86)(591) 7854548
OOCL (China) Ltd.
☎ (86)(591) 7547190
Schenker Stinnes Logistics
☎ (86)(591) 7855395
P&O Nedlloyd Ltd.
☎ (86)(591) 7800810

Xiamen
APC Asia Pacific Cargo (HK) Ltd.
☎ (86)(592) 6011500
APL Company Pte. Ltd.
☎ (86)(592) 2016683

Atlantic Forwarding (China) Ltd.
☎ (86)(592) 5087125
Barwil Agencies Ltd.
☎ (86)(592) 6019485
China Ocean Shipping (Group) Ltd
☎ (86)(592) 5310868
Cho Yang (HK) Ltd
☎ (86)(592) 6028358
Compagnie Maritime D'ffretement (CMA)
☎ (86)(592) 5098999
Danzas Z.F.Freight Agency Co. Ltd.
☎ (86)(592) 5068465
Dyna Int'l Shipping Ltd.
☎ (86)(592) 5620064
Euro-Asia Line (HK) Ltd.
☎ (86)(592) 5620064
Evergreen
☎ (86)(592) 5117877
Fritz Logistics Service
☎ (86)(592) 2960106
Hanjin Shipping
☎ (86)(592) 5091902
Hapag-Lloyd (China) Shipping Ltd.
☎ (86)(592) 5113562-4
J H Bachmann (HK) Ltd.
☎ (86)(592) 5310250
K Line (HK) Ltd.
☎ (86)(592) 2025326
Maersk (China) Shipping Co. Ltd.
☎ (86)(592) 5065011
Mitsui O.S.K. (Asia) Ltd.
☎ (86)(592) 5117818
NYK Line
☎ (86)(592) 6021666
OOCL (China) Ltd.
☎ (86)(592) 2394391
P&O Nedlloyd
☎ (86)(592) 2394018
Panalpina China Ltd.
☎ (86)(592) 2398879
Penavico (China Ocean Shipping Agency)
☎ (86)(592) 6016996
Zhonghang Scanwell Int'l Freight Agent
☎ (86)(592) 6037737
Schenker (HK) Ltd.
☎ (86)(592) 5064894

Sinoformosa Systems (HK) Ltd.
☎ (86)(592) 6027181

Guangdong

Dongguan
China Marine Shipping Agency
☎ (86)(769) 2461022
Hanjin Shipping
☎ (86)(769) 5103531
Jardine Logistics
☎ (86)(769) 2413376
Man On Shipping Co. Ltd.
☎ (86)(769) 2492200

Fushan
Hanjin Shipping
☎ (86)(591) 3354539

Guangzhou
APL Co. Pte. Ltd.
☎ (86)(20) 87664629
Bax Global
☎ (86)(20) 83634513
Ben Line Agencies (HK) Ltd.
☎ (86)(20) 85592433
Chinese-Polish Joint Stock Shipping Co.
☎ (86)(20) 83801197
Cho Yang (Hong Kong) Co. Ltd.
☎ (86)(20) 87520696
Clan S.A.
☎ (86)(20) 84328209
CMA CGM – The French Line
☎ (86 20) 87322815
COSCO Group, Guangzhou
☎ (86)(20) 87765567
Danzas AEI Ocean Services (HK) Ltd.
☎ (86)(20) 87358257
Damco Maritime (China) Ltd.
☎ (86)(20) 87310888
EAS Shipping
☎ (86)(20) 82304578
Evergreen
☎ (86)(20) 87320321
Fritz Logistics Service
☎ (86)(20) 38780566
Guangzhou-Penavico Transport Int'l Co.
☎ (86)(20) 83837954

Hanjin Shipping Co. Ltd.
☎ (86)(20) 83837400
Hapag-Lloyd (China) Shipping Ltd.
☎ (86)(20) 83850591
Hyundai Merchant Marine Co.
☎ (86)(20) 86661804
Jardine Shipping Agencies (HK) Ltd.
☎ (86)(20) 6675529
"K" Line (HK) Ltd.
☎ (86)(20) 87321699
Kuehne & Nagel
☎ (86)(20) 87786983
Lloyd Triestino Pacific Ltd.
☎ (86)(20) 82217422
Maersk (China) Shipping Co. Ltd.
☎ (86)(20) 38780571
Mediterranean Shipping Co. S.A. (MSC)
☎ (86)(20) 83581921
Merzario (HK) Ltd.
☎ (86)(20) 83864483
Mitsui O.S.K. Lines (Asia) Ltd.
☎ (86)(20) 83338999
Norasia (China) Ltd.
☎ (86)(20) 87604123
NYK Line
☎ (86)(20) 87554538
OOCL (China) Ltd.
☎ (86)(20) 38771688
OT Africa Line
☎ (86)(20) 87762888
P&O Nedlloyd
☎ (86)(20) 87311182
Pacific Int'l Lines (China) Ltd.
☎ (86)(20) 83843207
Pacific Star Line
☎ (86)(20) 83150577
Panalpina China Ltd.
☎ (86)(20) 87322132
Penavico
☎ (86)(20) 83808582
P&O Nedlloyd Ltd.
☎ (86)(20) 87311182
Regional Container Lines (HK) Ltd.
☎ (86)(20) 83633236
Scanwell Consolidators Ltd.
☎ (86)(20) 87609110

Schenker (HK) Ltd.
☎ (86)(20) 87255441
Sinotrans
☎ (86)(20) 83805661
Triple Eagle Container Line
☎ (86)(20) 83837899
WSA Lines
☎ (86)(20) 86682372
Zim Israel Navigation Company
☎ (86)(20) 83311145

Jiangmen
Hanjin Shipping
☎ (86)(750) 3100351

Shantou
Hanjin Shipping
☎ (86)(754) 8939753
Maersk Sealand
☎ (86)(754) 8164031
OOCL
☎ (86)(754) 8175061
P&O Nedlloyd Ltd.
☎ (86)(754) 8118909

Shenzhen
American President Lines
☎ (86)(755) 25353202
APL Co. Pte Ltd.
☎ (86)(755) 25181018
Barwil Agencies Ltd.
☎ (86)(755) 82205584
Ben Line Agencies (H.K.) Ltd.
☎ (86)(755) 25181193
Birkart Globistics
☎ (86)(755) 82350499
China Marine Shipping Agency (Sinoagent)
☎ (86)(755) 25290265
China Merchants Marine & Transportation
☎ (86)(755) 26692816
China Merchants Ocena Shipping Agency
☎ (86)(755) 26688750
Cho Yang (Hong Kong) Co. Ltd.
☎ (86)(755) 83694290
Clan S.A.
☎ (86)(755) 26696711

CMA CGM – The French Line
☎ (86)(755) 82350100
COSCO Container Lines
☎ (86)(755) 26695005
COSCO Group
☎ (86)(755) 83344836
COSCO Shenzhen Int'l Freight Co.
☎ (86)(755) 26689696
Dyna Int'l Shipping Ltd.
☎ (86)(755) 26688688
Eastern Worldwide Co. Ltd.
☎ (86)(755) 25290757
Evergreen
☎ (86)(755) 82461930
Fair Wind Shipping Co. Ltd.
☎ (86)(755) 26688500
Fritz Logistics Service
☎ (86)(755) 26851280, 27776788
Hanjin Shipping
☎ (86)(755) 82170918, 25290815
Hapag-Lloyd (China) Shipping Ltd.
☎ (86)(755) 26675657, 25291127
Hercules Logistics & Forwarding Ltd.
☎ (86)(755) 26813927
Hong Kong Ming Wah Shipping
☎ (86)(755) 6689968
Inchcape Shipping Service
☎ (86)(755) 83323804
Jardine Logistics
☎ (86)(755) 82181407
K-Line (HK) Ltd.
☎ (86)(755) 25290746
Lloyd Triestino Pacific Ltd.
☎ (86)(755) 82194884
Luen Tong Shipping Ltd.
☎ (86)(755) 26689228
Maersk (China) Shipping Co. Ltd.
☎ (86)(755) 82187770, 25352536
Mediterranean Shipping Co. S.A. (MSC)
☎ (86)(755) 26815568, 26694183
Merzario (HK) Ltd.
☎ (86)(755) 25569667
Norasia (China) Ltd.
☎ (86)(755) 26698867
NYK Line
☎ (86)(755) 82463226, 26851597

OOCL (China) Ltd.
☎ (86)(755) 82280552, 25290481
OT Africa Line
☎ (86)(755) 26689371
P&O Nedlloyd
☎ (86)(755) 26685803, 82366236
Panalpina China Ltd.
☎ (86)(755) 26672124, 82406275
Pacific Int'l Lines (China) Ltd.
☎ (86)(755) 82204804
Pacific Star Line
☎ (86)(755) 26691060
Penavico
☎ (86)(755) 26692257
Regional Container Lines
☎ (86)(755) 82170914
Schenker (HK) Ltd.
☎ (86)(755) 27398047
Sinotrans
☎ (86)(755) 25186815
Sun Hing Shipping Co. Ltd.
☎ (86)(755) 26851840
United Signal Cargo
☎ (86)(755) 26391099
United Transportation
☎ (86)(755) 26689371
Universal Shipping (Asia) Co. Ltd.
☎ (86)(755) 26826168
Wan Hai Lines Ltd.
☎ (86)(755) 82290858
WSA Lines Ltd.
☎ (86)(755) 25115831

Shunde
Evergreen
☎ (86)(765) 2212672
Maersk Sealand
☎ (86)(765) 2209090
P&O Nedlloyd Ltd.
☎ (86)(765) 6623603
Schenker Stinnes Logistics
☎ (86)(765) 6617863

Zhongshan
Evergreen
☎ (86)(760) 3326611

Maersk Sealand
☎ (86)(760) 8309042
NYK Line
☎ (86)(760) 5310123
OOCL
☎ (86)(760) 8381488
Zhongshan Marine Shipping Agency
☎ (86)(760) 5310668

Zhuhai
Evergreen
☎ (86)(756) 3328410
Maersk Sealand
☎ (86)(756) 3329740
NYK line
☎ (86)(756) 8153571
Penavico
☎ (86)(756) 3336431

Hainan
Hercules Logistics & Forwarding (Yangpu)
☎ (86)(898) 6114280

Heilongjiang
Harbin
APL Co. Pte. Ltd.
☎ (86)(451) 3605383
China Foreign Carry Harbin Corporation
☎ (86)(451) 4618779
China Foreign Carry Heilongjinag Corp.
☎ (86)(451) 2300878
Harbin United Transport Corp.
☎ (86)(451) 8686791
Heilongjiang Int'l Freightage Deputize General Corp.
☎ (86)(451) 2624115
Heilongjiang Ocean Shipping Corp.
☎ (86)(451) 8673949
Maersk Sealand
☎ (86)(451) 2613840

Hong Kong
Accord Container Line (HK) Ltd.
☎ (852) 28507100
American Consolidation Services Ltd.
☎ (852) 23027555

American Intermodal Container Line (HK)
☎ (352) 25112184
Ami-su Line S.A.
☎ (852) 23001380
APL-American President Lines.
☎ (852) 27387333
Bax Global Ltd.
☎ (852) 23799280
Blue Anchor Line
☎ (852) 28237688
CMA CGM (ASIA) Ltd.
☎ (852) 28653881
CMA-CGM (Hong Kong) Shipping Agencies
☎ (852) 31981688
Cosco Container Line Agencies Ltd.
☎ (852) 25890388
Damco (HK) Ltd.
☎ (852) 23694981
Danzas AEI (HK) Ltd.
☎ (852) 24811388
Evergreen Star Hong Kong Ltd.
☎ (852) 28258211
Expeditors Hong Kong Ltd.
☎ (852) 21903000
Freight Links Express (HK) Ltd.
☎ (852) 25458233
Gulf Orient Lines
☎ (852) 23697226
Hanjin Shipping Co. Ltd.
☎ (852) 25071100
Heung-A Line.
☎ (852) 25343700
Hub Line
☎ (852) 28153222
Hyundai Merchant Marine Co.Ltd.
☎ (852) 25144100
Jardine Logistics Services (HKG) Ltd.
☎ (852) 25904333
Jardine Shipping Agencies (HK) Ltd.
☎ (852) 25793579
Kintetsu World Express (HK) Ltd.
☎ (852) 27963340
Lloyd Triestino Pacific Ltd.
☎ (852) 27459123
Maersk Hong Kong Ltd.
☎ (852) 28372222

Maersk Logistics Hong Kong Ltd.
☎ (852) 28302999
Mediterranean Shipping Co. Ltd.
☎ (852) 29025555
Mitsui O.S.K. Lines (HK) Ltd.
☎ (852) 28236800
Mitsui-Soko Co. Ltd.
☎ (852) 23664378
Naigai Nitto Logistics (HK) Ltd.
☎ (852) 23686323
Nippon Express (HK) Co. Ltd.
☎ (852) 24081177
NYK Line (HK) Ltd.
☎ (852) 28645100
OOCL (HK) Ltd.
☎ (852) 25066888
OSL Orion Star Line Ltd.
☎ (852) 27900921
OT Africa Line
☎ (852) 28952569
P&O Nedlloyd
☎ (852) 28566100
Pacific International Shipping Co Ltd.
☎ (852) 26251911
Panalpina China Ltd.
☎ (852) 27602600
United Arab Agencies (Hong Kong) Ltd
☎ (852) 25793793
W S A (International) Lines Ltd.
☎ (852) 25598018

Hubei
Wuhan
APC Asia Pacific Cargo(HK) Ltd.
☎ (86)(27) 83634037
APL Co. Pte. Ltd.
☎ (86)(27) 8577808
Compagnie Maritime D'ffretement (CMA)
☎ (86)(27) 8574 3391
Danzas Z.F.Freight Agency Co. Ltd.
☎ (86)(27) 85729480
Maersk (China) Shipping Co. Ltd.
☎ (86)(27) 85473309
OOCL (China) Ltd.
☎ (86)(27) 85486863
P&O Nedlloyd
☎ (86)(27) 85743290

Penavico
☎ (86)(27) 82818988
Shanghai Chang Hang Transportation
Service Dept.
☎ (86)(27) 83776437
Sinotrans
☎ (86)(27) 83620268
WSA Lines Ltd.
☎ (86)(27) 82912113

Jiangsu
Lianyungang
COSCO Group
☎ (86)(518) 2341607
Hanjin Shipping
☎ (86)(518) 2310653
Maersk Sealand
☎ (86)(518) 2381527
Penavico (China Ocean Shipping Agency)
☎ (86)(518) 2312851
Sinotrans
☎ (86)(518) 2310653

Nanjing
AEI Ocean Services (HK) Ltd.
☎ (86)(25) 3322962
APL Co Pte Ltd.
☎ (86)(25) 4798700
Compagnie Maritime D'ffretement (CMA)
☎ (86)(25) 4799011
Danzas Z.F. Freight Agency Co. Ltd.
☎ (86)(25) 3311123
DSR Senator Lines (China) Co. Ltd.
☎ (86)(25) 4798595/6
Evergreen
☎ (86)(25) 4798760
Fritz Logistics Service
☎ (86)(25) 4529894
Hanjin Shipping
☎ (86)(25) 4799981
Hapag-Lloyd (China) Shipping Ltd.
☎ (86)(25) 4799458
Hyundai Merchant Marine Co. Ltd.
☎ (86)(25) 4700405
Jardin Logistics Nanjing Office
☎ (86)(25) 4524466

K Line (HK) Ltd.
☎ (86)(25) 4700200
Lloyd Triestino Pacific Ltd.
☎ (86)(25) 2267804
Maersk (China) Shipping Co. Ltd.
☎ (86)(25) 4799044
Mitsui O.S.K. (Asia) Ltd.
☎ (86)(25) 4528290
NYK Line
☎ (86)(25) 4516997
OOCL (China) Ltd.
☎ (86)(25) 4799655
P&O Nedlloyd
☎ (86)(25) 4799168
Panalpina China Ltd.
☎ (86)(25) 4799784
Penavico
☎ (86)(25) 8808308
Schenker (HK) Ltd.
☎ (86)(25) 3369651
Sinotrans
☎ (86)(25) 4543868
WSA Lines Ltd.
☎ (86)(25) 2256860

Nantong
APL Company Pte. Ltd.
☎ (86)(513) 3537585
Hanjin Shipping
☎ (86)(513) 3533397
Maersk Sealand
☎ (86)(513) 3558176
OOCL (China) Ltd.
☎ (86)(513) 3554811
Penavico
☎ (86)(513) 3518594

Suzhou
Fritz Logistics Service
☎ (86)(512) 5110840
OOCL (China) Ltd.
☎ (86)(512) 5113782

Liaoning
Dalian
APC Asia Pacific Cargo (HK) Ltd.
☎ (86)(411) 2719031

AEI Ocean Services (HK) Ltd.
☎ (86)(411) 2648088
APC Asia Pacific Cargo (HK) Ltd.
☎ (36)(411) 27 9031
APL Company Pte. Ltd.
☎ (86)(411) 2800158
Atlantic Forwarding (China) Ltd.
☎ (86)(411) 2721598
Birkart Globistics
☎ (86)(411) 2653712
Champ Express Ltd.
☎ (86)(411) 3645839
China Express Int'l Transportation Co Ltd.
☎ (86)(411) 2808010
China Ocean Shipping (Group) Co.
☎ (86)(411) 2636161
Chinese-Polish Joint Stock Shipping Co.
☎ (86)(411) 2642132
Cho Yang (HK) Co Ltd.
☎ (86)(411) 2715538
Compagnie Maritime D'ffretement
☎ (86)(411) 2728181
COSCO Container Lines
☎ (86)(411) 2626077
Danzas Z.F. Freight Agency Co. Ltd.
☎ (86)(411) 2805041
DTW Group
☎ (86)(411) 2798298
Evergreen
☎ (86)(411) 2800094
Exel
☎ (86)(411) 2821930
Fritz Logistics Service
☎ (86)(411) 2714068
GeoLogistics Ltd.
☎ (86)(411) 2798225
Hanjin Shipping Co Ltd.
☎ (86)(411) 2718188
Hapag-Lloyd (China) Shipping Ltd.
☎ (86)(411) 2819293
Hong Kong Ming Wah Shipping Co. Ltd.
☎ (86)(411) 2725304
Hyundai Merchant Marine Co. Ltd.
☎ (86)(411) 2800911
Inchcape Shipping Services (HK) Ltd.
☎ (86)(411) 2743798

Jardine Logistics
☎ (86)(411) 2656938
K Line (HK) Ltd.
☎ (86)(411) 2645836
Lloyd Triestino Pacific Ltd.
☎ (86)(411) 2551001
Maersk (China) Shipping Co. Ltd.
☎ (86)(411) 2714285
Mitsui O.S.K (Asia) Ltd.
☎ (86)(411) 2730696
NYK Line
☎ (86)(411) 3687879
OOCL (China) Ltd.
☎ (86)(411) 2715566
P&O Nedlloyd
☎ (86)(411) 2658649
Panalpina China Ltd.
☎ (86)(411) 2551345
Penavico
☎ (86)(411) 2639377
Rickmers Linie
☎ (86)(411) 2803981
Schenker (HK) Ltd.
☎ (86)(411) 2798233
Sinotrans
☎ (86)(411) 2703638
WSA Lines Ltd.
☎ (86)(411) 2592311

Shenyang
Danzas AEI
☎ (86)(24) 23341521
Hanjin Shipping
☎ (86)(24) 22791102
Maersk Sealand
☎ (86)(24) 25362902
WSA Lines Ltd.
☎ (86)(24) 22526163

Macau

Baltrans (Macau) Ltd, Macau
☎ (853) 786383
Kuehne & Nagel (Macau) Ltd
☎ (853) 704008
Panalpina China Ltd.
☎ (853) 703409

Schenker International (Macau) Ltd
☎ (853) 712687

Shaanxi

Xi'an
Bax Global
☎ (86)(29) 8408011
Danzas AEI
☎ (86)(29) 8311813
Maersk Sealland
☎ (86)(29) 7513771
OOCL (China) Ltd.
☎ (86)(29) 7203195
Shaanxi Int'l Freight Transport Comp. Ltd.
☎ (86)(29) 8311030
Xi'an Zhongyuan Int'l Freight Transport
☎ (86)(29) 3291906

Shandong

Qingdao
AEI Ocean Services (HK) Ltd.
☎ (86)(532) 5753016/7
APL Company Pte. Ltd.
☎ (86)(532) 5016777
Bax Global
☎ (86)(532) 5712329
Ben Line Agencies (HK) Ltd.
☎ (86)(532) 5021839
Chinese-Polish Joint Stock Shipping Co.
☎ (86)(532) 5841029
Cho Yang (HK) Co. Ltd.
☎ (86)(532) 2896581
Compagnie Maritime D'ffretement (CMA)
☎ (86)(532) 5027058
COSCO Container Lines
☎ (86)(532) 5716888
Danzas Z.F. Freight Agency Co. Ltd.
☎ (86)(532) 5718014
Euro-Asia Line (HK) Ltd.
☎ (86)(532) 5026269
Evergreen
☎ (86)(532) 5910398
Fritz Logistics Service
☎ (86)(532) 5729812
Hanjin Shipping
☎ (86)(532) 5717795

Hapag-Lloyd (China) Shipping Ltd.
☎ (86)(532) 2971738
Hyundai Merchant Marine Co. Ltd.
☎ (86)(532) 5847232
Inchcape Shipping Service (HK) Ltd.
☎ (86)(532) 2667691
Jardine Shipping Agencies (HK) Ltd.
☎ (86)(532) 5846264
K Line (HK) Ltd.
☎ (86)(532) 5729682
Lloyd Triestino Pacific Ltd.
☎ (86)(532) 2651688
Maersk (China) Shipping Co. Ltd.
☎ (86)(532) 3878052
Mediterranean Shipping Co. S.A.(MSC)
☎ (86)(532) 2972466
Merzario (HK) Ltd.
☎ (86)(532) 2686868
Mitsui O.S.K. Lines (Asia) Ltd.
☎ (86)(532) 2896303
Norasia (China) Ltd.
☎ (86)(532) 2665654
NYK Line
☎ (86)(532) 5027000
OOCL (China) Ltd.
☎ (86)(532) 5763833
P&O Nedlloyd Ltd.
☎ (86)(532) 5713205
Panalpina China Ltd.
☎ (86)(532) 5919925
Penavico
☎ (86)(532) 2651110
Regional Container Lines (HK) Ltd.
☎ (86)(532) 5026277
Schenker (HK) Ltd.
☎ (86)(532) 2665401
Sinotrans
☎ (86)(532) 3831193
Wan Hai Lines Ltd.
☎ (86)(532) 5716699
WSA Lines Ltd.
☎ (86)(532) 5763498

Yantai
Compagnie Maritime D'ffretement (CMA)
☎ (86)(535) 6233861

Fritz Logistics Service
☎ (86)(535) 6280145
Hanjin Shipping
☎ (86)(535) 6613949
NYK Line
☎ (86)(535) 5290979
Penavico
☎ (86)(535) 6243181

Shanghai

AEI Ocean Services (HK) Ltd.
☎ (86)(21) 62136445
APL Company Pte. Ltd.
☎ (86)(21) 63851551
Bax Global
☎ (86)(21) 52340505
Ben Line Agencies (HK) Ltd.
☎ (86)(21) 53850040
Birkart Globistics
☎ (86)(21) 65958940
Chinese-Polish Joint Stock Shipping Co.
☎ (86)(21) 63360108
Cho Yang (HK) Ltd.
☎ (86)(21) 64663518
Compagnie Martime D'ffretement (CMA)
☎ (86)(21) 63233813
COSCO Container Lines
☎ (86)(21) 65841888
Danzas Z.F. Freight Agency Co. Ltd.
☎ (86)(21) 63598140
Delmas HK Ltd.
☎ (86)(21) 63261491
Evergreen
☎ (86)(21) 53081080
Fritz Logistics Service
☎ (86)(21) 63865288
Hanjin Shipping Co. Ltd.
☎ (86)(21) 58201030
Hapag-Lloyd (China) Shipping Ltd.
☎ (86)(21) 64155170
Hyundai Merchant Marine Co. Ltd.
☎ (86)(21) 53854198
Inchcape Shipping Service (HK) Ltd.
☎ (86)(21) 63514756
Integra Shipping Pte. Ltd.
☎ (86)(21) 6357949

Islamic Republic of Iran Shipping Lines
☎ (86)(21) 58369264
Jardine Shipping Agencies (HK) Ltd.
☎ (86)(21) 62701598
K Line (HK) Ltd.
☎ (86)(21) 63229988
Lloyd Triestino Pacific Ltd.
☎ (86)(21) 53086690
Maersk (China) Shipping Co. Ltd.
☎ (86)(21) 63201326
Mediterranean Shipping Co. (MSC)
☎ (86)(21) 62881118
Merzario (HK) Ltd.
☎ (86)(21) 62491521
Mitsui O.S.K. Lines (Asia) Ltd.
☎ (86)(21) 53060088
Norasia (China) Ltd.
☎ (86)(21) 63644919
NYK Line
☎ (86)(21) 63851166
OOCL (China) Ltd.
☎ (86)(21) 62794567
P&O Nedlloyd
☎ (86)(21) 63912500
Pacific Int'l Lines (China) Ltd.
☎ (86)(21) 63936900
Panalpina China Ltd.
☎ (86)(21) 62726010
Penavico
☎ (86)(21) 63647688
Schenker (HK) Ltd.
☎ (86)(21) 54048087
TNT Logistics Co. Ltd.
☎ (86)(21) 64690615
Transoceanic Shipping Company Inc.
☎ (86)(21) 63620091
WSA Lines Ltd.
☎ (86)(21) 65461457

Sichuan

Chengdu

APL Co. Pte. Ltd.
☎ (86)(28) 86620216
Crown Worldwide
☎ (86)(28) 82952810
Dyna Int'l Shipping Ltd.
☎ (86)(28) 86642888

Maersk Sealand
☎ (86)(28) 86527677
OOCL (China) Ltd.
☎ (86)(28) 86528833
P&O Nedlloyd Ltd.
☎ (86)(28) 83192206
Panalpina China Ltd.
☎ (86)(28) 86673108
Schenker Stinnes Logistics
☎ (86)(28) 86626385
Sinotrans
☎ (86)(28) 86628759

Tianjin

AEI Ocean Services (HK) Ltd.
☎ (86)(22) 28364265
APL Company Pte. Ltd.
☎ (86)(22) 23302040
Bax Global
☎ (86)(22) 25324145
China Express Int'l Transportation Co. Ltd.
☎ (86)(22) 23398156
China Marine Shipping Agency
☎ (86)(22) 23317745
Chinese-Polish Joint Stock Shipping Co.
☎ (86)(22) 23306532
Cho Yang (HK) Co. Ltd.
☎ (86)(22) 23133033
Compagnie Maritime D'ffretement (CMA)
☎ (86)(22) 23307051
COSCO Bulk Carrier
☎ (86)(22) 24205188
Crown Worldwide
☎ (86)(22) 65298998
Danzas Z.F. Freight Agency Co. Ltd.
☎ (86)(22) 25324080
Evergreen
☎ (86)(22) 23133111
Fritz Logistics Service
☎ (86)(22) 27217071
Hapag-Lloyd (China) Shipping
☎ (86)(22) 27113380
Hanjin Shipping
☎ (86)(22) 23306958
Hyundai Merchant Marine Co. Ltd.
☎ (86 22) 23307368

Inchcape Shipping Service (HK) Ltd.
☎ (86)(22) 27831740
Jardine Shipping Agencies (HK) Ltd.
☎ (86)(22) 23923492/5
K Line (HK) Ltd.
☎ (86)(22) 27237077
Lian Huat Shipping Co. Pte. Ltd.
☎ (86)(22) 27114018
Lloyd Tristino Pacific Ltd
☎ (86)(22) 27826590
Maersk (China) Shipping Co. Ltd.
☎ (86)(22) 23303510
Mediterranean Shipping Co. S.S.(MSC)
☎ (86)(22) 24109866
Militzer & Munch Tianbao Int'l Fowarding
☎ (86)(22) 27118033
Mitsui O.S.K. (Asia) Ltd.
☎ (86)(22) 23398349
Norasia (China) Ltd.
☎ (86)(22) 23310841
NYK Line
☎ (86)(22) 23307115
OOCL (China) Ltd.
☎ (86)(22) 23307760
P&O Nedlloyd
☎ (86)(22) 24109787
Panalpina China Ltd.
☎ (86)(22) 23116756
Penavico
☎ (86)(22) 23191008
Schenker (HK) Ltd.
☎ (86)(22) 23304001
Sinotrans
☎ (86)(22) 23310746

Zhejiang

Hangzhou

APL Co. Pte. Ltd.
☎ (86)(571) 5153911
Exel
☎ (86)(571) 5304880
Maersk Sealand
☎ (86)(571) 8577738
NYK Line
☎ (86)(571) 7210607
OOCL
☎ (86)(571) 7085100

Schenker Stinnes Logistics
☎ (86)(571) 5096811

Ningbo
APL Co. Pte. Ltd.
☎ (86)(574) 7321148
China Ocean Shipping Company
☎ (86)(574) 7032229
Compagnie Maritime D'ffretement (CMA)
☎ (86)(574) 7730282
Danzas Z.F. Freight Agency Co. Ltd.
☎ (86)(574) 7296071
DSR Senator Lines (China) Co. Ltd.
☎ (86)(574) 7316025
Evergreen
☎ (86)(574) 7092724
Hanjin Shipping
☎ (86)(574) 7317737
Hyundai Merchant Marine Co. Ltd.
☎ (86)(574) 7328243
Lloyd Triestino Pacific Ltd.
☎ (86)(574) 7323387
Maersk (China) Shipping Co. Ltd.
☎ (86)(574) 4292777
Mitsui O.S.K. Lines (Asia) Ltd.
☎ (86)(574) 7262887
Norasia (China) Ltd.
☎ (86)(574) 7195523
NYK Line
☎ (86)(574) 7296696
OOCL (China) Ltd
☎ (86)(574) 7281098
P&O Nedlloyd
☎ (86)(574) 7296752
Panalpine China Ltd.
☎ (86)(574) 7243691
Penavico (China Ocean Shipping Agency)
☎ (86)(574) 7355372
Schenker (HK) Ltd.
☎ (86)(574) 7315500
Sinotrans
☎ (86)(574) 7292013

Wenzhou
Hanjin Shipping
☎ (86)(577) 8619030

Hotels

Anhui
Hefei
★★★★
Anhui Hotel
☎ (86)(551) 2811818
NOVOTEL QIYUN HOTEL
☎ (86)(551) 2887777
★★★
Anhui Overseas Chinese Hotel
☎ (86)(551) 2652221
Meiling Hotel
☎ (86)(551) 2887277

Huangshan
★★★
Cloudy Valley Hotel
☎ (86)(559) 5562456
Huangshan Taiping Int'l Hotel
☎ (86)(559) 8532888
Peach Garden Hotel
☎ (86)(559) 5562295

Wuhu
★★★
Yingkesong Hotel
☎ (86)(553) 3857788
Tieshan Hotel
☎ (86)(553) 3835981

Beijing
★★★★★
Beijing International Hotel
☎ (86)(10) 65126688
Beijing Hotel
☎ (86)(10) 65137766
Beijing New Century Hotel
☎ (86)(10) 68492001
China World Hotel
☎ (86)(10) 65052266
Diaoyutai State Guest House
☎ (86)(10) 68591188
Grand Hotel Beijing
☎ (86)(10) 65137788

Harbour Plaza
☎ (86)(10) 64362288
Hilton Beijing
☎ (86)(10) 64662288
Holiday Inn Crowne Plaza Beijing
☎ (86)(10) 65133388
Hotel Kunlun Beijing
☎ (86)(10) 65903388
Hotel New Otani Changfugong
☎ (86)(10) 65125555
Jing Guang New World Hotel
☎ (86)(10) 65978888
Kempinski Hotel Beijing Lufthansa Center
☎ (86)(10) 64653388
Prime Hotel
☎ (86)(10) 65136666
Shangri-La Hotel Beijing
☎ (86)(10) 68412211
ST Regis Hotel Former Int'l Club
☎ (86)(10) 64606688
Swissotel (Beijing Hong Kong Macau Center)
☎ (86)(10) 65012288
The Great Wall Sheraton Hotel Beijing
☎ (86)(10) 65905566
The Palace Hotel Beijing
☎ (86)(10) 65128899
★★★★
Beijing Continental Grand Hotel
☎ (86)(10) 64915588
Beijing Friendship Hotel
☎ (86)(10) 68498888
Beijing Grace Hotel
☎ (86)(10) 64362288
Bejing Mandarin Hotel
☎ (86)(10) 68319988
Beijing Telecom Hotel
☎ (86)(10) 63901166
Beijing Scitech Hotel
☎ (86)(10) 65123388
Capital Hotel
☎ (86)(10) 65129988
Central Garden Hotel
☎ (86)(10) 62178888
China Resources Hotel
☎ (86)(10) 85772233
China Travel Service Tower
☎ (86)(10) 64622288

Debao Hotel Beijing
☎ (86)(10) 68318866
Fragrant Hill Hotel
☎ (86)(10) 62591166
Gloria Plaza Hotel Beijing
☎ (86)(10) 65158855
Grand View Garden Hotel
☎ (86)(10) 63538899
Guangxi Plaza
☎ (86)(10) 67796688
Holiday Inn Downtown Beijing
☎ (86)(10) 68338822
Holiday Inn-Lido Beijing
☎ (86)(10) 64376688
Jianguo Hotel
☎ (86)(10) 65002233
Jinglun Hotel
☎ (86)(10) 65002266
Landmark Hotel
☎ (86)(10) 65906688
Movenpick Hotel
☎ (86)(10) 64565588
North Garden Hotel
☎ (86)(10) 65238888
NOVOTEL PEACE HOTEL
☎ (86)(10) 65128833
Oriental Garden Hotel
☎ (86)(10) 64168866
Radisson SAS Hotel Beijing
☎ (86)(10) 64663388
Sino-Swiss Hotel Beijing Airport
☎ (86)(10) 64565588
Tianlun Dynasty Hotel
☎ (86)(10) 65138888
Traders Hotel
☎ (86)(10) 65052277
Xindadu Hotel
☎ (86)(10) 68319988
Xiyuan Hotel
☎ (86)(10) 68313388
Yanshan Hotel
☎ (86)(10) 62563388
Zhaolong Hotel
☎ (86)(10) 65972299
★★★
Chongqing Hotel
☎ (86)(10) 64228888

Chongwenmen Hotel
☎ (86)(10) 65122211
COFCO Dragon Spring Resort
☎ (86)(10) 60811616
NOVOTEL XINQIAO BEIJING
☎ (86)(10) 65133366
Qianmen Hotel Beijing
☎ (86)(10) 63016688
Paragon Hotel Beijing
☎ (86)(10) 65266688
Ritan Hotel Beijing
☎ (86)(10) 65125588
Taiwan Hotel
☎ (86)(10) 65136688
Tiantan Hotel
☎ (86)(10) 67112277
Tibet Hotel
☎ (86)(10) 64981133

Chongqing
★★★★
Chongqing Guest House
☎ (86)(23) 63845888
Holiday Inn Yangtze
☎ (86)(23) 62803380
★★★
Chaotianmen Hotel
☎ (86)(23) 63712600
Chongqing Renmin Hotel
☎ (86)(23) 63851421
Chongqing Grand Hotel
☎ (86)(23) 65339888
Chongqing Hotel
☎ (86)(23) 63849302
Chongqing Milky Way Hotel
☎ (86)(23) 63808585
Southwest Hotel
☎ (86)(23) 62800009

Fujian
Fuzhou
★★★★★
Foreign Trade Centre Hotel
☎ (86)(591) 7523388
Fuzhou Lakeside Hotel
☎ (86)(591) 7839888

Hot Spring Hotel
☎ (86)(591) 7851818
★★★
East Lake Hotel
☎ (86)(591) 7557755
Minjiang Hotel
☎ (86)(591) 7557895

Quanzhou
★★★★
Quanzhou Hotel
☎ (86)(595) 2289958
★★★
Golden Star Hotel
☎ (86)(595) 2988888

Wuyishan
★★★
Jade Maid Hotel
☎ (86)(599) 5252988
Wuyi Mountain Villa
☎ (86)(599) 5251888

Xiamen
★★★★★
Xiamen Mandarin Hotel
☎ (86)(592) 6023333
★★★★
Holiday Inn Crowne Plaza
☎ (86)(592) 2023333
The Marco Polo
☎ (86)(592) 5091888
★★★
East Ocean Hotel
☎ (86)(592) 2021111
Huaxia Hotel
☎ (86)(592) 5159888
Miramar Hotel
☎ (86)(592) 6031666
Xiamen Lujiang Hotel
☎ (86)(592) 2022922
Xiamen International Airport Hotel
☎ (86)(592) 5736688

Gansu
Dunhuang

★★★
Dunhuang Hotel
☎ (86)(937) 8822538
Dunhuang Shazhou Hotel
☎ (86)(937) 8825031
Grand Sun Hotel
☎ (86)(937) 8829998

Jiayuguan
★★★
Great Wall Hotel
☎ (86)(937) 6226306
Jiayuguan Hotel
☎ (86)(937) 6226158

Lanzhou
★★★★
Lanzhou Legend Hotel
☎ (86)(931) 8882876
★★★
Lanzhou Hotel
☎ (86)(931) 8416321
Xibei Hotel
☎ (86)(931) 8413456

Guangdong
Dongguan
★★★★★
Yincheng Hotel
☎ (86)(769) 2818888
★★★★
Golden Palace Hotel
☎ (86)(769) 3326328
Huaqiao Hotel
☎ (86)(769) 2118888
★★★
Dongguan Hotel
☎ (86)(769) 2222222
Golden Lake Hotel
☎ (86)(769) 7721000
Oriental Hotel
☎ (86)(769) 2227788
Regent Hotel
☎ (86)(769) 2466888

Foshan

★★★★
Foshan Hotel
☎ (86)(757) 3353338
★★★
Foshan Huaqiao Hotel
☎ (86)(757) 2223828

Guangzhou
★★★★★
China Hotel
☎ (86)(20) 86666888
Dongfang Hotel
☎ (86)(20) 86669900
Guangdong Int'l Hotel
☎ (86)(20) 83311888
Garden Hotel
☎ (86)(20) 83338989
White Swan Hotel
☎ (86)(20) 81886968
★★★★
Baiyun Int'l Airport Hotel
☎ (86)(20) 86638838
Central Hotel
☎ (86)(20) 86578331
Citic Riverside Hotel
☎ (86)(20) 83839888
Friendship Hotel
☎ (86)(20) 86679898
Golden City Hotel
☎ (86)(20) 87754888
Guangdong Guest House
☎ (86)(20) 83332950
Guangdong Hotel
☎ (86)(20) 83339933
Guangdong Victory Hotel
☎ (86)(20) 81216688
Guangzhou Hotel
☎ (86)(20) 83338168
Holiday Inn City Centre
☎ (86)(20) 87766999
Hotel Landmark Canton
☎ (86)(20) 83355988
Hotel Royal
☎ (86)(20) 86622888
Liuhua Hotel
☎ (86)(20) 86668800

New Mainland Hotel
☎ (36)(20) 86678638
Oriental Silk Hotel
☎ (86)(20) 87762888
Overseas Chinese Hotel
☎ (86)(20) 86663488
Plaza Canton
☎ (86)(20) 84418888
Ramada Pearl Hotel Guangzhou
☎ (83)(20) 87372988
Rosedale Hotel & Suites Guangzhou
☎ (86)(20) 84418888

Huizhou
★★★
Huizhou Hotel
☎ (86)(752) 2232333

Shantou

★★★★★
Golden Gulf Hotel
96 Jinsha Road, Shantou
Guangdong, China 515041
☎ (86)(754) 8263263
🗐 (86)(754) 8265163
Toll Free Reservation: 800-810-5198
Email: stagghotl@pub.shantou.gd.cn
Web: www.goldengulfhotel.com
Hong Kong Office
☎ (852) 23014138

★★★★
Longhu Hotel
☎ (86)(754) 8260706
Shantou International Hotel
☎ (86)(754) 8251212

Shaoguan
★★★
Greenlake Villa
☎ (86)(751) 8774871
Yuetong Hotel
☎ (86)(751) 8229944

Shenzhen
★★★★★
Forum Hotel
☎ (86)(755) 25586333
Junhao Hotel
☎ (86)(755) 28020888
Nanhai Hotel
☎ (86)(755) 26692888
Shangri-la Hotel
☎ (86)(755) 82230888
Sunshine Hotel
☎ (86)(755) 82233888
The Landmark Hotel
☎ (86)(755) 82172288
★★★★
Century Plaza Hotel
☎ (86)(755) 82320888
Holiday Inn Donghua
☎ (86)(755) 26416688
Hotel Oriental Regent
☎ (86)(755) 82247000
NOVOTEL WATERGATE SHENZHEN
☎ (86)(755) 82137999
Shenzhen Bay Hotel
☎ (86)(755) 26600111
★★★
Ambassador Hotel
☎ (86)(755) 82258388
City Hotel
☎ (86)(755) 82257000
Far East Grand Hotel
☎ (86)(755) 82205369
Grand Skylight Hotel
☎ (86)(755) 83363698
Honey Lake Country Club Hotel
☎ (86)(755) 83708988
Kindlion Hotel
☎ (86)(755) 28289999
Shenzhen Lido Hotel
☎ (86)(755) 82259988
Shenzhen Lotus Hotel
☎ (86)(755) 82235966
Silver Lake Resort Hotel
☎ (86)(755) 82222827

Shunde
★★★★

Century Hotel
☎ (86)(765) 2293333

Zhanjiang
★★★★
Silver Sea Hotel
☎ (86)(759) 3380688
★★★
Zhanjiang Peninsula Hotel
☎ (86)(759) 3319168

Zhongshan
★★★★
Fuhua Hotel
☎ (86)(760) 8638888
Zhongshan International Hotel
☎ (86)(760) 8633388
Zhongshan Hot Spring Hotel
☎ (86)(760) 6683888

Zhuhai
★★★★★
Grand Bay View Hotel
☎ (86)(756) 8877998
Yindu (Grand Jasper) Hotel
☎ (86)(756) 8883388
Zhuhai Holiday Resort Hotel
☎ (86)(756) 3333838
★★★★
Gong Bei Palace Hotel
☎ (86)(756) 8886833
Grand Angel Hotel
☎ (86)(756) 3338899
The Greenery Hotel
☎ (86)(756) 3333968
The Guangdong Regency Hotel (Zhuhai)
☎ (86)(756) 8888128
Zhuhai Hotel
☎ (86)(756) 3333718
★★★
Garden Hotel
☎ (86)(756) 3333968
Paradise Hill Hotel
☎ (86)(756) 3337388

Guangxi
Nanning

★★★★★
Mingyuan Xindu Hotel
☎ (86)(771) 2830808
★★★★
Yongjiang Hotel
☎ (86)(771) 2808123
★★★
Mingyuan Hotel
☎ (86)(771) 2808923
Nanning Hotel
☎ (86)(771) 2618138

Liuzhou
★★★
Jingdu Hotel
☎ (86)(772) 2860188
Liuzhou Hotel
☎ (86)(772) 2824921

Guilin
★★★★★
Royal Garden Hotel
☎ (86)(773) 5812411
Sheraton Hotel
☎ (86)(773) 2825588
★★★★
Guilin Guishan Hotel
☎ (86)(773) 5813388
Guilin Park Hotel
☎ (86)(773) 2828899
Holiday Inn
☎ (86)(773) 2823950
★★★
Guilin Lijiang Hotel
☎ (86)(773) 2822881
Guilin Osmanthus Hotel
☎ (86)(773) 3834300
Guilin Plaza
☎ (86)(773) 5812488
Hotel Universal
☎ (86)(773) 2828228
Pine Garden Resort
☎ (86)(773) 5812311
Seven Star Hotel
☎ (86)(773) 5812311

Beihai
★★★★★
Shangri-La Hotel
☎ (86)(779) 2062288
★★★
Furama Hotel
☎ (86)(779) 2055588

Guizhou
Guiyang
★★★★
Guizhou Park Hotel
☎ (86)(851) 6822888
Holiday Inn
☎ (86)(851) 6771888
★★★
Guiyang Plaza Hotel
☎ (86)(851) 6827047

Hainan
Haikou
★★★★★
Golden Coast Lawton Hotel
☎ (86)(898) 6258888
Huandao Tide Hotel
☎ (86)(898) 6268888
★★★★
Baohua Harbour View Hotel
☎ (86)(898) 8536699
International Finance Hotel
☎ (86)(898) 6774099
★★★
Haikou Hotel
☎ (86)(898) 5351234
Peninsula Hotel
☎ (86)(898) 6265443
Wanghai International Hotel
☎ (86)(898) 6773381

Sanya
★★★★★
Gloria Resort
☎ (86)(899) 8568855
★★★★
Sanya Orient Hotel
☎ (86)(899) 8298080

Sanya Pearl River Garden Hotel
☎ (86)(899) 8211888
South China Hotel
☎ (86)(899) 8213888

Hebei
Baoding
★★★
Baoding Yanzhao Hotel
☎ (86)(312) 3027921

Chengde
★★★
Guesthouse For Diplomatic Missions
☎ (86)(314) 2021980

Handan
★★★
Handan Grand Hotel
☎ (86)(310) 3010951

Langfang
★★★
Tiandu Grand Hotel
☎ (86)(316) 2119998

Qinghuangdao
★★★
CNTIC golden Coast Resort
☎ (86)(335) 2081248
International Hotel
☎ (86)(335) 3083083

Shijiazhuang
★★★★
Hebei Grand Hotel
☎ (86)(311) 5815961
★★★
Shijiazhuang Int'l Hotel
☎ (86)(311) 6044321

Tangshan
★★★★
Tangshan Jinjiang Grand Hotel
☎ (86)(315) 2821611

★★★
Jinbin Hotel
☎ (86)(315) 2846711
Yuanyang Hotel
☎ (86)(315) 2914001

Heilongjiang
Daqing
★★★
Daqing Foreign Expert Hotel
☎ (86)(459) 6350270
Daqing Hotel
☎ (86)(459) 6103121

Harbin
★★★★★
Singapore Hotel
☎ (86)(451) 2336888
★★★
Friendship Palace Hotel
☎ (86)(451) 4618001
Harbin Int'l Hotel
☎ (86)(451) 3669698
Longmen Hotel
☎ (86)(451) 3639702
Modern Hotel
☎ (86)(451) 4615846
Power Hotel
☎ (86)(451) 3653378
Songhuajiang Gloria Inn
☎ (86)(451) 4638855
Swan Hotel
☎ (86)(451) 2311555

Henan
Kaifeng
★★★
Dongjing Hotel
☎ (86)(378) 3931075
Kaifeng Hotel
☎ (86)(378) 5955589

Luoyang
★★★
Luoyang Peony Hotel
☎ (86)(379) 4856699

Luoyang Friendship Hotel
☎ (86)(379) 4912780
Luoyang Int'l Hotel
☎ (86)(379) 3903888

Zhengzhou
★★★★★
SOFITEL ZHENGZHOU
☎ (86)(371) 5950088
★★★★
The Red Coral Hotel
☎ (86)(371) 6986688
Weilai Conifer Hotel
☎ (86)(371) 5612288
★★★
Asia Holiday Hotel
☎ (86)(371) 5728899
Dukang Hotel
☎ (86)(371) 7636888
Int'l Hotel Henan
☎ (86)(371) 5956600

Hong Kong
★★★★★
Conrad Int'l Hong Kong
☎ (852) 25213838
Gold Coast Hotel
☎ (852) 24528888
Grand Hyatt Hong Kong
☎ (852) 25881234
Grand Stanford Inter-Continental Hong Kong
☎ (852) 27215161
Harbor Plaza Hong Kong
☎ (852) 26213188
Hotel Inter-Continental Hong Kong
☎ (852) 27211211
Island Shangri-La Hong Kong
☎ (852) 28773838
JW Marriott Hotel Hong Kong
☎ (852) 28108366
Kowloon Shangri-La Hong Kong
☎ (852) 27212111
Mandarin Oriental Hong Kong
☎ (852) 25220111
Peninsula Hong Kong
☎ (852) 23666251

Regal Hong Kong Hotel
☎ (852) 28906633
Renaissance Harbor View Hotel
☎ (852) 28028888
Sheraton Hong Kong Hotel & Towers
☎ (852) 23691111
The Marco Polo Hong Kong
☎ (852) 21130088
The Ritz-Carlton Hong Kong
☎ (852) 28776666
★★★★
City Garden Hotel
☎ (852) 28872888
Eaton Hotel Hong Kong
☎ (852) 27821818
Grand Plaza Hotel
☎ (852) 28860011
Great Eagle Hotel
☎ (852) 23751133
Habor Plaza North Point
☎ (852) 21878888
Harbor Plaza Resort City
☎ (852) 21806688
Holiday Inn Golden Mile Hong Kong
☎ (852) 23693111
Hotel Miramar
☎ (852) 23681111
Hotel Nikko Hong Kong
☎ (852) 27391111
Hyatt Regency Hong Kong
☎ (852) 2311 1234
Island Pacific Hotel
☎ (852) 21311188
Metropark Hotel
☎ (852) 26001000
New World Renaissance Hotel
☎ (852) 23694111
NOVOTEL CENTURY HOTEL
☎ (852) 25988888
Novotel Century Harbourview Hotel
☎ (852) 29741234
Regal Airport Hotel
☎ (852) 22868888
Regal Kowloon Hotel
☎ (852) 27221818
Regal Riverside Hotel
☎ (852) 26497878

Rosedale on the Park
☎ (852) 21278888
Royal Park Hotel
☎ (852) 26012111
Royal Plaza Hotel
☎ (852) 2928 8822
The Emperor (Happy Valley) Hotel
☎ (852) 28933693
The Empire Kowloon Hotel
☎ (852) 26853000
The Excelsior Hong Kong
☎ (852) 28948888
The Kowloon Hotel
☎ (852) 29292888
The Marco Polo Gateway
☎ (852) 21130888
The Marco Polo Prince
☎ (852) 21131888
The Metropole Hotel
☎ (852) 27611711
The Royal Garden
☎ (852) 27215215
The Royal Pacific Hotel & Towers
☎ (852) 27361188

Hubei
Jingzhou
★★★★
Jingzhou Hotel
☎ (86)(716) 8467600

Wuhan
★★★★★
Oriental Grand Hotel
☎ (86)(27) 85888668
★★★★
Hubei White Rose Hotel
☎ (86)(27) 87893366
NOVOTEL XINHUA HOTEL
☎ (86)(27) 85551188
Wuhan Asia Hotel
☎ (86)(27) 83807777
★★★
Great Hankou Hotel
☎ (86)(27) 85797834
Hubei Hotel

☎ (86)(27) 87811311
Lijiang Hotel
☎ (86)(27) 87813668
New World Countyard Hotel
☎ (86)(27) 85787968
Wuhan Victory Hotel
☎ (86)(27) 82707241
Yangtze Hotel
☎ (86)(27) 83632828

Xiangfan
★★★
Nanhu Hotel
☎ (86)(710) 3513643
Railway Grand Hotel
☎ (86)(710) 3220454

Yichang
★★★★
Yichang Taohualing Hotel
☎ (86)(717) 6442244
★★★
Three Gorges Hotel
☎ (86)(717) 6739888

Hunan
Changsha
★★★★★
Huatian Hotel
☎ (86)(731) 4442888
Shennong Hotel
☎ (86)(731) 5218888
Tongcheng Int'l Hotel
☎ (86)(731) 4168888
★★★★
Hunan Furama Hotel
☎ (86)(731) 2298888
★★★
Lotus Hotel
☎ (86)(731) 4401888
Xiangjiang Hotel
☎ (86)(731) 4468888

Huaihua
★★★
Huaihua Int'l Grand Hotel
☎ (86)(745) 2238898

Huairong Hotel
☎ (86)(745) 2233850

Xiangtan
★★★
Xiangtan Hotel
☎ (86)(732) 8232600

Yueyang
★★★
Yueyang Hotel
☎ (86)(730) 8223011

Zhangjiajie
★★★★
Xianglong Int'l Hotel
☎ (86)(744) 8226888
★★★
Heaven Gate Hotel
☎ (86)(744) 8225588
Pipaxi Hotel
☎ (86)(744) 5718888

Zhuzhou
★★★
Zhuzhou Hotel
☎ (86)(733) 8216888

Inner Mongolia
Baotou
★★★
Baotou Hotel
☎ (86)(472) 5156655

Hailar
★★★
Hulunbeir Hotel
☎ (86)(470) 8222212

Hohhot
★★★
Inner Monglia Hotel
☎ (86)(471) 6964233
Pearl Inner Mongolia Hotel
☎ (86)(471) 6280088
Zhaojun Hotel
☎ (86)(471) 6962211

Manzhouli
★★★
Manzhouli Friendship Hotel
☎ (86)(470) 6223977
Manzhouli Int'l Hotel
☎ (86)(470) 6228888

Jiangsu
Changzhou
★★★★
Changzhou Grand Hotel
☎ (86)(519) 8109988
Changzhou Hotel
☎ (86)(519) 6600713
Jiangnanchun Hotel
☎ (86)(519) 6643663

Huaiyin
★★★
Huaihai Hotel
☎ (86)(517) 3930888

Jiangyin
★★★★
Jiangyin International Hotel
☎ (86)(510) 6815000
Jiangyin Jiyang Hotel
☎ (86) 510) 6810000

Kunshan
★★★
Huali Hotel
☎ (86)(520) 7310660
Kunshan Hotel
☎ (86)(520) 7553491

Lianyungang
★★★
Tianranju Hotel
☎ (86)(518) 5411688

Nanjing
★★★★★
Golden Eagle Plaza
☎ (86)(25) 4718888
Hilton
☎ (86)(25) 4808888

Jinling Hotel
☎ (86)(25) 4711888
Mandarin Garden Hotel
☎ (86)(25) 2202555
Sheraton Nanjing Kingsley
☎ (86)(25) 6668888
★★★★
Central Hotel Nanjing
☎ (86)(25) 4733888
Dingshan Garden Hotel
☎ (86)(25) 8802888
Gunandu Hotel
☎ (86)(25) 3311999
New Century Hotel
☎ (86)(25) 5408888
Ramada Plaza Yihua
☎ (86)(25) 3308888
Xuanwu Hotel
☎ (86)(25) 3358888
★★★
Central Hotel
☎ (86)(25) 4500888
Jinqiao Hotel
☎ (86)(25) 7711988
Kingdom Inn
☎ (86)(25) 3708888
Nanjing Hotel
☎ (86)(25) 3411888
Paradise Hotel
☎ (86)(25) 4209888
Pearl Hotel
☎ (86)(25) 7716088
Yangzi Guest House
☎ (86)(25) 7784888
Zhongshan Hotel
☎ (86)(25) 3361888

Nantong
★★★★
Nantong Hotel
☎ (86)(513) 3568989
★★★
Wenfeng Hotel
☎ (86)(513) 5517157

Suzhou

★★★★★
New Suzhou International
☎ (86)(512) 7616688
Sheraton Suzhou
☎ (86)(512) 5103388
★★★★
Aster Hotel
☎ (86)(512) 8291888
Bamboo Grove Hotel
☎ (86)(512) 5205601
Gloria Plaza
☎ (86)(512) 5218855
New City Garden Hotel
☎ (86)(512) 8250228
Suzhou Hotel
☎ (86)(512) 5204646
★★★
Royal Garden Hotel
☎ (86)(512) 5251621
Suzhou New Century Hotel
☎ (86)(512) 5338888
Suzhou Overseas Chinese Hotel
☎ (86)(512) 8264011

Taizhou
★★★
Taizhou Hotel
☎ (86)(523) 6226088

Taicang
★★★
Friend Hotel
☎ (86)(520) 3523711

Wuxi
★★★★★
Taihu Hotel
☎ (86)(510) 5517888
Sheraton Wuxi
☎ (86)(510) 2721888
★★★★
Hubin Hotel
☎ (86)(510) 5101888
The Pan Pacific Hotel
☎ (86)(510) 5806789
Xizhou Hotel
☎ (86)(510) 8702888

★★★
Canal Hotel
☎ (86)(510) 5806909
Concord Plaza
☎ (86)(510) 5887878
Lakeside Garden Resort
☎ (86)(510) 5996666
Ramada Hotel
☎ (86)(510) 2762888
Wuxi International Hotel
☎ (86)(510) 2718888
Wuxi Rome Hotel
☎ (86)(510) 5418989

Xuzhou
★★★
Garden Hotel
☎ (86)(516) 3738740

Yangzhou
★★★★
Garden International Hotel
☎ (86)(514) 7888333
Jinling West Lake Villa
☎ (86)(514) 7313888
Yangzhou Hotel
☎ (86)(514) 7342611

Zhangjiagang
★★★★
Xinyuan Holiday Hotel
☎ (86)(520) 8265188
★★★
Guomao Hotel
☎ (86)(520) 8687788

Zhenjiang
★★★
Zhenjiang Hotel
☎ (86)(511) 5236666

Jiangxi
Ganzhou
★★★
Gannan Hotel
☎ (86)(797) 8221888

Ji'an
★★★
Jingxiu Guest Villa
☎ (86)(796) 6555888

Jingdezhen
★★★
Jingdezhen Hotel
☎ (86)(798) 8225010

Jiujiang
★★★
Bailu Hotel
☎ (86)(792) 8222818
Jiujiang Hotel
☎ (86)(792) 8560018
Lushan Hotel
☎ (86)(792) 8282060

Nanchang
★★★★
Jiangxi Hotel
☎ (86)(791) 6221133
Jinfeng Hotel
☎ (86)(791) 6418888
★★★
Ganjiang Hotel
☎ (86)(791) 6221159
Hongdu Hotel
☎ (86)(791) 6829999
Poyang Lake Hotel
☎ (86)(791) 6471188
Qingshan Lake Hotel
☎ (86)(791) 6361162

Pingxiang
★★★
Anyuan Hotel
☎ (86)(799) 6848888

Yingtan
★★★
Yingtan Huaqiao Hotel
☎ (86)(792) 6221344

Jilin

Changchun
★★★★★
Noble Hotel
☎ (86)(431) 5622888
Shangri-La Hotel
☎ (86)(431) 8981818
★★★★
Paradise Hotel
☎ (86)(431) 2717071
★★★
Changbaishan Hotel
☎ (86)(431) 5643553
Changchun Hotel
☎ (86)(431) 8929920
Jilin Province Hotel
☎ (86)(431) 8973071
Lucky Grand Hotel
☎ (86)(431) 5620111
Traders Hotel
☎ (86)(431) 8966688

Jilin
★★★★
Wusong Hotel
☎ (86)(432) 3086200
★★★
Jiangcheng Hotel
☎ (86)(432) 2457721

Yanji
★★★
Baishan Hotel
☎ (86)(433) 2526666

Liaoning

Anshan
★★★★★
Anshan International Hotel
☎ (86)(412) 5555888
★★★
Tianhe Hotel
☎ (86)(412) 2237928

Dalian
★★★★★
Furama Hotel
☎ (86)(411) 2630888

★★★★
Dalian Regent Hotel
☎ (86)(411) 2892811
Dalian International Hotel
☎ (86)(411) 2638238
East Hotel
☎ (86)(411) 7612988
Holiday Inn
☎ (86)(411) 2808888
Kerren Hotel
☎ (86)(411) 7621188
★★★
Bohai Grand Hotel
☎ (86)(411) 2808999
Dalian Everbright Hotel
☎ (86)(411) 7615888
Dalian Hotel
☎ (86)(411) 2633111
Grand Hotel
☎ (86)(411) 2806161
Inn Fine Hotel
☎ (86)(411) 7612888

Dandong
★★★
Dandong Int'l Hotel
☎ (86)(415) 2137788
Yinxing Garden Hotel
☎ (86)(415) 2135555

Fushun
★★★
Fushun Friendship Hotel
☎ (86)(413) 2622181

Shenyang
★★★★
Gloria Plaza Hotel
☎ (86)(24) 22528855
Traders Hotel
☎ (86)(24) 23412288
★★★
The Rose Hotel
☎ (86)(24) 24841001
Liaoning Tiandu Hotel
☎ (86)(24) 23866939

Phoenix Hotel
☎ (86)(24) 86805858

Macau
★★★★★
Hyatt Regency Macau
☎ (853) 831234
Hotel Lisboa
☎ (853) 377666
Hotel New Century
☎ (853) 831111
Hotel Ritz Macau
☎ (853) 339955
Hotel Royal
☎ (853) 552222
Mandarin Oriental
☎ (853) 567888
Pousada De Sao Tiago
☎ (853) 378111
The Westin Resort
☎ (853) 871111
★★★★
Grand View Hotel
☎ (853) 837788
Hotel China
☎ (853) 851166
Hotel Grandeur
☎ (853) 781233
Holiday Inn Macau
☎ (853) 783333
Hotel Nam Yue
☎ (853) 726288
Hotel Presidente
☎ (853) 553888
Pousada Marina Infante
☎ (853) 838333

Ningxia
Yinchuan
★★★
International Hotel
☎ (86)(951) 6728688

Qinghai
Xining
★★★

Qinchai Hotel
☎ (86)(971) 6144888
Xining Hotel
☎ (86)(971) 8238701

Shaanxi
Baoji
★★★
Baoji Hotel
☎ (86)(917) 3513366
Taibai Vacation Village
☎ (86)(917) 5711090

Huayin
★★★
Huashan Financial Hotel
☎ (86)(913) 4612673

Hanzhong
★★★
Jinjiang Hotel
☎ (86)(916) 2238588

Xi'an
★★★★★
Chang'an Grand Castle Hotel
☎ (86)(29) 7231800
Golden Flower Hotel
☎ (86)(29) 3232981
Hyatt Regency Xi'an
☎ (86)(29) 7231234
Sheraton Xi'an Hotel
☎ (86)(29) 4261888
★★★★
Grand New World Hotel
☎ (86)(29) 7216868
Jianguo Hotel
☎ (86)(29) 3238888
Le Garden Hotel
☎ (86)(29) 4263388
Tangcheng Hotel
☎ (86)(29) 5255920
Xi'an Garden Hotel
☎ (86)(29) 5261111
Xi'an Hotel
☎ (86)(29) 5261351

★★★
Bell Tower Hotel
☎ (86)(29) 7279200
Dynasty Hotel
☎ (86)(29) 8626262
Empress Hotel
☎ (86)(29) 3232999
Holiday Inn
☎ (86)(29) 3233888
Longhai Hotel
☎ (86)(29) 7420093
New Era Hotel
☎ (86)(29) 8226699
Orient Hotel
☎ (86)(29) 5262211

Xianyang
★★★
Aviation Hotel
☎ (86)(910) 8707000
Caihong Hotel
☎ (86)(910) 3313472
Xianyang Imperial Hotel
☎ (86)(910) 3313388

Shandong
Jinan
★★★★★
SOFITEL SILVER PLAZA
☎ (86)(531) 6065666
★★★★
Century Run Hua Hotel
☎ (86)(531) 2901818
Qilu Hotel
☎ (86)(531) 2966888
Yuquan Simpson Hotel
☎ (86)(531) 6938888
Zhonghao Hotel
☎ (86)(531) 6968888

★★★
Guiyou Hotel
☎ (86)(531) 2980088
Quancheng Hotel
Tel: (86)(531) 6921911

Shandong Pearl Hotel
☎ (86)(531) 7932888

Qingdao
★★★★★
Grand Regency Hotel
☎ (86)(532) 5881818
Qingdao Haitian Hotel
☎ (86)(532) 3871888
★★★★
Huiquan Dynasty Hotel
☎ (86)(532) 2886688
Sea View Garden Hotel
☎ (86)(532) 5875777
Qingdao Dongfang Hotel
Tel : (86)(532) 2865888
★★★
China Travel Service Building
☎ (86)(532) 5828666
Huanhai Gloria Inn
☎ (86)(532) 3878855
Haidu Hotel
☎ (86)(532) 6896888
Qingdao Golden Beach Hotel
☎ (86)(532) 8897888
Qingdao Hotel
☎ (86)(532) 2879068
Sanfod Hotel
☎ (86)(532) 5897888

Qufu
★★★
Queli Hotel
☎ (86)(537) 4411300

Tai'an
★★★★
Taishan Overseas Chinese Mansion
☎ (86)(538) 8223852
★★★
Taishan Hotel
☎ (86)(538) 8224678

Weifang
★★★★★
Fuhwa Hotel
☎ (86)(536) 8881988

★★★★
Yuanfei Hotel
☎ (86)(536) 8236901

Weihai
★★★★
Weihaiwei Hotel
☎ (86)(631) 5232542
★★★
Haidu Hotel
☎ (86)(631) 5261339
White Swan Hotel
☎ (86)(631) 5231891

Yantai
★★★★
Shandong Pacific Hotel
☎ (86)(535) 6206888
★★★
Asia Hotel
☎ (86)(535) 6247888
International Trade Hotel
☎ (86)(535) 6217888
Yantai Peninsula Holiday Resort
☎ (86)(535) 6377333
Yantai Hotel
☎ (86)(535) 6888468

Zibo
★★★
Puquan Hotel
☎ (86)(533) 5177888
Zibo Hotel
☎ (86)(533) 2133418

Shanghai
★★★★★
Four Seasons Hotel
☎ (86)(21) 62568888
Grand Hyatt
☎ (86)(21) 50491234
Huating Sheraton Hotel
☎ (86)(21) 64391000
Inter-Continental Pudong
☎ (86)(21) 58318888
JC Mandarin
☎ (86)(21) 62791888

Jing'an Hilton
☎ (86)(21) 62480000
Jinjiang Tower
☎ (86)(21) 64151188
Marriott Hongqiao
☎ (86)(21) 62376000
Okura Garden Hotel
☎ (86)(21) 64151111
Oriental Riverside
☎ (86)(21) 50370000
The Portman Ritz-Carlton
☎ (86)(21) 62798888
Pudong Shangri-la
☎ (86)(21) 68828888
Radisson Plaza Xingguo Hotel
☎ (86)(21) 62129998
Ramada Plaza Pudong
☎ (86)(21) 50554466
Regal Int'l East Asia
☎ (86)(21) 64155588

SOFITEL JINJIANG ORIENTAL PUDONG
☎ (86)(21) 50504888
St. Regis Hotel
☎ (86)(21) 50504567
The Westin Taipingyang (Pacific)
☎ (86)(21) 62728888
Xinya Tangchen Hotel
☎ (86)(21) 58318888
★★★★
City Hotel
☎ (86)(21) 62551133
Crowne Plaza
☎ (86)(21) 62808888
Galaxy Hotel
☎ (86)(21) 62755888
Hotel Nikko Longbai
☎ (86)(21) 62689111

HOTEL SOF TEL HYLAND
☎ (86)(21) 63515888
Jianguo Hotel
☎ (86)(21) 64399299
Jing'an Hotel
☎ (86)(21) 62481888
Jinjiang Hotel
☎ (86)(21) 62582582

NOVOTEL ATLANTIS SHANGHAI
☎ (86)(21) 50366666

Ocean Hotel
☎ (86)(21) 65458888
Park Hotel
☎ (86)(21) 63275225
Peace Hotel
☎ (86)(21) 63216888
Radisson SAS Lansheng Hotel
☎ (86)(21) 65428000
Rainbow Hotel
☎ (86)(21) 62753388
Renaissance Yangtze Hotel
☎ (86)(21) 62750000
Shanghai Int'l Equatorial Hotel
☎ (86)(21) 62481688
Shanghai Mansion
☎ (86)(21) 63246260
Worldfield Convention Hotel
☎ (86)(21) 62703388

★★★
East China Hotel
☎ (86)(21) 63178000
Fareast Everbright City Hotel
☎ (86)(21) 63178900
Jiangsu Hotel
☎ (86)(21) 62051888
Jinqiao Hotel
☎ (86)(21) 58990890
Longhua Hotel
☎ (86)(21) 64570570
Magnolia Seaside Resort
☎ (86)(21) 58291000
New Asia Hotel
☎ (86)(21) 63242210
New Garden Hotel
☎ (86)(21) 62426688
Oasis Tower
☎ (86)(21) 62865888
Pacific Hotel
☎ (86)(21) 63276226
Pine City Hotel
☎ (86)(21) 64433888
Qingpu Hotel
☎ (86)(21) 59850688
SAIC Activities Centre
☎ (86)(21) 59161000

Shanghai Hengshan Hotel
☎ (86)(21) 64377050
Shanghai Hotel
☎ (86)(21) 62480088
Shanghai Hunan Hotel
☎ (86)(21) 62752468
Shanghai Int'l Airport Hotel
☎ (86)(21) 62688866

Shanxi
Datong
★★★
Datong Hotel
☎ (86)(352) 2032476

Taiyuan
★★★★
Shanxi Grand Hotel
☎ (86)(351) 4043901
Yingze Hotel
☎ (86)(351) 4043211
★★★
Bingzhou Hotel
☎ (86)(351) 4042111
Garden Holiday Hotel
☎ (86)(351) 2026688
Shanxi CITS Mansion
☎ (86)(351) 7232188
Shanxi Wulong Grand Hotel
☎ (86)(351) 4121318

Sichuan
Chengdu
★★★★★
Holiday Inn Crowne Plaza
☎ (86)(28) 6786666
Jinjiang Hotel
☎ (86)(28) 5582222
★★★★
Sichuan Hotel
☎ (86)(28) 6755555
Minshan Hotel
☎ (86)(28) 5583333
★★★
Chengdu Hotel
☎ (86)(28) 4448888

Quanxing Hotel
☎ (86)(28) 6259988
Lhasa Hotel
☎ (86)(28) 5198998
Tibet Hotel
☎ (86)(28) 3183388
Chengdu Grand Hotel
☎ (86)(28) 3173888

Emeishan
★★★
Emeishan Hotel
☎ (86)(833) 5526888
Jinding Hotel
☎ (86)(833) 5527077

Jiuzhaigou
★★★
Jiulong Hotel
☎ (86)(837) 7734155

Mianyang
★★★
Taoyuan Hotel
☎ (86)(816) 2338888
Fuleshan Int'l Hotel
☎ (86)(816) 2274888

Tianjin
★★★★★
Sheraton Tianjin Hotel
☎ (86)(22) 23343388
★★★★
Astor Hotel
☎ (86)(22) 23311112
Teda Int'l Hotel & Club
☎ (86)(22) 25326000
Hyatt Regency Tianjin
☎ (86)(22) 23318888
Geneva Hotel Tianjin
☎ (86)(22) 28352222
The Crystal Palace Hotel
☎ (86)(22) 28356888
★★★
East Asia Hotel Tianjin
☎ (86)(22) 27838888

Imperial Palace Hotel
☎ (86)(22) 22300888
The Park Hotel
☎ (86)(22) 28309818
Summer Holiday Inn
☎ (86)(22) 25319118
Tianjin View Hotel
☎ (86)(22) 25311301
Tianjin Golden Sail Hotel
☎ (86)(22) 25326666
Tianjin Huafu Palace Grand Hotel
☎ (86)(22) 27350066
Tianjin Friendship Hotel
☎ (86)(22) 23310372
Tianjin Hotel
☎ (86)(22) 28359000
Victory Hotel Tianjin
☎ (86)(22) 25345833
Yaoshun Grand Hotel
☎ (86)(22) 28897000

Tibet
Lhasa
★★★
Holiday Inn Hotel Lhasa
☎ (86)(891) 6832221
Tibet Hotel
☎ (86)(891) 6839999

Xinjiang
Altay
★★★
Xinjiang Altay Golden Bridge Hotel
☎ (86)(906) 2127588

Urumqi
★★★★★
Haide Hotel
☎ (86)(991) 2322828
Yindu Hotel
☎ (86)(991) 4536688
★★★★
Holiday Inn Urumqi
☎ (86)(991) 2818788
Hongfu Hotel
☎ (86)(991) 5881588

★★★
Islam Grand Hotel
☎ (86)(991) 2811017
City Hotel
☎ (86)(991) 2309911
Silk Road Hotel
☎ (86)(991) 2874999

Yunnan
Dali
★★★
Cangshan Hotel
☎ (86)(872) 2171999
Xiaguan Hotel
☎ (86)(872) 2125579

Honghe
★★★
Nanhu Hotel
☎ (86)(873) 3644145

Jinghong
★★★★
Dai Garden Hotel
☎ (86)(691) 2123888
★★★
Crown Hotel
☎ (86)(691) 2128888
Hotel Xishuangbanna
☎ (86)(691) 2130999
Golden Phoenix Hotel
☎ (86)(691) 2129888
Jinbanna Hotel Xishuangbanna
☎ (86)(691) 2124901

Kunming
★★★★
Golden Dragon Hotel
☎ (86)(871) 3133015
Holiday Inn
☎ (86)(871) 3165888
King World Hotel
☎ (86)(871) 3138888
Kunming Hotel
☎ (86)(871) 3162063
★★★

Guanguang Hotel Kunming Int'l Airport
☎ (86)(871) 7177038
Baoshan Hotel
☎ (86)(871) 3191988
Yaolong Hotel
☎ (86)(871) 3111166
Red River Hotel
☎ (86)(871) 3515666
Yuxi Hotel
☎ (86)(871) 7166888
Tea Garden Hotel
☎ (86)(871) 3139208
Xinfeng Hot Spring Resort
☎ (86)(871) 7671666

Lijiang
★★★★★
Guanfang Hotel
☎ (86)(888) 5188888
★★★
Lijiang Hotel
☎ (86)(888) 5121911
Senlong Hotel
☎ (86)(888) 5120666

Qujing
★★★
Stone Forest Int'l Hotel
☎ (86)(874) 3318888

Yuxi
★★★
Yuxi Hotel
☎ (86)(877) 2026416

Zhejiang
Hangzhou
★★★★
Dragon Hotel
☎ (86)(571) 7998833
Hangzhou Zhijing Holiday Resort
☎ (86)(571) 6696888
Hangzhouwan Hotel
☎ (86)(571) 6456688
Wanghu Hotel
☎ (86)(571) 7071024

Xiaoshan International Hotel
☎ (86)(571) 2656888
★★★
Friendship Hotel
☎ (86)(571) 7077888
Tianhong Hotel
☎ (86)(571) 8801234
Hangzhou Hotel
☎ (86)(571) 5166888
Qiangwang Hotel
☎ (86)(571) 3718888
Wangxiang Hotel
☎ (86)(571) 5102888
Zhejiang Hotel
☎ (86)(571) 797 7988
Meiyuan Hotal
☎ (86)(571) 8075524
Lily Hotel
☎ (86)(571) 7991188

Jiaxing
★★★
East Hotel
☎ (86)(573) 2070378
Jiaxing Hotel
☎ (86)(573) 2067788

Ningbo
★★★★
East Seaport Hotel
☎ (86)(574) 87373188
South Garden Hotel
☎ (86)(574) 87295678
Xinyuan Hotel
☎ (86)(574) 87321818
★★★
Asia Garden Hotel
☎ (86)(574) 87116888
Yunhai Hotel
☎ (86)(574) 87311543
Shaoxing
★★★★
Xianheng International Hotel
☎ (86)(575) 8068638

Wenzhou

★★★
Hubin Hotel
☎ (86)(577) 8227961
Wenzhou Hotel
☎ (86)(577) 8252525

Insurance Companies

FOREIGN FIRMS

Beijing

Allianz General Representative Office
☎ (86)(10) 64638052
Aetna Insurance Group
☎ (86)(10) 65012889
American International Group
☎ (86)(10) 65012889
Aon China
☎ (86)(10) 64603170
AXA China
☎ (86)(10) 65056172
Cigna Corporation
☎ (86)(10) 65182285
Chiyoda Fire Offshore Company
☎ (86)(10) 65978312
Chubb Federal Insurance
☎ (86)(10) 35057766
CNP Assurance BJ Rep. Office
☎ (86)(10) 65882150
Colonial Mutual Group
☎ (86)(10) 65055023
Continental Insurance Co.
☎ (86)(10) 64637972
Dai-Ichi Life Insurance
☎ (86)(10) 65139031
Eagle Star Insurance Co., Ltd.
☎ (86)(10) 65006050
E.W.Blanch Ltd.
☎ (86)(10) 65053833
Federal Insurance Company
☎ (86)(10) 65882050
Gerling Genera Insurance Company
☎ (86)(10) 64622083
ING Insurance Int'l B.V.
☎ (86)(10) 65900382

Lincoln National(China) Inc.
☎ (86)(10) 65263483
London Life Insurance
☎ (86)(10) 65903920
John Hancock Life Insurance Company
☎ (86)(10) 65056288
Mitsui Marine and Fire Insurance Company
☎ (86)(10) 65908360
New York Life Int'l
☎ (86)(10) 65171016
Nichido Marine and Fire Insurance
☎ (86)(10) 65908558
Pacific Century Insurance Co. Ltd.
☎ (86)(10) 65101988
Principal Insurance Company
☎ (86)(10) 64628820
Prudential Assurance
☎ (86)(10) 6463 7934
Royal & Sun Alliance Insurance Company
☎ (86)(10) 64660183
Samsung Fire & Marine Insurance
☎ (86)(10) 65101517
Sedgwick Group
☎ (86)(10) 65182670
Sumisei Life Insurance
☎ (86)(10) 65138510
Sumitomo Marine and Fire Insurance Co.
☎ (86)(10) 65051322
Singapore NTUC Income Insurance Corp.
☎ (86)(10) 66211880
Sun Life Insurance Co. of Canada
☎ (86)(10) 6510 2783
Swiss Reinsurance Company
☎ (86)(10) 65927760
The Maufacturers Life Insurance Co. of Canada
☎ (86)(10) 68038226
Toho Mutual Life Insurance Co.
☎ (86)(10) 65900834
Tokio Marine and Fire Insurance
☎ (86)(10) 65138789
Top Glory Insurance Co., Ltd.
☎ (86)(10) 65101988
Transamerica Occidental Life Insurance Co.
☎ (86)(10) 65881566
Winterthur Insurance Co.
☎ (86)(10) 65881281

Yasuda Marine & Fire Insurance
☎ (86)(10) 65908970
Zurich Insurance Company
☎ (86)(10) 65123562

Guangdong
Guangzhou
Aetna Insurance Company
☎ (86)(20) 83842193
Allianz Guangzhou Rep. Office
☎ (86)(20) 83864818
American International Assurance Co. Ltd.
☎ (86)(20) 87311888
AIU Insurance Company
☎ (86)(20) 87311888
AXA
☎ (86)(20) 83848268
ING General Insurance Int'l
☎ (86)(20) 83338989
Mitsui Marine & Fire Insurance Co. Ltd.
☎ (86)(20) 8667775
The Tokio Marine & Fire Insurance Co. Ltd.
☎ (86)(20) 83317388
Prudential Company
☎ (86)(20) 83338999
Sumitomo Marine & Fire Insurance Co. Ltd.
☎ (86)(20) 87780998

Shenzhen
ING General Insurance Int'l
☎ (86)(755) 82320888
Asahi Life Insurance Co.
☎ (86)(755) 25586333
Chubb China
☎ (86)(755) 82080845
Federal Insurance Co. Ltd.
☎ (86)(755) 82253324
Manulife Financial Co. Rep. Office
☎ (86)(755) 83351000
Mitsui Marine & Fire Insurance Co. Ltd.
☎ (86)(755) 82461263
Sumitomo Marine & Fire Insurance Co. Ltd.
☎ (86)(755) 82322840
Ming An Insurance Co.(H.K.) Ltd.
☎ (86)(755) 82170792
Tokio Marine & Fire Insurance Co. Ltd.
☎ (86)(755) 82227072

Yasuda Fire & Marine Insurance Co. Ltd.
☎ (86)(755) 25570521

Hong Kong
Charles Monat Ltd.
☎ (852) 25248176
Dah Sing Life Assurance
☎ (852) 25078989
GlobalHealth Asia Ltd.
☎ (852) 25260505
Grand Trust Underwriters
☎ (852) 25266674
Hong Kong Federation of Insurers
☎ (852) 25201868
ING General Insurance Int'l
☎ (852) 2850 3030
New York Life Insurance Company
☎ (852) 28949833
Pacific Int'l Insurance Company
☎ (852) 25910452
Winterthur Life Insurance Company
☎ (852) 21173000

Hubei
Wuhan
AXA
☎ (86)(27) 87303779

Liaoning
Dalian
AXA
☎ (86)(411) 2809963
Mitsui Marine & Fire Insurance Co. Ltd.
☎ (86)(411) 2652905
Royal & Sunalliance Insurance Company
☎ (86)(411) 4307156
Sumitomo Marine & Fire Insurance Co. Ltd.
☎ (86)(411) 2657849
Tokio Marine and Fire Insurance
☎ (86)(411) 2657042
Yasuda Fire & Marine Insurance Company
☎ (86)(411) 3623669

Shanghai
Aetna Life Insurance
☎ (86)(21) 62756785

AIA Shanghai Branch
☎ (86)(21) 63216698
Allianz Life Insurance Co. Ltd.
☎ (86)(21) 57898828
Allianz Insurance Shanghai Rep. Office
☎ (86)(21) 62488240
Aon Insurance Corp. (Group)
☎ (86)(21) 64267605
Cigna Corp. Shanghai Rep.
☎ (86)(21) 58826563
Cologne Reinsurance Co.
☎ (86)(21) 58761100
Colonial Mutual Group
☎ (86)(21) 63211523
Commercial Union Assurance Co. Ltd.
☎ (86)(21) 62491648
Continental Insurance Corp.
☎ (86)(21) 62497512
E. W.Blanch Ltd.
☎ (86)(21) 53069898
Federal Insurance Company
☎ (86)(21) 58415188
Generalcologne Reinsurance Company
☎ (86)(21) 58761122
Great Eastern Life
☎ (86)(21) 53301297
ING General Insurance Int'l
☎ (86)(21) 62756785
Japan Life Insurance Co.
☎ (86)(21) 62780441
John Hancock Tianan Life Insurance Co.
☎ (86)(21) 68816658
Kerry Insurance Co. Ltd.
☎ (86)(21) 65224273
Kyoritsu Co. Ltd.
☎ (86)(21) 62098086
Massmutual Insurance Asia Co. Ltd.
☎ (86)(21) 53965761
Mitsui Marine & Fire Insurance Co. Ltd.
☎ (86)(21) 68414998
Munich Reinsurance Co.
☎ (86)(21) 68411666
New York Life Insurance Company
☎ (86)(21) 62493541
Pacific Century Insurance Co. Ltd.
☎ (86)(21) 58401939
Royal & Sun Alliance Insurance

☎ (86)(21) 68411999
Samsung Fire & Marine Insurance
☎ (86)(21) 62080080
Standard Life Assurance Co.
☎ (86)(21) 68413311
Sumitomo Marine & Fire Insurance Co. Ltd.
☎ (86)(21) 68410515
Swiss Reinsurance Company
☎ (86)(21) 63916562
Transamerican Occidental Life
☎ (86)(21) 62195320
Yasuda Marine & Fire Insurance Co. Ltd.
☎ (86)(21) 68411199
Winterthur Insurance (Asia) Ltd.
☎ (86)(21) 58823351
Zurich Insurance Company
☎ (86)(21) 62798686

Sichuan
Chengdu
AXA
☎ (86)(28) 6513351

Tianjin
Chiyoda Fire& Marine Insurance
☎ (86)(22) 3320060
John Hancock Tianan Life Insurance Co.
☎ (86)(22) 23303995
Mitsui Marine & Fire Insurance
☎ (86)(22) 3304987
Nippon Mitsui Sea Fire Insurance Co.
☎ (86)(22) 23304986
Tokio Marine and Fire Insurance
☎ (86)(22) 3307387

Zhejiang
Ningbo
Swiss Reinsurance Company
☎ (86)(574) 7729953

SINO-FOREIGN JOINT VENTURES

Guangzhou
CITIC Prudential Life Insurance Co. Ltd.
☎ (86)(20) 87521966

Hong Kong
Manulife Financial
☎ (852) 25103200

Shanghai
Allianz Dazhong Life Insurance Company
☎ (86)(21) 58798828
AXA-Minmetal Assurance Co.
☎ (86)(21) 58792288
Pacific Aetna Life Insurance Company
☎ (86)(21) 62375666
Manulife-Sinochem Life Insurance
☎ (86)(21) 50492288

DOMESTIC FIRMS

Beijing
China Pacific Insurance Co. Ltd.
☎ (86)(10) 68525522
China Ping An Insurance
☎ (86)(10) 64073367
Hua Tai Insurance Co. Ltd.
☎ (86)(10) 88092222
People's Insurance Company of China
☎ (86)(10) 63034719
TaiKang Insurance
☎ (86)(10) 66426360
Tai Ping Life Insurance
☎ (86)(10) 85185665

Guangdong
Guangzhou
China Life Insurance
☎ (86)(20) 84628757
People's Insurance Company
☎ (86)(20) 83390599
Tai Ping Life Insurance
☎ (86)(20) 38804888
Hua Tai Insurance Co. Ltd.
☎ (86)(20) 38783999

Foshan
China Life Insurance
☎ (86)(757) 3202520

Shenzhen
Hua Tai Insurance Co. Ltd.
☎ (86)(755) 82137899
China Ping An Insurance Company
☎ (86)(755) 82262888

Jiangsu
Nanjin
Huatai Insurance Co. Ltd.
☎ (86)(25) 3302800

Liaoning
Dalian
Huatai Insurance Co. Ltd.
☎ (86)(411) 2557788

Shandong
Qingdao
Hua Tai Insurance Co. Ltd.
☎ (86)(532) 5028111
People's Insurance Company
☎ (86)(532) 2822877

Shanghai
China Ping An Insurance Company
☎ (86)(21) 62192022
Dazhong Insurance Co.
☎ (86)(21) 62581111
Hua Tai Insurance Co. Ltd.
☎ (86)(21) 68756699
China Pacific Insurance Company
☎ (86)(21) 63232488
People's Insurance Company
☎ (86)(21) 63765444
Sinosafe (Huan An) Insurance Co.
☎ (86)(21) 58219955
Tai Ping Life Insurance
☎ (86)(21) 58778888

Sichuan
Chengdu
Tai Ping Life Insurance
☎ (86)(28) 6957766

Tianjin
Huatai Insurance Co. Ltd.
☎ (86)(22) 23142187

International Accounting Firms

Beijing
Deloitte Touche Tohmatsu
☎ (86)(10) 65281599
Ernst & Young
☎ (86)(10) 65246688
Hua-Ander Certified Public Accountants
☎ (86)(10) 64627936
KPMG
☎ (86)(10) 65056300
LehmanBrown Int'l Accountants
☎ (86)(10) 85321720
Pricewaterhouse Coopers
☎ (86)(10) 65612233
Salustro Zhongrui
☎ (86)(10) 65263769

Guangdong
Guangzhou
Deloitte Touche Tohmatsu
☎ (86)(20) 83878555
Ernst & Young
☎ (86)(20) 83312788
KPMG
☎ (86)(20) 87322832
Pricewaterhouse Coopers
☎ (86)(20) 83633168

Shenzhen
Ernst & Young
☎ (86)(755) 82280788
KPMG
☎ (86)(755) 2173330
Pricewaterhouse Coopers
☎ (86)(755) 82461717
Hong Kong
Deloitte Touche Tohmatsu
☎ (852) 28521300
Ernst & Young
☎ (852) 28469888
KPMG
☎ (852) 25226022
LehmanBrown Int'l Accountants
☎ (852) 25371788

Pricewaterhouse Coopers
☎ (852) 22898888

Liaoning
Dalian
Deloitte Touche Tohmatsu
☎ (86)(411) 3609292
Pricewaterhouse Coopers
☎ (86)(411) 2714468

Macau
Ernst & Young
☎ (852) 26293888
Deloitte Touche Tohmatsu
☎ (853) 712998
Pricewaterhouse Coopers
☎ (853) 589589

Shanghai
Deloitte Touche Tohmatsu
☎ (86)(21) 63936292
Ernst & Young
☎ (86)(21) 62191219
KPMG
☎ (86)(21) 53594666
LehmanBrown Int'l Accountants
☎ (86)(21) 62881635
Pricewaterhouse Coopers
☎ (86)(21) 63863388
Salustro Zhongrui
☎ (86)(21) 50498176

Tianjin
Deloitte Touche Tohmatsu
☎ (86)(22) 23321671
Pricewaterhouse Coopers
☎ (86)(22) 23306789

International Schools

Beijing
Beijing BISS International School
☎ (86)(10) 64433151
Beijing Yew Chung International School
☎ (86)(10) 65941731

Children's House Montessori Kindergarten
☎ (86)(10) 650538069
International Montessori School of Beijing
☎ (86)(10) 65326713
International School of Beijing
☎ (86)(10) 64377119
Lido Kindergarten Beijing
☎ (86)(10) 64376688
New School of Collaborative Learning
☎ (86)(10) 62981620
Western Academy of Beijing
☎ (86)(10) 84564155

Fujian

Xiamen
Xiamen International School
☎ (86)(592) 6256583
Manila Xiamen International School
☎ (86) (592) 2089926

Guangdong

American International School
☎ (86)(20) 38810001
Utahloy International School
☎ (86)(20) 87703919

Shenzhen
Shekou International School
☎ (86)(755) 26693669

Hong Kong

American International School
☎ (852) 23363812
Australian International School
☎ (852) 23046978
Canadian International School
☎ (852) 25257088l
Carmel School
☎ (852) 29641600
Chinese International School
☎ (852) 25107288
Concordia International School
☎ (852) 27899890
Delia School of Canada
☎ (852) 28854786
Discovery Bay International School
☎ (852) 29877331

ESF International Kindergarten
☎ (852) 25400066
French International School
☎ (852) 25776217
German Swiss International School
☎ (852) 28496216
Glenealy Junior School (ESF)
☎ (852) 25221919
Highgate House School
☎ (852) 28496336
Hong Kong Academy Primary School
☎ (852) 25758282
Hong Kong International School
☎ (852) 28125000
Hong Kong Japanese School
☎ (852) 25747135
Hong Lok Yuen International School
☎ (852) 26586935
International Montessori School
☎ (852) 60801082
Island School (ESF)
☎ (852) 25247135
Jimmy's Int'l Nursery and Kindergarten
☎ (852) 28756501
Kellett School
☎ (852) 25518234
Kennedy School (ESF)
☎ (852) 28550711
Kiangsu & Chekiang School
☎ (852) 25704594
Korean International School
☎ (852) 25695500
Letterland Child Care Center and
International Pre-School
☎ (852) 28818717
Park View International Pre-School (PIPS)
☎ (852) 28126023
Peak School (ESF)
☎ (852) 28497211
Quarry Bay School (ESF)
☎ (852) 25664242
Sear Rogers International School
☎ (852) 25475479
Shatin College
☎ (852) 26991811
Singapore International School
☎ (852) 28720266

Sir Ellis Kadoorie Primary School
☎ (852) 25773489
Small World Christian Kindergarten
☎ (852) 25250922
Southside Kindergarten
☎ (852) 25927527
St. Stephen's College
☎ (852) 28130360
Starters School
☎ (852) 25278676
Sunshine House Int'l Pre-School and
Kindergarten
☎ (852) 28130713
Tutor Time Int'l Nursery and Kindergarten
☎ (852) 25291188
Watchdog Early Learning and Development
Center
☎ (852) 25217364
West Island School (ESF)
☎ (852) 28191962
Woodland Happy Valley Pre-School
☎ (852) 25750042
Woodland Montessori Pre-School
☎ (852) 25491211
Woodland Montessori Pre-school
☎ (852) 28031885
Woodland Pokfulam Panda Pre-School
☎ (852) 25517177
Woodland Pre-schools
☎ (852) 25594855
Woodland Repulse Bay Pre-School
☎ (852) 28120274
Woodland The Peak Pre-school
☎ (852) 28496192

Hubei
Wuhan International School
☎ (86)(27) 85763863

Jiangsu
Nanjing International School
☎ (86)(25) 8836545

Liaoning
Dalian

Dalian Maple Leaf International School
☎ (86)(411) 7900671

Shandong
Qingdao
Qingdao International School
☎ (86)(532) 8908000
Qingdao MTI International School
☎ (86)(532) 3895006

Shanghai
Concordia International School Shanghai
☎ (86)(21) 58990380
Shanghai American School
☎ (86)(21) 62211445
Yew Chung Shanghai International School
☎ (86)(21) 62423243

Tianjin
TEDA International School
☎ (86)(22) 25290140
Tianjin Rego International School
☎ (86)(22) 23343375

International Law Firms

Beijing
Adamas Law Firm
☎ (86)(10) 65975196
Allen & Overy
☎ (86)(10) 65102368
Baker & McKenzie
☎ (86)(10) 65050591
Becker & Poliakoff, P.A.
☎ (86)(10) 88092888
Blake, Cassels & Graydon LLP
☎ (86)(10) 65611515
Brand Farrar Buxbaum LLP
☎ (86)(10) 65052288
Bryan Cave LLP
☎ (86)(10) 65223061
Brown & Wood LLP
☎ (86)(10) 65055359
Coudert Brothers
☎ (86)(10) 65973851

David Ben Kay
☎ (86)(10) 65054891
Denton Wilde Sapte
☎ (86)(10) 65054891
Freshfields
☎ (86)(10) 64106338
Gide Loyrette Nouel
☎ (86)(10) 65974511
Goodman Phillips & Vineberg
☎ (86)(10) 65186210
Graham & James LLP
☎ (86)(10) 65918343
Herbert Smith
☎ (86)(10) 65056512
Livasiri & Co.
☎ (86)(10) 65052620
Morrison & Foerster LLP
☎ (86)(10) 65059090
Mallesons Stephen Jaques
☎ (86)(10) 65123565
Richard Butler
☎ (86)(10) 65992690
Rouse & Co. International
☎ (86)(10) 63103377
Sherman & Sterling
☎ (86)(10) 65053399
Sullivan & Cromwell
☎ (86)(10) 65056120
Torys LLP
☎ (86)(10) 65669088
Vovan & Associes Law Firm
☎ (86)(10) 64681348
Vinson & Elkins L.L.P.
☎ (86)(10) 64106300
Rouse & Co. International
☎ (86)(10) 68364235

Chongqing
Brand Farrar Buxbaum LLP
☎ (86)(23) 63828373

Fujian
Xiamen
Fujian Xiamen Mingjia Lawyer Office
☎ (86)(592) 2396769

Guangdong
Guangzhou
Deacons
☎ (86)(20) 87785678
Stephenson Harwood & Lo
☎ (86)(20) 83880590

Shenzhen
Henry & Co
☎ (86)(755) 3668592

Hainan
Haikou
Jun He Law Office
☎ (86)(898) 8512544

Hong Kong
AB Nasir & Co
☎ (852) 28775299
Allen & Overy
☎ (852) 29747000
Baker & McKenzie
☎ (852) 28461888
BBLP Beiten Burkhardt Mittl & Wegener
☎ (852) 25246468
Brown & Wood LLP
☎ (852) 25097888
Bruckhaus Westrick Heller Lober
☎ (852) 28463400
Bryan Cave LLP
☎ (852) 25222821
Clifford Chance
☎ (852) 28258888
Cleary, Gottilieb, Steen & Hamilton
☎ (852) 25214122
Clyde & CO
☎ (852) 28788600
CMS Cameron McKenna
☎ (852) 28469100
Coudert Brothers
☎ (852) 22189100
Davis Wright Tremaine
☎ (852) 28259211
Deacons
☎ (852) 28259211

Debevoise & Plimpton
☎ (852) 21609800
Denton Wilde Sapte
☎ (852) 28206272
Dewey Ballantine LLP
☎ (852) 25097000
Freshfields Bruckhaus Deringer
☎ (852) 28463400
Graham & James
☎ (852) 25099977
Herbert Smith
☎ (852) 28456639
Johnson Stokes & Master
☎ (852) 2843 2211
Kaye Scholer LLP
☎ (852) 28458989
Koo and Partners
☎ (852) 28679988
Linklaters
☎ (852) 28424888
Livasiri & Co.
☎ (852) 25253318
Maples and Calder Asia
☎ (852) 25229333
Minter Ellison
☎ (852) 28416888
Morrison & Foerster LLP
☎ (852) 25850888
O' Melveny & Myers LLP
☎ (852) 25238266
Richards Butler
☎ (852) 28103008
Sidey Austin Erown & Wood
☎ (852) 25097888
Simmons & Simmons
☎ (852) 28681131
Stephenson Harwood & Lo
☎ (852) 28680789
Wilkinson & Grist
☎ (852) 25246011

Macau
C & C Advogados
☎ (853) 372642

Shandong
Qingdao
Baker & Daniels
☎ (86)(532) 5751051

Shanghai
Adamas Law Firm
☎ (86)(21) 50368100
Allen & Overy
☎ (86)(21) 62883099
Altheimer & Gray
☎ (86)(21) 62890990
Blake Dawson Waldron
☎ (86)(21) 62798069
Brown & Wood LLP
☎ (86)(21) 53068966
Bruckhaus Westrick Heller Lober
☎ (86)(21) 50491118
Bryan Cave LLP
☎ (86)(21) 62798166
Bull, Housser & Tupper
☎ (86)(21) 64400015
Coudert Brothers
☎ (86)(21) 38784620
Davis Wright Tremaine LLP
☎ (86)(21) 62798560
Haarmann Hemmelrath
☎ (86)(21) 50498176
Haworth & Lexon
☎ (86)(21) 68767750
Holman Fenwich & Willan
☎ (86)(21) 68115647
Johnson Stokes & Master
☎ (86)(21) 62880688
Kaye Scholer LLP & Affiliates
☎ (86)(21) 52984266
Linklaters
☎ (86)(21) 68415858
Minter Ellison
☎ (86)(21) 28909049
O'melveny & Mayers LLP
☎ (86)(21) 52985600
Rouse & Co. International
☎ (86)(21) 63915368
Schulz Noack Barwinkel
☎ (86)(21) 62198370

Simmons & Simmons
☎ (86)(21) 62490700
Sidley Austin Brown & Wood
☎ (86)(21) 53062866
Thirffry & Associes
☎ (86)(21) 68411388
Wessing
☎ (86)(21) 684155 25
YISHI Law Firm
☎ (86)(21) 68754728

Sichuan
Chengdu
Brand Farrar Buxbaum LLP
☎ (86)(28) 6521316

Tianjin
Zhengda Lawyer Office
☎ (86)(22) 23126166
Thomas, Herbecq & Associes
☎ (86)(22) 23139763

Zhejiang
Ningbo
Zhejiang Haitai Law Firm
☎ (86)(574) 87195220

Medical Services

Beijing
Asia Emergency Rescue Center
☎ (86)(10) 64629100
Beijing First-aid Center
☎ (86)(10) 66098114
Beijing Hospital
☎ (86)(10) 65132266
Beijing Hospital of Chinese Traditional
Medicines
☎ (86)(10) 64040791
Beijing Obstetrics & Gynaecology Hospital
☎ (86)(10) 65250731
Beijing United Family Hospital
☎ (86)(10) 64333960
Beijing University People's Hospital
☎ (86)(10) 68314422

China-Japan Friendship Hospital
☎ (86)(10) 64221122
International Medical Center
☎ (86)(10) 64651561
SOS International
☎ (86)(10) 64629100
The International Medical Center (IMC)
☎ (86)(10) 64651561
The Medical Service of the French and
German Embassies
☎ (86)(10) 65323515

Chongqing
Chongqing First People's Hospital
☎ (86)(23) 63841324
Chongqing First-aid Medical Treatment
Center
☎ (86)(23) 63874000
Chongqing Harbor Hospital
☎ (86)(23) 62873235
Chongqing Surgical Hospital
☎ (86)(23) 63527121

Fujian
Fuzhou
Fujian Apitherapy Hospital
☎ (86)(591) 3789242
Fujian Provincial Hospital
☎ (86)(591) 7557768
Fuzhou Red Cross Hospital
☎ (86)(591) 3269925
Provincial Hospital for Women & Children
☎ (86)(591) 7505886
Xiamen
Xiamen Chinese Medicine Hospital
☎ (86)(592) 2022860
Xiamen First-aid Medical Center
☎ (86)(592) 2086707
Xiamen First Hospital
☎ (86)(592) 2137300
Xiamen Zhongshan Hospital
☎ (86)(592) 2211200

Guangdong
Guangzhou
Guangdong Traditional Chinese Medicine

Hosp tal
☎ (86)(20) 81863943
Guangzhou Medical College First Hospital
☎ (86)(20) 81340312
Guangzhou First People's Hospital
☎ (86)(20) 81089679
Guangdong People's Hospital
☎ (86)(20) 83868917

Shantou
Shantou Central Hospital
☎ (86)(754) 8550450
Shantou Traditional Chinese Medicine
Hospital
☎ (86)(754) 8981274
Shantou Women & Children Hospital
☎ (86)(754) 8549342

Shenzhen
Bo'ai Hospital
☎ (86)(755) 25890395
Emergency Medical Center
☎ (86)(755) 82430759
Red Cross Hospital
☎ (86)(755) 83365228
Shenzhen Central Hospital
☎ (86)(755) 33061341
Shenzhen Traditional Chinese Medicine
Hospital
☎ (86)(755) 3334055
Shenzhen People's Hospital
☎ (86)(755) 5531387

Zhuhai
Gongbei Hospital
☎ (86)(756) 8896430
Hongqi Hospital
☎ (86)(756) 7256255
Gold Coast First Hospital
☎ (86)(756) 7764190
Zhuhai Medical Center
☎ (86)(756) 2516197

Shanghai
Changzheng Hospital
☎ (86)(21) 63610109
Huadong Hospital
☎ (86)(21) 62483130

Huashan Hospital
☎ (86)(21) 62489999
International SOS Shanghai Alarm Center
☎ (86)(21) 62950099
Int'l Medical & Health Care Center
☎ (86)(21) 63240090
Ruijin Hospital
☎ (86)(21) 64370045
Shanghai First People's Hospital
☎ (86)(21) 63243852
World Link Hongqiao Clinic
☎ (86)(21) 64055788
🖳 (86)(21) 64053587
World Link Shanghai Center Clinic
☎ (86)(21) 62797688
🖳 (86)(21) 62797698
Zhongshan Hospital
☎ (86)(21) 64041990

Real Estate

Beijing
Beijing Bel-Property Investment Ltd.
☎ (86)(10) 64107078
Beijing Genti Property Management Co.
☎ (86)(10) 68319988
Beijing Sun Real Estate Adm. Center
☎ (86)(10) 68022702
Beijing Wanke Enterprise Co.
☎ (86)(10) 64902288
CB Richard Ellis
☎ (86)(10) 65391288
Chesterton Petty
☎ (86)(10) 65264146
China Everbright Real Estate Co.
☎ (86)(10) 62055864
China Real Estate Group Co.
☎ (86)(10) 68184422
Colliers Jardine International
☎ (86)(10) 84863099
Cushman & Wakefield
☎ (86)(10) 65915697
DTZ Debenham Tie Leung
☎ (86)(10) 65101388

FPDSavills
☎ (86)(10) 65052348
General Technology Group Estate
Management Co. Ltd.
☎ (86)(10) 68330675
Glorious Century Real Estate Development
☎ (86)(10) 82072288
Joanna Real Estate Consulting
☎ (86)(10) 64158179
Jones Lang LaSalle
☎ (86)(10) 65881300
Insignia Brooke
☎ (86)(10) 64625384
Kiu Lok Property Services (China) Ltd.
☎ (86)(10) 67029902
Maverick China Consulting (China)
☎ (86)(10) 65513520
Stanford Realty Service Co. Ltd.
☎ (86)(10) 64226422
Wanhai Real Estate
☎ (86)(10) 65991618

Chongqing

Bangxing Real Estate Corp. Ltd.
☎ (86)(23) 63829266
DTZ Debenham Tie Leung
☎ (86)(23) 63888405
Olympic (Group) Real Estate Corp.
☎ (86)(23) 68827964
Silver Star Real Estate Corp. Ltd.
☎ (86)(23) 63731627
Hongtai Real Estate Development
☎ (86)(23) 63507264

Fujian

Fuzhou
Taijiang District Real Estate Development
☎ (86)(591) 3267240
Huafu Real Estate Co.
☎ (86)(591) 3357679

Xiamen
Xiamen United Development(Group)
☎ (86)(592) 6023428
Century 21 China Real Estate (Xiamen)
☎ (86)(592) 5091262

XLG Properties Co.
☎ (86)(592) 2222488

Guangdong

Guangzhou
CB Richard Ellis
☎ (86)(20) 87322332
Chesterton Petty
☎ (86)(20) 38771477
Colliers Jardine International
☎ (86)(20) 86695176
DTZ Debenham Tie Leung
☎ (86)(20) 38770878
FPDSavills
☎ (86)(20) 81320107
Kiu Lok Property Services (China) Ltd
☎ (86)(20) 87732215
Zhujiang Real Estate Development Center
☎ (86)(20) 85560976

Shenzhen
Baoheng Real Estate Management Co.
☎ (86)(755) 27754521
DTZ Debenham Tie Leung
☎ (86)(755) 82125111
Fanhai Real Estate Management Co. Ltd.
☎ (86)(755) 26404491
Jindi Real Estate Management Co. Ltd.
☎ (86)(755) 83305795
Lushan Real Estate Co. Ltd.
☎ (86)(755) 82338899
Shenda Real Estate Management Co. Ltd.
☎ (86)(755) 83500030
Shenfang Real Estate Management Co.
☎ (86)(755) 82280078
World Union Properties consultancy
☎ (86)(755) 82080800
Zhonghang Real Estate Management Co.
☎ (86)(755) 83366419

Zhongshan
Hengmen Real Estate Development Co.
☎ (86)(760) 8850926
Songda Real Estate Consulting Co.
☎ (86)(760) 8852688

Zhuhai

Ancer Property Consultant
☎ (86)(756) 2226611
Guangxin Real Estate Co. Ltd.
☎ (86)(756) 8871166
Pingxin Real Estate Co. Ltd.
☎ (86)(756) 3369988
Zhuhai City Real Estate Co. Ltd.
☎ (86)(756) 8601380
Zhuhai Real Estate Development Corp.
☎ (86)(756) 2263102
Zhuhai SEZ Real Estate Co.
☎ (86)(756) 8883566

Guangx

Nanning

China Real Estate Group
☎ (86)(771) 5886870
Guangxi Commercial Real Estate
Development Corp.
☎ (86)(771) 5327585
Jiaan Realty Management Co. Ltd.
☎ (86)(771) 5314488
Nanning Dongya real Estate Development
Corp. Ltd.
☎ (86)(771) 4834039
Nanning Sanyuan Real Estate
Development Corp. Ltd.
☎ (86)(771) 5702333

Hainan

Changlong Real Estate Development Corp.
☎ (86)(898) 5362428
Funan Real Estate Development Corp.
☎ (86)(898) 8530929
Hongjian Real Estate Development Corp.
☎ (86)(898) 6251549
Hainan Real Estate Adm. Corp.
☎ (86)(898) 5338752

Hebei

Shijiazhuang

Jixing Real Estate Development Co. Ltd.
☎ (86)(311) 6984247
Yongxing Real Estate Development Co.
☎ (86)(311) 7012754

Dongxing Real Estate Co. Ltd.
☎ (86)(311) 6112054
Fudi Real Estate Co. Ltd.
☎ (86)(311) 6976257

Heilongjiang

Harbin

City Commerce House Development Corp.
☎ (86)(451) 4695294
City Land Development Corp.
☎ (86)(451) 4687364
City Realty Development Corp.
☎ (86)(451) 4687364
Tianding Realty Development Co. Ltd.
☎ (86)(451) 4609572
Longbang Realty Development Co. Ltd.
☎ (86)(451) 3603424
Longdi Realty Development Co. Ltd.
☎ (86)(451) 2702135

Henan

Zhengzhou

China Real Estate Development Co.
☎ (86)(371) 6963049
City & Town Construction Real Estate
Development Co.
☎ (86)(371) 2691305
Deyi Real Estate Development Corp.
☎ (86)(371) 5729666
Fudeng Real Estate Corp. Ltd.
☎ (86)(371) 5946200
Guanghui Real Estate Development Corp.
☎ (86)(371) 5958988
Guoxin Real Estate Corp. Ltd.
☎ (86)(371) 5717567
Huacheng Real Estate Development Co.
☎ (86)(371) 6251341
Henan Light Industrial Real Estate Co.
☎ (86)(371) 3829804
Zihua Real Estate Development Corp.
☎ (86)(371) 5713392
Jincheng Real Estate Co.
☎ (86)(371) 5970667
Overseas Chinese Friendship Real Estate
Development Corp. Ltd.
☎ (86)(371) 6984367

Hong Kong

CB Richard Ellis
☎ (852) 28202800
Chesterton Petty
☎ (852) 2840 1177
Colliers Jardine International
☎ (852) 28269166
Compass Worldwide Ltd.
☎ (852) 28695128
Cushman & Wakefield
☎ (852) 29563888
DTZ Debenham Tie Leung
☎ (852) 25070507
FPDSavills
☎ (852) 28424417
Hang Lung Properties
☎ (852) 28790370
Hutchison Whampoa Properties Ltd.
☎ (852) 21287500
Hysan Development Company
☎ (852) 28955777
Kerry Properties Ltd.
☎ (852) 29672300
Jones Lang LaSalle
☎ (852) 2846 5000
Insignia Brooke
☎ (852) 28791188
Kiu Lok Property Services (China) Ltd.
☎ (852) 28778802
Landmark Asia Realty
☎ (852) 25061008
Land & Fortune Realty Ltd.
☎ (852) 29157388
Sky Pacific Property Consultant Ltd.
☎ (852) 23889872
Sun Hung Kai Properties Ltd.
☎ (852) 28278111

Hubei
Wuhan

Wuhan Real Estate Development Co.
☎ (86)(27) 82649228
Wuhan Taihe Real Estate Development Co.
☎ (86)(27) 85414669
World Union Properties Consultancy
☎ (86)(27) 85561488

Hunan
Changsha

Hunan Changxin Real Estate Development
☎ (86)(731) 5821803
Hunan Guangshi Real Estate Development
☎ (86)(731) 5515365
Huaxia Real Estate Development Corp.
☎ (86)(731) 5220679
Hunan Int'l Real Estate Industrial Devt.
☎ (86)(731) 4436499
Jianxiang Real Estate Development Corp.
☎ (86)(731) 4113436
Nanfang Real Estate Development Corp.
☎ (86)(731) 8882054

Jiangsu
Nanjing

Dongheng Int'l Econ. & Trade Real Estate
Management Co. Ltd.
☎ (86)(25) 2254455
Fuyuhua Real Estate Development Co.
☎ (86)(25) 6526770
Huayang Real Estate Development Corp.
☎ (86)(25) 6633688
Xinghan Real Estate Co. Ltd.
☎ (86)(25) 6655888
Jieli Real Estate Econ. & Trade Co. Ltd.
☎ (86)(25) 6648376
Jincheng Real Estate Development Co.
☎ (86)(25) 4702278
Jitai Real Estate Development Co. Ltd.
☎ (86)(25) 4717757
Nanhai Real Estate Development Co. Ltd.
☎ (86)(25) 2601858
Guangxia Real Estate Development Corp.
☎ (86)(25) 3212929
Huaxia Real Estate Development Co. Ltd.
☎ (86)(25) 3214500
Jinbao Real Estate Development Co. Ltd.
☎ (86)(25) 4571186

Suzhou

Foreign Capital Weidi Real Estate Co. Ltd.
☎ (86)(512) 5271369
Jia'an Real Estate Development Co. Ltd.
☎ (86)(512) 5306632

Jiaxin Real Estate Development Co. Ltd.
☎ (86)(512) 7612128
Sino-Foreign Joint Venture Suzhou Taihua
House Property Co. Ltd.
☎ (86)(512) 5307963
Sino-Foreign Joint Venture Suzhou Taihua
House Property Co. Ltd.
☎ (86)(512) 5217947
Sino-Foreign Joint Venture Suzhou Yuehai
Real Estate Development Co. Ltd.
☎ (86)(512) 7282237

Jiangxi
Nanchang
HK Monopoly Capital Nanchang Jinchangli
Real Estate Co. Ltd.
☎ (86)(791) 6237919
Great Wall Estate Development Co. Ltd.
☎ (86)(791) 6784544
Hongcheng Real Estate Development Co.
☎ (86)(791) 6294757
Hongji Real Estate Development Co. Ltd.
☎ (86)(791) 6703025
Nanfang Real Estate Development Co.
☎ (86)(791) 6818318
Zhongda Rea Estate Development Co.
☎ (86)(791) 6400565

Jilin
Changchun
Dayu Real Estate Co. Ltd.
☎ (86)(431) 5607714
Changchun Real Estate (Group) Co. Ltd.
☎ (86)(431) 8944616
Futai Int'l Real Estate Development Co.
☎ (86)(431) 5636311
Jilin Guoji Real Estate Developement Co.
☎ (86)(431) 8948630
Huaxia Real Estate Development Co.
☎ (86)(431) 8743756
Zhengda Real Estate Development Co.
☎ (86)(431) 5954 91

Liaoning
Dalian

DTZ Debenham Tie Leung
☎ (86)(411) 2708800
Hualin Real Estate Development Co. Ltd.
☎ (86)(411) 2401241
New Type Real Estate Development Corp.
☎ (86)(411) 4403751
Wanda Real Estate Co. Ltd.
☎ (86)(411) 2819588
Yinhuan Real Estate Development Co. Ltd.
☎ (86)(411) 3693661

Shaanxi
Xi'an
Baijia Real Estate Agent Corp. Ltd.
☎ (86)(29) 7263064
Weiye Real Estate Development Co. Ltd.
☎ (86)(29) 7275990

Shandong
Jinan
Orient Real Estate Co. Ltd.
☎ (86)(531) 2958948
Taishan Real Estate Co. Ltd.
☎ (86)(531) 7968888
Tianfa Real Estate (Group) General Co.
☎ (86)(531) 5955624
Zhonghuan Real Estate Development Co.
☎ (86)(531) 6048347

Qingdao
Real Estate Development Co.
☎ (86)(532) 7611516
Qingdao Real Estate Development Co.
☎ (86)(532) 2667377
Taidong Real Estate Group Co.
☎ (86)(532) 3618297

Shanghai
Absolute Shanghai Home Realty
☎ (86)(21) 63857425
Adrienne Farrelly Shanghai Properties
☎ (86)(21) 62483336
Autumn Leaves Housing Consultants Ltd.
☎ (86)(21) 34060273
CB Richard Ellis
☎ (86)(21) 6289 1200

Chesterton Petty
☎ (86)(21) 6445 9967
Colliers Jardine International
☎ (86)(21) 62370088
DTZ Debenham Tie Leung
☎ (86)(21) 53061383
FPDSavills
☎ (86)(21) 63916688
Shanghai Centaline Property Agency Ltd
☎ (86)(21) 62086088
Shanghai Jinhai Real Estate Development
☎ (86)(21) 62980126
Shanghai Metropolis Real Estate
Consultants
☎ (86)(21) 62480245
Shanghai Xinjinqiao Property Management
☎ (86)(21) 58547356
Phoenix Property Consulting
☎ (86)(21) 64379891
The Emerald
☎ (86)(21) 68122222

Shanxi

Taiyuan
Guangxin Real Estate Corp. Ltd.
☎ (86)(351) 4077661
Jinjian Real Estate Development Corp.
☎ (86)(351) 4133337
Wanfeng Real Estate Development Corp.
☎ (86)(351) 4077181

Sichuan

Chengdu
Chengdu Holiday Real Estate Development
☎ (86)(28) 6698555
Chengda Real Estate Development Corp.
☎ (86)(28) 7786549
Chenggang Real Estate Development Co.
☎ (86)(28) 4334992
Shudu Real Estate Development Corp.
☎ (86)(28) 6628022
Far East Real Estate Joint Development
☎ (86)(28) 6943353
Guomao Group Real Estate Corp.
☎ (86)(28) 7640146

Guoxin Real Estate Corp. Ltd.
☎ (86)(28) 6262323
Jiarun Real Estate Corp. Ltd.
☎ (86)(28) 3319353
Tanghu Real Estate Development Corp.
☎ (86)(28) 5183957

Tianjin
Development Zone Fulu Real Estate Co.
☎ (86)(22) 28247307
DTZ Debenham Tie Leung
☎ (86)(22) 23139751
E-smart Relocation Consultants Co.,Ltd
☎ (86)(22) 28360997
Maigeli Housing Property Development &
Management Co. Ltd.
☎ (86)(22) 23130337
Tianjin City Real Estate Development Co.
☎ (86)(22) 23302145
Tianjin Port House Property Co.
☎ (86)(22) 25706753
Tianjin Winson Real Estate Development
☎ (86)(22) 88238011

Zhejiang

Ningbo
Commercial Real Estate Co. Ltd.
☎ (86)(574) 7754951
Haijian Real Estate Co, Ltd.
☎ (86)(574) 7293512
Hualian Real Estate Development Co.
☎ (86)(574) 7324812
Huaneng Real Estate Development Co.
☎ (86)(574) 7713238
Jianchang Real Estate Development Co.
☎ (86)(574) 7111764
Jianshe Real Estate Co. Ltd.
☎ (86)(574) 7313516
Ningxing Real Estate Development Co. Ltd.
☎ (86)(574) 7313239
Ningbo Real Estate Co.
☎ (86)(574) 7297470
Tuozhan Real Estate Development Co.
☎ (86)(574) 7215335
Ningbo United Real Estate Development
☎ (86)(574) 7216875

Securities Firms

Beijing

China Galaxy Securities
☎ (86)(10) 82579658
China Securities
☎ (86)(10) 65515588
Daiwa Securities
☎ (86)(10) 65126850
Goldman Sachs
☎ (86)(10) 65056888
Guotai Jun'an Securities
☎ (86)(10) 82080376
Haitong Securities
☎ (86)(10) 65087154
J P Morgan & Co.
☎ (86)(10) 65227488
Nomura International Securities
☎ (86)(10) 35908181
Merrill Lynch
☎ (86)(10) 65050290
Nikko Securities
☎ (86)(10) 65004402
SG Securities
☎ (86)(10) 65007510
Shenyin Wanguo Securities
☎ (86)(10) 67736289
Tai Fook Securities Group Ltd.
☎ (86)(10) 65973807

Guangdong
Guangzhou
China Galaxy Securities
☎ (86)(20) 83871427
Guangdong Securities Co. Ltd.
☎ (86)(20) 83270538
Guangfa Securities Co. Ltd.
☎ (86)(20) 87555888
Guotai Jun'an Securities
☎ (86)(20) 83606288
Gaungzhou Securties Co. Ltd.
☎ (86)(20) 83541137
Shenyin Wanguo Securities
☎ (86)(20) 84245766

Shenzhen
Celestial Asia Securities Holdings Ltd.
☎ (86)(755) 82364727
China Communication Securities
☎ (86)(755) 83796300
China Eagle Securities
☎ (86)(755) 82463388
China Southern Securities
☎ (86)(755) 83680023
Great Wall Securities
☎ (86)(755) 82416360
Ping'an Securities
☎ (86)(755) 83696036
Shenzhen SEZ Securities Co. Ltd.
☎ (86)(755) 82891536
V-Sun Securities Ltd.
☎ (86)(755) 83237698

Shanghai
Tai Fook Securities Group Ltd.
☎ (86)(21) 68419818
China Galaxy Securities
☎ (86)(21) 62188777
China Securities
☎ (86)(21) 63055812
Celestial Asia Securities Holdings
☎ (86)(21) 62881717
Daiwa Securities
☎ (86)(21) 63518888
Goldman Sachs
☎ (86)(21) 62797261
Guotai-Junan Securities
☎ (86)(21) 62580818
Haitong Securities
☎ (86)(21) 53594566
J P Morgan & Co.
☎ (86)(21) 62797301
Merrill Lynch
☎ (86)(21) 62797032
Nikko Securities
☎ (86)(21) 62798025
ING Baring Securities Ltd
☎ (86)(21) 68413355
Jardine Fleming Securities
☎ (86)(21) 64150828

Nomura International Securities
☎ (86)(21) 64151565
SG Securities
☎ (86)(21) 62798471
Shanghai Finance Securities
☎ (86)(21) 57334778
Shanghai Securitie Co. Ltd.
☎ (86)(21) 65223500
Shenyin Wanguo Securities
☎ (86)(21) 64158888

Tourism Services

Anhui

Hefei
Anhui Tourism Administration
☎ (86)(551) 2821906
Anhui Merchants Travel Services
☎ (86)(551) 2628011
China Youth Travel Service Co. Ltd.
☎ (86)(551) 429 1999
China Travel Service
☎ (86)(551) 2652017

Huangshan
China Travel Services
☎ (86)(559) 2525844
Huangshan Air Int'l Travel Service
☎ (86)(559) 2537790
China Comfort Travel Service
☎ (86)(559) 2411203
Huangshan Cultural Int'l Travel Service
☎ (86)(559) 2516778
Huangshan Financial Int'l Travel Service
☎ (86)(559) 2514768
Huangshan Straits Int'l Travel Service
☎ (86)(559) 2529988

Wuhu
Wuhu City Port Travel Service
☎ (86)(554) 3833780

Beijing
Beijing Tourism Administration
☎ (86)(10) 65158844

American Express
☎ (86)(10) 65052228
COSCO International Travel
☎ (86)(10) 65221871
Business Travel Service
☎ (86)(10) 63292244
CITIC Travel Company Ltd.
☎ (86)(10) 85263636
Beijing CTS Holiday Travel Service
☎ (86)(10) 65276909
China Education International Travel
☎ (86)(10) 62750708
China Int'l Travel Service (CITS)
☎ (86)(10) 65150218
China Kanghui Travel
☎ (86)(10) 65940881
China Air Int'l Travel Service
☎ (86)(10) 65673286
China Merchants Int'l Travel
☎ (86)(10) 65975588
China Peace Int'l Tourism Corp.
☎ (86)(10) 65122504
China Travel Service HQ
☎ (86)(10) 64622288
China Youth Travel Service
☎ (86)(10) 65137646
CTS Capital Agency
☎ (86)(10) 65284757
Diner's Club
☎ (86)(10 65101868
Mastercard International
☎ (86)(10) 65101090
Visa International
☎ (86)(10) 65064371

Chongqing
Chongqing Tourism Administration
☎ (86)(23) 63712358
China Int'l Travel Service
☎ (86)(23) 63850693
China Youth Travel Service
☎ (86)(23) 63832101
China Travel Service
☎ (86)(23) 63730046
Everbright Int'l Travel Service
☎ (86)(23) 65344531

Chongqing Travel Service
☎ (86)(23) 63502434
China Merchants Travel Service
☎ (86)(23) 69018667
Three Gorges Int'l Travel
☎ (86)(23) 58244880
Zhongtian Travel Service
☎ (86)(23) 63873993

Fujian

Fuzhou
Fujian Tourism Administration
☎ (86)(591) 7555148
China Int'l Travel Service
☎ (86)(591) 3370070
China Travel Service
☎ (86)(591) 3335590
China Youth Travel Service
☎ (86)(591) 7810001
Education Travel Service
☎ (86)(591) 3378557
Tianma Travel Service
☎ (86)(591) 7539298
Huaxia Travel Service
☎ (86)(591) 7557603

Xiamen
Xiamen Tourism Administration
☎ (86)(592) 5318858
American Express
☎ (86)(592) 2120268
China Youth Travel Service
☎ (86)(592) 2053188
China Travel Service
☎ (86)(592) 2032239
China Int'l Travel Service
☎ (86)(592) 5051825
Xiamen Tourism Group Corp.
☎ (86)(592) 2015482

Gansu

Lanzhou
Gansu Tourism Administration
☎ (86)(931) 8873901
China Youth Travel Service
☎ (86)(931) 8465965

China Travel Service
☎ (86)(931) 8416321
China Int'l Travel Service
☎ (86)(931) 8416638
Comfort Travel Service
☎ (86)(931) 8877803
Everbright Int'l Travel Service
☎ (86)(931) 8410953
Huaxia Travel Service
☎ (86)(931) 8816981
Silk Road Int'l Travel Service
☎ (86)(931) 8416638-6593

Guangdong

Guangzhou
Guangdong Tourism Administration
☎ (86)(20) 86666889
Amercian Express
☎ (86)(20) 83311611
China Travel Service
☎ (86)(20) 87556322
Fantasy Holidays
☎ (86)(20) 83874039
Guangdong Travel & Tourism Group Co.
☎ (86)(20) 86666889
Guangdong Zhujiang Int'l Travel Service
☎ (86)(20) 87550195
Southern Int'l Travel Service
☎ (86)(20) 85598190
Southern Air Int'l Travel
☎ (86)(20) 86129941
Sports Int'l Travel Service
☎ (86)(20) 81080906

Tianma Int'l Travel Service
☎ (86)(20) 86678334

Shantou
Shantou Tourism Corp.
☎ (86)(754) 8297612
China Int'l Travel Service
☎ (86)(754) 8230704
Tianma Travel Service
☎ (86)(754) 8896309
China Youth Travel Service
☎ (86)(754) 8465446

Shenzhen

Shenzhen Tourism Administration
☎ (86) (755) 82099972
Shenzhen Tourism Corp.
☎ (86) (755) 25108633
China Travel Service
☎ (86) (755) 82255888
China Int'l Travel Service
☎ (86)(755) 82329805
China Merchants Int'l Travel Service
☎ (86) (755) 83393798
Oriental Tourism Co.
☎ (86)(755) 82253180
Shenzhen Int'l Travel Service
☎ (86)(755) 83240480

Zhuhai

China Travel Service
☎ (86)(756) 8881981
China Int'l Travel Service
☎ (86)(756) 3321275
Pearl River Travel Service
☎ (86)(756) 8116117
Zhuhai Tourism Corp.
☎ (86)(756) 8895618
Zhuhai Gong Bin Int'l Tours
☎ (86)(756) 8886833-328/9

Guangxi

Nanning

Guangxi Tourism Administration
☎ (86)(771) 2808738
Guangxi Bagui Int'l Travel Service
☎ (86)(771) 5632087
China Travel Service
☎ (86)(771) 2833279
Nanning Travel Service
☎ (86)(771) 2420371
Tianma Travel Service
☎ (86)(771) 2804013
China Youth Travel Service
☎ (86)(771) 5860175

Guilin

Guilin Tourism Administration
☎ (86)(773) 2825890

Comfort Travel Service
☎ (86)(773) 3858280
China Int'l Travel Service
☎ (86)(773) 2827190
China Travel Service
☎ (86)(773) 3830270
Huaxia Travel Service
☎ (86)(773) 3830129
Guilin Global Travel Service
☎ (86)(773) 2813761
Lijiang River Int'l Travel
☎ (86)(773) 3849505
Ronghu Lake Travel Service
☎ (86)(773) 2806791
Xinhua Travel Service
☎ (86)(771) 5812380

Guizhou

Guiyang

Guizhou Tourism Administration
☎ (86)(851) 6817801
China Travel Service
☎ (86)(851) 5824139
China Int'l Travel Service
☎ (86)(851) 5816348
China Youth Travel Service
☎ (86)(851) 6850333
Guizhou Railway Travel Service
☎ (86)(851) 5797006
Tianma Int'l Travel Service
☎ (86)(851) 5814402-8241

Hainan

Haikou

Hainan Tourism Administration
☎ (86)(898) 6787224
China Travel Service
☎ (86)(898) 6778113
Hainan Tourism Corp.
☎ (86)(898) 5351679
Hainan Youth Travel
☎ (86)(898) 6760767
Pacific Int'l Travel Service
☎ (86)(898) 6791802
Hainan Aviation Int'l Travel Service
☎ (86)(898) 6769381

China Int'l Travel Service
☎ (86) 898) 5363161
Hainan China Youth Travel Service
☎ (86)(898) 536 5198
Pearl River Int'l Travel Service
☎ (86)(898) 6702642
Tianma Int'l Travel Service
☎ (86)(898) 5354677

Hebei
Shijiazhuang
Hebei Tourism Administration
☎ (86)(311) 5814405
China Int'l Travel Service
☎ (86)(311) 5814766
China Travel Service
☎ (86)(311) 5814570
Railway Travel Service
☎ (86)(311) 6074307
Tianma Travel Service
☎ (86)(311) 5819197

Chengde
China Travel Service
☎ (86)(314) 2030741
China Int'l Travel Service
☎ (86)(314) 2026418
China Youth Travel Service
☎ (86)(314) 2024049

Tangshan
China Travel Service
☎ (86)(315) 2847971
China Int'l Travel Service
☎ (86)(315) 2847971

Heilongjiang
Harbin
Helongjiang Tourism Administration
☎ (86)(451) 2311020
China Int'l Travel Service
☎ (86)(451) 3661191
China Travel Service
☎ (86)(451) 3640984
China Youth Travel Service
☎ (86)(451) 2644384

Songhuajiang Int'l Travel Service
☎ (86)(451) 8301947

Henan
Zhengzhou
Henan Tourism Administration
☎ (86)(371) 5955913
China Travel Service
☎ (86)(371) 6216898
Henan Friendship Int'l Travel Service
☎ (86)(371) 5948004
Railway Int'l Travel Service
☎ (86)(371) 6999480
Xinhua Travel Service
☎ (86)(371) 6229630
Zhengzhou Youth Travel Service
☎ (86)(371) 5712982

Hong Kong
Aero Int'l Ltd.
☎ (852) 25433800
All Nippon Air Service Co. Ltd.
☎ (852) 28484111
American Int'l Travel Ltd.
☎ (852) 28302828
Anglo-Eastern Travel Ltd.
☎ (852) 25272081
Asia Pacific Travel Resources Ltd.
☎ (852) 27361818
BSR Int'l Travel Ltd.
☎ (852) 27303626
COSCO Int'l Travel (H.K.) Co. Ltd.
☎ (852) 25590299
China Int'l Travel Service HK Ltd.
☎ (852) 27325888
Deks Air (HK) Ltd.
☎ (852) 28611811
Delight Air Transportation Ltd.
☎ (852) 25212307
Ever Sun Travel Ltd.
☎ (852) 28776683
Federal H. K. Holdings Ltd.
☎ (852) 23177313
Global Union Express (HK)Ltd.
☎ (852) 28454232

Great Eastern Tourist Ltd.
☎ (852) 23762588
Hong Kong Wing On Travel Service Ltd.
☎ (852) 28526868
Japan Travel Agency Ltd.
☎ (852) 23689151
Jardine Travel Ltd.
☎ (852) 28449668
Leburton Travel Services Ltd.
☎ (852) 28669033
Morning Star Travel Service Ltd.
☎ (852) 27230368
Norray Travel Co. Ltd.
☎ (852) 27393398
Pacific Ace Travel Agency Ltd
☎ (852) 25819281
Reliance Travel (HK) Ltd.
☎ (852) 7312098
Rosenbluth Int'l (Hong Kong) Ltd.
☎ (852) 28153263
Schenker Int'l (HK) Ltd. Travel Division
☎ (852) 25451611
Traveler Services (HK) Ltd.
☎ (852) 23752222

Hubei
Wuhan
Hubei Tourism Administration
☎ (86)(27) 84816530
Merchants Int'l Travel Service
☎ (86)(27) 85610180
Tianma Travel Service
☎ (86)(27) 82833517
Yangtze Int'l Travel Service
☎ (86)(27) 85823146
China Travel Service
☎ (86)(27) 82789269
Wuhan Travel Service
☎ (86)(27) 85861440
Wuhan Youth Travel Service
☎ (86)(27) 8579162
Zhongnan Int'l Tourism Co.
☎ (86)(27) 82844218

Hunan
Changsha

Hunan Tourism Administration
☎ (86)(731) 4720346
China Travel Service
☎ (86)(731) 2253422
China Int'l Travel Service
☎ (86)(731) 2280444
China Youth Travel Service
☎ (86)(731) 4441866
Comfort Travel Service
☎ (86)(731) 4441543
Huatian Int'l Travel
☎ (86)(731) 4119290
Southern Air Travel Service
☎ (86)(731) 4465212

Inner Mongolia
Hohhot
Inner Mongolia Tourism Administration
☎ (86)(471) 6965978
China Travel Service
☎ (86)(471) 6964233
China Youth Travel Service
☎ (86)(471) 6938326
China Int'l Travel Service
☎ (86)(471) 6929032
Minzu Travel Service
☎ (86)(471) 4954204

Jiangsu
Nanjing
Jiangsu Tourism Administration
☎ (86)(25) 341859
China Travel Service
☎ (86)(25) 3366582
China Youth Travel Service
☎ (86)(25) 6523344
China Int'l Travel Service
☎ (86)(25) 3428999
Comfort Travel Service
☎ (86)(25) 3413007
Nanjing Merchant Int'l Tourism Co.
☎ (86)(25) 4209837
Nanjing Friendship Int'l Travel Service
☎ (86)(25) 3311393
Nanjing Business Travel Service
☎ (86)(25) 3411888

Suzhou

China Int'l Travel Service
☎ (86)(512) 5223783
China Travel Service
☎ (86)(512) 5221918
China Youth Travel Service
☎ (86)(512) 5291746
Suzhou Business Travel Service
☎ (86)(512) 8272825

Wuxi

China Merchants Int'l Travel
☎ (86)(510) 2721226
Jiangnan Int'l Travel Service
☎ (86)(510) 2713084
China Int'l Travel Service
☎ (86)(510) 2705369
China Travel Service
☎ (86)(510) 2300584
China Youth Travel Service
☎ (86)(510) 2700738
Wuxi Travel Agency
☎ (86)(510) 2703351

Jiangxi

Nanchang

Jiangxi Tourism Administration
☎ (86)(791) 3295304
Comfort Travel Service
☎ (86)(791) 8322191
Nanchang Int'l Travel Service
☎ (86)(791) 6702443
Tianma Travel Service
☎ (86)(791) 6700066
China Youth Travel Service
☎ (86)(791) 6225541
Swan Int'l Travel
☎ (86)(791) 6256874

Jiujiang

COSCO Travel Service
☎ (86)(792) 8227285
Merchants Travel Service
☎ (86)(792) 8115889

Jilin

Changchun

Jilin Tourism Administration
☎ (86)(431) 5609250
China Int'l Travel Service
☎ (86)(431) 5656313
China Travel Service
☎ (86)(431) 5662997
China Youth Travel Service
☎ (86)(431) 8540522

Liaoning

Shenyang

Liaoning Tourism Administration
☎ (86)(24) 86807348
China Int'l Travel Service
☎ (86)(24) 23267507
China Travel Service
☎ (86)(24) 22710331
China Youth Travel Service
☎ (86)(24) 23904030
Shenyang Railway Int'l Travel Service
☎ (86)(24) 22510960

Dalian

China Everbright Travel Corp.
☎ (86)(411) 2824744
China Int'l Travel Service
☎ (86)(411) 3687606
China Travel Service
☎ (86)(411) 2381621
China Youth Travel Service
☎ (86)(411) 3686541
Int'l Business Travel Corp.
☎ (86)(411) 2647389
China Ocean Travel Service
☎ (86)(411) 2825947

Ningxia

Yinchuan

Ningxia Tourism Administration
☎ (86)(951) 5010397
China Travel Service
☎ (86)(951) 5044025
China Youth Travel Service
☎ (86)(951) 4104578
China Int'l Travel Service
☎ (86)(951) 5047228

Comfort Int'l Travel Service
☎ (86)(951) 5045678
Merchants Int'l Travel Service
☎ (86)(951) 6030583
Spring & Autumn Travel Service
☎ (86)(951) 6034998

Qinghai
Xining
Qinghai Toursim Administration
☎ (86)(971) 6157015
China Youth Travel Service
☎ (86)(971) 8127623
China Travel Service
☎ (86)(971) 8244074
China Int'l Travel Service
☎ (86)(971) 8133943
Kunlun Travel Service
☎ (86)(971) 6133844
Qinghai Tourism Corp.
☎ (86)(971) 6133643

Shaanxi
Xi'an
Shaanxi Tourism Administration
☎ (86)(29) 5261059
Comfort Int'l Tourism Service
☎ (86)(29) 5255550
China Int'l Travel Service
☎ (86)(29) 5262066
China Travel Service
☎ (86)(29) 5269464
CITIC Int'l Tourism Co. Ltd.
☎ (86)(29) 2221753
Everbright Int'l Tourism Service
☎ (86)(29) 8422705
Tianma Int'l Tourism Service
☎ (86)(29) 5257995
Merchants Int'l Travel Service
☎ (86)(29) 5229114
Northwest Travel Service
☎ (86)(29) 7435622
Peace Int'l Travel
☎ (86)(29) 7418440
Xi'an Tourism Corp.
☎ (86)(29) 7429365

Xinhua Travel Service
☎ (86)(29) 5382258

Shandong
Jinan
Shandong Tourism Administration
☎ (86)(531) 2965858
Aviation Int'l Travel Service
☎ (86)(531) 6034146
China Youth Travel Service
☎ (86)(531) 2065576
Comfort Int'l Travel Service
☎ (86)(531) 2967116
Confucius Int'l Travel Service
☎ (86)(531) 2951168
Cultural Int'l Travel Service
☎ (86)(531) 2960666
Jinan Tourist Service General Co.
☎ (86)(531) 2971304
Shandong Travel Service
☎ (86)(531) 6025270
Tianma Travel Service
☎ (86)(531) 2026948

Qingdao
Asia Pacific Travel Service
☎ (86)(532) 2965701
Continental Travel Service
☎ (86)(532) 5828064
Double Star Travel Service
☎ (86)(532) 2676007
Haier Int'l Travel
☎ (86)(532) 8938993
Seagull Travel Service
☎ (86)(532) 3031125
Yellow Sea Travel Service
☎ (86)(532) 2869488

Yantai
Friendship Travel Service
☎ (86)(535) 6249055
Tianma Travel Service
☎ (86)(535) 6612043
Yantai Travel Service
☎ (86)(535) 6265024
Xinhua Travel Service
☎ (86)(535) 6384475

Comfort Travel Service
☎ (86)(535) 6230141

Shanghai

Shanghai Tourism Administration
☎ (86)(21) 64391818
American Express
☎ (86)(21) 52798082
China Travel Service
☎ (86)(21) 63368800
China Youth Travel Service
☎ (86)(21) 64454583
CITIC International Travel Service
☎ (86)(21) 62793185
Jinjiang Travel Service
☎ (86)(21) 64662828
Hengshan Int'l Travel
☎ (86)(21) 62519335
Huaxia Travel Service
☎ (86)(21) 62159089
Shanghai Air Travel Service
☎ (86)(21) 62253687
Comfort Int'l Travel Service
☎ (86)(21) 63174049
Shanghai Merchants Travel
☎ (86)(21) 64470370
China Eastern Air Travel
☎ (86)(21) 62686268

Shanxi

Taiyuan
Shanxi Tourism Administration
☎ (86)(351) 4047525
China Travel Service
☎ (86)(351) 3531103
China Youth Travel Service
☎ (86)(351) 4048017
China Int'l Travel Service
☎ (86)(351) 7232188

Sichuan

Chengdu
Sichuan Tourism Administration
☎ (86)(28) 6671458
Business Int'l Travel Service
☎ (86)(28) 6606238

China Youth Tourism Service
☎ (86)(28) 6693482
China Travel Service
☎ (86)(28) 5562986
China Int'l Travel Service
☎ (86)(28) 5534128
CITIC Travel Service
☎ (86)(28) 3355924
Culture Tourism Service
☎ (86)(28) 6999111
Yangtze Int'l Travel Service
☎ (86)(28) 7606526

Tianjin

Tianjin Tourism Administration
☎ (86)(22) 28358812
China Int'l Travel Service
☎ (86)(22) 28358350
China Merchants Int'l Travel
☎ (86)(22) 28357483
China Travel Service
☎ (86)(22) 23535388
China Youth Travel Service
☎ (86)(22) 27423238
Comfort Travel Service
☎ (86)(22) 28371876

Tibet

Lahsa
Tibet Tourism Administration
☎ (86)(891) 6834331
China Youth Travel Service
☎ (86)(891) 6327414
Century Int'l Travel Service
☎ (86)(891) 6836784
Holiday Int'l Travel
☎ (86)(891) 6824305
Lahsa Tourism Service
☎ (86)(891) 6322944
Tibet Tourism Corp.
☎ (86)(891) 6832890

Xinjiang

Urumqi
Xinjiang Tourism Administration
☎ (86)(991) 2843662

China Travel Service
☎ (86)(991) 2854917
China Youth Travel Service
☎ (86)(991) 2818634
China Int'l Travel Service
☎ (86)(991) 2845947
Straits Travel Service
☎ (86)(991) 4813533
Oasis China Travel Service
☎ (86)(991) 4522946
Xinjiang Air Int'l Travel
☎ (86)(991) 3804770
Xinjiang Western Travel Service
☎ (86)(991) 2845953

Yunnan
Kunming
Yunnan Tourism Administration
☎ (86)(871) 3453560
China Youth Travel Service
☎ (86)(871) 4143188
Comfort Travel Service
☎ (86)(871) 7198626
COSCO Travel Service
☎ (86)(871) 3559377
China Merchants Int'l Travel
☎ (86)(871) 3354595
Taihe Travel Service
☎ (86)(871) 3130308
Yunnan Int'l Travel Service
☎ (86)(871) 3367526
Yunnan Air Int'l Travel
☎ (86)(871) 3637089

Zhejiang
Hangzhou
Zhejiang Tourism Administration
☎ (86)(571) 5150505
China Travel Service
☎ (86)(571) 7080888
Hangzhou West Lake Travel Service
☎ (86)(571) 7290017
China Youth Travel Service
☎ (86)(571) 7012333
China Int'l Travel Service
☎ (86)(571) 5152888

Ningbo
Ningbo Asia Travel Service Co. Ltd.
☎ (86)(574) 7314789
China Int'l Travel Service
☎ (86)(574) 7315317
China Travel Service
☎ (86)(574) 7329254
Ningbo Travel Service
☎ (86)(574) 7286617
Ningbo Youth Travel Service
☎ (86)(574) 7309182

Shaoxing
Shaoxing China Int'l Travel Service
☎ (86)(575) 5166965
Shaoxing City China Travel Service
☎ (86)(575) 5138349
Shaoxing City Youth Travel Service
☎ (86)(575) 5142926
Shaoxing City Straits Travel Service
☎ (86)(575) 5137355

Wenzhou
Wenzhou China Travel Service
☎ (86)(577) 8254384
Wenzhou Tourism Service
☎ (86)(577) 8813587

Trade Events

Beijing

07-10 Aug, 2002	2002 China International Clothing & Accessories Fair	China Int'l Exhibition Center
28-31 Aug, 2002	Water China 2002	China World Trade Center
01-04 Sep, 2002	The 6th China Int'l Fair on E-learning	China Int'l Exhibition Center
05 Sep, 2002	2002 Autumn Real Estate Trade Fair Beijing	China Int'l Exhibition Center
11-14 Sep 2002	International Fair for Technology of Environment Protection in China	China World Trade Center
17-20 Sep 2002	The 8th International Metallurgical Industry Expo.	China Int'l Exhibition Center
24-27 Sep, 2002	China Int'l Trade Fair for Sanitation, Heating, Air-Conditioning	China Int'l Exhibition Center
24-27 Sep, 2002	China Int'l Trade Fair for Windows, Walls, Doors & Roofs	China Int'l Exhibition Center
Sept-Oct, 2002	China Int'l Exhibition & Conference for Water Treatment Technology and Equipment	National Agriculture Exhibition Center
15-19 Oct, 2002	The 4th China Int'l Textile Chemicals Exhibition & Conference	China Int'l Exhibition Center
15-19 Oct, 2002	The 8th China Int'l Textile Machinery Exhibition	China Int'l Exhibition Center
19-21 Oct, 2002	Education Expo China 2002	Beijing Exhibition Center
22-25 Oct, 2002	IPP-International Exhibition for Intelligent Traffic Systems, Public Design and Parking	China World Trade Center
29 Oct-02 Nov, 02	PT/EXPO COMM China	China World Trade Center
Oct 2002	China International Watch & Clock Fair 2002	China Int'l Exhibition Center
Oct 2002	The 4th China Grain & Oil Fine Products Trade Fair	China Int'l Exhibition Center
Oct 2002	China Occupational Safety and Health Expo	China World Trade Center
4-5 Nov,2002	The 5th Annual Franchise China 2002 Conference & Exhibition	China Int'l Exhibition Center
06-09 Nov, 2002	2nd China Int'l Energy & Environment Protection Exhibition & Conference	China Int'l High-Tech CEC
06-09 Nov, 2002	3rd China Int'l Digitech & Palm Electronics Exhibition	China Int'l Exhibition Center
11-14 Nov, 2002	Scan-China 2002	Beijing Int'l Convention Center
13-16 Nov, 2002	The 9th Int'l Exhibition on Electric Power Equipment and Technology	China Int'l Exhibition Center
13-16 Nov, 2002	The 2nd Int'l Exhibition on Electrical	China Int'l Exhibition Center

	Engineering, Electrical Equipment and Contractors' Supplies	
13-16 Nov, 2002	Int'l Exhibition on Building Materials, Building Services and Interior Decoration	China Int'l Exhibition Center
13-16 Nov, 2002	Int'l Petroleum & Petrochemical Exhibition 2002	China Int'l Exhibition Center
19-22 Dec, 2002	2002 Winter Real Estate Trade Fair Beijing	China Int'l Exhibition Center
16-22 Apr, 2003	The China International Truck Exhibition 2003	National Agriculture Exhibition Centre
11-14 Mar, 2003	Automechanika China	China Int'l Exhibition Center
16-22 Apr, 2003	The China Int'l Truck Exhibition 2003	National Agriculture Exhibition Center

Chongqing

18-21 Sep, 2002	Medical Expo 2002	Chongqing Int'l Technology Exhibition Center

Fujian
Xiamen

08-11 Sep, 2002	The 6th China Int'l Fair for Investment & Trade	Xiamen Int'l Conference & Exhibition Center

Guangdong
Guangzhou

03-06 Aug, 2002	The 7th Guangdong Int'l Illumination Exhibition	Guangzhou China Export Commodities Trade Fair Exhibition Hall (GCECTFEH)
17-20 Sep, 2002	Int'l Pharmaceutical Trade Fair	GCECTFEH
18-20 Sep, 2002	China Int'l Exhibition on Animal Husbandry & Feed Industry	GCECTFEH
18-20 Sep, 2002	China Int'l Exhibition on Fishery	GCECTFEH
25-28 Sep, 2002	2002 Int'l Garments Festival	GCECTFEH
01-04 Nov, 2002	China Int'l Sporting Goods Fair	GCECTFEH
07-08 Nov, 2002	Franchise China Conference & Exhibition	GCECTFEH
07-10 Nov, 2002	The 5th Int'l Environment Protection Technology & Product Exhibition	GCECTFEH
21-24 Nov, 2002	Chian Int'l Foodstaff Industries Trade	GCECTFEH
07-11 Dec, 2002	The Fifth Guangzhou Int'l Automobile Exhibition (Auto South China 2002)	GCECTFEH
02-04 Apr, 2003	Food Ingredients China 2003	GCECTFEH
24-26 Sep, 2003	Electric South China 2003	GCECTFEH

| 26-28 Sep, 2003 | Energy/Electric South China | GCECTFEH |

Shenzhen

27-30 Aug, 2002	Microelectronics Shenzhen	China High-Tech Fair Exhibition Center (CHTFEC)
13-17 Sep, 2002	Int'l Jewelry Fair 2002	CHTFEC
12-17 Oct, 2002	The 4th China High Tech 2002	CHTFEC
Nov 2002	Electronics China 2002	CHTFEC

Zhuhai

| 04-10 Nov 2002 | 2002Airshow China | Zhuhai |

Guangxi

Guilin

| 29-31Oct, 2002 | China (Guilin) International Environment Fair | Guilin Int'l Exhibition Hall |

Nanning

| 16-31 Nov, 2002 | Guangxi Investment & Trade Fair | Guangxi Exhibition Hall |

Hebei

Qinghuangdao

| 25-28 Aug, 2002 | China (Qinghuangdao) Int'l Glass Fair cum Symposium | The Hebei Province Ceramic |

Heilongjiang

Harbin

| 16-20 Sep, 2002 | Harbin Int'l Fashion Fair | Heilongjiang Int'l Fair Center |

Henan

Zhenzhou

| 28-31 Aug, 2002 | Zhengzhou Fair | Zhenzhou Central Plains Int'l Exhibition Center |

Hong Kong

15-19 Aug, 2002	Food Expo 2002	Hong Kong Convention and Exhibition Centre (CEC)
10-14 Sep, 2002	Hong Kong Watch & Clock Fair	Hong Kong CEC
11-14 Oct, 2002	Hong Kong Electronics Fair	Hong Kong CEC
11-14 Oct, 2002	Hong Kong Lighting Fair	Hong Kong CEC
24-26 Oct, 2002	Hong Kong Int'l Hardware & Home Improvement Fair 2002	Hong Kong CEC
06-08 Nov, 2002	Hong Kong Optical Fair 2002	Hong Kong CEC
07-10 Jan, 2003	Hong Kong Toys & Games Fair	Hong Kong CEC
07-10 Jan, 2003	Hong Kong Int'l Stationery Fair	Hong Kong CEC

14-17 Jan, 2003	Hong Kong Fashion Week for Fall/Winter 2003	Hong Kong CEC
14-17 Jan, 2003	World Boutique, Hong Kong	Hong Kong CEC
20-23 Feb, 2003	Education & Careers 2003	Hong Kong CEC
04-07 Mar, 2003	Hong Kong International Jewellery Show 2003	Hong Kong CEC
21-24 April, 2003	Hong Kong Houseware Fair	Hong Kong CEC
28 Apr-01 May,03	Hong Kong Gifts & Premium Fair 2003	Hong Kong CEC
06-09 May, 2003	HOFEX 2003	Hong Kong CEC
06-09 May , 2003	Wine and Spirits Asia 2003	Hong Kong CEC
06-09 May, 2003	Bakery and Confectionery Asia	Hong Kong CEC
06-09 May, 2003	Asian International Seafood Show	Hong Kong CEC

Jiangsu
Changzhou

| 20-24 Sep, 2002 | China int'l Commodities Fair | Changzhou Int'l Exhibition Center |
| 08-11 Nov, 2002 | The 5th China Int'l Trade Fair for Electronic Information Industry | Changzhou Int'l Exhibition Center |

Liaoning
Dalian

07-10 Aug, 2002	Dalian Int'l Beauty & Hair Cosmetics Exhibition	Dalian Xinhai Convention and Exhibition Center (XHCEC)
07-11 Aug, 2002	Dalian Int'l Art Fair 2002	XHCEC
14-17 Aug, 2002	Dalian Int'l Exhibition for Medical Instruments and Medicine Health Care Products	XHCEC
22-26 Aug, 2002	The 7th Dalian Int'l Auto & Parts Exhibition	XHCEC
31Aug-01 Sep, 02	2002 Liaoning Int'l Education Exhibition	XHCEC
04-06 Sep, 2002	Dalian Int'l Industry Materials and Fittings Expo	XHCEC
04-07 Sep, 2002	2002 Int'l Turf & Golfing Conference Expo.	XHCEC
27-29 Sep, 2002	The 6th Dalian Int'l Food Processing & Packing Machinery Expo	XHCEC
27-30 Sep, 2002	2002 Int'l Radio & TV Broadcasting Equipment Expo.	XHCEC
27-30 Sep, 2002	Int'l Modern Agriculture Exhibition	XHCEC
Sep 2002	China Int'l EnvironmentProtection Fair	XHCEC
Sep 2002	The 14th Dalian Int'l Garment Fair & China Garment Export Fair	XHCEC

01-18 Oct, 2002	Dalian Tour Artware and Tour Commodities Fair	XHCEC
10-14 Oct, 2002	2002 Dalian Exhibition of Rehabilitation Articles for Mid-Old Age	XHCEC
31 Oct-05 Nov, 02	2002 Dalian Autumn Real Estate Exhibition	XHCEC
31 Oct-05 Nov, 02	The 4th China Int'l Building and Decorative Materials & Ware Exhibition	XHCEC
01-05 Nov, 2002	The 4th China Int'l Building Materials & Bath Facilities (Dalian) Exhibition; 2002 Dalian Autumn Real Estate Exchange Fair	XHCEC
14-19 Nov, 2002	The 6th Int'l Fur, Leather and Products Fair	XHCEC
21-26 Dec, 2002	The 7th Dalian Commodities Fair for the New Year	XHCEC

Shenyang

28-31 Aug, 2002	The 2nd Shenyang Int'l Fair for Auto Maintenance and Testing Equipment	Shenyang Science Palace CEC
07-11 Oct, 2002	China Shenyang Int'l Fair for Auto Parts and Equipment	Liaoning Industrial Hall
Aug 2003	The 3rd Shenyang Int'l Auto Industry Expo (Auto North China 2003)	Shenyang Automobile Center

Shaanxi

Xi'an

| 18-24 Aug, 2002 | Western China Medical Instruments Expo | Xi'an Int'l Exhibition Center |

Yangling

| 05-09 Nov, 2002 | The 9th China Yangling Agricultural Hi-Tech Fair | Int'l CEC, Yangling |

Shandong

Qingdao

| 29-31 Oct, 2002 | China Fisheries & Seafood Expo 2002; Aquaculture China 2002 | Qingdao Int'l Convention Center |

Yantai

06-09 Sep, 2002	Int'l Info Tach Expo	Yantai Int'l CEC
17-21 Oct, 2002	The 4th Int'l Fruit/VegetableExpo	Yantai
27-30 Oct, 2002	Public Security Expo	Yantai Int'l CEC

Shanghai

02-05 Sep, 2002	CeBIT Asia	Shanghai Int'l Exhibition Center (INTEX Shanghai)
03-06 Sep, 2002	Food & Drink 2002; Equipment & Hospitality	Shanghai Everbright CEC
03-06 Sep, 2002	Medical Technology Int'l Expo Shanghai 2002	Shanghai Mart
11-15 Sep, 2002	Furniture China 2002	New Int'l Expo Center
17-20 Sep, 2002	Marine Port China 2002	INTEX Shanghai
18-20 Sep, 2002	2002 Moda Shanghai	Shanghai Everbright CEC
18-20 Sep, 2002	All China Leather Exhibition	Shanghai Everbright CEC
18-20 Sep, 2002	The 8th China International Composite Materials, Industrial & Technical Exhibition	Shanghai Mart
18-21 Sep, 2002	The 6th DenTech China 2002	INTEX Shanghai
09-12 Oct 2002	The 10th China Int'l Industry Fair;	Shanghai Exhibition Center
09-12 Oct 2002	China International Industry Packaging Printing & Plastic Expo	INTEX Shanghai
09-12 Oct, 2002	InterElectronics China 2002; Productronics China 2002; Component & Industry Supply	Shanghai Exhibition Center
22-25 Oct, 2002	Interfood Shanghai 2002 PNP CHINA 2002	INTEX Shanghai
22-25 Oct, 2002	China Int'l Water Industry 2002	Shanghai Mart
24-27 Oct, 2002	The 60th National Electronics Fair; 2002 International Electronics Expo	Shanghai Everbright CEC
04-05 Nov, 2002	The World Property Show	Shanghai Four Seasons Hotel
Nov 2002	Shanghai Int'l AD & Print New Technology, New Material, New Equipment, New Media Exhibition	Shanghai Mart
Nov 2002	Shanghai Int'l Wire & Cable	Shanghai Mart
05-08 Nov, 2002	Metal Working China 2002	New Int'l Expo Centre
06-09 Nov, 2002	The 11th Shanghai Int'l Consumer Goods Fair	INTEX Shanghai
12-15 Nov, 2002	China Wine Italy	Shanghai Everbright CEC
26-29 Nov, 2002	China International Housing & Building Expo 2002	INTEX Shanghai
03-06 Dec, 2002	Auto Parts & Equip Shanghai; TYREXPO 2002	INTEX Shanghai
25-28 Feb, 2003	WoodMac China 2003; FurniTek China 2003; Woodbuild China 2003	INTEX Shanghai
05-07 Mar, 2003	Fi Asia - China 2003	Shanghai
21-24 Mar, 2003	Shanghai International Diamond Trade Fair 2003	INTEX Shanghai
03-06 Jun, 2003	Machine Parts 2003	Shanghai

Date	Event	Venue
03-06 Jun, 2003	Int'l Bearing Industry Exhibition	Shanghai
08-11 Jul, 2003	ProPak China 2003	Shanghai Everbright CEC
16-19 Sep, 2003	Food & Drink, Equipment & Hospitality	Shanghai Everbright CEC
17-20 Feb, 2004	WoodMac China 2004; FurniTek China 2004; Woodbuild China 2004	INTEX Shanghai
13-16 Jul, 2004	ProPak China 2004	New Int'l Expo Centre

Sichuan
Chengdu

Date	Event	Venue
09-12 Sep, 2002	The 8th Chengdu Int'l Exhibition for Power Supply Equipment	Chengdu Int'l CEC
23-26 Sep, 2002	Int'l Furniture Fair 2002	Chengdu Int'l CEC
14-17 Oct, 2002	2002 Chengdu Int'l Newspaper Industry & Magazine Fair	Sichuan Exhibition Hall
18-21 Oct, 2002	2002 Chengdu Int'l Exhibition for Goods & Popular Home & Living	Sichuan Exhibition Hall
02-05 Dec, 2002	The 5th Chengdu Int'l Environment Protection Industry Fair	Sichuan Exhibition Hall
21-24 Dec, 2002	Chengdu Int'l Textile Machinery & Technology Exhibition	Sichuan Exhibition Hall

Tianjin

Date	Event	Venue
18-21 Oct, 2002	National Building Materials Commodities Fair China 2002	Tianjin Sports Exhibition Center

Xinjiang
Urumqi

Date	Event	Venue
01-08 Sep, 2002	Urumqi (China) Foreign Economic Relations And Trade Fair	Xinjiang Int'l Exhibition Center

Zhejiang
Hangzhou

Date	Event	Venue
10-14 Oct, 2002	The 5th West Lake Art Expo	Zhejiang World Trade Center
1-14 Oct, 2002	The 5th China Int'l Tea Fair	Zhejiang World Trade Center
13 Oct, 2002	2002 China Internet Summit & 3rd West Lake Symposium	Zhejiang World Trade Center
18-21 Oct, 2002	2002 China Int'l Women's Dress Exhibition	Zhejiang World Trade Center
18-21 Oct, 2002	2002 China (Hangzhou) Int'l Intelligent House Appliances Exhibition	Zhejiang World Trade Center
19-22 Oct, 2002	2002 China (Hangzhou) Philatelic Culture Exhibition	Zhejiang World Trade Center
20-22 Oct, 2002	2002 Hangzhou Silk Fashion Festival	Zhejiang World Trade Center
21-23 Oct, 2002	The 23th China(Hangzhou) Bicycle, Auto-Bicycle and Parts Exhibition	Zhejiang World Trade Center

23-24 Oct, 2002	The 3rd China (Hangzhou) Int'l Auto Exhibition	Zhejiang World Trade Center
25-28 Oct, 2002	2002 China(Hangzhou) Jewelry and Cosmetics Exhibition	Zhejiang World Trade Center
28-29 Oct, 2002	2002 China (Hangzhou) Int'l Furniture Exhibition	Zhejiang World Trade Center
31Oct-04 Nov, 02	The 3rd China Int'l Silk Expo	Zhejiang World Trade Center
01-04 Nov, 2002	The 3rd China West Electronic Audio Video Expo	Zhejiang World Trade Center
01-03 Nov, 2002	2002 Hangzhou Int'l Education Exhibition	Zhejiang World Trade Center
07-10 Nov, 2002	2002 China (Hangzhou) Int'l Exhibition on IT Products	Zhejiang World Trade Center
07-10 Nov, 2002	2002 China (Hangzhou) Foreign Economic and Trade Conference	Zhejiang World Trade Center
22-25 Nov, 2002	The 4th Hangzhou High-Quality Farm Produce and New Technology	Zhejiang World Trade Center
25 Nov, 2002	2002 Hangzhou West Lake Flower Fair	Hangzhou Taiziwan Park

Ningbo

15-19 Nov, 2002	The Seventh Ningbo Int'l Expo on Housing Industry Products	Ningbo
28-31 Oct, 2002	The 4th China Plastics Exhibition	Yuyao City

Wenzhou

12-15 Nov, 2002	The 7th Int'l Shoe Machinery & Raw Materials Exhibition	Wenzhou

Index To Industrial Parks

PROVINCES

Guangdong

Guizhou

Hainan

Hebei

Heilongjian

Henan

Hubei

Hunan

Jiangsu

Jiangxi

Shanxi

Sichuan

Yunnan

Zhejiang

SPECIAL ADMINISTRATIVE REGIONS

Hong Kong

Macau

Map Your Business Direction. Embrace Your Core Competency

BEIJING   GUANGZHOU   HONG KONG   SHANGHAI   SINGAPORE

▶ **Direct Mail & Mailing list Rental**
Specially designed mailing lists can help you target the right customers. We can help you select and define your target, obtain lists, and produce mailing campaigns that deliver results.

▶ **Catalogs & Sales Literature**
We make sure your message effectively portrays what sets your company, products and services apart. You can leave us to create high quality marketing brochure, catalog and sales literature that deliver impact and communicate effectively.

▶ **Media Representation**
Our sales and client services professionals provide creative, innovative and value-added services that enhance our client's business.

www.mapplercore.com

CHINA

Business & Travel Guide 2002/3

中国

Gateway
to the Land of
Opportunities

ISBN 981-04-5962-9 US$35

Please indicate the titles and quantities that you want to order :

CKP TITLES (All Prices In US$)	Retail Price	Quantity
☐ **China Business & Travel Guide 2002/3**	US$35	
☐ **Building A Successful Plant in China 2002/3 Edition (An Insider's Guide)**	US$99	
☐ **(Insider's Guide) Doing Business in Shanghai**	US$49	
☐ **(Insider's Guide) Doing Business in Beijing**	US$49	
☐ **(Insider's Guide) Doing Business in Guangdong**	US$49	
☐ **(Insider's Guide) Doing Business in Jiangsu**	US$49	
☐ **(Insider's Guide) Doing Business in Shandong**	US$49	

Payment Method (Please tick one):   Total Amount: US$_____

☐ Telegraphic Transfer to ("**China Knowledge Press Pte Ltd**")
   A/c No. 0048-001013-01-3-022
   Swift code: DBSSSGSG

* Shipping & Delivery charges to:
Asia   US$15
Australia / New Zealand   US$15
US, UK & Europe   US$25
Other Countries   US$30
Shipping & Delivery charges are waived for orders above US$1000

☐ Charge my American Express Card

Card No: ☐☐☐☐☐☐☐☐☐☐☐☐☐☐☐☐☐☐

Expiry Date: ☐☐☐☐   Signature: _____

Below is my: ☐ Home Address   ☐ Office Address
Salutation   : ☐ Dr.   ☐ Mr.   ☐ Ms.   ☐ Mdm.
Family Name   :_____
Given Name   :_____
Job Title   :_____
Company Name   :_____
Address   :_____
                :_____
Country   :_____ Postal Code: _____
Telephone   :_____ Fax: _____
Email   :_____
Business Activity :_____ No. of Employees:_____

Please send your completed order form with payment to:
China Knowledge Press Pte Ltd
119 Genting Lane   Robinson Road
#05-01 H&H Building   P. O. Box 1362
Singapore 349570   Singapore 902712

For faster service, please fax this form to us at
Tel: (65) 6310 8737, Fax: (65) 6310 8738,
or email us at order @chinaknowledge-press.com

China Knowledge Press